Horace C. Hovey.

From a Photograph by Thompson 1897.

Henry E. Hovey

INTRODUCTION.

The HOVEY BOOK owes its existence to the wishes and combined efforts of many individuals. The materials have been drawn from all parts of New England, and even from distant regions of the Continent and from foreign lands. Here and there have lived men and women of today who longed to know more facts than were in their possession concerning their ancestors. They ransacked attics for ancient relics and old family documents. They frequented bookstores, and old curiosity shops. They tried to build up family traditions and records into consistent genealogies. They made scrap-books filled with clippings, often disconnected and less authentic than could be desired. They did not disdain any scrap of information that might come to hand concerning anybody by the name of Hovey.

Meanwhile the scattered branches of the family did not even know of each other's existence, much less of the kindred aims that led them to similar lines of independent research. It is impossible to do justice in these pages to every individual whose patient mind and diligent hand have wrought out the results now for the first time offered in a combined form to the public. Yet this passing recognition is due to those who have even secretly taken a wholesome and praiseworthy interest in their colonial ancestry.

By way of introduction the writer, who has from the first been honored as the President of the Daniel Hovey Association, desires to tell the story of its origin and aims, of its various annual and mid-winter meetings, of its officers and members, and also to give a few facts of interest that hardly seem germane to the body of the book.

In May, 1900, on a grassy knoll, under a gnarled and twisted apple-tree, near the spot where the Newbury pilgrims landed long ago, two families by the name of Hovey, one from Portsmouth and the other from Newburyport, picnicked together. They found the occasion so agreeable as to suggest a larger family gathering; to effect which the following circular was issued with a few additional names:—

DEAR COUSIN:

You are invited with kith and kin to Ipswich, the home of our common immigrant ancestor, Daniel Hovey. Let us meet at noon, on Tuesday, the twenty-first of August (or if stormy, the next fair day), at the rooms of the Ipswich Historical Society, near the railroad station in that city.

After a friendly interchange of greetings, we will visit the Public Library and other points of interest. Dinner will await us at 2 p. m., at fifty cents a plate, at the Agawam House.

At 3 p. m. we will proceed to the foot of Hovey street and cross the river by row-boats to the ruins of the Hovey Home and the remains of the Hovey Wharf, built 250 years ago. A delightful sail at high tide may follow; or carriages may be had at reasonable rates for a drive among the hills.

Ipswich may be reached by railroad, electrics, or steamboat, and the ride thither is a favorite one for wheelmen.

If you can come, please notify the chairman a week in advance, or as soon as possible. If you cannot come, please send a letter to your assembled cousins, addressing any member of the committee; saying who you are, and how related to Daniel Hovey. Valuable information, of interest to us all, may thus be gained.

Will you kindly extend this invitation to any other relatives of Daniel Hovey with whom you may be acquainted?

Sincerely yours,
    HORACE C. HOVEY, of Newburyport, Mass.
    HENRY E. HOVEY, of Portsmouth, N. H.
    GEORGE L. HOVEY, of Ipswich, Mass.
    LEWIS R. HOVEY, of Haverhill, Mass.
    EDMUND F. SLAFTER, of Boston, Mass.

Newburyport, Mass., July 20, 1900.

The program thus indicated was carried out with a degree of success beyond the expectations of the impromptu committee convening the assembly. After inspecting the rooms of the Ipswich Historical Society, the company repaired to the chapel of the First Church, and Rev. Henry Emerson Hovey, of Portsmouth, called the meeting to order, asked Dr. Alvah Hovey, of Newton, Mass., to offer prayer, and then moved that Dr. Horace C. Hovey, of Newburyport, take the chair. In answer to a roll-call seventy-six persons responded as present, and greetings came from others who were absent. On motion of Rev. Henry Emerson Hovey an organization was effected under the name of the Daniel Hovey Association, officers were duly elected, and a committee on genealogy was informally chosen, consisting of all who had been at work in that line: namely, Henry E. Hovey, Horace C. Hovey, Lewis R. Hovey, Henry Russell Hovey, Charles L. Hovey, Alvah Hovey, Augustine Caldwell, Edmund Slafter, William H. Ricker, Mrs. Gardner Chapin, Miss Caroline Hovey, and Miss Lefavour.

As a contribution to the family genealogy Dr. H. C. Hovey read a concise memoir of Daniel Hovey, our immigrant ancestor, a printed copy of which was presented with the author's compli-

ments, to every member of the association. At 2 P. M. dinner
was served at the Agawam House; after which came postprandial
speeches and letters from numerous absentees. Barges were then
taken to Town Hill, the old burying ground, Hovey Street, the
site of the ancient Daniel Hovey house, and the Hovey Wharf;
followed by a ride down the river on the steamer Carlotta, which
conveyed the party out to the Ipswich Bay, and brought them
back in time to witness a glorious sunset. On arriving again at
the Hovey Wharf the assembly dispersed, voting to meet again
the ensuing year.

Eleven annual meetings have been held, all at Ipswich, except one at Groveland Pines, and one at Ipswich Bluffs on Plum
Island. Six mid-winter meetings have been held; five of them in
Boston and one in New York City. The attendance has usually
been about the same as at the first meeting; varied, however, by
the absence of some of the original members and the advent of
new members. The ranks have also been thinned by the death of
some of the veterans: especially of Rev. Henry Emerson Hovey,
Dr. Alvah Hovey, Mr. George Hovey, Dr. Edmund F. Slafter and
Mr. Hamblin L. Hovey, all prominent as founders and able, generous supporters of the association. One of the most interesting
of the special meetings of the Association was held on November
18th, 1907, in Newburyport, in honor of the Golden Wedding of
the President and his wife; when the Vice-President, Rev. Henry
Emerson Hovey, modified the Episcopal marriage service to suit
the occasion, and the guests left a golden memorial of their esteem and affection.

Only a few of the more salient facts recorded by our secretary can be related in this introduction.

Mr. Hamblin L. Hovey, of Waltham, headed a subscription
for a memorial tablet to be erected at Ipswich in honor of Daniel
Hovey, which was placed on the south wall of the Historical reception room with appropriate ceremonies, August 6, 1903. Re-
gret was expressed that careful search had failed to locate the
last resting-place of our distinguished ancestor, but we rejoiced
to be able thus to show our veneration for his name and appreciation of his worth. The tablet of bronze was designed and cast
by Mr. George P. Tilton of Newburyport, and bears an inscription suggested by Rev. Henry Emerson Hovey.

Each member of the genealogical committee had previously
been at work, and some of them for many years, on different
branches of the family. Of course there were some discrepan-
cies, and not a few difficulties; data also accumulated rapidly.
It became evident that all material should be placed in the hands
of an expert, who should adjust what was on hand, correct errors,
and obtain as much additional material as possible. Mr. Sidney

Perley, of Salem, Mass., was accordingly employed as our historian and genealogist, to work under the supervision of our Executive Committee. Mr. Perley's familiarity with Essex county, and indeed with the entire State, and his exact and painstaking methods, led us to regard him as a responsible and conscientious man for the position; and the results have verified the wisdom of our selection

In order to get into touch with as many of the Hovey Family as possible, we employed an amanuensis, Miss Helen A. Pike, to examine the hundreds of domestic and foreign directories in the hands of Messrs. Samson and Murdock, and thus obtained a vast number of addresses in all parts of the continent and abroad, to which a circular was sent soliciting the fullest information. All replies were placed at Mr. Perley's disposal. Church records were searched and town records inspected; old family Bibles were examined, and many old tombstones visited, either by members or our committee or by our historian himself. It is our impression that, first or last, we came into touch with nearly 5,000 individuals, the majority of whom came from Daniel Hovey of Ipswich.

Our attempts to find an authentic coat of arms were too successful. We found too many coats; enough for a wardrobe. We assume that Daniel Hovey himself had none, or he would have used it. Evidently different branches of the family have exercised their right to adopt, or manufacture, armorial bearings to suit themselves. In this they simply followed the example already set by the American families of Adams, Franklin, Hancock and Paul Revere—none of which had any patent from Royalty, or grant from any College of Heraldry, but devised their own coats of arms. It is our impression that George Washington did the same.

At the outset we agreed to use, and have habitually done so, the crest of the English Hovey Family, namely, a hand holding a pen, with a scroll underneath, bearing the legend "Hinc Orior" (by this I rise); not inappropriate in view of the literary character of many of the family. In 1902 it was agreed to adopt a combination of two or more coats of arms known to have been granted to foreign branches of the Hovey Family by heraldic authority. But after all this composite design did not please us, and in 1903 it was voted to postpone the vexed subject indefinitely. In 1910 it was suggested that, unless serious objection was offered, we should make use of the duly recognized English coat of arms, honestly stating it to be such. It appeals to us more than any one of the five or more American coats of arms, whose history we have thus far been unable to verify.

To assist our Historian, and at his request, several special committees were appointed in 1906: namely, to examine Boston records, etc., Miss Shapleigh, Mrs. Ricker, and Miss Chapin; for those of Cambridge, Mr. Ricker, Miss Caroline Hovey, and H. N. Hovey; for Brookfield and Hadley, H. C. Hovey and Miss Amy Kenyon; for Lowell and vicinity, Mr. Grenville Hovey; for Dedham, Mrs. N. W. Davis and Mrs. Mildred Alexander; for Haverhill and Groveland, Mr. Lewis R. Hovey. Mr. Perley himself has visited numerous places to examine town, church and family records and inscriptions in cemeteries.

Our first aim was to get the facts; but when, in 1908, we found that we had a sum total of 1221 pages of MSS., we felt that the time was ripe for a Hovey Book. Accordingly we appointed a Comimttee on Publication, with full powers; of which Dr. H. C. Hovey was made chairman and treasurer; and Mr. Lewis R. Hovey was chosen as printer; and funds were provided by gift and by loan.

The materials amassed are as complete as possible under the circumstances. After all there may remain some differences of opinion. This remark applies to the identification of the old Hovey House. It is certain that Daniel Hovey, Sr., bought a home before his marriage in April, 1639, being one of a series of house-lots laid out along the south bank of the river. He added other lots bought of Wm. Holdred and Wm. Knowlton. Rev. T. F. Waters, president of the Ipswich Historical Society, gives a very full account of the various Hovey real estate transactions in early times. (See "Ipswich, in the Mass. Bay Colony," pp. 482-485.) By permission Daniel Hovey built a fence, made stiles at each end of his property, and in 1659 had leave to "build a wharf against his ground," and also "such building as may tend to the improvement thereof." Mr. Waters says, in a letter to us dated Jan. 13, 1911, "I see no reason to believe that Daniel Hovey ever lived in any other part of the town. The grant of wharf privileges, etc., indicates residence here." His migrations to other towns did not alienate him from Ipswich, which he still claimed as his settled residence." (See petition quoted pp. 11 and 12 of this book.) His will mentions his "dwelling-house"; and his inventory, in 1692, speaks of his "house and wharf," as if contiguous to each other. Thus he certainly had a house in 1639 and also in 1692; but we do not know them to be identical. He moved to Quabog in 1668, and thence to Hadley; but he seems to have returned to his Ipswich home in 1678. According to Mr. Perley he was at that time "in straightened circumstances, and there is no reason to think he built another house of which he died possessed." Our Historian also reasons that "when Daniel Sr. removed to Quabog, apparently Daniel Jr. lived on his father's homestead, and not being satisfied to have his new wife live in the old house, as soon as he obtained control of the premises, he got from the town the right to fell trees for a house." Hence the conclusion that what we have known as "The Old Hovey House" was built by him in 1668, and stood till 1894 when it was burned down. But some of us cling to the previously received idea that this ancient dwelling was the original home of our immigrant ancestor. It pleases our fancy to think of him as residing there, with his "loving and well-beloved" wife Abigail, and their six sons and "one dafter"; holding family councils under its rooftree; extending hospitality to their neighbors, and particularly honoring as a guest the learned teacher, Thomas Andrews, their "truly dear and well-beloved brother," who died July 10, 1683. The house was two story frame, with a "lean-to"; nine windows in front and four at the end, with small square panes, of which only those over the front door were "bullseyes." Around it were rocks and trees and in the distance Sagamore Hill was visible, overlooking the bay.

We cannot be denied a brief reference to the ancestry of Abigail Andrews, with whom Daniel Hovey says, "I did more than forty years ago match and by whom the Lord hath blessed me."

Our colonial ancestor, her father, retained the English way of spelling his name, signing it "Robert Andrewes"; the extra "e" in the final syllable being suggestive of the "ancient ancestry" of Suffolk County, England, that spelled it thus.

The widow of Thomas Andrewes, (Master of Trinity House), Mrs. Johane Andrewes, residing at London, on "Tower Hill, All Saints Barking," left a will which is found in "Genealogical Gleanings in England," Vol. I, p. 603. She mentions her son, Lancelot, the Bishop of Winchester, who lived in the reigns of Elizabeth, James I., (whom he assisted to crown), and Charles I. He was first in the list of fifty-four learned men selected to make what is known as King James' "authorized version" of the Bible. The will also mentions her son, Thomas; and her brother-in-law, William, to whom (along with Richard Ireland) she left "one-third part of the ship called 'the Mayflower,'" on certain conditions. It has pleased our fancy to imagine that this was the same ship on which the Pilgrims embarked for the New World, and on whose deck they made the celebrated Mayflower Compact. It is said that William afterwards, in 1633, came over and settled in Boston. This will likewise mentions a brother-in-law Robert Andrewes.*

---

* It is a curious fact that none of the earlier records of the Pilgrims ever mentioned the name of the vessel that brought them to these American shores. They always mentioned it as "the ship"—"the biger ship" or by some similar term, vague and uncertain, or else as the all-important ship to them. Antiquarians have identified twenty or thirty different vessels bearing the name "Mayflower." For a full discussion of this interesting subject, the reader is referred to "The Mayflower and her Log," by Azel Ames, Houghton-Mifflin Co., 1907, especially pages 94, 95 and 96.

The Bishop's will, found on pp. 609 and 610, of the same volume, names numerous relatives, among them his "cousin Robert Andrewes." Thomas and Richard Andrewes are mentioned in Bradford's Letter-Book, as among the forty-two merchant adventurers of London who financed the Plymouth Plantation; and Thomas at least belonged subsequently to the Massachusetts Company. Both names figure frequently on the pages of what is sometimes styled "The Log of the Mayflower."

How the foregoing persons stood related, if at all, to Captain Robert Andrewes, master and owner of the Angel Gabriel, we do not certainly know; but they shared in planting New England.

The Angel Gabriel was an armed ship that came as consort of the James, in August, 1635, and both were caught in a terrible thunder storm,* and had to part company. The James anchored near the Isles of Shoals, and the Angel Gabriel off Pemaquid, on the coast of Maine. The diary of Rev. Richard Mather, published by Dr. Young, in 1846, and republished by the Dorchester Antiquarian and Historical Society, gives an account of that disastrous gale, as it imperilled the James, which finally arrived "rent in sunder and split in pieces" in the Boston harbor. Mr. Mather remarks that "The Angel Gabriel was the first vessel which miscarried with passengers from Old England to New." It was built for Sir Walter Raleigh, and sailed from Bristol, England, and was of 240 tons burden, carrying sixteen guns. For a full account of the wreck of this gallant ship, we refer the reader to Chapter XI of a book entitled "Ten Years at Pemaquid," and to Vols. XXX, and XXXIX of the Massachusetts Archives. Omitting details it interests us that among the rescued passengers, besides Captain Andrewes and his family, were his three nephews, John, Thomas and Robert Burnham, sons of his sister Mary, who had been put under the charge of their uncle. These all, with a London merchant, named John Coggswell, afterwards settled in the town of Ipswich. From the town records it appears that large land grants were made in 1635 to Mr. Coggswell, and considerable grants were made to Robert Andrewes. The latter was also licensed to "keep ordinary (an inn) in the plantation where he lives during the pleasure of the court." It was agreed that he might sell wine, "if he do not unwittingly sell to such as abuse it by drunkenness." This was probably the first case of the kind in this region. Under the circumstances it proved the confidence men had in Mr. Andrewes as a man of discretion and integrity.

Consulting various histories and genealogies of the Andrews Family (e. g. the files of the Essex Antiquarian, the N. E. Hist.

---

* See "The Great Storm of 1635." Essex Antiq. Vol. I, p. 63.

and Gen. Register, the Andrews Memorial, by Rev. Alfred Andrews, the "History of the Andrews Family," by Hon. H. F. Andrews, etc.,) we find no little confusion as to the different dwelling-lots and land grants, owing to the fact that a number of representatives of the family with similar names, settled in Ipswich, Topsfield, Rowley and other adjoining places. Caldwell's "Antiquarian Papers" states that our Robert Andrews lived near the South Church, and he probably did.

In Waters's "Ipswich," p. 58, it is stated that road surveyors were appointed in January, 1640-1, and that Mr. Robert Andrews was one of the first four men designated for that responsible office. Their task was to transform crooked paths and grass-grown lanes into passable highways for ox-carts and primitive carriages. It was also their duty to detect encroachments on the roadways and to enforce the laws for repairing the same by the labor of all "youths above 14 years of age." They had power to call out all the Town for at least one day's work with men and teams for mending walls and wharves.

The will of Robert Andrewes, March first, 1643, mentions his wife, Elizabeth, his sons John and Thomas, his grandchildren, one of them being his "son-in-law Franklyn's daughter," and the other "my son Daniel Hovey's child, Daniel Hovey my grandchild." The mother of the former has been identified as Alice, and the mother of the latter was Abigail, as proved by Daniel Hovey's will. In order of age they were Alice, Abigail, John and Thomas. Robert Andrewes provided by his will for the education of his younger son, Thomas, who also had further aid by a legacy from John Ward, and became the school master of Ipswich, concerning whose estate Daniel Hovey made a certificate. (See pp. 12 and 13 of this book.) The will of Robert Andrewes names his nephews, John, Thomas and Robert Burnham, who were with him on the Angel Gabriel. The family of the Captain must have included our colonial grandmother, Abigail, who was married to Daniel Hovey six years later. John, mentioned in the will as the eldest son, must also have been a survivor of that shipwreck. Hammatt states that the latter was in the Pequot War, being first Corporal, then Lieutenant. He moderated the town meeting, August 23, 1687, when sturdy resistance was made to the tyrant, Sir Edmund Andros, who violated the terms of the charter of the colony by levying taxes without consent of the General Court. In memory of that event the seal of Ipswich bears the motto: "The Birthplace of American Independence, 1687." A memorial brochure of 16 pages has been published concerning this heroic Lieutenant, by Hon. H. F. Andrews, in 1909, expressing doubt as to his relationship to our Captain Robert Andrewes, of whom he may have been a brother instead of a son. Anyhow "it was all in the family." The authority above quoted is of the opinion that the name of Andrewes ceased with John Andrews of Salem, a shipwright, who was the grandson of Captain Robert, and had three daughters but no sons. We certainly hope this conjecture (which honesty requires us to give for what it may be worth) is groundless; for the descendants of Lieut. John Andrews now number many thousands, and have intermarried with many of the best families of Essex county and elsewhere.

Our conscientious genealogist has very wisely aimed to exclude conjectures from the body of this volume. Yet, in this introductory chapter it is not amiss to give brief room for some conjectures as to the origin of our ancestral name and allied lineage.

The name of "Hove," accented on the terminal syllable, is found in France, Holland, Norway and Sweden. So strongly was the late Rev. George L. Hovey, of Bricksburg, N. J., convinced of the identity of this name with his own, as to cause him to change the pronunciation accordingly. His theory was that the "y" was added to prevent the English name from being sounded as one syllable. This was also the theory of Gen. Charles E. Hovey, of Washington, D. C., and Prof. E. O. Hovey, of Newark, N. J.* The learned linguist, Dr. J. D. Butler, of Madison, Wis., derived our name from the Angle-Saxon words, "Hof," meaning a walled place, and the suffix "ey," meaning an island; the "f" being changed to "v" for euphony; the combination meaning "a walled island."

In my memoir of Daniel Hovey, published in 1900, another conjecture was offered, on the ground that "f" and "v" are often interchangeable; e. g. in the words "save" and "safe," "calf" and "calve," "half" and "halve," and in such proper names as "Farnam" and "Varnam." Possibly the "Hovey" of colonial days was identical with the "Hoffe" so frequently found in our early annals, and which Trumbull assumes to be the same as Goffe. Agawam (Ipswich) was settled in 1633 by John Winthrop, Jr., and twelve men, "the rest to be supplied at the coming of the next ships." The largest of these was the Griffin, on which Mr. Hoffe was a passenger. Winthrop's letters show that Hoffe and Goffe were not identical. In 1635, Winthrop, Dummer and Hoffe were chosen as assistants to Governor Haynes; and in 1637 Hoffe is again mentioned along with Dummer, Saltonstall and Wheelwright. It was in 1637 that the name of Hovey first appears in

* The fact is worth noting that the traditional original form of our family name, Hove, is given to a municipal borough of Sussex, England, with a population of about 37,000 souls, and an area of 1521 acres. It boasts a mayor, 10 aldermen and 30 councillors, and within its bounds is located the Sussex county cricket-ground. Although the parish of Hove is ancient, the incorporation of the borough only dates to 1898, having formerly been a part of Brighton, whose famous seawall continues along its border, forming a delightful promenade.

the records of Ipswich. Later Hovey's wharf is described as
Hoffe's wharf. These facts may not amount to proofs, but are
worth considering.

Our colonial sires were not exact spellers, and varied from
Hovey to Hovy, Hovie, Houey, etc. Mr. W. H. Ricker, an officer
of our Association, when in England, in 1910, gave this question
some attention. The rector of Waltham Abbey, Rev. J. M.
Stamp, suggested that the original name may have been "Tovi,"
dating back to the great Danish thane, Ralph de Tovi, the royal
standard bearer at whose wedding feast Hardicanute died, and on
whose land the famous Holy Cross was found which he brought
to Waltham and reared on a church built for its reception. Giving
this idea for what it may be worth, we are further assured by Mr.
Ricker that he had the satisfaction of seeing in the Waltham
Abbey vestment room the name of "Hovey," thus spelled, "in
bold, clear Saxon letters," thus proving that our own way is not
an American innovation. But he also says that "there is no place
yet known, except at Waltham, where the name was spelled
'Hovey' prior to 1590; but 'Houfe' was common in the older
Waltham MSS., and elsewhere. There was one Richard Houfe
in Lincolnshire in 1329, and another Houfe was buried in Westminster Abbey. The names of Houfe, Huffe and Huffee are
found in English history."

In our preliminary correspondence we have found only here
and there some one of our name in America who did not claim
descent from Daniel Hovey of Ipswich. Letters have come from
Canada, Ireland, Scotland and England sent by those of other
lines of ancestry. But the task has been sufficiently great to trace
the more immediate connections. And even here perfection in de-
tail must not be demanded. All we can say is that we have done
our best, and we hope that this volume may at least serve the purpose of bringing into better acquaintance the widely scattered
branches of our American family by the name of HOVEY.

Besides the tablet in memory of Daniel Hovey already mentioned, hundreds of monuments mark the resting-places of many
of his descendants. Among more public memorials may be spec-
ified the ornate oriel window over the main entrance to the
Centre Presbyterian Church at Crawfordsville, Indiana, for Professor Edmund O. Hovey, of Wabash College; the splendid window recently placed in St. John's Episcopal Church, Portsmouth,
N. H., in honor of its Rector, the Rev. Henry Emerson Hovey,
our beloved Vice-President; and the marble fountain also at
Portsmouth to commemorate his gallant son, Emerson Hovey,
Ensign in the U. S. Navy, who fell in battle in the Philippine
Islands.

As Ipswich has been the Mecca of our family pilgrimages, it is suggested that, ultimately, copies of all books and pamphlets published by any of our name; all available photographs and relics that may not be retained by private families; and all documents accumulated in the preparation of this Hovey Book, should be placed for safe-keeping and ready reference in the custody of the Public Library at Ipswich, in whose fire-proof building they may remain accessible to coming generations.

HORACE CARTER HOVEY.

ILLUSTRATIONS.

No fixed plan was adopted by the Publishing Committee concerning either the subjects or the styles of illustration. They simply sought to serve the tastes and wishes of the individual members of the Daniel Hovey Association, as far as these could be ascertained. A circular was issued opening the way for any member to send any material he pleased. Hence, there is much variety and individuality in the portraits to be found in this volume. Some portraits that might appropriately have place in it are missing merely because they were not offered, or else those offering them made no provision for meeting the expense of their insertion. Concerning views of historic localities and Hovey houses, a similar rule has been observed; and those used have been mainly such as were given and expense provided for by the interested parties.

Most of the engraving and printing of engravings has been done by the Walker Lithograph and Publishing Company of Boston, under the direction of our Publishing Committee.

The following is a list of the illustrations in the order in which they are introduced into these pages: —

1. Frontispiece. The Memorial Tablet of Daniel Hovey, in the Historical House at Ipswich; and the English Hovey Crest.

2. Horace Carter Hovey, D. D. President of the Daniel Hovey Association and one of the founders. (No. 1593.) Opp. page iv.

3. Rev. Henry Emerson Hovey. First Vice-President, and one of the founders of the Daniel Hovey Association. (No. 1558.) Opp. page viii.

4. Waltham Abbey, Essex county, England; exterior and interior views; and Waltham Abbey coat of arms. Opp. page 1.

5. Old Hovey Wharf at Ipswich (from photograph by H. C. Hovey). Built in 1659, and the oldest wharf existing in this region. Opp. page 9.

6. Old Hovey House in Ipswich; burned down in 1894. (From painting by E. Whitefield in 1888.) Opp. page 16.

7. Moulton-Hovey House, Mansfield, Conn. Home of the late Miss Julia Moulton, a recognized authority on Hovey genealogy. A Rev. Mr. Hovey also shared this home with her for several years. (No. 583—vi.—4.) Opp. page 24.

8. The Russell Church and the Elmwood House on the site of the old Russell home where the Regicides were hidden. In Hadley, Mass. Mr. Daniel Hovey lived in Hadley for two years and worshipped in this meeting-house. His son, Lieut. Thomas Hovey, was prominent in civil, military and church life in Hadley for many years. Opp. page 24.

9. Home of Rev. Dr. Ivory Hovey, at Mattapoisette, Mass. Built in 1740, and still standing as a relic of Colonial times. Opp. page 116.

10. Home of Aaron Hovey, who married Abigail Freeman, and his son, Edmund Hovey, at Mansfield, Conn. Opp. page 184.

11. Hovey-Farwell House, at Mansfield, Conn. Home of Aaron Hovey, who married Olive Farwell. Here also lived Roger Hovey in his youth. Now the property of Storrs Agricultural College. Opp. page 184.

12. Thomas Hovey, of Brighton, Mass. Drum-Major and Paymaster under Washington, in the Revolutionary Army. (No. 344.) Opp. page 200.

13. Home of George Hovey and his sister, Hannah Hovey. On Hovey Street, Ipswich, Mass. (Nos. 936 and 937.) Opp. page 232.

14. Rev. Aaron Hovey. Pastor at Saybrook, Conn., and Chaplain of the Seventh Regiment of Connecticut Militia. (No. 582.) Opp. page 246.

15. Mrs. Huldah (Ely) Hovey. Wife of Rev. Aaron Hovey. Opp. page 248.

16. Old Hovey Tavern, in Cambridge, Mass. Twice burned down, and rebuilt as now standing in 1728. Here the news was told of the Lexington alarm and of the Declaration of Independence. The early home of the Cambridge Free Masons. Opp. page 274.

17. The Dana Hovey Store, in Cambridge, Mass. Opp. page 274.

18. Hon. Alvin Peterson Hovey. Major General U. S. Volunteers. Member of U. S. Congress. Governor of Indiana. (No. 869.) Opp. page 286.

19. Edmund Otis Hovey, D. D. For 45 years identified with Wabash College, as founder, trustee and professor. (No. 1051.) Opp. page 306.

20. Henry Russell Hovey. Famous sea captain, and hero of many marine adventures. (No. 1068.) Opp. page 314.

21. Testimonial given to Captain Henry Russell Hovey by the City of New York. Opp. page 316.

22. Alvah Hovey, D. D., LL. D. Professor and president of the Newton Theological Institution, and author of numerous theological works. (No. 1081.) Opp. page 320.

23. Charles Edward Hovey, of Washington, D. C. Prominent educator. Major General U. S. Volunteers. (No. 1085.) Opp. page 324.

24. William Bowles Hovey, of Cambridge, Mass. Soldier in Mexican War. Popularly known as "Honest Hovey," and as "Butter Hovey." Deacon in Baptist Church. (No. 1204.) Opp. page 334.

25. Hovey House, at Crawfordsville, Indiana. Home for 60 years of the family of Prof. Edmund Otis Hovey, D. D. Opp. page 360.

26. Hovey House at Lowell, Mass. Home for many years of the family of Charles Hovey. Opp. page 366.

27. Memorial Drinking Fountain, at Portsmouth, N. H. Erected in honor of Ensign Charles Emerson Hovey, of the U. S. Navy. (No. 1959.) Opp. page 362.

28. Edmund Otis Hovey, Ph. D. For 20 years principal of the High School at Newark, N. J. (No. 1604.) Opp. page 370.

29. Richard Hovey. Poet, and Professor of English Literature in Barnard College, New York City. (No. 1655.) Opp. page 376.

30. Lewis Richard Hovey. Secretary of the Daniel Hovey Association and printer of this volume. Publisher of the Haverhill Record. (No. 1949.) Opp. page 394.

31. Edmund Otis Hovey, Ph. D. Geological Curator in the American Museum of Natural History, New York City; secretary of the G. S. A. A Vice-President of the Daniel Hovey Association. (No. 1997.) Opp. page 396.

32. Hamblin Levi Hovey. Banker and prominent in civic affairs at Waltham, Mass. A zealous and generous member of the Daniel Hovey Association. (No. 2225.) Opp. page 400.

Exterior and Interior views of Waltham Abbey, county of Essex, England, where Richard Hovey, and many of his family were baptized and worshipped, and in whose church-yard they were buried. Here his son, Daniel Hovey, was baptized, August 9, 1618. The town dates from the time of Ralph de Tovi, standard-bearer to Canute the Great, and the Abbey was originally built and adorned by Harold, and consecrated May 3, 1060. It is regarded as a noble specimen of the Northern Romanesque style of architecture.

PARENTAGE OF DANIEL HOVEY.

THE origin of Daniel Hovey, the ancestor of the American Hovey family, has hitherto been unknown to genealogists, and it would have continued to be a matter for investigation had it not been for a chance discovery in 1905 by John Albree of Swampscott, Mass. He was making a search in the Boston public library for a copy of a work mentioned in an account of the unfortunate Sir Henry Moody, son of Lady Deborah Moody, the versatile, interesting and almost forgotten English woman of noble birth and breeding who "was (good, poor lady) almost undone by buying Master Humphries farme. Swampscott." The library possesses four copies, and by chance the one Mr. Albree chose for examination proved to be the one with the record of the birth of Daniel Hovey. The title is : "G. de Saluste du Bartas: His Devine Weekes and Workes, with a Compleate Collection of all the other most delightfull Works Translated and written by y^t famous Philomusus Iosvah Sylvester Gent: London Printed by Humfrey Lownes, dwelling on Bread Street Hill, 1621."

The eye of the reader caught the following on page 200:—

> Daniel Hovey his boke hee was born in waltham aby ye 9th of Auguft 1618. Son of Richard Hovey of ye fam town. fent him by Mr John Gibons ye minifter of that town. fent him as a token from him in 37. ye yer of the pequod wars.   Daniel Hovey.*

This inspired further search, and on page 266 the record again appeared in different form:—

* See page 8.

I

Daniel Hovey
his Booke fent ouer
to him in 37 at y° pecod war
time
ffrom M' John Gibons
under hof miniftry he lived
at Waltham Abəy*

Could this be indeed fresh material ? Was it a fact that at
length had come to light a record made over two centuries ago ?
Was it an autograph ?   As to the last it was an easy matter to
verify the signature by that on the will at the Essex probate office
and other family papers.   It was also readily found that no
record was known as to the place of Hovey's birth, nor as to the
exact date.   Why should he have chosen this book for this
record?   The thought suggested itself to Mr. Albree that
some knowledge of the personality of the founder of the Hovey
family and his associates might be found in the book.

The volume itself is a large octavo of thirteen hundred
pages, bound in full leather.   In the middle of each cover are the
letters D and H. stamped deeply, each being separated with a
conventional bookbinder's design.   These are the initials of
Daniel Hovey's name; and does the fact that they are in so conspicuous a place indicate that he had a pride in the possession of
his books ?   Possibly these initial letters may have been stamped
on the covers in England as the book was about to be presented
to young Daniel, who was then but nineteen.   In his will he
makes specific bequests of books, and from their number and
character it is known that he had a good library.   This particular
book, however, is not mentioned by name.   But there is sufficient
internal evidence to trace the book into his possession, by the
entries in different styles of chirography and at various dates.

On the inside of the front cover is written:—

Mary Wise.

At page 155 is this orphic statement, not however in Hovey's
handwriting:—

Antoni cruden
40s Pope

On page 556 are written in different handwritings these
several statements:—

* See page 8.

Francis Wainwrights, Book: 1702-3
Bought of Dan¹¹ Hovey:
Feb 16ᵗʰ 1702/3 Pretium: 12ˢ; 06ᵈ; 00ˢᵗ

Daniell Hovey
His Booke:
Left him by his Grand
ffather
Witneſs Nath Ruſt juʳ
who borrowed this book of fᵈ Hovey
For
Francis Wainwrights, Book:
Anno: 1702/3

The second of these statements, that of the grandson, is
crossed out, perhaps by some later owner who thought that in this
way he could dispose of any evidence of possession or ownership
by another.

On page 1216 is found:—

Ex Libris F Wainwright

On another page is the record of still another transfer:—

5: 2: 17.
Joſepho Levallo*
Ex Dono D. Francifce Wainwright
Amici
(Januar: rio insunto)
Lectorib

The history of the ownership of the volume appears to be
complete and without a break from Daniel Hovey. It went first
by will to the grandson Daniel, then by sale to Francis Wainwright, and then, by gift, to Joseph Sewall, who was the pastor
of the Old South Church, in Boston. Thomas Prince, who accumulated the Prince library, was his associate, and a number of
Sewall's books are in the Prince library now, whether by gift or
purchase is not material at this late day.

Guillaume de Salluste du Bartas, the author of this book,
was a French poet, born in 1544, who died of wounds received in
the battle of Ivry, having commanded a troop of horse in Gas-
cony. His principal work, "La Divine Sepmaine," an epic poem
on the creation of the world, was so popular that thirty editions
were issued within six years after 1579, when it first appeared. It
was translated into Gascon French, Italian, Spanish, German,

* "Levallo" is probably intended for "Sevallo," i. e. "Seuallo," "Sewall."

English, Latin, and, later, Swedish and Danish.[*] Its style and religious tone made it a great favorite with English writers in his time, and was influential in forming English style. Joshua Sylvester, a Spenserian poet, translated this as well as the "Weekes and Workes" of Du Bartas into English. This poem is divided into portions for reading each week, hence the name "Weekes."

After the discovery of this book and the manuscript entries, Mr. Albree wrote to the clerk of the parish of Holy Cross, Waltham, England, requesting verification of the record. The curate, Rev. J. Henry Stamp, answered, saying that the parish registers were under his charge, and enclosing an attested copy of the record of baptism of Daniel Hovey, which corresponded exactly with the statement in the book. He, also, subsequently sent copies of all the Hovey baptisms, marriages and burials recorded in the register, copies of several issues of a monthly historical publication issued by the parish, and five views of the church. The publication contained much of the history of the parish and information concerning Rev. John Guibon, who gave the book to Daniel Hovey. The copies of records sent by Rev. Mr. Stamp are as follows:—

Extracted from the Parish Register in the Abbey Church of Waltham Holy Cross in the County of Essex: England on Oct. 28, 1905 by me.
J. Henry Stamp: Curate.

April 1597.
Burialls: Agnes Hovey the daughter of Rychard Hovey: Glover buried ye 13 dai.

October 1602
Baptizings: Margret Hovey daughter of Rychard Hovey bapt ye 10 daye

Febuarii 1604[-5]
Baptizings: Janne Hovey daughter to Rychard Hovey ye 3 daye

December 1607.
Baptizings: ffrancis Hovey son to Rychard Hovey ye 20 [day]

Aprill 1610.
Baptizings: Jeames Hovey son to Rychard Hovey ye 15 [day]

Aprill 1612.
Bapt: John Hovey, son to Rychard Hovey the 19 day

ffebruary 1614[-5].
Baptizings: Isabell Hovy daughter to Richard Hovy bapt[d] 26 day

September 1616
Baptizings: Katharin Hovey daughtr of Richard Hovy bap. 8 day

August 1618
Baptisings: Daniell Hovey, sonne too Richard Hovey, baptised 9 day.

[*] See Poetes Francais, by Philoxene Boyer, volume II, page 234; Fraser's Magazine, Neglected Poets.

October 1634

Marryages: Roger Coker and Katherine Hovey married the 5 day

March 1636[-7]

Burials: Richard Hovy a Glover was buried the 7 day

September 1637

Marriages: John Hovey and Joan ffowller married the 17 day

July 1638

Baptizings: Margret Hovy, daughter to John Hovy as all so to Joan the 22 day

October 1638

Burialls: Margret Hovey, the daughter of John Hovy the 20 day

May 1640.

Baptizings: Elizabeth Hovey daughter to John Hovey as well as to Joan the 10 day.

October 1641.

Burialls: a child of John Hovey's ye 24 day

November 1647.

Baptizings: Margret Hovy, daughter to John Hovy as all so to Joan the 13 day.

May 1649.

Burialls: Richard Hovey the sonne of John Hovey buried the 29 day

May 1651.

Burialls: A nurse Child of the widow Hovey's the 9 day

August 1653

Burialls: Widow Hovey the elder was buried the 29 day

August 1658

Burialls: Joan Hovey Wid Relict of John Hovey ye 23 day.

The certified copy of Daniel Hovey's baptism is as follows:—

August 1618.

Baptisinges:

Daniell Hovey, sonne too Richard Hovey, baptized 9 day.*

I hereby certify that the above is a true copy of the entry recorded in the Register of the Parish of Waltham Hily Cross, otherwise Waltham Abbey, in the County of Essex, England, as witness my hand this 3^d day of Novr 1905.

J. HENRY STAMP,
Curate.

| Revenue Stamp. |

Genealogically, these records constitute the following arranged families:—

RICHARD HOVEY[1], glover, lived at Waltham Abbey, in Essex; and died there, being buried March 7, 1636-7, probably at about the age of sixty-one or sixty-two. Children:—

1. AGNES[2], buried April 13, 1597.
2. MARGARET[2], baptized Oct. 10, 1602.
3. JANNE[2], baptized Feb. 3, 1604-5.
4. FRANCIS[2], baptized Dec. 20, 1607.
5. JAMES[2], baptized April 15, 1610.

* Volume III, page 137.

6. JOHN², baptized April 19, 1612. *See below (6).*
7. ISABELL², baptized Feb. 26, 1614-5.
8. KATHERINE², baptized Sept. 8, 1616; married Roger Coker Oct. 5, 1634.
9. DANIEL², baptized Aug. 9, 1618; emigrated to Ipswich, Mass., in 1635, at the age of seventeen.

(6) JOHN HOVEY², married Jane Fowler Sept. 17, 1637; he died before May 9, 1651; and Aug. 23, 1658, his widow, Joan Hovey, was buried. Children:—

1. MARGARET³, baptized July 22, 1638; she died, and was buried Oct. 20, 1638.
2. ELIZABETH³, baptized May 10, 1640.
3. ————³, buried Oct. 24, 1641.
4. MARGRET³, baptized Nov. 13, 1647.
5. RICHARD³, buried May 29, 1649.
6. ————³, "a nurse child" of the widow Hovey, buried May 9, 1651.

What is now the town or village of Waltham Holy Cross, known as Waltham Abbey, as far back as the days of Hardicanute, was the hunting lodge of the Danish thane Tovi or Tovius, known as Tovi the Proud. Tovi subsequently founded there a small convent; and, through the wastefulness of Tovi's son Atheston, his family lost the grant in the days of Edward the Confessor. Waltham reverted to the crown; and it was subsequently granted to Harold, who built a new church or enlarged the existing one, dedicating the foundation to the Holy Cross May 3, 1060. Harold's body was buried by the high altar in the church. After the Conquest, various benefactions were received. Queen Maud gave a mill and Queen Adeliza the tithes of Waltham to the abbey, while from Stephen was received the confirmation of all privileges.*

The great forest there was long known as the forest of Waltham, and the part yet remaining is called Epping forest.

At Waltham Cross is the beautiful cross erected between 1291 and 1294 by Edward I. at one of the resting places of the corpse of Queen Eleanor while on its way to burial in Westminster Abbey. It is of Caen stone, and is supposed to have been designed by Pietro Cavalini, a Roman sculptor.

Waltham Abbey, or Waltham Holy Cross, is a market town of Essex county, and lies thirteen miles north of the Liverpool street station, London, on the Cambridge branch of the Great Eastern Railway. The town lies in a hollow, and the streets are for the most part crooked and narrow.

Waltham was the home of John Fox, the martyrologist, and there a considerable portion of his work was written.

* See "Essex: Highways, Byways, and Waterways," second series, by C. R. B. Barrett, London, 1893, pages 198-208.

The parish has had several famous minisiters. Rev. John Guibon, who presented the copy of Du Bartas' "Weekes and Workes" to Daniel Hovey, was a resident of Waltham as early as 1629, and succeeded to the curacy of the Abbey church. He left Waltham in 1640, going to London, where he appears to have been preferred to the living of St. Anne's, near Aldersgate. He eventually became a member of the Westminster Assembly of Divines, and was elected chairman of one of the three committees into which the Assembly was divided. Like his great predecessor, Bishop Hall, Mr. Guibon retained his affection for his old parish. He was ejected from the living of St. Anne's, and soon after died of consumption, the burial taking place in Waltham.

The following is an exact copy of the autographic statement of Daniel Hovey on page 266 of Du Bartas' "Devine Weekes and Workes":—

[autographic handwritten statement]

The following is an exact copy of the autographic statement of Daniel Hovey on page 200 of Du Bartas' "Devine Weekes and Workes":—

[autographic handwritten statement]

DANIEL HOVEY
AND HIS DESCENDANTS.

 ANIEL HOVEY[1], the ancestor of the American Hoveys, was born at Waltham Abbey, in Essex county, England, Aug. 9, 1618, being son of Richard Hovey, a glover, of that place. He was apparently a man of education, and the fact that the curate of his parish church was friendly to and interested in him while he was in his teens and far away in a strange land, indicates that there were elements in his character which drew and held attention to him. He was one of the early settlers of Ipswich, Massachusetts, in 1635, at the age of seventeen. Feb. 5, 1637, the town granted to him six acres of land on Muddy creek; and also "Granted to Daniell Hovey, an house lott, 1 acre of ground on the South syde of the Town River, having a house lott, granted to William Holdred on the West, and a house lott granted to Thomas Sherman on the East. Also six acres of planting ground, lying on Sagamore Hill, having a planting lott, formerly granted Henry Wilkinson on the West, and a planting lott granted to William Holdred on the East: to enjoy the sayde Landes, to him, his heirs, or assigns forever. Entered this 27th day of March 1639."* The freemen of the town granted to William Holdred a house lot of half-an-acre adjoining Daniel Hovey's on the southwest, being on the south side of the river, and bounded by the house lot of Roger Preston on the southwest; also six acres of planting ground on Sagamore hill adjoining Daniel Hovey's planting lot west, and the planting lot of Roger Preston on the east; the grants being entered April 9, 1639; and both of these lots were conveyed by Mr. Holdred to "Daniel Hovey of Ipswich, planter," and, also, one dwelling house built on the house lot and all the fencing belonging to both lots. Entered April 10, 1639.*

* Town records.

9

Feb. 10, 1644, the town of Ipswich ordered that Mr. Hovey be paid three shillings for killing three foxes.

In 1648, he subscribed three shillings three times a year to Maj. Daniel Denison, "so long as he shall be their leader, to encourage him in his military helpfulness," the whole annual sum being twenty-four pounds and seven shillings, and the largest subscription ten shillings.

Mr. Hovey was somewhat prominent, and held several town offices in Ipswich, being chosen one of the selectmen Feb. 14, 1659; a surveyor of highways in 1648-9 and 1649-50; and a constable in 1658. In 1656, he was one of a committee to set up a saw mill on Chebacco river. The selectmen ordered, 12: 12: 1650, that Symon Tomson and Daniell Hovey shall view a certain parcel of land.* In 1649, he was a juror at Ipswich court.

In the county court which sat at Ipswich 29: 1: 1642, Mr. Hovey was plaintiff in three civil actions. One was against James Pitney and James Howe, in which he recovered judgment for nine bushels of corn; one against Jo: Lee, which was not tried; and the other was against George Varnham and Jo: North, which was continued.

Daniel Hovey was granted a highway to go to his lot in, by the town of Ipswich, March 4, 1650.*

22: 12: 1652, the town gave him liberty to set his fence down to the river at his ground which he bought of William Knowlton, making a stile at each end.*

At a town meeting held Feb. 14, 1659, Daniel Hovey was granted liberty to build a wharf against his ground that he bought of William Knowlton, and, also, such building as may tend to the improvement thereof.*

Mr. Hovey was living on his farm in Topsfield in 1663 and 1664. Jan. 15, 1663, he was chosen one of two persons to lay out some land.†

Mr. Hovey was complained of for speaking falsely to the prejudice of General Denison, and was fined twenty shillings in Ipswich court Sept. 24, 1667. The records show that in some case, in which evidently General Denison acted as magistrate, Mr. Hovey said that Major Denison did not write his determination nor state his sentence in public, and what was done occurred after he was gone, and that John Gould whispered in the major's ear as he was going away.‡ Magistrates did not allow themselves to be criticised in those days.

In May, 1660, a colony went from Ipswich to Quaboag,§ a place subsequently named Brookfield; and Daniel Hovey joined

* Ipswich town records.
† Topsfield town records.
‡ Court records and files.
§ Also, Quabeg and Quabaugh.

it in 1668. His sons James and Thomas went with him. The lots of land laid out to the father and sons adjoined, and were situated easterly of the little brook, on the north side of the road. Daniel Hovey was living in Quaboag in May, 1672, and settled in Hadley before the massacre at Quabog in 1675.

While in Hadley, he lived on a farm of Mr. Henry Clerke: and Mr. John Russell, jr., and Mr. Peter Tilton, sr., executors of the will of Mr. Clerke of Hadley, deceased, brought an action against Mr. Hovey, at the court in Springfield Sept. 26, 1676. for withholding rent due to said plaintiffs "for a ffarm or Land of yᵉ sayd Mr. Henry Clerkes which yᵉ sayd Hovey hath Occupyed as a tenement."* The jury found a verdict for the plaintiffs, and awarded them fourteen pounds damages, due in 1676.† At the succeeding term of court held at Springfield the same year, Mr. Hovey brought suit against Mr. John Russell, jr., being an "Action of unjust molestation in a Suite at yᵉ last Corte at Springfield & for uncharitable Charges to yᵉ defamation or Slandour of the sᵈ Danˡˡ Hovey & his Wife & Charging yᵉ sᵈ Danˡˡ to be a man of a Scandolous life in an Open Asembly & therefore was denyed Church Comunion & this threatened to be made Out to his Church and yᵗ he belonged too & all yᵉ Churches thereaboute." The jury found a verdict for Mr. Hovey.‡ Whether these proceedings and the unhappy contentions that must have been engendered by them had aught to do with his departure from Hadley or not the writer does not know; but Mr. Hovey returned to Ipswich in 1678.

While living in Hadley, he suffered much at the hands of the Indians, and was also a sharer in providing defence for the town. Three years after his return to Ipswich, he sent to the colonial council a petition, an exact copy of which, copied from the original instrument on file in the Massachusetts archives, at the state house in Boston, is as follows:—§

To the Honoured Council now sitting in Boston; the humble petition of Daniel Hovey of Ipswich,

Wheras your humble petitioner was an inhabitant of Hadly in the time of the late Indian warrs, and there expended (beside my losses) much of my Estate in the Countreys service against the common enemy; and since that time was removed thence by Providence to Ipswich, where I have remained now these three yeers last past; and by reason of the remote distance fro Hadly and want of intelligence thence I missed the opportunity of sending in my last accoᵗˢ together with my neighbours there, to the last Sessions of the Genˡˡ Court; which caused me much labour and long travell thither from Ipswich: yet at the last I have gained a certificate of those my Expences from the Committee of Militia in

* Records in probate office at Northampton, Mass., volume I, page 177.
† Records in probate office at Northampton, Mass., volume I, page 189.
‡ Records in probate office at Northampton, Mass., volume I, page 190.
§ Massachusetts Archives, volume LXX, document 58.

Hadley, being the last of mine Expences there on the Countreys service; amounting to 11ᵗᵇ 13ˢ 08ᵈ; as by the said Certificate doth fully appear : now my humble request and petition is, that yoʳ Honoʳˢ would be pleased to grant me an Order to the Constables of Ipswich that I may receive the said Sums there; where my setled residence is, and have no commerce or dealing at Hadley : that so I may discount my present Rates, and may have the residue for the relief of my family, which hath been much straitned by my losses and expences there in time of the warrs, and by rates both then and since. The Lord direct your counsells and afsist yoʳ endeavoʳˢ in all weighty transactions now in hand, that we may rejoice and blefs God under yoʳ good governmᵗ continued over us. so prayeth

Yoʳ humble petitioner,

DANIEL HOVEY.

The order thereon was as follows:—

28 ffebruary

It is ordered that the Trefurer pay vnto Daniel Hovey of Ipswich the Sume of Eleven poun[n]ds out of there Country Rate in full of all his Accounˢ in Controversy

p councill   EDW RAWSON Secreᵗʸ

Councils act to pay Danl Hovey 11ᵗᵇ 1681.

The selectmen of Ipswich granted to him six pine trees, presumably for timber, at two times, three on Jan. 2, 1678, and three Dec. 15, 1679.*

Daniel Hovey married Abigail, daughter of Robert and Elizabeth (Franklin?) Andrews of Ipswich, about 1641. Mr. Andrews died in 1643, having given to Mr. Hovey a legacy of ten pounds. In the settlement of the estate of Mrs. Hovey's brother Thomas Andrews, a prominent schoolmaster, Mr. Hovey certified to the county court as follows:—†

September 27. '83

Thefe may inform this Honored Cort. & may it pleafe your Honors. to take notis touching the relations of this worthy gentilman Mʳ Thomas Andrews. my truly louing dear & wel. beloved Brother &c.   I did more then forty years ago. match wᵗᵇ his Louing & welbeloved fifter Abigal Andrews. by home the lord bleft me wiᵗᵇ fix fons. & on dafter. five of which fons ar yet liuing fo that by thes it may apear that we ar fuerly related to this defefed gentlman. but in breif he hath fix nefews & two nefes. as. folows their is the fon and dafter of his brotheʳ as namly John. Andrews & fara Connant his fifter both which are Confiderably deters vnto his eftate as alfo Mʳˢ Elifibeth Glouer wo is married to Mʳ John Glouer formerly liuing at Bofton now at fwanfy wᶜᵇ alfo is deter to the eftate ther is myfelf alfo deter to yᵉ eftate five fhilins vpon the prifin of fom things he lent me for my prefent vs & gaue me order to vfe & kep them til he Caled for them. there is Daniel & John Hovey two of his nefews deter to the eftate for fcolin their Children about four pounds. their is alfo Thomas, Jofeph & nathaniel Hovey. thre of his nefews wᶜᵇ never had the value of on fhiling of the eftate of their unkls that I know of. I humbly draw your favor to ouerlook my weaknes in indevrin to lay this narative befor your Honors. yᵗ when their fhal aper a vifibl eftat of my Loving Brothers youe mav haue fo much as thef

* Town records.

† Court files, clerk of courts office, Salem, volume XL, leaf 63.

few lines may aford as touching the fetling of his eftat upon his relations
that we quietly & peafably wth ye lords bleſing may haue the benifit of the
vf of y^t his eſtate wch he left vndiſpoſed of now the good lord of
heven ſo influenſ your heads & hearts by ye lit of his holy ſpirit as that
a *Gevin* ſentans may proſed frome you as god may haue honor your-
felus ioy in the day of Chriſt & no perſons or perſon may haue cauſe of
complaint but that we may bleſ god for his merſy to ſe juſtis & judg^t
ſil runin in our ſtrets. ſo prays your humble petitioner.

Daniel Rypney, ſini.

　　The real estate transactions to which Mr. Hovey was a party
besides those that were grants from the town in the earlier
days are as follows: He owned, with others, twenty-five acres
of marsh, which was divided Jan. 30, 1658.* He bought seventy
acres of upland and meadow in Topsfield, bounded north and
northeast by the pond, east by a part of the Ipswich commons,
south by upland and meadow of Robert Andrews and west by
common land and meadow, June 12, 1660.† When he was living
at Quabog, he conveyed a piece of marsh and "my farm in Topsfield wch my son John now liveth in, to him he surrendering to me
his land in Ipswich," and paying forty pounds and allowing to
the grantor thirty shillings a year during the latter's life; and
also "my division of land at wheall brooke," June 13, 1671.‡
While Mr. Hovey was still at "Quabaugh," he conveyed one-half
of an acre of land in Ipswich, lying on the south side of the river,
together with the frame of a house standing on the adjoining
land of his son Daniel and some shingles at Topsfield, May 8,
1672.§ When Mr. Hovey lived at Hadley he sold twenty-four
rods of land in Ipswich, being part of that lot called Knowlton's
lot, on the south side of the river, May 1, 1677.‖ After Mr.
Hovey's return to Ipswich, he sold one and one-half acres of
plowing land lying on the south side of the river in Ipswich, Feb.
11, 1688-9.¶ He also conveyed six acres and seventy-one square
rods of pasture land in Ipswich April 23, 1689.** He also conveyed one and one-half acres of plowing land in Ipswich, lying
on the south side of the river, next to the lot last above described,
Oct. 12, 1689.††

　　Mrs. Hovey died between 1676 and 1683. He died in Ipswich April 24, 1692. His will was proved Oct. 31, 1692.

　　* Ipswich Deeds, book 1, page 245.
　　† Ipswich Deeds, book 1, page 239.
　　‡ Ipswich Deeds, book 4, page 114.
　　§ Ipswich Deeds, book 3, page 227.
　　‖ Ipswich Deeds, book 4, page 99.
　　¶ Ipswich Deeds, book 5, page 333.
　　** Ipswich Deeds, book 5, page 306.
　　†† Ipswich Deeds, book 5, page 334.

The following is a copy of the original document on file in the probate office at Salem: —

I Daniell Hovey fenier of Ipfidg Confidrin the changes of man doe defier by the help of the Lord to fetel my concerns as may be for the glory of god and the good of my family my fole I defir to resign and Comit unto the hand of my Lovin ffather in Jefus Chrift ho is the Lord my Ritofnis my body to be desently buried in erth in hop of a glorious and blefed reserectio by chrift amen

Itt The ftat which god of his grace hath giuen me I haue difpofd of af folows to my Eldest fonf Daniell and John houey and my daftor Airs I haue giuen them thire proptions of yt Eftat I had to our mutuall content y° one at Ipfig ye other in Topsfill Now in their pofefon Abigals paid by my fon John to my fon Airs:

Itt To my fon Thomas and James his fon Daniell I give all that my lland caled houeys lland which with the thatchbanks and Low marfh belongin to me on the other fid the crek which I a Lowed quarter mafter Perkins to improue holdin my pofefion till I had ocafion for fam alfo all y' houfe and Land in Ipfig y' I fhall not difpos of befor deth

Itt I giue to my fon Jofeph and Nathanil Houey one hundred rods of ground a pice Joseph bounded Next to m' Emersons Land from y° hiway to y' Land Daniell Ringes Nathanil one hundred rod of my Land Next to my fon Daniell with y° dweling hous Barn part of y° orchard to but on Danil Ring: half planting Lot a bout three acres w' a way to it or y° bridg I made to go to it three acrs at plum lland alfo: which Lands I Leaue in y° hands of my Executor and overfcars: y' if left after my deth To be difpofed of af folows: the Children of Jofeph Hovey: to haue an equall proporfhon of what if Left after my D:th: as to y' father Legaci: the children of my fon Nathaniell to haue an Equall proporfhon: amounxt y™ only Nathaniell Houey y° fon of Nathaniell Houey to haue a duble pro porfhon: if he Liue to y° eage of one and twenty if not y° to be diuided among y° other Children of y' family:

Itt my mouables to my fon Nathaniell thofe sheep he hath of mine to his children: my cart and plow Irons chains great tramill great braf cittell Iron Cettell Little Iron pot: my poutter poringer and drincking Cup with one chamber pot: and my wife wearing aparell to Nathaniell children: the other to Jofeph his brothers children all my wearing cloths my great braf pot and putter pot and my great bible an dbooks af faloweth: come to chrift and wellcom Cotten one y° Connant mader: 7: farmons to Nathaniell Children to Daniell gran child thofe fheep with w' hif mafter and books alfo Christian warfer Caluen one Job tenn deuins y° golden fepter with what other Books undefpofd by me of mine and fhuch towls for his trade as are futable of mine: to Abigel Hodgkins wife of Thomas Hodgkins y° brafe pan and a putter falfeller, my part of y° meare and colt to gran child Daniell and luory

Itt my entreit of brockfeld and fwampfeld I giue to my fon Jofeph and Nathaniell children

Itt I make my fon Thomas Executor and would haue his Nephu in cafe he Liues to eage if capable to Joyne in y° fame w' him and he to pay out of his part to his brother James and fister prafila and John Aires tenn pounds a pice within thre   after his pofefon and in Cafe of his deth I put James Houey in his Rome and Let y™ four Equally deuid hif part: my bed bolster and pillow w' my gren Rug a paier of 'lanckits. w' y° bedfted to Daniell gran child, I would haue my fon John of topsfeld to tack in to his pofefhon with his Books:

Itt I doe apoynt my Louing fons Daniell Houey: and John Hovey to be overfers: of this my Laft will; and fe: to difcharg my ffunerall Chargis which I alow four pounds Eftat: and to take any: inventary of my estate: and discharge all my dets and make probet of my will: and to fe his Nephnfe haue their equall proporfhon: Joseph and [torn] children how haue lately defefed: for which I a Low my our fears three pounds apice for their ceare and truble: This is my will: as witnes my hand and feal

wittnesis
PHILEMON DANE
THOMAS HODGKINS

Daniel Egovey foniur

aged fevnty three & goin to
fevnty fower this on &
twentieth day of march on
thoufand   fix   hundred
ninty on or two   (SEAL)

The following is a copy of the inventory of the estate of Daniel Hovey:—

An Inuentory of the Estate of Daniell Houey fener Defeafid The twenty forth of April (1692)

	£	s	d
Itam. The homfted w^t about three eacres Tilidg Land	50	00	00
Itam one eacer of Low ground w^t a bout 3 eacers Tilidg	24	00	00
Itm in Nolton Lot a bout one eacor w^t houfe and wharf	35	00	00
Itam: Iland of upland and faltmarfh Containing about 18 eacers y^t if caled Houey's Iland	80	00	00
Itam 3 ecors marfh at plum IlfLand by ye knobs	3	10	00
Itam about one Eacer of falt march	6	00	00
ffether beed a bolfter and pillow a gren Rodg and 2 blanckits	7	00	00
Itam Seuerall books y^t weare ualued at	5	00	06
Itam in Neat Cattell 3 bullock one cow	18	15	00
Itam in fheep 20^s half a mare half 2 yeareling Colt	3	10	00
Itam to Lining 34^s and wolling cloth much worne w^t feurall other old things	3	15	00
Itam to wolling cloathing one camblit fut 2 pearc of fhufe	3	16	00
Itam houfe hold goods nauily pcutter and braife	4	10	6
Itam husbandery tolef cart lorns and plow lorns whip faw	2	10	00
Itam armes and amanifhon	00	14	00
	248	01	00
Itam one brafe pot	001	00	00

may the 21: 1692 Leftenant Burnam and Philemon dane
we are ye prifers of ye a boufe Named preticulers

The children of Daniel and Abigail Hovey were born in Ipswich as follows:—

2—I.   DANIEL², born in 1642. *See family numbered "2."*
3—II.   JOHN², born in 1644. *See family numbered "3."*
4—III. THOMAS², born in 1648. *See family numbered "4."*
5—IV.   JAMES², born 1650. *See family numbered "5."*
6—V.   JOSEPH², born in 1653. *See family numbered "6."*
7—VI.   ABIGAIL², married John Ayers before 1692.
8—VII. NATHANIEL², born March 20, 1657. *See family numbered "8."*

2

DANIEL HOVEY[2], born in Ipswich in 1642. He was a husbandman, and always lived in his native town. He was made a freeman March 11, 1673-4; and held several offices in the town. He was a fence viewer in 1671, having been chosen by the commoners and confirmed by the selectmen; a surveyor in 1671; a tithing man in 1681; a constable in 1691 and 1693.

The selectmen of Ipswich granted to Mr. Hovey, Nov. 27, 1668, the right to fell trees for a house. This ancient Hovey house stood upon the south side of the river, and was burned July 17, 1894.‡ It had been untenanted since 1877, its great chimney had been torn down, and the building used as a hay-barn. Over the front door were bull's eye panes of glass. The engraving on the opposite page is the most picturesque picture of the old house extant. It was made by E. Whitefield in 1888. The house had been owned by strangers for about half a century.

March 2, 1670-1, the selectmen granted to Daniel Hovey timber for a neb and axletree. Jan. 17, 1680, the selectmen granted him liberty to fell some more trees. In 1683, the town paid him three pounds and eighteen shillings "for fetching the boat from ye Island."

Among the papers on file in the office of the clerk of courts at Salem, in the settlement of the estate of Thomas Andrews of Ipswich, the schoolmaster, is the following certificate of Daniel Hovey as to the heirs of the deceased:—

Thefe may Informe This Hon^rd Court held at Salem Novemb^r 1683. That the children of the sister of the deseafe m^r Thomas Andrews : vizt Abigaell Houy their names are as follow: vizt Daniell Houy Jno Houy Thomas: Jofeph & Nathaniell: m^r Andrews his sister Franklings daughters name is Elizabeth Glouer.

Nouemb^r 30. 1683
    p me

Daniell Hovey jun

The only real estate transactions recorded in the registries of deeds in which Mr. Hovey was a party was a deed, dated May 3, 1694, by which he conveyed twenty acres of upland and salt marsh in Labor-in-vain field in Ipswich, on the south side of the town river, and six acres of pasture at Heartbreak hill on the south side of the river;* and a conveyance from his brother Thomas of one acre of land in Labor-in-vain field in Ipswich, on south side of the river, March 23, 1694.†

Mr. Hovey married, first, Rebecca ———, who died, on the day her son Daniel was born, May 24, 1665. He married, second, Esther, daughter of Thomas Treadwell of Ipswich Oct. 8, 1666.

---

* Essex Registry of Deeds, book 9, leaf 277.
† Essex Registry of Deeds, book 39, leaf 27.
‡ See Introduction. (H. C. H.)

Mr. Hovey died in Ipswich May 29, 1695, at about fifty-three years of age.

The following is a copy of Mr. Hovey's will, which is on file in the probate office at Salem :—

This is the last Will of Danell Houey ayged a bout 53 yers

I give my sole to god who gave it mee and my bode my will is that it shold bee desent ly bered and I hope for a ioy full resaxsion throu the ritosnes of ieses christ my redeemer:

and as for my esteate that god hath ginen mee: I giue as foloeth

itin I giue onto Ester my wife one rume in the hous and the benefit of half the scler for her use during her natral life and allso I giue her all the mouobals goods in my house to my wife to bee at her one dissposing, and allso I giue her tow cows to be kept for her benifit yerly and sixe shep during her lif and all so my wil is that my excutors shall tend all my plouing land and bring into my wife own therd of the Corne yerly for her benifit and allso I giue my wife all the frut of the orchard during her lif:

ittam: I giue on to my son john twenty pounds to be paid by my excutors to be paid within thre yers after my deth in mercentabale corne or catell as gose between man and man:

I giue on to my son Ebenezer twenty pounds to be paid him by my excutars when he come to the ayg of on an twenty yers old

itom I giue onto my daftor Abigal ten pounds to be paid her by my excutars with in thre yers after mi deth:

Itom I giue on to my dafter mara twenty pounds to be paid her with in tow yers after my deth

and I do mack my tow sons Nathaniell Hofe and Thomas houe my excutars of this my wil as witnes my hand this 26 may 1695 and sele

I desier Decken foster and Nathaniell Tredwell: sen: to be my ouersers of this my will

witneses   DANILL HOVEY SE

PHILEMON DANE
OFFIN BOURMAN

This will was proved June 25, 1695.

The following is a copy of the inventory of Mr. Hovey's estate, which is also on file in the probate office at Salem :—

A True Inuentory of all & Singular y° Goods Chattels rights & Credits of Daniell Houey Seni° Deceased & Apprized in Ipswich as pay y° 15th of June 1695 by y° Subfcribers as ffollows

	l	s	d
Imp°mis His houfes & Lands	470	00	00
his Cattle horfes Sheep & Swine & ct	056	00	00
his wearing Apparrell	066	12	00
his houfhold Stufe & Vtensils of hufbandrey & ct	060	02	00
Totall is	592	14	00

JACOB FFOSTER SENER
PHILEMON DANE

Debts due to y° Estate   11¹: 13°:—
Debts due from the Estate
83 3 3

The inventory was sworn to by Thomas Hovey, executor, April 1, 1696.

Thomas Hovey, the surviving executor of the will of Daniel Hovey, with his mother and his brothers and sisters, viz.: John Hovey, Ebenezer Hovey, Abigail Hodgkins, Mary Hovey and Thomas Hodgkins, all of Ipswich, conveyed a six-acre lot of pasture land in Ipswich, in Labor-in-vain field, on the north side of Heartbreak hill, June 28, 1697.[*]

The same executor conveyed two acres of planting land in the same field, on the south side of the river, May 2, 1704;[†] and he also conveyed to his brother Ebenezer Hovey four acres of marsh on Barr island in Ipswich, bounded westerly by the river, July 20, 1704.[‡] The same executor also conveyed to his brother John Hovey of Ipswich, weaver, five acres of salt marsh, pasture and planting ground in Ipswich, on the south side of the river, in Labor-in-vain field; one acre of marsh and upland (the upland being an island in said acre) in Labor-in-vain field; and four and one-half acres of marsh at Barr Island, on Plum Island, in Ipswich, April 18, 1705.[§]

The same executor, for twenty-one pounds, conveyed to Joseph Fuller of Ipswich, carpenter, three acres of upland or pasture in Labor-in-vain field in Ipswich, April 23, 1712.[‖]

The same executor, for three pounds and ten shillings, conveyed to his brother John Hovey of Ipswich, weaver, half an acre of upland in Labor-in-vain field in Ipswich, Dec. 28, 1715.[¶]

Mrs. Esther Hovey survived her husband, and died in Ipswich, his widow, Jan. 4, 1730, at the age of ninety.

The children of Daniel Hovey were born in Ipswich as follows:—

9—I.   DANIEL[2], born June 21, 1665; probably died young, not being mentioned in his father's will.

10—II.   NATHANIEL[2], born Oct. 9, 1667. *See family numbered "10."*

11—III. ABIGAIL[2], married Serg. Thomas, son of William and Grace (Dutch) Hodgkins, of Ipswich Dec 12, 1689; they lived in Ipswich; he was born in 1668; and died Nov 16, 1710, aged fifty-one; his estate was valued at £625; she survived him, and died, his widow, Nov. 28, 1754. Children, born in Ipswich: 1. *Daniel*, born Oct. 14, 1690; lived in Ipswich; married, first, Abigail Hunt in 1714; second, Margaret Harris in 1737; he died June 1, 1773, aged eighty-two years; his wife Margaret survived him. They had ten children. 2. *Thomas*, born 1692; lived in Ipswich; married, first, Sarah Ayers of Ipswich Dec. 16, 1721; she died June 13, 1728; he married,

* Essex Registry of Deeds, book 12, leaf 14.
† Essex Registry of Deeds, book 16, leaf 195.
‡ Essex Registry of Deeds, book 36, leaf 198.
§ Essex Registry of Deeds, book 18, leaf 54.
‖ Norfolk Registry of Deeds, book 4, leaf 103.
¶ Essex Registry of Deeds, book 31, leaf 193.

second, widow Hannah (Warner) Stanwood Jan. 20, 1729;
he died Dec. 30, 1778, aged eighty-six. He had eight children,
one of whom was Col. Joseph Hodgkins of the army of the
Revolution, and another, Abigail, married, first, Thomas Ross,
and, second, Andrew Burley, and lived to be ninety-nine
years old. 3. *Hezekiah*², living in 1737. 4. *Esther*², living
in 1737. 5. *Ezekiel*², lived in Ipswich; married, first, Margaret
Lakeman Jan. 20, 1731; she died March 1, 1744; he married,
second, Deborah (Heard), widow of John Hovey (72) in
1740; and he died Sept. 13, 1777, having had eight children.
6. *Hannah*², married John Lakeman in 1735. 7. *John*², baptized Aug. 16, 1713; lived in Ipswich; married Elizabeth
Hovey (73) Oct. —, 1738. (See No. 73).

12—IV.   THOMAS², born May 28, 1673. *See family numbered "12."*
13—V.   JOHN², born Aug. 13, 1675. *See family numbered "13."*
14—VI.   MARY², born June 27, 1678; was unmarried in 1697.
15—VII. EBENEZER², born Jan. 11, 1680. *See family numbered "15."*

3

SERG. JOHN HOVEY², born in Ipswich, Mass., in 1644. He
lived in Ipswich until after 1607, and subsequently in Topsfield,
on the farm which his father conveyed to him by deed June 13,
1671.* The house was probably built before 1663, and was gone
in 1709. He built a new house near the old site before the latter
date, and lived in it. The new house measured forty feet long
and twenty-six feet wide. Before 1789, the place had come into
the ownership of Thomas Emerson, and while he owned it the
house was burned on the night of Jan. 2, 1821, having caught fire
from an oven.†

Mr. Hovey was a yeoman, and attained the rank of sergeant
in the militia. He was prominent in town affairs, being tithing
man in 1682; pounder, 1694; assessor, 1694; constable, 1672;
treasurer, 1672; selectman, 1678, 1680, 1684, 1686, 1680 and 1692.
He was a grandjuror in 1690, and representative to the general
court in 1704. March 2, 1676-7, he was one of two chosen by the
town to see to the mending of fences; in January, 1680, he was
one of a committee chosen to treat with a new minister; March 1,
1680-1, he was chosen to view some land; March 10, 1680-1, he
was chosen to erect a gallery in the meeting house; July 15, 1681,
he was chosen one of two to inform Rev. Mr. Danforth of the
invitation of the town to settle in the ministry in Topsfield; Sept.
1, 1681, he was chosen to view some land for the town; March 4,
1683-4, he was chosen one of a committee to lay out a highway
from Rowley to Topsfield; April 22, 1684, he was chosen one of a
committee to settle the town line with Ipswich; May 16, 1684, he
was chosen one of a committee to provide for the ordination of

* Ipswich Registry of Deeds, book 4, page 114.
† For a full and interesting account of the fire see *Salem Gazette*,
Jan. 9, 1821.

Rev. Joseph Capen; March 3, 1684-5, he was chosen with others to run the Salem line; March 2, 1685-6, he was chosen to lay out some land to Mr. Capen, and to renew the parsonage bounds; April 16, 1686, he was chosen to perambulate the Salem line; Jan. 25, 1686-7, he was chosen to repair the gallery in the meeting house; April 6, 1687, and Jan. 14, 1689-90, he was chosen to "seat" the meeting house; March 4, 1689-90, he was chosen one of a committee to settle the town line with Boxford; and March 7, 1692-3, he was chosen to view a highway, to lay out a highway, some land, etc.*

Mr. Hovey was a man of property, being the sixth on the list of those assessed for the minister's rate in 1681, that is, there were only five men that paid a larger tax. There are a number of transactions in real estate on record, in which Mr. Hovey appears as a party. He bought, with several other men, Mr. Nelson's farm in Rowley Village (Boxford), containing two thousand acres, July 17, 1683.† Of this large tract of land which was situated in the northwestern corner of Boxford, being bounded by the Andover and Bradford lines, various divisions were made, Jan. 1, 1701-2.‡ Jan. 13. 1709-10.§ Feb. 13, 1709-10.‖ One of the division deeds, dated Jan. 1, 1701-2, released to Mr. Hovey a lot on Rush pond, another on Walnut tree hill and on Maiden hill, on the Andover line and one on Philistine hill on the Bradford line; also, a part of rough meadow.¶ The deed dated Jan. 13, 1709-10, released to Mr. Hovey a part of maple meadow on the Andover line and a part of long meadow.§ All the other deeds were releases in which Mr. Hovey joined as grantor.

Mr. Hovey bought four acres of meadow in Rowley great meadow Sept. 26, 1684.** March 3, 1692-3, he conveyed twenty acres called the sticky meadow on the south side of Ipswich river, which his father had conveyed to him.†† Feb. 10, 1702-3, he conveyed seventeen acres of upland on the south side of the river between Smith's hill and round hill, and two and one-half acres on the same side of the river.‡‡ Feb. 19, 1702-3, he bought ninety-one acres of land in Boxford.§§ Jan. 24, 1703-4, he conveyed three and one-half acres in Fries' meadow in Boxford.‖‖

* Topsfield town records.
† Essex Registry of Deeds, book 7, leaf 142.
‡ Essex Registry of Deeds, book 22, leaf 56; book 33, leaf 16; book 33, leaf 186; book 38, leaf 146.
§ Essex Registry of Deeds, book 24, leaf 209.
‖ Essex Registry of Deeds, book 35, leaf 72.
¶ Essex Registry of Deeds, book 38, leaf 146.
** Essex Registry of Deeds, book 9, leaf 263.
†† Essex Registry of Deeds, book 9, leaf 129.
‡‡ Essex Registry of Deeds, book 15, leaf 120; book 19, leaf 9.
§§ Essex Registry of Deeds, book 15, leaf 137.
‖‖ Essex Registry of Deeds, book 16, leaf 163.

Aug. 28, 1706, he conveyed to his son Luke Hovey forty-three acres of upland and meadow in Boxford, on which Luke "has built and now dwells."* March 7, 1706-7, he conveyed to his son John Hovey forty-nine acres in Boxford on the Andover line adjoining Philistine hill, and a part of maple meadow.† He also conveyed to his son John five acres of meadow and upland at rough meadow in Boxford Nov. 22, 1708.‡ He conveyed to his sons John and Luke part of maple meadow in Boxford on Andover line and Wade's neck, Jan. 13, 1709-10.§ On the same day, he conveyed to his son Ivory thirty-two acres of upland and meadow in Topsfield, near his house, on Pye brook.|| March 26, 1715, for twenty pounds, he conveyed to his son Luke twenty-five acres in Boxford, known as the bush hill lot.¶ March 14, 1717-8, fifteen days before his death, Mr. Hovey divided the remainder of his real estate among his sons John, Luke and Ivory. To his son Ivory he conveyed one hundred acres being the remaining part of his homestead farm in Topsfield with dwelling house, barn, etc.; also, one half of his common rights; land bought of Col. John Wainwright in Boxford (except fifteen acres he gave to his son John) ; one-half of his part of Rowley great meadow ; and two-thirds of his marsh in Ipswich.** He conveyed to his son Luke one hundred acres of upland and meadow in Boxford, being the remainder of the farm on which Luke then lived; also, part of long meadow; part of little rock meadow; and one-half of his remaining interest in the Nelson farm in Boxford.†† To his son John, "for yᵉ Severall Duties that he Shall doe towards my maintainance if need Shall hereafter require & yᵉ payment of his part of Severall portions to his Sisters & Cousens as he is bound as he is with his brethren to me sᵈ John Hovey Senʳ as appeareth more at large in a bond from him & his bretheren to me," he conveyed fifty acres of land lying between Andover line and Philistine hill and Walker's hill; also, twenty acres lying between Bradford line and Philistine hill to Walker's hill; "my share" in ash swamp; fifteen acres "I bought" of Col. John Wainwright lying on the road from Rowley to Boxford; one-half of "my part" of Rowley great meadow ; one-half of "my interest" in the Nelson farm in Boxford; one-third of "my marsh" at Hovey's island in Ipswich; and "my land" in Topsfield next Baker's pond.‡‡

* Essex Registry of Deeds, book 18, leaf 201.
† Essex Registry of Deeds, book 20, leaf 115.
‡ Essex Registry of Deeds, book 21, leaf 150.
§ Essex Registry of Deeds, book 22, leaf 33.
|| Essex Registry of Deeds, book 22, leaf 117.
¶ Essex Registry of Deeds, book 31, leaf 1.
** Essex Registry of Deeds, book 33, leaf 299.
†† Essex Registry of Deeds, book 37, leaf 44.
‡‡ Essex Registry of Deeds, book 38, leaf 10.

Mr. Hovey was administrator of the estate of his brother Joseph Hovey in 1693, and the following is a copy of his signature on his official bond:

John Howey

March 18, 1717-8, Mr. Hovey, then called seventy years of age, testified relative to a certain salt house in Ipswich. This was only eleven days before his death, and his signature to the deposition is signed by mark; "Boo."*

A week before his death, Mr. Hovey made his will, which was proved in the probate court April 7, 1718. The following is a copy of the will as it is recorded in the probate records,† the original not having been found:—

In The Name of God Amen The Twenty Second of March 1717/18/ I John Hovey of Topsfeild in y⁰ County of Essex in New England being Weak of Body but of p'fect Mind & Memory Thanks be given To God Therefor I Calling To Mind The Mortality of my Body & knowing It Is Appointed for Man To Dye Doe make & Ordaine This my Last Will & Testam' That Is To Say principally & first of all I Give & recomend my Soul In to y⁰ hand of God y' Gave It mee hoping Thro° y⁰ Meritt of Jesus Christ To have full & free pardon of all my Sins & Inheritt Eternall Life; and my Body To be Decently bury⁴ In y⁰ Earth att y' Discretion of my Executo's afternamed

Item I Doe give To my Dear & Loveing Wife If Shee goe off & acquitt my Estate within Two months after my Decease five pounds a year To be payed her by my Three Sons John Luke & Ivory according as They are bound To pay it In a bond bareing Date y⁰ 14 of March 1717/8 as Shee & I have Agreed To be payd att Three Entire payments Annually att y⁰ End of Every fourth Month as appears by our hands & Seals y⁰ Sixth of March Aforesaid and I Doe give To My Wife one Cow & Two pair of Sheets & six pounds of flax Teers & three bush¹¹ˢ of In⁴ Corn & halfe a buf¹¹ of Rye halfe bu¹¹ Wheat & 70ᵗʰ of pork.

Item I Doe give To my son John all y⁰ Land I have made over To him by Deeds formerly & my brass Watch & abreaking up Share & Coult & halfe y⁰ Iron bars & half y⁰ Timber Chaine & The Book of Lives.

Item I Give To my Son Luke all his Land y' I have made Over To him by Deeds formerly & a Chaine & affoot y' he hath of mine and my Great Bef Bible

Item I Doe Give To my Son Ivory all y⁰ Land & Buildings mention⁴ In a Deed to him bareing Date y⁰ 14 Day of March 1717/8 and I Doe give To my Son Ivory my Great new Bible & my brass Scales & Wheights my Gun & Sword & half my Iron Barr & halfe my Timber Chaine & all y⁰ Rest of my Tools not before mentioned for y⁰ Carrying on of husbandry Together with my Stillyards & And Irons & all That Is Due from him To me upon Book.

Item I Doe give To my Daugh' Dorcas Jewett & my Dafter Eliz⁰ Uphams Children & my Dafter Abigaile Upham all my household Goods proper for Womens Improvement not before mentioned The y⁰ one Third part y'of To Dorcas & another Third part To Elizabeths Children & y⁰ other Third part To Abigail. I Doe Give To my Daughter Abigaile Upham my Cambridge Bible. and all y⁰ Rest of my Books not above men-

* Essex Registry of Deeds, book 34, leaf 162.
† Essex Probate records, book 312, page 267.

tioned my Will Is y' They fhall be Equally Divided among my Three Sons
& Two Daughters to my Dafter Eliz' Children one fixt part of Said
Books

Item. My Will Is y' my Exe[c]utors pay To my Granson Luke
Averhill y' Sum of Thirteen pounds If he Live To y' Age of Twenty one
years which was Due To his Mother att her Deceafe by her Grandfather
Ivorys Will

Item I Doe Give all my Moveable Estate not above mentioned To my
Three Sons abovesaid They paying my ffunerall Charges & all my Debts

Item I Doe Confititute & appoint my Two Sons John & Ivory Hovey
To be Exe[c]utors To This my Last Will & Testam' & In Confirmation of
what Is above written I y' aboves' John Hovey have Sett To my haud &
Seale This Twenty fecond Day of March In y' year of our Lord one
Thoufand Seven hundred & feventeen & Eighteen

Signed Sealed
publish' & Declared
In y' p'fence of us
  BENJ' HOW
  JACOB DORMAN   JOHN HOVEY (SEAL)
  JOSEPH DORMAN

Mr. Hovey married, first, Dorcas Ivory Aug. 13, 1665; and
she died there Nov. 5, 1711. He married, second, Mercy, widow
of Dea. Joseph Goodhue of Ipswich (published in Ipswich, Nov.
30, 1712). Mrs. Goodhue was daughter of John and Ellinor
(Pell) Boynton of Rowley, where she was born 5: 10 mo: 1651,
and married, first, Josiah Clarke of Ipswich Dec. 14, 1670. Mr.
Clark died, and she married Deacon Goodhue July 4, 1692. He
died in Ipswich Sept. 2, 1697; and she next married Mr. Hovey,
as above stated. Mr. Hovey died March 29, 1718, aged about
seventy-four. His wife Mercy survived him, and died in Rowley,
his widow, Dec. 22, 1730, at the age of seventy-nine.

Children, born in Topsfield :—

16—I.   JOHN⁴, born Dec. —, 1666. *See family numbered "16."*
17—II.   DORCAS⁴, born Jan. 16, 1668-9; married Isaac, son of John and
            Elizabeth (Cummings) Jewett of Ipswich June 12, 1695.
            They removed from Ipswich to Killingly, Conn., about 1714,
            and were living there in 1715. Children, born in Inswich:
            1. *Isaac*, baptized Feb. 5, 1698-9. 2. *Abigail*, born S: pt. 22,
            1705. 3. *David*, baptized Jan. 25, 1707-8. 4. ——— (dau.),
            baptized July 2, 1710.
18—III. ———⁴ (dau.), born Feb. 20, 1670-1; died March 2, 1670-1.
19—IV. ELIZABETH⁴, born Jan. 18, 1671-2; married Thomas, son of Lt.
            Phineas and Ruth Upham of Malden April 21, 1693. Thomas
            Upham was born in 1668, in Malden, where he lived. His
            wife Elizabeth died Feb. 16, 1703-4, at the age of thirty-two;
            and he married, secondly, Mary Brown of Reading Oct. 2,
            1704. His wife Mary died in 1707; and he married, thirdly,
            Ruth (Cutler), widow of John Smith of Charlestown. Mr.
            Upham died Nov. 26, 1735, at the age of sixty-six, in Read-
            ing (in that part now Wakefield), his farm having been an-
            nexed to Reading. Children of Thomas and Elizabeth
            (Hovey) Upham, born in Malden, except the first, which
            was probably born at Topsfield: 1. *Thomas*, born in 1694;

baptized in Topsfield Nov. 18, 1694; lived in Malden; married, first, Ruth Smith; she died in Weston in 1722, aged twenty-eight; he married, second, Elizabeth, widow of John Bullard, in 1723; he died Sept. 25, 1729-30; she died in 1753. He had four children. 2. *Elizabeth*[4], born in 1695; married Joseph Woolson in 1726. 3. *Abijah*[4], born in 1698; lived in Weston, Mass.; deacon nearly thirty years; representative to the general court several terms; married Elizabeth Spring in 1725; he died Dec. 3, 1775, at the age of seventy-seven; and she died, his widow, Feb. 18, 1794, aged ninety. They had six children; and among their descendants are Rev. Albert George Upham of Southbridge, Mass., and Montreal, Canada, and Hon. William E. Chandler, United States senator, secretary of the navy, etc. 4. *Nathan*[4], born in 1701; married first, Sarah Wesson of Reading June 5, 1728; she died in 1729; he married, second, Mary Brown of Weston in 1730; he died Sept. —, 1754. He had five children.

20—V.   SUSANNAH[4], born in 1674; married Ebenezer, son of William and Hannah (Jackson) Averill of Topsfield Nov. 30, 1697. Ebenezer Averill was born in Topsfield Oct. 14, 1669; was a husbandman; and lived in his native town. His wife Susannah died Nov. 11, 1699, at the age of twenty-five; and he married, secondly, Mehitable Foster of Ipswich Dec. 31, 1700. He died Dec. 22, 1717; and his wife Mehitable survived him, dying Nov. 19, 1740. The inventory of his estate says that some of the things were reserved for "Luke the sunn of Susannah his first wife that came from Engld." The only child of Ebenezer and Susannah (Hovey) Averill was born in Topsfield, as follows: 1. *Luke*[5], born Aug. 2, 1699; yeoman; lived in Topsfield; married Sarah Peabody; and died April 16, 1776. They had eight children.

21—VI.   LUKE[4], born May 3, 1676. *See family numbered "21."*

22—VII. ABIGAIL[4], born April 28, 1680; married Richard, son of Lt. Phineas and Ruth Upham of Malden May 19, 1698. He was born in Malden in 1675; and lived in Reading after 1727, when the neighborhood in which he lived in Malden was annexed to that part of Reading which is now Wakefield. He was a farmer; and died, of strangury, May 18, 1734, aged fifty-eight. His wife survived him, and died, his widow, Sept. 1, 1764, at the age of eighty-four. Their children were born in Malden as follows: 1. *Richard*[5], died Sept. 4, 1700. 2. *Ivory*[5], born June 16, 1701; settled in Killingly, Conn.; married, first, Tabitha ———, who died March 13, 1744; he married, second, Jane ———, probably from Sutton, Mass.; she died in Killingly, Conn., Jan. 23, 1750-1; he married, third, Mary Haskol of Beverly, Mass., July 2, 1752; he died about 1756, having had nine children. 3. *Abigail*[5], born April 19, 1703; died Jan. 7, 1715-6. 4. *Dorcas*[5], born May 19, 1707; died Jan. 22, 1715-6. 5. *Hepzibah*[5], born Feb. 29, 1711-2; married Nathaniel Longley of Derchester Jan. 29, 1756. 6. *Mary*[5], spinster, lived in Malden. 7. *Ruth*[5], born Dec. 3, 1714; died July 7, 1769. 8. *Richard*[5], born Dec. 3, 1716; lived in Onslow. N. S.; mariner; married, first, Elizabeth Hovey (   ): she died June 7, 1756, at the age of thirty-four; he married, second, widow Elizabeth Putnam of Danvers, Mass.; he died at Onslow about 1780, having had a large family. 9. *Luke*[5], born March 28, 1719; died May 6,

1719. 10. *Luke*⁴ (twin), born July 10, 1721; died April 23,
1731. 11. *Abigail*⁴ (twin), born July 10, 1721; died Nov. —,
1738. 12. *Susanna*⁴, married Ephraim Weston Dec. 5, 17:8.
23—VIII. IVORY³, born May 4, 1682. *See family numbered "23."*

4

LT. THOMAS HOVEY² was born in Ipswich, Mass., in 1648.
He was one of the grantees of Quabog (now Brookfield), but did
not settle there. He lived in Hadley as early as 1672, and was a
yeoman and a prominent man in the town. He served as representative to the general court in 1699 and 1703; and was a lieutenant in the militia.

Joseph Barnard brought a suit against Mr. Hovey in the
court held at Northampton March 25, 1672-3, for "unjust molestation."*

Mr. Hovey was bound over by the commissioners of Hadley
for resisting the constable of Hadley and fined twenty shillings
in 1676.†

Mr. Hovey was admitted freeman in the court at Springfield,
Mass., Sept. 27, 1681.‡ and was sworn in the court at Northampton March 28, 1682.§

Samuel Gardner, sr., brought a suit against Mr. Hovey about
some pork in the court at Northampton March 27, 1683.‖

Mr. Hovey was a party to several real estate transactions on
record, and probably there are others that are not recorded. He
bought of Thomas Dickinson of Hadley, for ninety pounds, Mr.
Dickinson's homestead, of house and eight acre lot and other
land April 22, 1679.¶ He also, bought eight and one-half acres
of land in Hoccanum meadow in Hadley of Caleb Watson of
Hartford, Conn., Oct. 10, 1680.¶

March 23, 1694, he conveyed one and one-half acres of land
in Labor-in-vain field on the south side of the river in Ipswich,
bounded by land of his father, etc.,** and on the same day he
conveyed to his brother Daniel Hovey one acre of land in the
Labor-in-vain field on the south side of the river in Ipswich,
bounded by his father's estate, etc.†† Oct. 18, 1697, with Daniel
Hovey of Ipswich, carpenter, he conveyed Hovey's island of

* Records in probate office at Northampton, Mass., volume I, page 144.
† Records in probate office at Northampton, Mass., volume I, page 179.
‡ Records in probate office at Northampton, Mass., volume I, page 217.
§ Records in probate office at Northampton, Mass., volume I, page 219.
‖ Records in probate office at Northampton, Mass., volume I, page 225.
¶ Hampden Registry of Deeds, book A, page 106.
** Essex Registry of Deeds, book 12, leaf 12.
†† Essex Registry of Deeds, book 39, leaf 27.

twenty acres of upland and salf marsh on Sagamore Hill creek in Ipswich.*

Mr. Hovey bought of James Smith, who had removed from Hadley to Haddam, Conn., a house and eight-acre lot of land in Hadley Jan. 23, 1705-6.†

Oct. 28, 1707, Mr. Hovey deposed in reference to land his father had bought of Deacon Lumpkins.‡ The following is his signature to this deposition:

Mr. Hovey again deposed, Feb. 17, 1712-3, as to bounds of the land his father bought of Deacon Lumpkin, that "his land was at y⁰ End of a great oake tree which formerly stood by a Swamp Side beyond a little Pond hole northeasterly from the place where John Hovey Junʳ his dwelling house in Topsfield now is wᶜʰ Tree is now fallen down."§ Feb. 13, 1722-3, was recorded another deposition of Mr. Hovey relative to the farm of his father, lying upon Pye brook in Topsfield, that he saw possession of it given to his father, and that it extended to Baker's pond.‖

For ninety pounds, Mr. Hovey conveyed an old common right in Ipswich, which had been granted to his father Feb. 14, 1664, and also other rights granted Feb. —, 1678, Jan. 25, 1702-3, and March 29, 1728.¶ He also conveyed to his grandson Thomas Austin of Suffield land in Hadley, on the south side of Mount Holyoke, Jan. 8, 1728-9.** He and his wife's brother Westwood Cook of Hadley released to each other, June 27, 1730, one hundred and sixteen acres of land in Hadley that had been laid out to them.††

Mr. Hovey married Sarah, daughter of Capt. Aaron and Sarah (Westwood) Cook Nov. —, 1677. She was born in Hadley Jan. 31, 1662; and she was his wife in 1734. He died March 4, 1739, at the age of ninety-one. His remains lie in the old burial place in Hadley, and his gravestone is inscribed as follows:

Lᴇɴᴛᴇɴ. THOMAⁿ Hᴼᴠᴇʏ

DYED ON MARCH Yᵉ 4, 1739,

AGED 91 YEAR.

* Essex Registry of Deeds, book 13, leaf 55.
† Hampden Registry of Deeds, book B, page 125.
‡ Essex Registry of Deeds, book 22, leaf 9.
§ Essex Registry of Deeds, book 25, leaf 174.
‖ Essex Registry of Deeds, book 40, leaf 228.
¶ Essex Registry of Deeds, book 31, leaf 243.
** Hampden Registry of Deeds, book E, page 442.
†† Hampden Registry of Deeds, book E, page 441.

The original will of Lieutenant Hovey is on file in the probate office at Northampton, Mass., and it reads as follows:—

In the name of God amen: the tenth Day of augst Seventeen Hundred and thirty four: I Thomas Hovey of Hadley In the County of Hampſhire In the province of the maſſechuſet Bay In new England; Knowing the unſertainty of my Life: and the fraility of my Bodey: yet thr^e Gods Goodneſs I haue at preſent the vſe of my Reſon and memory; and am willing while So to Diſpoſe of what eſtate God has Given me: Do make and ordain this my laſt will and Teſtament; that is to ſay Principally, and furſt of all I Giue and Recommend my ſole into the hands of God that gaue it: and my Body I Recommend to the Earth to be Buryed In Chreſtian or Decent maner: nothing Doubting but at the Generall Reſerrection I ſhall Reſeve the ſame again by the mighty power of God and as Touching ſuch worldly Eſtate God has Bleſed me with In this Life; I Giue Demiſe and Diſpoſe of the ſame In the following manner and forme.

Imp^{ts} I Giue and Bequeath to ſarah: my Beloued wife: twenty pounds value oute of my Parſionall Eſtate: ſuch as ſhe ſhall Chuſe to be at her own diſpoſe foreuer: as alſſo the uſe and Improuement of one thurd part of my Real Eſtate dureing the term of her naturall Life.

Item: I Giue and Bequeath unto my Grand ſon Benjamin Church (whoe now Liues with & takes Good Care of me & my Buſineſs) a Doble ſhear: (to my children) out of my whole Eſtate; as alſſo the ſume of ſixty pounds In or as mony ouer and aboue the Doble ſhear aſſoreſaid for the ſeruis allredey he hes downe (for the payment of which I haue giuen him a note of hand) all which I Giue to him his Heirs &c: for Euer. further I giue to my Grandſon aſſore ſaid to him and his Heirs foreuer all my houſings Buildings orchards and Lands: excepting onely my wood Lot In the thurd or laſt Deveſion of my Lands Eaſtward of the town: and allſſo my teem and teem tackling he paying back what the ſame may be ouer & aboue his Doble ſhear and the Sixty pounds before mentioned: within ſix years after my Deceas

Item: I Giue and Bequeath: To my Daughter Sarah Winchill: Including the thurty pounds I haue heretofore Giuen Her, a ſingel Portion or ſhear oute of my Eſtate: viz half ſo much as my Grand ſon Doble ſhear: before mentioned: to be paid her In ſix year^s after my deceas:

Item I Giue and Bequeath to may Daf^r Abigel auſtin; Including the thurty pound ſhe hes allredy had: a ſingel ſhear or portion (as aſſore^d) out of my Eſtate: to be paid her In ſix years after *after* my deceas:

Item I Giue and Bequeath to my Daf^r Johanah wodsworth: Including the thurty pounds ſhe hes alredy had: a ſingel ſhear or portion out of my Eſtate (as aſſore^d) to be paid her In ſix years after my Deceaſe:

Item: I Giue and Bequeath to my Daf^r Elizabeth ſmith Including the thurty pounds ſhe hes allrady had out of my Eſtate: a ſingel ſhear or Portion out of my eſtate (as aſſoreſaid) to be paid Her In Six years after my Deceas.

Item I Give and Bequeath to my daf^r Darkos a ſingel ſhear or Portion out of my Eſtate: thurty pounds of which to be paid her ſoon after my deceas: the Remainder In ſix years after my deceas: as allſo I Giue Her ſixty Pounds In or as money ouer and aboue her ſingell portion aſſoreſaid: to be paid her ſoon after my deceaſe: I allſſo Give and Bequeath to her, her Heirs & aſsigns for Ever my wood Lot In the thurd or Laſt deveſion of out lands Eaſtward of the town: which at a Juſt valuation is to be Reckened as ſo much In Part of the aſſore ſaid Legeſey given Her

Item: I Give and Bequeath to my Grand Daf⁴ marah Houey alies marah moody three Pounds In or as mony to be paid out of my Eftate

Item I Give to my Grand Daf⁴ martha Houey thurty fhillings to be paid out of my Eftate

Item I Give to my Grand Daf⁴ meriam Church four Pounds In or as money to be paid her out of my Eftate

Item my will is that if aney of my Legetees fhould Die before me or before they Receue there Refpectiue Legeties that there Heirs: Refpectively: or thofe that Legally Reprefent them fhall haue and Refeve the fame: and unto whome I will and Bequeath the fame In Cafe my affore i⁴ Legatees Die before me or before they Receve there Refpective Legefas: as affore faid

Item: I Doe by thefe Prefence conftitute make & ordain my wife farah to be my Executrix and my grand fon Benjemin Church (before mentioned) to be my executer: of this my laft will and Teftement and I Doe hereby Ratify and Conferm this and no other to be my laft will & Teftement In witnefs whereof I haue hereunto fet my hand & feal the Day and Date before mentioned aug⁴ 10ᵗʰ 1734.

figned fealled Publifhed
Pronounced and Declared by the
f⁴ Thoˣ Houey as his Laft
will & Teftement In the
Prefence of us the fubfcribers
ELEAZER PORTER
AARON WARNER
SARAH PORTER

Efornaf Hovey

Mr. Hovey's estate was appraised at £1.107, 1s, 11d. His real estate is described in the inventory of his estate, taken in May, 1739, as follows:—

the House lot and buildings,	£260.
a lot in ye pine plain, 8 acres,	40.
ye lower lot in Hawkanum, 9½ acres,	180.
a lot in great meadow at Cross path hill, 4½ acres,	80.
a lot at ye upper end of Ackenitee, 3½ acres,	70.
a lot at Plum brook, 72 acres,	85.
a lot in third division east of ye town,	40.
a lot on fort river, about 19 acres,	60.
also, 5 lots, aggregating 163 acres,	188. 3s

The estate owed eighty-seven pounds.
Children, born in Hadley:—

24—i.   THOMAS⁴, born in 1678. *See family numbered "24."*
25—ii.   SARAH⁴, born Dec. 25, 1680; married, first, Jonathan, son of Jonathan and Abigail (Bruson) Winchell of Suffield, Conn., June 21, 1704; he was born in Windsor, Conn., Feb. 14, 1669; and died in Suffield, where they lived, Dec. 13, 1714; she married, second, Ichabod Smith; and died June —, 1766, at the age of eighty-five. Her children, by her first husband, Jonathan Winchell, were born in Suffield as follows: 1. *Jonathan⁵*, born March 29, 1705; died in Springfield, Mass., July 13, 1729. 2. *Daniel⁵*, born Dec. 2, 1706; died Jan. 13, 1708. 3. *Daniel⁵*, born July 10, 1709; had eight children; died in Hadley, Mass. 4. *Sarah⁵*, born Oct. 14, 1711.

26—III. ABIGAIL², born Jan. 8, 1682; married Nathaniel Austin, jr., of Suffield, Conn., Jan. 27, 1701; and she was living in 1734. Their son, 1. *Thomas*³, lived in Suffield in 1729.

27—IV. JOANNA³, born about 1684; married Joseph, son of Joseph and Elizabeth (Barnard) Wadsworth of Hartford, Conn., about 1706; he was born in Hartford in 1682; and she was living in 1734. He died in 1778, at the age of ninety-six. Children, born in Hartford: 1. *Joseph*⁴, born in 1707; lived in Avon, N. Y.; married Elizabeth Cook in 1742; and died in 1758, having had six children. 2. *Joanna*⁴, born in 1710; married Timothy Goodman in 1735. 3. *Elizabeth*⁴, married R. Seymour in 1740. 4. *Daniel*⁴, born in 1720; had a son Daniel⁵, born in 1762. 5. *William*⁴, born in 1723; married Mary Cook in 1751; had two children; and he died in 1771.

28—V. ELIZABETH³, born about 1686; married Dea. John, son of Serg. Joseph and Rebecca (Dickinson) Smith of Hadley in 1709. He was a cooper by trade. They removed to Hartford in 1711, and in 1736 to Belchertown, where he died in 1777, at the age of ninety. His wife Elizabeth died in 1758, at the age of "seventy." Children: 1. *John*⁴, born Dec. 21, 1710; married Mary ———; lived in Hatfield; had nine children; and died in 1751. 2. *Abner*⁴, born Sept. 10, 1712; married, first, Martha Warner Oct. 2, 1736; and, second, Mary Pomeroy; removed to Springfield; and died Nov. 19, 1766, at the age of fifty-four. 3. *Elizabeth*⁴, born Sept. 19, 1714; married Walter Fairfield of Belchertown April 20, 1736. 4. *Daniel*⁴, born about 1716; married Abigail Sacket in 1742; and died in Belchertown May 31, 1800, aged eighty-four. 5. *Miriam*⁴, born Oct. 30, 1718; married Jesse Warner Oct. 3, 1739. 6. *Samuel*⁴, born in 1721. 7. *Joseph*⁴, married Eunice Bascom; and died in Lyme, N. H., in 1803. 8. *Elijah*⁴, born in 1723; served as captain in the French war in 1756; and was deacon in Belchertown; he married Sibyl Worthington of Colchester, Conn., in 1751; he died April 21, 1770, at the age of forty-seven; she married, secondly, Reuben Smith, and died May 26, 1828, at the great age of one hundred and one. Captain Smith had nine children; among them being Rev. Ethan Smith of Haverhill and Hopkinton, N. H., Hebron, N. Y., Poultney, Vt., Hanover and Boylston. 9. *Rachel*⁴, born Jan. 4, 1727; married Aaron Hannum of Belchertown; and died in 1811, at the age of eighty-five. 10. *Sarah*⁴, born Sept. 27, 1729; married Abner Dickinson of Whately. 11. *Rebecca*⁴, born May 4, 1732; married Oliver Graves of Whately.

29—VI. MIRIAM³, born Aug. 27, 1689; married Benjamin, son of Samuel and Mary (Churchill?) Church of Hadley Jan. 13, 1709. He was born Sept. 1, 1680. She died in 1713, at the age of twenty-four. He married, secondly, Hannah Dickinson Sept. 23, 1714; and, thirdly, Sarah, widow of Elisha Perkins May 29, 1724. He died Jan. 15, 1755, at the age of seventy-four. His children, by his first wife, Miriam Hovey, were born in Hadley, as follows: 1. *Benjamin*⁴, born Dec. 26, 1709; lived in South Hadley; married Ruth Kellogg; and had nine children, one of whom was Rev. Nathan Church of Bridgton, Me. 2. *Meriam*⁴, born May 12, 1712; married Joseph Smith May 24, 1739; and died in 1773.

30—VII. HANNAH³, born Nov. 5, 1691; buried March 7, 1694.

31—VIII.   ———⁵ (dau.), (triplet), born Nov. 12, 1693; died Nov. 12, 1693.
32—IX.   ———⁵ (dau.), (triplet), born Nov. 12, 1693; died Nov. 12, 1693.
33—X.   ———⁵ (dau.), (triplet), born Nov. 12, 1693; died Nov. 12, 1693.
34—XI.   DANIEL⁵, born Dec. 1, 1694; died Feb. 13, 1716.
35—XII.   DORCAS⁵, born Feb. 1, 1697-8; died, unmarried, March 3, 1795,
            at the age of ninety-seven.
36—XIII.   RACHEL⁵, born Jan. 20, 1699-1700; died Oct. 12, 1703.

5

JAMES HOVEY², born in Ipswich, Mass., in 1650. He was one
of the first settlers of Quabog, in Hampshire county, Mass., in
1668, and received a grant of a homelot, upon which he built a
house and lived.

He married Priscilla, daughter of John Dane of Ipswich in
1670.

Mr. Hovey was one of the signers of the petition to the general court dated Oct. 10, 1673, praying for the incorporation of
the settlement, and that it might
receive the name of Brookfield.
The following is a copy of Mr.
Hovey's   signature   to   this
petition:

The request was granted, and Quabog became a town, its
name being changed to Brookfield.

Mr. Hovey was killed by the Indians, when a considerable
number of his townsmen were massacred, Aug. 2, 1675.

Mr. Hovey's wife Priscilla survived him; and she returned
to the court an inventory which was taken Sept. 25, 1676. She
was appointed administratrix. The inventory states that "Only
yᵉ land at Brookfeild by Reafon of yᵉ Indian wars & the Defola-
tion at her dispofe for the bringing up of the Children & when
they Come to age to be devided amongst yᵐ according to law."
The following is a copy of the inventory:—

Inventory of the estate of James Hovey taken Septemb' 25 1676 by
Richd Goodman & Aaron Cooke Ju'
    Imp' to 2 Steers all 8ˡˢ to fmall yeareling Steers at ˡˢ   ˢ   ᵈ
3ˡˢ to I Bedd with yᵉ ffurneture   012 10 00
    to I horfe his part being half at 1ˡ 10ˢ 0ᵈ gun &
fword at 20ˢ; I Pott at 10ˢ   003 00 00
    The totall Sum of this Inventory is   015 10 00*

Children, born in Brookfield:—

37—I.   PRISCILLA³, married Samuel Smith Nov. 23, 1699, at Malden;
           and lived in Reading until after 1707, when they removed
           to Charlestown, and from there to Mansfield, Conn. July 7,

* Records in probate office at Northampton, Mass., volume I, page 170.

1703, when they were called of Charlestown, they joined with her brothers Daniel and James in conveying to Benoni Morse of Dedham, farmer, for eight pounds, thirty of upland and meadow in Brookfield.* Mr. Smith bought land in Mansfield in 1716-7, and they united with the church there in 1718. She died in Mansfield Aug. 9, 1720, and he died there July 15, 1730. Children, born in Reading: 1. *Samuel*², born in 1701. 2. *John*² (twin), born in 1707. 3. *Priscilla*² (twin), born in 1707. 4. *Mehitable*², baptized Oct. 11, 1713.

38—II. DANIEL², born in 1672. *See family numbered "38."*
39—III. JAMES², born in 1674. *See family numbered "39."*

6

JOSEPH HOVEY², born in Ipswich in 1653. He lived in Hadley, Mass., until 1690, when he removed to Milton. He married Hannah, daughter of Richard and Mary Pratt of Malden May 31, 1677; and died in the summer of 1693, administration upon his estate being granted to his brother John Hovey, sr., of Topsfield June 9, 1693. The inventory of his estate amounted to £11, 12s, 8d, being all personal. £1, 4s, of this amount was of "Things prized at Ipswich." The estate was declared insolvent; and Thomas Holman and Nathaniel Pitcher, both of Milton, were appointed commissioners to examine claims.

Children, born in Hadley :—

40—I. JOSEPH³, born Feb. 28, 1677-8. *See family numbered "40."*
41—II. EBENEZER³, born Nov. 5, 1680. *See family numbered "41."*
42—III. HANNAH³, born Nov. 21, 1682.
43—IV. JOHN³, born Aug. 21, 1684. *See family numbered "43."*
44—V. CALEB³, born June 4, 1687. *See family numbered "44."*
45—VI. THOMAS³, born June 6, 1689.
46—VII. JAMES³, born about 1691. *See family numbered "46."*

8

NATHANIEL HOVEY², born in Ipswich March 20, 1657. He lived in Ipswich; and married Sarah Fuller Nov. —, 1679. He died March 24, 1692, at the age of thirty-five. The following is a copy of the original inventory of his estate filed in the probate office at Salem :—

An Inuentory of yᵉ Eſtate of Nathˡˡ Houey Deceaſed this: 24ᵗʰ of march 1692.

		li	s
It 1 oxe: 5ˡⁱ: two Coues 6ˡⁱ: 1 mere 4ˡⁱ and: 13 ſheepe 5ˡⁱ 4ˢ A heffor: 1ˡⁱ 8ˢ		21	12 00
It 2 pegss: 12ˢ: yᵉ bede & bedding & 4: peir of ſheets and cloath for A ſhirt and Two bedstads: 7ˡⁱ 10ˢ: and 4 Cheares: 5ˢ: & Table 3ˢ		08	10 00

* Hampden Registry of Deeds, book C, page 458.

It : 3 : Traies : 2ˢ two poudering tubs : 2 Bear Beriles two pailes
     and A half Tube 12ˢ A ſtraining Dish 8ˢ & wormen
     pann 5ˢ   ᴄɪ ᴏᴏ ᴏᴏ
It wooding Dishes & porngers & arthan Dishes : 10ˢ 6ᵈ &
     Trenchors 4ˢ 6ᵈ & a peir of Tonges & ſlice 5 & : 2 : oyron
     poots & 1 peir of poot hooks   ᴏɪ 08 ᴏᴏ
It A Bras Kittle : 5ˢ & fiue pound of Linning yearne & 5 of
     Tooe yarn :   15 00
It A frien pann 5ˢ a tinn lamp & 1 peir of cerds : 2ˢ and
     Tramel 3ˢ   ᴏᴏ 10 ᴏᴏ
It Two Bibles : 6ˢ & : 2 : other Books : 3ˢ & mele ; troof & 2
     chists & 2 boxes   ᴏɪ 07 ᴏᴏ
It A musket : 1ˡⁱ & ammornition & wering clothes : 3ˡⁱ & 2
     forks : 2ˢ   04 02 ᴏᴏ
It A Credle 6ˢ & 3 Glas Boottles 3ˢ A Box oyron and hetors :
     3ˢ & fythe and fickle and tackling to it : 5 : A plow 3ˢ
     A nax 4ˢ : & 1 peir of Tracies   02 05 06

                                           41 09 6
It ther wafe ingageid to faid houfey defefid by his father on
     contrackt of marag the fume of fixty fix pounds   66 00 00
             Aprized by vs   Lᴇꜰᵗ : Tʜᴏᴍᴀꜱ Bᴜʀɴᴜᴍ Sᴇ
                                       Lᴇꜰᴛ Dᴀɴɪᴇʟ Rɪɴᴅɢᴇ

    Mrs. Hovey survived her husband, and married, secondly, as
his second wife, Christopher Bidlacke of Ipswich before Aug. 15,
1694, when a daughter, Mary, was born to them. Mr. Bidlacke's
first wife, Anna, died Dec. 13, 1692.

    Children, born in Ipswich :—

47—ɪ.   Sᴀʀᴀʜ², born Sept. 19, 1680 ; married Jonathan Remington of
          Rowley June 11, 1701 ; and removed to Suffield, Conn.

48—ɪɪ.   Eʟɪᴢᴀʙᴇᴛʜ², born March 25, 1681-2 ; married Joseph Ford of
          Ipswich Feb. 13, 1704 ; and removed to Hartford, Conn.,
          just before or in 1712. He was a yeoman.
             Mr. and Mrs. Ford, then of Ipswich, conveyed the estate
          that had been devised to her in the will of her grandfather
          Daniel Hovey, April 7, 1705 ;* and, for fifteen shillings, they
          conveyed the title to some marsh in Ipswich which had been
          granted by the commoners of Ipswich to her father's heirs,
          July 4, 1712.†

49—ɪɪɪ. Aʙɪɢᴀɪʟ², married Moses Stevens (published April 19, 1707).
          She conveyed the estate which was devised to her in the will
          of her grandfather Daniel Hovey, April 7, 1705.*

50—ɪᴠ. Mᴀʀɢᴀʀᴇᴛ², removed from Ipswich to Topsfield before June 7,
          1712, when she conveyed the real estate devised to her in the
          will of her grandfather Daniel Hovey ;‡ she then went to
          Windham, Conn., where she married Daniel Ross June 5, 1716 ;
          and she died there June 19, 1724, aged thirty-three years, lacking
          ten days. Their children were born in Windham, as follows :
          1. *Ruth*³, born May 7, 1717. 2. *Daniel*³, born June 13, 1719 ;
          died July 4, 1720. 3. *Jemima*³, born Aug. 31, 1721 ; died Dec.
          11, 1721. 4. *Margaret*³, born June 19, 1724.

      * Essex Registry of Deeds, book 18, leaf 189.
      † Essex Registry of Deeds, book 43, leaf 151.
      ‡ Essex Registry of Deeds, book 25, leaf 202.

51—v. NATHANIEL³, born June 29, 1691. *See family numbered "51."*

10

NATHANIEL HOVEY², born in Ipswich Oct. 9, 1667. He was a cordwainer by trade ; and always lived in Ipswich. He married Mary ———— about 1692 : and died in the winter of 1695-6, at the age of twenty-eight. The following is a copy of the inventory of his estate:—

A True Inuentery of all and fingalar the Goods Chattels Rights and credits of nathaniell Houey Cordwainer deceased Apriesed at Ipswich march 31 : 1695/6 as pay by thefubscribers as floll.

It part of A dwelling house	40	00	00
It fheepe swine and cowe	16	00	00
It wearing Apparell	08	00	00
It Houshold Stufe and leather	32	08	00

JACOB ffOSTER
PHILEMON DANE   Apris'⁸

ye marke X of mary Hovey

Mr. Hovey's widow, Mary, was appointed administratrix of his estate March 31, 1696. She married, secondly, John Brown of Ipswich before 1701, and was the latter's wife in 1718.

Children, born in Ipswich :—

52—i.   ESTHER⁴, born Dec. 22, 1693 ; died before 1701.
53—ii. NATHANIEL⁴, born in 1696. *See family numbered "53."*

12

THOMAS HOVEY³, born in Ipswich May 28, 1673. He was a yeoman, and was also called a fisherman in 1718. He lived in his native town until the spring of 1743, when he bought a farm in the West parish of Boxford, near what is now the residence of George B. Austin, where he afterward lived and died. Some of his children had already married and removed thither. In Ipswich, he held several minor offices, as hayward and field driver in 1699 and tithing man in 1709 and 1711.

The following is a copy of his autograph taken from the bond of the administrator of the estate of John Fisk, his son-in-law, in 1739, he being a surety :

Mr. Hovey was a party to a number of conveyances of real estate. He conveyed three acres of salt marsh on Plum island in Ipswich Nov. 6, 1699.* For sixty-five pounds, he conveyed "my now dwelling house" and about forty rods of land in Ipswich May 21, 1712.† For nineteen pounds, he conveyed about twelve acres of land in Chebacco woods, lot 413, April 3, 1714.‡ In

* Essex Registry of Deeds, book 15, leaf 55.
† Essex Registry of Deeds, book 26, leaf 167.
‡ Essex Registry of Deeds, book 27, leaf 142.

exchange for other land. Mr. Hovey conveyed his interest in the
estate of his father to his nephew Nathaniel Hovey of Ipswich,
weaver, April 10, 1718.* In exchange for the interest of Thomas
Hovey in the estate of his father, as stated above, his nephew
Nathaniel Hovey conveyed to him and John Hovey of Ipswich,
weaver, said Nathaniel's interest in the dwelling house of his
father on south side of Ipswich river in Ipswich, April 8, 1718.†
He, also, conveyed to them his interest in the estate of his grandfather Daniel Hovey of Ipswich, deceased, on the same day.‡
Thomas Hovey, for the rent of twenty-two shillings and six pence
yearly which "my deceased brother," John Hovey of Ipswich, had
agreed to pay our mother, to John's heirs a right of way to a
marsh Jan. 26, 1721.§ He conveyed the house that William Fuller
then lived in and one-half an acre of land lying on the river,
Jan. 19, 1719-20.‖ He also conveyed to his brother John Hovey
of Ipswich, weaver, ten acres of marsh and upland in Ipswich, on
Labor-in-vain creek, March 20, 1718.¶ For seven pounds, he also
conveyed lot 94 (one hundred and thirty-six square rods) on
Jeffries neck, and "my old thatch lot" 185, on Cross' bank
(one acre) in Ipswich May 21, 1713.** For forty-one pounds, he
conveyed three acres and ninety rods of marsh in Labor-in-vain
field in Ipswich May 29, 1724.†† He also conveyed, for eight
pounds, eighty-four rods of marsh in the same field May 22,
1721.‡‡ For fifteen pounds and ten shillings, he conveyed one acre
of planting ground in said field Dec. 2, 1724.§§ For four pounds,
he conveyed thirty-six rods of land in the same field Jan. 28,
1724-5.‖‖ For thirty-eight pounds, he conveyed one acre and one
hundred and forty-two rods of upland in the same field Jan. 29,
1724-5.¶¶ For seventy pounds, he conveyed one-half of an old
right in the junior division of the south-eight in Ipswich April 30,
1729.*** For thirty pounds, he conveyed one-half of a common
right in Ipswich that formerly belonged to "my father Mr. Daniel
Hovey, deceased," March 2, 1720-1.††† For fifty-five pounds, he
conveyed four acres of land, being an old common right in the

     * Essex Registry of Deeds, book 35, leaf 55.
     † Essex Registry of Deeds, book 36, leaf 115.
     ‡ Essex Registry of Deeds, book 36, leaf 125.
     § Essex Registry of Deeds, book 38, leaf 260.
     ‖ Essex Registry of Deeds, book 38, leaf 272.
     ¶ Essex Registry of Deeds, book 39, leaf 93.
     ** Essex Registry of Deeds, book 39, leaf 80.
     †† Essex Registry of Deeds, book 44, leaf 43.
     ‡‡ Essex Registry of Deeds, book 44, leaf 72.
     §§ Essex Registry of Deeds, book 44, leaf 73.
     ‖‖ Essex Registry of Deeds, book 45, leaf 18.
     ¶¶ Essex Registry of Deeds, book 45, leaf 83.
     *** Essex Registry of Deeds, book 56, leaf 53.
     ††† Essex Registry of Deeds, book 77, leaf 172.

south-eight in Ipswich, originally the lot of Daniel Hovey of
Ipswich, deceased, lying in Wilderness Hill division, March 12.
1738-9.* For four hundred and twenty pounds, he conveyed six
and one-half acres of land and buildings thereon, "formerly of
my father Daniel Hovey of Ipswich, deceased," Jan. 12, 1742.†
For one hundred and seventy-eight pounds and fifteen shillings,
he bought forty acres of upland and meadow in West parish of
Boxford, with the buildings thereon, May 18, 1743.‡

Mr. Hovey married Martha, daughter of Dea. Samuel and
Martha (Newmarch) Balch of Beverly about 1698. She was
born in Beverly Sept. 13, 1676. Mr. Hovey died in Boxford Feb.
16, 1748-9, aged seventy-five; and his wife Martha survived him,
dying in Boxford Aug. 16, 1761, at the age of eighty-four. Their
children were born in Ipswich as follows:—

54—I.   MARTHA², born Oct. 30, 1699; married John Fisk of Boxford
(published May 13, 1725); lived in Boxford until about 1737,
when he removed to Methuen. He died in 1739; administration being granted on his estate May 29, 1739. She returned
to Boxford; and died there, his widow, Sept. 19, 1746, aged
forty-six. Children: 1. *John*, born Sept. 28, 1727, in Boxford; was living in 1739. 2. *Mary*, born Oct. 8, 1729, in
Boxford; died in Boxford Sept. 5, 1736. 3. *Martha*, born in
173-; living in 1739. 4. *Sarah*, born in 173-; living in
1739. 5. *Abiah (Abiel)*, baptized in Boxford July 29, 1739.

55—II.   DANIEL², born Oct. 29, 1701. *See family numbered "55."*

56—III.   ESTHER², born Jan. 21, 1703; married, when she was of Rowley,
Stephen, son of Samuel and Abigail (Middleton) Runnells of
Bradford Nov. 20, 1728. He was born in Bradford May 14,
1703; and lived in Bradford, being a cooper, until 1736, when
they removed to Boxford, where he died suddenly March 10,
1753, at the age of forty-nine. The inscription upon his gravestone, in the ancient burial place at West Boxford, reads as
follows:—

HERE LIES BURIED
THE   BODY   OF
Mʳ   STEPHEN
RUNNELS WHO
DIED   MARCH
THE 10th 1753
AGED 48 YEARS.

His wife had belonged to the church in Bradford before
their removal to Boxford, and became one of the founders in
the Second church in Boxford. She married, secondly, Luke
Hovey (88) of Boxford April 24, 1755; and died Feb. 19,
1776, at the age of seventy-three. Her children were all by
Mr. Runnels, as follows: 1. *Stephen*, born in Bradford,
baptized Oct. 19, 1729; married Hannah Pearl of Boxford
April 11, 1754; lived in Boxford; yeoman; his farm being
that which was late of Miss Harriet Reynolds; he died in

* Essex Registry of Deeds, book 78, leaf 17.
† Essex Registry of Deeds, book 85, leaf 84.
‡ Essex Registry of Deeds, book 95, leaf 129.

Boxford June 23, 1771, aged forty-one; she survived him, and died, his widow, in 1789. They had nine children. Stephen Reynolds, who was so prominent at Honolulu nearly a century ago, was their grandson. 2. *Martha*[2], born in Bradford, baptized Dec. 31, 1732; probably died young. 3. *Esther*[2], born in Bradford, baptized Dec. 29, 1734; married Moses Sargent of Methuen Nov. 29, 1767, as his second wife; he was a farmer, and lived and died in Methuen. She had one child. 4. *Daniel*[2], born in Boxford in 1736, baptized Oct. 9, 1737; died Nov. 11, 1738, aged thirteen months. 5. *William*[2], born in Boxford, baptized Sept. 9, 1739; served in the Revolution. 6. *Daniel*[2], born in Boxford, baptized Sept. 12, 1742; settled in Londonderry, N. H., as early as 1765; married Hannah Spofford April 14, 1767; he was a carpenter, and a colonel in the Revolution; he died Dec. 13, 1795, aged fifty-three; and she died in Derry Jan. 23, 1829, at the age of eighty-three. They had ten children.

57—IV. THOMAS[2], born March 30, 1707. *See family numbered "57."*
58—V. ABIGAIL[2], baptized 14: 8: 1711;* married Job Runnels (brother of her sister Esther's husband) of Bradford Nov. 19, 1733. He was born in Bradford June 18, 1712. She died Oct. 14, 1753; and he married, secondly, Mary Woodman Oct. 5, 1758. He died in 1776. The children of Mrs. Abigail Runnels were born in Bradford as follows: 1. *Abigail*[2], born Oct. 12, 1734; married Jeremiah Kimball, jr., of Bradford Dec. 6, 1757; and they had five children. 2. *John*[2], born Feb. 27, 1736; was in the old French war and the Revolution; lived in Bradford; married, first, Sarah Kimball June 8, 1758; and, second, Mrs. Rebecca (Poor), widow of Moses Kimball of Boxford, Oct. 26, 1797. He died at the old homestead in 1821, at the age of eighty-five; and she died Nov. 3, 1821, at the age of seventy-nine. 3. *Mary*[2], born July 22, 1737; married Daniel Buswell of Bradford Jan. 25, 1759; and died Dec. 9, 1765, aged twenty-eight. He died Aug. 12, 1813, at the age of seventy-seven. They had four children, a grandson being Rev. Charles Spofford Buswell of West Fairlee, Vt., and Chicago, Ill. 4. *Phebe*[2], born May 8, 1739; married Abraham Kimball. 5. *Thomas*[2], born Feb. 26, 1741; lived in Methuen, and removed to Salem, N. H., in 1780; married Phebe ————; and had two children. 6. *Elizabeth*[2], born in 1743; baptized June 12, 1743; died young. 7. *Elizabeth*[2], born July 1, 1748; married Michael, son of Edmund and Dorothy (Kimball) Kimball of Bradford in 1763; he was born in Bradford April 21, 1745; lived in Pembroke, N. H.; she died, and he married, secondly, Anna ————; he died in 1803. They had children. 8. *Martha*[2], born July 3, 1750.

59—VI. PHEBE[2], baptized 20: 10: 1713;* was admitted to the Second church in Boxford (West parish) July 29, 1744.
60—VII. SAMUEL[2], baptized 22: 2: 1716* (born May 3, 1716?). *See family numbered "60."*
61—VIII. MARY (or MERCY)[2], baptized March 21; 1719;* married David Wood of Lunenburg Feb. 19, 1745-6. Their children were born in Lunenburg as follows: 1. *Mary*[2], born July 8, 1747. 2. *Martha*[2], born July 15, 1749. 3. *Bette*[2], born Oct. 21, 1751. 4. *Sarah*[2], born June 10, 1754. 5. *David*[2], born Dec. 6, 1756. 6. *Zephaniah*[2], born July 4, 1760.

* Their mother is called "Phebe" on the church records.

13

JOHN HOVEY[3], born in Ipswich, Mass., Aug. 13, 1675. He lived in Ipswich, and was a weaver by trade. He was possessed of a good estate, and his name appears in a number of real estate transactions.

For nine pounds, he conveyed four and a half acres of marsh on Plum island, at Bar island, April 3, 1705;[*] and, for eight pounds, he bought forty rods of land on the north side of the mill river in Ipswich, next to the land his shop then stood on, June 16, 1708.[†] For five pounds, he conveyed lot 294 in Chebacco woods, Dec. 11, 1712;[‡] and, for twenty-one shillings, he conveyed twenty-one rods of land in Labor-in-vain field, being part of his pasture, Dec. 28, 1712.[§] For eighteen shillings, he conveyed his new thatch lot of half an acre at "holl island" in Ipswich, being lot 317, on the south side of Rowley river, March 25, 1714;[||] and, for three pounds, he conveyed his new upland lot 44, at Jeffries' neck, in Ipswich, containing sixty rods, and being on Manning's hill, Jan. 12, 1715.[¶]

In exchange for other land, he bought of his brother Thomas Hovey ten acres of marsh and upland in Ipswich, on the west side of Labor-in-vain creek, March 20, 1718.[**]

With his brother Thomas Hovey, he bought of his nephew Nathaniel Hovey, the latter's interest in the dwelling house of the latter's deceased father, in Ipswich, on the south side of the river, April 8, 1718;[††] and, on the same day, the said Nathaniel also conveyed to his said uncles his interest in the estate of his grandfather Daniel Hovey.[‡‡]

Mr. Hovey married Mehitable Safford of Ipswich May 25, 1702; and died, "at his house in Ipswich," Aug. 17, 1720, aged thirty-five. His remains lie buried in the ancient cemetery at Ipswich, and his gravestone bears the following inscription:—

> JOHN HOUEY SON
> OF DANIEL HOU
> EY JUN DIED
> AUGUST Y[e] 17
> 1 7 2 0

[*] Essex Registry of Deeds, book 24, leaf 25.
[†] Essex Registry of Deeds, book 27, leaf 39.
[‡] Essex Registry of Deeds, book 32, leaf 248.
[§] Essex Registry of Deeds, book 25, leaf 253.
[||] Essex Registry of Deeds, book 29, leaf 77.
[¶] Essex Registry of Deeds, book 39, leaf 80.
[**] Essex Registry of Deeds, book 39, leaf 93.
[††] Essex Registry of Deeds, book 36, leaf 115.
[‡‡] Essex Registry of Deeds, book 36, leaf 125.

His widow was appointed administratrix of his estate Dec. 5, 1720. The following is a copy of the inventory of his property :—

A true Innentory of all & fingular yᵉ Goods Chattels and Creedits of John Houcy weeuer Late of Ipswich Decᵉ prifed the 14ᵗʰ Day of Decᵐ 1720 by Calib Kimbull Dillingham Caldwell and Thomas Staniford as followeth

	£	s	d
Impᵗᵃ His waring apparell	009	00	00
his arms 3ˢ 10ᵈ	003	10	00
Item Houfing & Land about it	110	00	00
thirteen acors & ½ of Land Marsh & upland	108	00	00
A new Right in yᵉ eights	020	00	00
to 4 Neete Cattell 8ˡ nine Sheep 58ˢ 6ᵈ	010	18	06
to two fwine	001	08	00
Itᵐ Two thirds of a fhaloop	013	06	08
Itᵐ two thirds of a floet 26ˢ 8ᵈ four lins & leads 18ˢ	002	04	08
Itᵐ a hogshead of falt 24ˢ & two flacks 12ˢ	001	16	00
to a wheel barow 3ˢ 6ᵈ	000	03	06
Item Indian Corn 40ˢ Pork & beff 90ˢ	006	10	00
Looms & tackling working bars & quill whell	009	00	00
Item 3 beeds & furnituer belonging to them	015	10	00
to a fmall trundel beed	001	05	00
Item to Linning	008	19	00
Item 5 Chefts & 2 boxes and ovell tabell	005	00	00
Item 14 Chairs 31ˢ to 2 tabels 2 Joynt Stools & meall trof	02	14	00
Item to two Looking Glafes 12ˢ	000	12	00
Item to putter	002	14	00
Item to 2 filluer Spoons 24ˢ	001	04	00
to earthen ware 19ˢ Tinware 7ˢ to Iron ware 3ˡ 13ˢ	004	10	00
Brafs ware 5ˡ 7ˢ to Books 30ˢ	006	17	00
Item to a pilyon 10ˢ	000	10	00
To old cask wooden ware & sundrey things	001	10	00
To six pounds of prouence bils	006	00	00
To on old plow	000	08	00
	353	06	02
The Reall Estate ::	238	0	0
the Parsonall	115	6	2
	353	6	2

CALEB KIMBALL
DILLINGHAM CALDWELL
THOˢ STANIFORD

Loſse vpon Sheep:

His brother Thomas Hovey, for rent of twenty-two shillings and six pence yearly payable to his mother, conveyed to the heirs of the deceased a right of way to his marsh Jan. 26, 1721.*

* Essex Registry of Deeds, book 38, leaf 260.

John Hovey's widow, as his administratrix, for one hundred and thirty-six pounds, conveyed thirteen acres of tillage, pasture and marsh land in Labor-in-vain field in Ipswich which belonged to the estate of the deceased, April 17, 1722.*

Mr. Hovey's daughter Mehitable, wife of James Moulton of Ipswich, conveyed to her brother Samuel Hovey her interest in her father's real estate, particularly in his homestead of a quarter of an acre, with the house and barn thereon, and a common right in Bush hill and at Birch island, in Ipswich, Jan. 7, 1733-4.†

His daughter Sarah and her husband, Bartholomew Pearson of Newbury, for twenty-seven pounds, conveyed her interest in the estate of her father to her brother Samuel March 25, 1734.†

Mr. Hovey's widow married, secondly, Ebenezer Browne of Rowley (published April 7, 1722). They apparently had no children; and he died in April, 1733, having devised to her half of his real estate, besides bequeathing to her all of his personal property. She married, thirdly, Lt. Jacob Perley of Boxford (published June 24, 1733). She died in Bradford in 1754, being the widow of Mr. Perley, who had died in the spring of 1751, in Bradford, where they then dwelt. Administration upon her estate was granted to her son Samuel Hovey March 23, 1754.

The children of John and Mehitable (Safford) Hovey were born in Ipswich as follows:—

62—1.   MEHITABLE⁴, born Aug. 11, 1703; married James, son of William Moulton of Ipswich March 10, 1721-2. He was a cordwainer. They lived in Ipswich until after 1735, when they removed to Windham, Conn., where they were living in 1755. Their son, 1. *Asa*⁵, lived in Mansfield, Conn.; married Lydia Freeman Jan. 26, 1769; she died Sept. 17, 1794; their son Daniel Moulton married Hannah Hovey (583).

63—11.   JOHN⁴, born Dec. 16, 1704; died Aug. 7, 1705.

64—111.   SARAH⁴, born June 9, 1706; married Bartholomew, son of Benjamin and Hannah (Thurston) Pearson of Newbury, millwright, Dec. 9, 1726. She died in 1736; and he married, secondly, Love Boynton of Bradford May 25, 1737. She died; and he married, thirdly, Lydia Randall of Lunenburg Nov. 3, 1763. He lived in Newbury until about 1746, when he removed to Shrewsbury. In 1759, he removed to Winchendon, and built the first mill on Miller's river. The children of Bartholomew and Sarah (Hovey) Pearson were baptized in Byfield parish as follows: 1. *John*⁵, baptized Oct. 22, 1727; and was living in Shrewsbury in 1754. 2. *Sarah*⁵, baptized April 5, 1730; living in Shrewsbury, unmarried, in 1754. 3. *Mary*⁵, baptized Nov. 12, 1732; living in Shrewsbury, unmarried, in 1754. 4. *Bartholomew*⁵, baptized June 29, 1735; living in Shrewsbury in 1754.

65—IV.   JOHN⁴, born July 11, 1708; died July 27, 1708.

66—V.   SAMUEL⁴, baptized 8: 2: 1711. *See family numbered "66."*

* Essex Registry of Deeds, book 38, leaf 237.
† Essex Registry of Deeds, book 69, leaf 82.

67—VI.   MARY⁴, baptized 23: 3: 1714; spinster; lived in Boxford in 1735;
         and in Bradford, unmarried, in 1757. When of Boxford, for
         forty pounds, she conveyed to her brother Samuel Hovey
         her (one-fifth) interest in the real estate of her father,
         particularly the homestead, house and barn and land, and
         three new common rights in Bush hill and at Birch island at
         Ipswich, Nov. 4, 1735.* When she was of Bradford, for
         eleven pounds and four shillings, she conveyed to her said
         brother two acres of land in Rowley by the grantee's house,
         Nov. 29, 1754.† For ten pounds, thirteen shillings and four
         pence, she sold two and a half acres of salt marsh in New-
         bury falls, on the west side of the falls river, July 5, 1757‡

68—VII. JOHN⁴, baptized July 6, 1718; died Aug. 14, 1719, about thirteen
         months old.

15

 EBENEZER HOVEY³, born in Ipswich, Mass., Jan. 11, 1680.
He was a weaver, fisherman and yeoman, and lived in his native
town. He was possessed of considerable property, and was a
party to a number of real estate transactions.

Mr. Hovey bought a house and barn and half an acre of
land in Ipswich, on the south side of Town river, Feb. 16,
1703-4.§ He,also, bought of his brother Thomas Hovey, surviving executor of Daniel Hovey, sr., of Ipswich, planter, deceased, for eight pounds, four acres of marsh in Ipswich, on Barr
island, lying on the easterly side of the river, July 20, 1704.
when he is called a laborer:‖ and, also, two acres of tillage land
in Labor-in-vain field in Ipswich April 30, 1708.¶ He bought
six acres of land in Labor-in-vain field, in Ipswich, Oct. 22,
1708;** and on the same day sold two acres of land in the same
field.††

For one hundred pounds, he conveyed his house and homestead, in Ipswich, "where I now live," and half an acre of land on
the southeast side of the Town river, northwest side of the highway, and southwesterly side of "ye proprietors' land of ye
wharfe"; and also six acres of pasture and tillage land in Labor-
in-vain field in Ipswich Sept. 20, 1714.‡‡

He mortgaged to his brother John Hovey and Thomas
Hodgkins four acres of salt marsh at Barr island on Plum island;

* Essex Registry of Deeds, book 105, leaf 203.
† Essex Registry of Deeds, book 104, leaf 261.
‡ Essex Registry of Deeds, book 107, leaf 132.
§ Essex Registry of Deeds, book 15, leaf 232.
‖ Essex Registry of Deeds, book 36, leaf 198.
¶ Essex Registry of Deeds, book 21, leaf 70.
** Essex Registry of Deeds, book 21, leaf 69.
†† Essex Registry of Deeds, book 21, leaf 123.
‡‡ Essex Registry of Deeds, book 30, leaf 127.

a new right, 130, in Jeffrey neck division; and a new right in the eighth or common lands in Ipswich, etc., Dec. 15, 1718.*

For fourteen pounds, he conveyed four acres of Marsh at Plum island in Ipswich on the northeast side of a creek next Sandy point, Feb. 8, 1719.†

For six pounds in money and seven cords of wood, he conveyed a five-acre woodlot in ye great swamp in Ipswich beyond Chebacco ponds, being lot 435, March 17, 1712-3.‡

For one hundred pounds, he conveyed his dwelling house in Ipswich on land of John Dennis opposite the dwelling house of John Potter, Jan. 1, 1719-20.§

For twenty-three pounds, he conveyed a common right in the Eighths in Ipswich Oct. 5, 1719.||

For six pounds, he sold an upland lot on Jeffries' neck in Ipswich, May 16, 1724.¶

Mr. Hovey was apparently not prominent in town affairs. He was a corder of wood, a town officer, in 1711 and until 1715.

He was engaged in fishing to a slight extent, having bought a small schooner the winter before his decease. His sons also became fishermen.

The following is a copy of his autograph, taken from his signature to a bond dated 1718:

Mr. Hovey married Elizabeth, daughter of Thomas and Grace (Searle) Dennis of Ipswich (published July 23, 1704) in 1704. When her father died, in 1706, he bequeathed to her one hundred pounds. A pillow-case possessed by her, having been spun, woven and sewed by her mother and embroidered with the maker's initials, is in the possession of Rev. Augustine Caldwell of Eliot, Me., a descendant of Mrs. Hovey.

Mr. Hovey died in Ipswich Aug. 8, 1729, at the age of forty-nine. His attending physician was Dr. Thomas Berry of Ipswich. His widow and their son Ebenezer Hovey were appointed administrators of the estate Dec. 22, 1729; and they duly returned the following inventory to the court:—

An Enuentory of the Estaite of Mr Ebenezer Hovey Laite of Ipswich Defesed taken this 4 Day of Defember 1730 viz

To 8 Books 50s/ to one Bead Bolster & furneture in the Lower
    Rome 10' 5s:s/ one Blonket 20s/   15   5

* Essex Registry of Deeds, book 35, leaf 81.
† Essex Registry of Deeds, book 35, leaf 258.
‡ Essex Registry of Deeds, book 36, leaf 24.
§ Essex Registry of Deeds, book 37, leaf 55.
|| Essex Registry of Deeds, book 39, leaf 118.
¶ Essex Registry of Deeds, book 45, leaf 1.

To one Ceuerlid 25*/ to one Cradell Cenerled 5*/ one pare
   of Sheets 16*/   2   6
To one Low Bead Bolster piler under Bead Bedstid & Cord   8 18
To one pare of Sheets 16*/ one Blankitt 10*/ Ceuerlide 12*/   1 18
To one Bead & Bolster in the Chamber 6 12   6 12
To one Beadstid & Cord under Bead 8*/ one peare of Sheets
   20*/   1   8
To two Ceuerlids 25*/ to 6 Black Chers 24*/ one Grate Chere
   5*/   2 14
To one pare of Sheets 30*/ to one pare of Sheet 10*/   2
To one Dofson of Napkins 36*/ half a Dofsion of Dieaper
   Ditto 12*/   2   8
To one table Cloth 4*/6* to 4 pelebers & one Napkine 35*/   1 19   0
To 7 pelebars 28*/ to 4 table Cloths 22*/ one Bolster Case 5   2 15
To one pilerber 4*/ one pare of Sheets 9*/ one Case of
   Drows 40*/   2 13
To 2 Caruide Boxis 20*/ to 2 Boxis 6*/ to one table 10*   1 16
To 2 Looking Glafsis 35*/ one Cradele Ceuerlide 3*/ one
   Cushing 3*/   2   1
To one Chist 15*/ to 2 tables 9* 2 joynt stools 5*/ to 2 Black
   Cheers 6*/   1 15
To 6 old Cheers 6*/ one Chist 20*/ one meet Chest 7*   1 13
To 2 Salt Boxis 3* to one old wheell 3*/ old Cask 9* & 2 old
   matures 3*/   18
To old Cradle 4*/ old Skals 4*/ & 3 Be hiues 4*/6* & 11
   pound of puter 33*/   2   5   6
To 17 pound of Puter 42*/6*   2   2   6
To ten ware 1*/ Erthing ware 12*/ to 11 Glafs Bottels 7*/8*
   13 trenchers 1*   1   1   8
To wood Uaffells 7* aboute an ounce of Siluer 17*/6   1   4   6
To 3 wine Glafis 2*/6 to 6 Brafs Kittels, 5£ 2*   5   4   6
To Blafs pane 16*/ & 3 jron potts 30*/ & 2 pare of pothooks 4*   2 10
To one pare of hand jrons 16*/ jron Spitt 5* & 2 jron
   tramils 10*/   1 11
To a Slice & tongs 8*/ Chafing Dish Gridiron tofter & flash
   fork 10*/   18
To one frying pan 10*/ one Bafkitt 2*/ to a Cow 90*   5   2
To two Box jrons & 4 heeters 16*/ to 2 Swine 20*/ Wheell
   Barrow 5*/   2   1
To a Small Skooner with Some Ridging Ankers & float   50
To 2 old Looms & other weuers tackling 45*   2   5
To an old Lamp 1*/6* Candle Stick 1*/ & a old puter pot 4*
   old stool 1*/6*   8
To one Bond Due to the Estaite by it yet   22
for Wagis for one of the Childrens Sarvice while his father
   Liued   17 10
for Wagis for one of the Children before his farthers Death 14 12   9
To ten pound of Bills of Crad*t   10
To 4 Shot of old Line & Leads 40*/
To a Swine houfe with bords aboute it 20*   1
To an owne 3* to 2 Cibe Skins 12*/   15
To 3 old Herrin Neatt 10*/ to a Cheese prafs 5*   15
To a Lewfitt 2*/6* old Skreen 2*/ to two Siues 2*/6*   7

       mark
ELIZA   X   HOVIE: JAMES fFOSTER
      her   AARON POTTER
EBENEZER HOUEY   Jofeph BOLLES

Ipsw^{ch}: Jan. 20th 1730: Then Eliz Hovie & Ebenez Hovie Admins made Oath to the truth of this Inventory
Before   JOHN APPLETON *J. Prob.*

The estate was represented insolvent and Richard Rogers and Aaron Potter of Ipswich were appointed commissioners to examine claims March 30, 1731. They met at the house of Samuel Staniford, innholder, in Ipswich. The order of distribution is dated March 1, 1731-2.

Mr. Hovey's widow was living in 1737, and probably deceased soon after.

Their children were born in Ipswich, and were as follows :—

69—I.   EBENEZER⁴, born Nov. 6, 1705. *See family numbered "69."*
70—II.   FRANCIS⁴, born Feb. 2, 1707-8; died June 19, 1710, aged two. The inscription on his gravestone in the ancient burial place is as follows :—

```
HERE  LYS  Y*
BODY  OF  FRAN
CSES    HOVEY
WHO  DIED  IVNE
Y*      19     1710
AGED    2   YEARS
4   MONTHS   &
20    D A Y S
```

71—III. THOMAS⁴, born May 9, 1710. *See family numbered "71."*
72—IV.   FRANCIS⁴, baptized 27 : 5 : 1712; drowned with six others at sea fishing on Canso Bank April 7, 1737.
73—V.   JOHN⁴, baptized March 28, 1714; he was a fisherman, and lived in Ipswich. For one hundred and fifty-five pounds, he bought a house and some land in Ipswich on the west side of the lane to Smith's shipyard, Oct. 16, 1736.* He married Deborah Heard of Ipswich Jan. 4, 1737-8; and apparently died before Aug. 30, 1746, when widow Deborah Hovey was published to Ezekiel Hodgkins, both of Ipswich. See No. 11.
74—VI.   ELIZABETH⁴, baptized 26 : 12 : 1715; married John, son of Thomas and Abigail (Hovey) [11] Hodgkins of Ipswich (published Oct. 21, 1738); lived in Ipswich. Their daughter Eunice married Isaac Stanwood of Ipswich; and the latter's great-grandson, Edward Stanwood of Boston, Bowdoin college, 1861, was editor of the Boston Advertiser in 1882 and 1883; and of the Youth's Companion from 1884.
75—VII. LYDIA⁴, baptized 21 : 9 : 1717; died young.
76—VIII. ABIGAIL⁴, baptized July 5, 1719; married John, son of John and Elizabeth (Lull) Caldwell of Ipswich (published Dec. 10, 1738); he was born July 11, 1717; she died of typhoid fever Nov. 7, 1770; he married, secondly, Ruth (Andrews), widow of Bemsley Wells (published Oct. 5, 1775); lived in Ipswich, for forty years on Turkey shore, opposite the old Hovey homestead; and the last few years of his life on the Argilla road. By his wife Abigail, he had the following children, born in Ipswich: 1. *Elizabeth⁵*, baptized Oct. 27, 1739; mar-

* Essex Registry of Deeds, book 71, leaf 236.

ried Daniel Rindge; and had five children. 2. *John*[2], baptized Aug. 30, 1741; married Abigail Hodgkins (published Jan. 19, 1763); and died of typhus fever July 26, 1771; they had three children: she married, secondly, Samuel Henderson, and died in Ipswich Dec. 17, 1733, aged ninety-three. 3. *Abigail*[2], baptized July 12, 1743; died July 7, 1747. 4. *Ebenezer*[3], born Sept. 21, 1745; married, first, Lucy Rindge Dec. 1, 1768; she died in 1772; he married, second, Mercy Dodge Dec. 9, 1773; he died Dec. 16, 1821, aged seventy-six; she died May 28, 1837, aged eighty-four; captain; Revolutionary soldier; he had twelve children; and was ancestor of Rev. Augustine Caldwell of Eliot, Me. 5. *Thomas*[4], baptized Oct. 1, 1747; Revolutionary soldier; married, first, Lucy Henderson Jan. 26, 1773; she died Sept. 18, 1788; he married, second, widow Mary (Ross) Sweet Feb. 14, 1793; and she died Sept. 19, 1833. He had eleven children. 6. *Stephen*[5], baptized Sept. 10, 1749; lived in Ipswich, Mass., Hampton Falls, N. H., and Augusta, Me.; married Abigail Low (published May 28, 1774); and she died in 1836, aged eighty-six. They had nine children. 7. *Abigail*[2], baptized Sept. 1, 1751; died of typhus fever May 12, 1771. 8. *Sarah*[3], baptized Dec. 2, 1752; died of typhus fever July 5, 1771. 9. *Sylvanus*[4], baptized May 10, 1756; died of typhus fever May 9, 1771. 10. *Lydia*[4], married (as his second wife) Benjamin Caldwell Dec. 31, 1789; and died in Derry, N. H., Feb. 12, 1835, aged seventy-seven. Their son Abel Caldwell, Dartmouth college, 1817, was a clergyman in Westford, N. Y., and a missionary. 11. *Francis*[4], baptized Sept. 1, 1760; Revolutionary soldier; married Abigail Merrifield June 1, 1793; he died Nov. 21, 1830; and she died Feb. 19, 1845, aged seventy-seven. They had no children. 12. *Mary*[3], baptized April 1, 1764; died at Ipswich March 2, 1835, aged seventy-two.

77—IX.   LYDIA[4], baptized Aug. 27, 1721; died July 18, 1737, aged fifteen.

16

JOHN HOVEY[3], born in Topsfield Dec. —, 1666. He lived in Topsfield, except for a few years beginning with 1711, when he lived in Boxford. He bought ten acres of land in Boxford on the Rowley town line June 29, 1706.* He also bought, of his father, forty-nine acres of land in Boxford, on the Andover town line, adjoining Philistine hill, and also a part of Maple meadow, March 7, 1706-7.† He also bought of his father five acres of land in Boxford Nov. 22, 1708.‡ With his brother Luke Hovey, he also bought of his father a part of Maple meadow in Boxford, on the Andover town line, Jan. 13, 1709-10;§ and, for seven pounds and ten shillings, he sold one-third of the meadow Jan.

* Essex Registry of Deeds, book 19, leaf 116.
† Essex Registry of Deeds, book 20, leaf 115.
‡ Essex Registry of Deeds, book 21, leaf 150.
§ Essex Registry of Deeds, book 22, leaf 33.

21, 1718.* He sold three acres of marsh in Ipswich, near Hovey's island, with Ivory Hovey of Topsfield, July 17, 1718.†

His father conveyed to him, for love and "yᵉ Severall Duties that he Shall doe towards my maintainance if need Shall hereafter require & yᵉ payment of his part of Severall portions to his Sisters & Cousens as he is bound or he is with his brethren to me sᵈ John Hovey Senʳ as appeareth more at large in a bond from him & his bretheren to me yᵉ sᵈ John Hovey Senʳ bearing Equall date with these presents," fifty acres, being the remainder of a lot lying all the way from Andover line to the top of Philistine hill and to Walker's hill and Walker's meadow, part of which he formerly conveyed to John (March 7, 1706-7); also, twenty acres extending from the Bradford line over Philistine hill to Walker's hill; also, the grantor's share in ash swamp; also, fifteen acres grantor bought of Col. John Wainwright, lying on the northwesterly side of the highway leading from Rowley to Boxford; also, one-half of a portion of great meadow in Rowley; also, one-half of the grantor's interest in Mr. Nelson's farm of two thousand acres; also, one-third of grantor's marsh by Hovey's island in Ipswich; also, grantor's land in Topsfield next Baker's pond; etc., March 14, 1717-8.‡

For one hundred pounds, he bought thirty acres of land on Pie brook, July 22, 1718.§ With Ivory Hovey of Topsfield he conveyed one and one-half acres of land in Topsfield, near Wenham meadows, Feb. 11, 1722,3.‖ For twenty-one pounds, he bought sixteen acres of upland, swamp and meadow in Rowley and Boxford Feb. 26, 1710-1;¶ and he bought some common land in Topsfield June 29, 1722.** He, also, bought, for ten pounds, three acres of swamp and meadow in Topsfield, on Pye brook, Feb. 8, 1724-5;†† and, also, for forty pounds and ten shillings, five acres of meadow, in two lots, in Poplar meadow in Topsfield Aug. 5, 1725.‡‡ For twenty pounds, he sold four acres in Satchwell's meadow in Topsfield July 21, 1718.§§ For sixteen pounds and five shillings, he sold ten acres of land in Boxford July 18, 1718.‖‖ Aug. 8, 1733, he joined with Luke Hovey and others in three deeds, conveying in each eleven acres of land in Boxford,

* Essex Registry of Deeds, book 37, leaf 63.
† Essex Registry of Deeds, book 36, leaf 35.
‡ Essex Registry of Deeds, book 38, leaf 10.
§ Essex Registry of Deeds, book 38, leaf 16.
‖ Essex Registry of Deeds, book 41, leaf 59.
¶ Essex Registry of Deeds, book 42, leaf 16.
** Essex Registry of Deeds, book 42, leaf 17.
†† Essex Registry of Deeds, book 48, leaf 21.
‡‡ Essex Registry of Deeds, book 48, leaf 22.
§§ Essex Registry of Deeds, book 49, leaf 141.
‖‖ Essex Registry of Deeds, book 51, leaf 61.

part of Nelson's farm.* He bought two or three acres of land in Ipswich, at Baker's pond, March 8, 1734-5.† For thirty-seven pounds, he sold fifteen acres of upland in Boxford and two acres in Rowley great meadows, which his father bought of John Parley, July 9, 1718.‡ For love, he conveyed to his son John Hovey of Boxford about seventeen acres of land in Boxford June 14, 1743.§

For eleven pounds, he bought two and three-quarters acres of land in Topsfield, being the first lot of the second division, "at or near the place called Wintrops Hills," and bounded on the northeast by the Ipswich line, Dec. 2, 1724.|| For six pounds, two shillings and six pence, he bought one and three-quarters acres, being the second lot in the above-mentioned division, May 1, 1724.||

Mr. Hovey was a husbandman all his life. He married, first, Mary, daughter of Michael and Mary Dwinnell of Topsfield Jan. 11, 1691-2. She was born in Topsfield Jan. 21, 1668-9. She died there May 7, 1737, at the age of sixty-eight. He married, second, Mary Abbot of Ipswich March 8, 1737-8; and she was living in 1743. He died in Topsfield May 31, 1751.

The following is a copy of his will:—

In the Name of God Amen: The ninth Day of February: 1739/40 I John Hovey of Topsfield in the County of Essex in yᵉ Province of Maſſachuſets Bay in New England: being Sickly and weak of body But of Perfect mind and memory: thanks be Giuen to God: Therefore Calling to mind the mortallity of my body, knowing that it is appointed for all men once to Die Do make and ordain this my Last Will and Testament: that is to say Principally and firſt of all I Give and Recommend my soul into the hands of God that Gave it, any my body I recommend to the Earth to be buried in Decent Chriſtian burial at the Diſcretion of my Executor: nothing Doubting but I shall Receive the same again, at the General Reſurrection by the mighty Power of God: and as for such worldiv Eſtate as it hath pleased God to bless me with in this Life I Give Demise and Dispose of the same in the following manner and form

Imprimes I Give and bequeath to my well beloved wife Mary one full third part of all my Real Estate as fully as if there were no will made and I Give to my said wife the use and benefit of one thirds of my Parſonal Estate During her natural Life and such Goods and Estate as my said wife brought with her which shall fall into her third she may Dispose of them as she shall see meet but the rest of my parſonal Estate that shall fall into her thirds shall return to my children at her Deceaſe.

Item I Give to my Son John all the Land which he now Lives on: viz all my Land in the farm former called mr Nelsons farm of Two thouſand acres being in Boxford and also that piece of salt marish which I

---

* Essex Registry of Deeds, book 66, leaves 51 and 267; book 67, leaf 273.
† Essex Registry of Deeds, book 69, leaf 45.
‡ Essex Registry of Deeds, book 77, leaf 279.
§ Essex Registry of Deeds, book 86, leaf 51.
|| Essex Registry of Deeds, book 121, leaf 114.

bought of Samuel Perley Lying in Ipswich hundreds so called and I Give to ‖my‖ Son John all my saws, and files, and setts belonging to them and my corn fan a sythe & a Gun; both which he shall chuse, and also my Great Bible.

Item I Give to my son Joseph all my Lands and buildings in Topsfield Lying on the North Eastwardly Side of Pie Brook so called and all my Lands Lying in Rowly and Boxford, Excepting what is above Given to my son John and I Give to my son Joseph my Book of Lives so called. and also a sythe & a Gun both which he shall chuse after his brother John has chosen his sythe & Gun. and I Give to my son Joseph all my Quick stock after his mothers third is taken out and all that shall be Left of her third of the stock at her Deceafe: and I Give to my said son all my instruments of Husbandry not other ways Given in this Will

Item I Give to my Daughter Mary Hale the fum of one hundred pounds to be paid by my Son Joseph Either in stock or money or other good pay Equevilent to bills of Publick Creditt of the old form and Tenor and to be paid as hereafter mentioned; namely Ten pound thereof within one year after my Decease and then fifteen pounds a year Every year after till whole be paid. and I give to my said Daughter my Book of Dr Prestons Entitled Gods Alsoficiency. I Give to my son Joseph Hale a sithe after my sons John and Joseph Hovey have had their choice.

Item I Give to my Daughter Susanna Scales all my Land in Topsfield Lying on the west of Southwesterly Side of Pie Brook so called. if she shall see Canfe to Live upon it. but if not then my son Joseph shall have said Land. and pay one hundred ‖pounds‖ to my said Daughter in manner and form as abovementioned to my Daughter Mary and my will is that my son Joseph shall allow a convenient way from the abovesaid Land to the country Road on pine Plain if my said Daughter Susanna shall come and Dwell on sd Land. and I Give to my said Daughter my Book of the London Ministers farewell Sermons and my will is that all my Books not above Given away shall be Equally Divided amongst all my Children.

And my Will is that my household Goods that shall be Left after my wifes thirds are taken out shall be Equelly Divided between my two Daughters. And I Give to my son in Law James Scales a Gun.

And I Do hereby Constitute make and ordain my Son Joseph Hovey to be the Sole Executor of this my Last Will and Testament Ratifying and confirming this to be my Last will and Testament and none other. In witness whereof I have hereunto set my hand and seal the Day and year above written

Signed Sealed Published & Declared
by the said John Hovey as his
Last Will and Testament
In presence of us yᵉ subscribers

John Hovey

Ivory Hovey
Jacob Dorman
Aaron Hovey
Jacob Peabody.

[SEAL]

The will was proved July 1, 1751.

The following is a copy of the original inventory on file in the office of the probate court at Salem:—

A True Inventory of all and singular the goods chattles and Eftate Both Real and personal of mr John Houey of Topsfield Late decᵈ ‖ In the county o Esex ‖ priesed at Topsfield yᵉ 25ᵗʰ day of July anno Domini

1751. By Jacob Dorman Joseph Robinson & Aron Houey as folloeth all
His Land in Topsfield with his Buildings theireon & all his Lands in
Boxford: and his Land & marsh in Ipswich and his Land L   s   d

	L	s	d
in Rowly at y* sume of	666	12	00
to his fire armes	01	01	04
to wareing aparil	06	18	08
to Hats	00	04	08
to shirts	00	10	00
to botes sohues stocking & buckiles	01	02	08
to Beads & beading	09	02	06
to chestes and other wooden wares	02	02	00
to Books	01	01	04
to a Came	00	08	00
to mony scailes and waites,	00	13	04
to shoue Leather	00	07	04
to a steele trape	00	10	08
to 4 old ougurs	00	03	00
to Brase wares	01	09	04
to old puter	01	04	04
to Ioron pots & cittles	00	06	09
to tramels and oirrons Slice & tongs & frying pan	00	08	00
to indian Corn 10 buchels	00	16	00
to sheps wool	00	07	06
to sider and caske	01	04	00
to Chains & plou iorns	00	04	08
to a paire of stilyards	00	04	08
to a brase watch	00	08	00
to a brase incken & a dial	00	02	08
to a pasel of old iron	01	12	00
to glase botels	00	02	08
to knifes & forcks	00	01	05
to 2 woolings wheles	00	02	08
to a pare of specttles	00	02	00
to chares	00	06	00
to a to Come or Hekel	00	04	08
to 2 pails & a pigen	00	01	10
to a plain jron shue mackers alls & shu heels and a tap boner			
& one busel of malt	00	03	04
to two bushels & a half of rye 1 bushel of otes	00	09	08
to a sadel & pilyon	00	18	08
to half a Bariel of porke	01	17	08
to 2 Horses	04	02	08
to one ox	02	13	04
to 3 Coues	06	18	08
to 2 yarlings & a Calf	02	08	00
to sheepe & Lambs	03	03	04
to seuen fwine	03	06	08
to files & a raspe	00	02	00
	730	09	10

By ous as abuf s^d y^r Day & Date abou wr[i]ten

JACOB DORMAN
AARON HOVEY   { Com
JOSEPH ROB[I]NSON   mitte

JOSEPH HOVEY EX^r

Efsex Ss. Ipswich July 24, 1751

Then Joseph Hovey made oath to the foregoing Inventory and if
anything further Appeared he would Cause it to be added

Before THO⁵ BERRY J⁴ Prob.

Mr. Hovey's children were born in Topsfield as follows:—

78—I.   DORCAS⁴, baptized Aug. 20, 1693; probably died young; not men-
        tioned in her father's will.

79—II. JOHN⁴, born May 29, 1695; died June 15, 1695.

80—III. MARY⁴, born Oct. 12, 1696; married Dea. Joseph, son of Joseph
        and Mary (Watson) Hale of Boxford Dec. 5, 1723. He was
        born in Boxford Aug. 23, 1694; and lived there, being deacon
        of the First church from 1759 until his death, twenty-nine
        years. She died May 25, 1753, aged fifty-six; and he married,
        secondly, Sarah (Rust), widow of Thomas Hovey (57) of
        Boxford Sept. 20, 1753. She died May 26, 1759; and he mar-
        ried, thirdly, widow Lydia Brown (published Sept. 23, 1759).
        He married, fourthly, widow Susanna Fellows of Ipswich
        Nov. 25, 1771. He died Oct. 5, 1778. Children of Joseph and
        Mary (Hovey) Hale, born in Boxford: 1. Mary⁵, born Jan.
        14, 1724-5; married Joseph, son of Isaac and Abigail (Board-
        man) Cummings of Ipswich Nov. 20, 1744. He was baptized
        in Topsfield May 20, 1722. She died; and he married, sec-
        ondly, Judith, daughter of Jonathan and Elizabeth Perkins of
        Topsfield March 21, 1758. She died March 30, 1791; and he
        married, thirdly, widow Lucy Knowlton June 21, 1791. He
        lived in Ipswich; and died Oct. 24, 1801. Joseph and Mary
        (Hale) Cummings had six children, the eldest of whom was
        Rev. Joseph Cummings of Marlboro, N. H. Among their
        grandsons are Hon. Isaac Cummings of Vermont, judge of
        probate, and Rev. Charles Cummings of Sullivan, N. H.; and
        among their great grandsons is Dr. Joseph Cummings Bach-
        elder of Topsfield and Templeton. 2. Joseph⁵, born Sept. 14,
        1727; built and lived in the "old Hale house" in Boxford;
        married Sarah Jackson of Topsfield Dec. 7, 1749; he died
        in 1795, aged sixty-seven; and she died April 24, 1813,
        aged eighty-four. They had six children. 3. Jonathan⁵, born
        Dec. 5, 1729; died June 24, 1731. 4. Sarah⁵, born Feb. 5,
        1731-2; married Thomas, son of Capt. Thomas and Sarah
        (Wade) Baker, jr., of Topsfield Feb. 26, 1752; he was born in
        Topsfield March 3, 1729-30; was a tanner, and lived in Tops-
        field until 1762, when they removed to Keene, N. H. They
        had several children. 5. Jonathan⁵, born Feb. 14, 1733-4; died
        of small pox Feb. —, 1757.

81—IV. JOHN⁴, born Aug. 27, 1699. See family numbered "81."

82—V.   JOSEPH⁴, born July 7, 1703. See family numbered "82."

83—VI. SUSANNAH⁴, born Aug. 22, 1710; married Rev. James, son of
        James and Sarah (Curtis) Scales of Rumford Sept. 10, 1736.
        He was born in Boxford May 21, 1707; and graduated at
        Harvard college in 1733. He settled in Concord, N. H., in
        1737; and was a physician there in 1746. He was the first
        preacher in Canterbury. He removed to Hopkinton, N. H.,
        between 1754 and 1757; and was ordained over the church
        there Nov. 23, 1757. He was dismissed July 4, 1770; and re-
        mained in the town being one of the selectmen, and a justice
        of the peace. He was a man of excellent ability, fertile in re-

sources, of a restless nature, and a natural pioneer. He
died in Hopkinton July 26, 1776, at the age of sixty-nine;
and his wife survived him until July 8, 1780, when she died in
Hopkinton, at the age of sixty-nine. Children: 1. *John*⁵, born
Oct. 4, 1737, in Rumford; died in Canterbury Oct. 13, 1752.
2. *Joseph*⁵, born April 15, 1740, in Rumford; died July 10,
1740. 3. *Stephen*⁵, born Oct. 16, 1741, in Rumford. 4. *Susanna*⁵, born Oct. 26, 1744, in Canterbury.

21

ENS. LUKE HOVEY³, born in Topsfield May 3, 1676. Mr.
Hovey lived in Topsfield until 1700, when he settled in Boxford.
On the land of his father, he built a house for himself across the
road from the present residence of John M. Pearl on the northern
shore of Mitchell's pond in the West parish of Boxford, where
an ancient cellar now marks the site. It is said that he and his
wife spent the last few years of their lives at the old Hovey house
which formerly stood near the brook on the west side of the highway between the houses of J. Warren Chadwick and the late Asa
Kimball, nearly on the opposite side of the pond from the house
he first built.

Mr. Hovey married Susannah, daughter of Moses and Susannah (Worth) Pillsbury of Newbury Oct. 25, 1698. She was
born in Newbury Feb. 1, 1677.

He was a husbandman; and held several offices in the town,
being one of the selectmen in 1708, 1709, 1719, 1736, 1743 and
1748. He was, also, ensign in the militia.

His father conveyed to him forty-three acres of land and
meadow in Boxford, on the northeast side of Mitchell's pond, including the sites of the two houses he had built, Aug. 28, 1706.*
It was bounded on the southwest by the pond, north and east by
the two roads, and on the southeast by the brook.

His father also conveyed to him and his brother John Hovey
his part of maple meadow on Andover town line, in Boxford, Jan.
13, 1709-10.† Mr. Hovey bought, for eleven pounds, thirteen
shillings and six pence, three acres of meadow "known as Mr.
Jewet's five-acre piece that is excepted out of Mr. Nelson's farm,"
March 9, 1714-5.‡ His father, for twenty pounds, also conveyed
to him twenty-five acres of land in Boxford, known as the Bush
hill lot, March 26, 1715;§ and, also, in consideration of love and a
bond, one hundred acres of upland and meadow in Boxford, part
of the farm Luke was living on; also, his undivided land in Mr.
Nelson's two thousand acres, March 14, 1717-8.‖

* Essex Registry of Deeds, book 18, leaf 201.
† Essex Registry of Deeds, book 22, leaf 33.
‡ Essex Registry of Deeds, book 28, leaf 235.
§ Essex Registry of Deeds, book 31, leaf 1.
‖ Essex Registry of Deeds, book 37, leaf 44.

For twenty pounds, Mr. Hovey sold three acres of meadow in Mr. Jewett's five acres that were excepted out of Mr. Nelson's farm, Sept. 14, 1722.* For fifty pounds, he bought ten acres of upland in Boxford March 2, 1730-1.† With his brother John Hovey he conveyed eleven acres of land in Boxford in three deeds, Aug. 8, 1733.‡ For love, he conveyed to his three sons, Luke, Joseph and Abijah, his interest in Walker's meadow in Boxford, March 8, 1748.§ With others, he bought a thatch bank on the long island in Parker river, Newbury, July 3, 1750.∥ He bought sixty acres of land in Oxford Jan. 6, 1723-4.¶

Mr. Hovey died Oct. 31, 1751, at the age of seventy-five. His remains lie buried in the ancient burial place in West Boxford, and his grave stone is inscribed:—

> HERE LIES BURIED
> THE BODY OF INSIN
> LUKE HOUEY WHO
> DEPARTED THIS LIFE
> OCTOBER 1751
> IN THE 76th YEAR
> OF HIS AGE

The following is a copy of his will on file in the office of the probate court in Salem:—

In The name of God Amen the Twenty first Day of October, AD: 1751; I Luke Hovey of Boxford in the County of Essex, in His Majesty's, provience of the Massachusetts-Bay, in New-England, gen'; Being very full of pain and weak in Body; but of perfect mind and memory. Thanks Be given unto God; Therefore Calling unto mind the mortality of my Body, and Knowing that it is appointed for all men once to Dye; Do make & Ordain this my Last Will and Testament: That is to say, principally, and First of all, I Give and recommend my Soul into the Hands of God that Gave it; and my Body I recommend to the earth, to be Buried in Decent Christian Burial, at the Discretion of my Executors; nothing Doubting but at the general resurrection, I Shall receive the Same again by the mighty power of God; and as Touching Such Worldly Estate wherewith it hath pleased God to bless me in this Life I Give Demise & Dispose of yᵉ Same in the Following manner and form:

Imprimis I give and Bequeath to my well-bloved wife Susannah, one third part of my Books and Household furniture to be at her Disposal; as she sees cause And as long as she shall Continue my widow, I Do hereby give her the use of the West room of my Dwelling house & one third part of the Cellcr, and one half of the West Chamber; and Liberty of yᵉ well & yard; and I Do hereby order & oblige my three sons. (ie) Luke Joseph & Abijah Them or their Heirs, to pay yearly to my aboves⁴ Wife as followeth (viz) Ten Bushels of Indian Corn, four bushels of

---

* Essex Registry of Deeds, book 41, leaf 68.
† Essex Registry of Deeds, book 55, leaf 218.
‡ Essex Registry of Deeds, book 66, leaves 51, 267 and 273.
§ Essex Registry of Deeds, book 95, leaf 204.
∥ Essex Registry of Deeds, book 97, leaf 217.
¶ Suffolk Registry of Deeds, book 38, page 45.

rie, one buiſhel of wheat, one buiſhel of malt; and Twelve pounds of
Sheeps Wool, Twelve pounds of flax, one hundred and Twenty pounds of
pork, & sixty pounds of beaf and as much Wood as she shall Have occaſion to burn, ready Cutt & brought into yᵉ yard, and what apples she
shall need for her Oun uſe in yᵉ Summer and four barils of Cyder & Six
buiſhels of apples for winter; and alſo to keep one Cow both in Summer
and Winter for the uſe of my said Wife, and Likewiſe find her a horſe to
go to meeting, or Carry her to meeting or or elſe where as she shall have
Occaſion, all theſe aboveſᵈ yearly payments are to be Well and Truly paid
by ‖my‖ three sons to my said Wife as long as she shall Continue my
widow & no longer:

Item I give & Bequeath to my Welbeloved wife the sum of Ten
Shillings and eight pence Lawfull money to be yearly paid her by my three
sons equally, During her natural Life:

Item I give and bequeath to my beloved Son Luke Hovey and to
his Hiers or aſsigns the several pieces or parcels of Land, herein hereafter mention'd withal the building thereon as a good and perfect eſtate
of Inheritance in fee simple, the first piece is bounded, as followeth beginning at a stake & stones by the way yᵗ goes from yᵉ homelots to yᵉ
hillots, Then Southarly as yᵉ fence now stands Down to yᵉ pond, Then
on yᵉ pond Westarly to runnels's, land & peabody's land, northarly,
Bounded on Woods land as yᵉ line goes on Woods & peabody land to yᵉ
aboveſᵈ Way then Eastarly on sᵈ way to yᵉ stake first mentioned, ——— and
₂ᵒᵈˡʸ a piece of mowing land in yᵉ hillots yᵉ First bounds is a stake &
stones in the Line that parts Thoˢ peabody Juᵗˢ land & said land then
westarly to a stake that stands in the line that parts the upland & meadow.
Then northarly to a stake & stones in Nathˡˡ peabody's line then eastarly
on Nathˡˡ land to tho's land, & then southarly to yᵉ first mention'd stake :
₃ʳᵈˡʸ Thirdly a piece of upland in the Hillots the first bounds is a stake
in or near yᵉ line of yᵉ land belonging to the Hiers of Danˡˡ Wood, Then
northarly as the fence now stands which fence parts yᵉ upland & madow
to a stake & stones, then westarly to a stake & stones, at yᵉ head of the
Hillots then southarly as yᵉ line of yᵉ Hillot's runs, to yᵉ Land of yᵉ
aforeſᵈ Woods Heirs, Then eastarly on sᵈ land to yᵉ stake first mention'd,
——— fourthly all my part of a lot of Land lying by Walkers meadow which
land was laid out to me & to my Brother John Hovey fifthly a Wood
lot in the rockey Woods, and to Contain fifteen acres and no more the
Northerly end is Bounded on yᵉ pond the Eastarly Side & southarly end
on Land I have lately sold to my son Joſeph Hovey yeᵉ Westarly side
Bounded on Land belonging to Porter & Eames, all the aboveſᵈ lands to
be freely poſſeſsed and Injoyed by him yᵉ said Luke Hovey his heirs or
aſsigns forever he or they paying out such sums as I have hereafter
herin order him to pay.

Item, I give & Bequeath to my beloved Son Joſeph Hovey all the
remainder of my lands meadows withal yᵉ Buildings standing thereon
excepting my now Dwelling Houſe the which he is to have no part of
although he is to Have the land it stands on after my Wives Deceſe—all
the aboveſᵈ Lands to be freely poſſeſsed and Injoyed by him the sᵈ Joſeph
Hovey his heirs or aſsigns forever as a good & perfect Eſtate of Inheritance in fee simple he or they paying out such sums as I Have or shall
hereafter herein order him to pay

Item I give and bequeath to my beloved son Abijah Hovey all my
Now Dwelling Houſe to him or his Heirs to be at his or their Diſpoſal
To remove of from yᵉ Land the sᵈ Houſe now stands on (after my Wives
Deceſe for he shall not Have Liberty to remove the same or any part
thereof before without her Conſent;) Himſelf or his heirs paying out
such sums of money or Dowrys as I Have or shall herein Hereafter Order

him To pay he having recciv'd, the most of His portion in money all ready:

Item I give and Bequeath to my Daughter Susannah Lakeman the sum of Thirteen pounds six shillings & eight pence Lawfull money to be paid To her Heirs within the Space of one year after my Decefe befides w iat I Have already given her.

Item I give and Bequeath to my Daughter Dorcas Foster the sum of Tw[e]lve pounds ten shillings & Eight pence Lawfull money which sum of money is To be for her Own ufe During her Natural Life; Then the principal sum given to her, I give to my grand Daughter Elizabeth Kimball y' She Has brought up if she shall survive my s' Dau'ter Foster which sum I order to be paid to her within the space of Two years after my Decefe, befides what I have already given her.

Item I give and Bequeath to my Daughter Mary Woster the sum of eight pounds Ten Shillings & Eight pence Lawfull money to be paid to her or her Heirs, within the space of three years after my Decefe befides what I Have already given Her:

Item I give and Bequeath to my three grand Children, Benjamin Hannah & Elizabeth y' Children of my Dau'ter Elizabeth Kimball Dece', the sum of Three pounds four shilling lawfull money to Each of them to be paid to them as they Come of age the Son to Twenty one, the Dau'ters to Eighteen or upon their marriage and in Cafe Either of them Die before y' said legacy be Due, Then my Will is y' y' Survivor or Survivors of my said Three grand children receive the sum or sums Due to y' Dece'

Item I give and Bequeath my grate English Bible to my Son Luke During His natural life & at His Dece' to His Son Luke and so to Continue in the Line to y' Latest poftritey.

Item I give and Bequeath to my three son's, all my wearing apparel, and the one Third part of the remainder of my Books, & the one third part of my Houfehold furniture to be equally Divided amongst them three

Item I give and Bequeath to my three Daughters, the one third part of the remainder of my Books, and the one third part of my Houfehold furniture to be Equally Divided amongst them three

And moreover, my Will is, That, that part of my Eftate which is in Trade whither it be in money or goods or whatfoever I pofsefs as original Stock with all my Bonds, notes of hand and Book Debts with what is Due to me from my Son Abijah on y' aco' of what money I paid for the negro man now in his pofseffion (which was thirty pounds old Tenor when I paid it) Shall be Equally Divided into Eight parts whereof my widow, if I Leave one shall have one part, and my six Children now Living, or their Heirs if any of them shall be Dece' shall Have one eighth a piece; and as to the Last Eighth, part remaining, my will is that it be Equally Divided into two parts, the one of which parts I give to my two grand, Children Benjamin & Hannah Kimball, to be Equally Divided between them, and my will is y' the Other Half of s' Eighth I give to the Reverend John Cushing if he Continue minister to y' Second Church in Boxford till after my Dece'

and I Do hereby order and Oblige my three sons Luke Jofeph and abijah To pay and Bare their Equal parts of my Debts, and funeral Charges and all other Charges, and alfo to pay their Equal parts Each of them of all Legacies by me given in this prefent Will—

And I Likewife Constitute make & ordain my Two Wellbeloved Sons Luke Hovey and Jofeph Hovey Sole Executors of this my Last Will and Testament and I Do hereby utterly diffalow, revoke & Difannul all and every other former Testaments Wills Legacies & Bequests & Executors, by me named before. Willed & bequeathed Ratifying & Confirming this & no other to be my Last Will & Testament. In Witnefs. Whereof I have hereunto set my hand and seal y* Day and year above Written

Signed   Sealed   Published
pronounced   &   Declared   by
the said Luke Hovey as his last
will   and   Testament   in   the
prefence of us the Subfcribers

Luke Hovey [SEAL]

EBENEZER SHERWIN
DANIEL SHERWIN
THO* PEABODY

Mrs. Hovey survived her husband, and died in Boxford, his widow, Dec. 22. 1767, at the age of ninety.

Their children were born as follows:—

84—I.   SUSANNAH*, born July 25, 1699, in Topsfield; married, first, Aaron Brown of Boxford in 1719; he died in 1724; his estate was valued at about £250; their children were born in Boxford as follows: 1. *Aaron*, born May 1. 1720; husbandman; was of Boxford in 1741. 2. *Daniel*, born May 21, 1722; was living in 1741. 3. *Abigail*, born March 12, 1723-4; married John Cole of Boxford April 14, 1746; she died, childless, March 8, 1747, aged twenty-three; he married, secondly, Eunice Spofford Dec. —, 1748; lived in Boxford until about 1763, when he removed to Amherst, N. H.; he was prominent in town and church affairs and a soldier in the Revolution in the company of Capt. Josiah Crosby, in Colonel Nichols' regiment in the Rhode Island campaign of 1777, his son John being killed at the battle of Bunker hill.

    Mrs. Susannah (Hovey) Brown married, second, William Lakeman of Ipswich Nov. 25, 1731; and they lived in the old Pearl house in West Boxford until 1738. He died in Boxford March 14. 1780, at the age of seventy; and she ("old M** Lakeman") survived him, dying, his widow, in Boxford June 10, 1782, aged eighty-two. The children of William and Susannah (Hovey) Lakeman were born in Boxford, and were as follows: 1. *Jedidiah*, born Aug. 20, 1732; died May 8, 1756, aged twenty-three. 2. *Elizabeth*, born Oct. 30, 1734; died Sept. 13, 1736. 3. *Elizabeth*, baptized July 30, 1738; died July 4, 1756, aged eighteen. 4. *Peltiah*, baptized Aug. 1, 1742; lived in West Boxford, in the old house that formerly stood opposite the house of the late venerable Daniel Wood, he having built the house; married Eunice Barker of Andover in 1767; had several children; and moved to Exeter, N. H., where they were living in 1793.

85—II.   DORCAS*, born May 10, 1701, in Boxford; married Capt. John, son of Ephraim and Hannah (Eames) Foster of Andover Nov. 23, 1732. He was born there March 26, 1690; and married, first, Rebecca Roe of Boxford Jan. 8, 1714-5. By his wife Rebecca he had three children. He died in Andover Oct. 28, 1778, aged eighty-eight; and his wife Dorcas survived him, dying his widow, at the age of ninety-two, and being buried Aug. 18, 1793. The children of John and Dorcas (Hovey) Foster were born in Andover as follows: 1. *Nathan*, born July 4, 1734; died in infancy. 2. *Rebecca*, born Nov. 20, 1735; died Jan. 18, 1736-7.

86—III. HANNAH[4], born July 18, 1703, in Boxford; married Samuel, son of Samuel and Martha Hale of the East parish of Bradford (now Groveland) Dec. 5, 1723, in Bradford, where he was born Oct. 23, 1699. She died, childless, Oct. 27, 1724, at the age of twenty-one. The following is the inscription on her gravestone in the Groveland burial ground :—

> HERE LYES BURIED
> the B O D Y O F
> HANNAH HALE
> the WIFE OF SAMUEL
> HALE IUN' WHO DIED
> OCtobEr the 27 &
> IN 1724 IN THE
> 22nd YEAR OF HER AGE

Mr. Hale married, secondly, Sarah Haseltine Dec. 13, 1725, at Newbury; had children, born in Bradford; and died there May 24, 1770, aged seventy.

87—IV. ELIZABETH[4], born Oct. 3, 1705, in Boxford; married Benjamin, son of Samuel and Elizabeth (Fowler) Kimball of Wenham Dec. 27, 1727. He was born in Wenham Jan. 30, 1705-6. She died Feb. 13, 1737-8, aged twenty-two. Her remains lie buried in the ancient Wenham cemetery, and the inscription on her gravestone reads as follows :—

> HERE LYES BURIED
> the BODY OF MRS.
> ELIZABETH KIMBALL
> the WIFE OF M'
> BENJAMIN KIMBALL
> WHO DEPARTED THIS
> LIFE FEB'' the 13, 1738
> IN Y* 33 YEAR
> OF HER AGE

Mr. Kimball married, secondly, Phebe Frye of Andover March 21, 1738-9; thirdly, Ruth Batchelder Nov. 18, 1747; and, fourthly, widow Hannah Gott of Salem Nov. 26, 1754. He died Dec. 29, 1776, aged seventy.

The children of Benjamin and Elizabeth (Hovey) Kimball were born in Wenham as follows: 1. ———, born Dec. 1, 1728; died Dec. 1, 1728. 2. *Hannah*[5], born Jan. 24, 1730; married Archelus Morrill of Salisbury May 21, 1752. 3. *Eunice*[5], born Oct. 30, 1731; died June 17, 1732. 4. *Benjamin*[5], born March 10, 1734; H. C., 1753; lived in Manchester, Mass.; was for many years town clerk; Revolutionary soldier; "Captain"; married Joanna Lee; and had nine children. 5. *Elizabeth*[5], born Feb. 13, 1737-8; was brought up by her aunt Dorcas Foster in Andover; married Richard Foster of Boxford Nov. 19, 1761. He died in Boxford Aug. 1, 1814, aged eighty-one; and she died, his widow, Feb. 15, 1821, aged eighty-three. They had children.

88—V. LUKE[4], born May 18, 1708, in Boxford. *See family numbered "88."*

89—VI. ABIGAIL[4], born July 6, 1710, in Boxford; probably died young, and unmarried, as her father does not mention her in his will in 1751.

90—VII.   JOSEPH⁴, born July 17, 1712, in Boxford. *See family numbered*
                "90."

91—VIII. MARY⁴, born in Boxford; married William Woster of Newbury
                Jan. 9, 1733-4. Their children were baptized in the West
                Boxford church as follows: 1. *Susanna⁵*, July 10, 1737.
                2. *Nathaniel⁵*, April 10, 1743; died, an infant, April 22, 1743.
                3. *Mary⁵*, Sept. 29, 1745. 4. *Abigail⁵*, May 15, 1748.

92—IX.   ABIJAH⁴, born Dec. 9, 1719, in Boxford. *See family numbered*
                "92."

23

CAPT. IVORY HOVEY³, born in Topsfield May 4, 1682. He
lived in Topsfield on the paternal homestead, which his father had
conveyed to him by deed dated March 14, 1717-8,* and confirmed
the gift in his will. The deed conveyed one hundred acres of
land, dwelling house and barn in Topsfield; land in Boxford
bought of Col. John Wainwright; meadow in Rowley great
meadows; and marsh in Ipswich. His father had conveyed to
him thirty-two acres of upland and meadow in Topsfield, being
part of the land which was granted by the town of Ipswich to
Richard Lumpkin, bounded on Baker's pond, Jan. 13, 1709.†
With his brother John Hovey, for twenty-one pounds, he conveyed three acres of marsh in Ipswich, near Hovey's island, July
17, 1718 ;‡ and, also with his brother John Hovey, one and one-
half acres of land in Topsfield, near the Wenham meadows, Feb.
11, 1722-3.§ For forty pounds, he bought some land lying on Pye
brook in Topsfield June 29, 1722;‖ and, for four pounds, he
bought two acres of land in Boxford May 9, 1722.¶ He also
bought three acres of marsh in Rowley Aug. 13, 1724.** For
twenty pounds, he sold two and three-quarters acres of land in
Topsfield, at ye sluice, on Pye brook, June 1, 1727.†† For sixty-
one pounds, he sold eight acres of land in Boxford Jan. 17,
1734-5.‡‡ For thirty pounds, he sold three acres of marsh in
Rowley Aug. 10, 1731 ;§§ and, for forty-seven pounds, he sold five
acres and thirty rods of upland in Boxford Oct. 17, 1737.‖‖ For
thirty-three pounds, nineteen shillings and six pence, he bought
two acres and one hundred and thirty-three rods of land at Bare

* Essex Registry of Deeds, book 33, leaf 229.
† Essex Registry of Deeds, book 22, leaf 117.
‡ Essex Registry of Deeds, book 36, leaf 35.
§ Essex Registry of Deeds, book 41, leaf 59.
‖ Essex Registry of Deeds, book 39, leaf 246.
¶ Essex Registry of Deeds, book 42, leaf 15.
** Essex Registry of Deeds, book, 51, leaf 101.
†† Essex Registry of Deeds, book 50, leaf 60.
‡‡ Essex Registry of Deeds, book 68, leaf 141.
§§Essex Registry of Deeds, book 72, leaf 233.
‖‖ Essex Registry of Deeds, book 74, leaf 49.

hill in Topsfield Feb. 13, 1734-5.* For thirty-three pounds, he bought three acres of land on Bare hill in Topsfield Oct. 28, 1737.† For sixty-four pounds, two shillings and ten pence, he sold five acres and one hundred and thirty-three rods of land in Topsfield May 16, 1740.‡ For forty-two pounds, he conveyed five and one-fourth acres of land in Topsfield Dec. 12, 1734.§ For one hundred and forty-six pounds. seven shillings and three pence he sold sixteen acres of land in Boxford Nov. 6, 1747.||

Captain Hovey was the commander of the miltary company of the town and deacon of the church in Topsfield from his election, Dec. 2, 1735, until his death. He was constable and treasurer of Topsfield in 1718 and 1729-1738, and selectman in 1720. 1721, 1728 and 1736.

In 1747, he wrote the following letter to his son Ivory and his wife:—

Topsfield August 29ᵗʰ 1747

Louing Son & Davghter after our Love remembered to you hopeing these lines may finde you in health as through the goodness of God to us we are at this time. we received youre letter yᵉ 24ᵗʰ of this instant which was dated yᵉ 29ᵗʰ of July Last: which we understand you are trobeled with yᵉ carker in youre throat: for which you may take a pece of alam and melt it with hot iron and drop it into honney which medison has helped me and many others for yᵗ ale: youre Brother Aaron & his wife remember their love to you: youre sister Kilborn has a davghter Anne yᵗ was born yᵉ third day of this instant: I heard Mʳ Whitefeild preach the same day at Ipswich: it is a time of sickness at Ipswich and many die of yᵉ nervios fevor and the feavor and flux: the docters recon the distemper very ketching: let us Endevor to commit ourselves and ours in to the hands of God and get our hearts fixed trusting in the Lord then we need not be afraid of evil tidings ; I remain youre

Loviig father

Jvory Hovey

Deacon Hovey married Anne, daughter of Aaron Pingree of Rowley Dec. 9, 1707; and died in Topsfield Jan. 21, 1759, aged seventy-six. His remains lie in the ancient burial place in Topsfield, and the stone at the head of his grave bears the following inscription :—

* Essex Registry of Deeds, book 75, leaf 130.
† Essex Registry of Deeds, book 78, leaf 249.
‡ Essex Registry of Deeds, book 84, leaf 251.
§ Essex Registry of Deeds, book 91, leaf 183.
|| Essex Registry of Deeds, book 97, leaf 157.

```
HERE LIES BURIED
THE BODY OF DEACⁿ
IVORY HOUEY WHO
DIED JANʳ THE 21ˢᵗ
A D 1 7 5 9 & I N
THE 7 7ᵗʰ YEAR
OF HIS AGE
HARK FROM THE TOMBS
A DOLFUL SOUND MINE
EARS ATTEND THE CRY
YE LIUING MEN COME
SEE THE GROUND
WHERE SHORTLY
YOU MUST LIE
```

Mr. Hovey left a will which is on file in the office of the probate court at Salem, and the following is a copy of it :—

In the Name of God Amen I Ivory Hovey of Topsfield in the County of Essex in the Province of the massachusets Bay in New England Gentleman being at this time in Perfect mind & memory thanks bee given to God therefor Calling to mind the mortality of my Body & knowing that it is Appointed for All Men once to Die do make and ordain this my last Will & Testament in the first Place I Comit my immortal foul into the Hands of God who gave it hopeing through Jesus Christ to obtain the pardon of all my sins & to obtain eternal Life whenever it Shall please God to take me out of this world and my Body I Recomend to the Earth to be Buried in a decent & Christian maner at the discretion of my Executer hereafter named || nothing doubting but I shall Receive the same at the general Resurection by the power of God ||, and as to Such worldly eastate as it hath pleased God to bless me with in this life my will is that it be disposed of as followeth

Firstly I give to my beloved Wife Anne Hovey all my quick Stock & Twenty pounds in mony to be paid by my son Aaron & I give her all my movibles excepting what is hereafter m[e]ntioned for my son Aaron Hovey that is all my household goods proper for womens improvement together with my wearing Cloaths of Apparil to be disposed of by her to my Children as She Shall See Cause & I give unto her the improuement of half my lands & buildings as long as She Shall Remain my widow & my will is that those Houshold goods above mentiond propper for womens improvement that she does not dispose of be equily divided after her decease to my two Daughters & grand-Daughter hearafter mentioned

Item I give to my son Ivory Hovey twenty shillings & no more I having given Him His portion already to his satisfaction,

Item I give to my son Aaron Hovey all my lands & buildings & all my tools for caring on husbandry & all my mony & all that is due to me by bonds or noates or otherwise due to me & my wood that I Reserved in Boxford he paying all my lawful debts & funeral charges he also paying the sums before & hereafter mentioned to be paid to my wife & Children in lawful money

Item. I give to my Daughter Abigal Kilburn twenty shilings & no more haueing given her her portion already in household goods & more to her Content

Item I give to my Daughter Anne Wilds twenty shilings & no more having given her her portion already in houshold goods & money to her satisfaction

Item I give to my grand Daughter Anne Easty if ſhe ſhall live to the Age of twenty years thirteen pounds ſix ſhillings & eight pence & my will is that my Executer deliver to her all thoſe houſehould goods that were her own mothers which I Received of her mother in law Jemima Easty of Beverly and if ſhe ſhall Die before ſhe is arived to the age mentioned then my will is the laſt mentioned thirteen pounds ſix ſhillings & eight pence be equily divided among all my grand Children

And I do hereby Conſtitute & Appoint my Son Aaron Hovey ‖ to be ‖ my ſole Executer of this my laſt Will and Teſtament And in Confirmation of all that above Written I the ſaid Ivory Hovey have Set hereunto my hand & Seal And have declared this to be my laſt Will and Teſtament this fifth Day of April in the year of our Lord Chriſt one thouſand Seven Hundred & fifty four And in the twenty ſeuenth year of the Reign of our ſoveraign Lord George the ſecond by the Grace of God of Great Brittain France & Ireland King &c Signed ſealed & Declared in the preſence of theſe Witneſſes

JOHN SMITH
EPHRAIM KIMBALL
JOSEPH HALE Yᵉ 3ʳᵈ

Jvory Hovey [SEAL]

The will was proved Feb. 19, 1759.

Mrs. Hovey survived her husband, and died in Topsfield, his widow, suddenly, March 10, 1776.

Their children were born in Topsfield as follows:—

93—I.　ANNE⁴, died July 17, 1709.

94—II.　ABIGAIL⁴, born June 20, 1709; died Aug. 14, 1709.

95—III.　ANNE⁴, born June 6, 1710; died Feb. 6, 1711.

96—IV.　DORCAS⁴, born Dec. 25, 1711; married Jacob, son of Jacob and Lydia (Elliot) Esty of Topsfield Nov. 15, 1733. He was born in Topsfield Jan. 29, 1711. Their daughter Anne was born in Topsfield Feb. 7, 1741-2; and died Feb. 25, 1839, aged ninety-seven.

97—V.　IVORY⁴, born July 3, 1714. *See family numbered "97."*

98—VI.　ABIGAIL⁴ born April 30, 1716; married Ebenezer, son of Joseph and Mary (Clark) Kilburn of Rowley Aug. 2, 1743. He was born in Rowley Feb. 11, 1720-1. She died Dec. 24, 1804, aged eighty-eight; and he died Nov. 24, 1808, aged eighty-seven. Children, born in Rowley: 1. *Joseph⁵*, baptized July 1, 1744. 2. *Mary⁵*, baptized July 7, 1745. 3. *Anne⁵*, born Aug. 3, 1747. 4. *Abigail⁵*, baptized Oct. 14, 1750. 5. *Anne⁵*, baptized Feb. 4, 1753. 6. *Ivory⁵* baptized April 6, 1755. 7. *Dorcas⁵* (twin), baptized May 22, 1757. 8. *Elizabeth⁵* (twin), baptized May 22, 1757.

99—VII.　AARON⁴, born Sept. 14, 1718. *See family numbered "99."*

100—VIII.　ANNE⁴, born Sept. 21, 1720; married Elijah, son of Ephraim and Mary (Howlet) Wildes of Topsfield May 15, 1744. He was born in Topsfield Jan. 4, 1717-8. They removed to Shirley, a part of Groton, Mass.; and when the Shaker religion was introduced into America by Ann Lee, Mr. and Mrs. Wildes were converted to it. The Shaker village was built on their estate. He died April 6, 1791; and she died March 16, 1806. Their children were born as follows: 1. *Elijah⁵*, born Nov. 10, 1745; died Dec. 27, 1745. 2. *Elijah⁵*, born Nov. 9, 1746, in Shirley; was a Shaker, being an elder; married Eunice Safford of Harvard July 4, 1771; she died Nov. 11, 1819; he died March 14, 1829; they had

five children. 3. *Anna*[4], born Feb. 15, 1749; married Elijah
Wheelock of Lancaster July 14, 1774; she was a Shaker;
and died Sept. 28, 1838. 4. *Ivory*[4], born Nov. 27, 1751, in
Shirley; a deacon of the Shakers; married Hannah Estabrook of Lancaster April 3, 1777; he died Sept. 13, 1817; they
had two children. 5. *Molly*[4], born Dec. 27, 1754; married
Samuel Randall of Stowe in 1774. 6. *Olive*[4], born April 5,
1757; died June 2, 1775. 7. *Phoebe*[4], born Feb. 15, 1761;
married Levi, son of John and Prudence (Wheelock)
Warner; he died June 27, 1825; she then left the Shaker
sect, and died Dec. 7, 1837, at the age of seventy-six.

24

THOMAS HOVEY[3], born in Hadley in 1678. He lived in the
"Swampfield" part of Hadley, which was incorporated as Sunderland in 1714. He sold land to his brother John Smith of Hatfield,
on the east side of Town street, Aug. 27, 1724.*

Mr. Hovey married, first, Mary, daughter of Thomas and
Abigail (Dickinson) Craft of Hadley about 1709. She was born
Feb. 3, 1687; and died Jan. 6, 1714, aged twenty-seven. He married, second, Hannah, daughter of Samuel and Martha (Bridg-
man) Dickinson of Hatfield Nov. 17, 1719. She was born April
4, 1689.

Mr. Hovey died in Sunderland March 30, 1728, aged forty.
His widow, Hannah Hovey, was appointed administratrix of his
estate May 8, 1728. The inventory of his estate amounted to
£667, 4s., 3d. The real estate was described therein as follows :—

"to one homlot with the building & the Crop att	£165	00	00
"to one Lott in the first Devition of plowland att	52	00	00
"to one Lot in the second Devition 28¹ 2 lots in y* third division 28¹	56	00	00
"to one Lot in flag Swamp att 40¹ one lot in Grate Swamp: att 18¹	58	00	00
"to one Lot in Litol medow at : 14¹ to two lots at hunting hil: 10	24	00	00
"to two Wood Lots at: 15¹ to one Lot cauld paftor lot at 3¹—10*	18	10	00
"to one hom Lot in hadly with all that is upon itt att	72	00	00

In the division of the real estate, Nov. 14, 1732, a houselot
in Hadley, with the orchard, a lot in the East swamp in Sunderland, and a lot in a division known as Pasture lots were assigned
to his daughter Mary; two adjoining lots of land in the South
field in Sunderland, in the third division of plowing land, a lot in
the second division of plowing land in the South field in Sunderland, and a lot in the division known as the flag swamp, were assigned to his daughter Hannah; and one-half of the homelot in
Sunderland, one-half of the barn, one lot in the little meadow,

* Hampden Registry of Deeds, book E, page 441.

and two lots in the commons known as Ten acre rights lying on the east side of the Hunting hill in Sunderland, were assigned to Martha, daughter of the deceased.

Dower had been assigned to the widow in one-half of the home lot, all the house, one-half of the barn, a lot in the first division of plowing land, and a whole right in the Hunting hill field, all lying in Sunderland.

Mrs. Hovey continued to live in Sunderland, and she conveyed one hundred and five acres and fifty-six rods of land in Sunderland Sept. 7, 1731.[*]

She became *non compos mentis* and a guardian was appointed Jan. 13, 1756. She apparently lived in Sunderland, at the old home, with her daughter Martha and her husband Nathaniel Barstow. Mr. Barstow represented that his wife's mother had become *non compos mentis*, by reason of age and infirmity, Nov. 4, 1755; and several persons certified "that She is no ways Capable to mannage any Affair fhe is reduced to Nothing and will hear no more to Reafon than the Seat fhe fits on and is a Woman of the Profaneft Language as Can be uttered with Tongue and it is her Common Practice to wifh the Divil would fetch them away alive and would be heartily Glad if yᵉ Houfe was of a Light fire & they fhut in meaning her fon & Daughter: this the Neighbourhood Dayly hear as they are Providentially in there," Jan. 10, 1756.

Her daughter Martha said that she had nursed her mother from 1740 to the year 1745.

The inventory of the estate of Mrs. Hovey amounted to £326, 0s., 10d. Of her own real estate were a house lot that was Dickinson's, a division lot that was Dickinson's, a flag swamp lot, a lot in the Sequestered land, six and one-half acres at Miller's plain, a lot at Juggle meadow, nine and a quarter acres in the Sequestered land, so called, twenty-one acres in the Sequestered land, formerly Dickinson's and four acres and thirteen rods of land at Miller's plain; and of land that was Mr. Hovey's she had one-half of the house lot, a first division lot, two lots in Hunting hill field, forty-five acres on the west side of Bald hill, forty-three acres on the northeast side of Bald hill, and twenty and three-fourths acres on the northeast side of the same hill.

Her guardian conveyed to her son-in-law Nathaniel Barstow land in the South field Feb. 12, 1759.[†]

Mrs. Hovey died soon afterward.

The children of Mr. Hovey were born in Sunderland as follows :—

[*] Hampden Registry of Deeds, book F, page 112.
[†] Hampden Registry of Deeds, book 2, page 939.

101—I.   MARY⁴, born Feb. 12, 1710; married Samuel, son of Samuel
         and Sarah (Lane) Moody of Granby Oct. 13, 1729. They
         lived in Hadley, and removed to Granby. He died Dec. 11,
         1765; and she died, his widow, Sept. 15, 1775, aged sixty-five.
         Children: 1. *Samuel⁵*, born July 2, 1730; died, unmarried,
         Dec. 4, 1820, aged ninety. 2. *Gideon⁵*, born March 24, 1733;
         died in 1755. 3. *Thomas Hovey⁵*, born Aug. 31, 1736; lived
         in South Hadley and Granby; married Eunice Chapin of
         Springfield; had four children; and died Sept. 8, 1822. 4.
         Elisha⁵, born Jan. 14, 1738; lived in Granby; married Eliza-
         beth Nash April 15, 1766; had eleven children; he died Jan.
         17, 1825, aged eighty-seven; and his wife died, his widow,
         July 3, 1833. 5. *Reuben⁵*, born Jan. 21, 1740; died, unmar-
         ried, Jan. —, 1831, aged ninety-one. 6. *Simeon⁵*, born July 4,
         1743; died in 1746. 7. *Simeon⁵*, born Oct. 30, 1747; lived in
         Granby; married Mercy ———; had eight children; he died
         July 16, 1815, aged sixty-seven; and she died Sept. 14, 1815,
         aged sixty-seven. 8. *Enos⁵*, born April 7, 1753.

102—II. THOMAS⁴, born Sept. 10, 1720; died Sept. 10, 1720.
103—III. HANNAH⁴, born Sept. 22, 1721; died March 30, 1730.
104—IV. MIRIAM⁴, born Aug. 1, 1723; died Aug. 1, 1723.
105—V.   MARTHA⁴, born Aug. 18, 1724; married, first, Nathaniel Barstow
         May 28, 1746; lived in Sunderland; he was a farmer and
         buckle maker; he was living in 1759; she married, second,
         Elijah Morton of Hatfield Nov. 12, 1789.
106—VI. SARAH⁴, born Aug. 4, 1726; died Sept. 9, 1726.

38

DEA. DANIEL HOVEY³, born in Brookfield in 1672. He was
brought up in the family of his grandfather Hovey in Ipswich.
His grandfather John Dane bequeathed to him, in 1684, thirty
pounds, payable when Daniel became of age.

There are two depositions on file in the probate office at
Salem relating to Daniel's relationship to his grandfather Daniel
Hovey, as follows:—

> this may fartifi whom it may Confarn y⁴ Daniel houey fun of James
> houey: to my knouledg by Information from his granfather houey w⁴
> brought him up from a Child and Did bind him to me an aprentis for
> Seuen yeres if now fum months aboue twenty on yers of Age: an to y⁴
> truth of what is aboue wrightin I have fet tow my hand this: 19 of feb-
> rawary: 169¾   DANIEL RINDGE

> John Ayres eageid aboute forty foure yeres faith that I am
> fartinly informed by my ffather in law that Danell Hufey fonn of James
> Hufey, that faid Danniell wafe twenty on yeres of eage the beginning of
> this Laft winter & I my felf knowe that he wafe a prity bige boye when
> the indians burnt quabago or Brookfeeld. af atest my hand
>   february the 23: 169¾   JOHN AYRES

Mr. Hovey was a carpenter, and lived in Ipswich, where he
held several minor offices, until 1722, when he removed to Oxford, Mass.

While he was living in Ipswich, with Thomas Hovey of Hadley he sold Hovey's island, of twenty acres of upland and salt marsh on Sagamore Hill creek, in Ipswich, Oct. 18, 1697;* with his brother James and sister Priscilla, he conveyed to Benoni Morse of Dedham, farmer, for eight pounds, thirty acres of upland and meadow in Brookfield July 7, 1703;† and, for forty shillings, he sold his old thatch lot at Chebacco in Ipswich, 471, of about one acre, June 15, 1715.‡

Mr. Hovey was called a yeoman Feb. 12, 1718-9, when he bought, for sixteen pounds, seven and one-half acres of salt marsh on the north side of Plum Island river.§ This was probably in Ipswich.

He conveyed, for twenty-eight pounds, an old right on Jeffries Neck July 8, 1721.‖

He bought of Ebenezer Learned of Oxford, yeoman, fifty acres of swamp and upland, lying between Long and Flat hills, partly on both, in Oxford, and half an acre in the great meadow, Feb. 11, 1722.¶ For thirty-four pounds, he conveyed one-half acre of his old division in the south-eighths, March 26, 1722.** He bought of Samuel Barton of Oxford, yeoman, a fifty-acre lot of land on Long hill, in Oxford, April 4, 1722;†† and on the same day he bought of David Town of Oxford, yeoman, twelve acres of upland on Long hill.‡‡ Two days later, he bought of Philip Amidown of Oxford, cooper, lot 10 in the great cedar swamp in Oxford Village.§§

After his removal to Oxford, when he is called a yeoman, for twenty-three pounds, he sold seven and a half acres of marsh on Plum Island river, in Ipswich, Dec. 27, 1725;‖‖ and, for sixty-three pounds, he conveyed to Joseph Pratt of Oxford, husbandman, twenty-five acres of land on Long hill, in Oxford Village, Jan. 9, 1734-5.¶¶ By deed, he gave to his son, Daniel Hovey, eighty-seven acres of land in Oxford Village on Long and Flat hills, April 7, 1735;*** and, on the same day, to his son James Hovey one-half of his farm, "whereon I now dwell," and

* Essex Registry of Deeds, book 13, leaf 55.
† Hampden Registry of Deeds, book C, page 458.
‡ Essex Registry of Deeds, book 61, leaf 183.
§ Essex Registry of Deeds, book 36, leaf 5.
‖ Essex Registry of Deeds, book 65, leaf 107.
¶ Suffolk Registry of Deeds, book 36, page 204.
** Essex Registry of Deeds, book 42, leaf 271.
†† Suffolk Registry of Deeds, book 36, page 204.
‡‡ Suffolk Registry of Deeds, book 36, page 205.
§§ Suffolk Registry of Deeds, book 37, page 53.
‖‖ Essex Registry of Deeds, book 54, leaf 172.
¶¶ Worcester Registry of Deeds, book 9, page 137.
*** Worcester Registry of Deeds, book 7, page 399.

one-half of his right in the great cedar swamp in Oxford.*

    March 25, 1736, for three pounds, he conveyed land in Ox-
ford Village to Joseph Rocket of Oxford, husbandman ;† and, on
the same day, for a similar consideration, he bought of Mr.
Rocket land in Oxford Village.‡

    The farm he bought in Oxford, on Long hill, was occupied
by him and his descendants for more than a hundred years.

    Mr. Hovey was one of the selectmen of Oxford in 1726 and
1727 ; and a deacon of the church from 1729 until his death.

    Mr. Hovey married Mercy ———— in or before 1697 ; and
died March 7, 1741-2, at about seventy years of age. She survived him, and died, his widow, March 30, 1743.

    Their children were born in Ipswich as follows :—

107—I.   ———— (dau.)⁴, born May 29, 1695; probably died young.

108—II.   MERCY⁴, born May 10, 1698; married, first, Thomas, son of
Thomas Gleason of Sudbury, as his second wife, June 10,
1729. He had married, first, Mary Mellen of Sherborn Dec. 6,
1695; they had fourteen children; and she died March 13,
1727. Mr. Gleason settled in Oxford, where he died Jan. 11,
1732. Mrs. Gleason married, secondly, John Wait of Sutton
Dec. 19, 1749; and died Dec. —, 1767. Mr. Gleason was a
man of means; he took up the lot on the southeast corner of
Main street and Sutton road; he bought, in 1722, the house
lot and water privilege at Augutteback falls (selling in
1723 his lot on the Plain to his son Thomas), and built the
first mill at that place. The children of Thomas and Mercy
(Hovey) Gleason were born as follows: 1. *Daniel*⁵, born
March 2, 1730; lived in the east part of Oxford; shoemaker;
married Martha Bartlett April 26, 1753; had eight children;
he died Dec. 8, 1794; and she died Dec. 7, 1809, aged eighty-
one. 2. *Priscilla*⁵, born May 10, 1731; married Levi, son of
Oliver and Sarah (Pratt) Shumway of Oxford June 30,
1752; and had five children.

109—III.   DANIEL⁴, born April 7, 1702. *See family numbered "109."*

110—IV.   JAMES⁴, born Feb. 23, 1705; died April 16, 1709.

111—V.   PRISCILLA⁴, born June 16, 1709; married, as his third wife, David,
son of John and Mary (Smith) Town of Oxford Dec. 28,
1737. He was born in Topsfield, where he was baptized Oct.
29, 1693. Mr. Town had married, first, Mercy Barton of Oxford Dec. 31, 1716; and she died Dec. 3, 1730, aged thirty-
seven, having had three children. He married, second, Sarah
————, who died June 24, 1737, having had two children. Mr.
Town lived in Oxford, where his children were born. The
only child of himself and his wife Priscilla (Hovey) was,
1. *Priscilla*⁵, born March 7, 1740; married Jacob Thompson
(published May 21, 1768).

112—VI.   JAMES⁴, born 14: 7: 1712; was a husbandman; and lived in Oxford, where he was a constable in 1750. His father gave to
him, by deed, one-half of his farm and one-half of his right

    * Worcester Registry of Deeds, book 10, page 326.
    † Worcester Registry of Deeds, book 8, page 81.
    ‡ Worcester Registry of Deeds, book 8, page 88.

in the great cedar swamp, in Oxford, April 7, 1735;* and he conveyed it to David Town of Oxford, husbandman, Sept. 9, 1740.† James Hovey and his father then lived upon the farm. David Town of Oxford, yeoman, for three pounds, sold to him fifty acres of land in Oxford Sept. 9, 1740.‡ For one hundred and sixty pounds, he sold fifty acres of land in Oxford to Israel Whitney of Oxford, cordwainer, April 17, 1741;§ and bought of Benjamin Davis of Oxford, husbandman, for one hundred and seventy-five pounds, forty acres of land in Oxford, Dec. 7, 1741.‖ With his mother, his sister, Mercy Gleason, and brother Daniel Hovey, he released to David Town of Oxford, husbandman, the real estate of his father, April 2, 1742;¶ and thus the paternal farm came into the possession of Mr. Town. For seventeen shillings, Mr. Hovey also conveyed to Benjamin Davis five and one-half acres of land in Oxford, Nov. 23, 1742.**

Mr. Hovey married Rebecca, daughter of Joseph and Hannah (Chamberlain) Rockett of Oxford April 1, 1740. She was born in Oxford Dec. 4, 1716. He died in Oxford May 1, 1752, at the age of thirty-nine, childless. She survived him.

The following is a copy of Mr. Hovey's will:—

In the Name of God Amen, This twenty ninth Day of January in ye year of our Lord one' thousand seven hundred & fifty two. I James Hovey of Oxford in ye County of Worcester in the Province of the Massachusetts Bay in New England yeoman labouring often under Bodily Indispessitions and weeknesses: Do make this my last will & Testiment as follows viz: First & principally I commit my Soul into the hands of Almighty God my Creator, hopeing in his mercy thro' the merrits Death & passion, and prevailing intercession of Jesus Christ my Lord & Saviour, and my Body, I desire may be decently interred at the Discretion of my Executor's hereafter named, in faith of the Resurrection of it at ye Last Day, and as Touching such Temporal estate as God hath betrusted me with (after my Just debts & funeral charges are paid) I will & bequeath ye same as follows, That is to say, Imprimis I give and bequeath unto my beloved wife Rebeccah Hovey all my personal and moveable estate whatsoever & wheresoever (excepting wearing apparell & arms) to be Disposed of as she pleaseth after my Just Debts & funeral charges are paid; I also give & bequeath unto my sd wife Rebecca Hovey all that piece of meadow which I bought of Seth Twitchel lying in the great meadow. & two acres & a half more lying on the Southermost part of my other right of meadow, lying in the uper end of the sd Great meadow, to be to her, her heirs & assigns forever. Moreover, I give and bequeath unto said wife Rebeccah Hovey, the free uses im-

* Worcester Registry of Deeds, book 10, page 326.
† Worcester Registry of Deeds, book 15, page 45.
‡ Worcester Registry of Deeds, book 15, page 103.
§ Worcester Registry of Deeds, book 15, page 84.
‖ Worcester Registry of Deeds, book 15, page 104.
¶ Worcester Registry of Deeds, book 16, page 171.
** Worcester Registry of Deeds, book 15, page 490.

provements & profits of all my houseings & Lands (not Given
& bequeathed hereafter in this Instrument) during her natural life, and at the expiration thereof, to be Distributed &
Disposed of as is hereafter expressed in this Instrument.

Item I give & bequeath unto my nephew Daniel Gleeson
a certain piece of my Land Lying & being in sd Oxford &
bounded as follows, viz: beginning at ye southermost appel
Tree Grooing by ye wall of my barn yard then runing est
till it comes North of ye est end of my Dwelling house then
Runing south to ye courner of sd house thence Runing
southesterly to ye southwestwardly courner of ye sd Danl
Gleesons Shop then westerly about 12 Rhods to a Chesnut
Tree mark & then South 15 Rhods then Est about 38 Rhods to
land of Samuel Davis Junr; thence Runing Northerly on sd
sd Davis's Land to ye Courner of Land of Benja Davis thence
on sd Benja Davis's Land till it comes Northerly of ye tree
Furst mencioned Reserveing a Rod & a half way for sd Benja
Davis his heirs & assigns through said Discribad piece of
Land also Reserveing ye apples Grooing thereon for my sd
wife Rebeccah Hovey During her natural Life, moreover I
give & bequeath unto ye sd Daniel Gleeson one moity of my
present Dwelling house & ye whole of ye shop standing &
being on said piece of Land. It is also my will & pleasure
that ye above named Daniel Gleeson pay unto my said wife
Rebeccah Hovey Five pounds Twe[l]ve Shillings Law: money
Immediately after my Decease to be Disposed of as she
pleaseth, moreover yt he ye sd Daniel Gleeson pay unto his
sister Prissilla Gleeson Four pounds Law: money of ye
Province aforesaid: in mannour & form following, viz: one
moiety thereof on or before ye expiration of one year after
my Decease & ye other moiety at ye expiration of Two years
after my decease

Item I give & bequeath unto James Hovey Davis, son
of Benja Davis & Sybel his wife a certain piece of my land
begining on ye brook in ye west line of sd Benja Davis's land
then runing northerly on sd Davis's land to ye courner then
westerly to a heap of stones on Thos Davis's land thence
south one Degree west down to ye brook & then runing est-
erly on sd brook to ye place first mentioned moreover I give
unto ye sd James Hovey Davis my arms.

Item I give & bequeath unto my brother Daniel Hovey
all my wearing apparal w'soever to be disposed of as he
pleaseth

Item I do hereby nominate desire and appoint my be-
love'd wife Rebeccah Hovey and my very good friend Saml
Davis Junr of sd Oxford yeoman to be executors of this my
last will & testiment and do by these presence fully impower
them & ither of them surviveing ye other to sell all my
housing & land (of which ye use & improvement is giveing
to my sd wife dureing her natural life) To the best ad-
vantage as soon as may be after her decease & the proseeds
thereof I hereby give & bequeath as is to be divided in mannour following vizt 2.9th to ye sd Daniel Gleeson 1.9th To ye
sd Prissillah Gleeson & five ninths I give & bequeath unto ye
children of my sd brother Daniel Hovey vizt To Mehitaball
Hovey 1.9th to Tabitha Hovey 2.9ths To Mercy Hovey 1.9th
& Sarah Hovey 1.9th

Finally I give & bequeat[h] unto my neese Prissallah Town ye daughter of David Town ye remaining ninth.

In witness whereof I the said James Hovey have hereunto set my hand & seal the Day & year first hereinbefore mentioned.

JAMES HOVEY [SEAL]

Sign'd seal'd & Dd in the presence of us by the said James Hovey & by him Declared to be his Last Will and testiment

JOSEPH DAVIS
JOHN BARTEN
THOMAS DAVIS

The will was proved May 13, 1752; and it is on file in the probate office at Worcester.

Mrs. Hovey married, secondly, William Lamb of Oxford (as his second wife) Feb. 12, 1753; and she died Sept. 30, 1791, childless.

39

JAMES HOVEY[3], born in Brookfield, Mass., in 1674. He was a weaver, and lived in Malden, Mass., until the summer of 1716, when he removed to Mansfield, Conn., where he was afterward a yeoman. He joined with his brother Daniel and sister Priscilla in conveying to Benoni Morse of Dedham, farmer, for eight pounds, thirty acres of upland and meadow in Brookfield, adjoining land laid out to Daniel Hovey, July 7, 1703.* He joined his wife and her sister, Mary, widow of John Chadwick of Bradford, in conveying to Thomas Pratt of Charlestown, boatman, for fifty pounds, a five-acre lot and one-half of a three-acre lot of upland, lying on the north side of the country road, and half of an acre lot of fresh meadow on the south side of the country road, all of it being in Charlestown, May 10, 1715.† Mr. Hovey sold his interest in seven acres of land in Charlestown, on Spot Pond brook, near Spot Pond mill, up stream, for seven pounds, May 5, 1716.‡ He conveyed his homestead of fifteen acres of land and five and one-half acres of woodland in Malden, for two hundred and twenty pounds, June 8, 1716;§ and a week later he bought of Bowley Arnold of Mansfield, Conn., one hundred acres of land in Mansfield.‖ Oct. 8, 1716, for three pounds and ten shillings, he bought of Jonathan Roode of Mansfield, husbandman, other land in Mansfield.¶ Feb. 6, 1716-7, he bought of Israel Foulsham one hundred acres of land in Mansfield.** For

* Hampden Registry of Deeds, book C, page 458.
† Middlesex Registry of Deeds, book 17, page 473.
‡ Middlesex Registry of Deeds, book 25, page 116.
§ Middlesex Registry of Deeds, book 23, page 6.
‖ Mansfield Registry of Deeds, book 1, page 465.
¶ Mansfield Registry of Deeds, book 2, page 39.
** Mansfield Registry of Deeds, book 1, page 477.

love he conveyed to his son James Hovey, jr., fifty acres of land
on Mount Hope river, being a part of the one hundred acres
bought of Bowley Arnold.* Jan. 25, 1721-2, for love, he conveyed to his son Edmond Hovey between forty and fifty acres
of the one hundred acres he bought of Israel Foulsham.† April
25, 1722, he exchanged with Thomas Storrs of Mansfield, husbandman, eight acres of land and meadow in Mansfield for seven
acres of land, in Mansfield, on Mount Hope river.‡ Sept. 28
1722, for love, he conveyed to his son John Hovey forty acres of
land, being part of the one hundred acres he bought of Bowley
Arnold ;§ and, for love, he conveyed to his son Daniel Hovey fifty
acres of land in Mansfield Feb. 16, 1732-3.‖

Mr. Hovey married Deborah, daughter of Edmund and
Mary (Pemberton) Barlow of Charlestown about 1694; and she
died in Mansfield May 15, 1749. He probably died in the spring
of 1760, as his will was proved May 6, 1760.

The following is an exact copy of his will, taken from the
original instrument on file in the probate office at Willimantic,
Conn. :—

In the Name of God Amen I James Hovey of Mansfield In The
County of windham and Coloney of Connecticutt, being In good health
of body and of perfect sound mind and memory praiſe be Therefore
given To Almighty God, but calling To mind The mortallity of my body
I do Therefore make and ordain This my last will and Teſtament In
manner & form following, that is to Say, first and principally I commend
my Soul Into The hands of God That gave it and my body I Commit
to The Earth to be decently buried att The diſcretion of my Executor
Hereafter named nothing doubting but att The General reſurection I
Shall receive The same again by The almighty power of God, and as
Touching Such worldly Eſtate wherewith it hath pleaſed God To bleſs me
In This life I give deniſe and diſpoſe of the same as followeth

Imprimis, I give all my goods and Chattels To be divided In Equal
proportion To Thoſe of my Children, That Shall Servive me only To my
Eldeſt Son a Double In Caſe he shall Servive me. This only To Contain
what is proper moveable Eſtate without rights Credits or monys

Item. I give and bequeath unto Daniel Dimmick Aſa Dimmick and
Abigail Dimmick the Children of my Daughter Priſcilla Dimmick To
Each of Them as They Come of age Twenty shillings old Tenᵣ bills
according To its preſent vallue

Item I give and bequeath unto my grand daughter Abigail Curtis
The Daughter of my daughter Abigail Curtis Deceaſ'd the sum of Ten
pounds old Tenᵣ bills according To its preſent value, To be paid her by
my Executor when she shall Come of age or marriage which shall first
happen.

Item I give and bequeath all the reſt reſidue and remainder of my
Eſtate real and perſonal Vizᵗ lands rights and Credits The whole vallue

* Mansfield Registry of Deeds, book 2, page 44.
† Mansfield Registry of Deeds, book 2, page 178.
‡ Mansfield Registry of Deeds, book 2, pages 207 and 209.
§ Mansfield Registry of Deeds, book 2, page 251.
‖ Mansfield Registry of Deeds, book 3, page 420.

Thereof to be Equally Divided between my five Sons viz[t] James Edmond John Jofeph and Daniel and my Two Daughters viz Deborah Huntington and Mary Auftin which are now liveing Togather with the Children of my late son Thomas Deceafd, who are To share Equale with one of my Children, In such proportion that the Children that he had by his first wife shall have the one half of his rights, and the Children he had by his second wife shall have the other half of his rights Each to receive Their part as They shall Come of age and my will further is that if any of my Children afforenamed shall die before me, Their Children shall receive their parents portion as They Shall Come of age

and my will further is that Such receits from my Children In part of their portions shall be In my hands att my Deceafe shall be Confidered allowed and accounted To them In part or In whole of Their portions

Finally I nominate and appoint Conftitute and ordain my beloved Son John Hovey of Mansfield To be The Sole Executor of This m[y] laft will and Teftament hereby giveing unto my s[d] Executor full power and authority after my Deceafe To sell and Convey my lands according To his Difcretion—To make and Execute good authentick deed or deeds of the same

And I do hereby Revoke and difanull all and Every other wills and Teftaments by me In any way before made, ratifying This and no other to be my laft will and Teftament In witnefs whereof I do hereunto sett my hand and Seal This ——— Day of April In the year of our Lord 1752 In the 25th year of his majefties Reign

Signed Sealed pronounced & Declard To be his laft Will In Prefence of

JOSEPH WALDEN
PAUL HEBARD
SAMUEL GRAY

James Hovey

[SEAL]

The inventory of the estate of James Hovey amounted to £329, 10s, 9d.; £53, 18s of which was real estate, and £275, 12s, 9d was personal.

The children of James and Deborah (Barlow) Hovey were born in Malden as follows :—

113—I. JAMES[3], born Sept. 24, 1695. *See family numbered "113."*
114—II. DEBORAH[4], born April 2, 1697; married Eleazer, son of Dea. Thomas and Elizabeth (Backus) Huntington Feb. 25, 1718-9; he was born in Windham July 28 (?), 1697; and died March 7, 1748-9. She died Feb. 26, 1784, at the age of eighty-six. They lived in Mansfield, Conn., where their children were born, as follows: 1. *Samuel[5]*, born Dec. 31, 1729; married Abigail, daughter of Samuel Backus of Windham May 7, 1752; and went west, after living in Mansfield eight or nine years. 2. *Eleazer[5]*, born Sept. 19, 1734; lived in Mansfield, being the captain of a noted military company; married Phebe, daughter of David Hartshorn of Norwich, Conn., Nov. 18, 1756; and died in Scotland parish, Windham, in 1808.
115—III. EDMUND[4], born July 10, 1699. *See family numbered "115."*
116—IV. JOHN[4], born Feb. —, 1700-1. *See family numbered "116."*
117—V. MARY[4], born Dec. —, 1702: married John Austin; and she was his wife in 1752. They lived in Mansfield, Conn., where their children were born as follows: 1. *David[5]*, born July 5, 1734. 2. *Agnish[5]*, born April 23, 1736. 3. *Philhs[5]*, born Jan. 8

1737-8. 4. *Ruth*², born Oct. 29, 1739; died April 10, 1748. 5. *James*², born Dec. 18, 1742; died May 22, 1748. 6. *Eunice*², born Oct. 11, 1744. 7. *Mary*², died Oct. 24, 1748.

118—VI.   JOSEPH⁴, born Feb. 6, 1704-5. *See family numbered "118."*
119—VII.   THOMAS⁴, born Feb. 15, 1706-7. *See family numbered "119."*
120—VIII. PRISCILLA⁴, born Dec. 11, 1708; married Shubael, son of Timothy and Abigail Dimmick Dec. 11, 1731. He was born in Mansfield May 27, 1707; and she died in Mansfield March 14, 1746-7. Children: 1. *Asa*⁵ (twin), born Aug. 14, 1732, in Mansfield; died Dec. 29, 1740. 2. *Anne*⁵ (twin), born Aug. 14, 1732, in Mansfield; died July 18, 1749. 3. *Abigail*⁵, born July 16, 1734, in Mansfield; died Dec. 11, 1737. 4. *Daniel*⁵, born Sept. 24, 1736, in Ashford; and he was living in 1752. 5. *Shubael*⁵, born July 16, 1737, in Ashford; died Nov. 8, 1740. 6. *Asa*⁵, born Oct. 18, 1740, in Ashford; and was living in 1752. 7. *Abigail*⁵, born Aug. 23, 1742, in Mansfield; and was living in 1752.
121—IX.   DANIEL⁴, born Dec. 7, 1710. *See family numbered "121."*
122—X.   SAMUEL⁴, born April 29, 1713; died March 17, 1713-4.
123—XI.   ABIGAIL⁴, born March 15, 1714-5; married Jonathan Curtis of Mansfield April 6, 1736; and she died in Mansfield July 2, 1747, at the age of thirty-two. Children, born in Mansfield: 1. ————⁵ (son), born March 22, 1736-7; died April 4, 1737. 2. *Abigail*⁵, born Jan. 8, 1737-8; and was living in 1752. 3. *Sarah*⁵, born July 22, 1744; died Aug. 15, 1746.

40

JOSEPH HOVEY³, born in Hadley, Mass., Feb. 28, 1677-8. Upon his marriage, in 1702, he settled in Cambridge, being a cooper by trade. Dec. 15, 1704, he mortgaged the estate known as the Sign of the Blue Anchor,* though his deed from the heirs of the former owner Capt. Jonathan Remington of Cambridge, deceased, viz.; his widow, Martha Remington, and children, Jonathan Remington of Harvard college, gent., Martha Remington, jr., Hannah Remington, Elizabeth Remington and Sarah Remington, is dated May 12, 1705.† This ancient tavern was situated near what was then the market place, and included the house and other buildings and land. It was then bounded on the south side by the "Lane that leads from the market place Towards Cooks Pond," and on the west side by "the Queens highway leading to the College." Mr. Hovey conducted the inn for about five years; and, April 1, 1709, conveyed the estate, for one hundred and forty-five pounds, to his brother John Hovey of Charlestown, baker.‡

July 13, 1711, Joseph Hovey joined with others of the heirs of his grandfather Daniel Hovey, sr., of Ipswich, deceased, in

* Middlesex Registry of Deeds, book 14, page 432.
† Middlesex Registry of Deeds, book 13, page 739.
‡ Middlesex Registry of Deeds, book 15, page 492.

conveying, for twelve pounds, one hundred rods of upland lying in Ipswich, on the southeasterly side of the highway.*

When he is called a laborer, Feb. 11, 1725-6, Mr. Hovey and his wife released a claim against Amos Marrit, sr., of Cambridge, yeoman.† This Amos Marritt was probably Mrs. Hovey's father.

When he is called a cooper, Aug. 29, 1729, he bought, for seventy pounds, a messuage in Cambridge, situated near the school house on the north side of Town street;‡ and, Aug. 24, 1730, he mortgaged the same property for sixty pounds.§

Mr. Hovey married Mary Marret of Cambridge Dec. 10, 1702; and she was his wife a third of a century. He died in the late summer of 1735, at the age of fifty-seven.

The following is a copy of his will, transcribed from the original instrument on file in the probate office at Cambridge:—

I Joseph Hovey of Cambridge in yᵉ County of Middˣ in the Province of yᵉ Maſsᵗˢ Bay in New England Cooper, do make & ordain this my Last Will & Testament And in the first place I Commend my Soul to Almighty God humbly intreating pardon and acceptance thruᵇ; the merritts of yᵉ Lord Jesus Christ, and my body to yᵉ earth to be buryed in a decent Christian manner at yᵉ discretion of my Exeᵗˣ hereaftr named And as to any Worldly Estate which it pleased God to bestow upon me (my Just debts and funeral charges being first Satisfied & paid) I dispose of the Same as follows Vizᵗ I give & bequeath to my beloved Wife Mary Hovey & to her hears forever my homested in Cambridge wᶜʰ we now dwell in and other my Real & personall estate Whatsoever, for ||her|| use & comfort and to dispose of as She pleases, puting that confidence in her yᵗ wᵗ of my sd estate She may leave at her decease She will dispose of amongst all or to Such of our Children as She Shall see meet. I also hereby Constitute & appoint my sd Wife Sole Exᵗˣ of this my Last Will In Wittneſs whereof I have hereunto Set my hand & Seal yᵉ Eight & Twentyᵗʰ day of June yᵉ ninth year of his majᵗˢ Reign Annoqᵉ Domini 1735.

Signed Sealed & published by yᵉ sd Jos Hovey as his Last Will & Testamᵗ In presence of us.

J MORRIS
FRANCIS MOOERS
EDMᵈ GOFFE JUN   *Joseph Hovey* [SEAL]

This will was proved and allowed in the court Nov. 18, 1735.

Mrs. Hovey survived her husband, and married, secondly, Nathaniel Parker of Newton, yeoman, Jan. 27, 1736-7. Mr. Hovey's mansion house and homestead, containing a quarter of an acre, were conveyed, under power to her given in his will, for

* Essex Registry of Deeds, book 31, leaf 188.
† Middlesex Registry of Deeds, book 24, page 587.
‡ Middlesex Registry of Deeds, book 29, page 229.
§ Middlesex Registry of Deeds, book 31, page 127.

sixty-six pounds and fifteen shillings, by Mr. and Mrs. Parker, to Edmund Trowbridge, esq., of Cambridge July 16. 1740.*

Mr. Parker died before 1758; and his wife survived him. She lived in Newton; and when she made her will, June 25, 1758, she said that she was then "well stricken in years." Her will was filed in court March 20, 1758, but was not proved until July 19, 1761. The original instrument is on file in the probate office at Cambridge. In it she gave her property to her Hovey children. The inventory of her estate amounted to fifteen pounds, four shillings and nine pence, being personal estate.

The children of Mr. and Mrs. Hovey were as follows:—

124—I. JOSEPH⁴, living in 1758.

125—II. MARY⁴, unmarried in 1758.

126—III. HANNAH⁴, born about 1706; married Dr. Samuel, son of Samuel Wheat of Newton in or before 1727. He was born in Water-town Oct. 2, 1703; and lived in Newton; dying Aug. 9. 1770. at the age of sixty-seven. She survived him, and died. his widow, July 6, 1792, at the age of eighty-six. Their children were born in Newton, as follows: 1. *Samuel*⁵, born Nov. 2, 1727; died June 5, 1745, at the age of seventeen. 2. *Lydia*⁵, born Nov. 14, 1729; probably married Lazarus Beal July 6, 1749. 3. *Jonathan*⁵, born Nov. 22, 1731; died Feb. 1, 1733-4. 4. *Mary*⁵, born Feb. 15, 1732-3. 5. *Hannah*⁵, born July 24, 1735. 6. *Jonathan*⁵, born Aug. 14, 1737; died Oct. 29, 1748, at the age of eleven. 7. *Moses*⁵, born July 20, 1739; was a physician; married Susanna Brown; and died in Newton March 23, 1770, at the age of thirty. 8. *William*⁵, born Aug. 21, 1741. 9. *Catherine*⁵, born July 11, 1743; married Capt. Thomas Eustis of Rutland. 10. *Jemima*⁵, born July 6, 1745; married Dr. Benjamin Parker Oct. 4, 1764; and she died, his widow, Oct. 2, 1779, at the age of thirty-four. 11. *Samuel*⁵, born March 13, 1746-7; married Jerusha Allen July 14, 1766; and lived in Newton. 12. *Martha*, born April 11, 1749. 13. *John*⁵, born July 31, 1751; died Aug. 29, 1751. 14. *Ann*⁵, born after 1751.

127—IV. DANIEL⁴, married Mary Tapley Dec. 30, 1736, in Cambridge; and was living in 1758.

128—V. AMOS⁴, born Jan. 26, 1711-2, in Cambridge; lived in Boston: married Hannah, daughter of Aaron Pratt of Cohasset July 22, 1737, in Boston, by Rev. Mather Byles; and died before 1758. His signature, written in 1735, is as follows:

Amos Hovey

129—VI. JOHN⁴, living in 1758. The following is his signature, as written in 1735:

John Hovey

* Middlesex Registry of Deeds, book 41, page 235.

41

DEA. EBENEZER HOVEY[a], born in Hadley Nov. 5, 1680. He was called a blacksmith in 1706, but subsequently was a yeoman. He settled in Weymouth as early as 1703, and ever afterward lived there. His wife and himself, for ten pounds and ten shillings, released to her brother Joseph Benson of Hull, cordwainer, all their interest in the real estate of her father (who had deceased), in Hull, Jan. 2, 1706.[*] June 5, 1710, Mr. Hovey sold, for ninety pounds, to Nathaniel Searle of Weymouth twenty-five acres of land on the north side of the highway in that town.[†] With his brothers he conveyed, for twelve pounds, one hundred rods of upland in Ipswich on the southeasterly side of the highway, July 13, 1711.[‡] For three hundred and eighty pounds, Mr. Hovey conveyed to Thomas Hunt of Weymouth, yeoman, fifty acres of land in Weymouth, called the Pond plain, on the south side of Pond river, April 18, 1739;[§] and on the same day, for one hundred and fifty pounds, he conveyed to Nathaniel White of Weymouth, gentleman, six acres of land in Weymouth, on the east side of the river.[||]

Mr. Hovey married, first, Joanna, daughter of Joseph Benson of Hull about 1702; and she died in Weymouth March 26, 1735. He married, second, widow Sarah King of Norton Nov. 13, 1735; and she was his wife in 1744.

Deacon Hovey made his will July 9, 1744, and the following is an exact transcript of the instrument on file in the probate court office in Boston :—

In the Name of God Amen. this Ninth day of July A. D. 1744: I Ebenezer Hovey of weymouth in the County of Suffolk: & Province: of the Maſachuſitts Bay in New England yeoman being very Sick & Weak in Body, but of perfect Mind and Memory, thanks be given to God: therefore calling unto Mind the Mortality of my Body and knowing that it is appointed for all men once to Dye, do Make and Ordain this my laſt Will & Teſtament, that is to ſay, Principally and firſt of all I give and Recommend my Soul into the hands of God that gave it; and my Body I Recommend to the Earth to be Buried in decent Chriſtian Burial at the discretion of by Executor; nothing doubting but at the General Reſurrection I Shall Receive that Same again by the mighty Power of God, and as touching Such worldly Eſtate wherewith it hath pleaſed God to Bleſs me in this Life, I give demiſe and diſpoſe of Same in the following Manner and form.

Imprimis I give and bequeath to my well beloved Wife all that She brought to me att the time of Mariage and alſo one third part ||to Improve|| of my Eſtate During her Natural Life and alſo my Will is

[*] Suffolk Registry of Deeds, book 26, page 181.
[†] Suffolk Registry of Deeds, book 25, page 150.
[‡] Essex Registry of Deeds, book 31, leaf 188.
[§] Suffolk Registry of Deeds, book 60, page 199.
[||] Suffolk Registry of Deeds, book 65, page 187.

that if my wife Should Marry that the abovesaid third part to go Immediately to my Executor he paying to her (that is now my Wife) yearly the Juſt yearly Income During the term above said: that is to Say her Natural Life

Item: I give and bequeath to my well beloved Daughter Hannah Snow the sum of twelve pounds ten Shilings Lawfull Money of New-England to be paid out of my Eſtate by my Executor at the End of one whole year after my Deceaſe which I think to [be] her part out of my Eſtate with what She hath already had

Item. I give and bequeath unto my well beloved Daughter Martha Pettengall the Sum of five pounds Lawfull Money of New England to be paid by my Executor out of my Eſtate at the End of one whole year after my Deceaſe which I think to be her part out of my Eſtate with what She hath already had   ..

Item: I give and bequeath unto my well beloved Son Samuel Hovey whom I likewiſe conſtitute make and ordain my Sole Executor of this my laſt Will and Teſtament, all and Singular my Lands Rights titles Intereſts whatſoever Real and Parſonal: he paying My Juſtes Debts and funeral Charges to him his heirs and aſsigns for Ever and alſo the one third that is allowed to my wife to be to him his heirs and aſsigns after the term or terms above Said and I do hereby utterly Diſsallo revoke and diſannul all and Every other former Teſtaments Legacies and bequeſts and Executors by me in any ways before Named, Willed and bequeathed Ratifying and Confirming this and no other to be my last Will and Teſtament: In Witneſs whereof I have hereunto Set my hand and Seal the Day and year above written

Signed Sealed Publiſhed Pronounced
and Declared by the said Ebenezer Hovey
as his laſt Will and Teſtament in the
preſence of us the Subscribers

JAMES BEAL   EBENEZER HOVEY [SEAL]
JACOB TURNER
EBEN' WHITE

Mr. Hovey probably died in the early spring of 1756, as his will was proved April 16, 1756.

The children of Deacon Hovey were as follows:—

130—I.   HANNAH⁴, born Feb. 4, 1703, in Weymouth; married James, son of Joseph and Hopestill Snow of Bridgewater Aug. 6, 1741; and she was his wife in 1744. They lived in East Bridgewater; and this was his second wife. He was born in 1693. They had one child: 1. *James⁵*, born in 1742.

131—II. MARTHA⁴, married Obadiah Pettingell of Abington Jan. 20, 1731-2; and she was his wife in 1744.

132—III. SUSANNA⁴, died June 29, 1717, in Weymouth.

133—IV. SAMUEL⁴, born Dec. 12, 1718, in Weymouth. *See family numbered "133."*

134—V.   EBENEZER⁴, baptized Dec. 27, 1724, in the Second church in Weymouth; and probably died before 1744.

43

JOHN HOVEY³, born in Hadley, Mass., Aug. 21, 1684. He was a resident of Cambridge, Mass., at an early age, being a baker. He bought of his brother Joseph Hovey the old Blue Anchor tavern, on the corner of Dunster (?) and Mt. Auburn

streets, in Cambridge, for one hundred and forty-five pounds.
April 1, 1709,* when he is called of Charlestown. He afterward
conducted the tavern.

Mr. Hovey joined with his brother in conveying, for twelve
pounds, to Rev. John Emerson of New Castle, N. H., one hundred rods of upland in Ipswich, on the southeasterly side of the
highway, July 13, 1711.†

May 6, 1714, Mr. Hovey bought of John Stedman of Cambridge, tailor, for one hundred and eighty-nine pounds, thirty-one
and one-half acres of land on the southwest side of Charles river,
and northwest side of the road leading towards Roxbury;‡ and,
May 22, 1714, when he is called a yeoman, he conveyed, for
fifteen pounds, one and one-half acres of marsh in Cambridge to
Richard Ward of Newton.§

Mr. Hovey married Abiel Watson of Cambridge in 1706
She was born about 1687. He died Sept. 13, 1714, at the age of
thirty. The following is a copy of the inscription on his gravestone in the old burial ground at Harvard square:—

> Here   Lyes   Buried
> The   B o d y   o f
> Mʳ   JOHN HOVEY
> Aged 30 Years 1 Month
> and 3 Weekes Decafed
> September The 13ᵗʰ 1714

Mr. Hovey's estate was valued at £389, 0s, 8d. The real estate included house, barn, etc. The house is mentioned as having
a hall, kitchen, parlor, hall chamber, kitchen chamber, parlor
chamber and garrets. The real estate was assigned by the probate court to the eldest son John Hovey. The widow was appointed administratrix of the estate Dec. 10, 1715.

Mrs. Hovey married, secondly, Edmund Angier of Cambridge April 9, 1717; and he died in Cambridge April 24, 1724,
at the age of thirty-nine. She married, thirdly, Isaac Watson of
Cambridge Aug. 27, 1725; and he perished in the conflagration
of his dwelling house Feb. 25, 1741, at the age of fifty-four. She
died, in Cambridge, his widow, Sept. 18, 1753, at the age of
sixty-six.

Mrs. Hovey and her then husband, Isaac Watson of Cambridge, yeoman, for thirty pounds, conveyed to her son John
Hovey of Cambridge her interest in the estate of her deceased

* Middlesex Registry of Deeds, book 15, page 492.
† Essex Registry of Deeds, book 31, leaf 188.
‡ Middlesex Registry of Deeds, book 16, page 555.
§ Middlesex Registry of Deeds, book 20, page 712.

husband John Hovey Nov. 1, 1736.* John Hovey, for seventy pounds, bought the interest of his brother Ebenezer Hovey of Cambridge, housewright, in the estate of his father and also of his brother Thomas Hovey, both real and personal, Nov. 1, 1736.*

For fifty pounds, Mr. and Mrs. Watson released her interest in thirty acres of land which had belonged to the estate of John Hovey, her first husband, Nov. 12, 1736.†

John Hovey, for seventy pounds, also bought the interest of his brother James Hovey of Plymouth, joiner, in the real and personal estate of his father and also of his brother Thomas Hovey, Nov. 1, 1737.‡

The children of John and Abiel Hovey were born in Cambridge as follows:—

135—I.   JOHN⁴, born June 12, 1707. *See family numbered "135."*
136—II.   SARAH⁴, born Feb. 28, 1708-9; died Oct. 11, 1720, aged eleven. The following is a copy of the inscription on her gravestone in the ancient burial ground at Harvard Square in Cambridge:—

> Sarah   Hovey,
> Daugͬ of Mͬ John
> &   Mͬˢ   Abiel
> Hovey;   Decͩ
> Oct͡b͡r 11ᵗʰ, 1720, in yᵉ
> 12ᵗʰ Yᵉʳ of Her Age

137—III.   THOMAS⁴, born Sept. 2, 1710; was a physician; sailed with Captain Deckerson as mate and physician to Africa; and died, unmarried, at the English Factory, on the river Gambia, in Africa, April —, 1732, at the age of twenty-one. His mother and stepfather, Isaac Watson of Cambridge, yeoman, were appointed administrators of his estate Oct. 28, 1734. In the administration papers he is called a resident of Charlestown, Mass.

138—IV.   JAMES⁴, born Dec. 1, 1712; was a joiner by trade; settled in Plymouth, Mass., and was a prominent town officer, justice of the peace and attorney. He conveyed, for seventy pounds, to his brother John Hovey of Cambridge his interest in the personal and real estate of his father and his brother Thomas Hovey, deceased, Nov. 1, 1737.‡ His real estate transactions were numerous, and principally connected with his professional business. He married, first, Lydia, daughter of John and Sarah Atwood of Plymouth March 20, 1734. She was born June 6, 1715. Mr. Hovey owned and occupied the house now known as the Central house on Main street. His wife Lydia died Feb. 23, 1771, at the age of fifty-five; and the

* Middlesex Registry of Deeds, book 37, page 609.
† Middlesex Registry of Deeds, book 38, page 7.
‡ Middlesex Registry of Deeds, book 38, page 429.

following is a copy of the inscription on her gravestone in the historic Burying Hill cemetery in Plymouth:—

> Here lies Buried y^e
> Body of Mrs Lydia Hou
> ey late wife of James
> Houey Esqr & Daughter
> of ye late Dec^d John
> Atwood dec^d she died
> Feb^{ry} ye 23^d 1771 In y^e
> 56th year of her age

Mr. Hovey married, secondly, Mrs. Mary, widow of Capt. Samuel Harlow of Plymouth June 2, 1771; and she died there June 2, 1774, at the age of forty-three. She is also buried by Mr. Hovey's side on Burying hill, and the following is the inscription on her gravestone:—

> Here lyes Buried ye body
> of Mrs Mary Hovey late
> wife of James Hovey *Esqr*
> fhe dyed on ye 2^d day of
> June Ad 1774, in ye 44th Year
> of her Age.

Mr. Hovey married, thirdly, Mrs. Margaret Connel (Correll?) of Boston (published Sept. 24, 1774); and she died at Boston in 1787.

Mr. Hovey settled in Cambridge in 1733; was a carpenter and joiner there from 1733 to 1742; and a preacher from 1742 to 1767. He was afterward a clerk for Edward and J. Winslow. He died in Plymouth Jan. 7, 1781, at the age of sixty-eight; and his remains lie by the side of the Pilgrim fathers on Burying hill, the inscription on his gravestone being as follows:—

> In Memory of
> JAMES HOVEY, *Esqr*
> who died Jany ye 7th 1781
> in ye 72^d year of his Age.

He made his will Jan. 1, 1761, and the following is a copy of the original instrument on file in the probate office at Plymouth:—

> In the Name of God Amen.
> I James Hovey of Plimouth in the County of Plimouth in New England Esqr being at this time on a sick Bed But through Gods Goodness of a sound and Disposing mind & memory & Desirous of Setting my House in Order before I die do make and ordain this my Last Will and Testament
> In the First place I Recomend my Soul into the hands of Almighty God & my body to a Decent burial at the discretion of my Excutrix hereafter named,
> And as To my Temporal Estate I dispose of the same in the following manner and Form, viz—
> Imp^s I Give to my Well beloved wife Lidia Hovey all my personal Estate whatsoever without Exception

I also Give to my said wife the Improvement of all my Real Estate without Impeachment of waste during her natural life—and after her Decease I give to my Brother John Hovey and his heirs & Assigns Three Seventh parts of my Real Estate

Item I Give To my Nephew Thomas Hovey the son of my Brother Ebenezer One Seventh part of my Real Estate to him his heirs & assigns forever.

Item the remaining three sevenths parts of my Real Estate I give to my nephew Francis Addams to him his heirs and Assigns forever. Finally I constitute my said wife Lidia Hovey Executrix of this my last will and Testament In Witness Whereof I have hereunto set my hand & Seal this first day of January Anno Domini 1761.

Signed Sealed Delivered Published
& Declared by said James Hovey to
be his last will and Testament
in presence of us.

EDWARD WINSLOW
SARAH SHURTLEFF   JAS. HOVEY [SEAL]
ELISEB HEARSEY

The will was proved April 11, 1781. The inventory of his estate amounted to £1,030, 6s., 2d.; of which £664, 17s., was real estate, and £275, 9s., 2d., was personal. He had two pews in the First Precinct meeting house. His list of property is long and interesting. There is furniture, household furnishings, cranes, hooks, trammels, skillets, creepers, lanthorn, all kinds of dishes and many books.

He had no children.

139—V.   EBENEZER⁶, born July 12, 1714. *See family numbered "139."*

44

CALEB HOVEY³, born in Hadley, Mass., June 4, 1687. He lived in Cambridge until 1730, when he removed to Newton.

July 13, 1711, he joined his brothers in conveying, for twelve pounds, to Rev. John Emerson of New Castle, N. H., one hundred rods of land in Ipswich, on the southeasterly side of the highway.*

He married Mary Winchester of Brookline in 1713; and she was living in 1724. He died just before Feb. 3, 1745, when his son Caleb Hovey of Newton, husbandman, was appointed administrator of his estate.

Their children were born in Cambridge, as follows:—

140—I.   MARY⁴, born April 11, 1714.
141—II.   ABIGAIL⁴, born April 20, 1716.
142—III.   CALEB⁴, born Dec. 21, 1717. *See family numbered "142."*
143—IV.   ESTHER⁴, born June 10, 1720.
144—V.   SARAH⁴, born May 21, 1722.

* Essex Registry of Deeds, book 31, leaf 188.

145—VI. JOSIAH⁶, born May 4, 1724; was an apprentice to Solomon
Townsend; and died at Cape Breton, in the expedition against
Louisburg, in 1745, at the age of twenty-one. His brother
Caleb Hovey was appointed administrator of his estate July
14, 1746, the deceased having lived in Malden at the time of
his death.

46

DEA. JAMES HOVEY⁵, born in Hadley, Mass., about 1691. He
was a sadler, called, in 1717, a saddle-tree maker, and in 1753 he
was called a yeoman. He lived in Charlestown until 1724, when
he settled in Malden, where he subsequently resided.

July 13, 1711, he joined with his brothers in conveying one
hundred rods of land in Ipswich, for twelve pounds, to Rev. John
Emerson of New Castle, N. H.* May 9, 1717, he and his wife
Elizabeth and John Brintnal of Charlestown, tanner, and wife
Deborah, divided between their wives eight acres of land and the
house and barn thereon, one and one-half acres of fresh meadow,
and one and one-half acres of salt marsh and upland, all situated
in Charlestown, which had been left to them by their fathers
John and William Mellins, both of Charlestown, mariners, deceased ;† and on the same day Mr. and Mrs. Hovey conveyed to
Mr. and Mrs. Brintnal their (James and Elizabeth) share of that
estate.‡

For twenty-eight pounds, he bought two acres of land in
Malden Dec. 1, 1722.§ He bought ten acres of upland and salt
marsh in Charlestown, lying on the north side of the country
highway, April 6. 1724.‖ For one hundred and twenty pounds,
he bought of John Townsend of Charlestown, sadler, eight acres
of land, in Charlestown, in two lots, one being on the east side of
the country road, and the other being salt marsh, Feb. 24, 1724.¶
He bought of Solomon Townsend of Malden, weaver, and another, for one hundred and twenty pounds, two acres of upland
on the south side of the road, and two acres of marsh, all lying
in Malden, May 22, 1739.**

Daniel Floyd of Malden, yeoman, gave a bond to James
Hovey of Malden, sadler, and another, in the sum of one hundred and twenty pounds, conditioned to pay legacies due from estate of said Floyd's father, Daniel Floyd, the bond being secured
by the conveyance to the obligees, three lots of land in Malden,

* Essex Registry of Deeds, book 31, leaf 188.
† Middlesex Registry of Deeds, book 24, page 241.
‡ Middlesex Registry of Deeds, book 20, page 356.
§ Middlesex Registry of Deeds, book 50, page 648.
‖ Middlesex Registry of Deeds, book 23, page 476.
¶ Middlesex Registry of Deeds, book 51, page 107.
** Middlesex Registry of Deeds, book 51, page 108.

viz: The homestead of forty acres, situated on the south side of the country road leading to Lynn, eleven and one-half acres of woodland and six acres of woodland, Nov. 17, 1752.* With another, for one hundred pounds, he bought of Daniel Floyd of Malden, yeoman, his interest in twenty-three acres of land in Malden, and half of the barn lying on the side of the country road leading to Lynn; six and one-half acres of woodland; and one acre of orchard lying on the north side of the country road, being the thirds of widow Mary Floyd, Feb. 23, 1753.† Mr. Floyd also conveyed to him and another, for two hundred dollars, the premises bounded as above Nov. 17, 1752, and also half an acre on the north side of the road to Lynn, Feb. 23, 1753.‡ For two hundred and ninety pounds, thirteen shillings and four pence, he sold to John Shute of Malden, yeoman, and others, his mansion house, barn and six acres of land under and adjoining them, lying on the north side of the country road; one acre of mowing land on the south side of the town road; fifteen acres of salt marsh, lying on the south side of the country road; twelve acres of woodland in the great swamp, so called; and ten and one-half acres of woodland, all in Malden, March 13, 1753.§ Sept. 1, 1753, for three hundred and thirty pounds, he bought of John Shute of Malden, yeoman, and others house and barn and eight acres of land on which they stood, lying on the north side of the country road; sixteen acres of orchard, marsh and upland, lying on the south side of the country road, and north side of the mill pond; one-half acre on the south side of the country road; twelve acres of woodland in the great swamp; and ten acres of woodland, lying on the north side of a road; all being situated in Malden.|| Mr. Hovey mortgaged the real estate he had purchased by the above deed to Owen Harris of Boston, schoolmaster, Sept. 3, 1753; and it was duly discharged Feb. 14, 1756.¶ For two hundred and thirty-three pounds, seventeen shillings and eight pence, Mr. Hovey and another conveyed to Thomas Pratt of Chelsea, gentleman, forty-four acres of land on the south side of the country road; eleven and one-half acres of woodland; six acres of woodland; and one-half acre of land on north side of the country road; all being situated in Malden, Dec. 24, 1753.** For sixty-six pounds, he conveyed to Richard Dexter of Malden, housewright, house and barn and eight acres of land on north side of the

* Middlesex Registry of Deeds, book 51, page 38.
† Middlesex Registry of Deeds, book 51, page 150.
‡ Middlesex Registry of Deeds, book 51, page 152.
§ Middlesex Registry of Deeds, book 51, page 195.
|| Middlesex Registry of Deeds, book 52, page 212.
¶ Middlesex Registry of Deeds, book 52, page 214.
** Middlesex Registry of Deeds, book 54, page 40.

country road; three-fourths of an acre of mowing land, lying on the south side of the country road; twelve acres of woodland in the great swamp, so called; ten and one-half acres of woodland; all being in Malden, Dec. 8, 1755*. He also conveyed to Mr. Dexter, for one hundred and forty pounds, fifteen acres of land in Malden, lying on the south side of the country road, including salt marsh, upland and fresh meadow, Dec. 8, 1755.† Mr. Hovey and another, for forty-five pounds, conveyed to Benjamin Blaney of Malden, tanner, three-fifths of four and one-fourth acres of land and house and barn, on the north side of the highway; and three-fifths of three-fourths of an acre of land, lying on the south side of the highway; all being in Malden, July 24, 1764.‡

Mr. Hovey married, first, Elizabeth, daughter of William Mellins of Charlestown, mariner, about 1718. She fell down on the ferry ways at Peney ferry, and died immediately Oct. 1,§ 1750, at the age of fifty-four. He married, second, Susannah Dexter of Malden May 7, 1751.

Deacon Hovey died in Malden July 13, 1765, aged about seventy-four.

The following is a copy of his will transcribed from the original instrument on file in the probate office at Cambridge:—

In the name of God Amen. the ſixteenth Day of February one Thouſand ſeven Hundred and ſixty two— I James Hovey of malden in the County of Middleſex in the Province of the Maſſachuſets Bay in New England being far advanced in years and often exerciſed with bodily inſfirmities but of perfect mind and memory thanks be given to God for it, and knowing that it is appointed for all men once to dye, do make and ordain this my laſt Will and Teſtament, princapaly and firſt of all I recommend my ſoul into the hands of God that gave it and my Body I recommend to the Earth to be Buried in decent Chriſtian burial at the decretion of my Exectrex nothing doubting but at the General Reſurecction I ſhall receive the ſame again by the mighty power of God and as touching Such worldly Eſtate wherewith it hath pleaſed God to bleſs me in this life I give and diſpoſe off in the following manner and form viz.

Imprimis. I give unto Suſannah my well beloved Wife all my Perſonal Eſtate to be at her diſpoſal for ever, except what I herein give to my ſon Joſeph Hovey. as for my ſon John loſt at ſea I have don a great deal for him, and my Daughter Mary Sprague I gave her about fore hundred pounds old tenner when ſhe was married and beſides what I have done for her and her brother John ſhe with her Brother Joſeph and Johns two Children will by Law have my Buildings which coſt me above a thouſand pounds old tenner becauſe I built on the Land that was my firſt Wife. their Mother. which will be equaly divided between them. as for my beloved ſon Joſeph Hove if he livs to com home again I give to him ‖my‖ Cain, Belt and ſword beſids what he will have of my build-

* Middlesex Registry of Deeds, book 53, page 304.
† Middlesex Registry of Deeds, book 53, page 305.
‡ Middlesex Registry of Deeds, book 62, page 311.
§ Gravestone says "October 4."

ings and Land that I am in the poffiffion of. I Conftitute make and
ordain fufannah my beloved wife Executrex and my Brother in Law
||ritchard Dexter|| Executor of this my laft Will and Teftament and I do
hereby utterly revoke and difanul all other former wills, Teftaments and
Bequeaft whatfoever by me before named, willed and bequeathed ratifying and confirming this and no other to be my laft will and Teftament
I Wittnefs whereof I have hereunto fet to my hand and Seal the Day
and year above written.

Signed, sealed, Publifhed, Pronounfed
and declaired by the faid James Hovey
to be his laft will and Teftament
in the prefents of us the fubfcribers

NATHAN DEXTER
SAMUEL BALDWIN
WILLIAM DEXTER   *James Hovey* [SEAL]

The will was proved and Mrs. Hovey appointed executrix
Oct. 22, 1765.

Mrs. Hovey died Feb. 14, 1768, at the age of fifty-seven.

Mr. Hovey's children were all by his first wife, Elizabeth,
and were born in Malden as follows:—

146—I.   JAMES[4], born June 21, 1719; this is probably the James Hovey
          of Roxbury, school master, who conveyed his dwelling house
          and three acres of land in Lynn, on the east side of Heart's
          lane, in Lynn, Aug. 10, 1744.* He probably died before his
          father.

147—II.   ELIZABETH[4], born Sept. 18, 1723; died June 28, 1736, aged twelve.

148—III. MARY[4], born Oct. 24, 1727; married Nathan Sprague of Malden
          April 17, 1750. Children, born in Malden: 1. *Elizabeth*[5],
          born Feb. 22, 1751-2; died March 28, "1751." 2. *Elizabeth*[5],
          born Dec. 14, 1753. 3. *Mary*[5], born April 7, 1756. 4. *Sarah*[5],
          born Oct. 12, 1759. 5. *James Hovey*[5], born April 1, 1765.
          6. *William*[5], born Aug. 26, 1766.

149—IV.   JOHN[4], born Oct. 23, 1730. *See family numbered "149."*

150—V.   JOSEPH[4], born June 10, 1739; lived in Malden; mariner. For
          forty-five pounds, he joined with his father in conveying to
          Benjamin Blaney of Malden, tanner, three-fifths of four and
          one-fourth acres of land and house and barn, on north side of
          the highway, and three-fifths of three-fourths of an acre of
          land on the south side of the highway, all in Malden, July
          24, 1764.†

51

NATHANIEL HOVEY[3], born in Ipswich, Mass., June 29, 1691.
He removed to Windham, Conn., when he became twenty, and
was a yeoman. He married Abigail Gennings Nov. 25, 1712.

For twenty-four pounds, he sold one-sixth of one hundred
rods of land, of three acres of upland, and of three acres of
marsh on Plum Island, all situated in Ipswich, June 7, 1712.‡

* Essex Registry of Deeds, book 86, leaf 270.
† Middlesex Registry of Deeds, book 62, page 311.
‡ Essex Registry of Deeds, book 25, leaf 221.

For nineteen pounds, he conveyed to Joseph Ford of Windham one hundred acres of land, lying on the west side of Little river. June 30, 1713.* For two hundred and fifty pounds, he bought of Robert Durke of Windham land on the west side of Little river, Jan. 13, 1739-40.† For one hundred pounds, he mortgaged land in Windham to the Government of Connecticut, March 19, 1744.‡

Mr. Hovey died in Windham June 26, 1761, aged seventy, lacking three days. The following is a copy of his will transcribed from the original instrument on file in the probate office at Willimantic, Conn. :—

In the Name of God Amen The second Day of August In the year of our Lord: 1756 I Nathaniel Hovey of Windham in the County of Windham in New England yeoman Being in a Comfortable mesure of helth and Perfect mind and memory thanks be Giuen to God But Calling to mind yᵉ mortality of my Body & Knowing yᵗ tis Appointed for all men once to Dye Do thenfforth make and Ordain this my Laſt Will and Teſtament That Is to say Principaly and firſt of all I Give and Recommend my soule Into the Hands of God yᵗ Gave it hoping thro yᵉ merits Death & Paſion of my sauiour Jeſus Chriſt to haue the full & free Pardon of all my sins and to Inherit Everlaſting Life and my Body I Commit to the Earth to be Decently Buried at the Diſcretion of my Executors hereafter named nothing Doubting But att yᵉ General Reſurrection I shall Receive yᵉ seame a Gain By the mighty Power of God And as Touching such Worldly Eſtate as it has Pleaſed God to Bleſs me With in this Life I Give & Diſpoſe of the same In the Following manner & Forme that Is to Say—

Imprimis I Will that all ‖my‖ Juſt Debts to any Perſon or Perſons and Funeral Charges be Paid By my Executors in Convenient Time &c

Item I Give to my Dearly Beloved son Nathaniel Hovey Fifty Pounds Lawfull money to be Paid Two years aftor the Longeſt Liver off me or my Wifes Deces to be Paid by my Executors Which is yᵉ full of his portion with what he has all Redy had this ‖ is ‖ to be pd by Luke

Item I give to my Dearly Belouid son John Hovey Fifty Pounds Lawfull money to be Paid Three years aftor yᵉ Longeſt Liver Deces by my Executors Which is yᵉ hol of his portion with what he has all Redy had and to be Paid by Jonathan Hovey

Item I Give to my Dearly beloved son Ebenezer Hovey Fifty Pounds Lawfull money to be Paid by my Executors Foor years aftor yᵉ Longeſt Liver Deces Which is the hol of his Portions With what he has all Redy had and to be paid by Luke Houey

Item I Give to my Dearly Beloved Daughters Abigal Durkee Sarah Genings mary Flint and Asa Dauiſon son to my Daughter Lyde Dauiſon Deceſt all my Endore movebels Equelly to be Diuided Between them all Foor Which is yᵉ hol of there Portion with what thay haue all Redy had: only I Giue to my Daughter Gennings one pare of Tongs one slice & a Trammil to be Deliverd by my Executors alſo I Referue my grate Trammil for Jonathan

Item I Give to my Dearly Belovid son Luke Hovey and his Heirs all the Eſt End of my Farme so far as os it was lately Diuided With all

* Windham Registry of Deeds, book D, page 328.
† Windham Registry of Deeds, book 8, page 26.
‡ Windham Registry of Deeds, book 9, page 84.

the Buldings on the same to him and his Heirs forever and my Iron Bar & half the out Dore movebels

Item I Give to my Dearly Belovid son Jonathan Hovey the Weſt End of my Farm so Far as it Was Lately Divided to him and his Heirs forever alſo I Give to Jonathan Hovey my Grate Tramil and half the out Dore movebels Excepting my Iron Bar

Item I Likewiſe Conſtitute make and ordain my soule Executors John Fuller Luke Hovey and Jonathan Hovey of this my Laſt Will and Teſtament all & singuler my Lands & Tenements ‖ not Disposed off ‖ by them Freely to be Poſſeſed and Enjoyed and I Do hereby uterly Diſ-allow Reuoke Diſanull all and Every other Former Teſtament Will Legeceis and Bequeſt and Executors by me in any Ways Before Named Willed and Bequeſted Ratifying and Confirming this and no other to be my Laſt Will and Teſtement In Witneſs Whereof I have hereunto sett my hand & seal

The Day and year above Riten signed sealed Published and Declared by the sd Nathaniel Hovey as his Laſt Will and Teſte-men In the Priſents of us the subſcribers

    SAMUELL FAULKNER
    THOMAS HODGKINS
    SAMUELL FULLER   *Nath.ll Hovy* [SEAL]

The will was duly proved July 24, 1761. His estate was appraised at £833, 11s., 1d.; personal estate £49, 16s., 1d.; and real estate, £783, 15s. He had a house and barn and one hundred and sixty-five acres of land.

Mr. Hovey's wife survived him and died Dec. 11, 1773, at the age of eighty.

The children of Nathaniel and Abigail Hovey were born in Windham as follows:—

151—I.   NATHANIEL* (twin), born Oct. 31, 1713; died Dec. 31. 1713.
152—II. ABIGAIL* (twin), born Oct. 31, 1713; married Capt. William, son of William and Rebecca (Gould) Durkee of Windham Feb. 8, 1732-3. He was born there Feb. 28, 1710; and died Jan. 15, 1795. She died May 30, 1791, at the age of seventy-seven. Mrs. Mary (Goodell) Bill of Connecticut had a crayon portrait of her. Children, born in Windham: 1. *Abigail*, born April 14, 1734; married Capt. Josiah Hammond. 2. *Sarah*, born Aug. 30, 1736; died June 15. 1742. 3. *Hannah*, born Jan. 26, 1738-9; married William Foster. 4. *Mary*, born Nov. 29, 1741; married Dr. John Brewster.
153—III. SARAH*, born Nov. 10, 1716; married Joseph Gennings, jr., April 15, 1735; and lived in Windham. He was living there in 1761; and she in 1762. Children, born in Windham: 1. *Abigail*, born Nov. 13. 1736. 2. *Mary*, born Nov. 15. 1738; died Aug. 13, 1753, aged fourteen. 3. *Sibel*, born Feb. 8, 1740-1; died Nov. —, 1741. 4. *Mary*, born Aug. 24, 1742. 5. *Sarah*, born July 17, 1746; died Aug. 20, 1753. 6. *Lydia*, born Sept. 11, 1748. 7. *Sybel*, born June 14, 1752.
154—IV. NATHANIEL*, born Oct. 23, 1717. *See family numbered "154."*
155—V.   JOHN*, born Jan. 16, 1719-20. *See family numbered "155."*
156—VI. EBENEZER*, born April 9, 1722; died March 9, 1723.
157—VII. EBENEZER*, born Feb. 21, 1723-4. *See family numbered "157."*

158—VIII.   MARY⁴, born May 15, 1726; married Nathaniel, son of Nathaniel
              and Sarah (Cutler) Flint of Windham July 3, 1751. He
              was born in Windham (in that part now Hampton) Sept. 5,
              1720; and died Jan. —, 1795, aged seventy-four. He married,
              fiirst, Sarah, daughter of Benjamin and Lydia Bidlack Jan.
              16, 1742; and she died Sept. 5, 1749, at the age of twenty-five.
              Mary Hovey was his second wife. She died in Braintree,
              Vt., Sept. 30, 1807, at the age of eighty-one. She had been
              living at Braintree with her sons Daniel and William since
              the summer of 1803. Children of Nathaniel and Mary
              (Hovey) Flint, born in Windham: 1. *Luke⁵*, born Dec. 20,
              1752; married Mary Slate, and removed from town about
              1785; they had children. 2. *Jonathan⁵*, born March 29, 1754;
              died April 14, 1754. 3. *Jonathan⁵*, born Nov. 22, 1755; mar-
              ried Mary Amidon; and removed to Vermont about 1800.
              4. *Phineas⁵*, born Feb. 23, 1757; removed to Braintree, Vt.,
              Jan. 25, 1796; married Hannah, daughter of Jeremiah and
              Hannah Clark Feb. 24, 1780; she was born Dec. 29, 1757.
              They had eleven children. 5. *Abigail⁵*, born May 29, 1758;
              married Shuball Martin April 19, 1779; he was born Dec 3,
              1757; and they had ten children. 6. *Zacheus⁵*, born April
              24, 1760. 7. *Daniel⁵*, born Dec. 7, 1761; removed to Brain-
              tree, Vt.; married Elizabeth, daughter of Joseph Martin; she
              was born Dec. 24, 1761; she died Oct. —, 1807; he died
              March 12, 1841; and they had nine children. 8. *Elisha⁵*,
              born Nov. 25, 1763. 9. *Mary⁵*, born April 28, 1765. 10.
              William⁵, born April 29, 1769; married Patty Randall; and
              died in 1850, having had twelve children.
159—IX.   JONATHAN⁴, born May 4. 1728; died Jan. 7, 1731-2.
160—X.   LUKE⁴, born Feb. 28, 1729-30. *See family numbered "160."*
161—XI.   PHINEAS⁴, born Dec. 6, 1731. Perhaps he went to Pennsyl-
              vania, and was never heard from.
162—XII.   JONATHAN⁴, born Dec. 2, 1734. *See family numbered "162."*
163—XIII. LYDIA⁴, born Jan. 15, 1736-7; married Asa Davison June 5,
              1755; and died in Windham April 8. 1756, at the age of
              nineteen. Child, born in Windham: 1. *Asa⁵*, born April
              1, 1756; living in 1762.

53

NATHANIEL HOVEY⁴, born in Ipswich, Mass., in 1696 He
was a weaver, and always lived in Ipswich.

For twenty pounds, he conveyed to his uncles Thomas Hovey
and John Hovey, both of Ipswich, his interest in the dwelling
house of his father, on the south side of the river, in Ipswich.
April 8, 1718 :* and on the same day, for forty-eight pounds, he
conveyed to his said uncles his interest in the estate of his
grandfather Daniel Hovey.† April 10, 1718, he bought of Thomas
Hovey of Ipswich, fisherman, by way of exchange, Thomas' interest in the estate of his father Daniel Hovey.‡ He bought, for

* Essex Registry of Deeds, book 36, leaf 115.
† Essex Registry of Deeds, book 36, leaf 125.
‡ Essex Registry of Deeds, book 35, leaf 55.

twenty-five pounds and five shillings, thirty-nine and one-fifth
rods of orchard land in Ipswich, lying next to Annable's lane.
Nov. 5, 1718.* Aug. 8, 1719, he bought, for fifty shillings, old
thatch or marsh lot, numbered 16, on Jeffries Neck in Ipswich.† For six pounds and fifteen shillings, he sold new woodlot
in Chebacco, numbered 350, Dec. 30, 1719.‡ For two pounds and
ten shillings, he bought old thatch lot, numbered 324, drawn by
John Pearly of Ipswich, in ye north common field, on Rogers
island, in Ipswich, Sept. 8, 1720.§ In 1722, for thirty pounds, he
bought a common right in the Bush hill and Turner's hill eighths,
on the north side of the Town river.|| Oct. 6, 1722, he made an
agreement with another person to support a well mutually.¶
For thirty pounds, he conveyed a right in the south eighths, on
the south side of the river, in 1722.** For thirty shillings, he
bought thatch lot, numbered 206, on Cross' banks, in Ipswich,
March 18, 1722-3 ;†† and, for twenty-five shillings, he bought lot
numbered 207 on the same banks, Nov. 19, 1723.‡‡ For four
pounds, he bought some marsh land in Ipswich Dec. 8, 1724 ;§§
having, also, for thirty-two shillings, bought some more marsh
there Dec, 31, 1722.§§ For forty-five shillings, he bought old
thatch lot, numbered 208, on Cross' bank, in Ipswich, Dec. 1,
1724.|||| For seven pounds and ten shillings, he bought half of
old common right, numbered 242, on Jeffries Neck, in Ipswich,
Dec. 9, 1726.¶¶ For five pounds, he bought one-half of new upland lot, numbered 124, and new marsh lot, numbered 35, on
Jeffries Neck, in Ipswich, May 5, 1726.*** For twelve pounds, he
bought one-half of a woodlot in the great meadow woods in
Rowley Jan. 24, 1731.††† For twelve pounds, he sold old common
rights, numbered 2 and 16, in Jeffries Neck marsh in Ipswich.
Oct. 31, 1735.‡‡‡ For twelve pounds and ten shillings, he sold
one-half of four and one-half acres of thatch bank on Plum
Island, in Ipswich, June 22, 1736.§§§ For eleven pounds and five

---

* Essex Registry of Deeds, book 33, leaf 260.
† Essex Registry of Deeds, book 37, leaf 36.
‡ Essex Registry of Deeds, book 37, leaf 256.
§ Essex Registry of Deeds, book 38, leaf 112.
|| Essex Registry of Deeds, book 38, leaf 277.
¶ Essex Registry of Deeds, book 39, leaf 203.
** Essex Registry of Deeds, book 39, leaf 221.
†† Essex Registry of Deeds, book 41, leaf 267.
‡‡ Essex Registry of Deeds, book 42, leaf 93.
§§ Essex Registry of Deeds, book 44, leaf 6.
|||| Essex Registry of Deeds, book 47, leaf 21.
¶¶ Essex Registry of Deeds, book 47, leaf 197.
*** Essex Registry of Deeds, book 48, leaf 9.
††† Essex Registry of Deeds, book 59, leaf 234.
‡‡‡ Essex Registry of Deeds, book 74, leaf 15.
§§§ Essex Registry of Deeds, book 80, leaf 226.

shillings, he bought eleven rods and four feet of land in Ipswich, Nov. 3, 1739.* For twenty-two pounds, he bought one-half of four and one-half acres of salt marsh and thatch bank on Plum Island, in Ipswich, June 30, 1746.† For twenty-five pounds, he bought four and one-half acres of salt marsh and thatch bank on Plum Island, in Ipswich, bounded northeast by the sea, July 7, 1735.‡ For thirty pounds, he bought about an acre of land in the north common field, in Ipswich, Nov. 3, 1735.§ For fourteen pounds, he bought old thatch lot, numbered 181, on Cross' bank in Ipswich, March 18, 1742.§ For fourteen pounds, he bought a new lot in the Birch Island division in the Bush Hill eighths, in Ipswich, new lot, numbered 18, etc., March 4, 1734-5.|| Nov. 18, 1747, he and another person bought two and one-half acres of tillage land, on Manning's Neck, in Ipswich.¶ For eight pounds, he sold one-half of old upland right, on Jeffries Neck, in Ipswich, numbered 242, and one-half of new right, numbered 124, Jan. 18, 1760.** For twenty pounds, he sold new right, numbered 15, in Turner's Hill pasture, in Ipswich, March 27, 1770.†† With his wife, for forty shillings, he conveyed to Moses Hazzen of Rowley, yeoman, woodlot, numbered 25, on letter R, in the great meadow woods, June 10, 1766.‡‡ For two pounds, thirteen shillings and four pence, he conveyed to Nathaniel Kimball of Ipswich, housewright, three old thatch lots on Cross' banks, in Ipswich, numbered 204, 206 and 208, and new lot, numbered 207, March 1, 1774.§§ For twelve pounds, he also conveyed to Mr. Kimball thatch lot, on Cross' banks, in Ipswich, numbered 180, old thatch lot, numbered 181, and new lot, numbered 182, May 26, 1774.§§

Mr. Hovey married Hannah Fosse (published in Ipswich 10: 8: 1719). He died in Ipswich Sept. 28, 1775.

His will is on file in the probate office at Salem, and the following is a copy of the original instrument:—

in the Name of God amen this twenty fifth day of September anno Domini one thousand seven Hundred and seventy five I Nathathaniel Hovey of Ipswich in the County of Essex and province of massachusetts Bay in New England weaver Being very sick and weak of Body but of perfect mind and memory thanks be Given unto God calling to mind the mortality of my Body knowing that it is appointed for all men once to

* Essex Registry of Deeds, book 88, leaf 277.
† Essex Registry of Deeds, book 88, leaf 282.
‡ Essex Registry of Deeds, book 88, leaf 283.
§ Essex Registry of Deeds, book 88, leaf 284.
|| Essex Registry of Deeds, book 89, leaf 253.
¶ Essex Registry of Deeds, book 90, leaf 206.
** Essex Registry of Deeds, book 110, leaf 97.
†† Essex Registry of Deeds, book 127, leaf 193.
‡‡ Essex Registry of Deeds, book 146, leaf 171.
§§ Essex Registry of Deeds, book 141, leaf 127.

Die Do make and ordaine this my Last will and testament principally
and first of all I Give and Recomend my soul to God that Gave it and
my Body to the Dust to Be Buried in Decent Christian Burial at the
Direction of my executor nothing Doubting But that I shall Recieve the
same again at the General Resurrection and as touching such worldly
Estate as it has pleased God to Bless me withal I Give Bequeath and
dispose of in the following manner and form—

imprimis I Give to ‖ my ‖ well Beloved wife hannah a Comfortable
and Decent Support out of my Estate to be provided for her and deliver'd
to her by my executor hereafter Named

item I Give to my son Joseph Hovey the improvement of all my
Real Estate and quick stock and Hay During the Natural Life of his
mother my aforsd wife hannah upon Condition that my sd Son (whom I
make and ordaine sole executor of this my Last will and testament) do
provide for and Deliver to his s⁴ mother a Comfortable and Decent support and Bury her at her Decease with Decent christian Burial and provided that s⁴ improvent be insufficient for the purposes afores⁴ and for
the discharging my Just Debts and funeral charges my will is that my
s⁴ son and Executor do fell and I do hereby authorise him to convey by
Good and Lawfull deed or deeds any part of my Real Estate also I Give
to my s⁴ son Joseph the whole of my marsh Lot at Plumb Island in Ipswich and his heirs forever

Item I Give to my Dau'ter Esther Treadwell and to my afores⁴ son
Joseph Hovey and to my Dau'ter Hannah wells and to my Daughter
Elizabeth martain and to my Grand Dau'ter Hannah Hovey to be equally
Divided Between them the whole of what shall Remain of my Estate
Real and perfonal at my wife's Decease excepting the marsh Lot before
mentioned only in Case my wife decease Before my Grand dau'ter arrive
at the age of twenty one or marriage my s⁴ Son and executor shall Detain
her share till such arrival and in case my s⁴ Grand Dau'ter Decease befor
such arrival her s⁰ share shall be Divided among and Between my afore⁴
Children and I do hereby Ratify and Confirm this and no other to be my
Last will and testament Revoking and Disannulling all former and others

Signed sealed published pronounced
and declar'd by the s⁴ Nathaniel Hovey
to be his Last will and testament

JOHN CALDWELL JR
JONATHAN LAKEMAN   NATHANLL HOVEY [SEAL]
NATHAN FOSTER

The will was proved Jan. 1, 1776. The inventory of his
estate amounted to £104, 3s., 4d.; personal, £20, 2s.; and real.
£84, 1s., 4d.

His wife Hannah survived him and died about June 1, 1783.

The children of Mr. and Mrs. Hovey were born in Ipswich.
as follows:—

164—I.   NATHANIEL⁵, baptized Dec. 8, 1723; died young.
165—II. JOHN⁵, baptized June 11, 1726; died Nov. 24, 1729.
166—III. ESTHER⁵, baptized Feb. 23, 1728; married Capt. Thomas, son of
         Thomas and Sarah (Goodhue) Treadwell of Ipswich Feb.
         19, 1752. He was born in Ipswich Aug. 6, 1732; and died in
         1766. She survived him, and died in Ipswich Oct. 5, 1809.
         He was a master mariner. Their children were born in
         Ipswich, and were as follows: 1. *Nathaniel⁶*, born Dec. 20
         1752; sea captain; lived in Ipswich; married, first, Elizabeth

Stone of Ipswich May 4, 1775; she died, in Ipswich, Dec. 25, 1808; he married, second, Elizabeth Fuller March 19, 1810; and she died, in Ipswich, Sept. 26, 1828. He had nine children. 2. *Hannah*⁵, baptized May 12, 1754. 3. *Esther*⁵, baptized Nov. 14, 1756.

167—IV. JOHN⁴, baptized Oct. 24, 1731; lived in Ipswich; married widow Rebecca Leatherland of Ipswich March 12, 1754; and died, probably without issue; she married, thirdly, William Pulcifer, jr., of Douglass (published in Ipswich March 14, 1761).

168—V. JOSEPH⁴, baptized Feb. 10, 1733. *See family numbered "168."*

169—VI. DANIEL⁴, baptized Aug. 22, 1736; died Oct. 25, 1736, aged two months.

170—VII. HANNAH⁴, baptized April 1, 1739; married, first, Ebenezer Smith of Ipswich Jan. 29, 1760; and, second, Jonathan Wells (published July 25, 1772); Mr. Wells died in Ipswich April 23, 1793; and she died there, his widow, March 21, 1818, aged seventy-eight. Children of Ebenezer and Hannah (Hovey) Smith: 1. *Ebenezer*⁵, baptized Dec. 28, 1760. 2. *Hannah*⁵, baptized Oct. 3, 1762. 3. *Sarah*⁵, baptized March 17, 1765. Children of Jonathan and Hannah (Hovey) Wells: 1. *John*⁵, born Dec. 10, 1772. 2. *Jonathan*⁵, born July 10, 1775.

171—VIII. ELIZABETH⁴, baptized Sept. 13, 1741; married David, son of Josiah Martin (published July 20, 1765); and was his wife in 1775. Their children were born in Ipswich as follows: 1. *David*⁵, baptized Sept. 28, 1766. 2. *Mary*⁵, baptized Nov. 6, 1768.

55

DANIEL HOVEY⁴, born in Ipswich, Mass., Oct. 29, 1701. He was a cooper, and lived in Boxford until the winter of 1741-2, when he married and settled in Bradford, having bought, for one hundred and ninety-five pounds, one and one-half acres of land, with the buildings thereon, in Bradford, Nov. 25, 1741.* He lived in Bradford six years; and, then removed to Sutton, selling his estate in Bradford for three hundred pounds, July 2, 1747.†

Mr. Hovey bought of Daniel Chase, jr., of Sutton, husbandman, for one hundred and six pounds, thirteen shillings and four pence, fifty acres of land with a house and barn thereon, in Sutton, Aug. 26, 1754.‡ This estate was situated in the northwesterly part of the town, now included in Oxford; and June 4, 1772, with his wife, he conveyed the same estate, valued at that time at two hundred and thirty pounds, to his son Moses Hovey.§ The property was conveyed upon condition that Moses support his parents as long as they lived, and pay certain sums of money to his brothers Daniel and Benjamin and sisters Anna and Mary.∥

* Essex Registry of Deeds, book 90, leaf 41.
† Essex Registry of Deeds, book 96, leaf 260.
‡ Worcester Registry of Deeds, book 34, page 541.
§ Worcester Registry of Deeds, book 68, page 194.
∥ Worcester Registry of Deeds, book 69, page 81.

Mr. Hovey thus settled his estate in his lifetime, and there appear in consequence no probate records concerning it.

Mr. Hovey married Ruth, daughter of Capt. John and Anne (Messenger) Tyler of Boxford March 31, 1742. She was baptized in Boxford June 30, 1728. He was admitted to the Second church in Boxford Jan. 1, 1737-8; and she was admitted June 13, 1742. They were dismissed to the Second church in Sutton March 8, 1761. Neither the places nor dates of their deaths are known.

Their children were as follows:—

172—I.   DANIEL[6], born Jan. 20, 1742-3, in Bradford; living in 1772; married Elizabeth, daughter of Rev. Thomas Green of Malden. Mr. Hovey died, and his widow married, secondly, Rev. Benjamin Foster, D. D.

173—II. ANNA[6], baptized Nov. 18, 1744, in Bradford; unmarried in 1772; married Thomas, son of Rev. Thomas Green of Malden, as his second wife; and died Aug. —, 1807, aged "sixty-three." He was born in Leicester in 1733.

174—III. JOSHUA[6], born Oct. 26, 1746, in Bradford; probably died before 1772.

175—IV. MOSES[6], born Oct. 28, 1748, in Sutton; baptized in Boxford Oct. 30, 1748. *See family numbered "175."*

176—V. THOMAS[6], baptized Feb. 10, 1750-1, in Sutton; probably died before 1772.

177—VI. JOHN TYLER[6], baptized May 20, 1753, in Sutton; probably died before 1772.

178—VII. MARY[6], born Sept. 16, 1755, in Sutton; married Stephen, son of Richard and Sarah (Williams) Hume, July 15, 1779. He was a farmer, and lived in Sutton and Windsor, Mass. He was born in Douglass, Mass., March —, 1764. He was a soldier of the Revolution from Aug. 1, 1775, to Nov. 29, 1777, and died in Windsor, Mass., April 24, 1843. She died in Windsor Sept. 27, 1837, aged eighty-two. Children: 1. *Stephen Tyler*[6], born July 30, 1780, in Sutton; was a farmer; lived in Windsor; married, first, Sally Buck; and, second, Lucy Baldwin; and died in Windsor Aug. 27, 1862. 2. *David*[6], born March 13, 1783, in Windsor; farmer; lived in Riga and Holly, N. Y.; married, first, —— Ford; and, second, Sarah, daughter of Jacob and Abigail (Deane) Spofford of Bergen, N. Y., and widow of —— Wilcox; he had several children; and died in Holly. 3. *Daniel*[6], born April 14, 1784, in Windsor; died March 21, 1785. 4. *Moses*[6], born June 14, 1787, in Windsor; was a carpenter; lived in Windsor, Mass., Riga, Monroe county, N. Y., and Hudson, Mich.; married Sarah Stewart Jan. 30, 1811, in Stephentown, N. Y.; and died in Hudson June 16, 1864, aged seventy-seven. Dr. Charles R. Hume of Anadaska, Oklahoma, is a grandson. 5. *Richard*[6], born May 25, 1780, in Windsor; lived in his native town; teacher; married Abigail Brown; and died in Windsor Dec. 15, 1859. 6. *Ruth*[6], born July 6, 1790, in Windsor; died Aug. 15, 1790. 7. *Mary*[6], born May 16, 1792, in Windsor; married Horace Johnson; and died in Hudson, Mich., Dec. 26, 1867.

179—VIII. BENJAMIN[6], born March 12, 1758, in Sutton. *See family numbered "179."*

57

THOMAS HOVEY⁴, born in Ipswich, Mass., March 30, 1707.
He lived in Ipswich until 1743, when he removed to Boxford
with his parents. He married Sarah Rust of Ipswich Dec. 17,
1729; and died (drowned?) in Boxford Aug. 9, 1747, at the age
of forty. She survived him; and married, secondly, Ens. Joseph
Hale, jr., of Boxford Sept. 20, 1753. She died in Boxford, his
wife, May 26, 1759. This was Mr. Hale's second marriage. He
married, first, Mary Hovey (80) Dec. 5, 1723; and she died May
25, 1753. He married, thirdly, widow Lydia Brown (published
Sept. 23, 1759); and, fourthly, Susanna Fellows of Ipswich
Nov. 25, 1771. Mr. Hale died Oct. 5, 1778, at the age of
eighty-four, having been deacon of the First church from 1759.

The children of Thomas and Sarah Hovey were born as
follows:—

180—I.   SARAH⁵, baptized Nov. 29, 1730, in Ipswich; married Ebenezer,
         son of Ebenezer and Hephzibah (Cole) Sherwin of Boxford
         (published Jan. 15, 1748-9); he was born in Boxford March
         12, 1728. Children, born in Boxford: 1. *Sarah*⁶, born March
         29, 1750. 2. *Ebenezer*⁶, born Oct. 16, 1752. 3. *Mehitable*⁶,
         born Nov. 16, 1754. 4. *Susannah*⁶, born July 17, 1757. 5.
         *Ahimeaz*⁶, born Aug. 7, 1759. 6. *Azariah*⁶, born Jan. 11, 1762;
         died Nov. 18, 1762. 7. *Rhoda*⁶, born Sept. 12, 1763. 8. *Sil-
         vanus*⁶, born March 2, 1766. 9. *Lemuel*⁶, baptized April 10,
         1768.

181—II. MARGARET⁵, baptized July 22, 1733, in Ipswich; married Asa
         Robinson of Andover May 4, 1756. Their children were born
         in Andover, as follows: 1. *Peter*⁶, born July 27, 1757. 2.
         *Lucy*⁶, born Feb. 6, 1760. 3. *William*⁶, born Feb. 2, 1762.
         4. *Asa*⁶, baptized Feb. 19, 1764.

182—III. THOMAS⁵, born Oct. 1, 1736, in Ipswich. *See family numbered
         "182."*

183—IV. JOHN⁵, baptized Oct. 14, 1739, in Ipswich. *See family numbered
         "183."*

184—V.   LYDIA⁵, baptized April 14, 1742, in Ipswich; married Benjamin
         Pindar of Ipswich (published Sept. 20, 1761). Children, born
         in Ipswich: 1. *John Hovey*⁶, baptized April 12, 1767. 2.
         *Katherine*⁶, baptized July 30, 1769. 3. *Deborah*⁶, baptized July
         21, 1771; married Benjamin Glazier Oct. 21, 1792.

185—VI. MARY⁵, baptized March 3, 1744-5, in Boxford; married James
         Crombie of Andover Aug. 18, 1767, in Andover. Child, born
         in Andover: 1. *Anna*⁶, baptized Aug. 28, 1768.

186—VII. PRISCILLA⁵, baptized Oct. 18, 1747, in Boxford.

60

SAMUEL HOVEY⁴, born in Ipswich, Mass. (May 3, 1716), and
baptized there 22: 2: 1716. He married Elizabeth Perkins of
Ipswich Oct. 10, 1737; and settled in Bradford. They became
members of the Second church in Boxford in 1738. They removed to Scotland Society, in Windham, Conn., in 1750, and afterwards lived there. She died March 22, 1788, at the age of
seventy; and he died July 26, 1806, at the age of ninety.

Their children were born as follows :—

187—I.   ELIZABETH[4], born Feb. 26, 1737-8, in Bradford; died Nov. 6,
         1740.
188—II. LUCY[4], born June 15, 1740, in Bradford.
189—III. SAMUEL[4], born Feb. 24, 1742-3, in Bradford. *See family num-
         bered "189."*
190—IV. JACOB[4], born Nov. 10, 1745, in Bradford. *See family num-
         bered "190."*
191—V.   ELIZABETH[4], born July 24, 1748, in Bradford.
192—VI. ABIGAIL[4] (twin), born March 9, 1751, in Windham; died Jan.
         23, 1839, aged eighty-seven.
193—VI. ———[4] (twin), still-born March 9, 1751, in Windham
194—VII. LYDIA[4], born Dec. 16, 1753, in Windham; died Oct. 17. 1826,
         aged seventy-two.
195—VIII. MARY[4], born April 8, 17—, in Windham; died April 11, 17—,
         aged three days.
196—IX. DAVID[4] (twin), born Aug. 5, 1757, in Windham. *See family
         numbered "196."*
197—X.   JONATHAN[4] (twin), born Aug. 5, 1757, in Windham.
198—XI. DUDLEY[4], born April 2, 1761, in Windham. *See family num-
         bered "198."*

66

SAMUEL HOVEY[4], born in Ipswich, Mass., and baptized there
8 : 2: 1711. He was at first a house-carpenter, and lived in the
Rowley part of Byfield parish until after the death of his wife;
removing to Mendon in 1754.

He was a grantee, in the right of Caleb Kimball, of Narraganset No. 1 in 1735, and a prominent promoter of the settlement of that town, which became Buxton. The meetings of the
proprietors were held at Newbury-falls (Byfield) for many years,
and Mr. Hovey was a usual attendant. April 11, 1739, he was
chosen one of the committee to build a meeting house for the new
town; and, June 20, 1774, a member of the committee chosen to
draw up resolves for the town.

For one hundred and eighty-two pounds, he sold a quarter of
an acre of land, lying on the north side of Ipswich river, in Ipswich, that John Hovey of Ipswich, deceased, bought of Thomas
Safford, Dec. 25, 1734.* For fifty pounds, he sold a new common
right in Bush hill eighths in Ipswich, being part of his father's
new common right, March 22, 1735.† He purchased of his sister
Mary Hovey, for forty pounds, her fifth interest in the estate of
her father, particularly the homestead, one-fourth of an acre of
land, house, farm, etc., also the new common right in Bush hill
and at Birch island at Ipswich, Nov. 4, 1735.‡ For eleven pounds
and four shillings, he bought of his sister Mary Hovey, he being

---

* Essex Registry of Deeds, book 69, leaf 79.
† Essex Registry of Deeds, book 72, leaf 135.
‡ Essex Registry of Deeds, book 105, leaf 203.

called a yeoman, two acres of land, in Rowley, near his house, Nov. 29, 1754.*

Mr. Hovey immediately removed to Mendon, in 1754, and became a weaver. Feb. 10, 1755, while living in Mendon, he bought, for fifty-three pounds, thirteen shillings and four pence, a house and some land in Rowley (in that part of the town which is now Georgetown), on the southwest side of Pentucket pond, between the pond and the road ;† and went there to live. Aug. 22, 1755, for twenty-six pounds, thirteen shillings and four pence, he sold the house and land to John Adams.‡

Upon his second marriage, in 1757, he again became a resident of Byfield parish. Jan. 27, 1759, being of Rowley and a stay-maker, for fifty-two pounds, he sold seven and one-half acres of land in Rowley, in Byfield parish, lying on the south side of the road "that leads to Andover spring," with the house, barn and orchard thereon.§

Mr. Hovey then removed to Cape Elizabeth, Me., where he resumed his trade of a housewright. He was of Falmouth in 1768; and, Dec. 13, 1768, when he is called of Cape Elizabeth, he bought of John Boynton six rods of land in Buxton, at the Lower corner.

Mr. Hovey removed to the new town, in which he was so much interested, Narraganset No. 1, in York county, now Buxton, Me., and again became a yeoman, before 1770. For sixty pounds, he sold six and three-fourths acres of land in the westerly part of Newbury and a right in a township bordering on Androscoggin river and New Gloucester, granted to the proprietors of Baker's town, etc., Sept. 28, 1770.§ Nov. 13, 1772, when he called himself a weaver, he sold, for eighteen pounds, six acres in Penny Ordinary pasture, in Newbury, that had been set off to his son John Hovey as a part of his share in the estates of Benjamin Ilsley and Sarah Ilsley of Newbury, deceased (probably parents of Mr. Hovey's first wife).‖ For twenty-nine pounds, six shillings and eight pence, he sold five and a half acres of marsh in Newbury, set off to John Hovey, as stated above, Nov. 8, 1773.¶ For six pounds, he sold two acres of marsh in Newbury, lying on the north side of Rowley great creek, Nov. 12, 1774.**

Mr. Hovey married, first, Mary, daughter of Joseph, jr., and Hannah (Pike) Ilsley, of Newbury Sept. 15, 1732. She was born

* Essex Registry of Deeds, book 104, leaf 261.
† Essex Registry of Deeds, book 106, leaf 14.
‡ Essex Registry of Deeds, book 137, leaf 183.
§ Essex Registry of Deeds, book 128, leaf 161.
‖ Essex Registry of Deeds, book 131, leaf 131.
¶ Essex Registry of Deeds, book 132, leaf 129.
** Essex Registry of Deeds, book 135, leaf 227.

in Newbury Oct. 6, 1707, and died in Byfield Parish, Rowley, of fever and dysentery, Sept. 18, 1753. The following is a copy of the inscription on her gravestone in the Byfield burying-ground:—

> Here Lies y*
> Body of Mrs
> M a r y H o v e y
> the Wife of Mr
> Samuel Hovey
> Who Died Sep**
> Y* 18** 1753 in
> the 46** Year
> o f H e r A g e

Mr. Hovey married, second, Lydia Langley of Chelmsford May 24, 1757, in Chelmsford. He died in Buxton in 1786, at the age of seventy-five. His wife Lydia was living in 1785, and probably survived him.

The following is a *fac simile* of the autograph of Mr. Hovey, being his signature to the inventory to the estate of Isaac Adams of Rowley, taken in 1738:

The following is a copy of the will of Samuel Hovey as it was printed in the published copy of the Records of the Proprietors of Narraganset Township, No. 1, in a note on page 248:—

In the name of God, amen, I Samuel Hovey of Buxton, in the county of York and commonwealth of Massachusetts, in New-England, yeoman, being infirm of body, but through the goodness of God of sound disposing mind and memory, not knowing how short my time in this world is do make and ordain this my last will and testament:—First of all, I do commit my Soul into the hand of God who gave it, hoping in his mercy through the merits of Christ for eternal life; and my body to the earth, to be buried in a decent manner, at the discretion of my executor hereafter named, in hope of its resurrection unto immortal life,—and respecting those worldly goods it hath pleased God to bestow upon me, I will and order the same to be disposed of in the mannare following; that is to say.

Imprimis. I will and order to my beloved wife, Lydia Hovey, the sole use tnd improvement of the westerly half of my house together with my household stuff properly so called, with one cow, for and during the term of her natural life: except two beds hereafter mentioned: which are given to my son Samuel, and daughter Lydia.

Item. I will and order to my son Samuel Hovey, after the decease of my wife, to him and his heirs forever, my homestead house, and land also the one half of my household stuff properly so called: together with half a right of the undivided land in said Buxton, originally the right of Caleb Kimball; and the residue or remainder of my personal estate after the legacies hereafter named are delivered to the legatees hereafter named. I will and order in case my said son shall pay all my just debts and

funeral expenses as soon as may be after my decease, and also the expences of the settlement of my estate, whom I here order so to do.

Item. I will and order to my six daughters, viz Hannah the wife of
Enoch Little; Mary the wife of Ebenezer Chaplain, Sarah the wife of
Wells Chase, Mehitable Hovey, Elizabeth the wife of Jonathan Thurston,
Phebe the wife of Stephen Jaques, to them & their heirs, to be equally
divided between them, the sum of one Pound ten Shillings lawful money:
to be paid in silver currency at six shillings and eight pence P ounce.

Item; I will and order to my daughter Lydia Hovey, my looms,
with all that appertains to them, for the business of weaving—which she is
to receive at my decease, with one bed and the furniture thereunto belonging; and one half of my household stuff, properly so called at the
decease of my wife.

Item; I will and order to my son John Hovey, who is absent, five
shillings lawful money; to be paid him by my executor, in case he makes
a demand of it within five years after my decease, but if he make no
demand of it within that term, he has received his full share of my estate.

Item; I do will unto my son Samuel Hovey, one bed with the furniture thereunto belonging, at my decease; also do appoint & constitute
my son Samuel to be executor to this my last will and testament.

In witness whereof I have hereunto set my hand & seal this the
thirteenth day of September 1785.

Signed, sealed, published pronounced &
declared by the testator, Samuel Hovey to
be his last will and testament in presence of

JACOB BRADBURY   SAM[l] HOVEY. [SEAL]
GERSHOM BILLINGS
SAM[l] KNIGHT

The will was proved Oct. 10, 1786.

The children of Mr. Hovey were as follows:—

199—1. HANNAH[4], born Feb. 27, 1733-4, in Rowley; married Enoch,
son of Tristram and Sarah (Dole) Little of Newbury June
5, 1759. He was born in Newbury May 21, 1728; and married, first, Sarah Pettingell Feb. 19, 1755. His wife Sarah
died March 10, 1758, at the age of twenty-six; and he married Hannah Hovey as his second wife. Mr. Little was a
weaver and shoemaker; and lived near the Upper Green in
Newbury until 1766, when he removed to Hampstead, N. H.,
and in 1774 to Boscawen, N. H., where he subsequently
lived. In Boscawen, he settled in an unbroken forest, and
endured all the privations of the wilderness. He had become a convert under the preaching of Rev. George Whitefield, at Newburyport, at the age of eleven, and was admitted a member of the old South church in Newburyport,
while living at Hampstead. After his removal to Boscawen,
he went annually to Newburyport to attend the August com-
munion until he became too feeble. She died March 15,
1801, aged sixty-seven; and he died Oct. 21, 1816, at the age
of eighty-eight. The children of Enoch and Hannah (Hovey)
Little were as follows: 1. *Benjamin*[5], born April 13, 1760,
in Newbury; lived upon the homestead in Boscawen, was a
man of sound judgment, and often settled estates and disputes; was a captain in the war of the Revolution, and took
part in the battle of Bennington; was a justice of the peace
forty years; selectman eight times; and representative four

years; married, first, Rhoda, daughter of Simeon Bartlett (brother of Gov. Josiah Bartlett) Nov. 25, 1790; she died Aug. 27, 1814, at the age of forty-six; he married. second. Persis Herbert of Concord March 5, 1816; and he died Aug. 30, 1846, at the age of eighty-six. He had five children, one of whom was Charles Herbert Little of the New Hampshire *Observer*. 2. *Joseph*[6], born May 30, 1761, in Newbury; lived on Little hill in Boscawen; was a selectman and representative to the legislature; served in the Revolution in the company of Captain Spurr, Colonel Nixon's regiment; married Anna, daughter of Rev. Robie and Elizabeth (Hobson) Morrill Nov. 30, 1784; she died Nov. 17, 1839, at the age of seventy-six; he died March 26, 1843; they had six children, a grandson being Rev. John M. Brown of Highland, Kansas. 3. *Enoch*[6], born Jan. 17, 1763, in Newbury; lived in Boscawen; deacon of the church; a man of remarkable mental and physical vigor, and an honor to his town and family; married Polly, daughter of Capt. James and Jane (Little) Noyes of Atkinson, N. H., Nov. 30, 1790; she died July 14, 1833, at the age of sixty-two; he died March 31, 1848, at the age of eighty-five; they had six children. 4. *Hannah*[6], born Sept. 3, 1764, in Newbury; died Oct. 17, 1764. 5. *Noah*[6], born Nov. 1, 1765; lived in Boscawen and Warner, N. H. and Chelsea, Vt.; married Ascenath, daughter of John Elliot of Boscawen; she died June 8, 1808, at the age of forty-one; he travelled extensively, and died in Cass county, Mich., Aug. 14, 1837, at the age of seventy-one; they had eight children. 6. *Jesse*[6], born July 30, 1767, in Hampstead, N. H.; was a farmer; lived on Little hill in what is now Webster, N. H.; was a good citizen and a consistent Christian; married Martha, daughter of Col. Henry and Martha (Clough) Gerrish of Boscawen; she died at New Buffalo, Mich., Aug. 28, 1855, aged seventy-eight; he died Aug. 19, 1840; they had ten children, two of whom were Rev. Jacob Little, D. D., of Granville, O., and Rev. Henry Little, D. D., of Madison. Ind. 7. *Phebe*[6], born Feb. 19, 1769, in Hampstead; died June 7, 1769. 8. *Sarah Ilsley*[6], born April 20, 1770, in Hampstead; married Moses, son of Col. Henry and Martha (Clough) Gerrish of Boscawen; lived in Boscawen; she died Dec. 10, 1836, at the age of sixty-six; he died Nov. 24, 1854, aged eighty-six; they had two children, Prof. Moses Gerrish Farmer of Salem, Mass., and Charles Carleton Coffin, the author, lecturer and journalist being two of their grandsons. 9. *John Hovey*[6], born March 12, 1772, in Hampstead; and died Aug. 29, 1773. 10. *Hannah*[6], born April 10, 1775, in Boscawen; married Moses Coffin Dec. 25, 1792; he was a tailor; early removed to Boscawen; she died Nov. 4, 1811; and he married, secondly, Ann Webster of Salisbury. N. H.; he died at Salisbury Feb. 3, 1843, aged seventy-five; and Hannah had two children.

300—II.   MARY[5], born Sept. 8, 1735, in Rowley; married Ebenezer Chaplin of Rowley Nov. 14, 1764; and she was his wife in 1785.

201—III.   SARAH[5], born Sept. 8, 1737, in Rowley; married Wells, son of Moses and Judith (Bartlett) Chase of Newbury Feb. 21, 1760; he was born in Newbury Sept. 9, 1737, and lived there until 1771, when he removed to Chester, N. H., where he died Dec. 28, 1824, at the age of eighty-seven. She was his wife in 1785. His only child: 1. *Benjamin Pike*[6] born June 28, 1762, in Newbury; lived on the homestead in Chester; married, first, Molly, daughter of Caleb Hall July 6, 1785; she died Dec. 18, 1790; married, second, Anna Blasdell Oct. 7, 1792; she died Feb. 22, 1808; married, third, Mary, daughter of Moody Chase Dec. 27, 1808; she died Feb. 15, 1823; and he died at Auburn, N. H., March 16, 1852, having had eleven children. John Carroll Chase of Derry, N. H., consulting engineer, is his great-grandson.

202—IV. MEHITABLE⁴, born March 31, 1739-40, in Rowley; living, unmarried, in 1785.

203—V. ELIZABETH⁴, born Sept. 23, 1741, in Rowley; married Jonathan, son of Nathaniel and Miner (Chase) Thurston of Plaistow, N. H., Oct. —, 1769; he was born in Plaistow Dec. 21, 1745; he was a farmer; lived in Boscawen, N. H.; a soldier in the Revolution; his homestead is now in the town of Webster; she died Aug. 14, 1823, aged eighty-one; and he died June 8, 1832, at the age of eighty-six. Their children were born as follows: 1. *Mary*⁵, born Aug. 18, 1770, in Newbury; married Ephraim, son of James and Jane Noyes of Newbury in 1794; he was a soldier in the war of 1812; a shoemaker; and lived in Boscawen, N. H.; he died May 11, 1856; and she died Sept. 5, 1857, aged eighty-seven; they had six children. 2. *Nathaniel*⁵, born Dec. 29, 1771, in Newbury, Mass.; farmer; lived in Boscawen; married Susanna Jackman of Boscawen May 17, 1792; she died May 8, 1842; and he died July 21, 1849, at the age of seventy-seven; they had fourteen children. 3. *Moses*⁵, born Sept. 27, 1773; teacher; died, unmarried, March 14, 1861, at the age of eighty-five. 4. *Ruth*⁵, born Oct. 12, 1775; died, unmarried, July 19, 1843, at the age of sixty-seven. 5. *Phebe*⁵, born May 30, 1778; teacher; died, unmarried, March 27, 1867, at the age of eighty-eight.

204—VI. JOHN⁴, born Oct. 19, 1743, in Rowley; he was absent from home in 1785, and apparently his family did not expect to see him again.

205—VII. PHEBE⁴, born June 29, 1746, in Rowley; married Stephen Jaques; and was his wife in 1785.

206—VIII. RUTH⁴, born Sept. 29, 1748, in Rowley; was living in 1768, when a guardian was appointed for her; and probably died before 1785.

207—IX. SAMUEL⁴, born Aug. 13, 1758, in Rowley; and was living in 1785.

208—X. LYDIA⁴, was living, unmarried, in 1785.

69

EBENEZER HOVEY⁴, born in Ipswich, Mass., Nov. 6, 1705. He was a fisherman, and lived in Ipswich. He married Hannah. daughter of Edward Dear of Ipswich Nov. 20, 1730; and he was drowned in Wells Bay Oct. 28, 1732, at the age of twenty-six. Thomas Lord of Ipswich was appointed administrator of his estate March 10, 1733. His property was all personal, and was appraised at £35, 16s. The estate was insolvent.

His widow continued to live in Ipswich; and with others she sold one common right in the Eighth division of land in Ipswich Nov. 23, 1733.* With others she conveyed her interest in the

* Essex Registry of Deeds, book 66, leaf 13.

real estate of her grandfather, Edmund Dear of Ipswich. deceased, July 12, 1733.* July 26, 1736, with others she sold an old upland lot, 81, on Jeffrey's Neck, in Ipswich, belonging to her said grandfather's estate.†

Mrs. Hovey married, secondly, Daniel Safford of Ipswich (published Oct. 30, 1736).

The only child of Ebenezer and Hannah (Dear) Hovey was born in Ipswich as follows:—

29—1. EBENEZER⁵, born Jan. —, 1731-2; baptized Jan. 23, 1731-2; drowned
        May 12, 1733, at the age of sixteen months.

71

THOMAS HOVEY⁴, born in Ipswich, Mass., May 9, 1710. He was a fisherman, and lived in Ipswich. For two hundred and seventy-five pounds, he bought a house, barn and two acres of land, in Ipswich, on the east side of Hog lane, March 31, 1741 ;‡ and Feb. 4, 1742, he bought, for one hundred and five pounds, three acres of tillage land in the North division of Turkey hill eighth and the eighth next Rowley.§ For forty-three pounds and fifteen shillings, he bought one acre and fifteen rods of upland and marsh in Manning's Neck field in Ipswich Feb. 25, 1743.‖ For twenty pounds, he bought one and one-half acres of upland and marsh in the same field Feb. 27, 1743.¶ April 7, 1744, when he is called a shoreman, he bought, for thirty-eight pounds, one-half of five and three-fourths acres of upland and marsh in the North field at Reedy marsh. in Ipswich.¶ For ninety-five pounds, he bought old lot 7, in the Booth hill pasture division, in Ipswich, Sept. 18, 1743.** For one hundred and thirty-eight pounds, he bought two acres of upland, in Ipswich, within the fields commonly called Manning's Neck, being the easterly side of a four-acre lot, Dec. 10, 1747.††

Mr. Hovey built a schooner, seventy-two feet long, of fifty-two tons burden, valued at six hundred pounds; and he became *non compos mentis* at that time, Aug. 30, 1749, when John Hodgkins, jr., of Ipswich, shipwright, was appointed his guardian. His estate was then valued at £1,040, 6s. His house, barn and land were appraised at £325.

For twenty-two pounds, his guardian sold old right 7. in Potter "Bushill Eighths" in Ipswich, drawn by Daniel Jordan's

---

* Essex Registry of Deeds, book 78, leaf 68.
† Essex Registry of Deeds, book 76, leaf 1.
‡ Essex Registry of Deeds, book 81, leaf 176.
§ Essex Registry of Deeds, book 84, leaf 148.
‖ Essex Registry of Deeds, book 86, leaf 183.
¶ Essex Registry of Deeds, book 86, leaf 184.
** Essex Registry of Deeds, book 86, leaf 185.
†† Essex Registry of Deeds, book 122, leaf 79.

original right, on the road leading from Ipswich to Topsfield, May 7, 1761.*

Mr. Hovey married Rebecca Lakeman of Ipswich (published Nov. 18, 1738); and died in 1771, at the age of sixty. His son John Hovey was appointed administrator of the estate May 7, 1771. Mr. Hovey was called a shoreman and yeoman. His estate was then appraised at £165, 8s., 8d., his house, barn and land being valued at £150, 16s., 8d. The estate was insolvent. His wife, Rebecca, survived him.

For sixteen pounds, five shillings and six pence, the administrator sold one acre and one hundred and fifty rods of land of said estate in Manning's field in Ipswich Oct. 10, 1771.† For ten pounds, eleven shillings, six pence and three farthings, he sold, as said administrator, two acres and one hundred and thirty-five rods of upland and marsh in the North field at Reedy marsh in Ipswich Oct. 10, 1771.‡ As said administrator, for fourteen pounds, fifteen shillings and ten pence, he sold one acre and one hundred and three rods of upland and marsh in Manning's Neck field in Ipswich, Oct. 10, 1771.§ As said administrator, for thirty-four pounds, thirteen shillings and four pence, he sold to Ebenezer Hovey of Ipswich, mariner, one-half of house and two-thirds of barn in Ipswich, at the easterly part of the town, being the easterly half of the house where the deceased dwelt, and a small piece of land adjoining, and one-half of the well, Jan. 27, 1773.‖

Dower was duly assigned to the widow of the deceased June 29, 1771; and the administrator sold, for sixty-five pounds, six shillings and eight pence, to Ebenezer Hovey of Ipswich, mariner, the easterly half of the house and barn and two acres of land adjoining, on the east side of Hog lane, that had been so assigned as dower, April 29, 1777.¶

Mrs. Hovey, the widow, died Nov. 20, 1785.

Their children were born in Ipswich, and were as follows:—

210—I.   REBECCA⁴, married Samuel Dennis of Ipswich (published July 3, 1762). Child, born in Ipswich: 1. *Rebecca⁵*, baptized Jan. 17, 1768.

211—II. ELIZABETH⁴, baptized Nov. 9, 1740; married, first, Thomas Newmarch, jr., of Ipswich (published Sept. 8, 1764); and, second, Capt. Gideon Parker May 30, 1782. Captain Parker was a soldier of the Revolution and a prominent man, and died in Ipswich Feb. 10, 1798. Children of Thomas and Elizabeth (Hovey) Newmarch, born in Ipswich: 1. ————⁵ (son), baptized Nov. 3, 1765. 2. *Thomas⁵*, baptized in 1767.

* Essex Registry of Deeds, book 117, leaf 74.
† Essex Registry of Deeds, book 130, leaf 52.
‡ Essex Registry of Deeds, book 135, leaf 150.
§ Essex Registry of Deeds, book 140, leaf 121.
‖ Essex Registry of Deeds, book 131, leaf 102.
¶ Essex Registry of Deeds, book 135, leaf 122.

212—III.   JOHN⁵, baptized Dec. 26, 1742; was a cooper, and lived in Salem.
           For sixty-five pounds, he conveyed to his brother Ebenezer
           Hovey his interest in the easterly half of house and barn
           and two acres of land lying on the east side of Hog lane,
           which was set off as dower to their mother in the estate of
           their father, April 29, 1777.*

213—IV.   EBENEZER⁵, baptized Sept. 30, 1744. *See family numbered "213."*
214—V.   FRANCIS⁵, baptized Jan. 25, 1746; died young.
215—VI.   FRANCIS⁵, born Feb. 24, 1747.   *See family numbered "215."*
216—VII.   SARAH⁵, married Philip, son of Arthur and Sarah (Will-
           comb) Abbott of Ipswich Dec. 6, 1773; he was born
           in Ipswich April 5, 1752; was a housewright; lived in
           Ipswich; he died Sept. 20, 1805; and she died July 25,
           1838. Their children were born in Ipswich as follows: 1.
           Daniel⁶, born Jan. 15, 1774; was a baker; lived in Salem;
           married Rebecca Allen of Salem Feb. 21, 1796; and had
           children. 2. *Philip⁶*, born Dec. 23, 1775; was a baker; lived
           in Salem; married Peggy Turner April 3, 1810; and had
           children. 3. *Thomas⁶*, born July 20, 1779; married Nabby
           Corbin May 9, 1810; died Aug. 14, 1818; and had children.
           4. *Arthur⁶*, born Jan. 24, 1782; died April 17, 1805. 5.
           Sally⁶, born March 18, 1784; died June 25, 1790. 6. *John
           Hovey⁶*, born June 17, 1787; died Dec. 24, 1805. 7. *Samuel
           N.⁶*, born Nov. 11, 1789; lived in Salem; married Mary A.
           Francis July 31, 1833; and had children. 8. *William⁶*, born
           Jan. 1, 1792; lived in Franklin, Ill.; married Mary Barry
           Dec. 2, 1824; and had children. 9. *Sally⁶*, born Oct. 5 1794;
           died Sept. 8, 1796.

81

JOHN HOVEY⁴, born in Topsfield, Mass., Aug. 27, 1699. He
was a farmer, and settled in Boxford upon his marriage, building
a house thirty-two feet long and twenty-four feet wide, two
stories in height, with a chimney of the large old-fashioned type,
in a pleasant, picturesque valley on the northern side of the road
leading from the house of George W. Chadwick to the North
Andover town line. June 14, 1743, his father conveyed to him,
for love, about seventeen acres of land in Boxford.†

Mr. Hovey married Mary Lakeman of Ipswich (published
April 17, 1725); and died March 14, 1778, at the age of seventy-
eight.

The following is a copy of his will, transcribed from the
original instrument on file in the probate office at Salem:—

In the name of God Amen

I John Hovey of Boxford in the County of Essex and Province of
the Maſachuſetts Bay in New-England Yeoman being thro' Divine Goodneſs favoured with the due exerciſe of my Reaſon have throught proper
to diſpoſe of my worldly Goods and Eſtate thereby diſcharge my Mind
from all Temporal Concerns that I may prepare for the future State

---

* Essex Registry of Deeds, book 135, leaf 122.
† Essex Registry of Deeds, book 86, leaf 51.

Commiting my Soul into the Hands of Jefus Chrift and my Body to the Duft to be decently buried by my Executors here after mentioned.

1ly It is my Will that my juft Debts and funeral Charges be paid in due Seafon by the Executors of this Teftament out of that part of my Eftate which I have here after given to them.

2ly I give to my well Beloved Wife Mary the Ufe of a full third part of my Lands during her natural Life, and my Will is that my Executors bring her a Sufficient Quantity of fire-Wood to her Door and cut it fit for the Fire yearly I also give to my beloved Wife the following Particulars for her own so that Shee may difpofe of them amongst my Children as Shee shall think fit (viz.) all my live Stock & all the eaft end of my dwelling Houfe & one third part of my Barn & all my Houfhold Goods that are Suitable for Womens Improvment

3ly I give to my Son John Hovey one half of my Lands in Boxford and Ipswich and all the west End of my dwelling Houfe & two Thirds of my Barn & half my Hufbandry Utenfels and half my wearing Apparral.

4ly I give to my Son Richard Hovey one half of my Lands in Boxford & Ipswich and the whole of that Houfe wherein he now dwells together with the Barn belonging thereto and half my Hufbandry Utenfels & half my wearing Apparral

5ly I give to my two Daughters Mary & Sarah Ten Shillings to be equally divided between then. & paid to them by my Executors at the Expiration of three years after my Deceafe and the Reafon why I give them no more is becaufe I have given them thirteen Pounds Six Shillings & eight Pence already a Piece

6ly I give to my Daughter Abigail Hovey thirteen Pounds Six Shillings and eight Pence to be paid to her by my Executors at the Expiration of three years after my Deceafe

7ly I give to my Daughter Efther Hovey Thirteen Pounds Six Shillings and eight Pence to be paid to her by my Executors at the Expiration of three years after my Deceafe

Laftly I Do hereby Conftitute make & ordain my aforefaid [sons] John and Richard Hovey the Sole Executors of this my laft Will & Teftament hereby making void all other Wills made by me heretofore, Ratifying and Confirming this and no other to be so. In Witnefs whereof I have hereunto set my Hand and Seal the firft Day of November in the Tenth year of the Reign of our Sovereign Lord George the Third of great Britain France and Ireland King &c. Anno Domini one thoufand feven Hundred and Sixty Nine

Signed Sealed and Delivered by the said John Hovey to be his laft Will and Teftament in Prefence of

JOHN PEABODY JU^r
JOHN PHILLIPS
JOHN HOVEY Y^e 3^d *John Hovey* [SEAL]

The will was proved April 13, 1778.

The inventory of his estate amounted to £2,453, 13s., 3d.; £2,186 of it being real estate, and £267, 13s., 3d., personal.

Mrs. Hovey survived her husband six months, and died Sept. 22, 1778, at the age of seventy-seven. She also left a will, a copy of which, transcribed from the original instrument on file in the probate office at Salem, follows:—

In the name of God Amen

I Mary Hovey of Boxford in the County of Efsex & State of the
Maffachufetts Bay in New England. Widdow. being left, (as appears by
the will of my Late hufband John Hovey of the town County and State
affore Said.) with Confidrable Eftate on my hands. & haveing a due
exercife of my Reafon. think it my Duty to Difpofe of my Eftate. that
my mind Difcharged from worldly things may be ingaged in preparation
for Eternity. Commiting my Soul into the hand of Jefus Chrift. and my
body to the Duft to be decently Buried by my Executor here after Mentioned imprimis

Item. it is my will that my Juft Debts and Funeral Charges be paid
& all the Charge attending the Setteling of my eftate by my Executor
out of my Live Stock

Item. I give to my Son John Hovey whom I appoint. Sole Executor
of this inftrument all my buildings except the Largeft lower rome in my
houfe I Referve for the ufe of my Daughter Efther

Item. I give to my two Sons John and Richard Hoveys all my Live
Stock at my Deceas. they being at equal Charge at maintaining my
weakley Daughter Efther, if She lives to be Chargable after my deceas

Item. I give to my two grandfons Daniel & Abraham Peabodys my
two beft peuter platers & two beft plates equal btwean them.

Item. I give to my only Surviveing Daughters (Viz) my Daughter
Barker and Eafther all my houfehold furniture, and all my wareing
apparel, to be equaly Devided between them.

Item. I give to my Daughter Efther the ufe of the Largeft lower
rome in my houfe Durcing her natural life or whilft. She Remain a
Single woman. & no longer. for the rome its Self or the property of it
I give to my Son John Hovey

Lastly I Ratify and Confirm this as my laft will and teftament.

in witnefs where of I have hereunto Set my hand and Seal this
Seventeenth Day of September anno Domini. one thousand Seven hundred & Seventy Eight.

Signed. Sealed & Delivered by the
s^d Mary Hovey to be her laft
will and testament in prefance of

STEPHEN BARKER   her
ASA PARKER   MARY X HOVEY [SEAL]
JOHN PEABODY JUN^r   mark

The will was proved Oct. 5, 1778. Her estate was appraised
at £491, 14s., 5d., 3f. The house and barn were valued at forty
pounds.

Their children were born in Boxford, and were as follows :—

217—L   MARY², born June 7, 1726; married Abraham, son of Ephraim
         and Hannah (Redington) Peabody of Boxford June 14,
         1753; he was born in Boxford Oct. 6, 1717; lived in Box-
         ford; he died April 24, 1773, at the age of fifty-five; and she
         died, his widow, in Boxford, Sept. 18, 1777, aged fifty-one.
         Children, born in Boxford: 1. *Daniel*, baptized July 13,
         1755; living in 1778. 2. *Abraham*, born June 15, 1762;
         married Elizabeth Marble Jan. 21, 1789.

218—II. JOHN², born Aug. 29, 1727. *See family numbered "218."*

219—III. SUSANNAH², born June 13, 1729; united with the Second church
         of Boxford April 25, 1756; and died, unmarried, Jan. 17,
         1757, at the age of twenty-seven.

220—IV. RICHARD⁴, born Aug. 3, 1733. *See family numbered "220."*
221—V. SARAH⁴, baptized Feb. 9, 1735, in Bradford; admitted to the
Second church in Boxford Oct. 10, 1756; and married Abiel,
son of Abiel and Hannah (Stiles) Barker of Andover Feb.
19, 1760. He was born in Andover May 14, 1736; and was
a yeoman. They lived in the North parish of Andover until
1777, when they removed to Pelham, N. H. She was dismissed from the Second church in Boxford to the church
in Pelham Sept. 20, 1778. Their children were born in Andover as follows: 1. *Hannah⁵*, born Jan. 5, 1762-3. 2.
John⁵, born Dec. 31, 1764; died Nov. 25, 1799, aged thirty-
four. 3. *Solomon⁵*, born May 6, 1767. 4. *Isaac⁵*, born Aug.
24, 1769. 5. *Sarah⁵*, born Feb. 4, 1772.
222—VI. ABIGAIL⁴, baptized Feb. 20, 1736-7; admitted to the Second
church in Boxford April 14, 1776; and died, unmarried,
Sept. 16, 1778, at the age of forty-one.
223—VII. ESTHER⁴, baptized April 19, 1741; she was never well or strong;
and died in Boxford, unmarried, Dec. 1, 1801, at the age of
sixty.

82

JOSEPH HOVEY⁴, born in Topsfield, Mass., July 7, 1703. He
was a husbandman; and lived in Topsfield. For fourteen pounds,
seven shillings and six pence, he bought a right of one and one-
fourth acres in the second division in Topsfield, on Ipswich line,
and "at or near the place called Wintrops Hills," April 12, 1729.*
For fifteen shillings and six pence, he sold some land in Topsfield
Nov. 20, 1751;† and for fifteen pounds, six shillings and eight
pence, he sold six acres and one hundred and seven rods of upland in Topsfield April 7, 1756.‡ For seventy-five pounds, three
shillings and four pence, he sold forty-one acres of pasture, woodland and meadow in Topsfield March 10, 1758.§ To secure a
certain man who had become bound for him, he conveyed to him
sixty acres of land in Topsfield, situated on the south side of
Pritchard's pond, and north side of Boxford road, Nov. 17,
1761;|| and this security was released June 3, 1766. For seven
pounds, five shillings and eight pence, he sold four and one-half
acres of swamp and upland in Rowley March 13, 1766;¶ and, for
eighteen pounds, he sold nine and one-half acres of woodland,
swamp and upland in Rowley and Boxford June 6, 1766.¶ April
1, 1766, when he is called yeoman, he sold, for two hundred and
forty pounds, his farm of land and buildings in Topsfield, lying
on the southeast side of the road, adjoining land of the heirs of

* Essex Registry of Deeds, book 121, leaf 115.
† Essex Registry of Deeds, book 98, leaf 54.
‡ Essex Registry of Deeds, book 103, leaf 239.
§ Essex Registry of Deeds, book 109, leaf 186.
|| Essex Registry of Deeds, book 110, leaf 70.
¶ Essex Registry of Deeds, book 117, leaf 159.

Ivory Hovey, deceased, and on the southeast side of Pritchard's pond so called, and four lots in the second division of common land in Topsfield, at the northwesterly end of Winthrop's hills, so called, lot 1, two acres and twelve rods; lot 2, one acre and one hundred and twenty rods; lot 4, one acre and thirty rods; and lot 5, one acre and forty rods, seventy-four acres in all, exclusive of one acre in Middle swamp belonging to the heirs of said Ivory Hovey.*

Mr. Hovey moved to Harvard, Mass., probably in June, 1766, and, for forty-six pounds, thirteen shillings and four pence, sold twenty acres of land in Topsfield, lying on the southwest side of the country road and on the northeast side of Pye brook, bounded northwesterly by land of the heirs of Deacon Hovey of Topsfield, deceased, June 25, 1766.† For twelve pounds, thirteen shillings and four pence, while he was still of Harvard, he sold four acres of marsh in the Hundreds in Ipswich Nov. 11, 1767.‡

After that date nothing is as yet known of Mr. Hovey. He married Abigail, daughter of Nathaniel and Sarah (Howlett) Averill of Topsfield Dec. 19, 1734. She was born in Topsfield Aug. 9, 1704; and was living in 1766.

Their children were born in Topsfield, as follows:—

224—I.   JOSEPH⁴, born Oct. 8, 1735; died Nov. 5, 1735.
225—II. ABIGAIL⁴, born Sept. 14, 1740; married Samuel Harris, jr., July 1, 1762. Children, born in Topsfield: 1. *Sarah*⁵, baptized April 15, 1764. 2. *Mary*⁵, baptized June 22, 1766.
226—III. MARY⁴, born Nov. 20, 1742; died Sept. 23, 1749, in Topsfield.
227—IV. JOSEPH⁴, born Nov. 19, 1748; died, "a student of yᵉ College," Aug. 29, 1766, at the age of seventeen.

88

LUKE HOVEY⁴, born in Boxford, Mass., May 18, 1708. He was a yeoman, and lived in the West parish of Boxford. The house stood across the road from the present residence of John Myron Pearl, on the northern shore of Mitchell's pond, so called, the location being high and beautiful. The farm consisted of forty-five acres, and had been devised to him by his father, it having been his father's homestead. His barn was struck by lightning in a thunder shower, July 14, 1772, and burned. The following notice of the fire appeared in the *Essex Gazette* the next week:—

SALEM, July 21.

A large Barn, belonging to Mr. Luke Hovey, of Boxford, was ſet on Fire, laſt Tueſday, by a Flaſh of Lightning, and entirely conſumed, with four Tons of Engliſh Hay.

* Essex Registry of Deeds, book 122, leaf 80.
† Essex Registry of Deeds, book 138, leaf 280.
‡ Essex Registry of Deeds, book 125, leaf 250.

Mr. Hovey belonged to the First church in Boxford until the Second parish church was organized, being dismissed to it in 1736.

Mr. Hovey, for three pounds, bought of Thomas Peabody of Boxford, yeoman, a quarter of an acre of land, in Boxford, on which his house now stands, Sept. 21, 1733.* For seventeen pounds, he bought eight acres of meadow in Walker's meadow, in Boxford, Sept. 17, 1747;† and, March 8, 1748, with his brothers Joseph and Abijah he received from his father, as a gift, the father's interest in Walker's meadow, in Boxford.‡ For forty-six pounds, thirteen shillings and four pence, he sold ten acres of upland and meadow on the south side of Johnson's pond, in Boxford, Jan. 31, 1764.§

Mr. Hovey married, first, Dorcas, daughter of Thomas and Elizabeth Kimball of Bradford, Oct. 10, 1732. She was born in Bradford Aug. 22, 1711; and died, in Boxford Sept. 16,|| 1752, at the age of forty-one. Her remains lie in the ancient burial place in West Boxford, and the gravestone above them is inscribed as follows:—

> HERE LIES BURIED
> THE BODY OF MR'
> DORCAS THE WIFE
> OF M' LUKE HOUEY
> WHO DIED SEP' 27ᵗʰ
> 1752 IN THE 42ⁿᵈ
> YEAR OF HER AGE

He married, second, Esther (Hovey) (56), widow of Stephen Runnels of Boxford April 24, 1755; and she died in Boxford Feb. 19, 1776, at the age of seventy-three. He married, third, Mehitable English May 30, 1776, in Boxford. Mr. Hovey died in the spring of 1787. His will was made Aug. 31, 1784; and the following is a copy of the original instrument on file in the probate office in Salem:—

In the Name of God amen the Thirty first Day of Aug' anno dom 1784 I Luke Hovey of Boxford in the County of Efsex in the State of mafsachufetts Bay in new England yeoman being att prefent, in a Comfortable meafure of health and soundnefs of mind Thanks to God for it, But, Calling to mind the mortality of my Body and *and* knowing that it is appointed for all men, once to Die do make and Ordain this my last will and testament, that is to Say Principuly and *and* first of all I Give

* Essex Registry of Deeds, book 68, leaf 197.
† Essex Registry of Deeds, book 95, leaf 203.
‡ Essex Registry of Deeds, book 95, leaf 204.
§ Essex Registry of Deeds, book 137, leaf 233.
|| Her gravestone says "27ᵗʰ."

and recommend my Soul, into the hands of God that Gave it, and my
Body I recommend to the Earth to be Buried in Decent Christian Burial,
at the Decrefion of my Executor nothing Doubting But at the General
Refurection I shall receive the same again by the mighty power of God
And as Touching such worldly Eftate where with it hath pleafed God to
Blefs ‖me‖ with in this Life I Difpofe of the same in the following
manner and form

Imprimus I Give to my welbeloved Wife mehitable Hovey the Improvement of one third part of all my real Eftate and alfo the wefterly
End of my Dwelling houfe with the Celler under it and alfo the ufe of my
back room Till Washington comes to the ‖of‖ age of one and Twenty
and to pafs & repafs to the well as She Shall have occation for it and
alfo one third part of my Barn with a Convenient Barn yard and Liberty
to pafs & repafs to it & from it and so much of the Door yard as She
Shall want for her own ufe all this Dowry so long as She Shall Continue
my widow and no longer and for her own property I Give her my horfe
if I Die Sezed of one with its furniture and alfo one of my cows that
She Shall Chufe & alfo one half all my Foultry and alfo all my houfehold furniture that I Shall Die Seized of and alfo all the Cloth & clothes
that we have made Since wee were married (Except my wearing apparel)
and alfo all her own wearing apparel that she brought with her when
she came to live with me and alfo all her houfehold furniture that ‖she‖
brought with her when She Came to live with me that Shall then be in
being and alfo Two pounds in Cash to be ‖paid‖ to her or her heirs in
three months after my Deceafe by my Executor

Item I Give to my Son Thomas Hovey or his Heirs two Pounds to
be paid to him or his heirs in two years after my Deceafe he haveing received most his portion already

Item I Give to my Son Phinnehas Hovey the Sum of Forty
two Pounds to be Paid to him or his heirs in the Space of one year after
my deacfe he having recued But Little of his portion as yet

Item I Give to my Son Luke Hovey and his heirs all my Lands with
all the Buildings thereon not euther wife difpofed off and alfo all my live
Stock ‖and‖ one half of ‖my‖ fowls and alfo I Give him all my Hufbandry utenfils and my Interest in the Andover Library and my Great
Englifh Bible to him and his heirs for ever he paying all my Juft Debts
and funeral Charges with all the Bequeathes and Legacies in this my
last will and Testament and further my will is Concerning my Son
Washington Hovey now on Infant that he be Put out to Learn some
Trade that he Shall Chufe or his friends shall Think most proper for him
as soon as he Shall be Capable for it and if he livs to the age of one and
Twenty Then I Give ‖to him‖ to be paid by my Executor the sum of
six pounds thirteen Shillings and four pence and alfo my Backroom when
his mother has Done with it alfo my writing Desk and my Little Gun or
Corbine and my walking Cane with all my Loofe money I Shall Die seiz[d]
of for his own ufe and Benefit

Item I Give to my Daughter Hannah Faulkner one Pound Befides
what I have already Given her to be paid to her or her Heirs in the
space [of] too years after my Deceafe

Item I Give to my Daughter Elizabeth ‖Brown‖ three Shillings on
Demand she haveing ‖received‖ her full portion of my Eftate already

Item I Give to my Daughter Abigail Baker Nine Pounds Befides
what I have already Givin her to be paid to her or her heirs in the space
of three years after my Deceafe by my Executor

Item. I Give to my Daughter Olive Gage one pound Six fhillings
and Eight pence to be paid to her or her heirs in the space [of] two years
after my Deceafe

Item I Give to my Daughter Mehitable Hovey the Sum of Eight Pounds to be paid to her at the age of one and Twenty or on marriage Day by my Executor

Item I Give and Bequeath to my four Sons Thomas Phinehas Luke and Washington, all my wearing apparel to be Equally Divided among them four further my will is that the remainder of my books & Phamphlets not already Difpofed of Shall be Equally Divided among my widow and all my Children, and further my will is that if anything apears to be my my Eftate not already Difpofed of it Shall be my Son Washingtons

and I Likewife Conftitute make and ordain my fon Luke Hovey Sole Executor of this my last will and Teftament and do utterly revoke Difannul all and Every outher former Teftament wills Legacies & Bequeathes Executors by me named willed and Bequeathed Ratyfing and Confirming this to be my last will and Tef[t]ament

In witnefs whereof I have Set to my hand and Seal the Day & year above writen

Signed Sealed Published and Declared by the Said Luke Hovey as his last will and Teftament in the prefents of us the Subfcribers as Witnefses

JOHN ROBINSON
LEMUEL WOOD
MOSES PLUMMER

Luke Hovey [SEAL]

The will was proved May 8, 1787.

Mrs. Mehitable Hovey survived him, and died in Boxford, his widow, Feb. 14, 1809, at the age of sixty-nine.

The children of Luke Hovey were born in Boxford, as follows:—

228—I.   THOMAS⁶, born Dec. 8, 1733; died in Boxford Aug. 21, 1736, aged two years.

229—II.   HANNAH⁶, born April 9, 1736; married Joseph Faulkner, jr., of Andover May 17, 1765; and she was his wife in 1784. He was a cordwainer; and they were living in Andover in 1782. Children, born in Andover: 1. *Dorcas⁶*, born Sept. 24, 1766. 2. *John⁶*, baptized Feb. 11, 1770.

230—III. THOMAS⁶, born Nov. 29, 1737. *See family numbered "230."*

231—IV.   ELIZABETH⁶, born Dec. 30, 1739; married William Brown; and was his wife in 1784. They were living in Falmouth, Me., in 1782, when he was a mariner.

232—V.   ABIGAIL⁶, born Feb. 26, 1741-2; married John Baker; and was his wife in 1784. He was a caulker, and they were living in Falmouth, Me., in 1782.

233—V.   OLIVE⁶, born Feb. 24, 1743; married Asa Gage Aug. 30, 1770, in Bradford; and was his wife in 1784. They were living in Pelham, N. H., in 1782.

234—VII. PHINEAS⁶, born Jan. 18, 1745-6. *See family numbered "234."*

235—VIII. LUKE⁶, born Feb. 26, 1747-8; died Sept. 12, 1748, in Boxford, aged six months.

236—IX.   LUKE⁶, born Sept. 13, 1749. *See family numbered "236."*

237—X.   WASHINGTON⁶, born March 7, 1777; lived in Newburyport; married Deborah, daughter of Abijah and Deborah (West) Gage of Bradford, Aug. 30, 1803. She was born in Bradford Nov. 27, 1779; and she died in Bradford, his widow, April 13, 1834.

238—XI. MEHITABLE[5], baptized May 2, 1779; married John Hovey, jr. (476), in Boxford, April 8, 1807.

90

DEA. JOSEPH HOVEY[4], born in Boxford, Mass., July 17, 1712. He was a yeoman, and lived in Boxford in the house which formerly stood near the brook, on the western side of the highway southerly from the house of J. Warren Chadwick. He came into possession of the estate upon the death of his father, in 1751. He was a deacon of the church in West Boxford from 1759 until his decease. He was also a lieutenant in the militia.

By deed, dated March 8, 1748, his father gave to him and his brothers Luke and Abijah the father's interest in Walker's meadow in Boxford.* For one hundred and forty pounds, he bought of Nathaniel Carlton of Bradford, cordwainer, two lots of land on Plum island, in Rowley, July 11, 1748.† With others of Boxford, proprietors of Nelson's farm, for eight pounds, three shillings and four pence, he sold seven and one-half acres of land in Walker's meadow, April 29, 1754.‡ He was called "gentleman," June 20, 1769, when, with his wife and others, he sold, for one hundred and fifty-two pounds, eighteen shillings and nine pence, their interest in fifteen and a quarter acres of land in Boxford, late of the estate of Joseph Mulliken of Bradford, deceased, and fifteen acres and one hundred and fifty-five rods of land in the three thousand acres of land in Rowley, the lots being numbered five and six on the letter S range.§ They, also, sold, on the same day, and for fifteen pounds, three acres and twenty rods of meadow in Bradford ;‖ and, also, on the same day, for one hundred and eleven pounds, eight acres and twenty-six rods of land in Bradford, late of said Joseph Mulliken, deceased, lying in the common field, on the south side of Merrimack river.¶ They, also, sold, on the same day, for one hundred and ninety-one pounds, six shillings and eight pence, house, etc., and one acre of land in Bradford, lying on the south side of Merrimack river.** They, also, sold, on the same day, for thirty pounds, nine shillings and eight pence, one acre and one hundred and ten rods of orchard land in Bradford, being part of the estate of Joseph Mulliken, deceased.†† They, also, on the same day, for sixty-three pounds and sixteen shillings, conveyed to Samuel

* Essex Registry of Deeds, book 95, leaf 204.
† Essex Registry of Deeds, book 148, leaf 86.
‡ Essex Registry of Deeds, book 124, leaf 71.
§ Essex Registry of Deeds, book 127, leaf 85.
‖ Essex Registry of Deeds, book 127, leaf 86.
¶ Essex Registry of Deeds, book 127, leaf 176.
** Essex Registry of Deeds, book 127, leaf 217.
†† Essex Registry of Deeds, book 138, leaf 11

Runnels of Boxford, gentleman, and others, six acres of woodland in Bradford, known as the Dismal hole, on the west side of the highway leading from Bradford to Boxford.* They, also, for twenty-four pounds, conveyed to widow Phebe Mulliken of Bradford their interest in Mulliken's ferry across Merrimack river between Bradford and Haverhill, lately the estate of Joseph Mulliken, deceased, Oct. 18, 1769.† They, also, for fifty-three pounds, six shillings and eight pence, conveyed to the said widow Phebe Mulliken one acre and ninety-four and a quarter rods of land in Bradford, on the north side of the new lane from Bradford to Rowley, April 25, 1774.†

Deacon Hovey married Rebecca, daughter of Thomas and Mary (Mulliken) Stickney of Bradford March 21, 1743-4. She was born in Bradford Oct. 3, 1724. He died Dec. 23, 1785, at the age of seventy-three ;‡ and his wife Rebecca, who survived him, died in Boxford Feb. 19, 1788, aged sixty-three.

in Boxford.

Their children were born in Boxford, as follows :—

239—I.   DOLLY[3], born Dec. 30, 1744; married Dea. Samuel Clark of Danvers July 25, 1775; he married, first, Hannah Gott of Wenham Feb. 12, 1756; and she died Oct. 23, 1773. They removed to Sterling, where she died June 21, 1816. The children of Dea. Samuel and Dolly (Hovey) Clark were as follows: 1.   *William*[4], born June 27, 1776; removed to Pittsfield, Mass., then to Albany, N. Y., finally settling in Utica, N. Y.; married, first, Beulah Allen of Northboro, Mass.; she died Feb. 10, 1827; he married, second, Mrs. Sarah Gridley; he died in Utica, N. Y., Aug. 3, 1841, having had four children, one of whom was Thomas Allen Clarke, esq., a lawyer of Albany, N. Y., and Rev. Anson Judd Upson, D. D., of Hamilton college, N. Y., was a grandson.   *2. Hovey*[4], born Oct. 9, 1778; lived in in Sterling; married Sarah Kilburn of Sterling; he died Feb. 20, 1812; she then removed to Utica, N. Y., and died there Sept. 12, 1827. They had three children, one of whom was Hovey Kilburn Clark, esq., a lawyer of Detroit, Mich.   3.   *Hobart*[4], born July 11, 1780; "Honorable"; lived in Andover, Mass.; was a trustee of Abbot academy from 1828, and a founder of the Protestant Episcopal church there; married Elizabeth Farwell in 1814; she died Feb. 6, 1862, aged seventy-one; and he died in Andover Aug. 3, 1870, at the age of ninety.   They had ten children, Rev. Hobart Clark of West New Brighton, Staten Island, N. Y., being a grandson.   4.   *Rebecca*[4], born May 14, 1783; died Oct. 12, 1837, unmarried, at the age of fifty-four.   5.   *Sarah*[4], born June 15, 1785; died at Sterling, Mass., unmarried, June 7, 1865, at the age of eighty, lacking eight days.

240—II.   JOSEPH[3], born Jan. 23, 1746.   *See family numbered "240."*

* Essex Registry of Deeds, book 142, leaf 92.
† Essex Registry of Deeds, book 143, leaf 23.
‡ A note says that he died in Warren, Me., but his death is recorded in Boxford.

241—III. LUCY[4], born March 15, 1748; married Dea. Thomas Cross of
          Bradford Nov. 17, 1767; lived in Bradford, until about 1796,
          when they removed to Gorham, Me. He was born Nov. 13,
          1741; and died in Gorham Feb. 15, 1819, at the age of sev-
          enty-seven. She died there May 21, 1821, at the age of sev-
          enty-three. Their children were born in Bradford as fol-
          lows: 1. *Joseph[5]*, born Dec. 31, 1768; married Betsey Dus-
          tin May 9, 1793; he died Oct. 29, 1819, aged fifty; she was
          born April 16, 1769, and died, his widow, Oct. 25, 1828. They
          had four children. 2. *Thomas[5]*, born March 3, 1770; mar-
          ried Laura Sandford Dec. 30, 1804 (5?); he died April 6,
          1833, at Portland, Me., aged sixty-three; she was born in
          Portland May 20, 1783, and after her husband's death was
          given a home at Springfield, Mass., with her sister Mary,
          wife of James S. Dwight, and died at Jackson, Mich., Oct. 26,
          1850, at the age of sixty-seven. They had four children. 3.
          Betsey[5], born Feb. 11, 1772; married Capt. Jonathan Stevens
          Oct. —, 1796 (4?); and died Nov. 13, 1838. They had six
          children. 4. *Rebecca[5]*, born Jan. 30, 1774; died, unmarried,
          April 11, 1794, aged twenty. 5. *Sarah[5]*, born Sept. 22, 1777;
          married Capt. Enoch Preble of Portland, Me., Sept. 14, 1800;
          lived in Portland; he was born on Falmouth Neck July 2,
          1763, and died in Portland Sept. 28, 1842, at the age of sev-
          enty-nine; she died, in Portland, his widow, June 20, 1848,
          aged seventy. They had four children, one of whom was
          George Henry Preble, rear-admiral in the United States
          navy. 6. *William[5]*, born Aug. 21, 1779; married Eliza
          Stevens Feb. 4, 1804; he died Feb. 14, 1819, at the age of
          thirty-nine; she married, secondly, Hon. Toppan Robie. Mr.
          Hovey had a daughter. 7. *Lucy[5]*, born March 7, 1782; mar-
          ried Dea. James Phinney, sr., of Gorham, Me., June 30, 1817;
          he was a farmer, and lived in Gorham; she died Jan. 30,
          1860, at the age of seventy-seven. They had a daughter. 8.
          Lois[5], born March 10, 1784; married Allison Libby of Gor-
          ham July 15, 1809; lived in Gorham, removed to Standish,
          Me.; she died March 26 (Feb. 25?), 1860, aged seventy-six;
          he was born in Gorham March 8, 1787, and died in Harrison,
          Me., Aug. 10, 1869, aged eighty-two. They had seven chil-
          dren. 9. *Leonard[5]*, born May 8, 1786; lived in Portland;
          and died, unmarried, March 20, 1867, at the age of eighty.
          10. *Amos Hovey[5]*, born April 22, 1788; died at Harrison,
          Me., unmarried, Sept. 27, 1842, at the age of fifty-four. 11.
          Harriet[5], born Oct. 20, 1790(4?); died March 11, 1798.

242—IV.   IVORY[4], born July 14, 1750. *See family numbered "242."*

243—V.   LOIS[4], born Sept. 24, 1752; died in Boxford Oct. 5, 1758, aged
          six.

244—VI.   REBECCA[4], born Dec. 15, 1754; married Amos, son of Capt.
          Francis and Huldah (Putnam) Perley of Boxford June 6,
          1775. He was born in Boxford Jan. 28, 1748-9. She died in
          Boxford April 10, 1776, at the age of twenty-one. He mar-
          ried, secondly, Sarah Smith Feb. 4, 1779. She was born in
          Newbury March 16, 1757. He lived in Boxford until about
          1790, when he removed to Winthrop, Me. He was a currier
          by trade, and probably continued his father's business in
          Boxford until his removal to Winthrop. He died Dec. 6,
          1830, at the age of eighty-one. His wife, Sarah, survived
          him, and died about 1833, at the age of eighty-six. The only

child of Amos and Rebecca (Hovey) Perley was: 1. *Rebecca*[5], born March 21, 1776, in Boxford; married Isaiah, son of Moses and Lydia (Waterman) Wood Jan. 6, 1799; he was a farmer and school teacher; and about 1805 had his name changed to Moses Wood, because of another Isaiah Wood. Upon his marriage he settled in Anson, Me., then practically a forest, and won by hard work a large and productive farm. They died in North Anson, he about 1832, and she in April, 1868, at the age of ninety-two. They had six children. Miss Marcia Louisa Wood of Amesbury, Mass., a granddaughter of Mrs. Wood, has an ancient highboy, which belonged to her great-grandmother Rebecca (Hovey) Perley. It is a handsome piece of furniture, and was made by Rebecca's brother as a wedding present to her.

245—VII.   Amos[5], born May 31, 1757. *See family numbered "245."*

246—VIII. Lois[5], born June 14, 1759; married Amos Gage of Bethel, Me., April 22, 1787. They lived in Bethel and Waterford, Me. Children: 1. *Thomas*[6], born June 8, 1789; married Frances C. Stockbridge of Bath, Me.; and had two children, Dr. Amos Leander Gage and Dr. Alexander Selkirk Gage, both of Baltimore, Md., being grandsons. 2. *Leander*[6], born Sept. 20, 1791; physician; lived in Waterford; married Anna B. Sargent in 1820; and died in 1842. They had eight children, one of whom is Dr. Thomas Hovey Gage of Worcester, Mass. 3. *William*[6], born March 15, 1795; died Jan. 1, 1820 (1842?); no children. 4. *Amos*[6], born March 2, 1797; deacon; married Mary Warren of Waterford; and died, leaving no children.

247—IX.   Thomas[5], born Feb. 9, 1762; lived in Portland, Me.; merchant, being of the firm of Stevens and Hovey; removed to Salem, Mass., a short time before his death, which occurred there in 1818. He had no children.

248—X.   Sarah[5], born in 176-; died June 26, 1764.

92

Abijah Hovey[4], born in Boxford, Mass., Dec. 9, 1719. He was yeoman, and lived in Boxford until 1750, when he removed to Lunenburg, where he afterwards lived.

March 8, 1748, his father gave to him and his brothers Luke and Joseph the father's interest in Walker's meadow in Boxford;[*] and he bought, for two hundred and fifty pounds, ten acres of upland and meadow, in Boxford, on the south side of Johnson's pond, May 10, 1748.[†]

Mr. Hovey bought, for two hundred and ten pounds, of Humphrey Holt of Andover, husbandman, seventy acres of land in Lunenburg, with the mansion house and barn thereon, March 18, 1750.[‡] He bought of Jonathan Willard of Lunenburg, gentleman, for ten pounds, five acres of land in Lunenburg, Feb. 18,

---

[*] Essex Registry of Deeds, book 95, leaf 204.
[†] Essex Registry of Deeds, book 109, leaf 6.
[‡] Worcester Registry of Deeds, book 33, page 512.

1754.* With his wife Lydia, he sold, for forty-three pounds, three shillings and two pence, woodland in Andover, May 27. 1762.† For one hundred and eighty-three pounds, six shillings and eight pence. he bought of Jonathan Holt of Fitchburg, yeoman, seventy acres of land, in Lunenburg, being a farm, with the house, barn and cooper's shop, Nov. 2, 1771.‡

Mr. Hovey was chosen surveyor of highways in Lunenburg in 1754. and constable in 1763.

He married, first, Lydia Graves of Haverhill March 21. 1744-5. She and her husband, Mr. Hovey, for one hundred and twenty-six pounds, conveyed to James Graves of Kingston, N. H., twenty acres of land in Kingston Feb. 10. 1747-8.§ She died in Lunenburg Nov. 28, 1760. He married, second, Lydia Ingalls of Andover Dec. 3, 1761; and she died before 1793. He married, third, Mary Ann Faulkner before 1793, when she was his wife. He died in the winter of 1794-5, at the age of seventy-five.

The following is a copy of his will taken from the original instrument which is on file in the probate office at Worcester :—

In the Name of God Amen this fifteenth Day of January one thousand seven Hundred & Ninety three

I Abijah Hove of Lunenburg in the County of Worcester in the Common Wealth of Massachusetts yeamon being of Disposeing mind & memory thanks be to God therefor Calling to mind the mortality of my Body Knowing that it is appointed for all men once to Die Do make and ordain this my Last will and Testament Principally and first of all I Recommend my Soul into the hands of God who gave it and my Body I Recommend to the Earth to be buried in a Decent manner at the Descretion of my Executor here after to mee [be?] named And as Touching that Estate where with it hath pleased God to bless me with in this Life I Giv and Dispose of it in manner as followeth

Imprimis To my Beloved Wife Mary Hovey I Giv and Bequeath all the Household Goods and furniture that She Bro' with her at the time of her marriage including Books allso my Great Bible to Her and her Heirs forever Furthermore I Giv to my Wife (So long as She remains my Widow) all the lower Rooms in my Dwelling House and the Cellar under the Same & the liberty of the well & half the Garden Allso two Good Cows Kept Summer and Winter and for ‖her‖ further yearly Support I giv her Ten Bushels of Indian Corn & four Bushels of Rye & one Bushel of Malt & Ten lb of Sheeps wool & Twelve lb of Flax one Hundred lb of pork & Ninety lb of Beef and five Barrels of Cyder & Casks to hold the Same & Six Bushels of Winter Apples and So many in the Summer as She needs allso So much fire wood as Shall be Necessary Brought to the House and Cut fit for the fire with convenient yard Room allso the privilege of a Horse to ride to Meeting & Elsewhere as She Shall have Occasion allso one Bushel & a half of Salt & four Bushels of potatoes & one Bushel of

---

* Worcester Registry of Deeds, book 39, page 332.
† Essex Registry of Deeds, book 119, leaf 252.
‡ Worcester Registry of Deeds, book 71, page 563.
§ Rockingham Registry of Deeds, book 50, page 378.

Wheat & one peck of Beans the above Bequeſt to be no Longer than
She Remains my Widow all the above Articles to be Rendered and paid
to my wife by my Executor She Quiting her Right of Dow⁴ to my
Eſtate Furthermore if my S⁴ Widow Should Marry I give her thirty
pounds to Her and her Heirs forever to be well and truly Paid by my
Executor

Item To my Beloved Daughter Sarah Farwell the wife of John
Farwell & Dorcas Weatherbee the wife of Paul Weatherbee & Liddya
Putnam and Miriam Paterson the wife of James Paterson I giv & bequeath beſides what I gave at the time of their Mariags to them and
their Heirs for Ever A Certain Tract of Land Suppoſed to be Twenty
two Acres (be the Same more or Leſs & is part of the Farm that I Now
Live on Lying at the Northweſterly Corner of s⁴ Farm which Land, was
taken out of Dorcheſter Farm So called & the bounds betwean my Farm
& the above s⁴ Twenty two Acres is the Boundary Line betwixt Dorchester & Woburn Farms So called—the above to be Equally Divided
between my above Named Daughters or their Heirs also I give to Each
of my Daughters & to my Son Solomon Hovey all my Houſehold goods
& furniture including Books Excepting my Apparil & what I have willed
to my wife to be Equally Divided betwean them

Item To my beloved Son Solomon Hovey in Consideration of that
Paren[t]al Affection & that Service a Labour that he hath performed for
me I giv & bequeath all my apparril and all my Land Except what is
above willed Buildings Quick Stock Huſbandry utenſels includeing all both
Real & personal Eſtate to Him and his Heirs forever he paying my Juſt
Debts Funerel Charges and the above Legacies

Furthermore I Do by theſe Preſants Conſtitute and appoint my
Beloved Son Solomon Hovey to be the Sole Executor of this my Laſt
will and Teſtament and I Do by theſe Preſants utterly Revoke and Diſ-
allow and Disannul all other former wills and teſtaments and Do Rattify
and this Only To be my Last Will and Teſtament

I[n] Witneſs here of I have here unto Sett my Hand and Seal the
Day and Year above mentioned

Signed Sealed Pronounc-
ed & Declared by the afors⁴
Abijah   Hovey   to   be
his Last will & Teſtament
in Preſents of us
    STEPHEN STICKNEY
    ZACHARIAH WHITNEY   *Abijah Hovey* [SEAL]
    RICHARD PEABODY

The will was proved March 3, 1795.
The children of Abijah Hovey were born as follows:—

249—I. SARAH⁸, born Nov. 19, 1746, in Boxford; married John Farwell
        of Fitchburg March 16, 1769; and died Aug. 19, 1779.
250—II. SOLOMON⁸, born Nov. 7, 1748, in Boxford. *See family num-
        bered "250."*
251—III. DORCAS⁸, born June 24, 1751, in Lunenburg; married Paul, son
        of Paul Wetherbee of Fitchburg Feb. 2, 1775. He was born
        in Lunenburg Aug. 12, 1749. He was a farmer; and lived in
        Fitchburg. He cleared his farm from a dense forest, about
        a mile south of the centre of Fitchburg, and now included
        in that city, and upon his marriage built a house. There they
        lived and died. Their daughter Salome lived with them

during their latter years, Mrs. Wetherbee being incapacitated
by paralysis after a life of activity and usefulness. The
house was standing and occupied in 1897. Mr. Wetherbee
was a "minute-man" in Capt. Ebenezer Bridge's company.
Col. John Whitcomb's regiment, and marched from Fitchburg
to Cambridge on the alarm of April 19, 1775, serving thirteen
days. He represented the town in the general court in 1810,
1811 and 1812. In politics he was a Jeffersonian, and in religion Unitarian. He was never a violent partisan, but held
all his opinions firmly. He was well-read for his times, and
a courteous, hospitable gentleman. With very limited means
and appliances, his house was the abode of quiet refinement
and intelligence. Mrs. Wetherbee died in Fitchburg Nov. 14,
1829, at the age of seventy-eight; and he died there April 24,
1834, aged eighty-four. Their children were born in what is
now the city of Fitchburg, as follows: 1. *Dorcas*[6], born
Nov. 29, 1775; married Daniel Farwell Dec. 18, 1797; and
died in Fitchburg Nov. 16, 1853. 2. *Paul*[6], born March 8,
1777; died in Troy, N. Y., Dec. 25, 1836, aged fifty-nine. 3.
Abel[6], born May 22, 1779; died in Fitchburg Sept. 25, 1801,
aged twenty-two. 4. *Abijah*[6], born July 20, 1781; married
Betsey Wilder in Boston in 1803; and died in New Ipswich,
N. H., July 21, 1835, aged fifty-four. 5. *Asa*[6], born Sept. 10,
1783; died Aug. 10, 1852, aged sixty-eight. 6. *Luke*[6], born
Nov. 14, 1786; died in Fitchburg April 24, 1823, aged thirty-
six. 7. *Salome*[6], born Dec. 7, 1788; married Jonas Fairbanks;
and died in Fitchburg Oct. 14, 1849, aged sixty. 8. *Sally*[6],
born May 24, 1791; married ———— Mosher; and died July 10,
1835, aged forty-four. 9. *Lucy*[6], born March 12, 1797; married ———— Beckwith; and died in Fitchburg March 7, 1828,
aged thirty.

252—IV. LYDIA[5], born Aug. 17, 1753, in Lunenburg; married Amos Putnam of Fitchburg (published May 2, 1781); and they were
living in 1793.

253—V. MIRIAM[5], born Oct. 8, 1758, in Lunenburg; married James Paterson of Fitchburg (published May 1, 1778); and they were
living in 1793. Children: 1. *Lovisa*[6], born July 4, 1779, at
Fitchburg. 2. *Lydia*[6], born Feb. 6, 1781, in Lunenburg; died
March 19, 1781. 3. *James*[6], born March 9, 1782, in Lunenburg.

254—VI. ALIJAH[5], born Oct. 16, 1760, in Lunenburg; died Nov. 29, 1760.

97

REV. IVORY HOVEY[4], born in Topsfield, Mass., July 3, 1714.
He was fitted for college under the instruction of Rev. John Rogers of Boxford, and entered Harvard college in 1731. Although
but thirteen years old, the great earthquake of 1727 so affected
him that he became a Christian, and was admitted to the Topsfield church Sept. 6, 1729. In college he joined a society of
students which met Sunday evenings for religious exercises. In
addition to the usual temptation of college life, he found great
difficulty in meeting the questions that arose relative to the
divine sovereignty in sin and redemption. He studied so hard
that toward the end of his third year his health gave way, and

he remained at home for nearly a year. Though he was disappointed at his forced retirement, he subsequently believed that his associations with his pastor, Rev. John Emerson, the privilege of private reflection and reading was more beneficial to him than what he would have otherwise gained in his regular studies. In the spring of 1735 he returned to college, and so good was his scholarship that he graduated with his class. He was then glad that he had escaped some of the "pernicious principles which prevailed at college about that time, whereby many were led astray." The next two years he taught a school in Marlborough. He lost a month of that time in consequence of breaking his leg by a fall from his horse. This was also a benefit to him, he said, as it gave him another season of reflection.

His religious character was now so pronounced that he was frequently called upon to officiate among the sick and at funerals. He believed in devotional meetings for young people, and drafted a plan of a society substantially like that of the modern Christian Endeavor society, with rules as to membership, time of meeting, order of exercises, behavior, fellowship, absences, fees, offerings, church loyalty, etc.

While a private tutor in a family in Biddeford, Me., in 1737, he became acquainted with Olive, daughter of Capt. Samuel Jordan of that place, and they were married Feb. 8, 1739. She was born in 1722.

Mr. Hovey studied divinity with his home pastor, Rev. Mr. Emerson. He wrote out, at this period, for his use, mostly in shorthand, some of Doctor Mather's "Directions to a Candidate for the Ministry—*Manuductio ad Ministerium,* or the Angels Preparing to Sound the Trumpets;" and under rules of prudence he wrote: "It is the observation of a very discrete man who said he had often got hurt by eating too much, rarely by eating too little; often got hurt by wearing too few cloathes, rarely by wearing too many; got hurt by speaking, rarely by holding his tongue. . . . Sometimes you will meet with unperswadable people. No counsel, no reason will do anything upon the obstinates. Throw them into the heap of the incurables." He concluded with a list of about twenty-five books for a young student's library.

Mr. Hovey preached his first sermon May 14, 1738, at Tewksbury. Though he was still in delicate health, he preached in Arundel, York and Biddeford during the next winter.

Harvard college conferred upon him the degree of Master of Arts in 1739.

He continued to preach in various places, until he was ordained, Oct. 29, 1740, at Mattapoisett, the Second parish in Rochester. Eighteen citizens of the town signed an agreement to give him one hundred and four dollars, in sums varying from two to twenty dollars toward his settlement, in addition to the rates. Two men agreed to give him two thousand great shingles, and another four gallons of rum, "if Mr. Hovey builds a house in said precinct, for raising." Mr. Hovey built a house, on the main street of Mattapoisett, water side, about a mile from where it now stands. It is a gambrel-roofed house, and shown in the engraving on the opposite page. The shingles and the rum were probably used in its construction.

Two years later his health had become so poor that he proposed to resign, but the people would not consent, and he continued their pastor twenty-nine years.

Because of his delicate health he paid much attention to the study of medicine, and he became the physician as well as minister of the parish. He was finally dismissed, by a council, Oct. 15, 1769; and the next Sunday was invited to preach at Manomet (South Plymouth). He soon had a call to settle there, and accepted it. The salary was fifty pounds a year and the use of a parsonage. He was installed April 18, 1770.

Mr. Hovey kept a diary during his long ministry, being contained in nine volumes, and aggregating seven thousand pages. Most of it was written in shorthand. Some extracts from it were published in the Piscataqua Evangelical Magazine in 1805 and 1807. Many of the entries refer to his spiritual and physical condition.

He was a small man, and wore the usual knee breeches and shoe buckles of the time.

He sat on most of the ecclesiastical councils that were held in the vicinity; and traveled very little at other times.

It was his practice to devote a tenth of his income to charitable uses.

Mr. Hovey published (1) A letter in the 24th Number of Prince's Christian History; (2) A sermon on the Duty and Privilege of Aged Saints; occasioned by the death of Lieut. John Hammond, of Rochester, Boston, 1749; (3) Farewell sermon at Mattapoisett, 1769; 2 Cor. xiii: 11; Boston, 1770; (4) A sermon on "Mortality," preached in the Second Parish in Plymouth, June 8, 1794, occasioned by the sudden death of two young persons . . and several aged persons. Isa. xl: 6-8; Boston, 1795; (5) A letter to Caleb Holmes, A. B., Oct. 24, 1803; in Piscataqua Evangelical Magazine, I: 90; also in Alden's Epitaphs, I: 246.

Sixty-three years of his life were spent in the gospel ministry, an experience not only of great length, but excelling in fruitfulness. He died on Friday, Nov. 4, 1803, at the age of eighty-nine. Five days later his funeral was held at the meeting house, and it was attended by a large concourse of people. Ministers from all the neighboring towns were present. The sermon was preached by Mr. Niles of Abington, Acts xx: 38 being the text. On the eight succeeding Sundays, the ministers who had attended the funeral, carrying out the custom of the times, preached in turn to his people.

Upon the church records were placed the following words as a testimony to the memory of Mr. Hovey: "The late reverend, worthy, highly esteemed and godly pastor, Ivory Hovey, was installed to the gospel ministry in this place April 18, 1770, deceased Friday, Nov. 4, 1803. and left behind as great an example of meekness, patience and Christian perseverance as ever shone perhaps in the character of a finite being, and it may with the greatest propriety as a just encomium to his memory, be said in the cause of Christ he eminently displayed the fortitude of the Christian, and the bravery of the hero."

His remains lie in the oldest burial ground in Manomet, in Plymouth, and his tombstone bears the following inscription:—

In memory of
Rev. IVORY HOVEY
who died Novr 4. 1803
in ye 90 year of his age.

By faith he lived, by faith he died,
CHRIST was his portion, theme and guide.
In precept and example shone.
With love to GOD and love to man
His daily course of action ran.
Till GOD, his Saviour, called him home.

Mrs. Hovey survived him, and died in Manomet, his widow, June 8, 1805, at the age of eighty-three. Her remains lie near his, and the memorial stone above them bears the following inscription:—

Mrs. OLIVE HOVEY
Wid^o of
Rev. IVORY HOVEY
died June 8 1805 in her
84 year

Thus long in wisdom's ways she trod
Bless'd with Christ's presence here.
Until prepar'd to meet her GOD
He call'd her to appear.

Their children were born at Mattapoisett, in Rochester, as follows:—

255—I.   Dominicus^8, born April 5, 1740. *See family numbered "255."*
256—II.   ————^{8}, died in infancy.
257—III.   ————^{8}, died in infancy.

258—IV.   OLIVE[5], born Aug. 8, 1746; married Maj. Isaac, son of Israel
          Pope of Dartmouth.
               It is said, that when the news of the Lexington alarm
          reached Dartmouth, Major Pope and another man were at
          work in the field, that they dropped their hoes and hurried
          home to take leave of their families. Mrs. Pope entreated
          her husband not to go; but he, burning with patriotism, said,
          "It is no time for tears now;" and, shouldering their muskets,
          the two men departed for the scene of conflict. He served,
          first, in Colonel Cotton's regiment, and subsequently with
          General Sullivan.
               They removed to Wells, Me., in 1779, sailing in a sloop
          May 4, and reaching their destination next day. The tide
          being out, she had to mount a horse and then ride four miles
          to their home. For a while they lived on greens and clams.
          In a letter to her father she wrote, "There is a Great plenty
          of woolves in these parts. They have been tract but a few
          rods from our hous, they have taken sheep out of barn &
          yards a great many times. The bairs was very plenty last
          fall. Some people was oblidged to watch their corn-fields
          all night. . . Mr. Pope came home for 7 weeks—the
          longest visit he had since he went into the army, . . We
          have lived without meat & I have had only ½ bushel of
          bread-corn for 2 months. I buy a few qts & pay for it in
          my work. We have bread but once a day. As to clothing I
          can't buy any, I am meeting with new trials from the
          family that came with us. You used to say that every
          trouble is to teach us some lesson, & when we have learned
          the trouble will be removed."
               Major Pope became a member of the Society of the
          Cincinnati. They were living in 1806. Their son, 1. *Domin-
          icus*[6], married Sally Tarbox.

259—V.   IVORY[5], born Dec. 29, 1748. *See family numbered "259."*
260—VI.   SAMUEL[5], born Dec. 6, 1750. *See family numbered "260."*
261—VII. ANNE[5], born Nov. 6, 1754; married Dea. Abner Bartlett of
          Plymouth, where she died Sept. 22, 1810, at the age of fifty-
          five. Her gravestone, in the old burial place at South Ply-
          mouth, bears the following inscription:—

                              There is rest in Heaven.
                                      Erected
                                 to the memory of
                              MRS. ANNE BARTLETT,
                                     Consort of
                               Deacon Abner Bartlett,
                                 & dau[tr] of the late
                                 Rev[d] Ivory Hovey;
                                 who died Sep[t] 22,
                                  1810, Aged 55
                                  years, 10 months,
                                       & 16
                                       days

                    The God who gave me children here,
                    And in affection made them near
                    With love toward my partner great;
                    Yet when my Jesus spake the word
                    I freely gave them back to God.

Deacon Bartlett died Oct. 28, 1813, at the age of fifty-eight. The inscription on the gravestone standing above his remains reads as follows:—

This
Stone is erected
to the memory of
DEACON ABNER BARTLETT
Who
was born March 2, 1755
and
Died October 28 1813

Mortals prepare eternity's at hand
GOD is your Judge, and you are in his hand
Be reconciled and own his ways are Just
Adore his will and on him lean and trust

Their children were born in Manomet (South Plymouth), as follows: 1. ————, died young. 2. ————, died young. 3. *Ivory Hovey*, born Sept. 21, 1794; finished his schooling at Sandwich, Mass., in 1814; and was appointed first lieutenant of Massachusetts militia Aug. 20, 1817. He moved to New Bedford, Mass., in the autumn of 1819, and was a merchant there, conducting a large whaling and commission business. He was alderman of the city from 1847 to 1851 inclusive; married Betsey Clark June 9, 1814, at Manomet; and died in New Bedford Feb. 6, 1871, aged seventy-six. She survived him, and died there March 31, 1874. They had nine children. Rev. Joseph B. Seabury, Rev. J. H. B. Headley and Ellis Bartlett were grandsons of Ivory Hovey Bartlett and his wife Betsey Clark, and Ellis Bartlett was the father of Ellis Ashmead Bartlett and William Lehman Ashmead Bartlett, both of England, and members of parliament. Ellis A. Bartlett was knighted by Queen Victoria, and William L. A. Bartlett married the Baroness Burdett Coutts.

99

AARON HOVEY[4], born in Topsfield, Mass., Sept. 14, 1718. He was a yeoman, and lived in Topsfield on his father's homestead, which had been devised to him, on Pye brook.

He married Sarah, daughter of Stephen and Hannah (Coker) Perley of Ipswich Dec. 23, 1740. She was born in Ipswich, on the ancient Perley homestead, Nov. 7, 1719.

With her husband and others, she conveyed land in Newbury which she inherited from Moses Coker of Newbury, yeoman, deceased. March 25, 1756;* and with several others she and her husband made partition of several lots of land in Newbury June 7, 1756.† With several other persons, she and her husband

* Essex Registry of Deeds, book 103, leaf 167.
† Essex Registry of Deeds, book 103, leaf 104.

sold four-sixths of three acres of land in Newbury, and four-sixths of six and one-half acres of salt marsh on Plum island, in Newbury, April 20, 1757.*

Mr. Hovey died in Topsfield May 4, 1759, at the age of forty; and his remains lie buried in the ancient burying ground in Topsfield. His gravestone bears the following inscription :—

```
                HERE LIES BURIED
            THE  BODY  OF
            Mr AARON HOUEY
            WHO      DECEASED
            MAY     THE    4th
            A  D     1759    &
            IN               THE
            41st          YEAR
            OF    HIS    AGE
```

Administration upon his estate was granted to his widow June 4, 1759. His estate was appraised at £685, 5s., 9d., 3 far. His personal estate amounted to £151, 19s., 1d., 3 far.; and the real estate to £533, 6s., 8d. He had one hundred and fifty acres of land and buildings. His real estate was divided among his heirs March 18, 1765, and, after dower had been assigned to the widow, the remainder was settled upon Stephen, the eldest son of the deceased.

His widow, Sarah Hovey, died in Topsfield Oct. 6. 1792, at the age of seventy-two. She was a woman of some education, and of strong mind and heart. Upon the return of her son Moses from the army, sick with small pox, she took care of him and became ill with the same disease herself. Her petition, given below, is interesting.

Their children were born in Topsfield, as follows :—

262—I. STEPHEN⁶, born Feb. 24, 1741-2. *See family numbered "262."*
263—II. MOSES⁶, born March 16, 1743-4; was a soldier in the expedition against Canada in 1760, in the company of Capt. Nathaniel Brown, in Colonel Willard's regiment, returning home in November; and died in Topsfield, of small pox, Nov. 27, 1760, a few days after his arrival, at the age of sixteen.

To obtain pay for the expense she had been to on her son's account, Mrs. Hovey sent the following petition to the governor and council and general court :—

To His Exelancy Francis Barnard Esqr Capt General and governor in Chief in and over his Majestys province of the Massachusetts Bay in New England &c. and to the Honourable his Majestys Councel and houfe of Reprefentatives in Generall Court afsembled

---

* Essex Registry of Deeds, book 108, leaf 194.

The Petition of Sarah Hovey of Topsfield Humbly Sheweth

That whereas her Son Mofes Hovey a Soldier in Cap⁺ Nathaniel Browns Company in Coll. Willards Reg⁺ in the Last Expedition against Canada was on his way hime in yᵉ month of November Last but was taken Sick on yᵉ way She hired a man and horfe to meet him and help him home who returned with him in nine days tho he was to appearence but Just alive She Sent for a Phyfician who made him two visits and applied medicins but on yᵉ third day after he gott home he broke out with the Small pox by which means She was O[b]liged to remove her Large family of Children and an Aged mother but She was Obliged to Stay with him her Self untill they Could procure Nurfes She tooke the Distemper which put [|her|] to greate Charges her Son also Died with the Distemper She therefor prays that your Exelency and hon⁺ˢ would take her poor Circumftances into your wife Consideration and make her Such reafonable allowence out of the province Treafury for the Charges of fetching her Son home and Other Charges by Reafon of his Sicknefs as you in your greate wifdom Shall think proper—and as in Duty bound Shall ever pray—The perticuler Charges by reafon of her Sons Sicknefs Exclufive of other Damages and greate Lofses Suftained in yᵉ time of his Sicknefs are as followeth (viz)

		£ s d
To Willm Hood 27ˢ/ to Doct^r Haile 14ˢ/		£2 1 0
To Joseph Leflie 58ˢ/ to Mary Edmunds 28ˢ/		4 6 0
To money Expended in bringing her son home		1 9 0
To Other Neceſarys in yᵉ time of his Sicknefs		0 14 9
		8 10 9

Topsfield March 2nd 1761.

SARAH HOVEY

Efsex ss march 12th 1761.
Then the above Named Sarah Hovey made oath to the Truth of what is above written
Before   JOHN HONFON Juˢ Peace

The Com^tee Report four pounds Sixteen Shillings In full to be paid to m^r Gould for yᵉ ufe of yᵉ Peti^r
W. LAWRANCE P order

264—III. SARAH⁸, born July 28, 1746; died, unmarried, in Topsfield, Sept. 30, 1766, aged twenty.

265—IV. DORCAS⁸, born April 18, 1749; married Joseph, sen of Nathan and Elizabeth (Palmer) Hood of Topsfield Oct. 13, 1767. He was born in Topsfield Feb. 2, 1746. They were living in Topsfield in 1774. Children, born in Topsfield: 1. *Sarah⁹*, baptized Aug. 14, 1768. 2. *Joseph⁹*, baptized Nov. 28, 1769. 3. *Huldah⁹*, baptized March 13, 1774.

266—V. HULDAH⁸, born Oct. 22, 1751; married Timothy Emerson of Nottingham-west (published June 4, 1775).

267—VI. THOMAS⁸, born April 20, 1754; and was living in 1776.

268—VII. IVORY⁸, born Sept. 16, 1756; married Anna Smith of Boxford April 28, 1778; and died in Topsfield Oct. 3, 1816, of fever, aged sixty.

109

DANIEL HOVEY⁴, born in Ipswich, Mass., April 7, 1702. He was a husbandman, and lived in his native town until 1724, when he settled in Oxford, where his father was then living. He was a constable of the town in 1738.

While he was living in Ipswich, for fifty-two pounds, he conveyed to James Burnam, jr., of Ipswich a common right in Ipswich, April 7, 1724;* and, for one hundred and twenty pounds, bought of Richard Moore of Oxford, yeoman, one hundred acres of land with meadow and swamp in Oxford, April 25, 1724.†

His father conveyed to him, as a gift, his farm of eighty-seven acres of land on Flat and Long hills in Oxford village, April 7, 1735‡ and the latter bought of Nathaniel Jones of Falmouth, Me., gentleman, for forty pounds, twenty acres of land in Oxford, March 4, 1739-40.§ With his mother, his sister and brother, he released to David Town of Oxford, husbandman, his interest in the real estate of his father April 2, 1742.‖ The house was standing in 1879.

Mr. Hovey married Mehitable, daughter of Benjamin and Elizabeth Bridges of Framingham Nov. 24, 1726. She was born in Framingham Oct. 17, 1706. He died in Oxford April 3, 1758.

Mr. Hovey's will is on file in the probate office at Worcester, and the following is a transcript of the original instrument:—

In the Name of God amen this Seuenth day of december, in the year of our Lord 1757 I Daniel Hovey of Oxford in the County of worcester in the province of the massachusetts Bay in new England yeoman being advanced in years and in a weak low Condition do make this my Last will and Testament as follows: viz first and principally I Commit my Soul into the hands of Almighty God my Creator, hoping in his mercy thro the merits death & passion and prevailing intercession of Jesus Christ my Lord & Saviour: and my body I desire may be decently Interred at the discretion of my Executors hereafter named, in faith of the Reserrection of it at the last day, and Touching Such temporal Estate as God hath betrusted me with (after my Just debts and funeral Charges are paid) I will and bequeath the Same as follows, that is to Say.

Impr I give and bequeath unto my beloved wife mehitabel Hovey one third Share of all my Stock of cattle whatsoever, as also all my houshold goods, furniture and moueables within doors, (Excepting my cash bonds notes and book accounts, my arms & wearing apparrel) to be disposed of by her as she pleaseth, moreover I give & bequeath unto my faid wife mehitabel Hovey one moiety of all my buildings & one third share of the improvement and profit of my farm whereon now we dwell. I alfo order and defire that my said wife have the free use & improvement of a horse kept on the said farm when she hath occasion for it the

* Essex Registry of Deeds, book 45, leaf 250.
† Suffolk Registry of Deeds, book 38, page 221.
‡ Worcester Registry of Deeds, book 7, page 399.
§ Worcester Registry of Deeds, book 11, page 570.
‖ Worcester Registry of Deeds, book 16, page 171.

moiety of the buildings, the third share of the improvement of the farm, is to be to her only while she remains my widow and no longer.

Item I give and bequeath unto my daughter mehitabel Hovey Sixteen pound lawful money of the said province to be paid to her, her heirs or assigns in the following manner viz four pound lawful money to be paid unto her or her aforesaids at the expiration of one year after my only Son Daniel Hovey arrives at lawful age; and So yearly until the whole sixteen pounds are paid at four pound per annum in four years commencing from the term above mentioned. I also give and bequeath unto my Said daughter mehitabel Hovey one cow as her part & portion of all my Estate all which is to be done & performed by my faid Son Daniel Hovey in ye manner and form herein prescribed.

Item I give and bequeath unto my daughter Tabitha Hovey Sixteen pound lawful money of the province aforesaid to be paid unto her, her heirs or assigns by my Said Son Daniel Hovey in the Same manner, at the respective terms as are expressed in the immediately proceeding paragraff of this Instrument. I also give and bequeath unto my said daughter Tabitha Hovey one cow, which together with the Said Sum of money is her part & portion of all my estate.

Item I give and bequeath unto my daughter mercy Hovey twelve pounds lawful money of the Said province to be paid unto her, her heirs or assigns in manner and form following, by my said Son Daniel Hovey viz four pound lawful money of the said province at the ex[p]iration of one year after She arrives at lawful age, and so on untill the twelve pounds are paid at four pound per annum in three years commencing from the term of her lawful age before mentioned, I also give and bequeath unto my Said daughter mercy Hovey one cow, to be delivered to her or her aforesaids by my Son Daniel Hovey which together with the Said Sum of money is her part & portion of all my Estate

Item I give and bequeath unto my daughter Sarah Hovey twelve pound lawful money of the said province to be paid unto her, her heirs or assigns at the expiration of one year after she arrives at lawful age by my Said Son Daniel Hovey in the Same manner, & at the Same terms as are expressed in the paragraff of this Instrument immediately preceding this. I also give unto her one cow to be delivered to her order aforesaids by my Said ||son|| Daniel Hovey, which together with the Said Sum of money is her part & portion of all my Estate and it is my will & pleasure, that each of my Said daughters make my house their home and place of residence untill they are married

Item I Give and bequeath unto my only Son Daniel Hovey all my Estate real & personal whatsoever & wheresoever not already disposed of in this my Last will & Testament to be to him, his heirs & assigns forever without any reservation or Condition. I also give and bequeath unto him and his aforesaids my two largest books and the bed which I bought out of my father's Estate after his mothers decease.

Item I Do hereby nominate, desire, and appoint my beloved wife mehitabel Hovey, and my good friend Thomas Davis of Oxford husband-man to be Executors of this my last will & Testament. In witness whereof I the Said Daniel Hovey have hereunto Set my hand & seal the day and year first written

Signed sealed & Delivered
in   presence   of   us   by   the
Said Daniel ||Hovey|| and by him
declared   to   be   his   Last
will & Testament.

WILLIAM WATSON
WILLIAM CAMPB[E]LL
MARY TOWN

DA[N]IEL HOVEY [SEAL]

The will was proved May 3, 1758, having been assented to by the widow and her daughters, Mehitable and Tabitha. The following are the signatures of the daughters:

Mr. Hovey's estate was valued at £363, 19s., 4d., of which £314, 6s., was real estate, and £49, 13s., 4d. was personal. The real estate consisted of one hundred and seven acres of land and the buildings and a tract of cedar swamp.

Mrs. Hovey died, his widow, Aug. 6, 1785, at the age of seventy-eight.

The children of Mr. and Mrs. Hovey were born in Oxford, as follows:—

269—V.　TABITHA[5], born April 17, 1728; died Nov. 5, 1731.

270—II.　BENJAMIN[5], born Jan. 25, 1730-1; died Oct. 6, 1741, in Oxford, aged ten.

271—III.　DANIEL[5], born Jan. 19, 1732-3; died Oct. 14, 1741, in Oxford, aged eight.

272—IV.　MEHITABLE[5], born Jan. 28, 1734-5; died, of dysentery, in Oxford, unmarried, Oct. 21, 1803, at the age of sixty-eight.

273—V.　TABITHA[5], born April 15, 1737; married Zebulon, son of Stephen and Katharine Streeter of Douglass July 16, 1760. He was born about 1737; was a soldier in the French war in 1758; a Baptist in his religious belief and later a Universalist preacher, being for several years president of the Annual Convention; and an amiable and excellent man. He died at Surrey, N. H., in 1808. Their child, baptized in Oxford, was, 1. *Benoni*[6], baptized Sept. 14, 1766.

274—VI.　MERCY[5], born March 19, 1739; died Oct. 24, 1741.

275—VII.　DANIEL[5], born Dec. 20, 1741. *See family numbered "275."*

276—VIII.　MERCY[5], born Dec. 9, 1743; married Ambrose Stone of Oxford Dec. 12, 1776, as his second wife. He came from Sutton; was a Revolutionary soldier; and married, first, Mary Everdan of Oxford May 12, 1768, subsequently removing to Oxford. He died Aug. 12, 1813, at the age of sixty-nine. The children of Ambrose and Mary (Hovey) Stone were born in Oxford, as follows: 1. *Mary*[6], born Oct. 5, 1777; married David Learned of Dudley (published Nov. 3, 1810). 2. *Mehitable*[6], born March 15, 1780; died, unmarried, in Oxford. 3. *Ruth*[6], born March 12, 1782; married Dr. Prentice Bugbee April 10, 1806; and settled at Montpelier, Vt. 4. *Daniel*[6], born April 29, 1784; settled on his father's homestead in Oxford; married Betsey, daughter of Andrew and Elizabeth (Wolcott) Sigourney (published Dec. 30, 1809); had three children; he died in Oxford Nov. 7, 1819, aged thirty-five; and she died, his widow, June 9, 1821, aged thirty-one, she having been born in Oxford Dec. 31, 1789.

277—IX.　SARAH[5], born Sept. 12, 1747; married Daniel Hood of Oxford April 23, 1767.

113

JAMES HOVEY[4], born in Malden, Mass., Sept. 24, 1695. He was a cordwinder, and lived in Mansfield, Conn. He bought of Nathaniel Bassett of Mansfield, blacksmith, one hundred acres of land in Mansfield Feb. 8, 1719-20;[*] and on the same day conveyed to him fifty acres of land there which he had of his father, James Hovey.[*] He conveyed to Mr. Bassett other land in Mansfield Dec. 18, 1720.[†] For forty-eight pounds, he conveyed to Nathaniel Hovey of Mansfield sixteen acres of land on Mount Hope river Aug. 5, 1740.[‡]

Mr. Hovey married, first, Joanna, daughter of Nathaniel and Joanna Bassett of Mansfield Feb. 4, 1717; and she died March 6, 1748-9. He married, second, Elizabeth Lyman of Lebanon Jan. 10, 1749-50.

Mr. Hovey's children were born in Mansfield, as follows:—

278—I.   NATHANIEL[5], born June 22. 1719. *See family numbered "278."*
279—II. DEBORAH[5], born Feb. 21, 1720-1; died Jan. 14, 1748-9, unmarried, in Mansfield, at the age of twenty-seven.
280—III. SAMUEL[5], born May 3, 1723.
281—IV. JAMES[5], born April 24, 1725; died Nov. 26, 1726.
282—V.   SOLOMON[5], born July 28, 1728; died Sept. 1, 1748, aged twenty.
283—VI. HANNAH[5], born Jan. 18, 1730-1; died March 6, 1748-9. Inscription on her gravestone in Mansfield: "Here Lyes ye Body of Hannah Hovey Who dyed March 7, 1748, Agd 17."
284—VII. JERUSHA[5], born March 5, 1733.
285—VIII. ABIGAIL[5], born Aug. 13, 1735; married Jeremiah Jennings Jan. 23, 1755; lived in Mansfield; and he died Nov. 6, 1759, in Mansfield. She survived him. Children, born in Mansfield: 1. *Irena[6]*, born June 6, 1756. 2. *Deborah[6]*, born March 20, 1758. 3. *Jeremiah[6]*, born March 27, 1760, posthumous.
286—IX. RUTH[5], baptized Sept. 24, 1738.
287—X.   PHEBE[5], born Dec. 11, 1742; died May —, 1748, aged five.
288—XI. SOLOMON[5], born March 27, 1751.

115

EDMUND HOVEY[4], born in Malden, Mass., July 10, 1699. He was a carpenter, and lived in Mansfield, Conn., until after 1766, when he moved to Norwich, Vt. He bought of John Agard of Mansfield, for one pound and ten shillings, land in Mansfield June 16, 1721.[§] His father conveyed to him forty or fifty acres of land in Mansfield Jan. 25, 1721-2.[||] On the same day, he bought of Thomas Storrs of Mansfield, for two pounds and three shillings, six acres of land in Mansfield;[¶] and of Thomas Hunt-

* Mansfield Registry of Deeds, book 2, leaf 47.
† Mansfield Registry of Deeds, book 3, leaf 38.
‡ Mansfield Registry of Deeds, book 3, leaf 968.
§ Mansfield Registry of Deeds, book 2, page 171.
|| Mansfield Registry of Deeds, book 2, page 178.
¶ Mansfield Registry of Deeds, book 2, page 174.

ington of Mansfield, for four pounds and eighteen shillings, fourteen acres of land in Mansfield.* The next day, he conveyed to John Slap of Salem, Mass., clothier, for eighty pounds, eighty acres of land in Mansfield.† For forty pounds, he bought of John Ross of Mansfield sixty acres of land in that town March 30, 1722.‡ For fifteen pounds, he bought of Samuel Storrs of Mansfield thirty-five and a quarter acres of land there Sept. 3, 1722.§ Jan. 1, 1723-4, he conveyed to Ens. John Sargeant of Mansfield, for fifty-four pounds, one hundred and three acres of land in Mansfield;† and the same estate was reconveyed to him for fifty-four pounds, Jan. 13, 1725-6.‖ He bought of Lt. Thomas Storrs of Mansfield, for one pound and ten shillings, six acres of land in Mansfield March 4, 1723-4.¶ For fifty-four pounds he conveyed to John Hovey of Mansfield one hundred and five acres of land in Mansfield (acknowledged Jan. 13, 1725-6).** For two pounds, he conveyed to Samuel Gurley of Mansfield forty acres of land in Mansfield April 2, 1727-8.†† He conveyed to his brother Joseph Hovey of Mansfield ten acres of land in that town March 7, 1728-9;‡‡ and on the same day his brother Joseph conveyed to him nineteen acres and twenty-five rods of land in Mansfield, northerly of Edmund's house.§§ For two pounds and thirteen shillings, he conveyed to John Hovey of Mansfield one and one-half acres of land in that town Dec. 10, 1731;‖‖ and, for forty pounds, he conveyed to Samuel Gurley of Mansfield thirty-one acres of land in that town Dec. 17, 1731.¶¶ For four hundred pounds, he conveyed to John Crane of Coventry one hundred and twenty acres of land in Mansfield April 4, 1733.*** For one hundred and twenty-two pounds and four shillings, he conveyed to Joseph Davis of Mansfield fifty-one acres and sixteen rods of land Feb. 13, 1734-5.††† He conveyed to Philip Turner of Mansfield, farmer, three acres and one hundred and fourteen rods of land April 15, 1735.‡‡‡ For two pounds and five shillings, he conveyed to Philip Turner of Mansfield one and one-half acres of

    * Mansfield Registry of Deeds, book 2, page 181.
    † Mansfield Registry of Deeds, book 2, page 175.
    ‡ Mansfield Registry of Deeds, book 2, page 205.
    § Mansfield Registry of Deeds, book 2, page 439.
    ‖ Mansfield Registry of Deeds, book 2, page 453.
    ¶ Mansfield Registry of Deeds, book 2, page 333.
    ** Mansfield Registry of Deeds, book 2, page 454.
    †† Mansfield Registry of Deeds, book 3, page 768.
    ‡‡ Mansfield Registry of Deeds, book 3, page 128.
    §§ Mansfield Registry of Deeds, book 3, page 166.
    ‖‖ Mansfield Registry of Deeds, book 3, page 387.
    ¶¶ Mansfield Registry of Deeds, book 3, page 376.
    *** Mansfield Registry of Deeds, book 3, page 334.
    ††† Mansfield Registry of Deeds, book 3, page 583.
    ‡‡‡ Mansfield Registry of Deeds, book 3, page 676.

land in Mansfield Feb. 19, 1736.* For one hundred and one pounds, three shillings and ten pence, he conveyed to Dr. Samuel Hare of Mansfield part of his farm Feb. 14, 1737-8.† For eighty pounds, he conveyed to Thomas Baldwin of Mansfield twenty-two acres and ninety-five rods of land in Mansfield June 19, 1738.‡

Mr. Hovey married, first, Mary, daughter of Isaac and Elizabeth Farwell Feb. 8, 1727-8, in Mansfield; and she died in Mansfield Jan. 27, 1746. He married, second, Anne, daughter of Thomas and Elizabeth (Arnold) Huntington of Mansfield April 16, 1747. She was born in Mansfield Nov. 15, 1714. He died at Norwich, Vt., Jan. 21, 1788, at the age of eighty-eight.

The remains of Mr. Hovey lie in the old burial ground in Norwich, and his gravestone is inscribed as follows:—

> In Memory of M^r
> Edmund Hovey
> Died January 21st
> 1788 in his 89 Year
> Depart My friends
> dry up your tears
> I Muſt Lie here till
> Chriſt   Appears

His wife Anne survived him, and died, his widow, —— 26, 1797, aged eighty-three. Her remains lie buried at Thetford, Vt. Mr. Hovey's children were born in Mansfield, as follows:—

289—I.   EDMUND[8], born Nov. 19, 1728. *See family numbered "289."*
290—II.   ISAAC[8], born Aug. 7, 1730; died Aug. —, 1761 (7?).
291—III. MARY[8], born Nov. 8, 1732; died Dec. 6, 1749.
292—IV.   AARON[8], born April 22, 1735. *See family numbered "292."*
293—V.   JAMES[8], born Aug. 14, 1737; lived in his native town; and died, of consumption, in South parish, Mansfield, where his father lived, Jan. 8, 1766, aged twenty-eight. He owned lot 35 in the lands of Norwich, Vt., which had been granted to Solomon Wales; and conveyed it, for four pounds, to Samuel Partridge, jr., of Preston, Conn., March 13, 1765.§ He bought share No. 27 in Hanover, N. H., lands Dec. 11, 1764;‖ No. 19, Dec. 29, 1764;¶ and on the same day No. 32, Dec. 29, 1764;‖ and his brother Aaron and sister Elizabeth conveyed land in Hanover, which they inherited from him, Feb. 4, 1767.**
294—VI.   WILLIAM[8], born May 29, 1740; died April 28, 1748.
295—VII. ELIJAH[8], born Sept. 30, 1741; died March 22, 1747-8.

* Mansfield Registry of Deeds, book 3, page 730.
† Mansfield Registry of Deeds, book 3, page 796.
‡ Mansfield Registry of Deeds, book 3, page 824.
§ Norwich Registry of Deeds, book 1, page 17.
‖ Grafton Registry of Deeds, book 9, page 377.
¶ Grafton Registry of Deeds, book 9, page 192.
** Grafton Registry of Deeds, book 9, page 271.

256—VIII. ELIZABETH[5], born June 22, 1744; married Dea. John, son of Samuel and Dorothy (Fenton) Slafter of Mansfield March 26, 1767. He was born in Mansfield May 26, 1739. At the age of sixteen he enlisted in the old French war as drummer boy in the company of Capt. Israel Putnam, in Lyman's regiment; and belonged to a company of rangers under Putnam and Rogers, which performed important services in the campaign for the reduction of Crown Point in 1755. The next year, he enlisted in the First regiment, Sixth company, Connecticut volunteers, commanded by Capt. Aaron Hitchcock; and he continued in the service until 1760, being present at the capitulation of the French at Montreal Sept. 8 of that year. Mr. Slafter made a journey through the forests of New Hampshire, in 1762, to examine the territory and report upon the advantages it might offer as a place of settlement; and in consequence of his favorable report a town was begun at what is now Norwich, Vt. His father transferred to him his right as proprietor in the new town June 7, 1763; and in company with Jacob Fenton, his mother's brother, and Ebenezer Smith, both being original proprietors, he set out for the township. They took with them a horse and necessary implements. His time was consumed that summer by felling trees, burning the wood, and clearing the ground for cultivation. In the autumn he returned to Mansfield. This was repeated successive summers until 1767, when he married and took his young wife to his forest home. The distance was one hundred and fifty miles, mostly through the primitive forest, and the road, for fifty miles at least, was scarcely passable except for footmen and packhorses. Other families went with them. They went up the Connecticut river in log canoes, leaving Mansfield on Thursday, April 23, and arrived at Norwich May 10. In several places, at that time of year, the rapids, or falls, could not be passed, and they were obliged to unship their goods and carry them and their boats around, and reload, before they could continue their journey. In the place of the rude cabin they found there, Mr. Slafter built, during the summer and autumn, a comfortable and substantial dwelling on the banks of the Connecticut. It was a loghouse, to be sure, but dry and warm. The furniture was equally primitive, the tables and chairs being made of logs split in the middle, with legs.

Mr. Slafter was one of the most prominent town officers, and deacon of the church. He was selectman, a member of many committees, especially the committee in 1776, and also frequently served as arbitrator. During the time of the Indian raids, he took his wife and two children back to Mansfield, Conn., leaving Norwich July 5, 1776. They reached Mansfield in safety, after their long and perilous journey on horseback, and remained there two years. He served in the Revolutionary war, and was present at the capitulation of Burgoyne Oct. 17, 1777. He also gave land for the benefit of Dartmouth college, which was located across the river.

May 4, 1784, he removed two miles inland, where two years later, June 8, 1786, he raised the frame of the house in which he afterward lived, and which belonged to Peter Johnson in 1869. It's chimney was of great dimensions, having three ovens, in which the family baking was done. About 1850, the chimney was removed, small ones being

erected in its stead, and the roof was changed to a pitch
roof. The lofty elm standing near the house was set out by
Mrs. Slafter when the house was built. In 1869, it measured,
one foot from the ground, sixteen feet in circumference.

Mrs. Slafter died Jan. 6, 1811, at the age of sixty-six;
and he married, secondly, her half-sister Priscilla, then the
widow Whittaker, Oct. 5, 1815. He died Oct. 8, 1819, at the
age of eighty. His wife Priscilla survived him, and died
May 1, 1847, aged ninety-six.

Mr. Slafter's children were born as follows: 1. *Chris-
tiana*[6], born Feb. 6, 1768, in Norwich, Vt.; married Dr.
Richard Crafts, son of Nathaniel and Judith (Treadway)
Seaver of Petersham, Mass., March —, 1793; he was born
Oct. 28, 1767; practised medecine at Norwich, Thetford and
Chelsea, Vt., and in Wayne, Me., where he died Oct. 5, 1821,
aged fifty-three. She died Feb. 17, 1815, aged forty-seven;
and he married a second wife. Mrs. Christiana (Slafter)
Seaver had six children, all born in Chelsea. 2. *Asahel*[6]
(twin), born May 6, 1770, in Norwich; died May 12, 1770.
3. *Asaph*[6] (twin), born May 6, 1770, in Norwich; died May
6, 1770. 4. *Farwell*[6], born June 13, 1771, in Norwich; died
June 22, 1771. 5. *Edmund Farwell*[6], born July 26, 1772, in
Norwich; married Clarissa, daughter of Peter and Elizabeth
(Hitchcock) Tolman of Guilford, Conn., Aug. 27, 1798. She
was born June 5, 1778; and lived in Norwich, where he died
March 17, 1812, aged thirty-nine. She survived him, and
married, secondly, Eliphalet Tenney of Corinth, Vt., July 17,
1814. She died Sept. 11, 1821, aged forty-three. Mr. Slafter
had six children. 6. *John*[6], born Oct. 31, 1776, in Mansfield,
Conn.; lived in Norwich until 1850, when he removed to
Worth, Mich.; married Persis, daughter of Rev. Timothy
and Phalle (Richardson) Grow of Hartland, Vt., Jan. 14,
1805; she was born June 17, 1783; he was a justice of the
peace, and influential and prominent in town affairs; and
died in Worth Nov. 21, 1856, at the age of eighty. They had
nine children, one of whom, William[7], born Oct. 1, 1807,
married Roisa Hovey, daughter of Samuel and Elizabeth
(Hovey) (588) Johnson of Norwich Feb. 4, 1830; she
was born March 17, 1809; and died Oct. 31, 1849. Another
son was Hon. David Grow Slafter of Tuscola county, Mich.
7. *Sylvester*[6], born June 30, 1780, in Norwich, Vt.; lived in
Thetford, Vt.; farmer; prominent in town affairs; married,
first, Mary Armstrong, daughter of Calvin and Sarah (Armstrong) Johnson of Norwich Jan. 20, 1803; she was born
March 25, 1783; she died Aug. 17, 1835, aged fifty-two; he
married, second, Anna, daughter of Nicholas and Deborah
(Ford) White of Bradford, Vt., April 9, 1836; she was born
Dec. 21, 1790; he died May 9, 1850, aged sixty-nine; and she
died April 1, 1867, aged seventy-six. He had ten children,
two of whom were Rev. Edmund Farwell Slafter, D. D.,
rector of St. John's church at Jamaica Plain, and secretary
of the New England Historic-Genealogical Society, and Rev.
Carlos Slafter, principal of the High school at Dedham. 8.
Elijah[6], born Jan. 9, 1784, in Norwich; lived in Norwich and
Orange, Vt., Lawrence, N. Y., and Genesee, Mich.; married
Olive, daughter of Rev. Timothy and Phalle (Richardson)
Grow of Hartland, Vt., Jan. 26, 1809; she was born Jan. 24,

1791; she died April 21, 1834, aged sixty-three; and he died July 29, 1884, aged eighty. They had ten children, one of whom was Rev. Coroden Hovey Slafter, a Baptist missionary to Siam, who was born at Norwich, Vt., Jan. 31, 1811.

297—IX.   ANNE[5], born Jan. 20, 1747-8; married Timothy Smith of Hanover, N. H.; and died March —, 1825.

298—X.   WILLIAM[4], born July 6, 1749. *See family numbered "298."*

299—XI.   PRISCILLA[5] born April 17, 1751; married, first, ——————— Whittaker; second, John Slafter of Norwich, Vt., the husband of her sister Elizabeth, Oct. 5, 1815; and died May 1, 1847, aged ninety-six.

300—XII.   AMOS[5], born April 9, 1753. *See family numbered "300."*

301—XIII.   MARY[5], born Sept. 24, 1755; married Josiah Hubbard July 19, 1781; lived in Thetford, Vt.; he died July 13, 1833, at the age of seventy-five; and she died, his widow, March 15, 1846, aged ninety-one; and their remains lie buried in the ancient cemetery at Thetford. Their children were born in Thetford, as follows: 1. *Mary[6]*, born May 2, 1782; died Feb. 6, 1790. 2. *Josiah[6]*, born Aug. 13, 1784. 3. *Anna[6]*, born Feb. 6, 1786; died Feb. 7, 1786. 4. *Orange[6]*, born April 9, 1787. 5. *Anna[6]*, born Feb. 16, 1789.

116

REV. JOHN HOVEY[4], born in Malden, Mass., Feb. —, 1700-1. He lived in Mansfield, Conn., where he was the owner of considerable land. For fifty-five pounds, he sold to Robert Arnold of Mansfield forty acres of land in Mansfield, which his father gave him by deed, June 26, 1724;[*] and, for fifty-four pounds, he bought of Edmund Hovey of Mansfield one hundred and five acres of land in Mansfield (acknowledged Jan. 13, 1725-6).[†] He bought of Edmund Hovey of Mansfield, carpenter, for two pounds and thirteen shillings, one and one-half acres of land in Mansfield Dec. 10. 1731.[‡]

The following is the autograph of Mr. Hovey, taken from his signature to a report upon his father's estate, in 1760:

John Hovey

The people in Woodstock invited Mr. Hovey to become their pastor in 1726, but he declined to do so. He and others withdrew from the church in Windham, and united with the Baptist church in Mansfield in 1745. Of this church he was elected teaching elder, and was ordained in February, 1746.

Mr. Hovey married, first, Mary, daughter of Ebenezer and Mary (Scott) Nash Nov. 18, 1730. She was born Oct. 29, 1704; and died in Mansfield Oct. 3, 1746. He married, second, Rebecca, daughter of Capt. William and Esther Hall of Mansfield

---

* Mansfield Registry of Deeds, book 2, page 372.
† Mansfield Registry of Deeds, book 2, page 454.
‡ Mansfield Registry of Deeds, book 3, page 387.

Jan. 19, 1748-9. She was born in Mansfield Feb. 10, 1716. Mr. Hovey died in 1775, at the age of seventy-four.

Mr. Hovey left a will, of which the following is a copy, taken from the probate records at Willimantic, Conn. :—

In the Name of God, Amen. The 23rd day of November Anno Dom: 1763. I John Hovey of Mansfield in the County of Windham & Colony of Connecticut in New England, being Infirm in Body but of Sound and disposing mind & Memory, Thanks be given to God therefor, calling to mind the Mortality of my Body & knowing that it is appointed for all Men Once to Die, do make and ordain this my Last Will & Testament, That is to Say, Principally and first of All I Give and Recommend my Soul to the Hand of God that gave it Hoping through the Merits Death & Passion of my Lord & Saviour Jesus Christ to have full & free pardon & forgivness of all my Sins & Inherit Everlasting Life and my Body I Commit to the Earth to be Decently Burried at the Discretion of my Executrix herein after named Nothing Doubting but at the General Ressurection I Shall receive the same again by the Mighty Power of God and as toutching Such Worldy Estate wherewith it hath pleased God to Bless me in this Life, Demise & Dispose of the Same in the following manner & form (viz)

First, I will that all those Debts & Duties as I do Owe in Right or Conscience to any Manner of Person or Persons Whatsoever, Only Excepting the Debt Due from me to my honored father in law William Hall of sd Mansfield be well and Truely Contented & paid or Ordained to be paid by my Executrix herin after named in Convenient Time after my Deceafe.

Item I Give & Bequeath unto my dearly beloued Wife Rebeckah (out of which I Will & Ordain, that She my sd Wife pay unto my sd Father in law ye whole of the Monies which I Owe unto Him & perform my Obligation for the support of my Father & Mother Hall if Living untill the month of October which will be in the Year of Our Lord 1774 and to enable my sd wife to bring up & suitable Educate my Children and the remainder to be to her in Lieu of Dower) the use improvement & whole profits of the farm which I have by Deed from my sd Father Hall untill the sd month of October A. D. 1774.

Also I Give & Bequeath unto my sd wife for her own disposal Five Cows, one Yoak of Oxen, my Riding Beast & Womens Riding Furniture, Twenty Sheep and all my cut Door Movables & Farming Utensils, also all my Household Stuff or Indoor Movables, only excepting my Writing Desk.

Also I give my sd Wife Twenty Pounds in Lawful Money and also I Give to my sd Wife the Use & Improvement of one third part of my sd farm from & after sd Term of October 1774, if she be then a widow in my name & so long as she shall continue to be my widow.

Item. I Give and Bequeath unto my well beloved son Johnathan Hovey to be & to remain unto him his Heirs & Assigns forever all & the whole of the sd Farm of Land Bought or Held by Deed from my Father in Law Hall as aforesd & also my writing Desk be from and after his coming to the age of twenty & one years which will be in the month of October 1774, fulfilling & performing My Obligations to my sd Father in Law & Mother in Law William & Esther Hall if then surviving, at which time, to wit on my sd sons arrival to the aforesd age of twenty & one Years. I Will that he Shall come into the Possession of Two third parts of sd Land & Buildings thereon and that he Come into the Possession of the other third part of sd Land & Buildings upon the marriage or deceas of my sd Wife whichsoever shall first happen only upon the Condition before expressed

Item. I Will as I have before the date of this Will advanced unto my well beloved Daughter Lowis to the amount of Forty pounds Lawfl money in Part of her Portion that before any further Dividend be made to and among the whole of my four Daughters there be by my Executrix of my estate set & divided unto my three well beloved Daughters to wit Deborah, Esther & Lydia the amount of the several sums following, to Deborah the amount of forty pounds lawfl money to be to her & her heirs forever. To Esther the amount of forty pounds lawfl money to be to her & her heirs forever and to Lydia the amount of Fifty pounds lawfl money to be to her & her heirs forever which advanced sum Bequeathed to Lydia is in Compassion for the Disability of her Right Hand; and I further Will & Bequeath all the Residue & Remainder of my Estate both Real & Personal of what nature or kind soever (after the Setting out of the aforesd legacies to my aforesd three Daughters & which is not otherwise in this Will before Bequeathed & Disposed of) unto my four well beloved Daughters, to wit Lowis, Deborah, Esther & Lydia, to be by my Executrix in equal parts Divided & Set out to them in Severalty to be and remain to them & their Heirs in Severalty forever, and my further Will is that if any or Either of my aforesd children Should Die before they arrive at the age of Twenty one Years & before they have Received or come into Possession of their Several & Respective Legacy or Legacies that would have come to such Dec'd. Child or Children, Shall by my Executrix be equally Divided to and among the Surviving Children and their Legal Representatives.

Finally, I Will, Constitute Ordain and make my sd wife Rebeckah Hovey my only and Sole Executrix of this my Last Will and Testament, and I Do hereby Utterly Disallow Revoke and Disannull all and every other former Wills Legacies Bequests and Executors by me before this time named, Willed or Bequeathed, Ratifying & Confirming this & no other to be my last Will & Testament.

In Witness Whereof, I have Hereunto Set my hand and Affixed my Seal the day and Year first before Written.

Signed, Sealed, Published,
Pronounced & Declared by the
sd   John   Hovey   as   his
Last   Will   &   Testament
in   ye   presence   of   us
Witnesses.
 RUTH CONANT   JOHN HOVEY [SEAL]
 RUTH CONANT, JUN.
 SARAH CONANT.

The will was proved Nov. 30, 1775. His estate was appraised at £1,135, 11s., 1d., of which £628, 19s., 7d., represented real estate, and £506, 11s., 6d., personal estate. His wife Rebecca survived him.

The children of Mr. Hovey were born in Mansfield, as follows:—

302—7. JOHN⁴, born Aug. 8, 1732; died Jan. 2, 1733-4.
303—11. LOIS⁵, born July 13, 1736; married Elijah, son of Francis and Ann Fenton of Willington, Conn., June 3, 1761. He was born in Willington Feb. 6, 1735-6; and died Oct. 10, 1776. She survived him. Children: 1. *Elijah*⁵, born March 9, 1762; lived in Willington; married Polly Storrs Jan. 18, 1777; and had five children. 2. *John*⁵, born July 8, 1763; lived in Willington; married Lucy Eldredge Dec. 1, 1785; he

died Dec. 13, 1807; she died May 28, 1850; and they had eight children. 3. *Lois⁵*, born Oct. 4, 1764. 4. *Roger⁵*, born May 2, 1766; married Sarah Hanks April 10, 1791. 5. *Ashbel⁵*, born Nov. 17, 1771.

304—III. JOHN⁴, born March 18, 1740-1; died Feb. 3, 1762, aged twenty.

305—IV. DEBORAH⁴, born Dec. 8, 1749; married Isaac Sargent Palmer Nov. 23, 1775. Children, born in Mansfield: 1. *Joshua⁵*, born Dec. 9, 1778. 2. *Aaron⁵*, born Aug. 25, 1780. 3. *Lydia⁵*, born June 17, 1783.

306—V. ESTHER⁴, born Oct. 14, 1751; living in 1776.

307—VI. JONATHAN⁴, born Oct. 10 (5?), 1753. *See family numbered "307."*

308—VII. LYDIA⁴, born Feb. 1 (5?), 1756; her father gave her in his will a legacy "in Compassion for the Disability of her Right Hand."

118

DEA. JOSEPH HOVEY⁴, born in Malden Feb. 6, 1704-5. He was a husbandman, and lived in Mansfield, Conn., where he was a deacon of the Baptist church for many years. For thirty pounds, he conveyed to Stephen Cross of Mansfield thirty acres of land in Mansfield Feb. 6, 1728-9.* He bought of his brother Edmund Hovey of Mansfield, carpenter, ten acres of land in Mansfield March 7, 1728-9;† and sold to him nineteen acres and twenty-five rods of land in Mansfield, northerly of Edmund's home, March 17, 1728-9.‡ He conveyed to Shubael Dimmick of Mansfield, for other land, eighty-two acres of land in Mansfield Nov. 29, 1732.§

Deacon Hovey married, first, Ruth, daughter of Nehemiah Closson of Lebanon Dec. —, 1731; and she died Dec. —, 1735. He married, second, Thankful ——— before 1739; and died Oct. 28, 1785, at the age of eighty. His remains lie buried in the Gurley burial ground in the northwest part of Mansfield, and the gravestone above them bears the following inscription: "In memory of Mr Joseph Hovey who died Oct[r] ye 28th A. D. 1785 In the 81st year of his age. Who was a Deacon of a Baptist Church for a number of years; & died in full belief of those Principles."

Mr. Hovey's will, dated Dec. 4, 1784, was proved Nov. 18, 1785. He lived in Windham the last two years of his life. His wife Thankful survived him, and died, his widow, May 13, 1791, at the age of eighty-eight. The gravestone over her remains, also in the Gurley burial place, bears the following inscription: "In memory of Mrs. Thankful wife of Deac[n] Joseph Hovey who died May 13th 1791 In Ye 89th year of her age."

---

* Mansfield Registry of Deeds, book 3, page 120.
† Mansfield Registry of Deeds, book 3, page 128.
‡ Mansfield Registry of Deeds, book 3, page 166.
§ Mansfield Registry of Deeds, book 3, page 320.

Mr. Hovey's children were born in Mansfield, as follows:—

309—I.   —— (son)⁵, born April —, 1733; died April —, 1733.
310—II.   JOSEPH⁵, born Sept. 9, 1734. *See family numbered "310."*
311—III. RUTH⁵, born May 28, 1739; died before 1791.
312—IV.   JACOB⁵, born Aug. 10, 1740. *See family numbered "312."*
313—V.   EUNICE⁵, born Dec. 24, 1742; married Seth, son of Seth and
          Judah (Paulk) Dunham of Mansfield May 31, 1764; he was
          born July 4, 1741; she died Feb. 28, 1789, aged forty-six; and
          he was living in 1791. Children, born in Mansfield: 1.
          Jacob⁶, born Jan. 6, 1765. 2. *Ruth⁶*, born March 24, 1766;
          married Simeon Allen of Mansfield. 3. *Eunice⁶*, born May
          12, 1768; and died unmarried. 4. *Enos⁶*, born April 6, 1770;
          died in Salisbury in 1792. 5. *Sarah⁶*, born Aug. 1, 1772; mar-
          ried Roswell Griggs of Tolland. 6. *Seth⁶*, born May 15,
          1774. 7. *Thankful⁶*, born April 15, 1776; married Zacheus
          Waldo. 8. *Marcia⁶*, born July 27, 1778; married Ambrose
          Hilliard. 9. *Cephas⁶*, born Feb. 12, 1781; married Polly
          Brigham. 10. *Ebenezer⁶*, born July 7, 1783. 11. *Elijah⁶*,
          born June 1, 1785; married. 12. *Mary⁶*, born Jan. 20, 1789.

119

THOMAS HOVEY⁴, born in Malden, Mass., Feb. 1, 1706-7. He
lived in Mansfield, Conn.; and conveyed to Mrs. Sarah Hobart
of Mansfield, for one hundred pounds, one hundred and thirty-
five acres and twenty-three rods of land Jan. 21, 1733-4.* May
26, 1735, he conveyed to Daniel Hovey of Mansfield, for two
hundred and thirty pounds, seventy acres of land in Mansfield;†
and on the same day, for five hundred and thirty pounds, he sold
to Jonathan Curtis of Lebanon three hundred and four acres of
land in Mansfield.‡

Mr. Hovey married, first, Abigail, daughter of Benjamin
and Deborah (Temple) Phelps Nov. 11, 1736. She was born in
Mansfield May 13, 1716. With her husband and other heirs of
her uncle John Temple of Concord, Mass., she released to John
Tullar of Mansfield, Conn., her interest in her said uncle's estate
Sept. 1, 1740.§ Mrs. Hovey died in Mansfield Feb. 22, 1741, at
the age of twenty-four; and he married, second, Abigail, daughter
of Jedidiah Phelps of Lebanon Oct. 22, 1741. He died in Mansfield Sept. 9, 1749, at the age of forty-two. Mr. Hovey left no
will, and his administrators charged in their account for the
maintenance of "old mʳ Hovey," who was probably his father,
James Hovey, who died in 1760, at the age of eighty-six.

Thomas Hovey's estate was appraised at £2,918, 6s., 8d.; real
estate, £2,350; and personal estate, £568, 6s., 8d.

* Mansfield Registry of Deeds, book 3, page 455.
† Mansfield Registry of Deeds, book 3, page 576.
‡ Mansfield Registry of Deeds, book 3, page 579.
§ Middlesex Registry of Deeds, book 44, page 374.

Mrs. Hovey survived him, and, having removed to Lebanon, married, secondly, Jabez Barrows of Mansfield May 15, 1771.

Mr. Hovey's children were born in Mansfield, as follows:—

314—I.   THOMAS[5], born Aug. 17, 1737; living in 1774.
315—II. ABIGAIL[5], born Jan. 30, 1738-9; died in Mansfield May 22, 1750, at the age of eleven.
316—III. NATHAN[5], born Dec. 22, 1740. *See family numbered "316."*
317—IV. ABEL[5], born Sept. 8, 1742; lived in Windham; and died before April —, 1774, when administration upon his estate was granted to Jonathan Clark of Lebanon. He was probably unmarried, as his brothers and sisters were named as his heirs.
318—V.   SETH[5], born June 6, 1744; living in 1774.
319—VI. JEMIMA[5], born April 20, 1747; married —— Clark before 1774.
320—VII. DEBORAH[5], born Feb. 10, 1749; died March 9, 1749.

121

DANIEL HOVEY[4], born in Malden, Mass., Dec. 7, 1710. He lived in Mansfield, Conn. His father gave him, by deed, fifty acres of land in Mansfield Feb. 16, 1732-3;* and he bought of Thomas Hovey of Mansfield, for two hundred and thirty pounds, seventy acres of land in Mansfield May 26, 1735.†

Mr. Hovey married Elizabeth, daughter of Lt. John and Elizabeth (Marble) Slap of Mansfield Dec. 6, 1732. She was born in Salem, Mass., April 25, 1714.

Their children were born in Mansfield, as follows:—

321—I.   ELIZABETH[5], born Nov. 1, 1734; married Nehemiah, son of Thomas and Abigail Wood March 5, 1752. He was born in Mansfield Jan. 16, 1727. Children, born in Mansfield: 1. *Ephraim[6]*, born Dec. 15, 1752. 2. *Desire[6]*, born Nov. 7, 1754; died July 8, 1755. 3. *Elizabeth[6]*, born Feb. 19, 1756. 4. *Daniel[6]*, born Jan. 17, 1758.
322—II. DANIEL[5], born Sept. 8, 1736. *See family numbered "322."*
323—III. ENOCH[5], born Nov. 10, 1738. *See family numbered "323."*
324—IV. ANNE[5], born Dec. 21, 1740; married Timothy Bibbens Aug. 15, 1773.
325—V.   JOSIAH[5], born Aug. 24, 1743. *See family numbered "325."*
326—VI. HANNAH[5], born June 15, 1745.
327—VII. SIMEON[5], born Oct. 15, 1747. *See family numbered "327."*
328—VIII. MIRIAM[5], born April 5, 1750; married Josiah, son of Joseph and Abigail (Ward) Southworth Aug. 18, 1773; he was born in Mansfield Dec. 20, 1750; lived in Mansfield, where their children were born, as follows: 1. *Lora[6]*, born April 4, 1774. 2. *Royal[6]*, born April 6, 1776. 3. *Gurdon Bibbens[6]*, born March 14, 1779. 4. *Alvin[6]*, born June 26, 1781.
329—IX. MARBLE[5] (son), born Nov. 22, 1752; died Nov. 12, 1754.
330—X.   ALICE[5], born Dec. 15 (10?), 1754.

* Mansfield Registry of Deeds, book 3, page 420.
† Mansfield Registry of Deeds, book 3, page 576.

133

CAPT. SAMUEL HOVEY[4], born in Weymouth, Mass., Dec. 12. 1718. He was a yeoman, and lived in Weymouth. He married Elizabeth Colson Sept. 2, 1741. in Weymouth; and, for seventeen pounds, six shillings and eight pence, they conveyed to John Hollis of Braintree two acres of salt meadow on the north side of the river in Braintree June 6, 1760.* Mr. Hovey bought; a tract of cedar swamp in Weymouth Jan. 2, 1786.†

He died Feb. 9, 1796. at the age of seventy-seven. The following is a copy of his will, which is on file in the probate office at Dedham, Mass.:—

In the Name of God Amen the Eighth Day of April in the year of our Lord one thousand seven Hundred and Ninety three I Samuel Hovey of Weymouth in the County of Suffolk yeoman being of Perfect Mind and Memory thanks be given to God therefor. Calling to Mind the Mortality of my Body Do make and ordain this my Last Will and Testament that is to say Principally and first of all I give and recommend my soul into the hands of God that gave it and for my body I Recommend to the Earth to be buried in a Decent manner and as touching such worldly Estate wherewith it has pleased God to bless me with in this Life I Give Devise bequeath and Dispose of the same in the following manner and form

First I give and bequeath to my beloved Wife Elisabeth all the Household furniture that now Remains that she brought to me at marriage and one third part of my other Household furniture and two Cows at her own Disposal also the Improvement of one half of my Real Estate During her Natural Life.

Item I give and bequeath to my Daughter Sarah Blanchard to her Heirs and Asigns four pounds at the Decease of my Wife

Item I give and bequeath to my Daughter Elisabeth Agar to her Heirs and asigns four pounds at the Decease of my Wife.

Item I give and bequeath to my Daughter Cloe Atwood to her heirs and asigns four pounds at the Decease of my Wife

Item I give and bequeath to my Daughter Joanna Hovey one Feather bed with suitable furniture for the same also Eight pound to be paid her after the Decease of my Wife for her support if she should stand in need of it if not I give and bequeath it to my son Samuel

Item I give and bequeath to the Legal Heirs of my son Ebenezer Hovey Deceased four pounds at the Decease of my Wife to be Equally Divided between them I also Discharg the Estate of any Debt now Due to me

Item I give and bequeath to my son Samuel Hovey his Heirs and asigns all the Remainder of my Estate both Real and personal not before given away and I Do hereby make Constitute and appoint my son Samuel my only and sole Executor of this my Last Will and Testament and I Do hereby utterly Revoke and Disallow all and every other former Testaments Wills and Legases by me in any waife before this time Named Willed & bequeathed Ratifing this and no other to be my last Will and Testament in witness whereof I have hereunto set my hand and seal the Day and year above written

* Suffolk Registry of Deeds, book 104, page 113.
† Norfolk Registry of Deeds.

Signed Sealed Publiſhed Pronounced and Declared by the said Samuel Hovey as his Last Will and Teſtament in Preſence of us the ſubſcribers

NATHANIEL BAYLEY
JOSIAH BLANCHARD   SAMUEL HOVEY [SEAL]
BETSEY BAYLEY

The will was proved May 10, 1796.

Mrs. Elizabeth Hovey survived her husband, and died, his widow, March 4, 1798, at the age of seventy-five. The following is a copy of her will, which is on file in the probate office at Dedham :—

In the Name of God Amen   The Twenty fifth Day of February in the year of our Lord one thouſand Seven Hundred and Ninety Six I Eleſabeth Hovey of Weymouth in the County of Norfolk Widdow being Weak in body but of Perfect mind and memory thanks be given to God. Calling to mind the mortallity of my body Do make and ordain this my Last Will and Teſtament that is to say Principally and first of all I give and Recomend my soul into the hands of God who gave it and for my body I Recommend it to the Earth to be buried in a Chriſtian like and Decent manner at the Direction of my Executor and as touching such Worldly Eſtate as it hath pleaſed God to bleſs me in this Life with I give Deviſe and Diſpose of the same in the following manner and form

Imprimis   I give and bequeath to my four Daughters Namely Sarah Blanchard Eliſabeth Agar Cloe Atwood and Joanna Hovey to be Equally Divided betwen them all my wareing apperril.

Item.   I give and bequeath to my three grand Children Namely Sarah Hovey Samuel Hovey and Ebenezer Hovey Children of my son Ebenezer Hovey Deceaſed To Each of them fifty Cents

Item   I give and bequeath to my Daughter Joanna the Remainder of my Eſtate to her own Diſpoſal Except fifty cents here after given to my son Samuel Hovey

Item   I give and bequeath to my aforeſaid son Samuel Hovey fifty cents whome I alſo make and ordain my Only and Sole Executor of this my last Will and teſtament in Witneſs whereof I the said Eliſabeth Hovey have hereunto set my hand and seal the Day and Year above written.

Signed sealed pronounced and Publiſhed and Declared by the said Eliſabeth Hovey as her last Will and Teſtament in preſence of us the Subſcribers

VINSON SIWELL   her
FRANCIS LOUD   ELISABETH   X   HOVEY [SEAL]
NATH¹ BAYLEY   mark

The will was proved May 8, 1798.

Their children were born in Weymouth, as follows:—

331—I.   JOANNA[4], born Aug. 17, 1742; never married, but lived at home, where she died Dec. 25, 1798, at the age of fifty-six.

332—II.   EBENEZER[5], born July 24, 1744. *See family numbered "332."*

333—III. SARAH[5], born Jan. 19, 1746-7; married Nicholas Blanchard of
Weymouth March 6, 1765; he died Jan. 28, 1801, aged sixty-
five; she died Aug. 8, 1803, aged "fifty-eight;" children, born
in Weymouth: 1. *Nicholas*[6], born July 26, 1766. 2. *Sarah*[6],
born June 21, 1769. 3. *Chloe*[6], baptized April 17, 1774; died
young. 4. *Nicholas*[6], born about 1776; died Sept. 23, 1791,
aged fifteen. 5. *Noah*[6], born April 4, 1777; died Sept. 23,
1791, aged fourteen. 6. *Chloe*[6], baptized July 17, 1785; died
Oct. 27, 1802, aged eighteen.

334—IV. ELIZABETH[5], married Ebenezer, son of Richard and Susannah
(Colson) Agar (also, Eager) of Weymouth Oct. 26, 1769.
He was born in Weymouth Aug. 7, 1744. She was his wife
in 1796. Children, born in Weymouth: 1. *Betsey*[6], baptized
July 9, 1782; died young. 2. *Ebenezer*[6], baptized July 9, 1782.
3. *Joel*[6], baptized July 9, 1782. 4. *Nathaniel*[6], baptized July
9, 1782. 5. *Richard*[6], baptized July 9, 1782. 6. *Susa*[6], baptized July 9, 1782. 7. *Betsey*[6], baptized Aug. 29, 1784. 8.
Polly[6], baptized April 16, 1786.

335—V. CHLOE[5], born Sept. 4, 1753; married Zaccheus Atwood of
Bridgewater Dec. 3, 1772; and was his wife in 1796.

336—VI. SAMUEL[5], born Dec. 28, 1761; married Molly Kingman of Abington Feb. 13, 1783, in Weymouth. Probably removed to
Barre, Mass., in 1799. Yeoman.

135

REV. JOHN HOVEY[4], born in Cambridge, Mass., June 12, 1707.
He graduated at Harvard college in 1725; and taught school a
number of years in Cambridge. Mr. Hovey married, first,
Elizabeth, daughter of John Muzzey of Lexington, about 1727.
She was baptized in Lexington April 23, 1710; and died in Cambridge Dec. 17, 1729, at the age of nineteen. The following is
the inscription cut upon her gravestone in the ancient burial
place at Harvard square :—

> Here Lyes y[e] Body of
> M[rs] Elizabeth y[e] Wife
> of M[r] John Hovey, who
> When Aged 19 Years
> & 8 M[s] Bid Farewell to
> This World on y[e] 17th
> Day of Decem[br] 1729

He married, second, Susannah, daughter of Joseph Levett
of York, Me., in or before 1736.

He subsequently taught school in York; and also preached
to the people as early as 1736. A professorship at cambridge
was offered to him at this time, but he declined it, and continued
his work at York. He was ordained over the church at Arundel,
York county, in 1741; and was dismissed in 1768.

Mr. Hovey bought his mother's interest in the estate of his father Nov. 1, 1736,[*] and, on the same day, he bought of his brother Ebenezer, for seventy pounds, the latter's interest in the real estate of their father and their brother Thomas.[*] For one thousand pounds, he sold thirty acres of mowing, pasture and marsh land, lying on the south side of Charles river and north-westerly side of the county road, in Cambridge, Nov. 12, 1736.[†] For five hundred and eighty pounds, he conveyed to John Gay of Cambridge, yeoman, one fourth of land and buildings, bounded south and east on highways, Nov. 20, 1736.[‡] He bought the interest of his brother James in the estates of their father and brother Thomas Nov. 1, 1737.[§] For one thousand pounds, he conveyed land in Cambridge, on the northwest side of the road leading toward Roxbury, and on the southwest bank of Charles river, Nov. 29, 1740.[||]

Mr. Hovey's son James was a soldier in the French and Indian war in 1760, and, on his way home from Fort Pownall, was taken sick at Maquoit with the small pox. He was brought home and treated by Dr. Phineas Neven of Georgetown, Me. The doctor brought suit against Mr. Hovey for attendance and medicine, the amount of the claim being £6, 17s., 2d. The writ was dated Dec. 8, 1760. Mr. Hovey asked the province to pay the claim out of its treasury, which was done.[¶] For the particulars of James' sickness see his sketch (339).

Mr. Hovey was a man of ability, and beside his work of teaching and preaching nearly all the deeds and other legal papers of his time and region were drawn by him. He was an excellent penman, as well as grammarian.

In returning from a visit to Plymouth, in 1773, he came to Biddeford by water and lodged at the house of Col. Richworth Jordan. Having been in his chamber some time without extinguishing the light, some of the family entered his apartment and found him sitting in his chair, partly undressed, and lifeless, having been dead for some time.[**] His age was sixty-six. Administration upon his estate was granted Sept. 10, 1773. His wife Susanna survived him.

The children of Mr. Hovey were born as follows:—

337—i.　SUSANNAH[*], baptized Sept. 18, 1737, in Cambridge; married, first, Thomas Perkins, jr.; and, second, Edward Emerson.

* Middlesex Registry of Deeds, book 37, page 609.
† Middlesex Registry of Deeds, book 38, page 7.
‡ Middlesex Registry of Deeds, book 81, page 257.
§ Middlesex Registry of Deeds, book 38, page 429.
|| Middlesex Registry of Deeds, book 41, page 312.
¶ Massachusetts Archives, volume 44, papers 438-445.
** Bradbury's History of Kennebunk Port.

338—II.   JOHN², baptized Jan. 7, 1738-9; married, first, Mary Barter;
          and, second, Esther Smith. He was a mariner, and lived in
          Arundel in 1773.
339—III. JAMES², born in 1740, in Cambridge. *See family numbered
          "339."*
340—IV.   EBENEZER², baptized in 1743; married Eunice Wiswall.
341—V.   HANNAH², baptized in 1746; married, first, James, son of Ben-
          jamin and Rebecca (Furbish) Gould, as his second wife.
          He was born in Kittery, Me., June 5, 1730; and married,
          first, Elizabeth Nason. He lived in Arundel; and was a
          soldier in Sir William Pepperrell's regiment in 1757 and in
          the expedition to Canada the same year. He died in Bidde-
          ford in 1810; and his widow married, second, Col. Caleb
          Emery in 1812. James Gould had twenty children.
342—VI.   SARAH², baptized in 1748; married James Perkins.
343—VII. ABIEL², baptized in 1751; married Nathaniel Sargent of York.

139

 EBENEZER HOVEY⁴, born in Cambridge, Mass., July 12 ,1714.
He was a housewright, and lived in his native town until his
marriage, when he removed to Watertown, where he afterward
lived. Nov. 1, 1736, he conveyed to his brother John, for seventy
pounds, his interest in the estates of their father and brother
Thomas.*

Mr. Hovey married Mary, daughter of Dea. Joseph and
Mary (Monk) Mason of Watertown April 7, 1737. She was
born in Boston Oct. 23, 1711. He died in Watertown April 11,
1742, at the age of twenty-seven. She survived him, and married, secondly, Caleb Fuller of Newton Dec. 27, 1750. He was a
weaver, and lived in Newton.

Mr. Hovey's child was born as follows:—

344—I.   THOMAS⁵, born Aug. 14, 1740, in Newton. *See family numbered
         "344."*

142

CALEB HOVEY⁴, born in Cambridge, Mass., Dec. 21, 1717.
He was a husbandman, and lived in Newton.

Mr. Hovey, with widow Margaret Eliott of Newton, for
forty-two pounds and ten shillings, bought thirty acres of land in
Newton, on the north side of "the road that leadeth from the
lower Falls to Watertown Bridge," July 1, 1743.† For thirty-
two pounds, they conveyed eight and three-fourths acres of land

---

* Middlesex Registry of Deeds, book 37, page 600.
† Middlesex Registry of Deeds, book 50, page 120.
‡ Middlesex Registry of Deeds, book 50, page 659.

in Newton April 25, 1750.‡ He mortgaged land and buildings on the westerly side of the country road, in Newton, Jan. 3, 1753.* the mortgage being discharged Dec. 18, 1767. For thirty-one pounds and three shillings, he conveyed to Joshua Fuller of Newton, gentleman. fifteen and one-half acres of land in Newton Jan. 3, 1753.†

Mr. Hovey married Margaret, daughter of Ebenezer and Margaret Elliot of Newton June 2, 1739. She was born in Newton March 1, 1717-8.

The following is a copy of his signature to the bond he gave to the probate court as administrator of the estate of his father in 1745:

Mr. Hovey enlisted as a soldier in the French and Indian war in 1759. Before leaving home he wrote and executed the following paper:—

will of Caleb Hovey of Newton.

NEWTON, april y 13 1759

thif Being my Laft will and Defire jf I Should not Return I Do here By giue unto you my Wife the Improuement of my Eftate Dureing my widdow and jf you marry your thirds and that all my Children Should Share Eqail of my Eftate and Jofeph Emery with them   af witnefs my hand   CALEB HOUEY

EBENEZER ELIOTT
HENRY SEGER

Mr. Hovey died in the service, at Fort Cumberland, Oct. 12, 1759, at the age of forty-one. This instrument was proved as his last will Feb. 18, 1760, and his widow. Margaret Hovey, was appointed administratrix of his estate. He had a house, barn and eight acres of land. in Newton, valued at thirty-seven pounds; and his personal estate was appraised at nine pounds, sixteen shillings and nine pence, the whole estate being £46, 16s., 9d. It was represented insolvent Sept. 30, 1766.

For the maintenance of their mother, who was still living and their father's widow. her son Moses Hovey and daughter Experience and her husband Ebenezer Prentiss, all of Cambridge, conveyed to their brother Caleb their interest in their father's estate April 1, 1795.‡ Mrs. Margaret Hovey died on the fifteenth of that month, at the age of eighty-seven.

Their children were born in Newton as follows:—

* Middlesex Registry of Deeds, book 50, page 622.
† Middlesex Registry of Deeds, book 71, page 358.
‡ Middlesex Registry of Deeds, book 119, page 552.

345—I. ABIGAIL[2], born June 6, 1741; married Ebenezer, son of Ebenezer
and Sarah (Pierce) Prentice of Menotony (Charlestown)
Dec. 9, 1762. He was a farmer. She died; and he married,
secondly, her sister Experience, widow of Josiah Williams of
Cambridge. Mr. Prentice died at Menotony April 23, 1803, at
the age of sixty-seven; and his widow Experience died Sept.
22, 1816. Children: 1. ————[3], died in infancy in 1763.
2. ————[3], died in infancy in 1767.

346—II. EBENEZER[2], born May 12, 1743. *See family numbered "346."*
347—III. CALEB[2], born March 21, 1746. *See family numbered "347."*
348—IV. MOSES[2], born May 11, 1753. *See family numbered "348."*
349—V. EXPERIENCE[2], married, first, Josiah Williams of Cambridge Dec.
17, 1776; and, second, her sister Abigail's husband, Ebenezer
Prentice of Menotony, in Cambridge; and she died Sept. 22,
1816.

149

JOHN HOVEY[4], born in Malden, Mass., Oct. 23, 1730. He
lived in Malden, and married Rachel, daughter of Thomas and
Rachel (Danforth) Kidder of Billerica July 8, 1751. She was
born in Billerica May 22, 1732. Mr. Hovey was lost at sea before
Feb. 16, 1762, as his father states in his will. She survived him,
and married, secondly, William Adams of Boston Nov. 5, 1766.
Mr. and Mrs. Adams lived in Boston, where several children
were born to them.

The children of Mr. and Mrs. Hovey were as follows:—

350—I. RACHEL[5], married Andrew, son of Neil and Esther McIntire of
Boston Oct. 7, 1779; he was born in Boston June 20, 1760; lived
there, being a stevedore; was a soldier in the Revolution, serving as a sergeant in the company of Capt. Jonathan W. Edes
and regiment (artillery) of Col. Thomas Crafts in 1777; was
promoted to lieutenant; Col. Paul Revere being commander
of the regiment, which rendered service in defence of Boston
harbor; he died Dec. 7, 1797, at the age of thirty-seven; she
survived him, and was his widow in 1803; children: 1. *Andrew[6]*, born Nov. 16, 1780. 2. *John Hovey[6]*, born March 5,
1782. 3. *William[6]*, born June 3, 1784. 4. *Betsey[6]*, born May
18, 1787; married William Eastie. 5. *Sarah[6]*, born Nov. 3, 1789.
6. *Nancy Hovey[6]*, born July 31, 1796; married Amos, son of
John Lewis of Boston Dec. 14, 1823; he was a member of the
Volunteer Home Guards, who constructed the fortifications
about Boston harbor in the war of 1812-15; and became a sail-
maker in the navy; lived in Boston and at Somers Point,
Atlantic county, N. Y.; she died Dec. 6, 1851; they had seven
children.

351—II. ————[5].

154

NATHANIEL HOVEY[4], born in Windham, Conn., Oct. 23, 1717.
He was a blacksmith and lived in his native town, in that part
which is now Hampton. For one hundred pounds, he bought of
William Durkee, jr., of Windham one acre of land in Wind-

ham April 28, 1750;[*] and, also bought land there Sept. 30, 1756.[†] With another person, he bought of Thomas Hall of East Haddam one hundred and seventy-one acres of land April 11, 1760;[‡] and bought out the other's interest May 5, 1760.[§] He bought of Christopher Davison of Windham, for twenty-four pounds, one and one-half acres of land in Windham Dec. 6, 1760;[||] and other land there of John Clerk, jr., of Windham Dec. 18, 1760.[¶] With Ebenezer Hovey of Windham, he bought land there, for seventy pounds, of Nathaniel Ford of Windham Feb. 21, 1761;[**] and released his interest in the land and buildings to Ebenezer June 10, 1761.[††] For fifty-six pounds, he sold land in Windham to Thomas Stedman, jr., of Windham April —, 1761.[‡‡] For sixty-two pounds, he conveyed to Isaac Rings of Windham house and three acres and one hundred and eight rods of land in Windham May 18, 1762.[§§] For one hundred pounds, he sold to Ezekiel Armstrong of Windham fifty acres of land in Windham Jan. 28, 1765;[||||] and some land to Thomas Arnold, jr., of Smithfield, R. I., for one hundred and two pounds and twelve shillings, May 22, 1765.[¶¶] With others, he conveyed to Ebenezer Hovey of Windham, for two pounds, land in Windham Oct. 30, 1765.[***] For thirty shillings, he conveyed to Luke Hovey of Windham one acre and fifty rods of land in Windham Feb. 21, 1767.[†††] For ninety pounds, he bought of Thomas Arnold of Smithfield, R. I., land in Windham May 24, 1770.[‡‡‡] For four pounds, he bought lot 8 in the "burnt cedar swamp," containing five acres and one hundred and fifty-two rods, Feb. 5, 1781.[§§§]

Mr. Hovey married Ruth Parker Jan. 21, 1747-8; and died in 1784, at the age of sixty-seven. His estate was valued at £395, 10s., 7d., of which £303, 10s., was real estate and £92, 0s., 7d., was personal. She was his widow in 1788.

Their children were born in Windham, as follows:—

352—I. NATHANIEL[5], born June 14, 1749. *See family numbered "352."*

* Windham Registry of Deeds, book L, page 431.
† Windham Registry of Deeds, book L, page 103.
‡ Windham Registry of Deeds, book L, page 261.
§ Windham Registry of Deeds, book M, page 154.
|| Windham Registry of Deeds, book N, page 19.
¶ Windham Registry of Deeds, book N, page 27.
** Windham Registry of Deeds, book M, page 156.
†† Windham Registry of Deeds, book M, page 238.
‡‡ Windham Registry of Deeds, book N, page 268.
§§ Windham Registry of Deeds, book Q, page 78.
|||| Windham Registry of Deeds, book N, page 209.
¶¶ Windham Registry of Deeds, book N, page 225.
*** Windham Registry of Deeds, book N, page 252.
††† Windham Registry of Deeds, book N, page 322.
‡‡‡ Windham Registry of Deeds, book O, page 216.
§§§ Windham Registry of Deeds, book Q, page 344.

353—II.   JOHN⁴, born Jan. 9, 1750-1; lived in Windham in 1786; and was
            alive in 1788.
354—III.   EBENEZER⁴, born Oct. 1, 1752. *See family numbered "351."*
355—IV.   RUTH⁴, born Aug. 28, 1754; married Dea. Abiel Abbot Nov. 13.
            1777; lived in Windsor, Willington and Tolland, Conn., and
            settled in Hatley, Stanstead county, Province of Quebec,
            going thither with her brother Ebenezer Hovey, in 1793, and
            settling about a mile from him. They began life there in a
            log cabin, four miles north of the village of Massawippi,
            upon a beautiful farm near Lake Massawippi. They erected
            a frame house later, which, now remodeled, gives shelter to
            their great-grandson. Deacon Abbot died in Hatley in 1838.
            Children: 1. *Abiel⁵*, born Aug. 15, 1778, in East Windsor,
            Conn.; farmer; lived in Hatley; was a conscientious and
            reputable citizen; in religion a Universalist; married Grace,
            daughter of Paul and Abigail (Pierce) Hitchcock Dec. 11,
            1800, in Hatley; she was born in Monson, Mass., Jan. 27,
            1778; he died in Hatley March 6, 1841, at the age of eighty-
            six; and she died there May 21, 1867, aged eighty-nine.
            One of their nine children, Philip James⁵, married Caroline
            Hovey (1234). 2. *John⁵*, born May 27, 1781, in Willington,
            Conn. 3. *Colbe⁵*, born May 21, 1783, in Willington; married
            Ester Oliver May 4, 1802; farmer; lived in Magog, Province
            of Quebec; and died Feb. 11, 1866. 4. *Augustus⁵*, farmer;
            lived in Magog.
356—V.   PHINEAS⁴, born April 12, 1756; probably died before 1788,
            without issue.
357—VI.   MARY⁴, born July 28, 1758; died Sept. 8, 1762, in Windham.
358—VII.   JACOB⁴, born May 16, 1760; living in 1788.
359—VIII.   ABEL⁴, born Jan. 3, 1763; died in Windham March 9, 1771.

155

JOHN HOVEY⁴, born in Windham, Conn., Jan. 16, 1719-20.
He lived in his native town; and married Susannah Ashley Nov.
8, 1742. For two pounds, with others, he conveyed some land
in Windham to Ebenezer Hovey Oct. 30, 1765.* He was living
in 1788.

    Child, born in Windham:—
360—I.   ELIZABETH⁵, born Jan. 15, 1743-4.

157

EBENEZER HOVEY⁴, born in Windham, Conn., Feb 21, 1723-4.
He lived in Windham, and removed from the state after 17—.
He married Dorcas Dwight in 175-. For ninety-eight pounds,
he conveyed to Edward Brown of Windham one-fourth of an
acre of land there Dec. 26, 1749.† For two hundred and twenty-
five pounds, he conveyed to Bartholomew Flint of Windham
land near the new meeting house in Windham Sept. 30, 1751 :‡

        * Windham Registry of Deeds, book N, page 252.
        † Windham Registry of Deeds, book L, page 168.
        ‡ Windham Registry of Deeds, book K, page 27.

and, for three hundred pounds, he conveyed some land to Elijah Simons of Windham Dec. 30, 1751.* For fifteen hundred pounds, he bought of Benjamin Abbot of Windham land and buildings in Windham Feb. 23, 1756;† and, for five hundred pounds, some other land there of the same grantor, on the same day.‡ For ten pounds, he sold to Elias Frink, jr., of Windham land there April 23, 1756.§ He bought of Delight Warren of Preston, for fifty-seven pounds, land in Pomfret April 21, 1758.‖ He bought of Thomas Pool of Pomfret, for fifty pounds, sixteen acres and forty-three rods of land in Windham Feb. 14, 1761 ;¶ and, with Nathaniel Hovey, jr., for seventy pounds, he bought some land in Windham of Nathaniel Ford of Windham Feb. 21, 1761.** He bought the interest of Nathaniel Hovey, jr., in the land above named and the buildings thereon June 10, 1761.†† With another man, for seventy-five pounds, he bought of Christopher Davison of Ashford a house and some land in Windham April 13, 1765.‡‡ He bought of his brothers, for two pounds, some land in Windham Oct. 30, 1765.§§ He bought of widow Mary Cabot of Killingly, for seven pounds and ten shillings, one-half of a house and some land in Killingly March 10, 1767 ;‖‖ and of the estate of Ezekiel Armstrong of Norwich, deceased, for thirty-five pounds, land in Windham May 4, 1767.¶¶ For twelve pounds and ten shillings, he conveyed to Samuel Badger, jr., of Windham rights of his brothers in farm of widow Mary Abbe of Windham, deceased, March 20, 1778.***

Their children were born in Windham, as follows :—

361—I. SALLY⁴, born Aug. 1, 1756.
362—II. DARIUS⁴, born March 24, 1758.
363—III. PATTY⁴, born March 12, 1760.
364—IV. OLIVE⁴, born Nov. 30, 1761; married Andrew Robinson March 10, 1785, in Windham; and she died, his wife, March 15, 1812. Children, born in Windham: 1. *Abigenn⁵*, (son), born Dec. 25, 1785; died July 15, 1788. 2. *Ebenezer⁵*, born Feb. 21, 1788. 3. *Albigenn⁵* (son), born Oct. 12, 1789. 4. *Elisha⁵*, born Dec. 4, 1791. 5. *Pamelia⁵*, born Aug. 18, 1793. 6. *Darius⁵*, born July 15, 1795. 7. *Lucinda⁵*, born July 22, 1798.

---

* Windham Registry of Deeds, book K, page 58.
† Windham Registry of Deeds, book L, page 350.
‡ Windham Registry of Deeds, book L, page 351.
§ Windham Registry of Deeds, book L, page 43.
‖ Windham Registry of Deeds, book L, page 491.
¶ Windham Registry of Deeds, book M, page 138.
** Windham Registry of Deeds, book M, page 156.
†† Windham Registry of Deeds, book M, page 238.
‡‡ Windham Registry of Deeds, book N, page 272.
§§ Windham Registry of Deeds, book N, page 252.
‖‖ Windham Registry of Deeds, book N, page 387.
¶¶ Windham Registry of Deeds, book N, page 365.
*** Windham Registry of Deeds, book Q, page 205.

8. *Tryphena*, born Feb. 18, 1800. 9. *Dorcas Dwight*, born
Dec. 15, 1801.   10. *Urbane*, born Sept. 14, 1804.
365—v.   SIMEON, born Dec. 10, 1763.
366—vi.   ACHSAH, born Feb. 21. 1766.
367—vii.   ASA, born May 3, 1769. *See family numbered "367."*

160

LUKE HOVEY, born in Windham, Conn., Feb. 28, 1729-30.
He lived in his native town; and, with several brothers, for two
pounds, he released land to his brother Ebenezer Oct. 30, 1765.[*]
He bought of Nathaniel Hovey of Windham, for thirty shillings,
one acre and fifty rods of land in Windham Feb. 21, 1767.[†]
For three hundred pounds, he conveyed to his brother Jonathan
land in Windham and Pomfret his father devised to him, Feb.
29, 1772;[‡] and on the same day Jonathan conveyed to him, for
two hundred pounds, eighty-two acres of land that his father had
devised to Jonathan.[§] He bought of Stephen Heth of Windham,
for one hundred and fifty pounds, forty-nine and one-half acres
of land in Windham July 9, 1777.[‖] For four hundred and seventy pounds, he conveyed to Joshua Lothrop of Norwich eighty-
seven acres of land in Windham Oct. 28, 1786.[¶]

Mr. Hovey married, first, Thankful Antizele of Windham
Oct. 31, 1754; and she died there Dec. 11, 1756. He married,
second, Elizabeth Armstrong of Windham May 26, 1757.

His children were born in Windham, as follows:—

368—i.   SARAH, born Nov. 11, 1755.
369—ii.   JONATHAN, born April 12, 1758.
370—iii.   THANKFUL, born Jan. 15, 1760.
371—iv.   NATHAN, born Oct. 7, 1761.
372—v.   FREDERICK, born Dec. 14, 1763.
373—vi.   LOVICY, born May 18, 1767.
374—vii.   PRISCILLA, born Jan. 8, 1772.
375—viii.   ELIZABETH, born July 9, 1775.

162

JONATHAN HOVEY, born in Windham, Conn., Dec. 2, 1734.
He lived in his native town, in that part incorporated as Hampton in 1——. He conveyed, with his brother, to Ebenezer Hovey
of Windham land there, for two pounds, Oct. 30, 1765.[*] He
bought of his brother Luke, for three hundred pounds, land in
Windham and Pomfret, devised to Luke by his father, Feb. 29,
1772;[‡] and, on the same day, for two hundred pounds, sold to

----

* Windham Registry of Deeds, book N, page 252.
† Windham Registry of Deeds, book N, page 322.
‡ Windham Registry of Deeds, book O, page 332.
§ Windham Registry of Deeds, book O, page 365.
‖ Windham Registry of Deeds, book N, page 252.
¶ Windham Registry of Deeds, book S, page 354.

Luke eighty-two acres of land in Windham that his father had
devised to him.* He bought some land in Windham of David
Ripley of that town, for thirty pounds, Sept. 10, 1778.† For five
pounds and ten shillings, he bought of Josiah Linken, jr., of
Windham seven and one-half acres of land there Dec. 6, 1790.‡

Mr. Hovey married Eunice Woodward of Windham Dec.
31, 1761. She was born April 5, 1744; and died May 17, 1810, at
the age of sixty-six. He died in Hampton May 31, 1811, at
the age of seventy-six. Administration on his estate was granted
to his son Frederick Aug. 23, 1811.

Children, born in Windham:—

376—I.   JACOB⁵, born March 23, 1762; died Oct. 23, 1822, aged sixty.
377—II.   ZACHEUS⁵, born Feb. 4, 1764; living in 1812.
378—III.   ELIJAH⁵, born Oct. 13, 1765. *See family numbered "378."*
379—IV.   EUNICE⁵, born Sept. 14, 1767; married ———— Fuller; and
      died before 1812, leaving an only son: 1. *Samuel⁶.*
380—V.   ABIGAIL⁵, born April 21, 1769; married —— Works before 1812.
381—VI.   ALICE⁵, born June 2, 1771; married ———— Sikes before 1812.
382—VII.   ABEL⁵, born Aug. 4, 1773; died in 1837.
383—VIII.   OLIVE⁵, born July 4, 1775; married John, son of John and Mary
      (Phelps) Dewey Feb. 18, 1798, at Hampton, Conn. He was
      born in Suffield, Conn., Aug. 4, 1773; and was a farmer and
      miller, living in Suffield until 1817, when he removed to
      Manchester, N. Y. She died in Manchester May 17, 1820;
      and he died there March 26, 1863. Children, born in Suffield:
      1. *Olive⁶*, born Dec. 27, 1799; died Nov. 6, 1800. 2. *John⁶*,
      born Aug. 24, 1801; died Aug. 10, 1805. 3. *Hiram⁶*, born
      Jan. 13, 1803; lived in Royalton, N. Y.; married Harriet
      Compton Oct. 17, 1839; she was born June 12, 1816; he died
      near West Shelby, N. Y., Dec. 25, 1843; and she died at
      Medina, N. Y., Oct. 30, 1893, at the age of ninety. They had
      three children. 4. *Eunice Woodward⁶*, born May 20, 1804;
      married Mowry Aldrich May 20, 1827, at Manchester; and
      he died in 1849. They had eight children. 5. *William
      Wyllis⁶*, born March 17, 1808; removed to Royalton, N. Y.,
      and lived for two or three years with his brother Hiram, and
      then bought a farm three or four miles from Hiram's. He
      was a member of the Baptist church, a successful and re-
      spected business man. He married Amanda, daughter of
      James and Betsey (McLouth) Harland Feb. 6, 1831, at
      Farmington, N. Y.; she was born at Farmington Sept. 21,
      1807; and died at Royalton July 3, 1889, at the age of eighty-
      one. They had eleven children. 6. *Joseph Howard⁶*, born
      Oct. 4, 1810; lived in Manchester on the paternal homestead.
      He married Mary H. Arnold May 23, 1843, at Farmington.
      She was born there Feb. 22, 1814. He died at Manchester
      March 30, 1885, at the age of eighty-four. She was living
      in 1897. They had four children. 7. *George Gordon⁶*, born
      Nov. 2, 1813; married Esther Swett; and died Sept. –,
      1841. They had one child.

* Windham Registry of Deeds, book O, page 365.
† Windham Registry of Deeds, book Q, page 258.
‡ Windham Registry of Deeds, book S, page 192.

384—IX.   JONATHAN⁵, born Sept. 21, 1777. *See family numbered "384."*
385—X.   DARIUS⁵, born Aug. 20, 1779. *See family numbered "385."*
386—XI.   CLARISSA⁵, born Sept. 13, 1781; married John Fitch Parsons;
           lived in Suffield, Conn.; and died Nov. —, 1830. Child, born
           in Suffield: 1. *Ralph⁶*, born in 1807; lived in Granville, O.;
           merchant; a man of influence, and an educated, refined
           christian gentleman; successful in business, and generous
           with his sympathy and purse; married Laura Thustead Case
           in 1835, at Granville. She was born in East Hartford, Conn.,
           in 1816. He died at Granville in 1875, and she died there
           in 1892.
387—XII.   FREDERICK⁵, born May 29, 1783; lived at Hampton in 1812; and
           died Nov. —, 1830.
388—XIII. ALFRED⁵, born April 10, 1785; died Aug. 22, 1804.
389—XIV.   ELETHEA⁵, born March 31, 1787; died Aug. 4, 1791.

168

JOSEPH HOVEY⁴, baptized in Ipswich, Mass., Feb. 10, 1733.
He was a weaver and yeoman, and lived in Ipswich until the
spring of 1783, when he removed to Londonderry, N. H., and
about 1800 to Salem, N. H. On or before Feb. 24, 1783, for
forty pounds, he sold four and one-half acres of salt marsh at
Plum Island, which had belonged to his father, and one and one-
quarter acres of upland on Manning's neck;* and, Feb. 28, 1783,
for six pounds, he conveyed to Thomas Caldwell and another of
Ipswich, husbandmen, two acres of land at the West meadows
in Ipswich.† March 1, 1783, for twelve hundred and fifty dollars, he bought of Samuel Pilsbury of Londonderry, N. H., yeoman, fifty-six acres of land, in two lots, in Londonderry.‡ For
one hundred and twenty pounds, he conveyed to Ebenezer Lakeman of Ipswich, mariner, his messuage in Ipswich, and one-half
of a well owned with the heirs of one Pinder, May 7, 1783.§
For two thousand pounds, he conveyed to Parker Stevens of
Hampstead, yeoman, forty acres of land on Island pond, in
Londonderry, Jan. 1, 1785;|| and, for one hundred and twenty-
three pounds and six shillings, he also conveyed forty acres on
the same pond, in Londonderry, Oct. 14, 1788.¶ He bought of
Dudley Currier of Salem, N. H., yeoman, for fifty-three pounds
and nine shillings, three acres of land in Salem, N. H., and
fourteen acres in Atkinson, N. H., April 27, 1790;** and sold
the fourteen acres in Atkinson to Edward Parker of Salem, N.
H., yeoman, March 13, 1805.††

          * Essex Registry of Deeds, book 140, leaf 121.
          † Essex Registry of Deeds, book 181, leaf 60.
          ‡ Rockingham Registry of Deeds, book 120, page 28.
          § Essex Registry of Deeds, book 141, leaf 229.
          || Rockingham Registry of Deeds, book 120, page 29.
          ¶ Rockingham Registry of Deeds, book 125, page 183.
          ** Rockingham Registry of Deeds, book 120, page 106.
          †† Rockingham Registry of Deeds, book 188, page 135.

Mr. Hovey married Elizabeth Caldwell of Ipswich (published Dec. 3, 1757) ; and she was living in 1783. He was living in 1805. Their children were born in Ipswich, as follows :—

390—I. ELIZABETH⁶, baptized Sept. 7, 1760.
391—II. HANNAH⁶, baptized July 19, 1761 ; living in 1775.
392—III. JOSEPH⁶, born Dec. 17, 1762. *See family numbered "392."*
393—IV. NATHANIEL⁶, baptized April 17, 1768.
394—V. ————⁶, died Nov. 2, 1773.
395—VI. LYDIA⁶, baptized Aug. 28, 1774.
396—VII. SARAH⁶, baptized Sept. 1, 1776.
397—VIII. ————⁶, died Jan. —, 1778

175

MOSES HOVEY⁶, born in Sutton, Mass., Oct. 28, 1748. He was a husbandman, and lived in Sutton on his father's farm, which his father conveyed to him June 4, 1772.* It consisted of fifty acres of land and the buildings in the northwest part of the town. The transfer was made upon the consideration that Moses would support his parents and pay to his brothers Daniel and Benjamin and sisters Annah and Molly certain sums of money. This was secured by a bond of the same date.†

He was a soldier of the Revolution.

In 1794, engaging in business, tradition relates of Mr. Hovey, that he became involved in debt, and as inprisonment awaited him, he sped to New York state, having first deposited his clothing on the bank of Town's pond, in Oxford, to give the impression that he had drowned himself. Travelling westward he came, after a few days to a town of large size, where a public sale of wild lands in that state was in progress. Although he had not five dollars in his pocket, he made a bid on a large tract of land, and to his surprise it was struck off to him. He obtained a few hours' time in which to make payment, and obtained lodging at Foster's tavern there. In the night he was awakened by some men clamoring for admission. He was alarmed, supposing that some of his creditors were in hot pursuit, and hurriedly dressed himself. Just as he was about to leave the house, the landlord met him, and told him that two men had arrived at the tavern ; that they had intended to have been at the auction, but were detained ; and that they wished to see him to know if he would sell the lot he had bid off. He replied that he might be induced to sell, if he obtained a sufficient bonus for his bargain. In the morning, he sold the land to them (except a good farm, which he reserved for himself out of the tract) for several hundred dollars more than he had bid. This land was in the new township of

* Worcester Registry of Deeds, book 68, page 194.
† Worcester Registry of Deeds, book 69, page 81.

Unadilla, in Otsego county, and there he afterward lived. It is said that his house was the only one between Cooperstown and Oswego.

Mr. Hovey married Phebe, daughter of Daniel and Rebecca (Dickinson) Tenney of Sutton Aug. 14, 1777. She was born April 22, 1759; and died April 25, 1813 (1810?). He died Oct. 29, 1813, aged sixty-five.

Their children were born as follows:—

398—I.   DANIEL⁶, born Oct. 29, 1778, in Sutton. *See family numbered "398."*

399—II. POLLY⁶, born Aug. 19, 1780, in Sutton.

400—III. REBECCA⁶ born Dec. 9, 1783, in Sutton.

401—IV. JOHN TYLER⁶, born Nov. 16, 1785, in Sutton; died Nov. 26, 1813, at the age of twenty-eight.

402—V.   EBENEZER B———⁶, born July 15, 1789, in Sutton; died Sept. —, 1826, aged thirty-seven.

403—VI. BENJAMIN⁶, born June 20, 1793, in Sutton. *See family numbered "403."*

404—VII. SIMON⁶, born July 19, 1795, in Unadilla. *See family numbered "404."*

405—VIII. WILLIAM⁶, born July 26, 1798, in Unadilla. *See family numbered "405."*

406—IX. RUTH⁶ born Dec. 18, 1800, at Unadilla; married Horace, son of Samuel and Hannah (Waters) Waters of Sutton (published Sept. 9, 1827); he was born in Sutton Aug. 28, 1799; and she died Feb. 8, 1878, aged seventy-seven. Their children were born in Sutton, as follows: 1. *Charles H.⁷*, born July 31, 1828; married Mary Farnsworth of Groton; and lived in Clinton, being a wire weaver. 2. *Cornelia⁷*, born June 14, 1833; married Royal Thayer. 3. *Osgood Herrick⁷*, born Oct. 13, 1836; married Ellen Crane. 4. *Horace Hovey⁷*, born Nov. 9, 1841; lived in Chicago.

179

GEN. BENJAMIN HOVEY⁵, born in Sutton, Mass., March 12, 1758. At the age of seventeen, he responded to the alarm of Lexington April 19, 1775, and served eighteen days. He was also in the company of Capt. Bartholomew Woodbury, in regiment of Colonel Learned, marching from home Dec. 9, 1775. He was also forty-three days in the company of Capt. Jeremiah Kingsbury, in Col. Jonathan Holman's regiment, at Providence, the roll being dated Jan. 20, 1777. He was also useful in procuring beef for the soldiers in the Revolution in 1781.

From 1782 to 1787, he was a deputy sheriff for Worcester county; and in the latter year he was conspicuous in quelling Shay's Rebellion.

Mr. Hovey owned an estate in Oxford; buying first the farm subsequently owned by George W. Gibson, and later the Doctor Learned place at North Oxford. He sold the latter estate in 1785.

In 1785, he was one of the signers of the compact for the formation of the Universalist society in Oxford.

A little before 1790, he removed to central New York, being among the pioneers of Chenango county. He was the first settler of the town to which he subsequently gave the name of Oxford, his old Massachusetts home. He cut the first tree to clear the ground where the village was built. He had purchased the land before he went there, and then started for New York, to lay his plans for the new settlement before the proprietors. He conducted the building of the village, and became the leading man of the region. He was a man of strong common sense and vigor of action and other personal qualities necessary for the arduous labors and hardships of pioneer life; but necessarily of limited education. He built his own log house, in 1790, on the site of Fort hill, so called from an old Indian fort, which overlooked the river. To this dwelling, he removed his family from Massachusetts the following year. The town was incorporated Jan. 19, 1793.

A grand-daughter, living at Syracuse, N. Y., wrote: "They chose with taste, as the Chenango river passes through the town. Grandfather's log hut was directly on its banks. There they fought the Indians, went forty miles to mill in a canoe and to Onondaga county for salt, and had a pioneer life, but men were men in those days, true to their time and men."

The first frame building erected in the town was the academy, an institution organized by Mr. Hovey in 1794, being the third in the state. Mr. Hovey's name headed the list of trustees, and he was their president as long as he remained there, about ten years. The academy held a festival Aug. 2, 1854, at which an address was delivered by W. H. Hyde, esq., from which the following paragraphs are quoted:—

"The shades of evening are gathering; what a sea of georgeousness on the autumn forest! We hear the light dip of paddles in the river and a canoe darts toward the landing on the shore. What strange beings are these? They seem regardless of the ruin that is gradually gathering over the race. Can it be that they do not think of the oncoming destruction that awaits them, while they see the little academy on the Common, the occasional dwelling, and hear the woodman's axe, whose strokes for them 'Like muffled drums are beating funeral marches to the grave?' That tall man with whom they are talking, bartering with at the loghouse, is Benjamin Hovey, the senior trustee of the academy. . . . Few men have passed a more eventful life. Having seen the fruition of his labors, and the harvest of his early toil and suffering, in the flourishing village around him, rapidly increasing in population and wealth, he looked for new projects with an ambition fed by its own innate energy and a spirit of enterprise faltering at no point beyond which were seen new fields open for its gratification."[*]

* History of Oxford, Mass., page 547.

Mr. Hovey was general of the militia, and judge of Chenango county. He took the contract for constructing the state road from Unadilla river, at what is now Rockdale to Cayuga lake, near Ithaca.

He was a member of the legislature of New York at the same time that Aaron Burr was a representative, and the two men became great personal friends. He joined Burr and General Wilkinson, in 1804, in a plan for canalling the Ohio river near Louisville, and went to Ohio in prosecution of the design. The restless ambition of Burr, however, led him to seek new objects on the lower Mississippi and amid the untold wealth and romance of Mexico, and the Ohio scheme, in which Mr. Hovey had embarked with ardor and had spent much of his property, was allowed to lapse. As Mr. Hyde stated, in his address, above mentioned, Mr. Hovey "retired at length in disgust . . . to find a grave on the shores of Lake Erie remote from the village he had founded and the friends of his manhood. A life of more romantic reality seldom occurs in the history of man."*

Mr. Hovey married Lydia, daughter of John and Susanna Haven of Sutton Oct. 24, 1775. She was born in Sutton June 8, 1755. No one knows the spot where Mr. Hovey was buried. She survived him, and died in March, 1827. G. N. Hartman, esq., Pomona, N. Y., has an oil painting of both Mr. Hovey and his daughter Alphena.

Their children were born as follows :—

407—I.   RUTH⁶, born Dec. 8, 1775, in Oxford; married Hon. Uri Tracy of Oxford, N. Y., Aug. 28, 1793. He was principal of the academy in Oxford for many years. He died ————; and she died, his widow, at Oxford, after a few hours' sickness, Jan. 30, 1847, at the age of seventy-one.

408—II.   ALPHENA⁶, born Jan. 22, 1778; married James Glover in 1795. Children: 1. *Katherine⁷;* married DeWitt C. Gage, a jurist of Michigan. Their son Henry T. Gage was governor of California in 1899. 2. *Justus S.⁷,* born in 1802; married Achsa Cornwall.

409—III.   NANCY⁶; married ———— Smith.
410—VI.   MARY⁶; married Nathaniel Locke.
411—V.   ALFRED⁶.
412—VI.   OTIS⁶.
413—VII.   SAMUEL⁶.

182

DEA. THOMAS HOVEY⁵, born in Ipswich, Mass., Oct. 1, 1736. After his father's death, when he was eleven years old, he was apprenticed to a man in Andover, where he attended school. He began to teach school in 1758, in Dracut, and two years later re-

* History of Oxford, Mass., page 547.

moved there with his wife and negro slave. He had force and good judgment, and was the leading man in Dracut in his time. He was often called upon to draw legal papers, and perform other duties requiring clerical knowledge. He took part in the French and Indian war as a lieutenant and his commission is in the possession of a descendant. He was commissioned captain to raise a company to march into Canada, was town treasurer and selectman during the Revolution, serving thirty years in all, and an active patriot. He was deacon of the church which worshipped in the old yellow meeting house in Dracut for fifty years. Many stories have been handed down showing his efficient work and amiable Christian spirit.

For twelve pounds and two shillings, he bought of Joseph Colburn of Dracut, husbandman, the frame of a house and twenty-seven rods of land in Dracut May 16, 1759.* He bought of Jonathan Jones of Dracut, husbandman, for twenty-six pounds, thirteen shillings and four pence, five acres of land in Dracut Nov. 9, 1764 ;† and of Elijah Hildreth of Dracut, gentleman, for fifty-six pounds, thirty-three acres in Blackbird swamp in Dracut June 20, 1766.‡ For seven pounds and four shillings, he conveyed to Jonathan Richardson of Dracut, gentleman, thirty acres of land on the north side of Merrimack river Aug. 21, 1765 ;§ and to Samuel Piper of Dracut, housewright, for four pounds and ten shillings, six acres of land in Dracut June 26, 1793.‖

Mr. Hovey married Mary, daughter of Lt. Henry and Mary (Platts) Abbott of Andover March 22, 1759. She was born in Andover Aug. 13, 1737 ; and died in Dracut Nov. 26, 1813, at the age of seventy-six. He died in Dracut July 29, 1826, aged eighty-nine. His grandsons, William, James, Horatio, Joshua, George and Cyrus, have placed a window in the church to his memory.

Their children were born in Dracut, as follows :—

414—I.   THOMAS⁴, born Jan. 15, 1762; died in Dracut Sept. 7, 1812, aged fifty.

415—II.   HENRY ABBOTT⁴, born Jan. 25, 1764. *See family numbered "415."*

416—III.   JOHN⁴, born March 24, 1765; died in Dracut March 4, 1782, aged sixteen.

417—IV.   JAMES PLATTS⁴, born July 21, 1767. *See family numbered "417."*

418—V.   MARY⁴, born Feb. 13, 1769; married Moses Whiting of Pelham, N. H., May 10, 1794; and died in Pelham in 1837.

419—VI.   ELIZABETH⁴, born Sept. 6, 1771; died in Dracut, unmarried, Dec. 6, 1845, aged seventy-four.

---

* Middlesex Registry of Deeds, book 69, page 456.
† Middlesex Registry of Deeds, book 69, page 457.
‡ Middlesex Registry of Deeds, book 69, page 458.
§ Middlesex Registry of Deeds, book 74, page 278.
‖ Middlesex Registry of Deeds, book 120, page 1.

420—VII.   SAMUEL[6], born Oct. 6, 1773.   *See family numbered "420."*
421—VIII. BENJAMIN[6], born May 9, 1775.   *See family numbered "421."*
422—IX.   JOSHUA[6], born Sept. 3, 1778; died in Dracut July 26, 1804.
423—X.   JOSEPH[6], born May 25, 1784.   *See family numbered "423."*

183

JOHN HOVEY[5], baptized in Ipswich, Mass., Oct. 14, 1739. He married Elizabeth Huse of Ipswich (published Oct. 3, 1761); and he died at sea in 1762, administration upon his estate being granted to his widow Nov. 22, 1762. His estate, which was all personal, was appraised at £10. 5s., 10d. She married, secondly, Nathaniel Perkins, jr., of Ipswich (published April 4, 1766).

Mr. Hovey's only child was

424—I.   HANNAH[6], baptized in Ipswich Dec. 5, 1762, having been born after her father's decease; married Nathaniel Fuller of Ipswich May —, 1781. He was a soldier of the Revolution, and died in Ipswich Dec. 29, 1842, at the age of eighty-two. Their son: I. *Nathaniel[7]*, born March 23, 1791, in Ipswich, was a captain; married Elizabeth Harris Oct. 2, 1820; and died at sea June 22, 1825, aged thirty-four.

189

ELDER SAMUEL HOVEY[5], born in Bradford, Mass., Feb. 24, 1742-3. He lived in Windham, Conn., until 1765, when he removed to Canterbury, Conn., where he lived until 1773. He was living in Weare, N. H., Jan. 31, 1777, when he conveyed lot 21, containing one hundred acres of land.* Later he settled in Lyme, N. H., upon Grant's island of sixty acres, in the Connecticut river. There were about thirty acres of fertile arable land, free from stones. He erected a comfortable dwelling house, barn and out-buildings, upon a slight bluff; and a canoe was kept fastened to the house or barn, as at times of high water the rest of the island was submerged. He was a soldier of the Revolution while living here; and continued his home on this island until about 1791, when the family removed to Norwich, Vt., and from thence, in 1794, to East Brookfield, Vt., where he remained during the remainder of his life.

Mr. Hovey and his wife were admitted to the church in Lyme, which was Presbyterian in its government, June 2, 1782; and he was chosen a ruling elder Nov. 11, 1784. He was not only a successful farmer, but preached the gospel, never taking anything for his ministerial labors in the way of compensation. After his settlement in East Brookfield, he was connected with the Baptists. Breadth seemed to mark their church relations. The record of dismissal of Mrs. Hovey from the church at Lyme is as follows:—

* Hillsboro Registry of Deeds, book 59, page 53.

Lime, Dec' 28, 1794, then Abigail Hovey, the wife of Samuel Hovey, by the consent of the Brethren was dismissed from this chh. to join any chh. of Christ which she might choose for her better edification.

Attest: Wm. Conant, Pas.

The record of Mr. Hovey's dismissal is as follows:—

Lime, April 13, 1795, then Samuel Hovey, a member of this chh. was recommended to the chh. of Christ in Brookfield.

Mr. Hovey married Abigail, daughter of Benjamin and Rachel (Hall) Cleveland of Canterbury, Conn., Sept. 29, 1763. She was born in Canterbury Aug. 13, 1746; and was remarkable for her truthfulness, patience and piety; a woman of amiable disposition, and a thrifty housewife. She had an intense love of music, and a voice remarkable for its sweetness, as well as for its sweetness, as well as for its power and compass. She watched over and nursed her aged parents in their old age most tenderly and untiringly. Mr. Hovey was naturally petulant, but became mild as he advanced in years; and in his old age his head was hoary. As a pastor, he had many admiring friends. Mrs. Hovey died at East Brookfield June 2, 1832, at the age of eighty-four. Her gravestone, standing over her remains in the burying ground on East hill, is inscribed as follows:—

Mrs. Abigail Hovey, wife of Elder Samuel Hovey, died June 2, 1832, aged 85 years and 10 mo.

Mr. Hovey died there May 12, 1833, at the age of ninety. He lies buried by the side of his wife, and his gravestone is inscribed as follows:—

Elder Samuel Hovey, Preacher of the Gospel, died May 12, 1833, aged 90 years and 2 mo.

In their old age and infirmities, they were tenderly cared for by their dutiful son Samuel Hovey.

Their children were born as follows:—

425—I.   DANIEL⁵, born July 24, 1764, in Windham, Conn. *See family numbered "425."*

426—II.   ABNER⁵, born Nov. 5, 1766, in Canterbury, Conn. *See family numbered "426."*

427—III.   MARY⁵, born May 26, 1768, in Canterbury; married Joseph, son of John and Ruth (Rogers) Lord of Lyme, N. H., Jan. 1, 1788; he was born in Vermont May 4, 1764; and removed to Ohio in 1806, dying near Jamestown, in that state, Aug. —, 1847. He was a farmer. She died in Germantown, O., April 10, 1859, at the age of ninety. Their children were as follows: 1. *Lucinda⁶*, born in 1789, in Windsor, Vt.; married William Fraser, a native of Scotland, in Green county, O.; and she died in Germantown in 1849. He also died

there. They had no children. 2. *Pamelia*[7] (twin), born
April 21, 1791, in Windsor; married John Crary, a native of
Vermont, about 1808, in Green county, O.; and she died in
1810. 3. *Mary*[7] (twin), born April 21, 1791, in Windsor;
married Josiah, son of David and Susannah (Craig) Bradbury of Warren county, O., in 1809; he was born in Essex
county, N. J., Dec. 9, 1785; she died in Wabash county, Ind.,
Aug. 15, 1871, aged eighty; and he died there June 20, 1872,
aged eighty-six. They had thirteen chi'dren, one of whom is
Rev. John Lord Bradbury of Grant county, Ind. 4. *Joseph
Tilden*[7], born April 14, 1793, in Windsor; married Maria.
daughter of William and Winnifred (Rector) Ross April
16, 1811, in Urbana, O.; she was born in Kentucky Jan. 13,
1793; he died in Cooper, Ill., July 21, 1845, aged fifty-two;
and she died there Oct. 17, 1852, aged fifty-nine. They had
nine children. 5. *John*[7] (twin), born Oct. 30, 1795, in
Windsor; married, first, Mary, daughter of Oliver and Jane
Bogart in Ohio Nov. 9, 1819; she died in Cincinnati, O., in
1828; he married, second, Verlinda, daughter of Richard and
Cynthia Ann Otwell in Danville, Ill., about 1832; and he
died in Ottawa, Ill., Oct. 20, 1860, aged sixty-four. He had
eight children. 6. *Alice*[7] (twin), born Oct. 30, 1795, in
Windsor; married, first, James Berryman in 1815; he died
in Cincinnati about 1819; she married, second, Samuel, son
of Adonijah and Abigail (Havens) Harrison Oct. 19, 1822,
in Cincinnati; he was born in Newark. N. J., July 20, 1791;
she died in Cincinnati Nov. 11, 1842; and he was living in
Elenor, O., in 1877. She had five children. 7. *Ruth*[7], born
July 25, 1797, in Windsor; married, first, Aaron, son of William and Mary Bennett in 1815; he was born near Richmond, Va., in 1793; he died in St. Louis, Mo., Nov. —, 1817;
she married, second, John Lewis, a native of Scotland, in
Cincinnati in 1819; he died in New Orleans, La., in 1821;
she married, third, Rev. William Fraser; she married,
fourth, Rev. John Kemp; she married, fifth, John Stout;
she died in Evansport, O., Oct. 31, 1873, having had two
children. 8. *David*[7] (twin), born Jan. 5, 1800. in Windsor;
died unmarried. 9. *Jonathan*[7] (twin), born Jan. 5, 1800. in
Windsor; married, first, Sarah, daughter of Alexander and
Sarah (McKibbin) Stewart Jan. 22. 1824. in Newtown, O.;
she died at Newtown about 1833; he married, second, Margaret, daughter of William and Nancy (Craig) Hatfield, and
widow of ———— Jones, Dec. 25, 1834; she was born in Virginia Nov. 13, 1802; he died in Newtown, O., in 1850; and
his widow Margaret died in Newtown Aug. 26, 1862, at the
age of fifty-nine. He had nine children. 10. *Abiel Hovey*[7],
born April 26, 1802. in Windsor; was a physician in Bellefontaine, O.; was three times elected treasurer of Logan
county; married Letitia, daughter of William and Elizabeth
(Boswell) McCloud May 27, 1824. in Bellefontaine; she was
born in Green county, O., Feb. 14. 1805; and she died in
Bellefontaine Aug. 22, 1875. Doctor Lord was living and
in active practice at Bellefontaine in 1879. They had four
children. 11. *Rhoda*[7], born in 1804; died in 1808. 12. *Rebecca*[7], born Jan. 10, 1807. in Hamilton county, O.; married
John, son of Rev. Josiah Hoskinson Sept. 20, 1827. in Cincinnati, O.; and she died at Portsmouth, O., Sept. 15, 1829.
aged twenty-two, having one child. 13. *Abigail*[7], born

April 30, 1811, in Hamilton county; married Protus, son of Joseph and Clara (Wyman) Hackenger Jan. 16, 1828, in Cincinnati; he was born in Baden, Germany, June 9, 1806; farmer; and they lived, in 1879, at Sedamsville, O. They had eleven children, all of whom were baptized into the Roman Catholic church.

428—iv.   RUFUS CLEVELAND[6], born Aug. 29, 1770, in Canterbury. *See family numbered "428."*

429—v.   REBECCA[6], born Sept. 6, 1772, in Canterbury; married James, son of James and Sarah (Powers) Sanderson Dec. 25, 1794, in Lyme, N. H.; he was born in Woodstock, Vt., June 6, 1772; removed to Huron county, O., in 1828; and died in Sherman (now Weaver's Corners), O., Sept. 2, 1828, aged fifty-six; she died in Newton county, Ind., Aug. 14, 1853, at the age of eighty. Their children were as follows: 1. *Lola[7]*, born Dec. 21, 1795, in Woodstock, Vt.; married Gurdon, son of Samuel and Prudence Lincoln Jan. 1, 1815, in Chelsea, Vt.; he was born in Windham, Vt., Jan. 25, 1787; and died in Madison, O., July 5, 1864; she died in Osakis, Minn., May 19, 1875. They had ten children. 2. *Electa[7]*, born July 16, 1797, in Woodstock; married Joshua, son of Daniel and Edith (Bakeman) Luce Dec. 26, 1822, in Williamstown, Vt.; he was born in Williamstown Dec. 7, 1796; and died in Lower Sandusky (now Fremont), O., Feb. 10, 1842; farmer. She died there Oct. 3, 1846, aged forty-nine. They had six children. 3. *Melissa[7]*, born Feb. 21, 1799, in Brookfield, Vt.; and died, unmarried, at Waterville, O., July 23, 1854, at the age of fifty-five. 4. *Rebecca[7]*, born Oct. 11, 1800, in Brookfield; married Brigham, son of Robert and Rachel (Lovell) McCrillis Nov. 1, 1818, in Brookfield; he was born in Corinth, Vt., April 18, 1796; and died in Sherman, O., June 17, 1864; farmer. She survived him; and was living at Weaver's Corners, O., in 1878. They had ten children. 5. *Minerva[7]*, born Aug. 4, 1802, in Brookfield; married Jeremiah, son of Israel and Hannah (Brown) Arling Aug. 4, 1806, in Williamstown, Vt.; he was born at Portsmouth, N. H., April 15, 1805; and died in Columbia City, Ind., Sept. 1, 1878. She was living in Columbia City in 1878. They had ten children. 6. *James[7]*, born April 13, 1804, in Morristown, Vt.; married, first, Sally Ann, daughter of Thomas and Sally (Worthington) Miller Sept. 28, 1830, in Berlin, O.; she was born in Michigan Oct. 16, 1808; and died in Hunt's Corners, Huron county, O., April 29, 1841; he married, second, Almira, daughter of Richard and Lucinda (Spaulding) Pattee July 4, 1841, in Lyme, O.; she was born in Derby, Vt., Jan. 21, 1814; he was a farmer; and lived in Pilot Grove, Newton county, O. He had five children, all being by his first wife. 7. *Sarah[7]*, born Feb. 19, 1806, in Morristown; and died, unmarried, in 1828. 8. *Asenath[7]*, born Aug. 16, 1808, in Morristown; married, first, Capt. Harvey Horton, son of Jesse and Annie (Horton) Hollister May 24, 1829, in Vermillion, O.; he was born in Vermont March 17, 1806; he was a shoemaker by trade, but followed the lakes during the season of navigation, being at one time commander of the *Louisa Jenkins*; and died, of cholera, at his home in Vermillion, Aug. 20, 1834, after an illness of ten hours. She married, second, Rev. Oliver, son of James and Elizabeth (McAllister) Atwood July 5, 1835,

in Oxford, O.; he was born in Vermont in 1808; was a
Methodist minister; he removed, in July, 1837, to Iowa, to
make a home and preach in that section of the then far
west. In the latter part of August, 1838, he left home to be
gone four weeks, and not then returning the neighbors went
in search of him, as the last trace was of his return about
ten miles away, having stopped at a store to make some
purchases. His body was found, bearing the mark of toma-
hawk and scalping knife, and torn by beasts of prey. The
date of his death was Sept. 20, 1838. His widow returned
to Ohio; and married, third, her second husband's brother,
Hiram Atwood, Aug. 21, 1839, at Sherman, O. He was a
tailor; was born in New Hampshire Jan. 30, 1816; and
died, of cancer in the stomach, in Bradford, Mass., April 20,
1873. She lived in Portland, Me., in 1878, having had eight
children. 9. *Benjamin*[7], born July 30, 1810, in Morristown;
married Mary Rose, daughter of Thomas and Rebecca
(Rose) Clay Aug. 30, 1835, in Vermillion, O.; she was born
in Sparta, N. J., Dec. 19, 1816; and removed with her parents
to Ohio in 1834; he died in Camden, O., of typhoid fever,
June 8, 1851, aged forty; and she married, secondly, John
Bassett, and was living in Vermillion in 1878. Mr. Sanderson had seven children. 10. *Joel*[7], born Dec. 26, 1816, in
Brookfield, Vt.; farmer; lived in Lima, Ind.; married Mary
Ann, daughter of Thomas and Ann (Purchas) Legg Aug. 7,
1842, in Sherman, O.; she was born in Somersetshire, England, Aug. 11, 1816. They had eight children.

430—VI.   SAMUEL[6], born Oct. 20, 1774, in Lyme, N. H. *See family num-
           bered "430."*

431—VII.   ARIEL[6], born Oct. 30, 1776, in Lyme. *See family numbered
           "431."*

432—VIII. ALVAN[6], born March 3, 1779, in Lyme. *See family numbered
           "432."*

433—IX.   ABIGAIL[6], born Dec. 25, 1780, in Lyme; married Oliver, son of
           Roger and Sarah (Davison) Hibbard Jan. 1, 1805, in Brook-
           field, Vt. He was born in Lebanon, N. H., Sept. 27, 1780;
           and was a farmer, living on a small place in Brookfield in its
           pioneer settlement. Religious services were held in the
           schoolhouse; and at first they traveled on horseback,
           but as the children increased in number and size they went
           in a common farm-cart, drawn by a yoke of oxen. She was
           a large woman physically, quick and sensitive in her feelings,
           and resembled her father more than her mother in features
           and mental characteristics. She was a neat and diligent
           housekeeper. Mr. Hibbard died, of dropsy, in East Brook-
           field July 29, 1833, at the age of fifty-two. She survived
           him, and died there, of bilious typhus fever, his widow,
           Oct. 11, 1851, at the age of seventy. Their children were
           born in Brookfield, as follows: 1. *Polly*[7], born Oct. 13,
           1805; married William Caldwell Clark, adopted son of Ed-
           mund Clark, Nov. 7, 1826, in Brookfield. He was born in
           Barre, Mass., in 1803; and died in Manchester, N. H., Nov.
           —, 1859. She died in Philadelphia, Pa., at the residence of
           her son, Daniel W. Clark, Jan. —, 1869, at the age of sixty-
           three, having had five children. 2. *Amanda*[7], born Aug. 14,
           1807; married John Alden, son of Jesse and Elizabeth
           (Wills) Wright Jan. 28, 1828, in Brookfield. He was born
           in Chelsea, Vt., Aug. 14, 1804; was a farmer; and lived in

East Brookfield. They had three children. 3. *Oliver Davison[7]*, born Oct. 12, 1809; was a clergyman of the Presbyterian denomination; resided at Wyandotte, Mich.; married, first, Maria Cornelia, daughter of Caleb and Polly (Bradley) Curtiss Nov. 27, 1837, at Evans. N. Y.; she was born in Evans May 1, 1819; and died there Feb. 23, 1840, at the age of twenty; he married, second, Catherine, daughter of John and Sarah (McFall) Barr, and widow of Jeremiah Platt Jolls; she was born in Ireland April 25, 1810. Mr. Hibbard was chaplain of the Sixty-fourth New York regiment in the Civil war. He had two children. 4. *Lewis[7]*, born Sept. 10, 1811; died in 1811. 5. —————[7] (son), born Jan. 12, 1813; died in 1813. 6. —————[7] (son), born May 20, 1814; died in 1814. 7. *William Lewis[7]*, born Aug. 6, 1816; teacher, and subsequently engaged in commercial pursuits; married Harriet Atwood, daughter of Edward and Asenath (Corliss) Sprague Sept. 23, 1836, in Brookfield; she was born in Randolph, Vt., Jan. 24, 1818; and he died, of bilious typhus fever, at Montpelier, Vt., Sept. 20, 1851, at the age of thirty-five. She died in North Stratford, N. H., Feb. 16, 1861, aged forty-three. 8. *Abigail Cleveland[6]*, born Dec. 31, 1818; died Feb. 16, 1835, at the age of sixteen. 9. *Almira[5]*, born Jan. 13, 1821; married Amos, son of Jonathan and Nancy A. (Eaton) Emery March 7, 1843, in Brookfield. He was born in Chester, N. H., March 27, 1820; was a farmer; and lived in Chelsea, Vt., in 1878. She died in Brookfield Nov. 24, 1856, at the age of thirty-five, having had two children. 10. *Sarah Marinda[5]*, born Sept. 23, 1826; married, as his second wife, her sister Almira's husband, Amos Emery, Oct. 9, 1859, in Brookfield; she lived in Chelsea, Vt., and had two children.

434—x. ELIZABETH[4], born April 15, 1783, in Lyme. She went to school in Brookfield, Vt., in the little log schoolhouse, which was afterwards burned. When young, it was supposed that she would die of consumption, but she became well and strong, being tall and weighing, at the time of her marriage, one hundred and sixty. She had deep blue eyes, dark brown hair, full forehead, and was fair. She was a beautiful singer. She married, after an engagement of seven years, Gurdon Hibbard, brother of her sister Abigail's husband, Dec. 25, 1808, in Brookfield. He was born in Lebanon, N. H., July 12, 1782. By constant labor as a carpenter, his health was injuriously affected; and his physician pronounced him a hopeless consumptive. He took a journey to Saratoga Springs, N. Y., against the wishes of his family; but there his racking cough and violent night sweats disappeared. After his recovery, he bought fifty acres of land near her father's house, built a barn, and set out an orchard. He then married; and lived in a part of her father's house until he could build a house. Her furniture consisted of two tables, two chests of drawers, six kitchen chairs, rocking chair, two bedsteads, large wheel, linen wheel, quill wheel, reel and swifts, made by her father, a looking glass and some necessary crockery. She had devoted some years to sewing, being a fine needlewoman, and making men's clothing. This was a lucrative employment for young women at that time. She was thus able to furnish beds with bedding, sheets and pillow cases, as well as beautiful table cloths and towels of her own handiwork. Her wedding cloak was very long and of scarlet broadcloth, being trimmed with silk velvet ribbon, nearly three inches wide. Her bonnet was of black velvet, with very little trimming. By economy, they were enabled to add to their farm from time to time until it contained between two and three hundred acres, and to build two additional barns and a convenient farmhouse. Mr. Hibbard introduced the first Spanish merinoes into the town, having bought a pair of lambs, for one hundred dollars, of the consul from the United States to Spain. Two spinners were hired two or three months in the summer, and, some years as many as two hundred pounds of wool were manufactured into cloth, Mrs. Hibbard doing the weaving; the cloth, when dressed, compared favorably with imported broadcloth, and brought from a dollar and a half to two dollars a yard. These spinners worked in the room where she and her little daughter performed the household work; and while the work went on beautiful hymns were sung. As the girls grew to womanhood, they took the place of the hired laborers. Mrs. Hibbard, after one day's sickness, folded her tired hands, gently closed her eyes, and slept the eternal sleep. This was in Brookfield March 6, 1864, at the age of eighty. Her husband survived her, and was unconsoled in his loss of her companionship. He died in Brookfield Sept. 27, 1871, at the age of eighty-nine. Their children were born in Brookfield, as follows: 1. *Mary*[5], born Oct. 24, 1809; married Ezra, son of Joel and Lois (Perigo) Wills Dec. 23, 1828, in Brookfield; he was born in Tunbridge, Vt., Oct. 1, 1808; and she died in Tunbridge May 27, 1859, at the age of forty-nine. He was living there in 1878. They had nine children. 2. *Gurdon Plummer*[5], born April 27, 1811; farmer; lived in East Brookfield, Vt.; married Isabella, daughter of Jonathan Wilder and Sylvia (Hastings) Hemenway Jan. 1, 1839, in Chelsea, Vt.; she was born in Chelsea Aug. 21, 1814. They had five children, the eldest of whom, Edwin Smiley Hibbard, married Amy Phyletta Hovey (860) Aug. 4, 1864. 3. *Ruth Hovey*[5], born Jan. 26, 1813; married John, son of Edward and Asenath (Corliss) Sprague Nov. 5, 1837, in Brookfield; he was born in Randolph, Vt., April 6, 1815; was a farmer; and lived in East Brookfield, Vt. They had two children. 4. *Eliza Matilda*[5], born May 28, 1815; and lived in Brookfield. 5. *Sarah Davison*[5], born Oct. 4, 1817; married Joseph, son of Joseph and Weltha (Strong) Newell Feb. 11, 1841; he was born in Oxford, N. H., Aug. 9, 1811; farmer; and lived in Brookfield. They had seven children, one of whom, Everett Clifton Newell, married Ida Alelia, daughter of Mary Ann (Hovey) Bixby (   ). 6. *Fanny Burnham*[5], born Sept. 10, 1819; married Nathan, son of Nathan and Lydia (Wentworth) Davis Sept. 10, 1844; he was born in Boston, Mass., Nov. 23, 1819; and she died in Washington, N. J., May 23, 1872, aged fifty-two. They had five children. 7. *Elizabeth Perkins*[5], born Sept. 5, 1821; married Solomon, son of Solomon and Mary (Buckland) Stoddard April 25, 1847; he was born in Washington, Vt., Dec. 27, 1801; and died in Methuen, Mass., Aug. 13, 1874, aged seventy-two. She was living in Methuen in 1878. They had three children, all born in Brookfield.

435—XI.   JOHN FAIRFIELD⁶, born April 11, 1785, in Lyme. *See family
            numbered "435."*
436—XII. LUCY⁶, born March 7, 1787, in Lyme; died in 1788.
437—XIII. LUCY⁶, born Oct. 17, 1789, in Lyme; married Lucius, son of
            Zachariah and Alice (Bingham) Howes July 7, 1811, in
            Brookfield; he was born in Windham, Conn., May 3, 1790;
            and she died in Chelsea, Vt., Feb. 19, 1847. He was a
            farmer; and died in Lowell, Mass., April 6, 1872, aged
            eighty-one. Their children were born as follows: 1. *Abner
            Hovey⁷*, born Dec. 23, 1811; died April 3, 1813   2. *Abigail
            Rosella⁷*, born Sept. 15, 1814; married Worcester, son of
            Pelatiah and Sally (Cook) Bugbee Nov. 23, 1831, in Chelsea,
            Vt.; he was born in Chelsea Feb. 5, 1805; a carriage maker;
            and lived in Chelsea, Vt., and Lowell. Mass. They had two
            children. 3. *Caroline Matilda⁷*, born Jan. 26, 1817; married,
            first, Joseph, son of Joseph and Mary (Sherman) Moore
            May 18, 1839, in Lowell, Mass.; he was born in Wayland,
            Mass., Feb. 15, 1812; was an engineer; and died, childless,
            in Lowell, Nov. 11, 1876, aged sixty-four; she married, sec-
            ond, Auford Coburn June —, 1878, in Lowell. 4. *Nancy
            Amanda⁷*, born Nov. 13, 1819; married Ora Kimball, son of
            Amos and Eunice (Crane) Goodale March 10, 1843, in Low-
            ell; he was born in Stoddard, N. H., Dec. 20, 1814; and died
            in Medford, Mass., Jan. 14, 1871. She lived in Medford in
            1878. They had two children.   5. *Lucius Edson⁷*, born
            Sept. 30, 1823; married Emily Melissa, daughter of Isaac
            Hurd and Sarah (Bowers) French Jan. 22, 1843, in Swanton,
            Vt.; she was born in Swanton June 27, 1823. He was a
            painter, and lived in Maquoketa, Iowa. They had three
            children.

190

JACOB HOVEY⁵, born in Bradford, Mass., Nov. 10, 1745. He
lived in Windham, Conn., in the Twelfth school district; and
hired the schoolhouse site for the benefit of the school Nov. 5,
1799.*

He married Lucy Manning, in Windham, Oct. 30, 1773.
Their children were born in Windham, as follows:—

438—I.   JACOB⁶, born Feb. 13, 1774; died Sept. 30, 1775, aged one year.
439—II.   JACOB⁶, born Aug. 6, 1776.
440—III. LUCY⁶, born Jan. 27, 1779; married Shubael Hebard Sept. 23,
            1798, in Windham. Child, born in Windham: 1. *Frederick
            Hovey⁷*, born Nov. 29, 1799.
441—IV.   JERUSHA⁶, born Sept. 1, 1780; married Dyer Treadway Sept.
            28, 1800, in Windham. Child, born in Windham: 1. *Lucy
            Manning⁷*, born Aug. 11, 1801.
442—V.   LOIS⁶, born Jan. 23, 1785.
443—VI.   FREDERICK⁶, born May 1, 1788; and died Oct. 18, 1793, in Wind-
            ham, aged five.

196

DAVID HOVEY⁵, born in Windham, Conn., Aug. 5, 1757. He
lived in Windham, hiring, in 1811, the farm of Stephen Brown.

* Windham Registry of Deeds, book W. page 242.

Mr. Hovey married Anna, daughter of Jacob and Anna (Tracy) Robinson Aug. 28, 1783, in Windham.

Children, born in Windham:—

444—I.   DAVID[4], born March 19, 1784.
445—II. SAMUEL TRACY[4], born Aug. 6, 1800, in Scotland parish. *See family numbered "445."*

198

DUDLEY HOVEY[3], born in Windham, Conn., April 2, 1761. He was a hatter, and lived in Scotland Society in Windham. In the early part of the nineteenth century, with his son Benjamin, he was engaged in the manufacture of wool hats for men and boys; and their goods were sold for many years to White Brothers, in New York. At that time it took a sloop a week, sometimes, to go from Norwich to New York. That was before the days of steamboats.

Mr. Hovey bought of Seth Grosvenor of Pomfret and another, for one hundred and thirty pounds, two acres of land in Scotland Society, in Windham, Feb. 10, 1795.* He bought twelve acres more of land there in 1801: and, Dec. 23, 1818, he bought of Warner Hebard of Windham a house, a shop and some land in Scotland Society.

Mr. Hovey married Mary, daughter of David and Mary (Roath) Moore Oct. 8, 1795. She was born Jan. 25, 1764; and was married in Norwich. Mr. Hovey died in Windham Aug. 14, 1844, at the age of eighty-three. He died testate, and his estate was appraised at $13,959.47, his real estate being valued at $6,650, and personal at $7,309.47. His wife survived him, and died, his widow, in Windham, Dec. 21, 1846, aged eighty-two.

Their children were born in Windham, as follows:—

446—I.   BENJAMIN[4], born Dec. 14, 1796. *See family numbered "446."*
447—II. FANNY[4], born Jan. 6, 1799; married Mason Manning, M. D., of Stonington, Conn., Nov. 20, 1821; and died Sept. 23, 1822, aged twenty-three. He died Feb. 10, 1883. Her only child was born as follows: 1. *Francis Mason[1]*, born Aug. 21, 1822; and was living in 1836.
448—III. CHARLES[4], born July 17, 1801; died March 2, 1804, in Windham.
449—IV. ELIZA[4], born July 29, 1804; married Erastus Tucker May 21, 1829, in Windham; and she died March 9, 1837. Their children were as follows: 1. *Mary Frances[1]*, born Aug. 18, 1830; died Aug. 16, 1879. 2. *Edwin[1]*, born Nov. 7, 1831; died Sept. 18, 1879. 3. *Henry[1]*, born March 11, 1834. 4. *George[1]*, born March 5, 1837. 5. *John D.[1]* 6. *Eliza E.[1]* 7. *William[1]*.

213

CAPT. EBENEZER HOVEY[3], baptized in Ipswich, Mass., Sept. 30, 1744. He was a mariner, and lived in Ipswich, on the corner

* Windham Registry of Deeds, book S, page 520; book U, page 520.

of Main street and Hog lane. For thirty-four pounds, thirteen shillings and four pence, he bought of his brother John, who was administrator of the estate of their father, one-half of their father's house and two-thirds of the barn, at the easterly part of the town, being the easterly half of the house in which their father had lived, and land adjoining, Jan. 27, 1773.* He, also, for sixty-five pounds, six shillings and eight pence, bought of his brother John Hovey the easterly house, barn and two acres of land, on the east side of Hog lane, which had been assigned as dower to their mother from the estate of their father, April 29, 1777.† For one hundred and sixty pounds, he conveyed to John Holmes of Ipswich, mariner, house, barn and two acres of land in Ipswich on the northeast corner of Main street and Hog lane, Dec. 21, 1785.‡

Michael Hodge of Newburyport, gentleman, brought suit against Captain Hovey, and recovered judgment in July, 1787, in the court of common pleas, for seventy-eight pounds, twelve shillings and three pence and costs. Mr. Hovey's house, barn and eighty-four square rods of land were set off to Mr. Hodge, in satisfaction of the judgment, Aug. 7, 1787.§ Mr. Hodge released the estate to Captain Hovey's son Ebenezer July 14, 1796.‖ Peleg Wadsworth, esq., of Portland, Me., also recovered judgment against Captain Hovey for sixty-five pounds and six shillings; and one hundred and thirty-four square rods of land on Hog lane, in Ipswich, was set off to Mr. Wadsworth, in satisfaction of his judgment, Oct. 23, 1787.¶

Mr. Hovey bought of Daniel Abbot of Salem, baker, for two hundred and forty-eight dollars, two-thirds of two acres and fifty-seven square rods of land in Ipswich on the southeast side of Newmarch's lane and on the southwest side of the highway leading to Dimon stage, with the house, etc., July 20, 1799.**

Captain Hovey married, first, Eunice Dutch of Ipswich Feb. 4, 1773; and she died Feb. 15, 1776, at "about 2 o'clock afternoon." He married, second, Sally, daughter of John and Sarah (Harris) Holmes of Ipswich Dec. 2, 1783; and she died Oct. 7, 1792, at the age of thirty-two. He married, third, Eunice Hodgkins Nov. 10, 1793. He died July 23, 1817, at the age of seventy-two; and his wife Eunice survived him, dying, his widow, Aug. 27, 1837, at the age of seventy-four.

Mr. Hovey's children were born in Ipswich, as follows:—

* Essex Registry of Deeds, book 131, leaf 102.
† Essex Registry of Deeds, book 135, leaf 122.
‡ Essex Registry of Deeds, book 145, leaf 174.
§ Essex Registry of Deeds, book 147, leaf 31.
‖ Essex Registry of Deeds, book 161, leaf 7.
¶ Essex Registry of Deeds, book 149, leaf 1.
** Essex Registry of Deeds, book 166, leaf 162.

450—I.   EBENEZER[6], born Nov. 19, 1773; was a mariner; and lived in
         Ipswich. For fifty dollars, he bought, of widow Sarah
         Holmes of Ipswich a quarter of an acre of land there
         Jan. 13, 1798.*
451—II. SALLY[6], baptized Sept. 4, 1785.
452—III. ————[6], died, in infancy, May 6, 1789.
453—IV. JOHN HOLMES[6], born Nov. 13, 1790; was a cordwainer in 1816
         and a mariner in 1827; lived in Ipswich; and died in 1884.
454—V.   ————[6], died, in infancy, Oct. 8, 1792.
455—VI. EUNICE[6], died Oct. 5, 1795.
456—VII. STEPHEN[6], born Dec. 16, 1795; cordwainer; lived in Ipswich;
         married Isette S. Hooke of Portsmouth, N. H., April 8, 1842;
         he died March 8, 1870, at the age of seventy-four; and his
         wife survived him. She was his widow in 1872.
457—VIII. EUNICE[6], born in 1798; lived in Ipswich; and died, unmarried,
         Oct. 20, 1819, at the age of twenty-one.

215

FRANCIS HOVEY[5], born in Ipswich, Mass., Feb. 24, 1747.
When a boy he lived with a Mr. Dodge in Wenham, and then
went to Boston, where he learned the trade of a bricklayer from a
Mr. Lewis, two of whose daughters he married. Jan. 24, 1775, he
was one of the minute-men of Ipswich. For forty-three pounds,
he bought of the estate of David Pulsipher of Ipswich, fisherman,
deceased, the eastern half of a house and land adjoining, on the
river, in Ipswich, May 13, 1788.†

Mr. Hovey brought suit against Benjamin Dutch of Bradford, yeoman, and recovered judgment, Sept. 28, 1789, for twenty-one pounds, eight shillings and nine pence; and to satisfy the
judgment part of an old dwelling house, etc., was set off to
the judgment creditor Nov. 16, 1789.‡ For twenty-four pounds,
Mr. Hovey conveyed to Rev. Ebenezer Dutch of Bradford the
part of the house and land thus set off to him, Dec. 11, 1792.§ He
bought of Richard Dummer Jewett of Ipswich, yeoman, for
twenty-one shillings, a house lot in Ipswich, on the north side of
the highway, Dec. 29, 1789.|| For two hundred and fifty dollars,
he conveyed to William Stone of Ipswich, fisherman, a dwelling
house and land, on the north side of the highway, in Ipswich,
Sept. 6, 1796.¶ For eleven dollars, he bought some land in Ips-
wich of Francis Pulsifer of Salem, cabinet-maker, May 6, 1799.||

Mr. Hovey married, first, Hannah Lewis of Boston about
1770. She was born in Boston Feb. 15, 1749; and died April 27,

---

* Essex Registry of Deeds, book 170, leaf 198.
† Essex Registry of Deeds, book 170, leaf 226.
‡ Essex Registry of Deeds, book 161, leaf 95.
§ Essex Registry of Deeds, book 160, leaf 257.
|| Essex Registry of Deeds, book 171, leaf 35.
¶ Essex Registry of Deeds, book 171, leaf 85.

1802, at the age of fifty-three. Her remains lie in the old cemetery in Ipswich, and her gravestone is inscribed as follows :—

In memory of
Mrs. Hannah Hovey,
wife of Mr. Francis Hovey,
who died April 26, 1802 ;
Aged 53.

Pafs on, my friend, dry up your tear*
I muſt lie here, till Chriſt appears ;
Death is a debt to nature due ;
I've paid the debt, and ſo muſt you.

Mr. Hovey married, secondly, his first wife's sister, Mrs.
Lydia (Lewis) Gray of Boston Aug. 31, 1803. She was born in
Boston Oct. 14, 1762 ; and died Feb. 12, 1826, aged sixty-four.
Mr. Hovey died Feb. 3, 1829, at the age of eighty-two. He had
but little property, and his estate was insolvent. He lived in the
house which stood at the head of Hovey's lane, in Ipswich.

Mr. Hovey's children were born in Ipswich, as follows :—

458—I.   FRANCIS*, born April 24, 1771 ; living in Ipswich, unmarried, in
          1827 ; died April 3, 1853, at the age of eighty-one.

459—II.   THOMAS LEWIS*, born Aug. 29, 1772. *See family numbered
          "459."*

460—III. HANNAH*, born Nov. 20, 1774 (baptized "June 16, 1774") ; died
          in 1775.

461—IV.   HANNAH*, born Dec. 16, 1776 ; died in Ipswich, unmarried,
          Aug. 26, 1836, at the age of fifty-nine.

462—V.   REBECCA*, born April 2, 1779 ; died in Ipswich, unmarried, Nov.
          19, 1836, aged fifty-seven.

463—VI.   MARY*, born June 30, 1781 ; married William, son of William
          and Sarah (Mansfield) Stone of Ipswich Sept. 12, 1802 ; he
          was born in Ipswich Jan. 26, 1778 ; they lived in Newbury-
          port. He was a gunner on the sloop-of-war Wasp ; and was
          lost on it in 1814. She survived him, and died Sept. 27,
          1853. Children, born in Newburyport : 1. *Mary Jane*, born
          Jan. 14, 1806 ; died young. 2. *Almira Lewis*, born June 11,
          1809 ; married Perley, son of Benjamin and Martha (Perley)
          Scott of Ipswich Nov. 7, 1839 ; he was born Jan. 6, 1804 ;
          lived in Ipswich ; he died Jan. 17, 1872 ; she died April 13,
          1895, aged eighty-five. 3. *William*, born Dec. 1, 1811 ; lived
          in Ipswich ; sold fish bait ; married L. Lord Nov. 28, 1832 ;
          and died April 19, 1899, in Ipswich. 4. *Elizabeth Pike*,
          born July 27, 1814 ; married Isaac Buzzell.

464—VII. JOHN*, born Nov. 26, 1783. *See family numbered "464."*

465—VIII. LYDIA*, born Aug. 26, 1785 ; married Francis, son of Thomas
          and Lucy (Henderson) Caldwell Jan. 16, 1812. He was
          born Sept. 12, 1788 ; and died Jan. 9, 1869, at the age of
          seventy-four. She survived him, and died, his widow, Oct.
          9, 1867, at the age of eighty-two. Their children were born
          as follows : 1. *Joseph A.*, born Aug. 2, 1814 ; married
          Cynthia Hovey June 17, 1841 ; she died Dec. 10, 1878, aged
          sixty-six ; and he died May 26, 1882, at the age of sixty-

seven. They had one child. 2. *John*[5], born March 10, 1816; was a reputable young man; and died, of typhus fever, Oct. 24, 1837, at the age of twenty-two. 3. *Tyler*[5], born Jan. 1, 1819; married Mrs. Frances A. Prince, a widow, of Shapleigh, Me.; and was a man of thrift and industry. His final sickness was only four days in length. She died Aug. —, 1876. They had two children. 4. *George Washington*[5] (twin), born March 24, 1821; was very retiring from society, and lived alone, hermit-like, had simple tastes, and was a good conversationalist. He was tall and strong. He dropped dead Jan. 9, 1896, at the age of seventy-four. 5. *Daniel A.*[5] (twin), born March 24, 1821; died Dec. 19, 1845, aged twenty-four. 6. *Joel*[5], born Aug. 11, 1824; married Margaret, daughter of Robert and Margaret (Smith) Kimball; was a quiet, unassuming man, diligent, faithful, honest. He was a daguerreotyper, and later a blacksmith, finally becoming night watchman at the woolen mills in Ipswich, where he lived. He dropped dead at the mills Jan. 10, 1883, at the age of fifty-eight. 7. *Elizabeth Boardman*[5], born May 7, 1827; and died Oct. 1, 1827. 8. *Lydia Ann*[5], born April 22, 1831; worked dressmaking for twenty-seven years, and was, for fifty years, a member of the Methodist church. She died Sept. 9, 1902, at the age of seventy-one.

466—ix.　Joseph[4], born Sept. 28, 1789. *See family numbered "466."*
467—x.　Levi[4], Born April 25, 1792. *See family numbered "467."*
468—xi.　George Lewis[4], born July 29, 1804; died at Batavia, on ship Merrimack, Captain Dennis, Aug. 9, 1826, at the age of twenty-two, unmarried.

218

John Hovey[5], born in Boxford, Mass., Aug. 29, 1727. He was a yeoman, and lived in Boxford, on the northern side of the road leading from the house of George W. Chadwick to the North Andover line, and near the town line. Mr. Hovey built the house, which was two stories in height, about thirty-two feet long and twenty-eight feet wide, and finished with dado boards. It faced the west, and the chimney was in the middle. The well was about three rods south of the house, near the road.

Mr. Hovey was one of the minute-men of Capt. William Perley's company, and with it marched to Lexington on the morning of April 19, 1775.

Mr. Hovey married, first, Mercy, daughter of Joshua and Sarah (Abbott) Jackson of Rowley Dec. 4, 1753. She was born in Rowley Feb. 12, 1730-1; admitted to the church of Linebrook parish, in Ipswich; dismissed to the Second church in Boxford May 19, 1754; and died at Boxford, in childbirth, May 19, 1755, at the age of twenty-four. He married, second, Mary, daughter of Samuel and Susanna Cole of Boxford Jan. 11, 1757.

For one hundred pounds, Mr. Hovey conveyed to his son-in-law, William Parker, one-third of his lands in Boxford April 18, 1788.*

* Essex Registry of Deeds, book 168, leaf 192.

Mrs. Hovey died May 26, 1802, at the age of seventy-one; and Mr. Hovey conveyed all his land and buildings to William Parker, his son-in-law, Oct. 25, 1802. Mr. Hovey died May 8, 1807, at the age of seventy-nine. The farm came into the possession of their only child.

Mr. Hovey's only child was born in Boxford, as follows:—

469—L MERCY[6], born May 11, 1755; married William Parker of Andover Aug. 30, 1781; he was a yeoman, and they lived on her father's farm in Boxford. After the decease of herself and husband in 1826, the place passed out of their possession. The house was taken down about 1853. Mr. Parker had a remarkable dream, which, unlike most dreams, came to pass. A man appeared to him near the barn and told him that he would lose his entire family, then consisting of himself and wife and four children, and named them in the order they would die. The dream was fulfilled soon after, and his wife and himself also died, he being the survivor but a few months. Mrs. Parker died March 10, 1826, at the age of seventy; and he died Nov. 23, 1826, aged seventy-two. Their children were born in Boxford, as follows: 1. William[7], born May 23, 1782; was admitted to the Second church on the day when all the family were baptized, Aug. 15, 1797, being then only fifteen years old, "upon condition of considering himself under the watch, and subject to the discipline of the church." He died Jan. 18, 1809, aged twenty-six. 2. Abigail[7], born Feb. 4, 1786; died Nov. 27, 1825, aged thirty-nine. 3. Hannah[7], born March 23, 1787; died Oct. 4, 1810, aged twenty-three. 4. Esther[7], born Nov. 5, 1789; married William Henry of Wells July 3, 1808. 5. Mary[7], born March 18, 1791; died Nov. 24, 1809, at the age of eighteen. 6. Susannah[7], born March 8, 1793; died March 16, 1826, at the age of thirty-three. 7. John[7], born Dec. 5, 1795; died June 9, 1826, at the age of thirty. 8. Benjamin[7], born about 1797; died Sept. 13, 1825, at the age of twenty-eight.

220

RICHARD HOVEY[3], born in Boxford, Mass., Aug. 3, 1733. He was a yeoman, and lived in West Boxford, on his father's farm, being noted as a bee keeper.

Dec. 25, 1778, he made a partition, with his brother John, of real estate devised to them by their father, and, also, a part of Walker's meadow.* This included land on Philistine hill, on Walker's hill, in Rough meadow and in common swamp, and the homestead. Richard received fifty-five acres and seventeen rods of the homestead land, and about twenty-two acres of other lands.

Mr. Hovey married Sarah Wood of Andover Nov. 10, 1757; and she died in Boxford Jan. 18, 1818, at the age of eighty-four. The inscription upon her gravestone is as follows: —

* Essex Registry of Deeds, book 186, leaf 130; book 188, leaf 32.

Mrs.
SARAH,
Relict of
Mr. Richard Hovey,
died March, 1818,
AEt. 84.

Mr. Hovey died in Boxford Feb. 14, 1818, at the age of eighty-four. The inscription upon his gravestone reads as follows :—

Mr.

RICHARD HOVEY
died
January, 1818,
AEt. 84.

Administration upon his estate was granted March 31, 1818. His property was appraised at $1,660.18, of which $1,386 was real estate, and $274.18 was personal.

Their children were born in Boxford, as follows :—

470—I. DAVID⁶, born July 30, 1758. *See family numbered "470."*
471—II. SARAH⁶, born March 1, 1760; died April 4, 1764, aged four years.
472—III. RICHARD⁶, born Feb. 4, 1762. *See family numbered "472."*
473—IV. ——⁶, died March 24, 1764.
474—V. SARAH⁶, born June 15, 1765; died in Boxford, unmarried, April 15, 1798, aged thirty-two.
475—VI. JONATHAN⁶, born Aug. 12, 1767; probably died before 1818.
476—VII. JOHN⁶ (twin), born Jan. 13, 1770. *See family numbered "476."*
477—VIII. BETTY⁶ (twin), born Jan. 13, 1770; died in Boxford, unmarried, Sept. 15, 1803, at the age of thirty-three.
478—IX. STEPHEN⁶, born Feb. 3, 1773. *See family numbered "478."*

230

THOMAS HOVEY⁵, born in Boxford, Mass., Nov. 29, 1737. He was a yeoman, and lived in Boxford until about 1770, when he removed to Beverly.

Mr. Hovey married Sarah Carlton July 21, 1762, in Boxford. He died in Beverly Feb. 9, 1820, at the age of eighty-two. His estate was very small, and proved to be insolvent. At that time, the probate papers state, Rebecca Hoyt was his only child living in Essex county. His wife survived him, and died in Beverly, his widow, July 20, 1826, at the age of eighty-three.

Their children were born as follows :—

479—I. DORCAS⁶, born Dec. 12, 1763, in Boxford; married Capt. Isaac, son of Lt. Joseph and Mehitable (Thorndike) Rea May 20, 1788; he was born in Beverly March 30, 1762; lived in Beverly; she died of dropsy in Beverly May 16, 1803, aged thirty-nine; he married, secondly, Lydia Symonds Oct. 7, 1804; and died there May 19, 1814, aged fifty-two.

480—II.   BILLY[6], born May 12, 1765, in Boxford.

481—III.   THOMAS[6], lived in Beverly; mariner; and died before Dec. 8, 1801, when administration upon his estate was granted to his father. His estate was appraised at $1,779.71, of which $1,200 was real estate and $579.71 was personal. He was probably unmarried.

482—IV.   ———[6], born about 1773; died, being buried June 8, 1776, aged three years.

483—V.   NATHAN[6], born March 8, 1775, in Beverly. He was a mariner, and at the age of sixteen was mate of the brigantine Hannah, sailing from Newburyport. While on a voyage to the West Indies, he disappeared, in February, 1802, and was supposed to have been murdered. The following affidavit, on record in the Essex County registry of deeds, gives interesting details of the matter:—

"I Jeremiah Brown J[r] of lawful age depose, that I was a foremast hand on board the Brig[e] Hannah, commanded by Charles Goodridge of Newburyport in faid county in her voyage from faid Newburyport to the West Indies, that Nathan Hovey of Beverly in s[d] county was our mate, and that we failed from Newburyport on faid voyage the twenty-fifth day of November eighteen hundred & one — that in February eighteen hundred & two when we were in Hispaniola at a Place called the great salt Plane, I faw faid Hovey lend faid Goodridge eighty two dollars, that I heard faid Goodridge fay that he fold three barrels of beef for faid Hovey at ten dollars p[r] Barrel, that I heard faid Goodridge promise to pay faid Hovey for the fame when the faid voyage fhould be ended, & I heard faid Hovey confent to wait till then, that I know faid Hovey had on board faid Brig[e] two bags of cotton, & two bags & part of a bag of coffee, That the captain fent faid Hovey to clear out the veffel & get a fum of money due the faid Goodridge, & we expected he would not be abfent more than two days but we never faw or heard of him afterwards, and fuppofe he was murdered, that I then took minutes of the contents of this Depofition in writing which I now have by me, That after faid Hovey had purchased two bags of cotton, faid Goodridge wished to purchase one of them, and faid Hovey faid he might have one if he would pay for it when we got home —That the night after the mate had left us in the morning, the Brig[e] ftruck a drift while the whole crew were afhore— That there being great confusion & we, being in great fear, went on board under pretence of bringing her in, & then made fail & came off, and further I fay not

"Jeremiah Brown J[r]

"Commonwealth of Mafsachufetts Efsex fs January 21st 1804 Perfonally appeared before us the subfcribers two Justices of the Peace in & for faid county of Efsex, quorum unus, the aforesaid Deponant; & after being carefully examined & duly cautioned to testify the whole & nothing but the truth, made Oath that the foregoing deposition by him fuhfcribed is true—Taken at the request of Levi Mills of Newburyport in faid county goldsmith, administrator on the

Eftate of Nathan Hovey late of Beverley in faid County mariner fuppofed to be deceased, to be preserved in perpetual remembrance of the thing, and we duly notified all perfons living within twenty miles of this place of Caption we knew to be interested in the property to which the s⁴ depofition relates, and Edw° Goodridge brother of the faid Charles Goodridge did attend

"Fees $2.
NIC° PIKE
EDWARD LITTLE"*

Nathan Hovey's father sent a note to the probate court, March 10, 1803, stating that "it is inconvenient for him to administer on the estate." The deceased left some personal property only. It was appraised at $184.83.

84—VI. JOSEPH⁶, born Aug. 18, 1777, in Beverly; died young.
485—VII. REBECCA⁶, born May 1, 1779, in Beverly; married Samuel Hoyt of Newburyport Sept. 26, 1799; and was his wife in 1820.
486—VIII. JOSEPH⁶, born Dec. 10, 1780, in Beverly. *See family numbered* "286."
487—IX. CHARLOTTE⁶, born Aug. 22, 1782, in Beverly; and died there Dec. 8, 1802, aged twenty.
488—X. STEPHEN SWEET⁶, born May 6, 1784, in Beverly.

234

PHINEAS HOVEY⁵, born in Boxford, Mass., Jan. 18, 1745-6. He was a yeoman, and lived in Beverly. He served in the army in the war of the Revolution, in Capt. Peter Shaw's company, of Beverly, at Lexington and in the battle of Bunker Hill. With others, he conveyed, for five hundred and ninety-two pounds and fifteen shillings, to Peter Russell of Bradford, gentleman, the homestead of Dea. Thomas Kimball of Bradford, deceased, April 5, 1782.†

Mr. Hovey married Miss Hannah, daughter of Thomas and Rebecca Preston of Beverly July 18, 1775. She was baptized in Beverly June 21, 1752. Mr. Hovey died Oct. 2, 1786, at the age of forty, and she survived him, being his widow, of Beverly, in 1807. For one hundred and ten pounds, with others, she conveyed to Phineas Foster of Boxford, yeoman, one acre of land with the house and barn thereon, and two other lots of land, all in Beverly, being formerly the property of Anna Preston of Beverly, deceased, Nov. 23, 1786.‡ For four pounds and ten shillings, her widowed mother conveyed to her one-fourth of an acre of land and eastern half of the house thereon March 15, 1788.§ For eighteen pounds, Mrs. Hovey conveyed the house, barn and land to Benjamin Foster of Beverly, cabinet-maker, Nov. 26, 1793.‖ Nov. 24, 1803, Mrs. Hovey bought back the

* Essex Registry of Deeds, book 173, leaf 173.
† Essex Registry of Deeds, book 141, leaf 31.
‡ Essex Registry of Deeds, book 147, leaf 233.
§ Essex Registry of Deeds, book 147, leaf 142.
‖ Essex Registry of Deeds, book 156, leaf 292.

house and barn, with the privilege of removing them within six months.

Their children were born in Beverly, as follows:—

489—I.   SUSANNA[4], born March 26, 1776; married Joseph, son of Ebenezer and Betsey (Dodge) Trask of Beverly, as his second wife, Oct. 11, 1804. He was born in Beverly April 21, 1776; and married, first, Sarah Dodge of Wenham Feb. 13, 1800. She died Dec. 30, 1802. Mr. Trask lost the sight of one eye by running a fork into it when he was two years old; and when about forty a fragment of a stone he was hammering struck him in the other eye, causing him to be totally blind for many years. He died at Gloucester May 8, 1855, at the age of seventy-nine. She died in Gloucester Dec. 12, 1832, aged fifty-six. They lived in Gloucester, where their children were born, as follows: 1. *Joshua Phippen[5]*, born July 23, 1805; wrote articles for the Gloucester papers, signed "Equal Rights," which led to the formation of the Gloucester lyceum; about 1837 they removed to Maine, where he was postmaster and a country-storekeeper; returned to Gloucester in 1847; was then deputy-sheriff, coroner, trial justice and judge of the police court; a Whig in politics; religious; an early abolitionist; a fearless leader, especially in temperance movements, founding temperance societies; a charter member of the Cape Ann Bank and secretary of the Fisherman's Insurance Company. He married Mary Ellery, daughter of William and Elizabeth (Low) Rogers Dec. 14, 1830. She was born in Gloucester April 29, 1803. He died in Gloucester Sept. 14, 1862, at the age of fifty-seven; and she died at Manchester, N. H., Nov. —, 1891, aged eighty-eight. 2. *Sarah Dodge[5]*, born Feb. 24, 1807; married Simeon Beckford of Beverly Aug. 19, 1832; he was born in Beverly, and lived there until 1860, when he removed to Gloucester; he was a master-builder, and went to California in 1849; she died in Gloucester Feb. —, 1888. 3. *Ebenezer[5]*, born Jan. 28, 1809; died Oct. 29, 1809. 4. *Ebenezer[5]*, born July 14, 1810; was educated at Dummer Academy and Phillips (Exeter) Academy; went to Bangor, Me., early and became a store-keeper with his brother; was cashier of the Traders' Bank in Bangor for thirty-four years; and a member of the Baptist church; married A. Delia Pool of Rockport Feb. 24, 1833; and died in Bangor Jan. 22, 1889, at the age of seventy-eight.

490—II. PHINEAS[4], baptized Sept. 7, 1777; died young.

491—III. SARAH LEACH[4], born about 1779; married, as his second wife, James, son of John and Nancy (Sparling) Bradburn April 1, 1804. He was born in Dublin, Ireland, Jan. 1, 1777, and came to America, with his parents, in 1787. He married, first, Miss Fanny Stetson of Wrentham June 4, 1797; and she died in Beverly Sept. 6, 1803, at the age of twenty-eight. He followed the business of his father, a manufacturer of woolen cloth, being among the earliest in New England; and had indomitable energy, individuality, wit and fine personal appearance. Sarah (Hovey) Bradburn was a very conscientious and strongly religious woman. They lived in Beverly, Attleboro, Waltham and Lowell. She died in 1814; and he died in Albany, N. Y., May 25, 1839, aged sixty-two. The children of James and Sarah Leach (Hovey) Bradburn were as follows: 1. *George*[5], born March 4. 1806, in Attleboro, Mass., having inherited from both parents many of their qualities, which permeated his whole nature. He was educated as a practical machinist, having a talent for that employment, but his inclination to the life of a student caused him to change his vocation, and he became a Unitarian clergyman. He was settled over a church in Nantucket; and while there, in 1836, married Lydia, daughter of Capt. Valentine Hussey, a lady of Quaker birth, of rare personal attraction, greatly beloved, and who had received her education at the Friends' college, in Providence, R. I. She died a year after their marriage, and their infant daughter a few months later. These losses shadowed his subsequent life. His second wife, Frances Stackpole Parker, whom he married in 1850, survived him. They had no children. For several years, he represented Nantucket in the legislature, as a Whig; was an editor at Lynn, Mass., and Cleveland, O.; but was best known throughout the North as an anti-slavery lecturer, being an intimate friend of Garrison. He was a delegate to the World's convention in London, in 1840, and is represented in the celebrated picture, now in London, of this famous anti-slavery gathering. As a speaker, he was witty and eloquent, his oratory being unique, picturesque and impressive. He was frank and sincere, his face and figure were of striking dignity and beauty, and he had courage that feared no antagonism. He died in Melrose, Mass., where he had lived for nearly a score of years, July 26, 1880, at the age of seventy-four. 2. *Charles*[5], born July 16, 1808, in Attleboro; was at first a resident of Lowell, Mass., then became a merchant in Cleveland, O., and always prominent. He married Eliza Stone Jan. 27. 1831. in Lowell. She was born in Chester, Vt., in 1807; and died in Cleveland Sept. 10, 1865. He was greatly interested in the cause of education, and organized the public schools of Cleveland, from which have been modeled most of our present school system, of which he is known as the father. His life-size oil portrait hangs in the old high school in Cleveland, having been painted and hung there by the board of education of that city. He died in Cleveland Aug. 12, 1872, at the age of sixty-four. He had six children.

492—IV.   DORCAS[5], baptized April 14, 1782; married Samuel Friend of Boston Oct. 14, 1804.

493—V.   PHINEAS[5], baptized July 26, 1784; mariner; lived in Beverly; married Betsey, daughter of Ebenezer and Betsey (Dodge) Trask of Beverly Dec. 26, 1805. She was born in Beverly Sept. 9, 1784; and died there May 16, 1810, at the age of twenty-five.

494—VI.   WILLIAM GROSS[5], baptized May 14, 1786; living in 1789.

236

LUKE HOVEY[5], born in Boxford, Mass., Sept. 13, 1794. He was a cordwainer and husbandman, and lived in Boxford. He was a soldier of the Revolution, being a minute-man, and served in the regiment of Col. Samuel Johnson.

With others, he conveyed, for five hundred and ninety-two pounds and fifteen shillings, to Peter Russell of Bradford, gentleman, the homestead farm of Dea. Thomas Kimball of Bradford, deceased, April 5, 1782;[*] and, for six pounds, he conveyed to James Kimball of Bradford, combmaker, one-sixteenth of eight square rods of thatch bank on Oldtown river, in Newbury, May 4, 1785.[†]

Mr. Hovey married Hannah, daughter of Nathan and Susanna (George) Kimball of Bradford March 2, 1775. She was born in Bradford Nov. 10, 1751. Mr. Hovey died in Boxford Dec. 8, 1798, at the age of forty-nine. His widow was appointed administrator of his estate Jan. 7, 1799. The inventory of his estate amounted to $3,554.16, of which $1,800 was real estate and $1,754.16 was personal. The children conveyed to Daniel Mitchell of Bradford, cordwainer, the homestead in Boxford and pew in the West Boxford meeting house, Dec. 17, 1812, on condition that he "truly and faithfully and decently support" their mother "Hannah Hovey in the place where she now dwells, accidents and casualties by fire excepted, and also provide her with board, lodging and apparel, nursing and medicine in sickness and health; and also furnish her with a seat in that pew in the meeting house in the West parish of Boxford that formerly belonged to Luke Hovey, late of Boxford, deceased; also pay her two dollars annually, and generally to take a prudent care of her through life, and at the close of life give her a decent burial."[‡] Mrs. Hovey died, his widow, in Boxford, March 8, 1831, at the age of seventy-nine.

The following copy of Mr. Hovey's signature has been made from that on his bond which he gave as executor of his father's will, the bond being dated in 1787:

The children of Mr. and Mrs. Hovey were born in Boxford, as follows:—

495—I.　HANNAH[*], baptized June 16, 1776; died July 22, 1777, aged one year.
496—II.　DORCAS[*], baptized March 30, 1777; living in Newburyport, unmarried, in 1812.
497—III.　BENJAMIN[*], baptized Jan. 31, 1779.
498—IV.　LEONARD[*], baptized Feb. 11, 1781. *See family numbered "498."*
499—V.　ISAAC[*], baptized April 13, 1783; cordwainer; and lived in Boxford in 1812.
500—VI.　HANNAH[*], born July 3, 1785; married Capt. Daniel, son of Daniel and Rebecca (Bailey) Mitchell of Boxford Nov. 29, 1804. He was born May 22, 1783; and was a farmer, and lived in Bradford until 1812, when he bought a farm on the northern shore of Mitchells pond, in West Boxford, his house standing across the road from the house of J. Myron

* Essex Registry of Deeds, book 141, leaf 31.
† Essex Registry of Deeds, book 185, leaf 266.
‡ Essex Registry of Deeds, book 199, leaf 84.

Pearl. Children: 1. *Ann*[7], born April 16, 1806, in Bradford. 2. *Emily*[7], born Dec. 9, 1809, in Bradford; married Robert McQuestion of Rowley (published March 22, 1834); he was born in Litchfield, N. H., March 20, 1802; lived in Newbury and West Newbury; she died June 13, 1847. 3. *Charlotte*[7], born Feb. 3, 1812, in Bradford; married Rev. Lewis F., son of Daniel Lane of Loudon, N. H., July 14, 1834; went west; she died in 1835. 4. *Rebecca*[7], born June 21, 1814, in Boxford; married John Blodget of Roxbury Aug. 19, 1833. 5. *Harriet*[7], born Aug. 17, 1816, in Boxford; married John L., son of John and Mary Platts of Georgetown Feb. 5, 1846; he was a shoe manufacturer. 6. *Daniel*[7], born Aug. 31, 1822; was a musician in Boston; married Maria Frances, daughter of Dea. O. Keech of Central Falls, Smithfield, R. I.; he died Jan. 7, 1853; she survived him, and married, secondly, Daniel Lee, a dentist.

501—VII.   SUSANNA[6], born about 1788; married John Barnes of Newburyport Nov. 7, 1810; and they were living in Deerfield, N. H., in 1812.

502—VIII. LUKE[6] (twin), baptized July 12, 1790; cordwainer; lived in Boxford in 1819.

503—IX.   ABIGAIL[6] (twin), baptized July 12, 1790; married Guy Carlton of Roxbury Dec. 8, 1811, in Bradford.

504—X.   CELINDA[6], baptized Aug. 19, 1792; married Amos Gage of Boxford Nov. 5, 1815. Their children were born as follows: 1. *Warren*[7], born March 17, 1816, in Bradford; was a contractor and builder; lived in Bradford; married Caroline B. ———; and had children. 2. *Abigail*[7], born March 21, 1818, at Pelham, N. H.; married James Carlton of Boxford April 27, 1838; he was a carpenter, and built and lived in the William R. Kimball house, in West Boxford, in 1840; bought the house now owned and occupied by Edward E. Pearl in 1860, and lived there until he moved to Georgetown in 1876; he died in Georgetown Jan. 6, 1886; and she died there, his widow, June 12, 1907. They had two children. 3. *Harriet R.*[7], born March 4, 1820, in Boxford; married Daniel Chamberlin; and lived in Auburndale, Mass., where she died, his widow, in 1906 or 1907. 4. *George*[7], born Aug. 26, 1822, in Boxford; died in 18—, leaving no children. 5. *Mary Ann*[7], born Nov. 24, 1824, in Boxford. 6. *Amos*[7], born March 20, 1827, in Boxford; died in Bradford July 2, 1830, aged three years. 7. *Celinda*[7], born June 1, 1829, in Bradford.

505—XI.   NATHAN[6], baptized July 26, 1795; died Aug. 29, 1797, aged two years.

240

JOSEPH HOVEY[5], born in Boxford, Mass., Jan. 23. 1746. He was a housewright, and lived in Boxford. He was a soldier of the Revolution, being a minute-man, and served in the regiment of Col. Samuel Johnson. In 1790, he was the lucky owner of ticket No. 760, in the Fifth class of the State lottery, which drew a prize of one thousand dollars.* With this money he purchased the farm which was afterward his son, Thomas S. Hovey's, the site of the house being now occupied by the Barker Free school

---

* Salem Gazette, Nov. 16, 1790.

in the West parish of Boxford, May 14, 1791.* The consideration was four hundred pounds, and the grantors were widow
Mercy Wood, Huldah Wood, singlewoman, and widow Mary
Boynton, all of Boxford. The farm contained one hundred acres
of land.

For sixty pounds, he bought of Amasa Peabody of Dracut,
yeoman, twenty acres and five rods of land in Boxford, on Rock
brook, May 4, 1790;† and on the same day conveyed one-half of
it, for thirty pounds, to John Pearl of Boxford, husbandman.‡
He bought of Asa Cole of Boxford, yeoman, for seventeen pounds
and ten shillings, four acres and twenty-one rods of salt marsh in
Newbury, on the northeast side of Long Point creek, Oct. 29,
1793.†

Mr. Hovey was called "gentleman" the latter part of his life.

He married Mary, daughter of Moses and Mary (Chadwick)
Porter of Boxford March 17, 1773. She was born in Boxford
July 20, 1754; and died in Boxford May 31, 1819, at the age of
sixty-four. Mr. Hovey died in Boxford Nov. 27, 1820, at the age
of seventy-four. His inventory shows a considerable library.
His son Thomas S. Hovey was appointed administrator of his
estate Feb. 6, 1821.

Their children were born in Boxford, as follows:—

506—I.   MOSES⁴, born April 7, 1773. *See family numbered "506."*
507—II.   JOSEPH⁴, born Oct. 31, 1776; was taught the trade of a clock
and watch maker, but being fond of reading he acquired a
taste for classical knowledge, and at maturity set about devis-
ing means to obtain a liberal education. He studied with his
pastor, Rev. Peter Eaton, and subsequently attended Phillips'
Academy at Andover, of which Mark Newman, esq., was
then principal. Mr. Newman was friendly to him, treating
him with great delicacy, and making his situation as pleasant
as possible. Though Mr. Hovey suffered on account of his
age, he persevered and made fair progress. He entered
Harvard college in 1800, and there won the respect and confidence of the few who really knew him, being retiring and
modest, and easily confused. He graduated in 1804.

After graduation, he taught school for a year or more,
and then entered the office of John Abbott, esq., a lawyer in
Westford, but soon removed to Haverhill, pursuing his legal
studies there with Hon. John Varnum until his admission
to the Essex bar in 1808. He opened an office in Haverhill,
and began his professional career. Mr. Varnum was his
friend, furnishing him with means of subsistence in such a
delicate and kindly manner that it could not be refused or
noticed. The society of Haverhill was social, intelligent and
refined, and in it Mr. Hovey was as happy as his nature,
disposition and habits permitted.

* Essex Registry of Deeds, book 154, leaf 222.
† Essex Registry of Deeds, book 162, leaf 199.
‡ Essex Registry of Deeds, book 173, leaf 53.

He had a good classical education, and excelled in mathematics and metaphysics, having a fondness for books which required mental exercise. His chief delight was in works of eloquence, poetry and able essays, quoting from them readily. But the more he read and the better he understood them the less he seemed qualified to speak himself. The sight of an audience withered all his faculties and dulled his brain, being spellbound before a small number of hearers even.

He wrote verses of merit, always chaste and delicate, but wanting in force and passion. He played the flute with some skill, and found consolation in music; when fretful and moody, his flute and little harpsichord were successfully used "to charm away the fiends."

In his religious belief he became an Episcopalian. Although many of his views of society were probably erroneous, his observations on characters were generally shrewd, learned and novel, frequently tinctured with corrosive and sickly impressions incident to chafed spirits. If his remarks were sometimes bitter, he had no permanent malice in his nature. His sarcasms were only the feverish breath of the moment, and passed away like the vapors of the morning.

He had read law with diligence, and was well acquainted with its principles, but he had no readiness in practice, hesitating, reflecting and doubting, until his client lost all confidence in his knowledge. Still, he was a safe counselor. Had he acted as well as he reasoned he would have had much to do.

Morbidness conjured for him evils which in reality he never had to bear. He was a friend and admirer of ladies, but fear of rivalry caused him to withhold advances; and in every amusement or entertainment a death's head rose before him.

In person he was tall, thin and pale, and was singularly abstemious, fearing that he should be plethoric by indulgence, while he was wasting away in a settled consumption.

In the summer of 1815 he was scarcely able to walk; but he was not in the slightest degree disturbed by the approach of death, and his nature seemed to wholly change. All soreness left him, all wounds of pride were healed. The disease of his disposition and fancy passed away. A pure serenity of soul—high and holy, philanthropic and devotional—beamed from his sunken eye, and was made manifest in every aspiration. All his enmities were forgotten, and injuries forgiven. His friends glowed with new life. As the hand of death pressed harder upon his brow, hope and joy beamed brighter in his countenance, free from all doubt or fear. He died May 6, 1816, at the age of thirty-nine; and his remains lie in the ancient burial place in West Boxford.[*]

508—III. AARON[6], born Feb. 3, 1778. *See family numbered "508."*

509—IV. MARY[6], born Nov. 1, 1781; married Benjamin, son of John and Eunice (Kimball) Pearl of Boxford May 7, 1807. He was born in Boxford Sept. 3, 1774. She died Dec. 27, 1819, aged

[*] Acknowledgement is due to Sketches of Lawyers, Statesmen and Men of Letters, by Samuel L. Knapp, for much of the material of this sketch.

thirty-eight years. He married, secondly, Sally Ayer of
Haverhill (published Dec. 1, 1820); and died Sept. 3, 1840,
on his sixty-sixth birthday. He lived in West Boxford; and
was one of the selectmen of the town in 1826. Their children were as follows: 1. *Ann Matilda*[8], born Nov. 3, 1809,
in Bradford; married, first, Joseph Hall of Bradford,
farmer, June 18,1841; and, second, Joseph Howe of Methuen.
She died April 25, 1882, at the age of seventy-two. 2. *Rebecca Hovey*[8], born Sept. 30, 1814, in Boxford; died young.

510—v.   HANNAH[6], born Oct. 16, 1783; never married; lived in Boxford; had daughter Olinda Ann Hovey born Sept. 20, 1808;
and died Jan. 1, 1815, at the age of thirty-one. Olinda Ann
married Amzi Camp of New York city, a missionary at Five
Points, May 22, 1835; and had three children. Mrs. Camp
died Jan. 23, 1884, at the age of seventy-five.

511—vi.   REBECCA[6], born April 17, 1788; died, unmarried, in Boxford,
Sept. 10, 1818, at the age of thirty.

512—vii.   RUFUS PORTER[6], born Feb. 5, 1790; graduated at Harvard college in 1813; and became a lawyer, first, in Lynn, and soon
afterward removed to Haverhill, where he was in 1816. He
died, unmarried, May 14, 1820, at the age of thirty.

513—viii.   THOMAS STICKNEY[6], born Sept. 8, 1792. *See family numbered
"513."*

242

CAPT. IVORY HOVEY[5], born in Boxford, Mass., July 14, 1750.
He was a yeoman, and lived in West Boxford. For one hundred
pounds, he bought his brother Thomas' interest in the estate of
their father June 23, 1788,* and in 1802, of his brother Amos the
Hill lots, so called, in Boxford, and salt marsh. In the latter part
of his life he was called "gentleman" and "esquire." He was a
captain in the militia, and orderly sergeant in the Revolutionary
war, being in the hottest of the fight in the battles at Bunker hill,
Trenton and other places. He was a pensioner.

Mr. Hovey married Lucy, daughter of John and Mary
(Chadwick) Peabody of Boxford July 23, 1772. She was born in
Boxford March 23, 1753. Captain Hovey and his wife and her
sister, for ninety pounds, conveyed their interest in that part of
the estate of their father, John Peabody, that was set off to his
widow Dec. 4, 1781.†

Captain Hovey died in Boxford Aug. 27, 1832, at the age of
eighty-two. In a petition to the probate court, his widow, Lucy
Hovey, stated that she was "married to him in July, 1773, and
lived with him as his lawful wife until the day of his death which
was the twenty-seventh of August last, and that he was a pensioner of the United States, having been a sergeant in the army
of the Revolution."

* Essex Registry of Deeds, book 169, leaf 265.
† Essex Registry of Deeds, book 148, leaf 93.

The following notice of his death appeared in the Salem Gazette :—

In Boxford, August 27, Capt. Ivory Hovey, aged 82. An ardent patriot and revolutionary soldier—who was in the hottest of the battle of Bunker Hill—sustained the office of orderly Sergeant under Capt. Robinson in the trying scenes in New Jersey and Long Island—was in the battle of Trenton and distinguished himself at sundry times by many fearless and heroic deeds—was a man of noble and generous heart—an obliging personal friend, and an active friend of humanity.*

Captain Hovey lived on the paternal homestead ; and a few years after his death there remained no vestige of the home but the narcissus of the old garden, which still springs up near the brook.

Mrs. Hovey survived him, and died, his widow, in Boxford, Jan. 2, 1835, at the age of eighty-one.

Their children were born in Boxford, as follows :—

514—I.   ISRAEL⁶, born Oct. 9, 1772. See family numbered "514."
515—II.   LUCY⁶, born March 5, 1774; died in Boxford April 2, 1778,
           aged four.
516—III.   REBECCA⁶, born Aug. 3, 1776; married James Platts Hovey
           (417) of Dracut May 13, 1801.
517—IV.   WILLIAM⁶, born Jan. 7, 1778. See family numbered "517."
518—V.   CHARLES⁶, born Jan. 11, 1780; removed to Warren, Me., in 1803,
           and established the tanning business there; but soon returned
           to Massachusetts; and was a soldier in the war of 1812. He
           died in New York.
519—VI.   MARY⁶, born Aug. 9, 1781; married Joseph Hovey (423) of
           Dracut July 23, 1812.
520—VII.   IVORY⁶, born July 31, 1783. See family numbered "520."
521—VIII. LUCY⁶, born March 12, 1785; died, unmarried, in Boxford,
           March 26, 1809, aged twenty-four.
522—IX.   ALFRED⁶, born Dec. 12, 1788. See family numbered "522."
523—X.   EDWARD⁶, born May 16, 1793; died in Boxford Aug. 24, 1797,
           aged four years.

245

GEN. AMOS HOVEY⁵, born in Boxford, Mass., May 31, 1757. He was at first a cordwainer, and lived in Boxford. He removed to Salem in 1783, and became a merchant. While living in Boxford, for one hundred and thirty pounds, he bought of Seth Ring a shop in Salem, standing on land of Joseph Chipman, April 26, 1783,† and sold it to William Phippen of Salem, trader, for thirty pounds, May 17, 1786.‡ On the latter date, Mr. Phippen conveyed to Mr. Hovey a shop for seventy-three pounds and ten shillings.§ Mr. Hovey disposed of land in Boxford in 1802 and 1809.

* Salem Gazette, Sept. 4, 1832.
† Essex Registry of Deeds, book 137, leaf 126.
‡ Essex Registry of Deeds, book 144, leaf 114.
§ Essex Registry of Deeds, book 144, leaf 115.

He bought of Joseph White of Salem, merchant, the house and lot in Salem, next east of the Franklin building, on the northern side of Essex street, Oct. 15, 1805;* and this was his permanent residence.

General Hovey was a soldier in the war of the Revolution; and major-general in the Second Division of the state militia. He was also one of the selectmen of Salem. He met with losses in business, and in his old age was obliged to fail.

Mr. Hovey married Deborah Steward of Nova Scotia Dec. 4, 1791; and he died in Salem Oct. 17, 1838, at the age of eighty-one. His wife survived him, dying his widow Dec. 21, 1841, at the age of seventy-six.

Their children were born in Salem, as follows:—

524—I.   REBECCA⁶ (twin), baptized March 17, 1793; and died before 1838.
525—II. DEBORAH⁶ (twin), baptized March 17, 1793; she entered the Salem hospital for inoculation from the small pox June 29, 1798, putrid spots appeared, and she died there July 11, 1798, at the age of five years.
526—III. SARAH⁶, baptized Oct. 16, 1796; she entered the Salem hospital for inoculation in the same class as her sister Deborah and died there July 20, 1798, at the age of twenty-two months.

250

SOLOMON HOVEY⁵, born in Boxford, Mass., Nov. 7, 1748. He married Jerusha Wyman of Burlington about 1780, and lived in Lunenburg, Mass. She was born Feb. 20, 1754. He was the executor of the will of his father and the following is his signature to his official bond dated March 3, 1795:

Solomon Hovey

Mr. Hovey died Sept. 19, 1825, at the age of seventy-six; and his widow died June 28, 1831, aged seventy-seven.

Their children were born in Lunenburg, as follows:—

527—I.   SOLOMON⁶, born Aug. 14, 1781. *See family numbered "527."*
528—II. ABIJAH⁶, born June 20, 1783. *See family numbered "528."*
529—III. RUTH⁶, born Oct. 18, 1784; died June 18, 1786.
530—IV. WILLIAM⁶, born Dec. 27, 1785. *See family numbered "530."*
531—V.   JOSEPH F.⁶, born June 18, 1787; married Sally Randall in 1810.
532—VI. JAMES⁶, born March 10, 1789; died, unmarried, Sept. —, 1807, aged eighteen.
533—VII. JERUSHA⁶, born Jan. 29, 1792; married Thomas Goodhue Dec. —, 1832 (1822?).

255

LT. DOMINICUS HOVEY⁵, born in Rochester, Mass., April 5, 1740. He was a soldier, in 1758, from Mendon, in Capt. Gamaliel

* Essex Registry of Deeds, book 177, leaf 63.

Bradford's company in the French war. He was a soldier of the
Revolution, being at the New York evacuation Sept. 15, 1777,
and at Valley Forge, in want of clothing, May 1, 1778. The following is an extract from one of his letters from the army,
written to his father:—

CAMP AT HARLAM, Oct. 7, 1776.

I desire your prayers for me that I may be kept from sin, and if
called to battle again that God would cover all our heads in the day of
battle and that he would give us courage and conduct that I may fight
manfully for our People and Country and the Cities of God. In General
Fellows' Brigade.

He held a lieutenant's commission.

He lived in Rochester; and married, first, Ruth Hammond
of Rochester (published Oct. 12, 1760). He married, second,
Mehitable ————, before 1811.

Mr. Hovey's children were born in Rochester, as follows:—

534—I.   OLIVE[6], born Oct. 17, 1761; married Roger Hammond Oct. 2,
          1792.
535—II.   EZRA[6], born Sept. 6, 1763; lost at sea in his teens.
536—III. SARAH[6], born Sept. 9, 1765; married John Blackmer of Ply-
          mouth in 1789.
537—IV.   RUTH[6], born July 11, 1767; married, first, Thomas Clark of
          Plymouth (published May 20, 1794); and, second, James
          Winslow.
538—V.   ELIZABETH[6], born May 21, 1769.
539—VI.   AARON[6], born May 16, 1771. *See family numbered "539."*
540—VII. IVORY[6], born March 16, 1773.
541—VIII. DOMINICUS[6], born March 3. 1775. *See family numbered "541."*
542—IX.   GIDEON[6], born Aug. 31, 1777; published to Betsey Clark of
          Plymouth before 1807.
543—X.   SAMUEL[6], born March 6, 1780.

259

DR. IVORY HOVEY[5], born in Rochester, Mass., Dec. 29, 1748.
He was a physician, and lived and practised his profession in
South Berwick, Me. From the following petition, it would seem
that he was a member of the house of representatives in 1775:—

To the Honourable the Counsel of the House of Representatives, of
the Colony of the Maſsachuſets bay Octo' 3[th] 1775.

The petition of Ivory Hovey in behalf of his Conſtitiants, humbly
prays, (that where as Powder Cannot be Obtained to fix out priviteers
in the Eastern settlements, at the Expence of the Colony at present), your
peti[o]ner therefore prays that the Committees appointed by this Honourable Court for the Eastern districts may *may* be directed to take into
their Cair, the veſſel or veſſels that are allready Detaind in their districts,
by this Honourable Court, and that thay be authoriz[d] (If thay Can procure
the Neceſſaries at their own Expence to fix them out as priviteers, your
petitioner forthermore pray as it will be attended with a great expence to
send up to their Honourable Court, If they Should fix said veſſels out),
that your Honoures would be pleaſ[d] to grant him, Two Commiſſions to be
laft a Blank, that the Committee may appoint Commander[s], whome thay
Shall think most Capable, & worthy, of such a Trust, forthermore your

petiti[o]ner would be glad, of your written Orders, that is to say, weather the Commanders, of the Vefsels. shall take all British, nova scotia, or Newfoundland, Bottoms, afsiating our unnatural Enimies with supplys, that the Commanders may Justly know how far their Commifsions extend your petiti[o]ner, prays that your Honours would be pleased to dispach him with their orders as Soon as may be: which he will Strictly Obey and your petiti[o]ner as in duty bound will ever pray

IVORY HOVEY

Your Petitioner farthermore prays that either of his Constituants may have Liberty of sending where they may think proper for Powder provided He, or they first obtain a *permit* from the Committee whom your Hon[rs] have appointed in the eastern Districts.

This petition was entered Oct. 5th., and it was ordered that it "lie till y* Com⁹ on Armed Vefsels report."*

Doctor Hovey served as surgeon in the Revolution, and was stationed at Fort Miller, Ticonderoga, having been appointed surgeon of Colonel Scammul's battalion April 12, 1777. A letter to his father, written by him at Fort Miller and dated July 27, 1777, says: "I am naturally a Great Coward, and all that quiets me is I am in the way of Duty."

Dr. Hovey married, first, Mary, daughter of William and Elizabeth Hight, who died Nov. 7, 1770, at the age of twenty-five. Her remains lie in the old burial place at South Berwick, and the epitaph upon her gravestone is "Blessed are the dead who die in the Lord." He married, second, Frances ————, who died Feb. 3, 1816, aged sixty-eight. He is also said to have married, third, Jenette Winslow.

A. C. Stearns of Watertown, Mass., has in his possession an interesting paper of Doctor Hovey. It is an agreement made with John and Alexander Cambell of Tobago, in 1789, that Doctor Hovey shall send in the brigantine Tryall, a cargo of boards, joists, scantling, staves, clapboards, shingles, beef, cod fish, horses, etc., to be exchanged for rum.

Doctor Hovey died in Wiscasset, Maine, Oct. 17, 1818, at the age of sixty-nine. His children were born as follows:—

544—I.   TEMPLE⁴, born about 1775; died Aug. 23, 1811, aged thirty-six.
545—II.   FANNY⁴, born Feb. 7, 1779; died, unmarried, May 3, 1799.

The following obituary notice is taken from the *Newburyport Herald*, issue of May 17, 1799:—

> "On the evening of Friday, May 3, fell afleep in death, Mifs *Fanny Hovey*, in the 21ft year of her age, the eldeft daughter of Dr. Ivory Hovey, Efq. of Berwick, Maine. Poor is thought and impotent is language to pourtray a character like hers. The focial fphere is enveloped in gloom by the deprivation of one, who irradiated it by her matchlefs beauty, enlivened it by her fprightly converfe, and charmed is by her improved underftanding. But in the do-

---

* Massachusetts Archives, volume CLXXX, leaf 182.

mestic circle inconfolable muſt be the diſtreſs, for irreparable is the loſs. Her ſerene temper, amiable diſpoſition, and active virtue, were eminently calculated to delight as a daughter and to bleſs as a SISTER. As her life was purity, her death was peace. She ſupported a long and tedious illneſs, with the compoſure of philoſophy, and met the laſt ſtruggle with the fortitude of chriſtianity.

> *"Here reſts what once was beauty, once was grace,*
> *Grace, that with tenderneſs and ſenſe combin'd,*
> *Here reſts what once was beauty, once was grace,*
> *To form that harmony of ſoul and face,*
> *Where beauty ſhines the mirror of the mind.*
> *While friendſhip's eye diſtills the copious tear,*
> *Faith lends her aid to eaſe affliction's load,*
> *Mortals may weep upon her hallowed bier,*
> *Chriſtians muſt yield an angel to her GOD."*

Her remains lie in the old graveyard at South Berwick, and the epitaph upon her gravestone is as follows:—

> "Parents ne'er lost a child more justly dear,
> A lovelier sister ne'r resided here;
> Her Heavenly Father called her from our love
> To join His family of saints above.
> Let then each tear be dry'd, each sigh supprest,
> Why should we mourn since she's supremely blest?
> Let us like her a spotless course pursue,
> Then we shall meet again no more to bid adieu."

546—III.   DOMINICUS[3], born July 11, 1783; died July 12, 1783.
547—IV.   DOMINICUS[4] (twin), still born March 4, 1790.
548—V.   SAMUEL[5] (twin), still born March 4, 1790.

260

CAPT. SAMUEL HOVEY[5], born at Rochester, Mass., Dec. 6, 1750. He lived in Plymouth, Mass.; and was a soldier of the Revolution, being at the evacuation of Boston March 17, 1776, and at New York at the reading of the Declaration of Independence to the army July 9, 1776. The following are parts of two letters, written by him to his father:—

ROXBURY CAMP, March 30, 1776.
And so I must conclude, begging an interest in your prayers that I may be kept from the sins and vices that are so ust to the Camp. And so I remain your dutiful son till death.

NEW YORK, July 10, 1776.
And so I must conclude, begging your prayers for me—that if I am called to the field of Battle that I may Play the Man. And so I rest your dutiful son till death.

Mr. Hovey married, first, Keturah Foster of Tisbury, Mass. (published March 30, 1777). She died Feb. 14, 1790, at the age of thirty-six. Her remains lie on the ancient burying hill in

Plymouth, by the side of the Pilgrim fathers, and her gravestone bears the following inscription: "In Memory of Mrs. Katurah Hovey wife of Capt. Samuel Hovey who died Feb. 14, 1790 in ye 37 year of her age. Also in Memory of Rachel, their Daughter who died Octr. 1790 aged 8 months & 5 days." He married, second, Cath ————.

Mr. Hovey was called of Wells, Me., in 1806.

Children :—

549—I. OLIVE⁶, born May 26, 1779.
550—II. MARY⁶, born Nov. 25, 1780; married Jesse, son of Sylvanus and Martha (Waite) Bartlett May 28, 1809. He was born in 1772; and married, first, Betsey Drew. The children of Jesse and Mary (Hovey) Bartlett were born as follows: 1. *Sylvanus⁷*, married Sarah Loring. 2. *.William D.⁸* 3. *Catherine⁷*.
551—III. JANE⁶, born Nov. 17, 1782, in Plymouth; married Jacob, son of Isaac and Sarah (Doten) Howland in 1798. Child: 1. *Pamelia⁷*, born Nov. 22, 1805, in Plymouth; married Thomas, son of Ichabod and Jerusha (Doten) Bearce of Plymouth April 6, 1825. He was born in Plymouth March 3, 1806; was an iron worker and farmer; and lived at Chiltonville, in Plymouth. She died in Plymouth May 14, 1876; and he died there April 16, 1883. They had nine children.
552—IV. CATHERINE⁶, born June 2, 1785; married Isaac Jackson Lucas in 1819.
553—V. SAMUEL⁶, born Oct. 7, 1787.
554—VI. RACHEL⁶, born Feb. —, 1790; died Oct. —, 1790, aged eight months and five days.
555—VII. SYLVANUS JOURDAINE⁶, born July 28, 1791.

262

STEPHEN HOVEY⁵, born in Topsfield, Mass., Feb. 24, 1741-2. He was a yeoman, and lived in Topsfield until about 1768, when he settled at Maugerville, on the St. John river, in New Brunswick. For one hundred and twenty-one pounds, he conveyed sixty acres and one hundred and thirty rods of land in Topsfield May 3, 1765.* For eight pounds, he conveyed to Allen Pearly of Ipswich, yeoman, two acres of meadow in Topsfield, on Pie brook, April 10, 1767.†

The following is a copy of Mr. Hovey's signature on a bond given in the course of settlement of the estate of his father in 1765:

Stephen Hovey

Mr. Hovey married Abigail, daughter of Nathaniel and Abigail (Potter) Hood of Topsfield (published July 18, 1761). She was baptized in Topsfield May 24, 1741. She was his wife

---

* Essex Registry of Deeds, book 115, leaf 223.
† Essex Registry of Deeds, book 158, leaf 76.

in 1767. The dates of their deaths have not come to the knowledge of the writer; he was dead in 1793, however.

Their children were born as follows:—

556—I. AARON⁶, baptized March 14, 1762, in Topsfield. *See family numbered "556."*

557—II. MARY⁶, baptized March 4, 1764, in Topsfield.

558—III. ABIGAIL⁶, baptized Sept. 29, 1765, in Topsfield.

559—IV. SARAH⁶, married Malachi Orcutt of Penobscot, Me., yeoman, and she probably died, childless, before 1793. Mr. Orcutt, for six pounds, conveyed to John Tibbits of Bangor, Me., yeoman, the estate "coming to me or my wife Sarah Orcutt by heirship out of my father Stephen Hovey's estate, late of Topsfield, deceased, he being heir to his father Aaron Hovey's estate, of Topsfield, deceased," July 24, 1793.* For seven pounds and three shillings, Mr. Tibbits conveyed to Ivory Hovey of Topsfield, yeoman, Timothy Emerson, yeoman, and Joseph Hood, yeoman, both of Hollis, N. H. all the estate of Stephen Hovey, late of Majorville, Cumberland, Nova Scotia, yeoman, and also said Sarah's interest in the estate of Aaron Hovey of Topsfield, deceased, Sept. 10, 1793.†

275

LT. DANIEL HOVEY⁵, born Dec. 20, 1741, in Oxford, Mass. He lived in Oxford, having his father's farm; and was one of the selectmen and constables, and also served in other capacities. He was a lieutenant in Captain Town's company, and marched on the Lexington alarm. With Ebenezer Shumway he purchased sixteen acres of land in Oxford, with the brickyard and clay pits, for thirty pounds, Jan. 25, 1773 ;‡ and they carried on the brickyard as long as Mr. Hovey lived. It was located northward of Town's pond.

Mr. Hovey married Content Ramsdell of Abington Dec. 31, 1759, in Abington; and died in 1776, his widow, Content Hovey, being appointed administratrix of his estate Feb. 6. 1777. The inventory of his estate amounted to £528. 16s., 4d., of which £382 was real estate, and the balance, £146. 16s., 4d., personal.

Mrs. Hovey married, secondly, Charles Cudworth of Freetown (published May 6. 1782).

Mr. Hovey's children were born in Oxford, as follows:—

560—I. SARAH⁶, born Dec. 23, 1760; married Moses Nelson of Sutton, husbandman, Aug. 19, 1779; and they were living there Feb. 21, 1784, when they, for twenty-eight pounds, released to her brother Gideon Hovey one-half of their father's homestead.§

561—II. GIDEON⁶, born Nov. 22, 1762. *See family numbered "561."*

562—III. LYDIA⁶, born April 6, 1765; living at Putney, Vt., unmarried, in 1792.

* Essex Registry of Deeds, book 157, leaf 55.
† Essex Registry of Deeds, book 157, leaf 56.
‡ Worcester Registry of Deeds, book 68, page 488.
§ Worcester Registry of Deeds, book 91, page 524.

563—IV. DANIEL[6], born May 7, 1767; died Nov. —, 1768.
564—V. MIRIAM[6], born Aug. 30, 1769; married Amos, son of Amos and Ruth (Parker) Shumway of Oxford (published June 7, 1788); and lived in Oxford. He was a Revolutionary soldier; and died in Oxford Dec. 18, 1816. She died Aug. 2, 1842, at the age of seventy-two. Their children were born in Oxford, as follows: 1. *Urania*[7], born Nov. 15, 1788; married Josiah Stone of Windsor, Vt., Jan. 1, 1817; settled at Petersham, where he died Feb. 10, 1823, aged thirty-four. She died at Oxford Feb. 10, 1880, at the age of ninety-one. They had one child. 2. *Sophia*[7], born Nov. 1, 1790; married Peter Kidder. 3. *Lewis*[7], born Nov. 20, 1792. 4. *Perez*[7], born Dec. 3, 1794; married Catherine Daniels of Connecticut; and had no children. 5. *Betsey*[7], born Sept. 26, 1796; married Josiah McFarland Feb. 15, 1818. 6. *Ruth*[7], born Feb. 13, 1799; married Richard Gleason April 19, 1819. 7. *Polly*[7], born Aug. 28, 1801; married Dr. Erastus Richardson of Eastport, Me., April 12, 1845; and she died at Augusta, Me., April 13, 1885. 8. *Amos*[7], born June 23, 1805; married Rosalinda Davis Feb. 28, 1833; lived at Webster; and had three children. 9. *Phila*[7], born Nov. 6, 1807; *married* James D. Tourtellotte of Pomfret, Conn., Jan. 24, 1827; settled at Tolland, Conn.; and removed to Willimantic, Conn., where he died May —, 1889. They had children. 10. *Celia*[7], born Nov. 29, 1813; married Jared Lilley of Woodstock, Conn., May 18, 1841; and removed to Rockford, Ill. They had no children.
565—VI. CONTENT[6], born March 10, 1772; married Obadiah Joy of Putney, Vt.
566—VII. MARY[6], born Dec. 6, 1774; living at Putney, Vt., unmarried, in 1795.

278

NATHANIEL HOVEY[5], born in Mansfield, Conn., June 22, 1719. He lived in Mansfield; and married Abigail ————. He bought of James Hovey, jr., of Mansfield, for forty-eight pounds, sixteen acres of land on Mount Hope river Aug. 5, 1740.* They were living there in 1752.

Children, born in Mansfield:—

567—I. NATHANIEL[6], born May 18, 1746.
568—II. EUNICE[6], baptized March 11, 1749-50 (daughter of "Nathaniel and Elizabeth Hovey").
569—III. JOANNA[6], born June 24, 1752.

289

EDMUND HOVEY[5], born in Mansfield, Conn., Nov. 19, 1728. He was a cordwainer and yeoman, and lived in Mansfield until 1760, when he settled in Manchester, Mass., having married a second wife from that town. In Manchester, he held several town offices, as hayward in 1762, and hogreeve and tithingman in 1764.

* Mansfield Registry of Deeds, book 3, page 968.

Mr. Hovey owned several lots of land in Manchester, having bought, for seven pounds, six shillings and eight pence, five acres and twenty rods of land there, near "Jabeshes Bridge so called," Dec. 15, 1763.* For thirty shillings, he bought thirty rods of land in Manchester on the road to Chebacco, March 15, 1765.†

Mr. Hovey married, first, Mary, daughter of Noah Gilbert of Mansfield Dec. 15, 1749; and she died there Nov. 3, 1754. He married, second, Margaret, daughter of Ezekiel and Emma (Foster) Knowlton of Manchester, Mass., May 16, 1758. She was born in Manchester Nov. 5, 1735. He died in Manchester Feb. 14, 1767, at the age of thirty-eight.

Mr. Hovey left a will, of which the following copy is taken from the original instrument on file in the probate office at Salem:—

In the name of god amen the first Day of Janary 1767 I Edmond Hovey of manchester in the County of Essex Cord winder being of perfect mind & memory thanks be unto god But Knowing this Body of mine is Subject to mortality have therefore Concluded while my memory & Reafon Remained Entire to make And ordain this my Last will and testament in the following manner and forme that is to Say principably & first of all all I giue and recommend my Immortal Soul into the Hands of god that gaue it and my Body I recommend to the Earth to be Buried in decent Christian manner Doutting Not But at the general Refurrection I Shall Receiue the Same again By the power of almighty God

and as to my worldly Estate wheurewith it hath pleafed God to Blefs me in the following manner & form I Difpose of the Same

Impr I giue and bequeath to margreet Houey my Dearly Beloued wife my House & Barn & all my Land thereto adjoyning & all other Real Eastate that appertaineth to me at the time of my Deceafs to gather With all my houshold goods Depts and moueable Eastate of what Nature foeuer She paying all my just and honest Debts & funeral Charges to will and Difpose of as She thinks proper.

Itam I make & ordain deen Jonathan Harick & margreet my wife my Sole Executris of this my Last will & testament & I Do hereby utterly Disallow Revock & Difannul all other wills testaments Legacies & Bequests By me in any ways Before named willed & bequeathd Ratifying And Confirming this and No other to be my Last will and testament.

In Witnefs where of I haue hereunto Set my hand and Seal the Day and year aboue written

Signd Seald & Deliuered by the
Said Edmond Houey as & for his
Last Will & testament in the prefance
of us who were prefent at the Signing
& Sealing thereof

Nath'l Lee
Benj's Craft
James Lee

[Edmund Hovey]   [SEAL]

The will was proved April 7, 1767. The inventory of his estate amounted to £55, 18s., 4d., of which £36, 13s., 4d., was real

* Essex Registry of Deeds, book 120, leaf 99.
† Essex Registry of Deeds, book 118, leaf 60.

estate, and £19, 5s., was personal. The real estate included a house and barn.

Mr. Hovey's wife Margaret *Margaret Hovey* survived him. The following is her signature to the probate papers:

She joined with her husband and other heirs of her father in a conveyance of four acres of swamp and upland in the Great Neck in Manchester, on the south side of the road leading to Lobster cove, and bounded southerly by the sea, Oct. 31. 1765.* She was still living in Manchester Feb. 13. 1778. when, for twenty-six pounds, thirteen shillings and four pence, she sold the small dwelling house and one-fourth of an acre of land, lying on the south side of the highway, in Manchester.† Her subsequent history is unknown, except that she died, his widow, in Norwich, Vt., Oct. 2, 1798, aged "61."

Mr. Hovey's children were as follows :—

570—I. MARY⁴, born Oct. 29, 1750, in Mansfield, Conn.; died Oct. 15 (19?), 1754, in Mansfield.

571—II. ELIJAH⁴, born April 17, 1752, in Mansfield; died Oct. 25 (21?), 1754, in Mansfield.

572—III. SARAH⁴, born Jan. 2, 1754, in Mansfield; died Oct. 22, 1754.

573—IV. ROGER⁴, born Feb. 20, 1759, in Mansfield. *See family numbered "573."*

574—V. NATHANIEL⁴, born Jan. 25, 1761, in Manchester, Mass. *See family numbered "574."*

575—VI. ISAAC⁴, born Oct. 24, 1763, in Manchester. *See family numbered "575."*

576—VII. JAMES⁴, born in 1765, in Manchester; died Sept. —, 1765, aged two months.

577—VIII. SARAH⁴, born Oct. 22, 1766, in Manchester.

292

AARON HOVEY³, born in Mansfield, Conn., April 22, 1735. He was brought up on the farm; and was a true type of the New England farmer, of strong personality, devoted to his family and devout in his religion. He lived in his native town, in a good-sized house of one story in height, with hip roof, which is still standing and substantially the same as when occupied by him.

Mr. Hovey conveyed his interest in some land in Hanover, N. H., which he inherited from his brother James Hovey, Feb. 4, 1767.‡ He bought, for thirty pounds, one acre of land in Norwich, Vt., being part of lot eleven in the first range of hundred-acre lots on Beaver meadow brook, Oct. 30, 1784 :§ and on the same day he also bought one hundred and thirty-six acres and one hundred and twelve rods of land in Norwich.§ For seventy

* Essex Registry of Deeds, book 126, leaf 217.
† Essex Registry of Deeds, book 138, leaf 66.
‡ Grafton Registry of Deeds, book 9, page 271.
§ Norwich Registry of Deeds, book 1, page 197.

pounds, he bought fifty-three acres of land in the east part of
Norwich Oct. 30, 1786;* and on the same day he also bought
forty-nine acres and seventy-five rods of land in Norwich, being
part of the Governor's lot so called.† For forty pounds, he sold
twenty-three acres of land in Norwich, being part of lot ten in
the first range of lots. Oct. 4, 1793.‡

Mr. Hovey married, first, his cousin Olive, daughter of John
and Dorothy (Baldwin) Farwell Jan. 15, 1761. She was born in
Mansfield July 24, 1740; and died there July 29, 1764. He married, second, Abigail, daughter of Dea. Edmund and Martha
(Otis) Freeman of Mansfield Feb. 18, 1768. She was born in
Mansfield May 20, 1743. He died in Mansfield March 10, 1812;
and his remains lie in the cemetery by the church which is near
the agricultural college. His wife Abigail survived him, and
died in Mansfield, his widow, in 1831, at the age of eighty-seven.

Mr. Hovey's children were born in Mansfield, as follows:—

578—i.   Olive[5], born Oct. 30, 1761; married Elijah, son of Prince and
          Rebecca (Johnson) Freeman of Mansfield Dec. 27, 1781.
          He was born in Mansfield Nov. 3, 1757; and they lived in
          Waterford, Vt., in 1810. She died Oct. 21, 1820, at the age
          of fifty-eight. Their children were born as follows: 1.
          Elijah[6], born Nov. 23, 1782, in Mansfield; and died April —,
          1869. 2. Aaron[6], born Dec. 31, 1784; and died Nov. 12, 1864.
          3. Arad[6], born Dec. 24, 1788. 4. Isaac Farwell[6], lived in
          Ogden, Utah; and died in 1844. 5. Olive Hovey[6], born June
          23, 1799, in Lebanon, N. H.; married Winslow Farr in 1816;
          lived in Ogden, Utah; and died at "Big Cottonwood," in
          Ogden, March 10, 1893, at the age of ninety-three.

579—ii.   Mary[5], born April 11, 1764; married Calvin Seaver of Nor-
          wich, Vt., Feb. 16, 1786; lived in the northeastern part of the
          town; and died July 4, 1857, at the age of ninety-three. Their
          children were born in Norwich, as follows: 1. Calvin[6],
          born Jan. 6, 1787. 2. Luther[6], born May 2, 1789. 3. Mary[6],
          born May 6, 1790. 4. Aaron[6], born April 19, 1793. 5. Olive[6],
          born Sept. 10, 1794. 6. Elizabeth[6], born Dec. 25, 1797. 7.
          Otis[6], born Jan. 5, 1801; lived in Norwich.

580—iii. Martha[5], born Dec. 9, 1768; married Jesse Waldo of Mans-
          field in 1786; they lived in Mansfield until about 1810, when
          they removed to Prattsburg, N. Y., where he died. She died
          April 17, 1849, at the age of eighty. Their children were
          born as follows: 1. Martha[6], born March 5, 1788, in Mans-
          field; married Isaac Pardee; and lived in Batavia, N. Y.
          2. Jesse[6], born May 6, 1790, in Mansfield; married Mary
          Fay; and lived in Prattsburg. 3. Aaron[6], born May 24,
          1792; married Mary Davenport; and lived in Prattsburg.
          4. Otis[6], born Dec. 28, 1794; married Fanny Cock; and lived
          in Prattsburg. 5. Albigence[6], born Feb. 23, 1797; married
          Elizabeth Williams; and lived in Prattsburg. 6. Henry
          Hovey[6], born Oct. 21, 1799; married Mary Clarg; and lived
          in Prattsburg. 7. Lucius[6], born June 25, 1802; married

* Norwich Registry of Deeds, book 1, page 268.
† Norwich Registry of Deeds, book 1, page 289.
‡ Norwich Registry of Deeds, book 2, page 22.

Rebecca Hearvy; and lived in Prattsburg. 8. *Charles[7]*, born Nov. 2, 1805; married Elizabeth E. Parmalee; and lived in in Prattsburg. 5. *Albigence[7]*, born Feb. 23, 1797; married *Freeman[7]*, born June 21, 1811. in Prattsburg; married, first, Elisabeth C. Holmes; and, second, Eliza Bass. He was a Presbyterian minister; and died at his home, Harbor Springs, Mich., Jan. 16, 1893.

581—IV. ABIGAIL[4], born May 9, 1770; married Rev. William, son of Joseph and Experience (Gurley) Storrs of Ashford, Conn., Dec. —, 1790. He was born in Mansfield Aug. 20, 1760, and was pastor of the church of Westford, in Ashford, for thirty-four years, it being his only pastorate. He died in his parish of Westford Nov. 30, 1824, at the age of sixty-four. She survived him, and died in the same parish May 17, 1850, aged eighty. Their children were born in Westford parish as follows: 1. *Abigail[5]*, born Sept. 15, 1791; married Ichabod Ward Jan. 11, 1811; lived in Westford; and died there Sept. — 1854, aged sixty-three. 2. *Crissa[5]*, born March 15, 1793; married Zewinglius Judson Dec. 1, 1840; lived in Eastford and Canterbury, Conn.; and died in Canterbury Sept. 22, 1848. 3. *William[5]*, born Sept. 2, 1796; married Harriet E. Woodward Oct. 14, 1822; lived in Westford and Mansfield, Conn.; and died at Hartford, Conn., May 11, 1887, at the age of ninety. 4. *Lucius[5]*, born Feb. 28, 1800; left home about 1824, and was heard from but once afterward. 5. *Aaron Hovey[5]*, born Jan. 20, 1806; married Mary A. Cady Nov. 2, 1827; lived in Brooklyn, Conn., where he died March 8, 1878. 6. *Rosetta Cecelia[5]*, born July 23, 1813; married Amos Wood April 18, 1837; and lived in Worcester, Mass.

582—V. AARON[4], born June 22, 1774. *See family numbered "582."*

583—VI. HANNAH[4], born Nov. 17, 1778; married Daniel, son of Asa (son of 62) and Lydia (Freeman) Moulton of Mansfield May 29, 1803. He was born in Mansfield June 15, 1773. She died at Mansfield Oct. 7, 1840; and he died there May 14, 1859, at the age of eighty-five. Their children were born in Mansfield, as follows: 1. ——————[5] (dau.), born Aug. 27, 1804; died Sept. 16, 1804. 2. *Lydia[5]*, born Sept. 6, 1808; lived in Mansfield; and died, unmarried, Jan. 13, 1899, at the age of ninety. 3. *Abigail[5]*, born Dec. 14, 1811; married James Chapman, jr., of Mansfield, Nov. 22, 1837; lived in Mansfield; and died there Feb. 20, 1888, at the age of seventy-six. 4. *Julia[5]*, born April 8, 1819; lives in Mansfield, unmarried, at the age of ninety-two.

584—VII. EDMUND[6], born Nov. 23, 1782. *See family numbered "584."*

298

WILLIAM HOVEY[6], born in Mansfield, Conn., July 6, 1749. He lived in Norwich, Vt., where he bought, for sixty pounds, one-half of lot 13 in the first range of Hundred-acre lots in Norwich, containing fifty acres, March 18, 1782.[*] July 19, 1783, for one pound, he bought one-half of an acre of land in Norwich, being part of the twelfth lot in the first range of the Hundred-acre lots.[†]

* Norwich Registry of Deeds, book 1, page 84.
† Norwich Registry of Deeds, book 1, page 191.

For four pounds and ten shillings, he conveyed six acres of the thirteenth lot, Feb. 11. 1785.* He bought one acre of the twelfth lot above-mentioned, for three pounds, in 1786 ;† and he sold parts of the twelfth and thirteenth lots, for one hundred and twenty pounds, March 29, 1793.‡ Mr. Hovey was a yeoman.

He married Lucinda Downer Dec. 7, 1780, in Norwich; where he died Oct. 14, 1834, at the age of eighty-five.

Their children were born in Norwich, as follows:—

585—I.   WILLIAM⁶, born Dec. 24, 1781.
586—II. LUCINDA⁶, born July 3, 1783.
587—III. JAMES⁶, born Jan. 22, 1785.
588—IV. ELIZABETH⁶, born Oct. 27, 1786; probably married Samuel John-
         son of Norwich May 26, 1808; lived in Norwich; children,
         born in Norwich: 1. *Roisa⁷*, born March 17, 1809; married
         William, son of John (son of No. 296) and Perrins
         (Grow) Slafter of Norwich Feb. 4, 1830; he was born Oct.
         1, 1807; and she died Oct. 31, 1849. 2. *Elizabeth⁷*, born
         April 11, 1811; died April 12, 1811. 3. *Samuel⁷*, born March
         30, 1812; died March 31, 1812. 4. *Martha Diana⁷*, born
         June 13, 1813. 5. *Calvin S.⁷*, born Dec. 4, 1820.
589—V.   ROXELENA⁶ (dau.), born Sept. 7, 1788.
590—VI. LEVINA⁶, born June 27, 1790.
591—VII. HANNAH⁶, born Feb. 22, 1792.

300

AMOS HOVEY⁵, born in Mansfield, Conn., April 9, 1753. He was a yeoman, and lived in Norwich, Vt., until about 1784, when he settled in Thetford, Vt., where he afterwards resided.

He bought, for sixty pounds, one-half of lot 13, in the first range of Hundred-acre lots in Norwich, containing fifty acres, March 18, 1782.§ For one hundred and sixty pounds, he sold seventy-seven acres of land, in Norwich, on the ast side of the highway leading from Unpompanusuck to the meeting house, Jan. 1, 1787.‖ He bought, for twenty pounds, one-fifth of lot 14, in the first range of Hundred-acre lots, in Norwich, Dec. 5, 1786.¶

Mr. Hovey married, first, Clara Amelia Calkins Jan. 22, 1781, in Norwich. She died in Thetford July 21, 1813, at the age of fifty-seven. He married, second, Mrs. Deborah (Ford), widow of Nicholas White Dec. 21, 1814; and she died March 25, 1837, at the age of seventy-two. He died July 11, 1840, at the age of eighty-seven. His remains lie buried in the ancient burial ground at Thetford Centre, and his gravestone is inscribed as follows:—

* Norwich Registry of Deeds, book 1, page 206.
† Norwich Registry of Deeds, book 1, page 283.
‡ Norwich Registry of Deeds, book 1, page 435.
§ Norwich Registry of Deeds, book 1, page 84.
‖ Norwich Registry of Deeds, book 1, page 281.
¶ Norwich Registry of Deeds, book 1, page 280.

MR.
AMOS HOVEY
Died July
11, 1 8 4 0 ,
Aged 87 years.

Mr. Hovey's children were born as follows :—

592—i.   LEANTHA[6], born Dec. 15, 1781, in Norwich; died in Thetford, unmarried, Sept. 15, 1807, aged twenty-five.

593—ii. AMOS[6], born about 1784; died April 10, 1786, aged twenty-one months.

594—iii. CLARA AMELIA[6], born Aug. 21, 1786, in Thetford, Vt.; died Jan. 19, 1809, aged twenty-two.

595—iv. AMOS[6], born Nov. 19, 1788, in Thetford; died March 5, 1790.

596—v.   ALFRED[6], born April 26, 1791, in Thetford. *See family numbered "596."*

597—vi. ELEAZER[6], born Oct. 26, 1793, in Thetford; died June —, 1861, at the age of sixty-seven.

598—vii. ALVA[6], born May 8, 1796, in Thetford; died March 29, 1804.

307

REV. JONATHAN HOVEY[5], born in Mansfield, Conn., Oct. 10, 1753. He lived in his native town and Piermont, N. H. He bought seven and one-half acres of land in the First Society, in Windham, Conn., for five pounds and ten shillings, Dec. 6, 1790.* For six pounds, nine shilling and fourteen pence, he bought two acres and twenty-five rods of land in New Boston, in Windham, May 28, 1791.† and twenty-three acres in Windham, for thirty-four pounds and ten shillings, Oct. 12, 1791.‡

He was at first a lawyer, and was ordained a minister of the gospel, at Piermont, N. H., in 1803.

Mr. Hovey married Mary Storrs March 27, 1777, in Mansfield; and died in Piermont Aug. 23, 1825.

Their children were born in Mansfield, as follows :—

599—i.   ROSETTA[6], born June 9, 1779; married James Weaver (Weber?). They lived in West Almond, N. Y., in 1832, and in Munsair, Graque county, Ohio, in 1840.

600—ii. ANNE[6], born Dec. 1, 1780.

601—iii. JONATHAN[6], born July 8, 1782; late of Winfield, N. H.; but residence unknown in 1832; lived in Conneant, Ashtabula co., Ohio, in 1840.

602—iv. LYDIA[6], born Sept. 26, 1784.

---

* Windham Registry of Deeds, book U, page 192.
† Windham Registry of Deeds, book U, page 193.
‡ Windham Registry of Deeds, book U, page 191.

603—v.   MARY⁶, born Sept. 20, 1788; married Jabez Spicer; and lived in
          Andover, N. Y., in 1832.
604—vi.   JOHN⁶, born March 27, 1791; died Aug. 4, 1792.
605—vii. SELENE⁶, born Jan. 1, 1793.
606—viii. HANNAH⁶, born in 1795 (?).
607—ix.   OLIVE⁶, born April 13, 1797.

310

JOSEPH HOVEY⁵, born in Mansfield, Conn., Sept. 9, 1734. He
lived in his native town, owning part of the Durkee farm. He
married Eunice, daughter of Capt. William and Experience Williams May 28, 1761, in Mansfield. She was born there March 6,
1742. He died in Mansfield July 7, 1797, at the age of sixty-two;
and the inscription upon his gravestone, in the Gurley burial
place, at Mansfield, reads as follows:—

In Memory of Mr. Joseph Hovey who died July 7ᵗʰ 1797 In ye 63ʳᵈ
year of his age.

Mr. Hovey's estate was appraised at £2,598, 14s., 10d., of
which £2,066, 15s., was real estate, and £531, 19s., 10d., was
personal. Administration was granted to his sons Joseph Hovey
and Elisha Hovey Aug. 4, 1797. His wife survived him, and
removed to Bridgewater, Oneida county, N. Y., where she died
May 5, 1801, her will, dated April 8, 1801, being proved June 13,
1801, in Mansfield, her old home. She bequeathed her great
bible to her son Oliver Hovey. She was sixty years of age.

Their children were born in Mansfield, as follows:—

608—1.   RUTH⁶, born Jan. 6, 1763; and died, unmarried, in Mansfield,
         March 17, 1796, at the age of thirty-three. The following is
         the inscription upon her gravestone in the Gurley burial-
         place, in Mansfield:—

         "In Memory of Mrs Ruth daughter of Mr Joseph &
         Eunice Hovey, who died March 17, 1796 In ye 34ᵗʰ year of
         her age."

609—ii. ————⁶, born Jan. 26, 1765; died Jan. 26, 1765.
610—iii. EXPERIENCE⁶, born April 8, 1766; married Zenas Gurley of
         Mansfield in 1793. He married, first, Lavina Dimock of
         Mansfield April 9, 1789; and she died Dec. 7, 1791, at the age
         of twenty-two. Mr. Gurley removed to Bridgewater, N. Y.;
         and died Dec. 18, 1800, at the age of thirty-five. His wife
         Experience survived him. Children of Zenas and Experience
         (Hovey) Gurley: 1. Henry⁷, born Oct. —, 1794. 2. Eunice⁷,
         born in 1796. 3. Lavina⁷, born April 3, 1799. 4. Zenas
         Hovey⁷, born May 17, 1801.
611—iv. JOSEPH⁶, born March 24, 1768. See family numbered "611."
612—v.   EUNICE⁶, born Sept. 19, 1770; and died, unmarried, Feb. 15,
         1795, at the age of twenty-four. The inscription on her
         gravestone in the old Gurley burial ground in Mansfield is
         as follows:—

"In Memory of Eunice, daughter of Mr. Joseph & Mrs.
Eunice Hovey, who died Feb. 15ᵗʰ 1795, In ye 25ʰ Year of
her Age."

613—VI.   JACOB⁶, born April 16, 1773; and died Feb. 11, 1776, aged two
          years.
614—VII. ELISHA⁶, born Aug. 3, 1775. *See family numbered "614."*
615—VIII. ———⁶, born Dec. 28, 1777; died Feb. 15, 1778.
616—IX.   OLIVER⁶, born June 3, 1780; died Feb. 9, 1803, at the age of
          twenty-two. The following is a copy of the inscription upon
          his gravestone in the ancient Gurley burial-place in Mans-
          field :—

"In Memory of Mr. Oliver Hovey who died Feb* 9ᵗʰ
1803, In ye 23ᵈ Year of his Age.
"Thus one by one we daily fall away:
Till all at length the debt of nature pay."

Oliver Hovey left a will, which was proved and his
brother Isaac Hovey appointed executor March 22, 1803.
617—X.   ISAAC⁶, born Oct. 4, 1782. *See family numbered "617."*

312

CAPT. JACOB HOVEY⁵, born in Mansfield, Conn., Aug. 10,
1740. He lived in his native town until about 1809, when he
removed to New York state. In Mansfield his father gave him a
farm. He is said to have served at Sackett's creek or harbor, in
the regiment of his son, Col. Jacob Hovey, in the war of 1812.
He married, first, Elizabeth, daughter of Peter Dimmick of Mansfield Dec. 25, 1760; and she died in Mansfield June 17, 1774. He
married, second, Abial, daughter of William Smith of Mansfield May 5, 1777. Some writers say that he was dead in 1805,
leaving a will, and that his wife Abial survived him.

The children of Mr. Hovey were born in Mansfield, as follows :—

618—I.   DINAH⁶, born Feb. 25, 1767; married Ethan, son of John and
          Mary (Cross) Barrows of Mansfield April 15, 1784; he was
          born in Mansfield Jan. 18, 1761; and he died there July 12,
          1809. Children, born in Mansfield: 1. *Elisha⁷*, born Sept. 8,
          1784. 2. *Huldah⁷*, born July 26, 1786. 3. *Orpha⁷*, born Dec.
          27, 1788. 4. *Ira⁷*, born April 26, 1791. 5. *John⁷*, born Jan.
          17, 1800. 6. *Sally⁷*, born July 28, 1804. 7. *Marcus⁷*, born
          Sept. 2, 1806. 8. *Symon⁷*, born Jan. 18, 1809.
619—II.   WILLIAM⁶.
620—III. JACOB⁶, born Feb. 16, 1778; went to Sackett's Harbor in war of
          1812, in the command of a regiment; colonel.
621—IV.   LEARNED⁶, born March 30, 1780.
622—V.   ELIZABETH⁶, born May 16, 1782; married Joel Dodge of Mans-
          field Nov. 25, 1802. Children, born in Mansfield: 1. *Eliza-
          beth⁷*, born May 25, 1804. 2. *Lucretia⁷*, born March 25, 1806.
          3. *Harry⁷*, born Aug. 27, 1808. 4. *Caroline⁷*, born July 1,
          1810; died May 10, 1811. 5. *Lucetta⁷*, born June 3, 1812.
          Mary Meria⁷, born Sept. 3, 1814. 7. *Joel⁷*, born March 16,

1816. 8. *Frederick Plummer*[7], born April 16, 1818; died July
2, 1818. 9. *Leonard Hovey*[7], born Sept. 22, 1821. 10.
Origen Stedman[7], born Dec. 19, 1823; married Abigail Ann
Parker Dec. 30, 1850. 11. *General Lafayette*[7], born July
6, 1827.

623—VI.   LUCRETIA[6], born March 2, 1784.
624—VII.   BELA[6], born Sept. 23, 1786. *See family numbered "624."*
625—VIII. ENOCH[6], born March 7, 1789. *See family numbered "625."*
626—IX.   ALVA[6], born Dec. 16, 1790. Isaac Hovey of Mansfield was
           appointed his guardian April 13, 1808.
627—X.   EUNICE[6], born Dec. 24, 1795.

316

NATHAN HOVEY[5], born in Mansfield, Conn., Dec. 22, 1740.
He lived in his native town; and married Jemima, daughter of
Paul Phelps of Lebanon Nov. 11, 1762.

Their child was born in Mansfield, as follows:—

628—I.   AZEL[6], born Nov. 5, 1763.

322

DANIEL HOVEY[5], born in Mansfield, Conn., Sept. 8, 1736.
He lived in his native town; and married Kezia ——————.

Their children were born in Mansfield, as follows:—

629—I.   ANNA[6], baptized Oct. 9, 1771.
630—II.   EZRA[6], baptized Oct. 9, 1771.
631—III.   LUCY[6], born Aug. 3, 1769.
632—IV.   VINE[6], born June 8, 1771.
633—V.   DAN[6], born Feb. 17, 1774.

323

ENOCH HOVEY[5], born in Mansfield, Conn., Nov. 10, 1738.
He lived in his native town; and married Hannah, daughter of
Dea. Cordial and Hannah (Woods) Storrs of Mansfield April 24,
1771. She was born there April 15, 1732. He died in 1805, ad-
ministration upon his estate being granted to his son, Cordial
Storrs Hovey, Nov. 13, 1805.

Their children were born in Mansfield, as follows:—

634—I.   CORDIAL STORRS[6], born Jan. 31, 1772. *See family numbered "634."*
635—II.   HANNAH[6], born Nov. 14, 1773.

325

JOSIAH HOVEY[5], born in Mansfield, Conn., Aug. 24, 1743. He
lived, until 1795, at Lebanon, N. H., after which he resided at
Whitestown, N. Y., Tioga, Pa., and Leicester, N. Y., finally
settling at the northern part of Warsaw, N. Y., where he remained the rest of his life. He served in the war of the Revolution, at Ticonderoga; and was one of the founders and original
members of the Methodist church at Warsaw.

He married Theodora Downer, a native of Mansfield, Conn., and died at Warsaw, N. Y., April 24, 1820, at the age of seventy-six. She survived him, and died at the age of a century, lacking a few months, but so close to that age that the bell was tolled a hundred times.

Their children were born as follows:—

636—I.   SIMEON⁶, born July 6, 1776, in Lebanon, N. H. *See family numbered "636."*
637—II.   GUPDON⁴, born June 6, 1778, in Lebanon. *See family numbered "637."*
638—III.   JOSIAH⁶, born Jan. —, 1780, in Lebanon. *See family numbered "638."*
639—IV.   JOHN⁶. *See family numbered "639."*
640—V.   SUEL⁶, married Lucinda Holmes, and removed to Michigan.
641—VI.   ORRE⁶, born July 23, 1788, in Plainfield, N. H. *See family numbered "641."*
642—VII.   ELIPHALET⁶, born in 1791. *See family numbered "642."*
643—VIII.   ALVIN⁶. *See family numbered "643."*
644—IX.   LURA⁶, born Sept. 23, 1797, at Whitestown, N. Y.; married Nathan Snow of Ellington, Conn., March 18, 1813, at Warsaw, N. Y. He was in the war of 1812, at Black Rock, under General Porter, and was promoted to captain. They lived in Warsaw, N. Y., until 1827, at Conewango, N. Y., till 1835, and removed to Randolph, Vt. Children: 1. *William⁷*, born Dec. 27, 1813, in Warsaw, N. Y. 2. *Suel H.⁷*, born Sept. 20, 1815, in Warsaw. 3. *Chauncey A.⁷*, born Oct. 12, 1817, in Warsaw; married his cousin Laura P. Hovey (1177). 4. *Filura⁷*, born Nov. 8, 1819, in Warsaw. 5. *Sylvanus⁷*, born Aug. 11, 1822, in Warsaw; died Sept. 28, 1822. 6. *Alvira⁷*, born Oct. 22, 1823, at Warsaw. 7. *Orre⁷*, born March 9, 1826, at Warsaw; lived in Conewango, N. Y.; was in the Civil war, in the Ninth New York volunteer cavalry, company E, under Benjamin F. Chamberlain; married Elizabeth Smith Aug. 16, 1854; and had three children. 8. *Edward⁷*, born Sept. 8, 1828, at Conewango, N. Y. 9. *Melvin⁷*, born March 8, 1830, at Conewango. 10. *Roselia⁷*, born Sept. 26, 1834, at Conewango.
645—X.   FINA⁶, married Lewis Alverson of Perry; and removed to Michigan.
646—XI.   MELINDA⁶, married Richard Jackson; and lived in Warsaw, N. Y., for many years. Children: 1. *Adelia⁷*. 2. *Z. Paddock⁷*; married in Steuben county. 3. *James⁷*; married, and went to Michigan. 4. *Calvin⁷*. 5. *Emery⁷*; served in the war, was taken sick, and died at his home in Michigan.
647—XII.   ZIBA⁶. *See family numbered "647."*
648—XIII.   THEODORA⁶, married Noah Willis; and removed to Missouri.

327

SIMEON HOVEY⁵, born in Mansfield, Conn., Oct. 15, 1747. He lived in his native town until 1801, when he removed to Lima, Livingston county, N. Y. He married, first, Joanna, daughter of Col. Shubael and Ruth (Conant) Conant of Mansfield Oct. 10, 1773. She was born in Mansfield Sept. 21, 1753; and died Nov.

8 (26?), 1783, at the age of thirty. He married, second, Lovisa Bloss Jan. 22, 1784; and she died Aug. 31, 1799. He married, third, Florilla Sargent April 17, 1805; and she died Feb. 4, 1809, at half-past eight o'clock in the morning. He survived her only twenty-four days, dying Feb. 28, 1809, at the age of sixty-one.

The children of Mr. Hovey were as follows:—*

649—I.	SHUBAEL CONANT[4], born Feb. 21, 1777, in Mansfield, Conn. *See family numbered "649."*	
650—II.	ENOCH[6], born June 15, 1779; and died Aug. 24, 1799, at the age of twenty.	
651—III.	JOHN[6], born Oct. 8, 1781; died Sept. 27, 1799.	
652—IV.	JOANNA[6] (Anna), born Sept. 8, 1783; died Nov. 26, 1783.	
653—V.	PARNESA[6], born Jan. 11, 1785.	
654—VI.	SAPETA[6], born Sept. 1, 1786; died Dec. 23, 1794.	
655—VII.	ELIHU[6], born July 23, 1788.	
656—VIII.	ABILENA[4], born May 3, 1790; and died Dec. 18, 1794.	
657—IX.	LEVI[4], born Jan. 16, 1792. *See family numbered "657."*	
658—X.	DANIEL[6], born Aug. 25, 1793.	
659—XI.	ZEBINA CURTIS[4], born May 22, 1795.	
660—XII.	ZELOTES[6], born Nov. 10, 1796.	
661—XIII.	HORATIO NELSON[6], born Feb. 24, 1799.	
662—XIV.	ADELINE[6], born Jan. 19, 1806.	
663—XV.	JOHN LANGDON[6], born June 28, 1807.	
664—XVI.	FLORILLA[6], born Jan. 14, 1809, at five o'clock in the morning.	

332

EBENEZER HOVEY[5], born in Weymouth, Mass., July 24, 1744. He lived in his native town, being a "laborer." For thirty-two pounds, five shillings and eight pence, he bought seven acres of land and buildings, in Weymouth, on the east side of Cedar swamp, Feb. 2, 1767;† and ten days later, for thirteen pounds, six shillings and eight pence, he bought twenty acres of land in Cedar swamp, in Braintree, on the Weymouth line.‡

He married Reliance Pratt of Abington Sept. 11, 1766; and died before 1793.

Their children were as follows:—

665—I.	SARAH[6]; unmarried in 1796.	
666—II.	SAMUEL[6]; living in 1796.	
667—III.	EBENEZER[6]; living in 1796.	

339

CAPT. JAMES HOVEY[5], born in Cambridge, Mass., in 1740. He was a soldier in the company of Captain Been,§ when he was under age, and was taken sick on his return home from Fort

---

* Most of the sons removed eventually to Vincennes, Indiana, and, with the exception of Levi, were carpenters.
† Suffolk Registry of Deeds, book 110, page 186.
‡ Suffolk Registry of Deeds, book 115, page 259.
§ The selectmen of Arundel, in their certificate on the next page, state that he was in the company of Capt. Johnson Moulton of York.

Pownal. He was then living with his father in Arundel, in York county. He was attended at Brunswick, in Lincoln county, while sick by Dr. Phineas Nevers of Georgetown, and Dixey Stone brought him home from Maquoit, arriving Dec. 3, 1760. His disease was small pox, which manifested itself as such five days afterward. On the next day Jeannet Averell was engaged to nurse him, and she continued in that service until Jan. 21, 1761. She states that during that period "he was bereaved of his Senſes generally far near a fortnight." Joseph Miller and James Deshon also nursed him. Mr. Miller sent to the father of the soldier the following bill for his service as nurse:—

ARUNDE Feb[r] 1761

Rev[d] M[r] Hovey D[r] to Joseph Miller, for Nursing James Hovey his Son, who got Home from the army on the 3[d] of December last, was sick of the Small Pox & with the Pleuriſe, for which I bled him twice, once on the 15 of Jan[y] about midnight, & on the Next Day P. M.; & attended him while sick with the Small Pox from the 12 to the 25th of December 14 days at half a Dollar a Day & one Dollar for bleeding in which Time he was dangerouſly ill, as witneſs my Hand.   JOSEPH MILLER.[*]

The following is a copy of a certificate of the selectmen of Arundel:—

ARUNDEL Feb[r] 21 1761

These may Certify whom it may concern that James Hovey of Arundel who was an enliſted Soldier under Captain Johnſon Moulton of York, & in the Service of the Province the laſt year among the weſtern Forces upon his Return to his Hon[d] Fathers Houſe who is our Rev[d] Paſtor which was on the 3[d] of December laſt in the evening, was on the 8th Day of s[d] month taken down with the Small Pox upon which the Family were obliged to move & that Jennet Averel, Joseph Miller & James Deſhon attended him in his Sickneſs time & that he was so dangerouſly ill that for near a week, there was little or no hopes of his Recovery as witneſs our Hands

DIXEY STONE)
THOMAS PERKINS } Select Men.[*]
MOSES FOSTER)

The following is a copy of the bill of Dixey Stone for bringing the soldier home from Maquoit:—

ARUNDEL Feb[r] 25 1761

the Rev[d] M[r] Hovey D[r] to Dixy Stone for himself & Boat three Days viz from August 28, 1759, going to Maquoit for James Hovey his Son that was then, a Soldier sick at Brunſwick, Thirteen Shillings & four pence
DIXEY ſTONE[*]

The father thought that the province should bear the charges of James' sickness, and the outcome was a suit brought by the

[*]Massachusetts Archives, State House, Boston volume XLIV., leaves 438-445.

doctor against the father Dec. 8, 1760, and the latter petitioned
the general court for relief the next February. The claim was
duly allowed, and paid from the province treasury.

Mr. Hovey became a sea-captain, securing two commissions,
from the continental congress, as captain in the privateer service.
He was the commander of the schooner Swallow of ten guns and
sixty men.*

He owned three vessels. He sailed from Stratford, Conn., in
August, 1784, on the day of birth of his eldest son, was ship-
wrecked and absent from home six years. He had a vessel built
of mahogany, and returned in it, entering the port of New Haven,
Conn. This is said to have been the first vessel, built entirely of
mahogany, to enter that port.

He lived at Huntington and Stratford, Conn.; and married
Hannah, daughter of Joseph Tomlinson of Huntington April 9,
1783. She was born in Huntington in 1763. He died at Stratford June 15, 1829; and she died there in 1831 or 1832, both
being aged.

Their children were born as follows:—

668—I. JAMES[2], born Aug. —, 1784; captain; died, unmarried, on the
island of Curracoa Feb. 3, 1806, at the age of twenty-one.
The following is a copy of the inscription on his gravestone:—

"James, son of Capt. James and Hannah Hovey, de-
parted this life on the Island of Curracoa, Feb. 3rd 1806, aged
21 years 6 months.
"By foreign hands his dying eyes were closed
By foreign hands his decent limbs composed,
By foreign hands his humble grave adorned
By strangers honored and by strangers mourned."

669—II. CATY[2], born Dec. 23, 1791; married Daniel Bennett of Huntington Feb. 6, 1814. He was born in Huntington July 20, 1784;
was a farmer; and lived at Long hill, in Huntington, where
he died May 21, 1849. She died at Bridgeport, Conn., Aug.
18, 1886, at the age of ninety-four. Their children were as
follows: 1. *Daniel Hovey*[3], born March 18, 1815; married,
first, Martha Ann Gould; and, second, Mrs. Eliza Heath
Millington; and lived and died in New Jersey. 2. *Hiram
Curtis*[3], born Jan. 16, 1817; married Cynthia J. Hawley; and
lived in New York and Stratford, Conn., where he died.
3. *Isaac Lewis*[3], born Feb. 1, 1820; died in Huntington. 4.
Henry[3], born Jan. —, 1824; married Emily Shelton; and
lived and died in Huntington. 5. *Jane*[3], born Feb. 17, 1829;
married Philip L. Smith; and lived in Bridgeport, Conn.

670—III. MARIA[2], born Oct. —, 1793; married Dr. Elbert Curtis of
Ithaca, N. Y.; and died at Ithaca.

* Connecticut Men in the War of the Revolution, page 606; List of
Privateers, 1775-1783, in The Navy of the United States by Lt. George F.
Emmons, U. S. N.

671—IV.   THOMAS[6], born Sept. 4, 1795; died Sept. 13, 1795, in Huntington.
672—V.   SUSAN[6], born Dec. 25, 1798; died, unmarried, in Ithaca, N. Y.
673—VI.   JAMES A.[6], born in 1810. *See family numbered "673."*

344

MAJ. THOMAS HOVEY[5], born in Newton, Mass., Aug. 14, 1770. He was probably brought up in Watertown, and lived there until 1762, when he moved to Cambridge, and settled in Brighton in 1776. He taught school in Brighton for about twenty winters, and also in Watertown and Newton. He was in the Battle of Bunker Hill, and subsequently served in Washington's army as a major drummer. He lived in Newton from 1792, and at other times resided in Cambridge, Roxbury, Lunenburg, and finally in Brighton. He was of Lunenburg, currier, in 1770.

Mr. Hovey married Miss Elizabeth, daughter of Joseph Brown of Brighton April 21, 1763.

He died in Brighton May 8, 1807, at the age of sixty-six. He died of consumption, and from Thanksgiving day in 1806, until he died, because of the peculiar nature of his disease, he could not lie down. If he tried to secure rest in that manner a severe coughing would ensue. All his sleep was obtained by some one rubbing his head. Often he remarked, "How good that bed looks. Oh! if I could lie down but one hour, but that is impossible, it distresses me. No one can tell but myself." At first he was irreconciled to leaving this attractive world, not that he was afraid to die, but his love for his family was so strong he could not bear to break the tie. He looked upon his wife with most lamentable sighs, saying, "How can I leave you; how can I leave my dear children. This world looks beautiful and pleasant to me, and I know that I am attached to it and my family." "Oh!" said he, "if it could be consistent with the Lord to spare me a few years longer, that I might see my children settled around me, it would be exceedingly pleasant, but if God has otherwise determined, I hope and pray that I may be reconciled." He truly saw that happy day and often said, "Forever, oh! Lord, thy word is settled in Heaven." A few minutes before he died he was asked where those words were that he so often repeated, and replied, "You will find them in Psalms. 119, v. 89."

His wife joined the Baptist church in Newton after the death of her husband; and she died Jan. 14, 1821, in Rutland. Mass., at the age of seventy-four. Her death was peaceful and happy. Rev. Mr. Clark said to her, "You will soon go to Jesus." She replied, "Oh! yes, I shall soon see Him as he is." Being asked if she had peace, she said, "Perfect peace. I feel happy,— happy,—happy;" and then closed her eyes, dying without a sigh or groan.

Their children were as follows:—

674—I. JOSIAH⁶, born Dec. 24, 1763, in Brighton. *See family numbered "674."*

675—II. MARY⁶, born July 1, 1765, in Brighton (baptized in Watertown July 14, 1765); married Benjamin Hammond, jr., (only son of Col. Benjamin Hammond of East Newton) Dec. 26, 1793; he was born June 12, 1768; he died Aug. 19, 1838, at the age of seventy; and she died at Roxbury Dec. 19, 1846, at the age of eighty-one, of consumption. Their children were born as follows: 1. *William⁷*, born Sept. 27, 1794; drowned at Rutland, Mass., July 5, 1825, aged thirty. 2. *Matilda⁷*, born July 23, 1796. 3. *Stephen⁷*, born Dec. 31, 1798; married Sarah M. Haskell Oct. 26, 1831; and she died April 25, 1851, aged thirty-eight. They had three children. 4. *Sarah⁷*, born Feb. 14, 1801. 5. *Mary P⁷*, born Sept. 14, 1803; died Sept. 26, 1833, at the age of thirty. 6. *Josiah⁷*, born Oct. 20, 1806; married Anna G. Warren of Grafton in 1829; lived in Grafton; and he died March 19, 1860. They had two sons and five daughters.

676—III. THOMAS⁶, born Aug. 8, 1766, in Roxbury. *See family numbered "676."*

677—IV. JAMES⁶, born Feb. 8, 1768, in Roxbury. *See family numbered "677."*

678—V. EBENEZER⁶, born June 8, 1769, in Lunenburg. *See family numbered "678."*

679—VI. PHINEAS BROWN⁶ born Nov. 8, 1770. *See family numbered "679."*

680—VII. ELIZABETH JOHNSON⁶, born July 4, 1772, in Lunenburg; married, first, John Royal Barlow of Cambridge Sept. 6, 1792; and they had one child: 1. *John R.⁷* She married, second, Daniel Johnson July 4, 1808. He died Aug. 29, 1848, at the age of eighty. She survived him, and a month before her death was taken sick at Cohasset and three weeks later removed to Boston, as it was thought that the change would be beneficial. She died at her son Andrew's house, on Pitts street, in Boston, Sept. 30, 1850, at the age of seventy-eight. The children of Mr. and Mrs. Johnson were as follows: 1. *Rebecca⁷*, born Oct. 29, 1809; died Sept. 1, 1815. 2. *William Bowls⁷*, born Aug. 27, 1811; and settled in Boston. 3. *Andrew J.⁷*, born Jan. 24, 1815, in Boston; was educated in the public schools of Boston, graduating from the English high school. On leaving school, he entered the hardware firm of Butler, Keith & Hill, where he learned the business. Later he came into the firm, and the firm name was changed to Butler, Sise & Johnson. The store was on Milk street, and was burned in the great fire of 1872. Mr. Johnson then retired from active business. He took an active part in local affairs; and was a prominent member of the Methodist church. He died at his home, 310 Vinton street, Melrose Highlands, of heart disease, after a short sickness, May 16, 1905, at the age of ninety. He left two daughters.

681—VIII. STEPHEN⁶, born June 23, 1774, in Lunenburg. He possessed an amiable disposition and a thoughtful mind. He believed that he could make his fortune upon the sea, and embarked to Canton, China, suddenly, to the surprise of the family. He arrived home in August, 1796, after an absence of twenty-two months, having enjoyed a healthy and pleasant voyage. He liked the sea so well that three weeks later he embarked for England. He had a pleasant voyage over, but on the return a terrific gale was experienced. In the midst of it, the captain called to the crew to go aloft, but as the hazard was so great they refused, with the exception of Stephen Hovey, who said, "Here I am; I will go, sir." "No, no," replied the master, "by no means. You must not go aloft." Then, a young man, a passenger and particular friend of Stephen's, stepped up, and said, "If you will go first, I will follow." They immediately began their dangerous tour in the dreadful midnight darkness and the roar of the storm. The waves dashed high and violently, and amid the awful commotion, the young men climbed courageously and cautiously up and up toward the top-gallant yard arm, which was finally reached and the task accomplished. Some of the rigging then gave away, and Stephen fell upon the deck, and a moment later was lifeless. This was on Christmas day, 1796, when he was twenty-two. The next day his remains were consigned to the deep. On Saturday, March first, following, his father heard that the brig had arrived in Boston, and went thither to meet him. When he reached home he sat down in silence, but his countenance was an index to the report he had to make and to what his heart felt. When Mrs. Hovey was told of the melancholy event, she clasped her hands together, saying, "The will of the Lord is done, why should a living man complain."

682—IX. WASHINGTON[6], born Aug. 26, 1777, in Brighton. He lived in Cambridge. He started on a journey to the South, to be absent six months or a year, and was never heard from. He is supposed to have perished in the conflagration that destroyed the Richmond theatre in 1811. He was unmarried, and thirty-four years of age.

683—X. ELEANOR DANA[6], born Feb. 23, 1779; married Rev. Abisha Samon (Simpson) May 13, 1807, and settled in Tisbury, on Martha's Vineyard. They removed to Harvard Sept. 8, 1812; and she died there Feb. 15, 1813, at the age of thirty-three. She died of bilious fever, and was sick but a few days, suffering intense bodily pain. Though weak, her senses remained, and she was capable of conversation as in health. She spoke calmly of dying, and said to her sister Elizabeth, "You see me here upon this bed of sickness. You behold me languishing away, but let me tell you, it is my body that languishes, for my flesh profiteth me nothing, but my soul is filled with God. It is impossible to describe the joy that I feel. It is more than I can express. I have food to eat that the world knows not of. I must exclaim as did Thomas, 'My Lord and my God!' Oh! is not this worth dying for, to enjoy so much of Heaven. I would not exchange my situation for a thousand such worlds as this." Her mother said to her, "My dear child, we think the symptoms of death are upon you." She replied, "Oh! good news to me, it is like cold water to a thirsty soul, or as good news from a far country. My dear mother, you see death depicted in my face, but glory is in my soul." She then closed her eyes in death. Their children were born as follows: 1. *Abisha Wheeler*[7] (twin), born May 20, 1808. 2. *Thomas Hovey*[7] (twin), born May 29, 1808. 3. ———[7] (son), born Dec. 26, 1809; died Dec. 27, 1809. 4. *Stephen Dana*[7], born June 26, 1811.

684—XI. JOHN[6], born Jan. 23, 1781; married Anna Greenwood; and died Dec. 11, 1853, at the age of seventy-two.

685—XII. SARAH[4], born Sept. 26, 1782; married Washington Lee; and died Jan. 7, 1862, at the age of seventy-nine.

686—XIII. ANNA[4], born Sept. 3, 1784; married Ephraim Chamberlain; and died May 10, 1860, at the age of seventy-five.

687—XIV. WILLIAM[4], born Aug. 4, 1786; and died of measles, after a sickness of six weeks, May —, 1790, aged three years.

688—XV. ————[4], died young.

689—XVI. SUSANNAH JORDAN[4], born April 5, 1791, in Brighton; married Elisha Brimhall, a United States officer. She died in Boston, of "congestive fever," Feb. 9, 1828, at six o'clock in the morning, at the age of thirty-six. Her sickness from stoppage proved fatal in eight days. In taking leave of her husband, she said to him, "My husband, my case is unalterably fixed, we must part, the cold hand of death is upon me, which will soon separate us forever in this world. Oh! my dear husband let me tell you, except Jesus Christ is formed in your soul as he is in mine, you never can enter into the Kingdom of Heaven, for Jesus Christ has said, where I am ye cannot come." She remarked to her sister Elizabeth, "I do believe that I am a child of God, and that Jesus Christ is mine, and I am His." With a sweet smile, she continued, "What can I desire besides. I can look beyond Jordan with as much pleasure as I ever eat when I am hungry." Children: 1. *Anna Eliza[5]*, who married Samuel Harward of Boston. 2. *Matilda[5]*, married ———— Hammond before 1838.

690—XVII. ————[4], died young.

346

EBENEZER HOVEY[3], born in Newton, Mass., May 12, 1743. July 4, 1763, he went to Medford to work out, being still under age, and lived in the family of Timothy Tufts, for whom he worked. He became a husbandman, and married Elizabeth, daughter of William and Elizabeth (Wiswall) (Fuller?) Baldwin of Newton April 5, 1768. She was born in "Narraganset No. 2," Oct. 17, 1742. They lived in Newton; and May 10, 1774, for fifty pounds, he conveyed to his brother Moses Hovey his interest in the homestead of their family.* He entered the army of the Revolution, and died in the service, at Naragansett, of smallpox, July —, 1776, at the age of thirty-three. She died, his widow, in Newton, Sept. 24, 1777, at the age of thirty-four.

Their children were born in Newton, as follows:—

691—I. HENRY[4], born Jan. 23, 1769; merchant; lived in Boston, Mass.; married Miss Welch of Charlestown. She lived only five years after their marriage.

692—II. ABIGAIL[4] (twin), born Sept. 29, 1770; married Oliver Houghton of Lancaster, Mass., where he was born Jan. 19, 1765. Their children were born as follows: 1. *Emeline[5]*, born July 3, 1792. 2. *Eliza[5]*, born May 22, 1794, in Lancaster; married Ezra Sawyer of Lancaster Feb. 7, 1821; lived in Newton a year or two, and then removed to Lancaster. They had seven children, one of their grandchildren being Dr. William

* Middlesex Registry of Deeds, book 76, page 322.

Brewster Sawyer of California. 3. *Jeffery Atherton*[1], born April 27, 1796; died at sea. 4. *Edmund Winchester*[1], born May 10, 1798; married and lived in Arkansas; had a large family, a grandson, Henry Hovey Houghton, being postmaster at Jonesboro, Ark. 5. *Oliver*[1], born Nov. 26, 1806; died Oct. 3, 1809.

693—III. SARAH[4] (twin), born Sept. 29, 1770; married Capt. ——— Jenkins; and had a daughter: 1. *Elizabeth*[1], married Rev. Henry Hersey of Hingham, and had no children.

694—IV. FRANCIS[4], born Aug. 3, 1772; went into the service in the War of 1812, and never returned.

695—V. PATTY[4], born March 14, 1774; married Aaron, son of Elisha and Mary Hyde of Newton May 22, 1794. He was born in Newton Feb. 15, 1770. She died Jan. 31, 1860, at the age of eighty-five. Their children were born in Newton, as follows: 1. *Aaron*[1], born Feb. 15, 1795. 2. *Henry Hovey*[1], born Feb. 6, 1796. 3. *Hosea*[1], born July 20, 1797; died Feb. 1, 1820, in Newton, aged twenty-two. 4. *Martha*[1], born May 14, 1800. 5. *John*[1], born Aug. 3, 1803. 6. *Mary*[1], born April 15, 1805; married Prescott Rice of Boston (published April 21, 1839); and had a daughter. 7. *Elizabeth*[1], born Sept. 15, 1807. 8. *Francis Hovey*[1], born Feb. 26, 1809. 9. *Ebenezer*[1], born Dec. 9, 1810. 10. *Horatio Nelson*[1], born Jan. 26, 1814; married Olive W. ———; and lived in Newton.

347

CALEB HOVEY[5], born in Newton, Mass., March 21, 1746. He was a husbandman, and lived in Cambridge. His residence was in that part of the town called West Cambridge, which is now the town of Arlington. He was called a victualer Jan. 12, 1778, when, for five hundred and forty pounds, he bought of Philip Bemis of Cambridge, yeoman, two lots of land in the northwest parish in Cambridge, one of the lots containing twenty-four acres and situated on the north side of the Concord road with the house, barn, etc., thereon, and the other lot containing six acres and lying on the south side of said road.* April 1, 1795, in consideration of the maintenance of his widowed mother, during the remainder of her life, his brother Moses Hovey and sister Experience and her husband Ebenezer Prentiss conveyed to him their interest in the estate of their father.† For sixty pounds, he sold to Benjamin Gardner of Watertown, tallow chandler, three shares in twelve acres of land in Newton which his father (Caleb Hovey) devised to his mother for her life, June 8, 1795.‡ For two hundred and twenty dollars, he conveyed to his son Caleb four acres of land on the north side of the Concord road, in Cambridge, Jan. 22, 1798.§

* Middlesex Registry of Deeds, book 79, page 195.
† Middlesex Registry of Deeds, book 119, page 552.
‡ Middlesex Registry of Deeds, book 116, page 367.
§ Middlesex Registry of Deeds, book 128, page 274.

Mr. Hovey married Rebecca Robbins of Cambridge Dec. 9, 1770; and they attended the Baptist church. She died Nov. 4, 1798, at the age of forty-two. He died just two weeks later, at the age of fifty-two. Administration upon his estate was granted to Benjamin Willington of Lexington, gentleman, Dec. 5, 1798. His estate was appraised at \$1,812.96, and included his farm in Cambridge, consisting of a house, barn and homestead of twenty-five acres, lying on the north side of the Concord road, and a pasture of eleven acres on the other side of the road. For fifteen hundred and fifty dollars, the administrator conveyed to Joseph Lock, 3d, of Cambridge, yeoman, ten acres of pasture land on the south side of the Concord road, in Cambridge, and thirty-one acres of land in Cambridge on the north side of the Concord road, and on road leading to Burlington, May 15, 1799.[*]

Their children were born in Cambridge, as follows:—

696—i.   REBECCA[4], born April 13, 1771; married Thomas Swan of Cambridge Dec. 12, 1793; and was living in 1798.

697—ii.   SUSANNA[4], born May 18, 1773; living in 1798.

698—iii.   CALEB[4], born Jan. 24, 1775; was a laborer, and lived in Watertown in 1798, and in Cambridge in 1799. His father conveyed to him, for two hundred and twenty dollars, four acres of land in Cambridge lying on the north side of the Concord road, Jan. 22, 1798;[†] and he conveyed the same lot, being pasture and orcharding, for one hundred and eighty-three dollars, to the administrator of his father's estate, April 13, 1799.[‡]

699—iv.   SARAH[4], born Jan. 27, 1777; she had a child die Oct. 30, 1801, a year and a half old.

700—v.   JOHN[4], born Dec. 5, 1778; living in 1798.

701—vi.   NATHAN[4], baptized Jan. 10, 1779.

702—vii.   AARON[4], living in 1798.

348

SERG. MOSES HOVEY[5], born in Newton, Mass., May 11, 1753. He was a victualer, and lived in that part of Cambridge which was subsequently incorporated as West Cambridge and is now Arlington. For fifty pounds, he bought of his brother Ebenezer Hovey the latter's interest in the homestead of their father, May 10, 1774.[§]

Mr. Hovey was a sergeant in the company of Capt. Benjamin Locke of Menotony, minute-men, in 1775, in the Revolution.

In 1784, he was a defendant in a civil suit brought by Ephraim Cock of Cambridge, victualer; and the judgment obtained by the plaintiff therein was satisfied by the assignment to him of twelve acres of land lying in Newton, on the west side of the

* Middlesex Registry of Deeds, book 134, page 127.
† Middlesex Registry of Deeds, book 128, page 274.
‡ Middlesex Registry of Deeds, book 132, page 221.
§ Middlesex Registry of Deeds, book 76, page 322.

country road leading to Sherburn, Sept. 7, 1784.* April 1, 1795, he conveyed his interest in his father's estate to his brother Caleb Hovey for support of his mother.†

Mr. Hovey married Love, daughter of Ebenezer and Sarah (Pierce) Prentice of Menotony (now Arlington) March 14, 1776. She was born March 22, 1755. He died there Nov. 19, 1805, at the age of fifty-two; and she died, his widow, in West Cambridge, May 10, 1824, at the age of sixty-eight.

Their children were born in West Cambridge, as follows:—

703—I. ———— (son)⁴, born Sept. 3, 1776; died Aug. 16, 1778.

704—II. MOSES⁴, born June 20, 1778. *See family numbered "704."*

705—III. SARAH⁴, married ———— Weld.

706—IV. HANNAH⁴, born June 25, 1794; married Zechariah, son of Zechariah and Abigail (Blodgett) Hill April 10, 1814. He was born in West Cambridge Oct. 16, 1790; was a farmer; and lived in his native town until 1823, when he removed to Woburn, where he died April 3, 1840. She survived him, and died in Waltham, Mass., Oct. 27, 1869, at the age of seventy-five. Their children were born as follows: 1. *Hannah⁵*, born Sept. 25, 1814, in West Cambridge; married Richard Sowdon Jan. 31, 1836; lived in Boston, Mass., and New York; and died in New York City Dec. 23, 1868. 2. *Zechariah⁵*, born Jan. 31, 1816, in West Cambridge; married Jane ————. 3. *Andrew Jackson⁵*, born May 12, 1817, in West Cambridge; lived in Boston; married Elizabeth W. Jones. 4. *Samuel⁵*, born Oct. 5, 1818, in West Cambridge; lived in Woburn; married Martha Wyman. 4. *Sarah Weld⁵*, born June 29, 1820, in West Cambridge; married Joseph Oliver Wellington April 15, 1841; lived in Belmont, where she died June 4, 1898, at the age of seventy-seven. 5. *Charles⁵*, born Dec. 25, 1821, in West Cambridge; was a farmer; lived in Belmont; married Cordelia ————; and died in Belmont July 10, 1882. 6. *George⁵*, born Aug. 6, 1823, in Woburn; died Sept. 22, 1824. 7. *George⁵*, born Oct. 2, 1825, in Woburn; died Jan. 12, 1826. 8. *Louise⁵*, born June 19, 1827, in Woburn; died, unmarried, in Belmont, April 5, 1896. 9. *Joseph Bennett⁵*, born April 13, 1832, in Woburn; lived in Waltham and Newton, Mass.; was a dry-goods salesman; married Grace M. Bigelow June 6, 1860; and died in Newton March 4, 1883.

707—V. MARY PRENTISS⁴, born Jan. 2, 1798; was admitted to the Unitarian church, Pleasant street, in West Cambridge, Aug. 4, 1816; married Thomas, son of Zechariah and Abigail (Blodgett) Hill of Cambridge Nov. 16, 1817. He was born in West Cambridge April 26, 1793; and lived in Cambridge, where she died Sept. 17, 1828. Her daughter, Mrs. Sarah F. Bird of 31 Beech Street, Waverley, Mass., has her silhoutte, taken about 1825. He died in Weymouth, Mass., Aug. 8, 1859. Their children were born in Cambridge, as follows: 1. *Mary⁵*, died in infancy. 2. *Thomas⁵*, born Aug. 19, 1820; hardware merchant; lived in South Boston; married Ellen Chapin; and died in South Boston Dec. 15, 1896. 3. *Ira Weld⁵*, born Aug. 11, 1823; dealer in provisions; lived in

Dorchester; married Caroline C. Walbridge Jan. 9, 1849; and died in South Boston July 29, 1868. 4. *Mary Caroline*[6], born Nov. 22, 1826; married Charles F. Lemon Oct. 6, 1852; lived in South Boston; and died in Belmont Dec. 13, 1898. 5. *Sarah Frances*[6], born Sept. 7, 1828; married Jason Wilson Bird Aug. 21, 1849; formerly lived in Dorchester, and now lives at 31 Beech street, in Waverley.

352

NATHANIEL HOVEY[5], born in Windham, Conn., June 14, 1749. He lived in Windham; and married ———— ————. He died before Jan. 21, 1788.

His children were as follows:—

708—I.   HANNAH[6], born Feb. 9, 1776, in Windham; and was living in 1788.
709—II.   PHINEAS[6], born Dec. 22, 1778, in Windham; and was living in 1788.
710—III. ORRIN[6], born Feb. 15, 1780, "att Willington" (recorded at Windham).
711—IV.   NATHANIEL[6], living in 1788.

354

CAPT. EBENEZER HOVEY[5], born in Windham, Conn., Oct. 1, 1752. He lived first in Tolland, Conn., and soon removed to Charlotte, Vt. In 1793, he took up some government land in what is now Hatley, in Stanstead county, Province of Quebec, Canada, and was one of the associates and first settlers of the town. After making a small clearing on the eastern shore of Lake Memphremagog, at the place now known as Judd's point, he put up a log shanty and returned to his home in Vermont. The next March he set out for Magog, as his new home was at first called, with an ox team, carrying his wife and eight children and bedding, provisions, etc. They were accompanied by Joseph Ives, Isaac Rexford and David Chamberlin, with their wives and children. They went by the way of Missiquoi Bay, and were seven days getting through the woods from Frulighsburg to Memphremagog Lake. The snow was deep, and the women and children suffered from cold and fatigue.

Mr. Hovey was, for many years, captain of the militia and actively employed in public affairs.

He married Rebecca Simmons; and died April 24, 1836, at the age of eighty-three, leaving sixty-two grandchildren.

Their children were born as follows:—

712—I.   POLLY[6], married David Chamberlin in Connecticut; and settled in Hatley, Canada, in 1794. She was burned to death at her flax wheel, in 1836. It was thought that a spark from the fire on the hearth might have set on fire the inflammable pile of flax around her. Mr. Chamberlin died in 1847. Their children were as follows: 1. *Olive*[7], married John S. Merry. 2. *Ira*[7], married Mary Erwin. 3. *David*[7], married Thankful Whitcomb. 4. *Polly*[7], born Jan. 20, 1799, in Hatley; married Abel B., son of Jonathan Johnson; and removed to Magog in 1832. They had four children, one of whom was Edwin R. Johnson, a brilliant lawyer. 5. *Arvilla*[7], married George, son of Dr. William Oliver. 6. *Matilda*[7], married Arthur Johnson. 7. *William*[7], married Ester Abbott. 8. *Fanny*[7], married John Emory. 9. *Lucy*[7], married Lyman Rexford. 10. *Sylvia*[7], married Calvin Abbott. 11. *Sarah*[7], married John Sweeney. 12. *Aaron*[7], married and settled in the West.

713—II. CHESTER[6], born Jan. 20, 1778. *See family numbered "713."*

714—III. EBENEZER[6], married Mary Cox, and settled in Canada.

715—IV. CHAUNCEY[6], went West when a young man, and remained there.

716—V. JOHN[6], married, first, Ruth Kezar from New Hampshire; and, second, Ann McLean. He had no children.

717—VI. ROXANNA[6], married, first, T. McConnell; and, second, P. Flanders.

718—VII. CLARISSA[6], married Abraham Rexford.

719—VIII. PERSIS[6], born Aug. 15, 1788; married Capt. Simon, son of Simon and Mehitable (Foster) Kezar. He was born in Sutton, N. H., July 21, 1772; and died in Hatley Jan. 10, 1833. She died in Hatley Aug. 28, 1783, at the age of eighty-five. An excellent daguerrotype of her is in the possession of her granddaughter Mrs. Burton H. Kezar, "Hillside," Massawippe, Quebec. He was captain of the local militia and a farmer, and lived in Hatley. Their children were as follows: 1. *Sherburn*[7], died young. 2. *Prasana*[7]. 3. *Simon*[7]. 4. *Sherburn*[7]. 5. *Lucinda*[7]. 6. *Hollis*[7]. 7. *Maria*[7]. 8. *Helen M.*[7], born April 5, 1828, in Hatley; married Burton F., son of Lemuel P. and Charlotte (Fletcher) Harvey May —, 1849, in Hatley. He was born in Compton, Quebec, May 22, 1828; was a farmer; and lived in Compton most of his life. She died at Ayers' Cliff, Quebec, April 4, 1910, at the age of eighty-two. They had four children.

720—IX. LAURA[6], born July 9, 1795, being the first child born in Hatley; married Zacheus H. Johnson. He was born July 9, 1793; settled number sixteen, third range, Hatley; and died Sept. 24, 1834. She survived him, and married, secondly, W. Cox. The children of Mr. and Mrs. Johnson were born as follows: 1. *Zacheus H.*[7], born Jan. 15, 1818; married Maria L. Kezar; and died in 1847. 2. *Laura*[7], born July 8, 1819; married Squire Colby. 3. *Sarah*[7], born Feb. 28, 1823; died March 12, 1824. 4. *Rebecca*[7], born Jan. 20, 1825; married Solon Shurtleff, M. D. 5. *Jonathan*[7], born Dec. 30, 1827; married Harriet Sweet. 6. *William E.*[7], born April 24, 1831; married Elizabeth Saddler. 7. *John H.*[7], born Aug. 6, 1834; married, first, Eleanor Kezar; and, second, Celina Sterling; and had two daughters.

721—X. SARAH[6], married John Wadleigh.

722—XI. HORACE[6], born Dec. 21, 1798, in Hatley. *See family numbered "722."*

367

ASA HOVEY[5], born in Windham, Conn., May 3, 1769. He lived in Hampton, Conn., until 1801, when he removed to Waterford, Vt. He married Mary Alworth; and died Sept. 9, 1818.

Their children were born as follows:—

723—I.   ACHSAH[6], born Oct. 1, 1793, in Hampton, Conn.
724—II.   MARY[6], born June 19, 1795, in Hampton; died in infancy.
725—III. WILLIAM[6], born Oct. 8, 1797, in Hampton. *See family num-
          bered "725."*
726—IV.   SALLY[6], born Dec. 5, 1799, in Hampton.
727—V.   IRENA[6], born June 21, 1802, in Waterford, Vt.
728—VI.   REBECCA[6], born May 12, 1805, in Waterford.
729—VII. ASA[6], born Sept. 16, 1807, in Waterford.
730—VIII. LUCIUS MOSLEY[6], born Aug. 13, 1810, in Waterford.
731—IX.   ————[6] (dau.), born Feb. 2, 1815, in Waterford; died in
          infancy.

378

ELIJAH HOVEY[5], born in Windham, Conn., Oct. 13, 1765.
He lived at first at Pomfret, Conn., and, in 1791, removed to
Hampton, in 1793 or 1794 to Monson, Mass., and finally removed
to Ohio in 1818. The family went overland, and experienced the
hardships and discomforts subject to a journey of months through
an almost unbroken wilderness. Mr. Hovey purchased three
hundred acres of land at what was then called "McDonough,"
and commenced work erecting a log cabin and clearing land for
their future home. In 1821, they decided to build a frame house,
and proceeded to carry out his plan at once, producing the first
frame house in the town. At the raising of this building, it was
proposed that the name of the town be changed from McDonough
to Monson, after Mr. Hovey's former home in Massachusetts.

Mr. Hovey married Wealthy Utley about 1789, in Massachusetts. She was discontented in Ohio, and longed to return to her
old home in Massachusetts. They went back to the old place,
and after a while again took the journey to Ohio. In 1830, Mr.
and Mrs. Hovey once more started for Massachusetts, and he
was taken sick on the way, dying in New York Sept. 18, 1830, at
the age of sixty-four. Mrs. Hovey continued on the way, and
afterward lived in Monson, Mass., where she died among her own
kindred, at the home of her son Oren Hovey, May 4, 1842.

Their children were born as follows:—

732—I.   WEALTHY[6], born Oct. 27, 1790, at Pomfret, Conn.; married
          Henry Graves; he was living in 1832; and she died June 23,
          1856, at the age of sixty-five.
733—II.   ELIJAH[6], born Dec. 7, 1791, in Hampton, Conn.; and died
          March 9, 1820, aged twenty-eight.
734—III. OLIVER[6], born Jan. 11, 1793, in Hampton. *See family numbered
          "734."*
735—IV.   ORRIN[6], born Dec. 11, 1794, in Monson, Mass. *See family num-
          bered "735."*
736—V.   HORACE[6], born June 24, 1796, in Monson. *See family num-
          bered "736."*
737—VI.   SALLY[6], born Nov. 18, 1797, in Monson; married Lyman Shaw;
          and they were both living in 1832.

738—VII. HARRIETT⁶, born Feb. 25, 1798, in Monson; married Lorin Par-
          sons; he was living in 1832; and she died in Ohio July 21,
          1872, at the age of seventy-five.
739—VIII. ALMIRA⁶, born May 22, 1801, in Monson.
740—IX.   HIRAM⁶, born Jan. 12, 1803, in Monson. *See family numbered*
          "740."

384

JONATHAN HOVEY⁵, born Sept. 21, 1777. He married Patience
Griffin of Hampton, Conn., April 16, 1802. She was born July
27, 1781; and died Feb. 4, 1835, at the age of fifty-three. He
died Aug. 11, 1840, aged sixty-two.

Their children were born as follows:—

741—I.   ANNA FULLER⁶ born Nov. 3, 1802; married William Kimball.
742—II.   JAMES STEDMAN⁶, born June 10, 1804; died March 1, 1810.
743—III. DANIEL ALFRED⁶, born Feb. 24, 1806; physician in Killingly,
          Conn.
744—IV.   ALBERT GRIFFIN⁶, born July 27, 1808; died Dec. 21, 1810.
745—V.   ————⁶, born July 2, 1810; died July 2, 1810.
746—VI.   CHLOE LOVINA⁶, born March 27, 1811; married William Clark of
          Hartford, Conn.
747—VII. EUNICE WOODWARD⁶, born Feb. 27, 1813; married Mr. Church.
748—VIII. JAMES ALBERT⁶, born April 29, 1815, in Hampton. *See family*
          numbered "748."
749—IX.   HIRAM⁶, born in 1817; died in 1818.
750—X.   FRANCES⁶, born in 1819; died in 1820.
751—XI.   ELIZA ANN STEDMAN⁶ born Sept. 8, 1822; died at Killingly in
          1856.

385

DARIUS HOVEY⁵, born in Windham, Conn., Aug. 20, 1779.
He lived in Brookfield, Mass. He married Sarah Crosby Horne;
and died Oct. 1, 1818.

Their children were born as follows:—

752—I.   CHARLES FOX⁶, born Feb. 28, 1807, in Brookfield. *See family*
          numbered "752."
753—II.   GEORGE OTIS⁶, born Feb. 22, 1809, in Brookfield. *See family*
          numbered "753."
754—III. FREDERIC⁶. *See family numbered "754."*

392

JOSEPH HOVEY⁴, born in Ipswich, Mass., Dec. 17, 1762. He
lived in Londonderry, N. H. He married, first, Sarah, daughter
of Isaac and Hannah (Smith) Burnham of Ipswich, Mass., June
2, 1783. She was born in Chebacco parish, in Ipswich (now the
town of Essex), Sept. 8, 1761; and died Oct. 5, 1804, at the age
of forty-three. She was a beautiful woman, with a delicate constitution. He married, second, Ruth ———— before 1810; and
died in 1825, at the age of sixty-three. His will, dated Oct. 1,
1825, was proved Jan. 3, 1826. His wife Ruth survived him.

Mr. Hovey's children were born as follows:—

755—I.   JOSEPH BURNHAM[7], born Sept. 7, 1783. He was a master mar-
          iner, and lived in Newburyport, Mass., until after 1811, sub-
          sequently living in Londonderry, N. H.
             In 1811, while master of the schooner Julian of New-
          buryport, he was wrecked at Currituck, on the coast of
          North Carolina; and on his return home, a year and a half
          later, on account of some legal complications which arose
          respecting the cargo, he made the following deposition:—*

          "I Joseph B. Hovey of Newburyport in the County of
          Essex of lawful age, testify and say, that in the year
          1811, I was master of the Schooner Julian, of and be-
          longing to s⁴ Newburyport and owned by Mess⁵⁵ Moses
          Brown John Coombs Leonard Smith Jeremiah Nelson
          Thomas M. Clark Richard Bartlet John Boardman Wil-
          liam Eaton Edm⁴ Bartlet Philip Coombs Paul Thurlo and
          Eben⁵ Wheelwright—That in the month of April of that
          year I was with said schooner at winsor in the State of
          North Carolina, and let said Schooner to charter to Mess⁵⁵
          Joseph Blount Kenneth Clark and Joseph H. Bryan for a
          voyage from said winsor to Lisbon, and entered into articles
          of agreement with the said Blount Clark and Bryan to charter
          said Schooner after she should be discharged at said Lisbon,
          for a return cargo to the United States, if the supercargo
          who went out in said Schooner and returned in her, should
          require it—that accordingly we took on board at Winsor
          aforesaid, a cargo of corn, staves, peas and naval stores, and
          sailed from Ocrecock in the month of May, and arrived with
          the same at Lisbon, the third day of July following and de-
          livered he said cargo there to M⁵ Kenneth Clark the said
          supercargo, all in good order who paid me the freight, but
          not according to Charter party, having kept from me
          about one hundred and eighty dollars: after the schooner
          was unloaded, I agreed with s⁴ Clark to take on board a
          cargo of salt, on their account, sufficient for ballast, as it
          would save us the expence of buying ballast: after we took
          the salt on board, we agreed with s⁴ Clark to take on board
          one hundred merino sheep, at two dollars each, and he was
          to find their living, and provide every thing for them, and fix
          the vessel to receive them on board; and I agreed to let him
          have a black man, which we had on board, to take charge of
          them; and take the necessary care of them on the voyage.
          Clark to have liberty to put them in such part of the vessel
          as he thought proper: accordingly we took on board eighty
          four sheep one of which died the next day, and sailed from
          Lisbon the nineteenth or twentieth of August following
          bound for North Carolina: the sheep were stowed in the
          hold of the Schooner by Mr. Clarks exprefs direction; he
          had at first determined to place them on deck and build
          suitable places for them there, but enquiring for lumber he
          found it scarce and dear, and concluded to put them under

          * This deposition was taken June 12, 1813, at the request of Moses
          Brown and other owners of the vessel, by Joseph Dana and William
          Woart, two justices of the peace and of the quorum for the county of
          Essex. The deposition was recorded in Essex registry of deeds, Execu-
          tions, book 2, leaf 8.

deck; I made only a verbal agreement for the freight home,
as the Charter party shew the cargo out to be on their account and a condition to load home if required—before we
left Lisbon I had the Schooners upper works caulked and
her bottom cleaned, and when we satled she was in good
order, and continued so on the voyage untill the 23ᵈ September, when we experienced a heavy gale of wind, in which
we lay too fourteen hours, after which she leaked a little
but not to do any damage; afterwards about the tenth of
October we experienced another Gale of wind; in one of
these gales a part of the hay which was stowed loose in bulk
and in the bows of the vessel, was injured; and the sheep
suffered considerably, for we had to keep the hatches down,
which increased the heat in the hold;—in one of the gales
the hatches were closed twenty four hours—after we left
Lisbon, and about a week after we left the Port, the sheep
began to die, and it appeared to me were diseased: I cut
several after they were dead in the back of the neck, and
found them filled with worms; more or less, died almost
every day for about thirty days, after which they appeared
to be very well; I am not able to recollect how many died,
but I think twenty-five or twenty-six in all—After the gales
they were kept on shorter allowance than usual, and as well
before as after were managed entirely under said Clarks direction—On the 23ᵈ of October we were driven on shore in
a gale of wind on Currituck, and the Sea breaking over the
Schooner, Mʳ Clark requested the hatches should be closed,
and they were accordingly kept closed until the sheep were
taken out and set on shore—I think fifty six or eight were
landed alive—after the sheep were landed. and the materials
saved, and the vessel and the sheep were sold, a difficulty
arose with the supercargo, and he seized our effects — we
were strangers in the place, and had with us ten or eleven
hundred dollars only—considerable of which was due to the
people for wages—All this was attached by a writ at Clark's
suit, but afterwards given up, all but one hundred dollars,
which he said he would retain to pay the expences; I con-
sented to this to save the remainder from their hands and to
get away; about thirty six hours after the schooner was
driven on shore she bilged, and about a third part of the salt
was wet and lost—the remainder of the salt and lemmons
were got on shore and sold—the lemmons were much rotten
—when we had saved all we could, I advised with Mʳ Clark
about what was necessary to be done, and he told me I
must proceed according to Law, and that he had nothing
more to do about it I accordingly applied to Samuel Salyer
Esq. wreck master, and had all sold under his direction, and
paid over to said Clark his proportion, after deducting expences—I noted my protest the day after we got on shore,
or shortly after, before a Justice of the Peace; the proper
Officer as I understood lived at a distance of twelve miles;—
the Justice gave me a certificate, and I went with it and carried with me all the crew, except one, to his residence—at
a place called Notts Island, in order to extend it—but he
had gone to Norfolk I was therefore obliged to wait untill I
could go to Norfolk to extend it, which I afterwards did on
the eleventh of November

"JOSEPH B. HOVEY"

Other vessels were driven on shore in the same storm, and all the people on one of them were lost.

Captain Hovey married, first, Margaret Stacey March 26, 1806; and she died in Newburyport May 19, 1809. He married, second, Rebecca Roger; and was living in Londonderry in 1825.

756—II.   SALLY⁷, born Jan. 15, 1785; married ———— Danforth before 1825.

757—III.   JOHN⁷, born Oct. 15, 1786, in Londonderry. *See family numbered "757."*

758—IV.   LUCY⁷, born Nov. 27, 1787; married ———— Boyd; and died before 1825.

759—V.   ISAAC BURNHAM⁷, born May 1, 1790, in Derry. *See family numbered "759."*

760—VI.   BETSEY⁷, born Feb. 22, 1792; after her father's second marriage, she went to live with John Pinkerton, founder of the Pinkerton academy in Derry. She married Ezekiel Cleasby before 1825. Children: 1. *Sarah Frances⁸*, married ———— Riley; and died in ————. 2. ————⁸, married Edward L. Tead; and was living in 1884. Mr. Tead was president of the National Exchange Bank of Boston for many years, and is now deceased. 3. ————⁸ (dau.). 4. ————⁸ (dau.).

761—VII.   LUCRETIA⁷, born May 8, 1794; owned a house in Derry, with her sister Charlotte, and lived there for many years. She was unmarried in 1825.

762—VIII.   JAMES⁷, born April 25, 1796; and died before 1825.

763—IX.   CHARLOTTE⁷, born May 20, 1798; owned a house in Derry with her sister Lucretia, and lived there many years. A sampler worked by her, when she was thirteen years of age, is in the possession of her grandniece Nellie F. Riley, Jamaica Plain, Mass. She was unmarried in 1825.

764—X.   EUNICE⁷, born June 7, 1800; unmarried in 1825.

765—XI.   LOIS⁷, born Dec. 14, 1803; died Sept. 8, 1804.

766—XII.   ROBERT H.⁷, was a minor in 1826.

767—XIII.   CHARLES⁷, was a minor, under fourteen, in 1826.

393

DANIEL HOVEY⁶, born in Sutton, Mass., Oct. 29, 1778. He lived in his native town, owning the old red house, which had a long back roof and a back basement. The house afterward became the property of his brother Benjamin Hovey; and it was taken down by S. H. Stockwell about 1876. Mr. Hovey subsequently lived in the house he bought of Joseph May 27, 1811. This house was originally built as a parsonage by Rev. John McKinstry about 1720. In 1876, it was occupied by Mr. Hovey's son Marius. Mr. Hovey was a very enterprising business man, conducting at one time a store at the end of the long shed at the tavern.

He married, first, Susanna, daughter of Jonas and Lydia (Rice) Sibley July 3, 1808. She was born in Sutton June 27, 1786; and died Aug. 25, 1811, at the age of twenty-five. He married, second, Miss Susan Jacobs of Millbury Nov. 10, 1813. She was born Dec. 15, 1793; and was one of the most worthy of women.

Mr. Hovey died in Sutton Jan. 10, 1839. His wife Susan survived him, and died March 25, 1850, aged fifty-six.

Mr. Hovey's children were all born in Sutton, as follows:—

768—I. JONAS AUGUSTUS[7], born Sept. 16, 1809. He was a fine looking man; and in early life kept a little store, subsequently becoming one of the most enterprising, wealthy and successful of the cotton manufacturers of Sutton. He married Miss Fidelia, daughter of Elijah and Lydia (Whittemore) Waters of Sutton, and then lived for several years in Millbury. He then removed to Ballston, N. Y., where he owned several factories, and built a mansion house, costing, it is said, when finished and furnished, one hundred thousand dollars. Afterward, he had unfortunate litigation concerning some of his titles, and this, together with the severe pressure of the times, fell heavily upon him, somewhat reducing his wealth. But his perseverance was wonderful. His business took him frequently to New York and other cities, and in the daytime he attended to business, but depending upon sleep obtained at night while traveling in sleeping cars for his chief rest. From this practice, he became insane, and finally died, in an asylum, where he had been under treatment for a few weeks, Jan. 22, 1875, at the age of sixty-five. She died at Ballston Spa April 12, 1878. They had no children.

769—II. ————[7], died Aug. 28, 1811.

770—III. JOHN JACOBS[7], born Aug. 31, 1814; went to Virginia; and was a wealthy planter and merchant there in 1876.

771—IV. DANIEL TYLER[7], born Oct. 19, 1815, went to college at Amherst, and studied medicine. He went to California, in search of gold, and had returned as far as New York, when he died, Jan. 31, 1851, at the age of thirty-five. He was not married, but was engaged to Miss Lydia Bishop, sister of Doctor Bishop of Worcester. She taught school in Sutton, and was a fine lady. She afterward married ——— Lanman, and died in Norwich, Conn.

772—V. SUSAN SIBLEY[7], born April 12, 1817; was a fine young lady, and died, of consumption, unmarried, Aug. 12, 1847, at the age of thirty.

773—VI. MARIUS MILNER[7], born Aug. 17, 1818. *See family numbered "773."*

774—VII. WILLIAM HENRY[7], born June 29, 1822. He was engaged in trade in Grenville, S. C., for several years, being worth upwards of a hundred thousand dollars before the war of the Rebellion broke out. He lost heavily by the war; and to regain his fortunes he started stores in different places, overworked, became insane, came home, and soon after died in the asylum at Worcester, May 11, 1871, aged forty-eight. He was loyal to his country, yet retained the love and respect of his Southern neighbors. He is gratefully remembered for his friendliness to the young men he employed, setting them up in business for themselves

775—VIII. ERASTUS FRANKLIN[7], born July 8, 1824. He went into the flax business, in New York state, in early life, and was burned out, losing everything. In 1876, he was in business in Philadelphia; and died in Richmond, Va., Aug. 21, 1898, aged seventy-four. He married Margaret ———; but had no children.

776—IX. CHARLES HARRISON[7], born July 17, 1826; died Sept. 9, 1848.

777—x.   MARY ELIZABETH[7], born Sept. 17, 1829; married Col. Asa
Holmes, son of Asa and Susan (Holman) Waters of Millbury June 27, 1849. He was born in Sutton (now Millbury)
Feb. 8, 1808; graduated at Yale college in 1829; studied law
at Harvard college; became a Massachusetts state senator,
president of a bank, and held many offices of honor and
trust. He was also engaged in the manufacture of guns, for
the United States government, and cotton and woolen goods.
Colonel Waters died in Millbury Jan. 17, 1887; and Mrs.
Waters died there March 5, 1892, at the age of sixty-two.
Their children were born in Millbury, as follows: 1. *Isabel
Holman[8]*, born July 31, 1850; lived in Millbury; and died,
unmarried, in Amherst March 16, 1909, at the age of fifty-
eight. 2. *Lilian Hovey[8]*, born Feb. 9, 1852; married Prof.
Edwin Augustus Grosvenor Oct. 23, 1873. He was born in
Newburyport, Mass., Aug. 30, 1845. He graduated at Amherst college in 1867; and afterwards studied for the ministry, graduating at Andover Theological Seminary in 1872.
He subsequently received degrees of A. M. and LL.D. from
his alma mater. For seven years, he was professor of history in Roberts college, Constantinople, in Turkey; and is
now professor of European history at Amherst college. He
has published several volumes on "Constantinople," "The
Permanence of the Greek Type" and "Contemporaneous History of the World." Their children were born at Constantinople. 3. *Florence Elizabeth[8]*, born March 12, 1854; married
Henry Ayling Phillips Oct. 4, 1888; and lives at Millbury.
Mr. Phillips received the degree of S. B. at the Massachusetts Institute of Technology; and is now an architect in
Boston.

403

BENJAMIN HOVEY[6], born in Sutton, Mass., June 20, 1793.
He lived in Sutton, buying the homestead of Peter Marsh for
his residence. A picture of this house is given in the History
of Sutton, at page 260. He subsequently sold the estate to Silas
Merriam, about 1818, and removed to Oxford. He married
Julia, daughter of Asa and Hannah (Dudley) Walker Feb. 16,
1813. She was born in Sutton July 21, 1794. Mrs. Calvin
Whipple of Syracuse, N. Y., has her picture. Mr. Hovey died
Dec. 19, 1865, at the age of seventy-two.

Their children were born as follows:—

778—I.   MOSES EDWIN[7], born Aug. 29, 1813, in Sutton, Mass.
779—II. MARY TYLER[7], born Nov. 24, 1814, in Sutton; married George
Washington, son of George and Leah (Newkirk) Smith of
Mamakating (near Bloomingburgh), Sullivan county, N. Y.,
Nov. 7, 1836. He was born Sept. 6, 1809. They lived first
at Mamakating until 18—, when they removed to McDon-
ough, N. Y. He was a singing master. He died at Mc-
Donough June 22, 1861, at the age of fifty-one; and she died
there March 11, 1885. Children: 1. *Satira Augusta[8]*, born
Nov. 8, 1837, at Mamakating, N. Y.; married Calvin, son of
Mason and Lydia Whipple of McDonough May 5, 1861.
He was born at McDonough Nov. 22, 1829; and was a
carpenter. They removed to Syracuse, N. Y., upon their

marriage. He died in Syracuse March 27, 1882, at the age of fifty-two; and she lives at Syracuse. They had four children. 2. *Ophelia Jane*[8], born Sept. 17, 1839; married Orson P. Beardsley of McDonough, N. Y.; he died about 1904; and she lives at Portland, Ore. They had children. 3. *Mary Catharine*[8], born Sept. 9, 1843; married Albert L. Field; and died at Glen's Falls, N. Y., Jan 9, 1884. They had one child. 4. *Julia Frances*[8], born March 28, 1848; married Sanford Worden Greene of East German (near McDonough), N. Y., Nov. —, 1870. They still live at East German, and have four children. 5. *Marius Decatur*[8], born April —, 1851; died Oct. 4, 1861. 6. *William Augustus*[8], born Sept. 25, 1854; died Sept. 24, 1861. 7. *George Edwin Lewis*[8], born May 23. 1858; married Virginia M'Guire, at Silverton, Ore., where they live. They have five children.

780—III.   JULIA EMELINE[7], born May 23, 1816, in Sutton.
781—IV.   ELIZA JANE[7], born June 21, 1817, in Sutton; married William Kendall of Woonsocket and Providence, R. I. Children: 1. *William Albert*[8]. 2. *George*[8], is a prominent man in New York, being a bank note engraver, etc.
782—V.   HANNAH W.[7], born March 23, 1820, in Oxford; died Oct. 8, 1848, at the age of twenty-eight.
783—VI.   RUTH AUGUSTA[7], born Aug. 19, 1826, in Oxford.
784—VII.   SIMON AUGUSTUS[7], born Dec. 21, 1828, in Oxford. *See family numbered "784."*
785—VIII.   CATHARINE CHASE[7], born May 31, 1832, in Oxford; married William Gordon of Oxford, where some of the family now live.

404

SIMON HOVEY[6], born in Unadilla, N. Y., July 19, 1795. He lived at Guilford Centre, N. Y. He married Betsey Ann Cornwall.

Child, born in Guilford Centre:—

786—I.   HORACE WATERS[7], born Aug. 16, 1827. *See family numbered "786."*

405

WILLIAM HOVEY[6], born in Unadilla, N. Y., July 26, 1798. He lived in Sutton, Mass., where he was cashier of the Sutton bank, serving until it closed its business, about 1830. He married Mary W. ————; and died Aug. —, 1838, at the age of forty.

Child, born in Sutton:—

787—I.   SALLY ADELIA[7], born Nov. 19, 1828.

415

HENRY ABBOTT HOVEY[6], born in Dracut, Mass., Jan. 25, 1764. He lived in his native town and in Milford, Mass., being a farmer. He married Hannah Bradley May 29, 1791, in Dracut. She was born in Dracut Feb. 29, 1772. He died July 26 (28?), 1829 (1830?); and she died May —, 1855, at Boston.

Their children were born in Dracut as follows:—

788—I.   HANNAH[1], born Oct. 15, 1791; married Reuben Reed of Boston May 2, 1813; and died in Boston Nov. 10, 1872. He died there in 1873. Child: 1. *Reuben Augustus*[2], born March —, 1817; died in Boston June 2, 1830.

789—II.   PAMELIA[1], born Oct. 10, 1795; married ———————— Nov. 28, 1816; and died in Providence, R. I., Aug. 17, 1835.

790—III.   RHODA BRADLEY[1], born Oct. 17, 1795; married Simeon Spalding of Chelmsford July 21, 1816; and died in Lowell Oct. —, 1877.

791—IV.   MARY[1], born Dec. 26, 1797; married Joseph Swan March 27, 1824; and died in Roxbury Jan. 18, 1876.

792—V.   ELIZABETH PAGE[1], born June 11, 1800.

793—VI.   HENRY ABBOTT[1], born June 22, 1802. *See family numbered "793."*

794—VII.   ANGELINE[1], born June 28, 1804; married Nathaniel Sylvester Oct. 5, 1837, in Charlestown, Mass. He was born in Hanover, Mass., Aug. 12, 1797; and removed from Westminster, Vt., to Boston. Mass., about 1845, dying there July 8, 1856, aged fifty-eight. He was a grocer. His widow died in Roxbury Jan. 27, 1887, at the age of eighty-two. Their children were born as follows: 1. *Mary Angelina*[2], born Sept. 10, 1838, in Charlestown, Mass.; married ———————— May —, 1865; and died in Boston April —, 1876. 2. *Adaline Louisa*[2], born Feb. 3, 1843, in Westminster, Vt.; graduated from the four years' course of the Girls' high school in Boston in 1860; and was immediately appointed to the position of a teacher in the same school. She remained in this school forty-seven years, and then resigned. She never married, and now resides in Roxbury, Mass. 3. *Horace Clapp*[2], born Sept. 16, 1842, in Westminster. He was educated in the public school system of Boston,—from primary to the English high school. He enlisted in the 13th Unattached Massachusetts volunteers, and joined his regiment at Rockville, Md., Sept. 10th. He was in the battle of South Mountain four days later, and was wounded three times in the battle of Antietam on the 17th. While in Boston, on sick leave, because of his wounds, he was detailed for duty in the war department, by special order of the war department, No. 36, Dec. 3, 1863; and was discharged from the army by order of the secretary of war to accept a first-class clerkship. A little later he was assigned to duty as private secretary to Gen. E. D. Townsend, acting adjutant-general of the United States army, and remained in that position until the war was over, resigning in November, 1865. He returned to Boston. In 1870, he became connected with the business house of A. T. Stewart & Co., in New York City; and in June, 1873, was sent to Paris, France, where he remained ten years, liquidating the firm's European business. He then became senior partner of their successors, Sylvester, Hilton & Co.; and remained as such about ten years. He withdrew from the firm, and formed the firm of Sylvester, Bell & Co., which was forced to liquidate. He has been in the importing wholesale or retail dry-goods business ever since, and is now merchandise manager of the house of McCreery & Co., in Pittsburg. Pa., one of the chain of stores organized by the H. B. Claflin Co. of New York City. He was one of the organizers of Post 15, G. A. R., Boston; was the first junior vice commander, and was afterward elected senior vice commander. He married Ada Mosher of New

York City June 21, 1873. She was born there Feb. 18, 1857. He lives in Pittsburg. They have had six children. 4. *Henry Abbott*[5], born Oct. 4, 1844, in Westminster; married ———— June 4, 1867, in Georgetown, D. C.; enlisted in a Wisconsin regiment in the Civil war, and was detailed as a clerk in the quartermaster's office. He was subsequently a clerk in the office of the adjutant-general in Washington. He died at Roxbury, Mass., in 1880, when he was engaged in the dry-goods business. 5. *George Bardin*[5], born Aug. 6, 1846, in Boston, where he lives, unmarried.

795—VIII. ALFRED[5], born Feb. 24, 1807; died in New York City Sept. 22, 1825.

796—IX. ELBRIDGE AUGUSTUS[5], born Jan. 28, 1811; married ———— ———— April 2, 1835; was a harness maker in Roxbury, and died there Jan. —, 1894.

797—X. CHARLES[5], born Oct. 3, 1813; died in Dracut Aug. 4, 1817.

417

JAMES PLATTS HOVEY[5], born in Dracut, Mass., July 21, 1767. He lived in Dracut, and married Rebecca Hovey (516) of Boxford May 13, 1801. She was born in Boxford Aug. 3, 1776. He died in Dracut Nov. 30, 1831, at the age of sixty-four. She survived him, and died in Lowell Jan. 31, 1853, at the age of seventy-six, being buried at Dracut.

Their children were born in Dracut, and were as follows:—

798—I. WILLIAM[7], born Sept. 10, 1802. *See family numbered "798."*
799—II. JAMES[7], born March 8, 1804. *See family numbered "799."*
800—III. HORATIO NELSON[7], born Dec. 8, 1805. *See family numbered "800."*
801—IV. JOSHUA[7], born Jan. 8, 1808. *See family numbered "801."*
802—V. GEORGE[7], born Nov. 26, 1810. *See family numbered "802."*
803—VI. CYRUS[7], born July 14, 1813. *See family numbered "803."*

420

SAMUEL HOVEY[6], born in Dracut, Mass., Oct. 6, 1773. He lived in Dracut; was a house carpenter; and married Martha Bradley Sept. 19, 1795, in Dracut. He died in Cambridge.

Their children were born in Dracut, and were as follows:—

804—I. GILBERT[7], born Oct. 12, 1797; died Jan. 22, 1798.
805—II. GEORGE[7], born Oct. 26, 1801.
806—III. JULIA[7], born April 10, 1805.
807—IV. MARTHA[7], born Nov. 26, 1801 (7?).

421

BENJAMIN HOVEY[6], born in Dracut, Mass., May 9, 1775. He lived in his native town, and married Lois ————. She died in Dracut Oct. 8, 1846; and he died there March 30, 1866, at the age of ninety.

Their children were born in Dracut, and were as follows:—*

808—I.   MARY[7], born Nov. 29, 1796; married ———— Emerson. Chil-
          dren: 1. *Mary*[8]; living, unmarried, in 1860. 2. *Minnie*[8];
          living, unmarried, in 1866.
809—II.   BENJAMIN[7], born Nov. 6, 1800; died Dec. 12, 1801.
810—III. BENJAMIN[7], born June 7, 1804; died May 2, 1805.
811—IV.   LOUISA[7], born Aug. 30, 1806; died Oct. 1, 1829, at the age of
          twenty-three.
812—V.   NANCY HEATH[7], born Nov. 13, 1808; and lived in Dracut, un-
          married, in 1866.

423

JOSEPH HOVEY[6], born in Dracut, Mass., May 25, 1784. He
lived in Dracut, and married Mary Hovey (519) of Boxford
July 23, 1812. She was born in Boxford Aug. 9, 1781. He died
Aug. 29, 1860, at the age of seventy-six.

Their children were born as follows:—

813—I.   JOSEPH[7]. *See family numbered "813."*
814—II.   AUGUSTUS V.[7] (twin), born Sept. 26, 1812, in Dracut. *See fam-
          ily numbered "814."*

425

DANIEL HOVEY[6], born in Windham, Conn., July 24, 1764.
He removed to Lyme, N. H., with his parents in childhood.
Near the close of the war of the Revolution his father was
drafted into the army, and although little more than a boy Daniel
was accepted in his father's place. Oct. 16, 1781, while acting as
a scout, with four others, from a fort in Corinth, they were fired
upon in Jericho by a party of sixteen tories, some of whom were
acquainted with Daniel and had partaken of the hospitality of the
family. One of the scouts was mortally wounded and died the
next day. The scouts jumped into some high brakes and thick
bushes and hid. Four of them were soon discovered. Three of
them stated that their number was four, but one of them, more
honest than the three said that there were five. Thereupon search
resulted in the discovery of Daniel, whom the leader of the tories
recognized, taking him by the hand, and inquiring after the health
of his father, and said if he had him there he would treat him.
It appeared that this tory was supposed to be a patriot, and had
so learned of the contemplated expedition of the scouts. They
were taken to Quebec and imprisoned, for eleven months, in the
same cell with an educated Englishman, who took pleasure in
instructing Daniel in arithmetic and surveying. Sometimes, when
he had no ink, he used blood from his wrist for writing out

* Mr. Hovey had two grandsons, Joseph C. Swan and Edward P.
Swan, living in Lowell, in 1866.

mathematical problems. His papers, written in blood, are in the possession of his grandson Fred Hovey Allen of Boston, and the writing in blood is bright, though that written with ink is much faded. This new-formed friend awakened in Daniel a thirst for learning; and he determined to pursue his desire when he was exchanged, after eleven months' imprisonment. He started for his home on foot, leaving his teacher friend and the charitable lady who had occasionally sent in to them food dainties. He become extremely foot sore, and about a day's journey from home his father met him on horseback. Daniel rode the remainder of the way, while his father walked by his side. In due time Daniel began to study with Rev. Dr. Burton of Thetford, Vt., with a view of entering Dartmouth college, but was prevented by the failure of his health from securing a liberal education.

Mr. Hovey lived on the river road in Lyme, near the Hanover line, during the remainder of his life. He received a pension from the government on account of his services in the war, and this was continued, after his decease, to his widow.

He taught school for twenty-five years, during the winter; and held many offices of honor and trust. He was active in establishing a circulating library; and frequently settled estates and disputes of his neighbors and friends. Though not joining the church until late in life, he always had family worship, and was among the first Sunday-school superintendents in New Hampshire. He remained, as superintendent or teacher, in the Sunday-school as long as he lived. His love for children increased with his years, and they were as fond of him. He was one of the first in his region to become a total abstainer from the use of intoxicating drinks. He was honest, good, just and unselfish, and his memory is precious.

He was short in stature, having dark brown hair and blue eyes, unassuming in his appearance, though a man of more than ordinary ability. He was known as "Master Hovey," because of his long service as teacher.

Mr. Hovey married Beulah, daughter of Sylvanus and Mary (Sawyer) Pingree of Hanover Feb. 18, 1789, in Lyme. She was born in Coventry, Conn., Feb. 1, 1769. Mr. Hovey died in Lyme March 2, 1850, at the age of eighty-five. Upon his monument, in the cemetery at Lyme, is the following inscription, prepared in accordance with his wish:—

Daniel Hovey, born in Windham, Conn., July 24, 1764, married Beulah Pingree of Hanover, Feb. 18, 1789—by whom he had four sons and six daughters. Died March 2, 1850, aged 86.

Mrs. Hovey survived her husband, and died at Lyme Nov. 26, 1857, at the age of eighty-eight.

Their children were born in Lyme, as follows:—

815—I.   BEULAH[1], born March 17, 1790; died, unmarried, May 29,* 1817, aged twenty-seven.

816—II. DANIEL[1], born March 25, 1792.   *See family numbered "816."*

817—III. MARY[1], born June 19, 1794; died, unmarried, Nov. 27, 1819, at the age of twenty-five.

818—IV. ABIGAIL[1], born Jan. 31, 1797.   She married Col. Jesse, son of Jesse and Miriam (Fairfield) Carpenter of Lyme Jan. 2, 1823.   He was born in Lyme April 5, 1796; and died in Windsor, Conn., July 4, 1876.   She died in Hartford, Conn., June 3, 1862, aged sixty-five.   Their children were born as follows: 1. *Daniel Hovey*[6], born April 19, 1824.   He was a farmer, and lived in Brooklyn, N. Y., Chelsea, Vt., and Wallingford, Wethersfield and Collinsville, Conn.   He married Ruth Estabrook, daughter of John and Hannah (Estabrook) Carleton Nov. 26, 1850, in Brookfield, Vt.   She was born in Brookfield July 15, 1824.   They had five children, one of whom is Harriet Abbey Carleton of Geneva, Switzerland, authoress and correspondent.   2. *Elizabeth*[6], born Oct. 9, 1825; married Franklin Joshua, son of Solomon and Betsey (Flint) Forbes May 6, 1846, in Hartford, Conn.   He was born in East Hartford, Conn., May 6, 1818; and was a merchant tailor.   He lived in Hartford, and New Britain, Conn., Springfield, Mass., and subsequently at Windsor Locks, Conn.   They had five children, one of whom is Rev. Jesse Franklin Forbes of Warren, Mass.   3. *Fairfield*[6], born March 15, 1828; died May —, 1832.   4. *Harriet*[6], born Dec. 5, 1834; married Solomon Augustus, son of Dea. Solomon Holt Oct. 1, 1851, in New Britain, Conn.   He was born in Andover, Mass., Jan. 3, 1832; and resided in Brooklyn, N. Y.   They had three children.

819—V.   SARAH[1], born June 29, 1799.   She married, first, Alpheus, son of Roger and Sarah (Davidson) Hibbard March 1, 1820, in Lyme.   He was born in Brookfield, Vt., July 12, 1795; and died there July 14, 1832.   She married, second, Daniel, son of Jesse and Eleanor (Welch) Cheeney April 3, 1837, in Brookfield.   He was born in Washington, Vt., Nov. 7, 1815.   They were divorced about 1855; and she died in Rockland, Mass., Feb. 20, 1876.   Her children by Alpheus Hibbard were born in Brookfield, as follows: 1. *Sylvanus Hovey*[6], born Dec. 16, 1820; married Philena A., daughter of Obed and Philena (Bennett) Allen April 3, 1844, in Chelsea, Vt.   She was born in Chelsea Jan. 6, 1822; and they lived there, having had two children.   2. *Franklin*[6], born Aug. 20, 1823; died Oct. 12, 1840.   3. *Rhoda Luthera*[6], born Oct. 11, 1829; married Charles Mann, son of Henry and Abigail (Mann) Burrell July 27, 1853, in Chelsea.   He was born in East Abingdon (now Rockland), Mass., July 15, 1830; and resided there.   They had two children.   4. *Alma Elizabeth*[6], born Oct. 20, 1832; married her second cousin Joseph Milton Hovey (1340) Jan. 20, 1850, in Brookfield.   Children by her second husband, Daniel Cheeney: 1. *Alpheus Hibbard*[6], born May 12, 1838; married Emma, daughter of Daniel and Julia (Hall) Whitney March 19, 1863, in Chelsea.   She was

* Her gravestone in Lyme says that Beulah died on the "30"th of May, 1817.

born in Tunbridge, Vt., Dec. 18, 1841. He was a farmer, and lived in Buck Creek, Bremer county, and Spencer, Iowa. They had four children. 2. *Ellen Delia*[7], born Feb. 21, 1841; married John, son of Adna and Mary Miller (Crocker) Burrell Jan. 3, 1860, in Rockland, Mass., where he was born Dec. 12, 1833. He resided in Rockland. They had four children.

820—VI. SAMUEL SYLVANUS[7], born Sept. 1, 1801; died Nov. 5, 1819, aged eighteen.

821—VII. ELIZABETH PERKINS[7], born Oct. 22, 1803; died, unmarried, Aug. 15, 1847, at the age of forty-three.

822—VIII. RHODA LORD[7], born April 14, 1806; married Philander, son of Ebenezer and Anna (Bennett) Allen June 3, 1832, in Lyme. He was born in Chelsea, Vt., May 19, 1807; and died at Lyme Feb. 16, 1851. She lived in Hartford, Conn., in 1878; and died Aug. 11, 1891, at the age of eighty-five, being buried at Lyme, N. H. Their children were born in Lyme as follows: 1. *Mary Elizabeth*[8], born Aug. 2, 1834; married Warren, son of Reuben Butterfield and Sarah Rackleffe (Staples) Sherburne Oct. 1, 1871, in Lexington, Mass. He was born in Charlestown, Mass., April 21, 1833; and was a merchant in Boston, residing in Lexington. 2. *George Lewis*[8], born June 25, 1836; married Albina, daughter of Ezra and Ann (Borden) Marble Dec. 25, 1865, in Lawrence, Mass. She was born in Fall River, Mass., March 30, 1844. He was a farmer, and lived in Lawrence, Mass., and Windsor, New Britain and Farmington, Conn. They had seven children. 3. *Edwin Bennett*[8], born Dec. 28, 1839; was a private in Company I, First regiment, Rhode Island cavalry volunteers, and was killed at the retaking of Front Royal, Warren county, Va., May 2, 1862, at the age of twenty-two, being unmarried. His remains still rest near the place where he was killed. 4. *Sylvanus Frank*[8], born Aug. 3, 1843; an insurance agent, residing at Hartford, Conn. He married Eliza, daughter of William and Mary (Hirstwood) Leyland Oct. 21, 1869, at Lawrence, Mass. She was born in York, England, Nov. 10, 1840. 5. *Frederic Hovey*[8], born Oct. 1, 1845. He was a clergyman, and resided in Boston.

823—IX. JOSIAH FAIRFIELD[7], born May 31, 1808; died June 2, 1808.

824—X. GEORGE LEWIS[7], born Aug. 20, 1810. *See family numbered "824."*

426

ABNER HOVEY[6], born in Canterbury, Conn., Nov. 5, 1766. He was a miller, and lived in Middlebury, Vt., until about 1825, when he removed to Indiana, settling eight miles up the Wabash river from its emptying into the Ohio. He married Lois, daughter of Capt. Stephen and Lois (Lyon) Tucker Feb. 17, 1790, in Woodstock, Conn. She was born in Woodstock Oct. 20, 1769; and died in Lyme, N. H., July 6, 1848. He died in Lyme Jan. 12, 1842, at the age of seventy-five.

Their children were born in Lyme, as follows:—

825—I. LYDIA[7], born May 15, 1791; died Nov. 19, 1810, aged nineteen years.

826—II.   ABIGAIL[2], born March 14, 1793; married Joshua, son of Jacob
and Sarah (Copp) Rouen Dec. 10, 1811, in Wentworth, N. H.
He was born in Rouen, France, Jan. 23. 1790; and died in
Wentworth, from injury received by the falling of a tree,
Oct. 16, 1816. She died in Wentworth Jan. 1, 1816, at the
age of twenty-two. Children, born in Lyme: 1. *Lydia
Elmina[3]*, born June 14, 1813; married, first, Thomas Carmel.
son of Leavitt and Abigail (Morrill) Clough Oct. 28, 1838,
in Solon, O.; he was born in Canterbury, N. H., Feb. 16.
1812; and died in Solon Oct. 14, 1839, having been a farmer.
She married, second, Benjamin, son of Luther and Elizabeth
(Wilbur) Crawford April 3, 1842, in East Cleveland, O. He
was born in Tolland, Conn., April 24, 1794; and died in East
Cleveland July 29, 1863. He was a farmer and lumberman.
She was living in Painesville, O., with the widow of her
eldest son in 1878. She had one child by her first husband,
and two by the second. 2. *Sarah Abigail[3]*, born April 21,
1815; married, first, Moses, son of Ethan and Caroline Atwood April 1, 1835, in Charlotte, Vt. He was born in Charlotte April 4, 1814; and died in Harbor Creek, Pa., Sept. 14,
1848. She married, second, Charles, son of John Taylor,
May —, 1819; and was divorced from him within a year
thereafter. She married, third, Sidney Huntley Dec. 5, 1853.
in Cleveland, O. He was born in 1810, and died March 29,
1868. She died in Cleveland April 14, 1874.

827—III.   SAMUEL[2], born March 9, 1795. *See family numbered "827."*
828—IV.   DUDLEY[2], born Jan. 31, 1797. *See family numbered "828."*
829—V.   DANIEL[2], born March 20, 1799; died March 20, 1799.
830—VI.   ESTHER[2], born March 11, 1800; married John, son of Daniel
and Margaret (McAdams) Clyde Jan. 22, 1828, in Lyme.
He was born in Windham, N. H., Nov. 6, 1791; and died in
Lyme Oct. 9, 1858. She died there Nov. 27, 1849, at the age
of forty-nine. Their children were born in Lyme as follows:
1. *John Downer[3]*, born Jan. 2, 1829; farmer; lived in Fremont and Argo, Minn.; married Sarah Amelia, daughter of
Charles and Caroline (Robinson) Hendershott Dec. 1, 1862,
in Fremont. Minn.; she was born in Hornersville, N. Y.,
April 20, 1844. They had six children. 2. *Samuel Syl-
vester[3]*, born March 11, 1830; died March 9, 1833. 3. *Abner
Hovey[3]*, born Oct. 8, 1831; never married; was drowned
near Cairo, Ill., by sinking of the steamer "Odd Fellow,"
Aug. 1, 1871, when he was thirty-nine years old. 4. *Moses
Sylvester[3]*, born Nov. 18, 1833; married Ellen E. Taylor in
1862; and died soon afterward in California. 5. *Hannah
Louisa[3]*, born Jan. 18, 1836; married Samuel Willard, son of
William and Anna (Clyde) Colburn March 4, 1861, in Troy,
Vt.; he was born in Lyme, N. H., June 29, 1827; was a
builder and contractor; lived in Troy, Vt., and Saratoga,
Minn. They had three children.

831—VII.   ————[2] (son), born March —, 1802; died March —, 1802.
832—VIII.   ————[2] (son), born March —, 1802; died March —, 1802.
833—IX.   RACHEL[2], born April 5, 1803; married Josiah, son of William
and Rachel (Searls) Burroughs Nov. 20, 1835, in Enosburgh,
Vt.; he was born in Nottingham, N. H., Dec. 28, 1809; they
lived in Belvidere, Vt., where she died June 5, 1838, at the
age of thirty-five. Children: 1. ————[3] (son), born Sept.
20, 1836; died Sept. 20, 1836. 2. ————[3] (son), born June
2, 1838; died June 2, 1838.

834—x. Lois[1], born May 24, 1806; married George, son of Sylvanus
and Tamasin (Nevins) Woodworth Aug. 14, 1825, in Canaan,
N. H.; he was born in Dorchester, N. H., Oct. 5, 1793; and
died in Hebron, N. H., April 18, 1864; she died in Concord,
Mass., Dec.. 2, 1877, of heart disease, after many weeks of
acute suffering, borne with much fortitude. Their twelve
children were born in Grafton county, N. H., as follows:
1. *Leigh Richmond*[2], born Aug. 7, 1826; married Hannah
Mather, daughter of James and Susan Hill (Cranmer)
Lamb June 18, 1862, in Springfield, Ill.; she was born in
Springfield July 6, 1838; and he died there May 28, 1865.
They had one child. 2. *William Henry*[2], born Jan. 14, 1828;
married Caroline Matilda, daughter of Adin and Martha
(Gee) Balch Dec. 8, 1849; she was born in Lunenburgh, N.
H., April 21, 1824; he is judge of probate; and lived in
Salmon Falls, N. H., and Pewamo and Ionia, Mich. They
had three children. 3. *Esther Tamasin*[2], born Dec. 14, 1829;
married Benjamin Franklin, son of Joseph and Elizabeth
(Atwood) Ellis Sept. 17, 1860, in Peoria, Ill.; he was born
in Middletown Point, N. J., Jan. 21. 1826; and lived in
Peoria, where their six children were born. 4. *John Ball*[2],
born Jan. 25, 1832; died in Hebron, N. H., Jan. 23, 1853.
5. *George Thornton*[2], born Aug. 2, 1834; married Frances
Cecilia, daughter of Samuel and Theodosia (Littlefield)
Wallace Oct. 31, 1859, in Concord, N. H.; she was born in
Homer, N. Y., Feb. 28, 1837. They had one child. 6. *Sarah
Frances*[2], born June 21, 1836; lived in Concord, Mass., un-
married, in 1878. 7. *Elizabeth Kimball*[2], born April 2, 1839;
married Peter, son of Caleb and Dorcas (Taylor) Whitte-
more March 19, 1862, in Concord, N. H.; he was born in
Bridgewater, N. H., May 28, 1821. They had four children.
8. *Artemas Brooks*[2], born April 15, 1841; married Lucia
Mahala, daughter of Artemas Lysias and Sarah (Phelps)
Brooks Dec. 25, 1865, in Lowell, Mass.; she was born in
Lowell July 5, 1840; and they lived in Lowell. They had
four children. 9. *Albert Bingham*[2], born April 7, 1843;
married Mary Angeline, daughter of Charles and Amelia
Emily (Bennett) Parker Sept. 30, 1873, in Lisbon, N. H.;
she was born in Lisbon May 15, 1849. He was a merchant,
and lived in Concord, N. H. 10. *Grace Lowella*[2], born
June 14, 1845; married Daniel Quincy, son of Moses Williams
and Tamar (Little) Clement Jan. 22, 1870, in Hebron, N. H.;
he was born in Warren, N. H.; and they were living in
1878. 11. *Edward Baker*[2], born March 27, 1847; married
Helen, daughter of John Milton and Fidelia (Wilson)
Whiton Sept. 9, 1875, in Franklin, Conn.; she was born in
Stoddard, N. H., May 3, 1849; and they lived in Concord,
N. H. 12. *Louisa Maria*[2], born May 17, 1850; married
Lucius Alfred, son of James Riley and Amelia Emily (Harris) Young May 15, 1872, in Lisbon, N. H., where he was
born July 10, 1850.

835—xi. ABNER BINGHAM[1] (twin), born March 12, 1809; died March
16, 1809.

836—xii. AREA GREEN[2] (twin), born March 12, 1809; died March 26, 1809.

837—xiii. NANCY BINGHAM[1], born Sept. 22, 1812; married Rev. Moses,
son of Capt. Moses and Elizabeth (Spaulding) Flint June 5,
1834, in Lyme. He was born in Lyme Jan. 17, 1811; and
died there, being a Baptist clergyman, April 5, 1842. She

died there, of pneumonia, May 26, 1843, at the age of thirty.
She was possessed of great personal beauty and loveliness
of character, and her death was greatly lamented.   Their
children were born in Lyme, as follows: 1.   *Elizabeth
Spaulding*[9], born March 17, 1835; married Johnson Colby,
son of Timothy and Martha (Colby) McIntyre Sept. 1, 1859,
in Dunbarton, N. H., where he was born Aug. 4, 1827.   They
lived in Goffstown, N. H.   2.   *Moses Attwood*[9], born Jan. 31,
1837; married Hannah Sophronia, daughter of Theodore and
Sally (Lovejoy) Balch March 19, 1861, in Manchester, N. H.
She was born in Lyme June 25, 1843.   He was a farmer,
and lived in Monroe, Iowa, Indianapolis, Ind., and Keokuk
and Deep River, Iowa.   They had a large family.

428

RUFUS CLEVELAND HOVEY[6], born in Canterbury, Conn., Aug.
29, 1770.   He was a farmer, and lived in Brookfield, Vt.   He
married Grace, daughter of Benjamin and Amy (Darby) Billings
July 17, 1794, in Lyme, N. H.   She was born in New London,
Conn., Nov. 22, 1777.   He died in Brookfield July 5, 1817, at
the age of forty-six; and she died there July 29, 1819, aged
forty-one.   Their children were born in Brookfield, except the
eldest, who was born in Lyme, as follows:—

838—I.   RUFUS BILLINGS[7], born Nov. 17, 1794.   *See family numbered
           "838."*

839—II.   AMY[7], born Dec. 7, 1795; married David, son of Timothy Bur-
           roughs Nov. 29, 1816, in Brookfield; and died there May 9,
           1818, at the age of twenty-two, childless.   He was born in
           Alstead, N. H., in 1793; and died in Brookfield, Vt., Jan.
           17, 1845.

840—III.   ORANGE[7], born Feb. 5, 1797.   *See family numbered "840."*
841—IV.   RUTH[7], born Nov. 2, 1798; died May 12, 1812, aged thirteen
           years.

842—V.   SILAS[7], born March 5, 1801.   *See family numbered "842."*
843—VI.   RHODA[7], born April 25, 1803; married Moses, son of Moses and
           Nancy (Bean) Ordway Nov. 27, 1823, in Brookfield; he
           was born in Tunbridge, Vt., July 7, 1798; died in Williams-
           town, Vt., Nov. 26, 1866; and she died in Chelsea, Vt., June
           22, 1878.   He was a farmer.   Children: 1.   *Charlotte Eliz-
           abeth*[8], born Aug. 31, 1824; married John Haskell, son of
           Dr. John and Susannah (Haskell) Edson March 18, 1868,
           in Williamstown, Vt.; he was born in West Randolph, Vt.,
           Sept. 12, 1827; and died in Northfield, Vt., Sept. 13, 1872.
           He was a foundryman, and lived in Northfield, where she
           was living in 1879.   They had no children.   2.   *Franklin*[8],
           born Jan. 19, 1826; married Maria Hatch, adopted daughter
           of Asa Hatch, of Williamstown, Vt., Nov. 14, 1850.   She
           was born in Williamstown Oct. 25, 1832; and he died in
           Chelsea, Vt., June 26, 1865.   She married, secondly, Elisha
           G. Lougee of North Tunbridge, Vt.   She had three chil-
           dren, all by her first husband.   3.   *Martin Frederic*[8], born
           Dec. 11, 1827; married Diana, daughter of Ariel and Sally
           (Paine) Burnham June 7, 1852, in Brookfield; she was born
           Aug. 18, 1833; he was a farmer, and lived in Chelsea, Vt.
           They had five children.

844—VII.   SIMEON SKINNER[2], born April 9, 1805; died Aug. 28, 1808.
845—VIII.   BETSEY[2], born May 2, 1807; died Sept. 3, 1808.
846—IX   SIMEON SKINNER[2], born Nov. 13, 1809. *See family numbered "846."*

847—X.   ASAHEL KING[2], born May 25, 1811. He was a farmer, and lived in Chelsea, Vt. He married, first, Martha, daughter of Rufus and Mary (Wells) Downing March 17, 1836, in Williamstown, Vt. She was born in Brookfield, Vt., June 1, 1813; and she died in Albany, Vt., Oct. 4, 1839. He married, second, Rocina Chastina, daughter of Daniel and Betsey (Moseley) Martin April 9, 1845, in Chelsea, Vt. She was born in Williamstown April 13, 1813. He had no children; and was living in 1878.

848—XI.   LAURA[2], born May 6, 1813; married Seth, son of Joshua and Hannah (Fowler) Phelps Dec. 13, 1831, in Albany, Vt. She died in Albany Jan. 12, 1868, at the age of fifty-four. He was born in Pembroke, N. H., April 6, 1804; was a farmer; and lived in Albany in 1878. Children: 1. *Simonds Fowler[2]*, born March 17, 1834; married Susan Jane, daughter of Aaron and Mahala (Noyes) Critchett Dec. 15, 1860, in Newport, Vt. She was born in Epsom, N. H., March 11, 1839. He was a farmer, and they resided in Lowell, Vt., in 1878. They had two children. 2. *George Hovey[2]*, born Feb. 13, 1838; died Jan. 2, 1862, unmarried, at the age of twenty-three. 3. *Betsey Grant[2]*, born March 31, 1843; unmarried in 1878.

849—XII.   HORACE NELSON[2], born Jan. 28, 1815. *See family numbered "849."*

850—XIII.   GRACE[2], born Jan. 26, 1817; died Aug. 10, 1819.

430

SAMUEL HOVEY[6], born in Lyme. N. H., Oct. 20, 1774. He was a man of ordinary stature, with blue eyes and brown hair; a farmer; and lived in Brookfield, Vt., being a Baptist in religious belief. He was social and friendly, and much respected, being a justice of the peace. He married, first, Amy, daughter of Benjamin and Amy (Darby) Billings Nov. 15, 1798, in Brookfield. She was sister of his brother Rufus C. Hovey's wife, and was born in New London, Conn., May 5, 1780. She died in Brookfield Feb. 13, 1836; and he married, second, Phyletta, daughter of Timothy and Eunice (Houghton) Kendall Dec. 7, 1836. She was born in Williamstown, Vt.. Oct. 7, 1800; and died in Brookfield July 22, 1872. He died July 25, 1856, at the age of eighty-one.

Mr. Hovey's children were born in Brookfield, as follows:—

851—I.   GRACE[2], born Dec. 3, 1799; died Sept. 4, 1802, at the age of two.
852—II.   SAMUEL WILLIS[2], born Sept. 25, 1801. *See family numbered "852."*
853—III.   ABIEL[2], born Nov. 25, 1803; died Nov. 25, 1805.
854—IV.   ALVAN[2], born Dec. 4, 1804. *See family numbered "854."*
855—V.   GRACE[2], born in 1807; died in 1807.
856—VI.   PERMELIA[2], born Oct. 4, 1809; married Bela, son of Rufus and Mary (Wells) Downing March 17, 1833, in Brookfield. He

was born in Chelsea, Vt., Dec. 12, 1804; was a mechanic; and lived in Brookfield and Hartford, Vt. Their children were born in Brookfield, as follows: 1. *Mary Hovey*, born Nov. 20, 1833; married Dennison Goodrich, son of Elijah and Nancy (Clifford) Crain March 5, 1857, in Chelsea, Vt.; he was born in Brookfield March 27, 1827; was a trader; and lived in Fort Atkinson, Wis. They had one child. 2. *Samuel Hovey*, born Oct. 27, 1835; died March 17, 1836. 3. *Alvan Hovey*, born June 27, 1837; mechanic; lived in Fort Atkinson; married Lizzie Phyletta, daughter of Hubbard and Phyletta (Page) Case March 4, 1861. She was born in Barnard, Vt., July 13, 1839. They had several children. 4. *Martha Minerva*, born Feb. 16, 1840; died April 16, 1856, at the age of sixteen. 5. *Luna Estella*, born Sept. 7, 1842; married Hazen Moses, son of Hazen Moses and Mary Ann (Cloud) West March 22, 1865, in Sharon, Vt. He was born in Norwich. Vt., April 13, 1842; was a farmer; and lived in Hartford, Vt. They had one child, who died young. 6. *Lydia Permelia*, born Feb. 12, 1844; married Nelson Walter, son of Ethan and Rosetta (Cummings) White Jan. 15, 1870, in Hartford, Vt. He was born in Dorchester, N. H., Feb. 21, 1838; was a mechanic; and lived in Hartford, having no children. 7. *Edward Blake*, born Feb. 9, 1846; merchant; lived in Grand Rapids, Mich.; married Hortense, daughter of Leonard and Matilda Olney Oct. 29, 1875, in Hillsdale, Mich., where she was born April —, 1848. 8. *Eliza Maria*, born July 1, 1848; married Alonzo Chapin, son of Allan and Hannah (May) Martin Sept. 2, 1873, in Norwich, Vt. He was born in Barnston, Province of Quebec, Canada, March 23, 1843; was a merchant; and lived at Hartford, Vt.

857—vii.	JAMES HARVEY[7], born July 28, 1811. *See family numbered "857."*
858—viii.	RUFUS CLEVELAND[7], born Oct. 15, 1816. *See family numbered "858."*

859—ix.	AMY BILLINGS[7], born Aug. 5, 1821; died Feb. 16, 1837, at the age of fifteen.
860—x.	AMY PHYLETTA[7], born July 7, 1838; married Edwin Smiley, son of Gurdon Plummer and Isabella (Hemenway) Hibbard (son of Elizabeth Hovey, 434), Aug. 4, 1864, in Brookfield. He was born in East Brookfield Oct. 13, 1839; was a builder; a man of earnest and active Christian character; and a deacon in the Baptist church. He died in Montpelier, Vt., Nov. 22, 1876. They had no children.
861—xi.	ALTHEA LORETTA[7], born Feb. 17, 1840; married James Alexander, son of James Gray and Eliza Melvina (Alexander) Trask March 27, 1861, at Brookfield, where he was born March 1, 1836. He was a farmer, and lived in East Brookfield. They had one child: 1. *James Edgar*, born March 9, 1865, in East Brookfield.

431

ARIEL HOVEY[6], born in Lyme, N. H., Oct. 30, 1776. He was a farmer, and lived in Rutland, Vt., until 1812, then in Montpelier until 1814, then in Middlebury until 1818, when he removed to Indiana, settling at Mount Vernon, in Posey county.

He was an active and energetic man, possessed of sound judgment and good principles.

Mr. Hovey married Frances, daughter of John and Frances Peterson about 1802. She was born in Vermont May 20, 1780(?). He died in Posey county July 17, 1823, at the age of forty-six; and she died there Sept. 6, 1836.

Their children were as follows:—

862—I.   JOHN[5], born Feb. —, 1803; died April —, 1803.

863—II. FRANCES[5], born Aug. —, 1806, in Rutland; married John Mitinger May 17, 1831, in Mount Vernon, Ind. They died, childless, in 1836.

864—III. ELIZA[5], born Aug. —, 1809, in Rutland; married Andrew Suter, son of Joseph and Martha (Crabtree) Gamble June 17, 1829, at Mount Vernon. He was born in Christian county, Ky., March 10, 1808; and she died at Mount Vernon Nov. —, 1834, at the age of twenty-five. He died there June 20, 1838, at the age of thirty. Their children were as follows: 1. ———[6] (daughter), born April 16, 1830; died April 16, 1830. 2. *Joseph Hovey*[6], born April 16, 1832; died Aug. 8, 1864, unmarried, being killed in a political quarrel.

865—IV. AMANDA[5], born June 11, 1811, in Rutland; died at Mount Vernon, unmarried, Sept. —, 1839(?).

866—V.   CHARLOTTE[5], born Oct. 15, 1813, in Montpelier; married, first, George LaFarry July 13, 1829, at Mount Vernon. He died the next year, childless; and she married, second, Thomas Stone Veatch Aug. 18, 1831, at Mount Vernon. He was born in Hagerstown, Md., Jan. 5, 1810. She was divorced from him (who went to California about 1842), and married, third, Aaron Culbertson Moore Oct. 12, 1837, at Mount Vernon. She married, fourth, Jacob, son of Jacob Fisher Feb. 21, 1851, at Mount Vernon. He was born in Philadelphia, Pa., Jan. 5, 1806; and died at Mount Vernon Aug. 16, 1877, having been a farmer. She died at Mount Vernon Jan. —, 1858.

Her children by Thomas S. Veatch were as follows: 1. *Virgil Stone*[6], born July 23, 1832, at Mount Vernon; married Margaret Abigail, daughter of Jesse and Abigail Oatman June 23, 1858. She was born in Floyd county, Ind., June 28, 1840. They lived in Evansville, Ind., and had five children. 2. *Charles*[6], born about 1834.

Her children by Aaron C. Moore were as follows: 1. *Mary*[6], born about 1839; married Seth Spanton about 1860; and died in Paterson, N. J., in 1876. 2. *Alvin*[6], born about 1843; married a widow Bradley; and lived in Terre Haute, Ind. 3. *Lucy*[6], born about 1845; lived, unmarried, in Paterson, N. J.

Her child by Jacob Fisher was as follows: 1. *Esther*[6], born Oct. 7, 1856; married Charles H., son of John H. and Mary (Ashworth) Barter Dec. 13, 1877. He was born at Mount Vernon June 28, 1854. She died at Mount Vernon Nov. 8, 1878, leaving one child.

867—VI. CHARLES[5], born April 19, 1815, in Middlebury. *See family numbered "867."*

868—VII. MINERVA[5], born Oct. 18, 1819, in Mount Vernon, Ind.; married, first, as the second wife of the husband of her sister Eliza (864), Andrew Suter Gamble March 10, 1836, at Mount Vernon. After his death, she married, second, Edmund, son of Charles Bacon in 1842, at Mount Vernon. He was born Feb. 25, 1812. She died Aug. 16, 1846, at the age of twenty-six.

Her children by Andrew S. Gamble were as follows: 1. *Martha*[6], born Jan. 19, 1837; died Oct. 20, 1838. 2. *Andrew Suter*[6], born Feb. 10, 1839; married Celia, daughter of Aaron and Elizabeth (Noel) Lichtenberger Oct. 25, 1866, at Mount Vernon. She was born in New Harmony, Ind., Nov. 6, 1845. He was a commission merchant; and resided in Evansville. They had three children.

Her children by Edmund Bacon were as follows: 1. *Charles*[6], born Nov. 2, 1844; died in Hindman, Ky., Nov. 10, 1862. 2. ———[6] (daughter), born Aug. 16, 1846; died Aug. 30, 1846.

869—VIII. ALVIN PETERSON[7], born Sept. 6, 1821, at Mount Vernon. *See family numbered "869."*

432

DEA. ALVAN HOVEY[6], born in Lyme, N. H., March 3, 1779. He lived in East Brookfield, Vt.; and married, first, Nancy, daughter of Benjamin and Lucretia (Kingsbury) Seabury April 3, 1803, in Brookfield. She was born in Connecticut Aug. 8, 1780; and died in Brookfield Nov. 27, 1856. He married, second, his cousin, Mrs. Nancy Bean, daughter of Oliver and Rachel (Cleveland) Hamblin Oct. 12, 1857, in Brookfield. She was born in Brookfield March 8, 1791. Having no sons who grew to adult age, he received into his family sons of several other people, and educated and supported them during their minority, receiving their labor on the farm. He invented a horse-rake which was patented. He was, also, a sweet singer, a handsome man, with a sedate smile on his face, and long white hair curling over his shoulders. He was a deacon of the Baptist church for many years; and died in Brookfield Jan. 29, 1864, at the age of eighty-four. She died at Enfield, N. H., Aug. 15, 1868, aged seventy-seven.

Deacon Hovey's children were born in East Brookfield as follows:—

870—I.   ALVAN[7], born Jan. 12, 1804; died Jan. 30, 1804.
871—II.   NANCY[7], born Feb. 20, 1805; died Feb. 20, 1805.
872—III. BENJAMIN[7], born June 15, 1806; died June 15, 1806.
873—IV.   NANCY SEABURY[7], born Dec. 6, 1807; married Andrew, son of Enoch and Ennice (Martin) Burnham April 3, 1827, in Brookfield. He was born in Williamstown, Vt., Jan. 10, 1799; was a farmer; and lived in Washington, Vt. Their children were born as follows: 1. *Nancy*[8], born Nov. 28, 1827; died Nov. 29, 1827. 2. *Nancy Luthera*[8], born March 29, 1829; died April 23, 1829. 3. *James*[8], born June 23, 1831; was a farmer; and lived in Washington, Vt. He married Abbie, daughter of John and Abigail (Abbott) Thompson Nov. 5, 1854, in Barre, Vt., where she was born May 1, 1837. They had three children. 4. *Alvin Hovey*[8], born Dec. 15, 1833; and died March 17, 1841, at the age of seven. 5. *Har-*

riet *Hovey*[6], born June 29, 1835; married Asa Herbert, son of Williard and Rachel (Taylor) Pepper Sept. 8, 1861, in Williamsburgh, Vt. He was born in Washington, Vt., Dec. 28, 1835; was a farmer; and lived in that town. They had three children. 6. *Fanny Flavilla*[6], born May 8, 1837; married John Ryland, son of Alvan and Amanda (Farnham) Seaver Feb. 17, 1856, in Barre, Vt. He was born in Williamstown, Vt., Feb. 17, 1831; was a farmer; and lived in Montpelier, Vt. She died Feb. 27, 1862, at the age of twenty-four. They had one child. 7. *Andrew*[6], born Oct. 19, 1838; married Mary Elizabeth, daughter of Hyde and Mary (Wiggin) Cabot June 14, 1860, in Chelsea, Vt., where she was born May —, 1842. She died May 1, 1871. He was a farmer, and lived in Braintree, Vt. They had two children. 8. *Lucretia Elizabeth*[6], born Dec. 7, 1840; married Thomas Warren, son of Joseph and Sarah (Glidden) Goodrich May 5, 1869, in Williamstown, Vt. He was born in Brookfield, Vt., March 19, 1838; was a farmer; and lived in Williamstown. They had one child. 9. *Luther*[6], born Sept. 7, 1842; lived in Washington, Vt.; entered the Union army Sept. 1, 1862, and participated in numerous engagements; was wounded June —, 1864, and sent to the hospital in August; remained there till December; was afterwards captured by Mosby, but escaped at great peril; was at the surrender of General Lee; and was discharged July 3, 1865. 10. *.William Pride*[6], born May 11, 1844; died April 10, 1845. 11. *Walter*[6], born Dec. 9, 1846. 12. *Emily Frances*[6], born May 24, 1850; married Charles Albert, son of Eli and Mary (Wright) Rich Jan. 22, 1876, in Williamstown, where he was born April 22, 1849. He was a farmer; and lived in Washington, Vt., having children.

874—V. ALVAN SEABURY[5], born March 27, 1809; died of fever July 15, 1821, aged twelve.

875—VI. LUCRETIA KINGSBURY[5], born Sept. 9, 1813; married Joseph, son of David and Sarah (Douglas) Perkins April 4, 1834, in Brookfield. He was born in Chelsea, Vt., May 17, 1806; was a farmer; and lived at Barre Village, Vt. She died in Barre May 7, 1838, at the age of twenty-four. They had one child: 1. *Joseph L.*[6], born Feb. 9, 1835, in East Brookfield; was a dentist; and lived in St. Johnsbury, Vt. He married Abbie Jane, daughter of Jonathan J. and Maria Jane (Tucker) Peck Nov. 6, 1862, in Barre. She was born in Groton, Vt., Feb. 12, 1838. They had three children.

876—VII. HARRIET ATWOOD[5], born Nov. 29, 1815; married George Dewham, son of Ebenezer and Elizabeth (Austin) Bacon June 27, 1838, in Brookfield. He was born in Washington, Vt., April 4, 1807; was a farmer; and lived in Chelsea, Vt. Their children were born in Chelsea as follows: 1. *Lucina Victoria*[6], born May 10, 1839; died Sept. 12, 1856. 2. *George Hovey*[6], born Sept. 16, 1840; was a farmer; and lived in Chelsea; married Sarah Eudora, daughter of Daniel and Hannah (Hackett) Cram March 22, 1866, in Chelsea, where she was born March 22, 1846. They had several children. 3. *Julia Elizabeth*[6], born March 17, 1842; married John Hibbard, son of John and Ruth Hovey (Hibbard) Sprague March 17, 1860, in Chelsea. He was born in East Brookfield, Vt., Nov. 5, 1838; was a farmer; and lived in Brookfield. They had several children. 4. *Erdix Newton*[6], born

April 20, 1844; was a farmer; and lived in Chelsea; married Mary Mehitable, daughter of David Joseph Farnham and Adaline Electa (Wells) Goodwin June 14, 1870, in Chelsea. where she was born Nov. 3, 1847. They had several children. 5. *Nancy Maria*[8], born June 29, 1853; married Oliver Dutton, son of Jackson Dickerson and Hannah Elizabeth (Dutton) Metcalf April 19, 1874, in Williamstown, Vt. He was born in Chelsea, Vt., Oct. 20, 1848; was a farmer; and lived in Brookfield, Vt. They had no children.

877—VIII.   EMILY ANN[7], born Feb. 12, 1808; married David, son of Jonathan and Nancy (Eaton) Emery Jan. 26, 1842. He was born in Grantham, N. H., Dec. 5, 1817; was a farmer; and lived in East Brookfield and Chelsea, Vt. Their children were born in East Brookfield as follows: 1, *Frederic Wilbur*[8], born Aug. 15, 1843; was a physician; resided in Chelsea; married Sarah Maria, daughter of Dr. George King and Susan Maria (Worthley) Bagley of Ware, Mass., Dec. 31, 1869, in Chelsea, Vt. She was born in Topsham, Vt., Dec. 21, 1851. They had several children. 2. *Walter Hovey*[8], born Oct. 14, 1847. 3. *Rosette Emily*[8], born April 9, 1852. 4. *Albert Bigelow*[8], born May 6, 1859.

435

JOHN FAIRFIELD HOVEY[6], born in Lyme, N. H., April 11, 1785. He was a farmer, and lived in Milton, Vt., and Camden, O. He married Elizabeth, daughter of Benjamin and Elizabeth (Owen) Hill Sept. 16, 1813, in Milton, Vt., where she was born Jan. 25, 1794. She died in Camden, O., April 14, 1864; and he died there Feb. 8, 1870, at the age of eighty-four.

Their children were all born in Milton, except the youngest, as follows:—

878—I.   SAMUEL BENJAMIN[7], born Sept. 27, 1814; died March 20, 1817.
879—II.   ABIGAIL ELIZABETH[7], born July 21, 1816; married Daniel, son of Daniel and Irene (Smedley) Waugh Jan. 1, 1837, in Camden, O. He was born in Camden Aug. 21, 1801; was a farmer; and lived in McPherson, Kansas, where he died Oct. 2, 1878. She survived him. Their children were born as follows: 1. *Albert Freeman*[8], born Oct. 17, 1837; farmer; lived in Jackson, Kansas; married Lena, daughter of John and Elizabeth (Reoser) Beeler June 3, 1868, at Onion River, Sheboygan county, Wis.; she was born in Volksberg, Unter Alsasz, Germany, Feb. 2, 1844. They had several children. 2. *Clarissa Elizabeth*[8], born March 24, 1840; died in Camden, O., Sept. 3, 1842. 3. *Sydney Horace*[8], born Dec. 21, 1841; died at Sheboygan Falls, Wis., Aug. 22, 1860. 4. *Emma Letitia*[8], born Sept. 6, 1843; married Alvin Birney, son of David and Jane (Lay) Bliss Feb. 11, 1864, in Sheboygan Falls, Wis.; he was born in Lorain, N. Y., April 15, 1839; was a farmer; and lived in McPherson, Kansas. They had several children. 5. *Lurena Elizabeth*[8], born June 4, 1847; died in Sheboygan Falls, Wis., Oct. 21, 1861. 6. *Frances Emily*[8], born Sept. 9, 1850; died Oct. 13, 1861, in Sheboygan Falls.
880—III. SAMUEL BENJAMIN[7], born Sept. 21, 1818. *See family numbered "880."*

881—IV.   JOHN KEAN⁷, born March 3, 1821. *See family numbered "881."*
882—V.   ALVAN SEABURY⁷, born March 31, 1823. *See family numbered "882."*

883—VI.   PHILEMON HENRY⁷, born March 17, 1826. *See family numbered "883."*

884—VII. DANIEL HILL⁷, born March 23, 1828. *See family numbered "884."*

885—VIII. CHARLES CARROLL⁷, born July 3, 1831; died April —, 1832.
886—IX.   JAMES MONROE PROUTY⁷, born Oct. 29, 1833. *See family numbered "886."*

887—X.   RUFUS CLEVELAND⁷, born Dec. 15, 1836; died July 1, 1863, at the age of twenty-six.

445

SAMUEL TRACY HOVEY⁶, born in Scotland parish, Windham, Conn., Aug. 6, 1800. He married Rachel E. Comer in Milford Center, Ohio. She was born in Rockingham county, Va., Jan. 24, 1805. He died in Urbana, O., Jan. —, 1886; and she died there Sept. 3, 1890.

Their children were born as follows:—

888—I.   LAURA⁷, born Aug. 1, 1825; died July 1, 1829.
889—II.   ANNA⁷, born Sept. 6, 1827; died June 28, 1829.
890—III. HARDEN⁷, born Jan. 15, 1829, in Woodstock, Champaign county, O. *See family numbered "890."*
891—VI.   VINE⁷, born July 22, 1832; married Elizabeth Goheen.
892—V.   WILLIAM WIRT⁷, born Nov. 8, 1835, in Champaign county, O. *See family numbered "892."*
893—VI.   LEWIS COOK⁷, born Dec. 2, 1837, in Urbana, O. *See family numbered "893."*
894—VII. EDWARD HARMON⁷, born Aug. 9, 1840; died while serving in the Union army, at Murfreesboro, Tenn., March 23, 1863, from the effects of a wound received at the battle of Perryville, Ky., aged twenty-two.
895—VIII. ALBERTINE RACHEL⁷, born Jan. 22, 1845; married William Edward Martin April 5, 1866, in Urbana, O. He was born in Macomb, Ill., Feb. 3, 1842. He was an undertaker. Children: 1. *Harry Hovey*⁸, born April 29, 1867; died Oct. 28, 1868. 2. *Charles Elmer*⁸, born Jan. 27, 1869; married Edith Zimmerman. 3. *Samuel Walter*⁸, born Jan. 23, 1872; married Nancy Aldridge. 4. *William Benjamin*⁸, born Oct. 3, 1877. 5. *Edgar Lewis*⁸, born Sept. 8, 1879.
896—IX.   SAMUEL COMER⁷, born Feb. 26, 1847; married Georgia Taylor.
897—X.   SOLON GILBERT⁷, born Feb. 10, 1851. *See family numbered "897."*

446

BENJAMIN HOVEY⁶, born in Windham, Conn., Dec. 14, 1796. He lived in Scotland Society in Windham; and was a farmer and hatter. In the manufacture of hats, he was engaged with his father. When Scotland Society was set off from Windham and incorporated as a separate town, Mr. Hovey was chosen the first town clerk, treasurer and register, in 1857. He was then sixty years old, but he served nearly twenty years, until declining years compelled him to relinquish the offices. He was a fine penman.

Mr. Hovey married Fanny Baker Feb. 5, 1822, at Scotland
Society. She was born Aug. 31, 1798. He died at Scotland Nov.
29, 1877, at the age of eighty. She survived him, and died at
Norwich, Conn., Jan. 27, 1890, at the age of ninety-one.

Their children were born in Windham, as follows:—

898—I.   CHARLES[7], born Nov. 22, 1822. *See family numbered "898."*
899—II.   GEORGE[7], born July 10, 1824. *See family numbered "899."*
900—III.   JOHN DUDLEY[7], born May 14, 1826; lived in Scotland; married
           Mrs. Marcella Bingham Reynolds; was a private in the
           Civil war, serving in Co. D., Twenty-first regiment Connecti-
           cut volunteers, being seriously wounded; and died in Scot-
           land March 26, 1897, at the age of seventy. They had no
           children.
901—IV.   LEWIS[7], born May 20, 1828. *See family numbered "901."*
902—V.   EDWARD HURLEY[7] (twin), born Oct. 1, 1830; served in the
           Civil war as artificer in the First Connecticut heavy artillery;
           and died, unmarried, July 11, 1867, at the age of thirty-six.
903—VI.   CATHERINE ELIZABETH[7] (twin), born Oct. 1, 1830; married
           William H. Page Nov. 20, 1855; and lives in Norwich, Conn.
           Their children were born as follows: 1. ———[8], born
           Nov. 26, 1856; died Nov. 28, 1856. 2. *William Edward*[8],
           born July 9, 1859. 3. *Lewis Hovey*[8], born July 14, 1861.
           4. *Hattie Luella*[8], born Aug. 27, 1863; died Aug. 31, 1864.
           5. *Inez Louise*[8], born Aug. 5, 1865; died Oct. 11, 1865.
           6. *Frederick Arden*[8], born April 11, 1867. 7. *Charles
           Greenleaf*[8], born Feb. 27, 1871; died Aug. 23, 1871. 8. *Helen
           Inez*[8], born Sept. 4, 1872.
904—VII.   FANNY[7], born March 1, 1833; married Edmund Lee Champlin
           Nov. 21, 1860, in Scotland; and is living at Tacoma, Wash.
           Children: 1. *Fanny Mansfield*[8], born July 18, 1862. 2.
           Edmund Lee[8], born Oct. 24, 1865.
905—VIII. ELIZA[7], born Oct. 28, 1837; married Henry Freeman Oct. 28,
           1857, in Scotland; and lives in New York City. Children:
           1. *Ida Fanny*[8], born Jan. 10, 1859. 2. *Anna Eliza*[8], born
           May 3, 1860.
906—IX.   HENRY[7], born Dec. 18, 1839. *See family numbered "906."*
907—X.   MARY[7], born Oct. 9, 1842; married David P. Walden Dec. 13,
           1877, in Scotland, Conn.; and died in Norwich, Conn., Dec.
           20, 1883. Their children were born as follows: 1. *Benja-
           min Hovey*[8], born June 3, 1879. 2. *Mary Hovey*[8], born Dec.
           20, 1883.

459

THOMAS LEWIS HOVEY[6], born in Ipswich Aug. 29, 1772. He
lived in Hallowell, Me.; and married, first, Mary Perkins Dec.
30, 1794. He married, second, Cynthia Markoe; and died May
—, 1857.

His children were as follows:—

908—I.   ———————[7].
909—II.   ———————[7].
910—III.   ———————[7].
911—IV.   ———————[7].
912—V.   ———————[7].
913—VI.   ———————[7].

914—VII.   ————.'
915—VIII.   ————.'
916—IX.   ————.'
917—X.   ————.'
918—XI.   ————.'
919—XII.   ————.'
920—XIII.   ————.'
921—XIV.   ————.'
922—XV.   ————.'
923—XVI.   ————.'
924—XVII.   ————.'
925—XVIII.   ————.'
926—XIX.   ————.'

464

JOHN HOVEY⁶, born in Ipswich, Mass., Nov. 26, 1783. He was a bricklayer, and lived in his native town, in the house with his father, at the head of Hovey's lane. He married Elizabeth Fuller Oct. 28, 1810; and she was his wife in 1856. He died Oct. 23, 1865, at the age of eighty-one.

Their children were born in Ipswich, as follows :—

927—I.   JOHN⁷, born March 17, 1811. *See family numbered "927."*
928—II.   ELIZABETH⁷, born Dec. 28, 1812; died, unmarried, Nov. 7, 1837,
          aged twenty-four.
929—III. ABIGAIL MANSFIELD⁷, born Jan. 26, 1814; died April 19, 1815.
930—IV.   THOMAS⁷, born May 2, 1816. His whereabouts were unknown
          in 1809.
931—V.   FRANCIS⁷, born July 20, 1818. He was a farmer, and lived on
          East street, in his native town. He married, first, Hannah
          Lewis; second, Elizabeth Lewis; and, third, Harriet Lewis,
          from Boston, before 1877. He died June 3, 1899, at the age
          of eighty. His wife Harriet survived him. Mr. Hovey had
          no children.
932—VI.   ABIGAIL M.⁷, born March 18, 1821; married Charles, son of
          Silas and Sarah Estes of Danvers Nov. 17, 1844. He was
          born in 1814; and was a leather dresser.
933—VII. NATHANIEL FULLER⁷, born Jan. 27, 1824. *See family num-
          bered "933."*
934—VIII. ————⁷ (twin), born Jan. 17, 1826.
935—IX.   ————⁷ (twin), born Jan. 17, 1826.
936—X.   HANNAH LEWIS⁷, born Sept. 20, 1827; she was living in Ips-
          wich, unmarried, in 1899.
937—XI.   GEORGE LEWIS⁷, born Nov. 11, 1830. He was living in Ipswich
          in 1899; and was never married.

466

JOSEPH HOVEY⁶, born in Ipswich, Mass., Sept. 28, 1789. He was a farmer, and lived in his native town. He married Mary Andrews Feb. 26, 1837, in Ipswich. She was born in Parsonsfield, Me., Dec. 6, 1813. He died in Ipswich June 1, 1872, at the age of eighty-one; and she died there, his widow, April 9, 1890, at the age of seventy-six.

Children, born in Ipswich:—

938—I.   MARY ELIZABETH[7], born Feb. 15, 1838; died in Ipswich Nov. 28,
          1840, aged two.
939—II.   RUTH ANN[7], born Aug. 16, 1840; lived in Ipswich, unmarried,
          until after 1880, when she removed to Lake Mohonk, N. Y.,
          where she resides.
940—III. MARY ELIZABETH[7], born Aug. 31, 1843; married, first, George
          W. Otis June 22, 1861, in Ipswich. He died Nov. 19, 1853;
          and she married, second, John Roberts May 13, 1868, in
          Ipswich.

467

LEVI HOVEY[6], born in Ipswich, Mass., April 25, 1792. He
was a laborer, and lived in Ipswich. He married Sarah Chase
Nov. 20, 1817; and was living in Ipswich in 1848. He died Sept.
—, 1854. She died Aug. 2, 1871.

Their children were born as follows:—

941—I.   ELIZA H.[7], married William Kingsford June 7, 1840, in Ipswich;
          and she died, of consumption, in Ipswich April 11, 1845, at
          the age of twenty-four.
942—II.   LYDIA[7], born in 1825; died May 9, 1840, aged fourteen.
943—III. SARAH[7], married ———— Parsons.
944—IV.   JOSEPH[7], born in 1827; died in 1851, aged twenty-four.

470

DAVID HOVEY[6], born in Boxford, Mass., July 30, 1758. He
was a yeoman, and with his brother Richard bought a tract of
land in Peterborough, N. H., in 1782. The land was located in
the northeastern part of the town. They made a division, David
taking the western portion. For sixty pounds, he bought, with
his brother Richard, a tract of one hundred acres, being lot fifteen
in the East range of lots in Peterborough, of John Penhallow,
esq., of Portsmouth, Sept. 15, 1790;[*] and he released his part of
the land to his brother Richard March 11, 1799.[†] He bought of
Robert Rand of Washington, N. H., for one hundred pounds, one
hundred and fifty acres of land in Washington, Oct. 19, 1796.[‡]
He removed to Ackworth in 1800; and was living in Washington,
N. H., in 1802.

Mr. Hovey married, first, Phebe Farnham of Andover,
Mass., March 30, 1784. She was born in Andover. He married,
second, Anna (Durant), widow of James Davidson of Ackworth
Feb. 21, 1802, in Charlestown, N. H. He married, third, Elizabeth Chambers.

Mr. Hovey's children were born as follows:—

945—I.   DAVID[7], born Feb. 28, 1785, in Peterborough. *See family num-
          bered "945."*

          * Hillsborough Registry of Deeds, book 31, page 21.
          † Hillsborough Registry of Deeds, book 51, page 244.
          ‡ Cheshire Registry of Deeds, book 71, leaf 381.

946—II.   PHEBE[7], probably died, unmarried, before 1865.
947—III. SALLY[7], probably died, unmarried, before 1865.
948—IV.   LYDIA[7], lived in Cambridge; and died, unmarried, Dec. 24, 1864.
949—V.   ELIZABETH[7]; married Iddo Church (as his second wife); he
          was born in Gilsum, and married, first, Emeline Kemp.
          Mr. Church died before 1865, when she lived, his widow, in
          Ackworth, N. H. Elizabeth had one child: 1. *Azil*[8]; mar-
          ried Lydia Symington.
950—VI.   STEPHEN[7], probably died before 1865.
951—VII. FARNHAM[7], probably died before 1865.
952—VIII. MARY[7], married Rufus Bruce of Wolcott, Vt., where they lived
          in 1865; and had three children: 1. *Louisa*[8]. 2. *Milton*[8].
          3. *Ryland*[8].

472

RICHARD HOVEY[6], born in Boxford, Mass., Feb. 4, 1762. He
was a yeoman, and lived in Peterborough, N. H. With his
brother David, he released to his brothers John and Stephen his
interest in the homestead of their father in Boxford Oct. 27,
1819. With his brother David, he bought a tract of land in
Peterborough in 1782. The land was located in the northeastern
part of the town; and they made a division of it, Richard taking
the eastern portion. For sixty pounds, he bought, with his
brother David, a tract of one hundred acres, being lot fifteen in
the East range of lots in Peterborough, of John Penhallow, esq.,
of Portsmouth, Sept. 15, 1790;* and he bought out David's interest March 11, 1799.† For sixty pounds, while he was living
in Boxford, he bought of Ephraim Stimson of Frankford, Me.,
yeoman, fifty acres, being lot numbered one hundred and six, in
Peterborough, N. H., April 5, 1784.‡

Mr. Hovey served in the Revolution three months, though
being quite young, and was at West Point at the time Colonel
Arnold attempted to deliver up to the British the American forces
stationed there.

He married, first, Rebecca Roberts Dec. 17, 1789, in Peterborough; and she died May 25, 1807, at the age of thirty-seven.
He married, second, Mrs. Asenath Hall, widow of ———— Hall,
of Francestown, and daughter of Jonathan and Mary (Lovejoy)
Baxter, May 20, 1811. She was born in Methuen, Mass., Nov.
10, 1768. He died May 10, 1842, at the age of eighty. His wife
Asenath survived him, and died, his widow, Nov. 28, 1853, at
the age of eighty-five.

The children of Mr. Hovey were born in Peterborough, as
follows:—

953—I.   SARAH[7], born Dec. 10, 1790; married Thomas Carter in 1810;
         and lived in Windham. They had eight children. She was
         living in 1836.

---

* Hillsborough Registry of Deeds, book 31, page 21.
† Hillsborough Registry of Deeds, book 31, page 244.
‡ Hillsborough Registry of Deeds, book 51, page 237.

954—II.   STEPHEN[7], born June 19, 1794. *See family numbered "954."*
955—III. JOSEPH[7], born Oct. 19, 1800. *See family numbered "955."*
956—IV.   JONATHAN[7], born July 10, 1803; lived in Acworth; married
          Betsey Persons of Acworth in 1828; and died in Lancaster
          June 5, 1851, at the age of forty-seven.
957—V.   ROBERTS[7] (twin), born May 17, 1807. *See family numbered
          "957."*
958—VI.   REBECCA[7] (twin), born May 17, 1807; married Isaac Clarke;
          lived in Barnstead; and died Sept. 17, 1845, at the age of
          thirty-eight. They had three children.
959—VII. TIMOTHY L.[7], born Aug. 9, 1813. *See family numbered "959."*

476

JOHN HOVEY[6], born in Boxford, Mass., Jan. 13, 1770. He
was a yeoman, and lived in Boxford. With his brother Stephen,
he purchased the interest of his brothers David and Richard in
the estate of their father in Boxford Oct. 27, 1819, and lived on
the old homestead. He was a man of great strength and endurance. He married, first, Hannah Weed of Haverhill June 10,
1796; and she died in Boxford July 10, 1805, at the age of thirty-
two. He married, second, Mehitable Hovey (238) April 8, 1807;
and she died in Boxford Nov. 29, 1811, at the age of thirty-two.
Mr. Hovey was living in Boxford in 1822.

Mr. Hovey's children were:—

960—I.   RICHARD[7].
961—II. MOSES[7].

478

STEPHEN HOVEY[6], born in Boxford, Mass., Feb. 3, 1773. He
was a yeoman, cordwainer and laborer; and lived in Bradford
until 1800, and afterward in Haverhill. He married Sarah Kelley
Feb. 11, 1800; and died between 1845 and 1857. She survived
him, and was living in Haverhill, on Washington street, in 1857.
Their children were born in Haverhill, as follows:—

962—I.   WILLIAM[7], born Dec. 13, 1802; died in Haverhill, of typhus fever,
          Oct. 7, 1820.
963—II. ANN[7], born Oct. 22, 1807; living in Haverhill, unmarried, in 1858.

486

JOSEPH HOVEY[6], born in Beverly, Mass., Dec. 10, 1780. He
lived in Beverly, and married Rebecca Homan Dec. 11, 1804.

Children, born in Beverly:—

964—I.   MARY HALE[7], born Sept. 27, 1805.
965—II.   REBECCA[7], died of fits and decline, in Beverly, and was buried
           Dec. 19, 1820, aged fifteen years.
966—III. NANCY HOMAN[7], born Sept. 6, 1808.
967—IV.   WILLIAM[7], born April 14, 1811.

498

LEONARD HOVEY[6], baptized in Boxford, Mass., Feb. 11, 1781.
He was a cordwainer, and lived in Boxford until about 1810,

when he removed to Bradford. He married Sally, daughter of Samuel and Susanna (Morse) Carlton Aug. 28, 1803, in Boxford, where she was born June 24, 1782. He died in Bradford, of fever, April 12, 1836, at the age of fifty-five; and she survived him, dying Jan. 14, 1860.

Their children were born as follows:—

968—I.   BENJAMIN K.[7], born Oct. 27, 1803, in Boxford; shoemaker, and lived in Bradford till 1845; trader, of Haverhill in 1845; trader, of Lawrence in 1849; shoemaker, of Groveland from 1858 to 1878; married Abigail, daughter of Moses and Rebecca (Tenney) Foster June 23, 1839. She was born in Bradford May 14, 1803, and died Sept. 26, 1871. He died April 14, 1878. They had no children.

969—II.   SAMUEL C.[7], born July 16, 1805. *See family numbered "969."*

970—III.   NATHAN[7], born Oct. 30, 1807; died, unmarried, May 25, 1843, at the age of thirty-five.

971—IV.   CHARLES[7], born Nov. 24, 1871. *See family numbered "971."*

972—V.   MARY J.[7], born March 10, 1815; died, unmarried, Jan. 18, 1879, aged sixty-three.

973—VI.   WILLIAM C.[7], born Dec. 19, 1820, in Bradford. *See family numbered "973."*

506

CAPT. MOSES HOVEY[6], born in Boxford, Mass., April 7, 1773. He was a tanner, and lived in East Machias, Me. He married Mary Foster of East Machias, where she lies buried. When in Salem, Mass., he died Sept. 8, 1827, at the age of fifty-four, and his remains were interred at West Boxford.

Their children were born in East Machias, as follows:—

974—I.   MARY[7], born about 1808; married Rev. ———— Ward; and died about 1835. He died about 1860. Their children were as follows: 1. ————[8] (daughter), died before her mother. 2. ————[8] (daughter), died before her mother.

975—II.   HENRY PORTER[7], born Sept. 4, 1810. *See family numbered "975."*

508

AARON HOVEY[6], born in Boxford, Mass., Feb. 3, 1778. He lived in Norwalk, Conn. He married ———— ————, and died in New York May 16, 1818, at the age of forty. His granddaughter, Mrs. Morris M. Norton, has his family bible.

Mr. Hovey's children were as follows:—

976—I.   MARY[7], born Sept. 14, 1805; married David Low; and died Feb. 29, 1864. Their children were as follows: 1. ————[8]. 2. ————[8]. 3. ————[8]. 4. ————[8]. 5. *Margaret*[8]; married Morris M. Norton of Norwalk, who resided at 88 West street, South Norwalk, Conn. He died July 5, 1909.

977—II.   MARGARET MCLAIN[7]; married Amizi Camp of South Norwalk; and died there Dec. 11, 1831. Their children were born as follows: 1. *Ann Eliza*[8], died, unmarried, many years ago. 2. *Mary Frances*[8], born Feb. 28, 1827; married Lawrence P. Mott of New York City; and she died Feb. 6, 1867. They had several children.

978—III.   ABBY[7], died, unmarried, in 1853.
979—IV.   HARRIET[7], died, unmarried.
980—V.   RUFUS[7], died in infancy.
981—VI.   RUFUS PORTER[7]. *See family numbered "981."*
982—VII.   CHARLES[7], married ――――― ――――――, an actress; and lived in
           New York City. He died in Brooklyn, N. Y., in the winter
           of 1856; and his wife died soon after.

513

THOMAS STICKNEY HOVEY[6], born in Boxford, Mass., Sept.
8, 1792. He was a farmer, and lived on the homestead of his
father in West Boxford. He married Sarah Chadwick, daughter
of Jacob and Sarah (Smith) Parker of Boxford Nov. 4, 1822.
She was born in Boxford Jan. 10, 1795. He died in Boxford
Feb. 3, 1869, at the age of seventy-six; and she died there, his
widow, Oct. 6, 1888, at the age of ninety-three.

Their children were born in Boxford, as follows:—

983—I.   ORVILLE LAURISTON[7], born Feb. 28, 1823; wheelwright; lived in
           Boxford; married Larissa Clark, daughter of Phineas Parker
           and Sarah (Day) Tyler. She was born Aug. —, 1829. He
           bought the Foster house in front of the meeting house in
           1857, and lived there. He died July 1, 1872, at the age of
           forty-nine. She survived him. They had no children.
984—II.   LUCY PORTER[7], born Oct. 6, 1826; lived in Haverhill; teacher;
           and died, unmarried, in Boxford, Feb. 13, 1894, at the age
           of sixty-seven.
985—III.   ALBERT PARKER[7], born Nov. 23, 1828; carpenter; lives in West
           Boxford; married Mary Ann Kimball before 1877. He was a
           soldier in the Civil war from July, 1861, to July, 1864, en-
           listing as a private in Company F., Twelfth Massachusetts
           regiment. The first year he was regimental wagon master,
           and the last two years brigade forage master. They had no
           children.
986—IV.   JOSEPH HENRY[7], born April 30, 1830. *See family numbered
           "986."*
987—V.   EDWARD BEECHER[7], born April 3, 1832. *See family numbered
           "987."*

514

ISRAEL HOVEY[6], born in Boxford, Mass., Oct. 9, 1772. When
a young man, he went to East Machias, Me., where he settled,
married and died. The old homestead is now owned by his
grandson, Frederic E. Hovey.

Children:—

988—I.   CHARLES P.[7] *See family numbered "988."*
989—II.   STEPHEN[7]. *See family numbered "989."*
990—III.   WARREN F.[7]. *See family numbered "990."*
991—IV.   ―――――[7].
992—V.   ―――――[7].
993—VI.   ―――――[7].
994—VII.   ―――――[7].
995—VIII. ―――――[7].
996—IX.   ―――――[7].

997—X. ——————'.
998—XI. ——————'.
999—XII. ——————'.
1000—XIII. ——————'.
1001—XIV. ——————'.
1002—XV. ——————'.
1003—XVI. ——————'.

517

WILLIAM HOVEY⁶, born in Boxford, Mass., Jan. 7, 1778. He was a merchant and tanner in Warren, Me., where he lived.

He bought the old homestead in Boxford in 1815, and sold it to Dea. Johua T. Day in 1835.

Mr. Hovey married, first, Angelica G. Head Dec. 3, 1806. He married, second, Hannah Rice of Wiscasset, Me., before 1835, when she was his wife.

Children :—

1004—I. SARAH FRANCES H.⁷, baptized Aug. 14, 1808; married Thomas Hodgman May 19, 1829; he was a merchant, and lived in Warren; he was born about 1798, and died Feb. 7, 1843; she died March 12, 1876. Their children were as follows: 1. *Frances Maria⁸*, born June 28, 1831; married Edwin Smith of Thomaston, Me.; she died March 24, 1899, at the age of sixty-seven; and left no children. 2. *Martha D.⁸*, born Feb. 13, 1836; died Oct. 1, 1844. 3. *William H.⁸*, born in 1840; lives at 53 Wareham street, Medford, Mass.
1005—II. ANGELICA H.⁷, baptized July 24, 1813; married Warren F. Hovey (990) of Machias, Me., May 11, 1835.

520

IVORY HOVEY⁶, born in Boxford, Mass., July 31, 1783. He was a tanner, and lived in Warren, Me.

He married Elizabeth Lermond Nov. 30, 1812; and died before 1845.

Children :—

1006—I. ELIZA D.⁷, born April 30, 1813; married Caleb Noyes Page Jan. 1, 1833; lived in Warren; he was born July 13, 1801; and she died in Warren Sept. 19, 1895, at the age of eighty-two. Their children were born in Warren, as follows: 1. *Elizabeth Jarvis⁸*, born in 183-; died in Warren in 1857, at the age of eighteen. 2. *Emily Eaton⁸*, born May —, 1838; died May 20, 1839. 3. *George Hovey⁸*, born about 1840; lives in Appleton, Me. 4. *Mary Ellen⁸*, born Jan. —, 1844; lives in Warren, unmarried.
1007—II. GEORGE KIMBALL⁷, born Feb. 16, 1815; lived in Warren; married Lucy Cornelia Cobb Oct. 13, 1846; and died in Warren May —, 1883, at the age of sixty-eight. They had an adopted daughter, Lizzie C., born in Camden, Me., July 29, 1854, who married ———— Dows, a druggist, and lives in Lowell, Mass.
1008—III. MARIA⁷, born July 28, 1818; married Elijah W. Hawkes of Windham, Me., Oct. —, 1848; and she died in Lowell, Mass., Feb. 11, 1893, at the age of seventy-four. Their children were born in Windham, as follows: 1. *Edith⁸*, born April

4, 1854; married E. W. Thompson; and lives at The Oaklands, in Lowell. 2. *Lewis W.*[5], born Dec. 19, 1855; lives on Middle street, in Lowell.

1009—IV.   MARTHA[7], born in 1823; died Sept. 17, 1826.

522

ALFRED HOVEY[6], born in Boxford, Mass., Dec. 12, 1788. He was a merchant, and lived in Warren, Alna and Waldoboro, Me., living at the town last named in 1854.

Mr. Hovey married Eliza Sampson.

Children:—

1010—I.   SARAH ELIZABETH[7], married ———— ————; and died in Bangor Dec. 15, 1896. They had one child: 1. *Delia F.*[8], married ———— Chamberlain; and lived at Newton, Mass.
1011—II.   CHARLES[7], merchant; lives in Waldoboro.
1012—III.   CAROLINE[7], married ———— Jarvis; and died in Castine, Me., Jan. —, 1899. She left one son: 1. *William H.*[8]; lives in Brewer, Me.

527

SOLOMON HOVEY[6], born in Lunenburg, Mass., Aug. 14, 1781. He married Sarah Johnson Jan. 5, 1806. She was born Nov. 26, 1784. They lived in Lunenburg until they settled in Charlestown, in the Neck district, on the north side of Main street. He was a tall, dignified and fine-looking man; and died July 21, 1842, at the age of sixty. She died May 18, 1873, aged eighty-eight.

Their children were born in Charlestown, as follows:—

1013—I.   SOLOMON[7], born Nov. 6, 1806. *See family numbered "1013."*
1014—II.   WILLIAM[7] (twin), born July 3, 1808; died July 7, 1808.
1015—III.   JAMES[7] (twin), born July 3, 1808; died July 8, 1808.
1016—IV.   SARAH CAROLINE[7], born June 19, 1809; married, first, Dea. John Doane; and, second, Dea. George Rogers.
1017—V.   MARTHA STORY[7], born Sept. 14, 1811; married Samuel Putnam Skilton of Charlestown; and died March —, 1889.
1018—VI.   JAMES[7], born Aug. 16, 1815; graduated at Amherst college; and was for many years the successful master of the Phillips school in Boston. He married Arria Saville of Chelsea; and died March 16, 1889, at the age of seventy-three.
1019—VII.   HARRIET J.[7], born Aug. 21, 1818; married Richard Saville of Chelsea.
1020—VIII.   JOSEPH FAULKNER[7], born Sept. 18, 1821; was widely known as the president of the insurance agency of Hovey & Fenno, in Boston. He married Elizabeth A. Frothingham in 1847.

528

ABIJAH HOVEY[6], born in Lunenburg, Mass., June 20, 1783. He was a victualer, and lived at Charlestown, in the Neck district, on the south side of Main street, a short distance from Charles street.

Mr. Hovey married Martha Story of Lunenburg June 11, 1809; and died Aug. 29, 1842, at the age of fifty-nine. His estate was appraised at seven thousand dollars. She survived him, and died Aug. 3, 1863.

Their children were as follows:—

1021—I.   MARTHA ANN⁷, unmarried in 1847.
1022—II. ABIJAH⁷, living in 1847.
1023—III. ALBERT⁷, living in 1847.
1024—IV. WILLIAM⁷, living in 1847.

530

WILLIAM HOVEY⁶, born in Lunenburg, Mass., Dec. 27, 1785. He lived in Lunenburg; and married Sally, daughter of Isaac and Hannah (Fay) Howe April 10, 1810. He died in Cambridge Feb. 19, 1852, at the age of sixty-six. She was born in Northboro, Mass., Sept. 24, 1792; and died at Cambridge Dec. 15, 1874, at the age of eighty-two.

Their children were born as follows:—

1025—I.   WILLIAM⁷, born Dec. 3, 1812, in Cambridge. *See family numbered "1025."*
1026—II. SARAH FULLER⁷, born June 9, 1815; married Leonard F. Markham; and died in Cambridge Aug. —, 1863. Children: 1. *Charles Leonard⁸*, lived in Sherburne, Mass.; married, first, Emma Howe; and, second, ——— ———. He died April —, 1903, in Auburndale, Mass.; and his widow lives in Portland, Me. 2. *Sarah⁸*, married William Lamoreaux; lived in Grand Rapids, Mich., where she died.
1027—III. CHARLES⁷, born Nov. 17, 1817, in Acton, Mass. *See family numbered "1027."*
1028—IV. ALBERT HENRY⁷, born Oct. 5, 1820, in Acton. *See family numbered "1028."*

539

AARON HOVEY⁶, born in Rochester, Mass., May 16, 1771. He married Sarah Griffith.

Children:—

1029—I.   JOSEPH⁷.
1030—II. RUTH⁷, married Spooner Cornish in 1817. Children: 1. *Aaron Hovey⁸*, born in 1818. 2. *Ivory Spooner⁸*, born in 1820. 3. *Theodore O.⁸*, married Louisa Bois. 4. *Francis⁸*, born in 1827. 5. *Sarah S.⁸*, born in 1829. 6. *Susan B.⁸*, born in 1834.
1031—III. FRANCIS⁷.
1032—IV. SARAH C.⁷.
1033—V.   ELIZA⁷, married Hosea Bartlett.
1034—VI. AARON⁷.
1035—VII. SAMUEL TEMPLE⁷.

541

DOMINICUS HOVEY⁶, born in Rochester, Mass., March 3, 1775. He married Elizabeth, daughter of Thomas and Elizabeth (Cornish) Clark of Plymouth (published June 6, 1799); and lived in Plymouth. He died at sea, at the West Indies, in 1806. She was born in 1777, and died in 1866.

Their children were born in Plymouth, as follows:—

1036—I.   DOMINICUS[7], born April 28, 1800; drowned at sea.
1037—II. ELIZABETH[7], born March 15, 1802; married James Pickett; and
          lived and died in California. He died in the West Indies.
1038—III. JOSIAH CLARK[7], born June 25, 1806, posthumous. *See family
          numbered "1038."*

556

AARON HOVEY[6], baptized in Topsfield, Mass., March 14,
1762. He lived in Houlton, Me. He married ——————— Kinney.
Child:—

1039—I.   EDMUND[7]. *See family numbered "1039."*

561

GIDEON HOVEY[6], born in Oxford, Mass., Nov. 22, 1762. He
was a soldier of the Revolution, serving thirteen days in the
company of Capt. Ebenezer Humphrey, and regiment of Col.
Jacob Davis, and having marched to Rhode Island on the alarm
of July 30, 1780. He was a yeoman; lived in Oxford on the old
homestead, which he owned, having bought one-half of it of his
sister Sarah Feb. 21, 1784;* and was a constable of the town in
1791.

Mr. Hovey married, first, Hannah, daughter of Lemuel and
Bathsheba (Gilbert) Crane May 1, 1784. She was born Sept. 26,
1765; and died April 5, 1785, at the age of nineteen. He married, second, Mary Crane, his first wife's sister, March 17, 1789.
She was born Jan. 10, 1772.

Mr. Hovey died Aug. 11, 1801, at the age of thirty-eight.
His wife Mary survived him, and married, secondly, Jeremiah
Dana of Oxford Nov. 27, 1804. She died Feb. 26, 1842, at the
age of seventy.

The children of Mr. Hovey and his wife Mary were born as
follows:—

1040—I.   HANNAH[7], born Nov. 15, 1789; died at Bristol, Ill., unmarried,
          after 1809.
1041—II. DANIEL[7], born May 26, 1793. *See family numbered "1041."*
1042—III. PEREZ G.[7], born Sept. 25, 1795. *See family numbered "1042."*

573

ROGER HOVEY[6], born Feb. 20, 1759, in Mansfield, Conn.
He twice enlisted as a soldier of the Revolution. The first enlistment was in February, 1776, at the age of seventeen years,
when he marched on foot to join the army encompassing Boston.
As he used to tell his children: "It was a downfall to be told to
cut beanpoles. I could have done that at home. But a soldier
must obey orders. Thousands of beanpoles were stacked near

* Worcester Registry of Deeds, book 91, page 524.

the old church in Roxbury ready for use." Then came that eventful night of March 4th, when three hundred wagons, loaded with those beanpoles, were hauled up Dorchester Heights, amid dead silence, except as broken by the crunching of the wheels over the frozen ground, and the brisk cannonading from another quarter to divert the enemy's attention. The poles were bound into fascines and with other materials were made into impregnable redoubts held by two thousand men. The "evacuation of Boston" followed on March 17th, and when Roger Hovey saw the British transports, crowded with eleven thousand red coats, sail away for Halifax, he said to his comrades, "Those 'beanpoles' drove them out." Mr. Hovey's second enlistment was for one year, during which he fought at the Battle of White Plains and elsewhere. He was granted a pension in his declining years.[*]

Mr. Hovey married Martha, daughter of Edmund and Martha (Otis) Freeman, Feb. 6, 1783, in Hanover, N. H.; of which town her brother, Col. Edmund Freeman, was the first settler. Mr. Hovey was the only blacksmith in the colony, and the legend is that he bought his first stock of iron with the continental money paid as his wages in the army. He not only shod horses and oxen, but did more ornate iron-work, and made all the hinges, latches, bolts and bars of old Dartmouth Hall, relics of which are treasured by his descendants. The fac-simile of his signature is taken from an indenture dated June 18th, 1801, binding Chester Bixby to him as an apprentice during minority. It is a formidable document, and well preserved.

Roger Hovey

In 1813, Mr. Hovey removed with his family to Thetford, Vt., where he built a house and shop and bought a farm of 160 acres. He spent his old age with his eldest son, Frederick, at Berlin, Vt., where he died, May 19, 1839, at the age of eighty years. His wife survived him and died at Berlin, April 6, 1841, aged eighty-two years. While at Hanover, N. H., they were members of the Presbyterian church, of which Dr. Eden Burroughs was pastor, by whom all their children were baptized.

Mrs. Hovey was the youngest daughter of Edmund Freeman of Mansfield, Conn., to whom, as a reward for services, the Hanover charter was granted, July 4th, 1761, conveying to him and ten others by the name of Freeman and others a tract of land including twenty-two thousand and four hundred acres, for which,

---

[*] See Vermont Pension Roll, page 113. See also U. S. Senate Papers, 8th part, Report of Secretary of War, 1835. "Roger Hovey. Rank, private. Annual allowance $33.37. Service in Conn. Militia. Placed on Pension Roll, Oct. 3, 1833."

December 25th of each year, each settler was to pay to the Crown, if demanded, one ear of Indian corn.* Edmund Freeman was the fifth in succession to bear that name, each being a deacon in his church.† Mrs. Hovey's mother, Martha Otis, was a daughter of Nathaniel Otis, son of Hon. John Otis, for twenty-one years member of His Majesty's Council at Plymouth; and her uncle, Col. James Otis, divided with Patrick Henry the distinction of setting in motion the American Revolution. Her maternal grandmother, Abigail (Russell) Otis, was the daughter of Rev. Jonathan Russell of Barnstable, son of Rev. John Russell of Hadley (who shielded the Regicides for ten years), and his wife, Martha (Moody) Russell, was the daughter of Rev. Joshua Moody, son of William Moody, who came to Ipswich in 1634-5, and was one of the first settlers of Newbury.‡

The children of Roger and Martha Hovey were born in Hanover, N. H., as follows:—

1043—I.   ————ⁱ (son), born Dec. 25, 1783; died Dec. 26, 1783.
1044—II.   NANCY¹, born Feb. 17, 1785; died of an epidemic Oct. 9, 1786, in Hanover.
1045—III. NANCY¹, born Dec. 24, 1786; married Israel Dewey March 1, 1809. He was born in Hanover Jan. 26, 1777; and married, first, Betsey Baldwin of Norwich, Vt., March 1, 1801. They had four children; and she died Oct. 27, 1807, at the age of thirty. After his marriage to Nancy Hovey he lived in Lunenburg, Vt., where she died Aug. 7, 1859. The children of Israel and Nancy (Hovey) Dewey were born as follows: 1. *Harry Hovey*⁶, born Dec. 30, 1809. 2. *Betsey Baldwin*⁶, born Sept. 4, 1811. 3. *Anna Maria*⁶, born Feb. 3, 1813; died June 30, 1824. 4. *Martha Louisa*⁶, born Aug. 10, 1816, in Berlin, Vt.; married Horace Pineo Coleman Jan. 25, 1843; she died at Norwich, Vt., April 26, 1886, at the age of seventy. They had six children, all born in Lunenburg, Vt.: Abbie Maria⁶, born March 16, 1844, married Charles D. Hazen; William Otis⁶, born March 13, 1846, died Feb. 2, 1884; Martha Louise, born Oct. 16, 1848, died Aug. 25, 1892; Charles Frederick⁶, born May 28, 1852, died Feb. 15, 1863; Zenas Milton, born Dec. 26, 1855, married Celia Estell Hurlbutt, Nov. 9, 1893; Lucia Annette⁶, born Feb. 4, 1859; and the children of Charles D. Hazen and Abbie Coleman Hazen are: Allen¹⁰, born Aug. 28, 1869; Annah Putnam¹⁰, born Sept. 22, 1872; Louise Coleman¹⁰, born Jan. 21, 1877; Charles Dana, Jr.¹⁰, born Feb. 3, 1881; Richard¹⁰, born July 14, 1887, died Aug. 13, 1911. 5. *Eunice*⁶, born Aug. 24, 1817. 6. *Frederick Freeman*⁶, born March 26, 1886. 7. *Mary Eliza*⁶, born May 31, 1822. 8. *Israel Otis*⁶, born March 9, 1824; was member of the New Hampshire legislature, aid to Gov. William Haile, with rank of colonel, and paymaster in the U. S. army, with rank of major, from 1864 till his death, May 12, 1888. He married Susan Augusta, daughter of Gen.

---

* See N. H. State Papers, XXV, pages 79-81, for charter in full.
† See Freeman Genealogy, by Rev. Frederick Freeman, Boston, 1875.
‡ Rev. Horace Carter Hovey, D. D.

Henry Sweetser July 29, 1851. Their children were as follows: Henry[9], judge of municipal court, Boston, and judge-advocate under Governors Crane and Bates, with rank of brigadier-general; Frank Otis[9]; and Annie Hovey[9]. 9. *John Calvin[8]*, born May 23, 1826. 10. *Nancy Maria[8]*, born March 12, 1828; married Cornelius Field; and had six children: Harriet[9], married Prof. Charles W. Scott; Edwin Dewey[9]; Cornelia[9]; Elizabeth[9]; Helen Emerson[9]; Alice Hovey[9]. The children of Charles W. Scott and Harriet (Field) Scott are: Charles Field[10]; Susan Helen[10]; and Alice Hovey[10].

1046—IV.   MARTHA[3], born Feb. 7, 1789; married Noah Coleman June 24, 1840; he died May 6, 1867, at the age of seventy; and she died in Norwich, Vt., July 6, 1873, aged eighty-four. Her remains were buried at Lunenburg, Vt. They had no children.

1047—V.   ABIGAIL[3], born May 6, 1791; died of an epidemic July 29, 1800. The following is a copy of the inscription on the stone at the head of Nabby's grave in Hanover:—

In memory of
Nabby, daughter of
Mr. Roger Hovey and
Mrs. Martha, his wife,
who died July 29th
1800, in the tenth year
of her age.

Adiew thou dear departed soul, adieu,
Yet short the term, for soon we follow too.

1048—VI.   EDMUND[3], born Jan. 14, 1794; died of an epidemic July 18, 1800, in Hanover, aged six.

1049—VII.   FREDERICK[3], born Aug. 2, 1796. *See family numbered "1049."*

1050—VIII.   OTIS[3], born June 26, 1799; died July 21, 1800, of the epidemic.

1051—IX.   EDMUND OTIS[3], born July 15, 1801. *See family numbered "1051."*

1052—X.   HORACE[3], born Aug. 1, 1805. *See family numbered "1052."*

574

NATHANIEL HOVEY[4], born in Manchester, Mass., Jan. 25, 1761. He was a blacksmith, and in 1785 the town of Manchester granted to him liberty to set a blacksmith's shop on the town's land near the mill bridge for ten years.

He removed to Norwich, Vt., before March 21, 1789, when he bought, for ten pounds, part of the eleventh lot on the west side of the highway, being one acre.* With his brother Isaac Hovey, for thirty pounds, he bought about forty acres of land in Norwich, part of lot twelve, on the south side of the school lot or highway, opposite said Nathaniel's house, where he then lived.† He leased for nine hundred and ninety-nine years, from James Johnson, part of the eleventh lot in the second range, on

* Norwich Registry of Deeds, book 1, page 354.
† Norwich Registry of Deeds, book 1, page 361.

the west side of the highway, April 22, 1790.* He pursued his trade of a blacksmith in Norwich.

Mr. Hovey married Elizabeth Seaver; and was living in Norwich in 1810.

Their children were born in Norwich, as follows:—

1053—I.   NATHANIEL⁷, born June 16, 1794; died young.
1054—II. ISAAC⁷ (twin), born Feb. 20, 1797.
1055—III. SUSAN⁷ (twin), born Feb. 20, 1797.
1056—IV. NANCY⁷, born Aug. 2, 1805.

575

ISAAC HOVEY⁶, born in Manchester, Mass., Oct. 24, 1763. He was a tailor, and lived in Norwich, Vt., as early as 1789, and until after 1810, removing to Craftsbury.

With his brother Nathaniel Hovey he bought forty acres of land in Norwich, opposite Nathaniel's house, Oct. 27, 1789.†

Mr. Hovey married Elizabeth Clark Oct. 23, 1790, in Norwich.

Their children were born in Norwich, as follows:—

1057—I.   EDMUND CLARK⁷, born Oct. 16, 1791. *See family numbered "1057."*
1058—II. FANNY⁷, born Oct. 28, 1793; married Simeon Culver of Norwich Nov. 21, 1811.
1059—III. ISAAC⁷ (twin), born Feb. 20, 1797.
1060—IV. SUSANNA⁷ (twin), born Feb. 20, 1797; died, unmarried, in Norwich Sept. 21, 1861, at the age of sixty-four.
1061—V.   OLIVER KNOWLTON⁷, born Aug. 25, 1799. *See family numbered "1061."*
1062—VI. BETSEY⁷, born Feb. 17, 1802; died, unmarried. Her journal was published in 1826.
1063—VII. ANDREW L.⁷, born July 11, 1805. *See family numbered "1063."*
1064—VIII. LEANTHA⁷, born March 20, 1808; married Samuel Blood.

582

REV. AARON HOVEY⁶, born in Mansfield, Conn., June 22, 1774. His boyhood days were passed upon the farm; and he was educated at Dartmouth college, from which he graduated in 1798. In his early days his conduct was unusually regular, and in college he was orderly, obedient to authority and diligent in his studies. He was early interested in religious matters, but did not unite with the church of his boyhood until the summer after he graduated from college. He taught school a year at Northampton, Mass., and entered the law office of Hon. Thomas R. Gold at Whitesborough, N. Y., as a student. He was soon convinced that the legal profession was not what he would care to adopt. His talents, tastes and feelings were more adapted to the

---

* Norwich Registry of Deeds, book 1, page 383.
† Norwich Registry of Deeds, book 1, page 361.

ministry; and, in 1801, he began the study of theology with Rev.
Charles Backus, D. D., of Somers, an eminent theologian, who
had directed the studies of many candidates for the ministry.
There were, at that time, no theological seminaries in the country. In 1802, he was licensed to preach by the association of
Windham county, and supplied vacant pulpits, but declined several invitations to settle. In the autumn of 1803, he was engaged
in the Second society of Saybrook (now Centerbrook), Conn.,
where "by reason of the advanced age of the pastor," Rev. Richard Ely, the people were disposed to employ a candidate to assist
him and "should his services be acceptable to settle him as colleague pastor." According to the custom of those prudent times
he preached several months, finally receiving a call. He was ordained as colleague with Mr. Ely Sept. 5, 1804. Mr. Ely immediately removed, and the full duties of pastor and preacher
devolved upon Mr. Hovey, who loved his work and devoted his
life to the service of the people. His sermons were sound in
doctrine and correct in argument and style, though he attempted
no display. In the early years of his ministry he instructed a
large number of young people in literature, science and navigation, and fitted several of them for college. The prominent at-
tribute of his mind is said to have been good sense, which enabled him not only to discern what was right but what was ex-
pedient. Discretion marked his domestic arrangements, his pastoral visits and his actions on all occasions. Few were as cautious
in avoiding everything in conversation, writing and conduct by
which the ministry might be blamed, and few were as studious
of peace and order. As a counselor he excelled. For thirty-four
years he was registrar of the Middletown (Conn.) Association.
He was interested in general affairs, and was chaplain of the
Seventh regiment of militia in Connecticut, having been appointed
by Col. Joseph Hill Aug. 22, 1809.

Mr. Hovey married Mrs. Huldah (Ely) Hayden, daughter
of Rev. Richard Ely and widow of Uriah Hayden, of Essex,
Conn., Sept. 9, 1804. She was born in Lyme, Conn., July 21,
1772; and was a woman of character, eminently domestic and
devoted to her family. She was generous to the poor, conscientious in all her life, noble, faithful and affectionate.

He died Sept. 9, 1843, on the anniversary of his wedding
day. His funeral was held on Sunday, when the churches of the
Episcopal, Baptist, Methodist within the limits of the Second society of Saybrook, and the Congregational church at Deep River
were closed that the people might attend the funeral services.
His remains were buried in the family lot in the Centerbrook
cemetery. His tombstone represents a full-sized pulpit, in marble,
with an open bible upon it, on the face of which is carved the

text of the last sermon he preached to his congregation: "Peace I leave with you, my peace I give unto you; not as the world giveth give I unto you. Let not your heart be troubled, neither let it be afraid."[*]

Mr. Hovey's wife survived him and died Jan. 22, 1844, at the age of seventy-one. She lies buried at his side.

Their children were born in Saybrook, as follows:—

1065—I.   AARON ELY[1], born June 20, 1805; married, first, Martha Ann Vincent of Washington, D. C., in 1832; she was born in 1810, and died in New York in 1847; he married, second, Mary Elizabeth Gilman of Gilmanton, N. H.; she was born in Gilmanton in 1826, and died there May 19, 1879. Mr. Hovey died in Hartford, Conn., Aug. 12, 1888, at the age of eighty-three, leaving no children.

1066—II.   GEORGE FREEMAN[1], born in 1807. He was playing marbles with some boys in his father's barn when he was accidentally jumped on by another boy, and injured so badly that he died the next day, Oct. 7, 1817, at the age of ten.

1067—III. RICHARD ELY[1], born in 1813; died Sept. —, 1832.

1068—IV.   HENRY RUSSELL[1], born Jan. 27, 1816. *See family numbered "1068."*

584

EDMUND HOVEY[6], born in Mansfield, Conn., Nov. 23, 1782. He was a farmer, and lived in his native town until about 1816, when he removed to Berlin, Conn., where he lived during the remainder of his life.

Mr. Hovey married Sophia, daughter of Justus and Mabel (Boardman) Bulkley of Rocky Hill, Wethersfield, Conn., April 13, 1806. She was born at Rocky Hill May 19, 1782; and died at Berlin Dec. 9, 1863, at the age of eighty-one. He died at Berlin Oct. 13, 1870, aged eighty-seven.

Their children were born in Mansfield, as follows:—

1069—I.   SOPHIA[1], born July 9, 1807; married Benjamin G., son of Selah and Roxa (Galpin) Savage of Berlin Dec. 1, 1834. He was born in Berlin May 25, 1809. They lived in Berlin, where he died Oct. 31, 1869. She survived him, and died in Berlin, his widow, July 31, 1899, at the age of ninety-two. Their children were born in Berlin, as follows: 1. *Frederic Benjamin[8]*, born Oct. 18, 1840; lived in Ivoryton, Conn.; married Jerusha Schofield May 14, 1865; had two children; and died at Ivoryton Feb. 16, 1910. 2. *Philip Melancthon[8]*, born Jan. 23, 1843; lives in Berlin. 3. *Julia Sophia[8]*, born April 23, 1847; died Dec. 18, 1853, in Berlin, at the age of six.

1070—II.   OLIVE[1], born Jan. 24, 1810; died at Berlin, where she lived. Oct. 23, 1886, at the age of seventy-six. She was never married.

1071—III. AARON[1], born March 31, 1812. *See family numbered "1071."*

1072—IV.   EDMUND BULKLEY[1], born Aug. 3, 1814. *See family numbered "1072."*

* John XIV: 27.

1073—v. HARRIET[7], born Nov. 8, 1817; married Samuel Merritt, son of
Samuel and Rebecca (Carter) Comstock of Saybrook,
Conn., Nov. 29, 1838. He was born in Saybrook Aug. 14,
1809; and lived in that part of Saybrook which was subsequently incorporated as Essex, the homestead being near
the Ivoryton post office. He was an ivory worker, and
built up the ivory manufacturing concern of Comstock,
Cheney & Co. She died at Ivoryton Oct. 10, 1877; and he
died at Wilmington, N. C., Jan. 18, 1878. Their children
were born at Ivoryton, as follows: 1. *George Hovey[9]*, born
Oct. 24, 1839. He is connected with the Comstock, Cheney
& Co. business; and lives near the Ivoryton post office in
Essex. He married Caroline M., daughter of Charles S.
and Sarah A. (Wilcox) Spencer Nov. 16, 1869, at Westbrook, Conn. She was born at Westbrook Aug. 17, 1843.
They had two children. 2. *Elizabeth Almira[9]*, born Dec. 3,
1840; married John Edward, son of John Odel and Char-
lotte (Giddings) Northrop Jan. 24, 1872. He was born in
Sherman, Conn., Feb. 1, 1837; and died at Ivoryton Feb. 9,
1897. They lived at Ivoryton, and he was treasurer of
Comstock, Cheney & Co. She still lives at Ivoryton, his
widow. They had no children. 3. *Samuel Carter[9]*, born
Feb. 26, 1843; died July 5, 1851. 4. *Edmund Hovey[9]*, born
June 14, 1845; died May 6, 1848. 5. *Harriet Sophia[9]*, born
Feb. 16, 1848; died April 12, 1891. 6. *Walter Merrit[9]*, born
Nov. 10, 1849; died Sept. 14, 1868. 7. *Frederic[9]*, born Nov.
25, 1851; died May 26, 1852. 8. *Robert Henry[9]*, born June
27, 1853, in Centrebrook. He is president of Comstock,
Cheney & Co., and lives at Ivoryton. He married Rachel
Cleveland, daughter of Charles and Belinda (Cleveland)
Kelsey June 2, 1880. She was born at Deep River, Conn.,
March 1, 1858. They live in Ivoryton, and have two children. 9. *Willis[9]*, born Sept. 7, 1855; died June 24, 1857.
10. *Elliott Bulkley[9]*, born Aug. 24, 1857; died May 2, 1890,
at the age of thirty-two. 11. *Archibald Welch[9]*, born May
25, 1860. He is treasurer of Comstock, Cheney & Co., and
lives at Ivoryton. He married Harriet Willard, daughter
of George and Sarah A. (Comstock) Mooar April 22, 1889,
at Oakland, Cal. She was born in Oakland Nov. 9, 1866.
Their only child, Elliott, was born at Ivoryton, Oct. 20, 1891.

1074—VI. ABIGAIL[7], born June 21, 1820; married Rev. Aaron, son of
Freeman Gross and Jane (Read) Snow Nov. —, 1846, at
Westford, Conn. He was born at Centerbrook, Conn.,
June 26, 1804; and died at Ivoryton, March 1, 1880, at the
age of seventy-five. They lived at Ivoryton, where she died
Aug. 19, 1906, at the age of eighty-six. Their only child
was born at Glastenbury, Conn., as follows: 1. *Jane
Sophia[9]*, born Feb. 20, 1848; married Nathaniel Miller Dec.
29, 1869; live at Ivoryton; and have two children.

1075—VII. CLARISSA[7], born Oct. 31, 1822; married Jedidiah, son of Elisha
and Hephzibah (Cornwall) Wilcox Sept. 6, 1848, in Berlin.
He was born in Westfield, Conn. They lived in Meriden,
Conn., and she died at Berlin Feb. 20, 1892. Their only
child was born at Meriden, as follows: 1. *Erving Cleveland[9]*, born Dec. 11, 1858; died at Meriden March 15, 1863.

1076—VIII. JULIA[7], born June 2, 1826; taught for eighteen years in the
Eaton school, at New Haven, Conn.; and lives in Berlin,
Conn., unmarried.

596

ALFRED HOVEY[6], born in Thetford, Vt., April 20, 1791. He was reared on a farm in his native town, and lived there until he became of age. He married, first, Abigail, daughter of Abijah and Priscilla (Cushman) Howard of Thetford Nov. 26, 1812. She was born in that town May 18, 1792. She had a good common school education, and excelled in vocal music. Her voice had compass, purity and sweetness. She was a social favorite, especially among the Baptists.

After his marriage, Mr. Hovey lived in Thetford for about six years, and then removed to Greene, N. Y. He remained in Greene about three years, and then returned to Thetford.

We was a sparely built man, about five feet and ten or eleven inches in height, with black hair and eyes, of nervous temperament, and decided will power. None would think of questioning his Puritan origin or convictions. He was of an inconstant disposition, desiring to move about and changing his business, but, through the influence of his wife, finally settled down to farming. He went in debt for his farm, worked hard, ran a large dairy, raised cattle and sheep, and paid for it.

Mrs. Hovey died in Thetford July 5, 1837, at the age of forty-five. After her death, Mr. Hovey sold the farm, and engaged in other pursuits.

He married, secondly, Sarah Hendricks of Hartland, Vt., Nov. 12, 1839. She was born there April 4, 1807. He was engaged in the lumber business at Dorchester, N. H., and finally removed to Darlington, Wis., where he died April 5, 1872, at the age of eighty. His wife Sarah survived him, and died at Centralia, Ill., April 14, 1882, at the age of seventy-five. She had no children.

The children of Alfred and Abigail (Howard) Hovey were as follows:—

1077—I. CLARA MILLY[7], born Aug. 13, 1813, in Thetford; married Solomon Chaffee Oct. 25, 1849; and died Sept. 22, 1851, at Richland City, Wis. He was born in Connecticut May 4, 1799; and died at Richland City March 25, 1857, at the age of fifty-seven. Child: 1. *Clara Pamelia*[8], born Sept. 1, 1850, in Richland City; and lived in Bristol Springs, N. Y., in 1893.

1078—II. MARY ANN[7], born Nov. 4, 1814, in Thetford; and died there Oct. 11, 1828, aged thirteen.

1079—III. LEANTHA[7], born March 10, 1816, in Thetford; she was a woman of sympathy and judgment; married Z. Ormond Paddock July 27, 1849. He was born in Woodstock, Vt., March 5, 1804; and died in Darlington, Wis., March 5, 1884, just eighty years of age. Mrs. Paddock lived at Darlington in 1893. Their children were born in Linden, Wis., as follows: 1. *Frances Harriet*[8], born April 7, 1855; married Sephus Smith Driver Dec. 27, 1873; lived in Darlington, where he was born Aug. 29, 1853. 2. *William Or-*

mond[6], born Feb. 25, 1857; married Martha Alice Houck April 5, 1883, in Darlington; he was born in Linden, Wis., Feb. 25, 1857. They reside at Holbrook, Arizona.

1080—IV.   AMOS WHITE[7], born July 5, 1818, in Greene, N. Y. *See family numbered "1080.*

1081—V.   ALVAH[7], born March 5, 1820, in Greene. *See family numbered "1081."*

1082—VI.   WILLIAM ASHLEY[7], born Sept. 30, 1821, in Thetford, Vt. *See family numbered "1082."*

1083—VII.   LELAND AARON[7], born Sept. 21, 1823, in Thetford. *See family numbered "1083."*

1084—VIII. ORAMAL FLETCHER[7], born July 11, 1825, in Thetford. *See family numbered "1084."*

1085—IX.   CHARLES EDWARD[7], born April 26, 1827, in Thetford. *See family numbered "1085."*

1086—X.   ELEAZER[7], born June 8, 1829, in Thetford. *See family numbered "1086."*

1087—XI.   FRANCES MARY ANN[7], born Aug. 18, 1834, in Thetford; married David Woodard Chapman Sept. 20, 1855, in Shullsburgh, Wis. He was born in Lyme, N. H., May 20, 1832. They lived in Centralia, Ill., in 1893. Child, born in Darlington. Wis.: 1. *Leantha Frances*[8], born Jan. 31, 1857; married John Henry Harsha Dec. 13, 1875, in Centralia, Ill., where they reside. He was born in Washington, Pa., Sept. 7, 1852. They have three children.

611

JOSEPH HOVEY[6], born in Mansfield, Conn., March 24, 1768. He lived in his native town; and married Mary, daughter of Rev. John Storrs of Mansfield Dec. 24, 1795. He died in Woodstock, Vt., Aug. 11, 1800, at the age of thirty-two. His estate was valued at $7,132.96.

Their child was born in Mansfield, as follows:—

1088—V.   SYLVESTER[7], born June 17, 1797. *See family numbered "1088."*

614

ELISHA HOVEY[6], born in Mansfield, Conn., Aug. 3, 1775. He lived in his native town; and married Martha Shepard of Plainfield Feb. 11, 1798. He died in Mansfield March 31, 1800, at the age of twenty-four. The following is a copy of the inscription upon his gravestone, in the Gurley burial-place in his native town:—

In Memory of Mr. Elisha Hovey who died March 31st 1800, In ye 25th year of his age.

> This dark abode proclaims the truth,
> To bending age & blooming youth;
> You must your active powers resign,
> And be a mouldering corpse like mine.

His will, dated March 5, 1800, was proved April 30, 1800. In it he gave one-half of his estate to his wife and the other half to his daughter. The estate was valued at $2,730.03. His wife survived him, and was his widow in 1801.

Their only child was born in Mansfield, as follows:—

1089—I. MARIA SALLY[7], born Feb. 17, 1799; was living in 1800.

617

DR. ISAAC HOVEY[6], born in Mansfield, Conn., Oct. 4, 1782. He was a physician; and died Oct. 24, 1865, at the age of eighty-three.

Child:—

1090—I. ————[7]. *See family numbered "1090."*

624

BELA HOVEY[6], born in Mansfield, Conn., Sept. 23, 1786. He lived in his native town; and married Deborah Tillinghast Nov. 27, 1808.

Mr. Hovey died in Mansfield in 1841, at the age of fifty-five. Their children were as follows:—

1091—I.   WILLIAM HENRY[7], born Oct. 17, 1809, in Mansfield.
1092—II.   MARY ANN[7], born July 11, 1812, in Mansfield.
1093—III. DANIEL T.[7], born Sept. 8, 1814.
1094—IV.   ELVIRA[7], born July 6, 1817.
1095—V.   CAROLINE[7], born Nov. 29, 1820.
1096—VI.   EUNICE[7], born March 1, 1823.
1097—VII. LUCIEN[7], born Feb. 6, 1825; married Lydia, daughter of James and Annah (Gray) Hempstead in 1851. She was born in Mansfield Nov. 10, 1825; and he died in 1895, at the age of seventy. She survived him. They had no children.
1098—VIII. PHILURA[7], born April 30, 1827.
1099—IX.   PHILO[7], born Feb. 23, 1830.
1100—X.   JOHN[7], born April 19, 1833.

625

ENOCH HOVEY[6], born in Mansfield, Conn., March 7, 1789. He married Martha Fay in Connecticut; and lived and died in New York state.

Children, born in New York state:—

1101—I.   EMELINE[7], died at the age of seventy-two.
1102—II.   EDWARD M.[7], died at the age of eighty-one.
1103—III. SOPHIA[7], died at the age of twenty-four.
1104—IV.   MARIA[7], died at the age of seventeen.
1105—V.   LOUISA[7], died at the age of forty-eight.
1106—VI.   NORMAN[7], died at the age of twenty-two.
1107—VII. GEORGE R.[7], born about 1830; living.

634

CORDIAL STORRS HOVEY[6], born in Mansfield, Conn., Jan. 31, 1772. He was a farmer; and lived in his native town. He married Olive, daughter of Capt. James and Abigail (Grow) Royce Dec. 22, 1796. She was born in Mansfield Dec. 6, 1773.

Their children were born in Mansfield, as follows:—

1108—I.   CORDIAL STORRS[7], born March 16, 1798; married Esther Coggs-
            hall; was a farmer; and lived in Mansfield, where he died.
1109—II.   ENOCH[7], born Jan. 18, 1800. *See family numbered "1109."*
1110—III.   JULIUS[7], born May 29, 1805. *See family numbered "1110."*
1111—IV.   OLIVE[7], married Hiram Newell; and lived and died in Rock-
            ville, Conn.

636

SIMEON HOVEY[6], born in Lebanon, N. H., July 6, 1776. He
married Jerusha Lamb Aug. 31, 1800; and with his brothers,
Gurdon and Josiah, bought lot 24 in the town of Warsaw, N. Y.,
in the autumn of 1803. He built a house upon this lot, and removed thither the next March. All three families occupied the
house until they had time to build houses for Gurdon and Josiah.
Mr. Hovey built, in 1805, for Judge Webster, the first saw mill in
the town.

With his wife, he was among the founders of the Methodist
Episcopal church there. A few years before his death, he removed to Monroe county, where he died April 25, 1862, at the
age of eighty-five. His wife survived him, and was living with
one of her sons, at the age of eighty-four.

Their children were born in Warsaw, as follows:—

1112—I.   HENRY[7], born Sept. 1, 1804, being the first white male child
            born in Warsaw. *See family numbered "1112."*
1113—II.   MARTHA E.[7], married Rev. Carlos Gould of Parma, N. Y.
            Children: 1.   *LeRoy H.[8]*, married Amelia Standish; and
            lives in Michigan. 2. *Mary[8]*. 3. *Francis[8]*, married —— ——.
1114—III.   DELOS[7], was a physician; and lived in Ohio.
1115—IV.   LEROY[7], married Deborah Smith; and died two monthslater.
1116—V.   SIMEON[7], born Feb. 7, 1813; never married; lived in Warsaw.
1117—VI.   EUNICE[7], married Daniel P. Sewell of Middlebury; and lived
            in Parma. Children: 1. *Charles[8]*. 2. *Mary[8]*.
1118—VII.   MARY A.[7], married Gideon H. Jenkins; and had two children.
1119—VIII. LAURA J.[7], died, unmarried, in 18—, about twenty-two years
            old.
1120—IX.   ENOCH WHITE[7], born in 1819. *See family numbered "1120."*

637

GURDON HOVEY[6], born in Lebanon, N. H., June 6, 1778. He
married Anna Starkweather; resided for many years at Warsaw,
N. Y., and finally removed to Michigan.

Children, born in Warsaw:—

1121—I.   ————[7].
1122—II.   ————[7].
1123—III.   ————[7].
1124—IV.   ————[7].
1125—V.   ————[7].
1126—VI.   ————[7].
1127—VII.   ————[7].
1128—VIII. ————[7].

638

JOSIAH HOVEY[6], born in Lebanon, N. H., Jan. —, 1780. He married Sally Lamb; and removed to Warsaw, N. Y., in 1804, living at first on a farm, and later in the village. He and his wife were among the founders of the Methodist church there, and in 1869, she was the only survivor.

The contract for the erection of the court house at Warsaw was let to Mr. Hovey, and built under the superintendence of his son-in-law Philander Pixley.

Mr. Hovey, after some years, removed to Buffalo, where they both died.

Children:—

1129—I.	ALFRED[7].	*See family numbered "1129."*
1130—II.	HORACE[7],	died in Warsaw at the age of nineteen.
1131—III.	JULIA ANN[7],	married Linus Crittenden.
1132—IV.	AMANDA[7],	lives in Buffalo, unmarried.
1133—V.	LOIS[7],	lives in Buffalo, unmarried.
1134—VI.	JUSTUS[7].	*See family numbered "1134."*
1135—VII.	ADALINE[7],	married Philander Pixley; and resides at Buffalo. Children: 1. ———[8] (daughter). 2. ———[8] (son). 3. ———[8] (son). 4. ———[8] (son).
1136—VIII.	DWIGHT R.[7],	married, first, ———————; and second, ——————. He resides in Kansas.
1137—IX.	ALMON[7],	married ——— ———; and lived in Washington, Del.
1138—X.	NANCY ;	married ——— Brown; and lives in Buffalo.
1139—XI.	SALLY[7];	married ——— ———; lived in Buffalo; and subsequently removed to the West.
1140—XII.	CLARISSA[7];	married Roswell Gardner of Attica.
1141—XIII.	DARIUS[7];	married ——— ———; and lives in Buffalo.

639

JOHN HOVEY[6], married, first, Elizabeth Brooks of Tioga, Pa. She died; and he married, second, ——— ———. He subsequently removed to the West, where he died.

Children:—

1142—I.	———[7]	(son).
1143—II.	———[7]	(son).
1144—III.	———[7]	(son).
1145—IV.	———[7]	(daughter).
1146—V.	———[7]	(daughter).
1147—VI.	———[7]	(daughter).

641

ORRE HOVEY[6], born in Plainfield, N. H., July 23, 1788. He married Azuba Root; and lived in Whitestown, N. Y., where he died in 1844.

Children:—

1148—I.	JOHN SUMNER[7].	*See family numbered "1148."*
1149—II.	———[7]	(son).
1150—III.	———[7]	(son).

1151—IV.   ————⁷ (son).
1152—V.   ————⁷ (daughter).
1153—VI.   ————⁷ (daughter).
1154—VII.   ————⁷ (daughter).

642

ELIPHALET HOVEY⁶, born in 1791. He married Sally Knapp.
Mr. Hovey died Dec. 18, 1843, at the age of fifty-two; and
his wife survived him, dying Nov. 18, 1848, aged fifty-six.
    Children:—

1155—I.   SALVIRA⁷; married Wright Blackmer.
1156—II.   BLEECKER⁷; married and practiced medicine in Rochester.
1157—III.   MARIA⁷; married ———— Mowry.
1158—IV.   JULIET⁷; married Jedediah Gordon of Rushford.
1159—V.   LOUISA⁷; married ———— Crane of Dansville.
1160—VI.   NINA⁷; married Ira Gifford.
1161—VII.   SPENCER⁷; lives at Linden.
1162—VIII. ALPHEUS⁷; lives in Rushford.

643

ALVIN HOVEY⁶; married Calista Roberts; and removed to
Michigan.
    Children:—

1163—I.   ————⁷.
1164—II.   ————⁷.
1165—III.   ————⁷.
1166—IV.   ————⁷.
1167—V.   ————⁷.
1168—VI.   ————⁷.
1169—VII.   ————⁷.
1170—VIII. ————⁷.
1171—IX.   ————⁷.

647

ZIBA HOVEY⁶. He removed, in 182-, from Genesee, now
Wyoming county, N. Y., to Chenango, where he carried on farming. He soon removed to Randolph, where he kept a hotel in
each of the villages. In 1836, he started to move his family down
the Alleghany and Ohio rivers on a raft, but navigation gave out,
and he landed at Cold Spring, where he built and kept a hotel,
returning to Randolph after two years. He finally went back to
Cold Spring.
    Mr. Hovey married Sophia Metcalf of Bethany Dec. 15,
1810. She was born in 1789, and died Feb. 17, 1873. He died
at the residence of his son LaFayette, in Cold Spring, Feb. 17,
1879, at the age of nearly ninety-one.
    Children:—

1172—I.   CHAUNCEY A.⁷, died in ————.
1173—II.   SOPHRONIA S.⁷, died in ————.

1174—III. ANDREW J.⁷, died in ——.
1175—IV. ZIBA M.⁷, born July 1, 1816; and lived in E. Randolph,
          N. Y.
1176—V.   EMILY⁷, born April 5, 1818; married D. B. Spaulding of Cold
          Spring.
1177—VI. ALTA M.⁷, born Nov. 29, 1819; died in ——.
1178—VII. LAURA P.⁷, born Oct. 20, 1821; married her cousin Chauncey
          A. Snow (son of No. 644) of East Randolph.
1179—VIII. FRANKLIN C.⁷, born Oct. 21, 1823; lived in E. Randolph, N. Y.
1180—IX. AMELIA A.⁷, born July 23, 1827.
1181—X.   LAFAYETTE⁷, born March 15, 1831; lives in Cold Spring.
          P. O. Address: Randolph, N. Y. He is a well-to-do
          farmer; and has a family.
1182—XI. CLARISSA⁷; lived in Iowa.

649

SHUBAEL CONANT HOVEY⁶, born in Mansfield, Conn., Feb.
21, 1777. He was a bridge builder and carpenter, and moved to
Lima, N. Y., after his marriage. He subsequently removed to
LeRoy, Ohio, in 1822.

Mr. Hovey married Mary Hovey (   ) Nov. 16, 1800, in
Lima. She was born in Brimfield, Mass., April 16, 1782; and
lived in Whitestown, N. Y. He died in LeRoy March 3, 1848,
at the age of seventy-one. She survived him, and died April 9,
1866(4?), in LeRoy.

Their children were born in Lima, as follows:—

1183—I.   MARLOW⁷, born Dec. 5, 1801. *See family numbered "1183."*
1184—II. JOANNA CONANT⁷, born Jan. 7, 1804; married Daniel Warner
          June 14, 1818; and died in Painesville, Ohio, April 16, 1888,
          at the age of eighty-four. Their children were born as
          follows: 1. *Mary Ann⁸*, born April 12, 1819; married Con-
          stantine Cephas Field May 3, 1838; and died Jan. 19, 1876,
          aged fifty-six. 2. *Martin Jonathan⁸*, born Jan. 6, 1821; mar-
          ried Marcia Beckwith June 24, 1842; and died Jan. 25, 1873,
          aged fifty-two. 3. *Daniel⁸*, born July 5, 1823; married Nancy
          Judd Dec. 3, 1846; and died April 2, 1886, aged sixty-two.
          4. *Asher⁸*, born Jan. 24, 1825; married, first, Hester ——
          July 23, 1846; second, Kate Field Nov. 6, 1861; and died
          Jan. 21, 1903, aged seventy-seven. 5. *Hannah Cornelia⁸*,
          born Oct. 23, 1826; married Benezette Aylworth Nov. 12,
          1845; and died Feb. 18, 1864, aged thirty-seven. 6. *Eliza-
          beth⁸*, born Sept. 7, 1828; married Lorenzo Sisson Oct. 14,
          1847. 7. *Field D.⁸*, born July 4, 1830; married Celestia
          Bushnell June 27, 1849; and died July 10, 1898, aged sixty-
          eight. 8. *Eliza⁸*, born April 30, 1832; married Charles
          Stewart Field Aug. 17, 1851. 9. *Calista I.⁸*, born Oct. 22,
          1835; married Dexter Wempole March 12, 1853; and died
          Sept. 17, 1864, at the age of twenty-eight. 10. ——⁸
          (twin), born June 26, 1837; died June 26, 1837. 11.
          ——⁸ (twin), born June 26, 1837; died June 26, 1837.
          12. *Jane Maria⁸*, born Oct. 16, 1839; married DeWitt Beck-
          with Nov. 6, 1861; and died Oct. 19, 1869, aged thirty.
1185—III. PHILETUS⁷, born May 12, 1808. *See family numbered "1185."*
1186—IV. SYLVANUS⁷, born June 6, 1810. *See family numbered "1186."*

1187—v.   ELIZA[7], born Oct. 25, 1812, at 2 A. M.; married Otis Warner
           July 3, 1828. He was born Jan. 29, 1800; and died Jan. 25,
           1885, at the age of eighty-four. She survived him, and
           died at Madison, Ohio, March 29, 1888, at the age of sev-
           enty-five. Their children were born in LeRoy, Ohio, as
           follows: 1. *S. Elmyra*[8], born June 14, 1834; married James
           Warren Sept. 23, 1858. He was born Aug. 29, 1820; and
           died June 2, 1894, aged seventy-three. She survives him,
           and lives in Madison. They had an adopted son. 2. *Halina
           R.*[8], born April 9, 1836; married Francis M. Scott March 11,
           1874. He was born May 16, 1823; and died Aug. 5, 1896,
           aged seventy-three. She survives him, and lives in Madison.
           They had one child, which died in infancy.

1188—vi.   SIMEON[7], born Aug. 12, 1814. *See family numbered "1188."*

657

HON. LEVI HOVEY[6], born Jan. 16, 1792. He began life as a
carpenter in Lima, N. Y.; but soon drifted to Genesee, N. Y.
There he studied law and became a lawyer and judge of a court
in Batavia, N. Y. He was the owner of a book store, and became
publisher and editor of the *Genesee Democrat*, the county organ
of the Democratic party. He invested in a new printing press,
and before he was able to pay for it a note he had given was
protested. Feeling disgraced, he went to New Orleans, La., and
died. It was learned, upon examination of his business affairs
that the books in his store would have been ample security for
his debt.

He married Betsey, daughter of Asa and Christiana (Dart)
Bishop Sept. 22, 1816. She was born in Genesee Sept. 20, 1792,
and died May 1, 1819.

Their children were born in Lima, N. Y., as follows:—

1189—I.   AUGUSTINE WASHINGTON[7], born June 19, 1817. *See family
           numbered "1189."*
1190—II.   CHARLES[7], born Aug. 2, 1821. *See family numbered "1190."*
1191—III. JANE ELIZABETH[7], born March 10, 1825; married Isaac I. Voor-
           heis April 24, 1867, in Pontiac. He was a farmer and cap-
           italist; and lived at Lapeer, Mich., where she died Sept. 30,
           1884.

673

DR. JAMES A. HOVEY[6], born in 1810. He was a physician;
and married Gloriance Phillips. He died in Ithaca, N. Y., many
years ago.

Child:—

1192—I.   LOUISE[7].

674

JOSIAH HOVEY[6], born in Brighton, Mass., Dec. 14 (24), 1763.
He was a soldier of the Revolution, being a pensioner; and re-
sided in Cambridge, where he was a merchant and innholder.
During the latter part of his life he was a merchant in Boston.

Mr. Hovey married, first, Miss Isabelle Winship, sister of Hon. Jonathan Winship, March 31, 1789; and she died Nov. 24, 1821. He married, second, Mrs. Mary Forbes in 1822. She was a school teacher in Cambridge. He married, third, widow Susan ———; and, fourth, Mrs. Elizabeth (Ingalls) Greenwood of Boston in 1838. Mr. Hovey died in Cambridgeport March 29, 1847, at the age of eighty-three. Eight days before his decease he was stricken with paralysis, remaining conscious, but unable to speak. He devised the residue of his estate to the Newton Theological Institution and the Baptist General Convention in the United States for Foreign Missions. His wife Elizabeth survived him, and died, his widow, her will, dated Feb. 28, 1849, being proved June 10, 1856. She possessed an estate of about twenty thousand dollars, and in her will she gave to the Northern Baptist Education Society, the Massachusetts Baptist State Convention and the American Tract Society, for the support of colporteurs in the West, one thousand dollars each; the Baptist Home Missionary Society in New York, three thousand dollars; the Boston Baptist Bethel Society, the New England Sabbath School Union and the American and Foreign Bible Society, five hundred dollars each; and the residue of her estate to the American Baptist Missionary Union.

Child:—

1193—i.   ISABELLA[7], bon Dec. 29, 1789; married William Leathe July 4, 1811; and died Aug. 9, 1875, at the age of eighty-five. Children: 1. *Mary Ann*[8]. 2. ———[8].

676

DEA. THOMAS HOVEY[6], born in Roxbury, Mass., Aug. 8, 1766. He was a blacksmith, and lived at first on the south side of the main road from Roxbury to Watertown, in Cambridge, until 1809, when he removed to Newton. He married Elizabeth, daughter of Capt. Ebenezer and Sarah (Coolidge) Seaver of Brighton Sept. 22 (30?) 1793. She was born Jan. 31, 1770.

Mr. Hovey, for fifty-seven pounds, bought of Lois Baker of Needham, widow, one-eighth of an acre of land in the South precinct of Cambridge, with the house thereon, Feb. 30(?), 1795;[*] and sold it, for nine hundred and fifty dollars, to Elijah White of Cambridge, victualer, Oct. 28, 1797.[†] The buildings on the lot were then described as a mansion house and barn. He bought, for two hundred dollars, of Benjamin Capen of Cambridge, yeoman, one acre of land in Cambridge, on the south side of the country road, June 10, 1799.[‡]

* Middlesex Registry of Deeds, book 116, page 551.
† Middlesex Registry of Deeds, book 127, page 513.
‡ Middlesex Registry of Deeds, book 134, page 30.

After his removal to Newton, Deacon Hovey became a yeoman; and was killed instantly while driving his team with a load of lumber which he was hauling for a barn he was building for himself, Nov. 19, 1829, at the age of sixty-three. It was supposed that he fell off the load, and that the wheels passed over his head. He was a consistent Christian, and a deacon of the Baptist church at Newton. Mrs. Hovey survived him, and died, in a fit, his widow, Aug. 4, 1843, at the age of seventy-three. Their children were born as follows:—

1194—I.   ELIZA ANN[7], born July 6, 1794, in Brighton; married Ebenezer, son of Jeremiah Fogg of Hancock, N. H., Dec. 25, 1814, at Cambridge. He was born in Hancock Oct. 25, 1788; and died at Cambridge, where they lived, May 18, 1836. She died April 8, 1869. Their children were born as follows: 1. *Eliza Ann*[8], born Oct. 25, 1815; died Aug. 15, 1817. 2. *William S.*[8], born April 26, 1817; married Mary S. Wood in New York City. 3. *Ebenezer*[8], born April 19, 1819; died Nov. 12, 1821. 4. *Sarah C.*[8], born Dec. 13, 1821; died Aug. 5, 1849. 5. *Caroline*[8], born Oct. 21, 1824; married Robert McLeod Nov. 27, 1843, at Cambridge; and had two children. 6. *Jane E.*[8], born Feb. 13, 1826; married Waldo W. Smith of Chicago, Ill., July 6, 1848; and had several children. 7. *Hannah M.*[8], born July 15, 1828; married John H. Dodge of Littleton, Mass., Oct. 15, 1855; and died Nov. —, 1899. 8. *Abigail S.*[8], born Dec. 30, 1829; married Edward Thorndike of Boston, Mass., Nov. 2, 1854; and had two children. 9. *Charles E.*[8], born Oct. 7, 1832; married Caroline Bristol July 3, 1862; and she died March 1, 1873. 10. *Stephen L.*[8], born Feb. 8, 1835; married Marian Auld of New York City Nov. 29, 1863; and has two children.

1195—II. THOMAS[7], born Jan. 7 (20?), 1796. *See family numbered "1195."*

1196—III. STEPHEN[7], born Feb. 8, 1799; and was living in 1829.

1197—IV. LUCY[7], born Oct. 3, 1800; married Ephraim Ward; lived in Cambridge, and died July 25, 1863, at the age of sixty-two. Their children were born as follows: 1. *Thomas A.*[8], born Dec. 18, 1830; married Hannah Morrison. 2. *Elijah L.*[8], born Aug. 11, 1833, in Newton. 3. *Ephraim*[8], born Dec. 29, 1834. 4. *Joseph Grafton*[8], born Aug. 5, 1837; died in the War of the Rebellion in 1863. 5. *Lucy E.*, born Aug. 20, 1840. 6. *Annie Caroline*[8], born Aug. 21, 1841.

1198—V.   SAMUEL SPARHAWK[7], born March 16, 1802, in Newton. *See family numbered "1198."*

1199—VI. ANNA SEAVER[7], born March 20, 1804.

1200—VII. EBEN SEAVER[7], born Dec. 16, 1805.

1201—VIII. ALLEN DANA[7], born Sept. 12, 1807.

1202—IX. ALMIRA COOLIDGE[7], born Oct. 31, 1809; married John Robinson; lived in Cambridge; and died in California.

1203—X.   JOSEPH GRAFTON[7], born Nov. 17, 1812; married Miss ———— Webster; lived in Cambridge; and died in California.

677

MAJ. JAMES HOVEY[6], born in Roxbury, Mass., Feb. 8, 1768. He was a yeoman, and lived at first in Cambridge and afterwards

in Brighton. He was a founder of the First Baptist church at
Central square, in Cambridge. He married Anna, daughter of
John Wilson of Cambridge Nov. 11, 1794. She was born in 1774.

Major Hovey died in Brighton, of consumption or a can-
cerous stomach, Sept. 21, 1831, at the age of sixty-three. His
will, dated July 18, 1831, was proved Nov. 8, 1831. He was a
kind and indulgent husband, and an affectionate father. She
survived him, and died in Brighton Dec. 2, 1865, at the age of
eighty-one.

Their children were born as follows:—

1204—I. WILLIAM BOWLES[7], born Sept. 3, 1795, in Newton. *See family
numbered "1204."*

1205—II. ABIGAIL [ABIA] WILSON[7], born July 27, 1797; lived in Quincy,
Mass. She early embraced the Christian faith. The latter
part of her life she was paralyzed, and never again spoke,
though with one hand she made clothing for the poor. She
died, unmarried, Sept. 2, 1869, at the age of seventy-two.

1206—III. ELEANOR[7], born Oct. 5, 1803; died Oct. 6, 1803.

1207—IV. MARTHA TURPIN[7], born Oct. 3, 1804, in Brighton; married Horatio Nelson, son of Benjamin Wadsworth and Mehitable
Willard (Baxter) Glover of Quincy Dec. 14, 1826. He was
born in Quincy March 6, 1801; and lived there, being a man
of moral worth, esteemed by his fellow-citizens, who elected
him to various offices of trust and honor, in which he served
faithfully. He was a promoter of education, and happy in
his domestic relations. He died in Quincy Dec. 28, 1863; and
she survived him, living there, his widow, in 1865. Their
children were born in Quincy, as follows: 1. *Horatio N.[8]*,
born Sept. 14, 1827; lived at Neponset village, in Dorchester;
merchant; married Anne Augusta, daughter of Nathan Holbrook of Dorchester Aug. 2, 1855; and had three children.
He died at Neponset May 22, 1905, at the age of seventy-
seven. 2. *James Hovey[8]*, born May 9, 1829; drowned in
Quincy bay by the upsetting of a new boat, which he had
built, Oct. 8, 1850, at the age of twenty-one. 3. *Anna
Hovey[8]*, born March 25, 1831; died, unmarried, Feb. 14, 1863,
aged thirty-one. 4. *Martha Maria[8]*, born July 8, 1833; died
March 16, 1835. 5. *William Bowles[8]*, born Sept. 20, 1835;
merchant in Boston; lived on the homestead in Quincy. 6.
Abby Caroline[8], born Feb. 16, 1838; died May 25, 1839. 7.
Harriet Lincoln[8], born Jan. 5, 1840; died in ———. 8.
Julia Elizabeth[8], born Feb. 13, 1843; lives on Atlantic avenue,
Atlantic, Mass. 9. *Emily Caroline Lincoln[8]*, born July 9,
1845; died in ———. 10. *Sarah Wadsworth[8]*, born Oct. 5,
1847; died in ———.

1208—V. JULIA ANNA[7], born Feb. 21, 1810; married, first, Rev. Valentine
Cushman, a Baptist clergyman, and lived in South Boston.
He died; and she married, second, John Russell of Natick
before 1865. After Mr. Russell's death, she lived in Ha-
verhill, being interested in the Second Advent people. Mr.
Russell died June 1, 1885, at the age of eighty-seven; and
she died Jan. 3, 1901, aged ninety. She had no children by
Mr. Russell.

1209—VI. JAMES GARDNER[7], born April 14, 1813. *See family numbered
"1209."*

678

EBENEZER HOVEY[6], born in Lunenburg, Mass., June 8, 1769. He was a yeoman, and lived in Cambridge, on the south side of the causeway leading to the West Boston bridge. He bought a pew in the Baptist meeting house in Newton in 1804, and probably attended church there. He married Sarah, daughter of Nathaniel Greenwood of Cambridge Nov. 28, 1799; and died in Cambridge May 5, 1831, at the age of sixty-one. His wife survived him, and died June 27, 1863.

Their children were born in Cambridge as follows:—

1210—I.	EBENEZER[7], born March 24, 1801. *See family numbered "1210."*
1211—II.	JOSIAH[7], born Nov. 1, 1802; instantly killed Sept. 19, 1803.
1212—III.	ELIZABETH[7], born June 10, 1804; unmarried in 1834.
1213—IV.	SARAH[7], born June 28, 1806; died May (March) 1, 1807.
1214—V.	ELEANOR[7], born Nov. 19, 1807; married Lorenzo Willis June —, 1829; and died Feb. 2, 1830, aged twenty-two. They had one child: 1. *Lewellyn[8]*, living in 1849.
1215—VI.	SARAH ANN[7], born Feb. 2 (22), 1809; died, unmarried, Nov. 23, 1830, at the age of twenty-one.
1216—VII.	FREEMAN[7], born March 1, 1811. *See family numbered "1216."*
1217—VIII.	SUSANNA[7], born Nov. 23, 1812; married Nahum Stone Jan. —, 1832; and died Aug. —, 1887, aged seventy-four. They had five or six children.
1218—IX.	GEORGE[7], born Aug. 5, 1814. *See family numbered "1218."*
1219—X.	THOMAS GREEN[7], born Jan. 23, 1816. His name was originally Thomas Hovey, and he had it changed by an act of the legislature of Massachusetts April 19, 1837. *See family numbered "1219."*
1220—XI.	JOSIAH[7], born June 3, 1819; married twice; and probably had no children. He was a druggist in Winchester, Mass., in 1849.
1221—XII.	STEPHEN DANA[7], born March 20, 1823; died Feb. 24, 1838, aged fourteen.

679

PHINEAS BROWN HOVEY[6], born Nov. 8, 1771. He lived in Cambridge, Mass., where he was probably born, and owned pew numbered twenty in the Cambridgeport meeting house. He conducted a grocery store at the western corner of Main and Brookline streets, in Cambridgeport, for many years; and was succeeded by his youngest son.

Mr. Hovey married, when he was of Watertown, Sarah Stone of Newton Dec. 5, 1792; and she died Dec. 9, 1846. He died April 19, 1852, at the age of eighty.

Children:—

1222—I.	SALLY[7], born April 10, 1795; married Samuel Foster of Greenwich Nov. 19, 1817; and died Dec. 10, 1819, aged twenty-four. Child: 1. *Sarah H.[8]*; married George W. Colburn of Cambridge; and died in or before 1884.

1223—II. EUNICE[7], born May 31, 1797; married Isaac Livermore of Cambridge; and died June 11, 1871, at the age of seventy-three. Children: 1. *Charles F.[8]*, lived in Detroit, Mich., in 1852 and 1885. 2. *Edward M.[8]*; lived in New York City in 1885. 3. *Jane E.[8]*; married ———— Burlingame; he died ————, and she lived at Syracuse, N. Y., in 1885. 4. *Sarah Elizabeth[8]*; married ———— Briggs; she lived in Pittsfield, Mass., his widow, in 1885.

1224—III. ELIZABETH[7], born March 17, 1799; lived in Cambridge, unmarried, in 1885.

1225—IV. PHINEAS BROWN[7], born Sept. 3, 1803; was a horticulturist; married Mary L. Cook Nov. 10, 1828; and died about 1885 She survived him.

1226—V. CAROLINE[7], born April 14, 1807; unmarried in 1852.

1227—VI. CHARLES MASON[7], born Oct. 3[1], 1810; graduated at Cambridge academy in 1824; and married Ann Maria Chaponil Dec. 25, 1835. He lived in Cambridge; was interested in fruits and flowers at an early age; became a horticulturalist; and had in his grounds on Cambridge street the largest cultivation of different varieties of trees in the United States. He originated many and fine kinds of fruit. He was a member of the principal horticultural societies of America, and corresponding and honorary member of the Royal societies of London and Edinburgh. He was president of the Massachusetts Horticultural Society, 1863 to 1867 inclusive. With his brother Phineas he edited and published the *American Gardner's Magazine*, in Boston, in 1835 and 1836. The name of this periodical was then changed to the *Magazine of Horticulture*, and it was edited and published by Charles alone from 1837 to 1869 inclusive. He published *Fruits of America*, with colored plates, in two volumes, in New York, in 1854. He died in Cambridge Sept. 2, 1887, at the age of seventy-six.

1228—VII. JOSIAH DANA[7], born March 31, 1813; married Atlantic Pierce Dec. 27, 1835; and conducted his father's old corner grocery in Cambridgeport, where he was living in 1885.

713

CHESTER HOVEY[6], born Jan. 20, 1778. He married Olive Rexford; and lived in Hatley, in the Province of Quebec, Canada. She died Aug. 21, 1833.

Children:—

1229—I. MALINDA[7]; married Capt. Taylor Wadleigh; and lived in Hatley. Their children were born in Hatley, as follows: 1. *Horatio[8]*, born Feb. 7, 1821; farmer; justice of the peace; school teacher; school commissioner; and municipal councilor; in every way a loyal British subject; married Matilda Gould June 2, 18—. She was born in Boston Nov. 1, 1828; and died in Lynn, Mass., in 1895; he died in Hatley Dec. 10, 1900, at the age of seventy-nine. They had four children. 2. *Alice J.[8]*; unmarried.

1230—II. MARY[7]; married Seth Huntingdon, esq.

1231—III. ELMIRA[7]; died at the age of twenty-eight.

1232—IV. LUCY[7]; married Charles Wallace.

1233—V. SOPHRONIA[7]; married Nathaniel Hawes.

1234—VI.   OLIVE[7]; married Russell Rexford.
1235—VII. CAROLINE[7]; married, first, Philip James, son of Abiel and
           Grace (Hitchcock) Abbott (grandson of Ruth Hovey, 355)
           Oct. 22, 1841. He was born Feb. 17, 1816; lived in Hatley;
           and was a farmer. She married, second, Simon Bean; and
           died Sept. 6, 1857. She had no children.
1236—VIII. CHESTER[7]; died at the age of thirty.
1237—IX.   ALONZO[7], born June 11, 1818, in Hatley. *See family numbered*
           "1237."
1238—X.   HESTER[7]; married George Oliver.

722

HORACE HOVEY[6], born in Hatley, Canada, Dec. 21, 1798.
He was a farmer, and lived in his native town. He married, first,
Pamelia, daughter of Jesse and Lucy (Turner) Wadleigh in
1829, in East Hatley. She was born in Hatley June —, 1808;
and died there Dec. 18, 1844. He married, second, Mary
Flanders in 1864; and died in Hatley Dec. 11, 1871, at the age
of seventy-two. His wife Mary survived him, and died Oct. 27,
1876, aged fifty-seven.

Mr. Hovey's children were all by his first wife and born in
Hatley, as follows:—

1239—I.   WRIGHT[7], born July 23, 1833. *See family numbered "1239."*
1240—II.   ALICE JANE[7], born Nov. 24, 1836; married, first, Horace, son of
           Jacob and ————— (Haines) Taylor Sept. 28, 1858. He
           was a farmer; and lived in Stanstead, Province of Quebec,
           where he died April —, 1861. They had one child, born in
           Stanstead: 1. *Minnie*[8], born Sept. 28, 1860; married Harry
           Hobbs Oct. —, 1884; and they live in Chicago, Ill., where he
           is manager of a manufacturing company.
               Mrs. Taylor married, second, William Miller, son of
           Joseph and Anna C. (Miller) Atwood June —, 1865, at
           Magog, Province of Quebec. He was born in Magog Nov.
           12, 1829; and lived there. He died in Magog Sept. 1, 1872.
           She survived him, and died in Clyde, Kansas, Jan. 17, 1904.
           Mr. and Mrs. Atwood had one child, born in Magog: 1.
           Don H.[8], born March 5, 1867. He is a banker, and resides
           in Clyde.
1241—III. HORACE MELVIN[7], born Dec. 15, 1838. *See family numbered*
           "1241."
1242—IV.   LESLIE PIERPONT[7], born Oct. 29, 1842. *See family numbered*
           "1242."

725

WILLIAM HOVEY[6], born in Hampton, Conn., Oct. 8, 1797.
He married ————— —————; and resided in Waterford,
Vt.

Child:—

1243—I.   JACOB G.[7], born June 24, 1834, in Waterford. *See family*
           numbered "1243."

734

OLIVER HOVEY[6], born in Hampton, Conn., Jan. 11, 1793. He married ———————— ————————; and died Sept. 18, 1840, at the age of forty-seven.

He had one child :—

1244—I. ANNA DEWEY[7]; married Sidney McBride; and died at Beloit, Iowa.

735

ORRIN HOVEY[6], born in Monson, Mass., Dec. 11, 1794. He married Sally, daughter of Dea. Daniel and Sally (Hatch) Childs of Becket, Mass., April 17, 1832. She was born in Becket May 7, 1806. They lived in Monson; and he died Nov. 28, 1861. She survived him, and died March 20, 1879, at the age of seventy-two.
Children :—

1245—I. GEORGE C.[7], born June 27, 1833; died May 27, 1846, aged twelve.

1246—II. WILLIAM OREN[7], born Dec. 16, 1834, in Monson, Mass. *See family numbered "1246."*

1247—III. SARAH E.[7], born June 26, 1836, in Monson; lived in Monson in 1862, at Milford, Conn., in 1865, and at Wilbraham, Mass.; married John L. Chaffee Jan. 30, 1883. He was born in Monson May 2, 1816; and died March 26, 1903, aged eighty-six.

1248—IV. DANIEL O.[7], born May 18, 1838; lived in Monson in 1862; served in Washington, in the Seventh company of artillery in 1865; and now resides in Massachusetts, unmarried.

1249—V. ALBERT HENRY[7], born March 22, 1840, in Monson. *See family numbered "1249."*

1250—VI. CHARLES LOUIE[7], born Nov. 29, 1842, in Monson. *See family numbered "1250."*

1251—VII. LAURA ELMIRA[7], born Dec. 22, 1845; married James K. Butler April 7, 1870; he was born March 18, 1845; and she died at Wilbraham, Mass., Jan. 19, 1907, at the age of fifty-one. Their children were born as follows: 1. *Adella E.*[8], born Aug. 2, 1871; died Feb. 14, 1872. 2. *Benjamin O.*[8], born Oct 1, 1873; died Feb. 4, 1875. 3. *Albert H. H.*[8], born Oct. 30, 1874. 4. *Blanche B.*[8], born Nov. 19, 1876.

736

HORACE HOVEY[6], born in Monson, Mass., June 24, 1796. He married ———————— ————————; and died Oct. 29, 1873, at the age of seventy-seven.

Children, all living at Vernon, Mich. :—

1252—I. ————————[7].
1253—II. ————————[7].
1254—III. ————————[7].
1255—IV. ————————[7].
1256—V. ————————[7].
1257—VI. ————————[7].

740

HIRAM HOVEY[6], born in Monson, Mass., Jan. 12, 1803. He was a farmer, and lived in Munson, Ohio. He married Abigail Foster of Monson, Mass., in 1827, at Munson, O. She was born Dec. —, 1812. He died at Munson, O., July 1, 1849, at the age of forty-six. She survived him, and died at Munson, O., Jan. 23, 1892, at the age of seventy-nine.

Their children were born at Munson, O., as follows:—

1258—I.   LOUISA[7], born May 28, 1831; married George Wheeler in 1849, in Newbury, Ohio. He was born in Munson, O., June 2, 1829. She died at Painesville, O., May 25, 1900, at the age of sixty-eight. They had no children.

1259—II.   ELISHA FLINT[7], born Dec. 6, 1832. *See family numbered "1259."*

1260—III.   HIRAM ALMON[7], born Nov. 18, 1835. *See family numbered "1260."*

1261—IV.   ELVIRA[7], born June 29, 1837; married Frank Loveland Feb. 14, 1856. He was born in Newbury, O., Oct. 5, 1824; was a farmer; and died in Geauga county, O., June 26, 1886, at the age of sixty-one. She lives, his widow, in Newbury, O. Children, born in Newbury: 1. *George F.*[8], born Feb. 11, 1857; lives at Newbury; married Elizabeth Walters Sept. 24, 1885. She was born at Sugar Creek, O., Sept. 28, 1868. They have three children. 2. *Nellie*[8], born April 25, 1870; married Hiram Carlton Aug. 4, 1897; and lives at Newbury. He was born at Burton, O., Nov. 15, 1870. They have three children.

1262—V.   ORRIN UTLEY[7], born Oct. 2, 1841. *See family numbered "1262."*

1263—VI.   ALBERT D.[7], born Nov. 7, 1845. *See family numbered "1263."*
1264—VII.   HORACE[7]; died young.
1265—VIII. MARY[7]; died young.

748

HON. JAMES ALBERT HOVEY[6], born in Hampton, Conn., April 29, 1815. He was educated in the common and private schools of his time, and chose the law as a profession. His life was spent in the towns of Hampton, Windham and Norwich. From 1830 until 1842 he was connected with the state militia. He was assignee in bankruptcy for New London county under the act of 1841, executive secretary in 1842 and 1843 under Gov. Chauncy F. Cleveland of Hampton, member of the board of aldermen in Norwich from 1849 till 1853, and judge of the New London county court from 1850 until 1854. He was vice-president and trustee of the Chelsea savings bank and trustee of the Norwich savings society. He was also president of the Uncas bank of Norwich from 1852 to 1872.

Judge Hovey was a member of the general assembly in 1859 and 1886; and mayor of Norwich in 1870 and 1871. He was always a Democrat in politics.

He married Miss Lavinia J. Barber; and she died before 1891.

Child:—

1266—1.   ————¹ (son) ; died before 1891.

752

CHARLES FOX HOVEY⁶, born in Brookfield, Mass., Feb. 28. 1807. He lived in Boston, and was the founder of the great dry-goods house of C F. Hovey & Co., on Summer street. He re-sided in Gloucester, Mass., in 1851 and 1854. He married Jus-tine Watts de Peyster, who was born in New York April 1, 1820. He died in Boston April 28, 1859, at the age of fifty-two; and she died there July 7. 1891, at the age of seventy-one. His estate was appraised at $167,086.

Mr. Hovey was an ardent supporter of all reforms, and in the anti-slavery movement was a follower of the Garrisonian wing of that party. In his will, he makes liberal provision for his wife and children, and gives to William Lloyd Garrison and his wife Helen E. Garrison, Parker Pillsbury, Stephen S. Foster and his wife Abby R. Foster one thousand dollars each; and to Henry Clarke Wright of Philadelphia, "an itinerant and independent lecturer and writer on moral reforms," two thousand dollars. The residue of his estate amounted to about sixty-five thousand dollars; and relative to this he made the following provision: "I direct my said trustees to hold all the rest and residue of my estate, real, personal and mixed, in special trust, for the following purposes, namely, to pay over, out of the interest and principal of said special trust. a sum of not less than eight thousand dollars annually, until the same shall be exhausted, to said Wendell Phillips. William Lloyd Garrison, Stephen S. Foster, Abby R. Foster, Parker Pillsbury, Henry C. Wright. Francis Jackson and Charles H. Whipple and their survivors and survivor, for them to use and expend, at their discretion, without any responsibility to any one, for the promotion of the anti-slavery cause, and other reforms; such as woman's rights, non-resistance, free trade and temperance, at their discretion; and I request said Wendell Phillips and his said associates, to expend not less than eight thousand dollars annually by the preparation and circulation of books, newspapers, employing agents and the delivery of lectures that will. in their judgment, change public opinion, and secure the abolition of slavery in the United States, and promote said other reforms. Believing that the chain upon four million slaves, with tyrants at one end. and hypocrites at the other. has become the strongest bond of the Union of the States. I desire said Phillips and his associates to expend said bequest by employing such agents as believe and practise the doctrine of 'Non union with slave holders, religiously or politically,' and by circulating such publications as tend to destroy every pro-slavery institution."

At the end of this interesting will Mr. Hovey requests that "No prayers be solicited from any person and that no priest be invited to perform any ceremony whatever, over or after my body. The priesthood are an order of men, as I believe, falsely assuming to be reverend and divine, pretending to be called of God; the great body of them, in all countries, have been on the side of power and oppression; the world has been too long cheated by them; the sooner they are unmasked, the better for humanity."

Mr. Hovey's children were born as follows:—

1267—I.   WILLIAM ALFRED[7], born Dec. 21, 1841, in Boston. *See family numbered "1267."*

1268—II.   EDWARD CLARENCE[7], born April 13, 1854, in Paris, France. *See family numbered "1268."*

753

GEORGE OTIS HOVEY[6], born in Brookfield, Mass., Feb. 22, 1809. He was reared in the household of his uncle Jabez C. Howe in Sterling, Mass., and when the family removed to Boston George went with them. When he became of age he was made a member of his uncle's firm, J. C. Howe & Co., Samuel R. Payson of Roxbury being one of the partners. He married Mary Ann Levley, daughter of Joseph Cotton March 19, 1835, in Boston, where she was born March 25, 1809. In the interests of the firm, he spent several years of his life following his marriage in France, his eldest two children being born in Paris. His winter home was 100 Beacon street, Boston. He was a pioneer of the North Shore summer residents, spending his first season at Fresh Water cove, in Gloucester, in 1843. He spent every summer there after that as long as he lived, building his home there in 1846. His wife died in Boston Oct. 29, 1873, at the age of sixty-four. He died at his summer home in Gloucester July 18, 1877, at the age of sixty-eight.

Their children were as follows: —

1269—I.   MARIAN[7], born Dec. 29, 1835, in Paris France. She died in Gloucester, unmarried, Aug. 28, 1898, at the age of sixty-two.

1270—II.   HELEN ELISE[7], born July 18, 1838, in Paris; died, unmarried, Feb. 8, 1870, at Pau Basses, Pyrenies, France, at the age of thirty-one.

1271—III. FANNY POPE[7], born May 27, 1840, in Roxbury, Mass.; married John T. Morse, jr., June 10, 1865, in Boston; and lives at 16 Fairfield street, Boston, Mass.

1272—IV.   GEORGE OTIS[7], born Jan. 6, 1842, in Boston; and died at Brookfield, Mass., Aug. 25, 1843, aged one year.

1273—V.   HENRY STONE[7], born Jan. 30, 1844, in Boston. He was for many years owner of the Pittsfield Cotton Mills at Pittsfield, N. H., but retired from the business a number of years before his death; and then gave a large part of his time to his favorite sport of yachting, being the owner of the sloop Fortuna, winner of many races at Marblehead. He was three times elected commodore of the Eastern Yacht Club, at Marblehead; and was a member of many other prominent yacht clubs. He was also a member of the Somerset Club and of other clubs in Boston and New York.

Mr. Hovey was a bachelor, and for many years lived with his father at their old home on Beacon street, in Boston. After his father's death, he continued to reside there with his sister, and when she died, in 1898, he gave up the house and lived at Hotel Chesterfield, 371 Commonwealth avenue, Boston, where he died Nov. 19, 1900, at the age of fifty-six. His funeral was held at his winter apartments, with the utmost simplicity. Many prominent men were present, and the interment was at Mt. Auburn.

1274—VI.   JOSEPH COTTON⁷, born June 20, 1816, in Boston. He was a commission merchant, and lived in Boston. He died unmarried, in Lowell, Mass., Oct. 9, 1874, at the age of twenty-eight.

754

FREDERIC HOVEY⁶; married Sally Judd.

His children were born in Hampton, Conn., as follows:—

1275—I.   BETSEY⁷, born Oct. 1, 1816; married Reuben Calkins Sept. 20, 1838, in Suffield, Conn. He was a farmer, and lived in Gaines, N. Y., where she died May 4, 1875. Child: 1. *Clarissa S.*⁸, born Dec. 28, 1841, in Milford, Mich.; and lives in Gaines, N. Y., unmarried.

1276—II.   DOUGLASS⁷, born Feb. 22, 1828. *See family numbered "1276."*

757

JOHN HOVEY⁷, born in Londonderry, N. H., Oct. 15, 1786. He was a house-carpenter, and lived in his native town until 1839, when he emigrated to Marietta, O. He married, first, Eleanor White of Chester, N. H., Sept. 27, 1810; and she died March 29, 1812. He married, second, his first wife's sister, Betsey White of Londonderry Dec. 16, 1813; and she died May 29, 1819. He married, third, Abigail, daughter of Timothy Dustin of Haverhill, Mass., June 29, 1820. She was born in Manchester, N. H., Jan. 14, 1798. He died in Marietta July 20, 1851, at the age of sixty-four; and she died there May 10, 1883, at the age of eighty-five.

The children of Mr. Hovey were born as follows:—

1277—I.   JOHN DUSTIN⁸, born June 19, 1821, in Londonderry, N. H. *See family numbered "1277."*

1278—II.   ALBERT GALETON⁸, born July 11, 1824, in Londonderry, N. H.; lived in Eugene, Ore.; married, first, Mary Ellen Mulkey in 1853, in Oregon; second, Emily Humphrey in 1866; was state senator of Oregon, and one of the most prominent citizens, being a banker. He died in Eugene Nov. 27, 1898, at the age of seventy-four.

1279—III. JAMES BURNHAM⁶, born July 1, 1826, in Londonderry; was a merchant, and president of the Marietta city council; married Virginia A. Rowland Oct. 9, 1849, in Newport, O., and died at Marietta April 25, 1897, at the age of seventy.

1280—IV. MILTON⁶, born Sept. 11, 1828, in Londonderry; was a carpenter and builder, and noted for his fine workmanship; married Elizabeth Hayes Dec. 24, 1857, in Marietta, where he died April 1, 1861, at the age of thirty-two.

1281—V. FRANKLIN STARK⁶, born Sept. 22, 1830, in N. H.; merchant; married Mary Kuntz Feb. 5, 1861; and died in Salem, Ore., March 31, 1877, at the age of forty-six. "An honest man."

1282—VI. ANN DUSTIN⁶, born May 26, 1834; died Aug. 15, 1835, aged one year.

1283—VII. GEORGE THEODORE⁶, born July 23, 1837, in Manchester, N. H.; lives in Marietta, O., being an architect of note. He is a distinguished Free Mason, having been Worshipful Master of American Union Lodge, No. 1, for sixteen years. He married Julia M. Sprague Oct. 12, 1864, in Marietta.

1284—VIII. ABIGAIL DUSTIN⁶, born Feb. 18, 1839; married J. S. Sprague May 5, 1857; and died March 1, 1895, at the age of fifty-six.

759

DR. ISAAC BURNHAM HOVEY⁷, born in Derry, N. H., May 1, 1790. He was a well-known physician, residing in Atkinson, N. H. He married Miss Eliza, daughter of Joseph and Lucy (Belknap) Richards of Atkinson Oct. 6, 1828. She was born in Atkinson Nov. 26, 1805; and died there, of fever, June 15, 1866. Doctor Hovey died there Jan. 6, 1872, at the age of eighty-one.

Child :—

1285—I. ISAAC R.⁸, born Dec. 30, 1830, in Atkinson, N. H.; farmer; lived in Atkinson; and died there, of heart disease, Dec. 29, 1895, at sixty-five years of age. He was never married.

770

JOHN JACOBS HOVEY⁷, born in Sutton. Mass., Aug. 31, 1814. He went to Virginia, and was a wealthy planter and merchant in York county. He married Alice Post Feb. 25, 1871, in York county. She was born in New York City Jan. 17, 1853. He died in York county Dec. 5, 1881, at the age of sixty-seven.

Their children were born in York county, as follows :—

1286—I. ELIZABETH WATERS⁸, born March 13, 1872; married James E. Wilkins Sept. 25, 1898; and lives in Virginia.

1287—II. JOHN JACOBS⁸ born Jan. 21, 1875; lived in Virginia; and married Mary Emeline Ewan Feb. 1, 1899.

1288—III. MABEL ALICE⁸, born Nov. 15, 1877; married R. E. Wilkins Feb. 18, 1893; and lives in Virginia.

1289—IV. CHARLES MARIUS⁸, born Aug. 28, 1880; lives in Virginia, unmarried.

773

MARIUS MILNER HOVEY⁷, born in Sutton, Mass., Aug. 17, 1818. He lived in his native town, and was largely engaged in the wood and lumber business, running a saw-mill for several years principally to saw his own lumber. He cleared much wood-land, and became an extensive landholder. His farm was one of the finest cultivated in the state, having on it some of the best stock. He also had a store in Greenville, S. C., where, in 1876, he was doing an extensive business under the firm name of Hovey & Town. He represented Sutton in the legislature, and held other offices of trust and honor. He made money, and accumulated a fortune.

Mr. Hovey married, first, Louisa L. Sabin of Plainfield, Conn., June 18, 1851; and she died in Sutton Sept. 24, 1860. He married, second, Ellen Douglas, daughter of Dr. Leonard and Mary LeBaron (Putnam) Pierce of Sutton Nov. 16, 1864. She was born in Sutton Aug. 22, 1836. He died in Sutton Feb. 16, 1898, at the age of seventy-nine. His wife Ellen survives him.

Mr. Hovey's children were born in Sutton, as follows:—

1290—I.   JOHN WILLIAM⁸, born Aug. 24, 1865; died, of diphtheria, in his
           third year at Harvard University, Jan. 13, 1889, aged twenty-
           three.
1291—II.   MARIUS MILNER⁸, born June 15, 1875; married Annie Hall May
           1, 1899.

784

SIMON AUGUSTUS HOVEY⁷, born in Oxford, N. Y., Dec. 21, 1828. He was a farmer, and lived in his native town. He married Harriet Amanda, daughter of John and Polly (Hackett) Gordon Nov. 16, 1853, in Oxford, where she was born May 9, 1831. He died at Oxford Jan. 7, 1868, at the age of thirty-nine.

Their children were born in Oxford, as follows:—

1292—I.   ELLEN ADELLA⁸, born Jan. 25, 1855; married Robert Gilson of
           Deposit, N. Y., May 6, 1873; he was a farmer, and lived in
           Deposit, where she died May 15, 1880.
1293—II.   FRANK ADELBERT⁸, born Feb. 28, 1859. *See family numbered
           "1293."*
1294—III. HENRY MORRIS⁸, born Aug. 2, 1860. *See family numbered
           "1294."*

786

HORACE WATERS HOVEY⁷, born in Guilford Centre, N. Y., Aug. 16, 1827.* He was brought up on a farm, and attended the village schools, then Oxford (N. Y.) Academy for two years, and the State Normal college at Albany for two years, graduating

* The record of the family of the father of Mr. Hovey was received too late for insertion in its proper place. Simon Hovey, the father, died Sept. 2, 1874; and Betsey, the mother, born May 28, 1799, died July 20,

from the latter school in 1851. He also studied at Albany University for a year. While he was pursuing his studies in these various institutions, he taught school three years. He subsequently taught in Wayne county, Pa., one year, in Chenango county, N. Y., seven years, in Millbury, Mass., one year, at Richmond, Va., five years, at Ironton, O., one year, in Shelton college, at St. Albans, W. Va., ten years, at Cedar Grove, two years, and at Hampton, London, Fair-View and other places in Kamawha county, twenty-five years in all in West Virginia,—and a teacher for forty years in all, generally as principal of graded schools. He conducted many county and state teachers' institutes in West Virginia and elsewhere.

He was elected surveyor of Henrico county, Va., in 1870, and was a railroad contractor eight years. He was also a justice of the peace at St. Albans, W. Va., several years, and a member of the city council, etc. He was connected with the Christian and A. W. commissions and other societies during the war and rendered valuable assistance. He oversaw the work of fitting up confiscated buildings and erecting new ones for educational purposes, and taught the first school for white boys and the first free night schools for colored men and boys, besides aiding in establishing libraries for prisons.

Mr. Hovey was, also, greatly interested in horticulture.

He wrote, in a letter, in 1901: "From what I have learned I am glad that I am a Hovey, for I find they have a remarkably good record for enterprise, industry, honor, loyalty, &c. No traitors in the Civil War, but many of them rendered valuable and valiant services in crushing secession."

Mr. Hovey married, first, Julia Allie, daughter of Hiram and Salma (Barnes) Brown Aug. 21, 1853, at Whitney's Point, N. Y.; and they separated five years later. She died Dec. 24, 1904. He married, second, Martha Jane, daughter of Dr. Thacher, in Richmond, Va., about 1870. She was born in Newburgh, N. Y., Dec. 28, 1835. Mr. Hovey died at St. Albans Oct. 30, 1903, aged seventy-six. She survived him, and lived with her son.

Mr. Hovey's children were born as follows:—

1295—1.   CORA LUCILLE⁶, born July 26, 1854, at Whitney's Point, N. Y.; married Charles Wyre, son of Nathaniel and Jane LeGarde (Hill) Vickery Feb. 21, 1871, at LaPorte, Ind. He was born in Unity, Me., March 22, 1840; and attended school at Bellows Falls, Vt., and later removed with his father to Chicago, Ill. He entered the army in May, 1861, as a private in the

1873. Their children were born as follows: 1. John Tyler, born April 27, 1818. 2. William Moses, born July 23, 1823; died Oct. 2, 1850. 3. Horace W., born Aug. 16, 1827. 4. Albert C., born April 17, 1829. 5. Hiram P., born Jan. 8, 1832; died Sept. 19, 1900. 6. Ransom, born June 22, 1834. 7. Nancy J., born Jan. 24, 1837; died Nov. 27, 1897. 8. Mary Anne, born Jan. 14, 1842.

Sturgis Rifles; served until April, 1863, when he was discharged with the rank of first sergeant. He was in the grocery business in Chicago from 1863 to 1867, and afterward was employed in the railway mail service, being promoted until, in 1881, he became superintendent of the Third division. He has held the latter position ever since. He is an important factor in all parts of the service. They live at 415 Third street N. W., Washington, D. C. Their children were born in Chicago as follows: 1. *Cora Tanetta*[8], born July 28, 1872; married William W. Horton Jan. 20, 1892, in Washington. He was a merchant, and lived in Washington. They had two sons. 2. *Alla LeGarde*[8], born Oct. 3, 1875; married J. Stewart Gass Dec. 11, 1905. He is a civil engineer, and lives in Washington. 3. *Ono Melita*[8], born Jan. 2, 1878; married Fred Elliott Healy Oct. 29, 1900. They live in Washington, where he is a merchant engineer. They have a daughter. 4. *Meta Inga*[8], born July 8, 1880; married, first, Charles Frank Hastings Dec. 31, 1896. He was an agent, and lived in Washington. They had a daughter. She married, second, James B. Archer, esq., Feb. 28, 1905. He is a lawyer, and they live in Washington.

1296—II.   FRANK EUGENE[8], born March 14, 1856, in Scranton, Pa.; died in Chicago, Ill., Oct. 20, 1872, at the age of sixteen.

1297—III.   HOWARD WILSON[8], born March 22, 1873; was agent for the Royal Baking Powder Co., at Albany, N. Y., and later engaged in the bicycle business, and is now a merchant in Tampa, Fla., where he resides.

793

HENRY ABBOTT HOVEY[7], born in Dracut, Mass., June 22, 1802. He lived in Boston, on Boylston street, opposite the common, where the Colonial Theatre now stands. He was a carriage builder, and built the old stage coaches until the introduction of railroads ruined his business as a coach builder. He then removed to St. Louis, Mo.

Mr. Hovey married, first, Rebecca Francis April 6, 1826, in Boston. She was born June 27, 1800; and died in Boston Nov. 28, 1833. He subsequently married twice; and the third wife had no children. He was a very hospitable man, and always had a house full of guests. He died in St. Louis Nov. 1, 1854, at the age of fifty-two.

Mr. Hovey's children were born as follows:—

1298—I.   REBECCA FRANCES[8], born June 21, 1827, in Boston; married George Sampson June 19, 1855, in Boston. He was the publisher of the Boston Directory for many years; and died in 18—. She lives at 31 Winthrop street, in Roxbury, now a part of Boston.

1299—II.   CHARLES HENRY[8], born March 28, 1830, in Boston. *See family numbered "1299."*

1300—III.   ALFRED AUGUSTUS[8], born Oct. 13, 1831, in Boston; died, unmarried, in Boston, from wounds received in the Civil war, May 8, 1863, aged thirty-one.

1301—IV.   LOUISA JANE[8], born March 2, 1835, in Boston; died in Boston Feb. 8, 1837.

1302—v. LOUISA JANE[6], born April 18, 1840, in Woodstock, Vt.; married Ernest H. de Sasseville Nov. —, 1891, in London, England; and lived in Boston, and in Denver, Col. She died in Denver in 1903.
1303—vi. GEORGE ABBOTT[6], born Feb. 18, 1844, in Boston; and died Feb. 22, 1845, in Boston, aged one year.

798

WILLIAM HOVEY[7], born in Dracut, Mass., Sept. 10, 1802. He lived in Lowell; and married Hannah Carhart July 5, 1832, in New York, where she was born Feb. 2, 1813. She died in Lowell June 17, 1892, at the age of seventy-nine. He died in Lowell March 21, 1893, at the age of ninety.

Their children were born as follows:—

1304—i. REBECCA FRANCES[8], born July 26, 1833, in New York; married ———— Webb Oct. 26, 1856, in Lowell; and died in Waldoboro, Me., June 21, 1861, at the age of twenty-seven.
1305—ii. HENRIETTA FAILING[8], born April 26, 1836, in Dracut, Mass.; married William T. Shapleigh June 8, 1858, in Lowell. They resided in Brookline, Mass., where she died Nov. 19, 1909, at the age of seventy-three.
1306—iii. HARRIET CAROLINE[8], born Aug. 23, 1838, in Dracut; resides at 18 Fourth street, Lowell, Mass., unmarried.

799

JAMES HOVEY[7], born in Dracut, Mass., March 8, 1804. He was a merchant; lived in Waldoboro, Me.; and married Eliza Ann, daughter of Samuel and Olive (Pond) Morse Aug. 31, 1835, at Waldoboro; where she was born March 4, 1809. He died in Waldoboro Sept. 1, 1855, at the age of fifty-one; and she died in Boston, Mass., June 10, 1872, at the age of sixty-three.

Their children were born in Waldoboro, as follows:—

1307—i. GRENVILLE[8], born June 3, 1837; clerk; lives in Lowell, Mass.; married Annie B., daughter of Thomas and Rebecca (Vollentine) Thompson of Boston Feb. 12, 1873. She was born in Boston Oct. 14, 1841; and died in Lowell Nov. 4, 1896, at the age of fifty-five. They had no children.
1308—ii. MYRON M.[8], born April 19, 1839; lives in Nashua, N. H.; acting paymaster of the United States navy; and married Minnie E., daughter of Stephen W. and Miranda B. (Knox) Eaton of Gorham, Me., June 2, 1869. She was born in Portland, Me., in 1842; and died in Boston, Mass., April 11, 1873. They had no children.
1309—iii. LEROY FARLEY[8], born Nov. 19, 1847. See family numbered "1309."

800

HORATIO NELSON HOVEY[7], born in Dracut, Mass., Dec. 8, 1805. He went to East Cambridge when nineteen years of age, and was employed as a clerk in the grocery store of Atherton H. Stevens until 1839, when he began to conduct for himself a store

at the corner of Third and Gore streets in a humble way. There
he remained for thirty-six years, and then built the present building at the corner of Cambridge and Third streets, moving into it
in 1876. He retired from business in 1886, when eighty years of
age, having been sixty-two years in the business. He was succeeded by his son-in-law George W. Dearborn.

Mr. Hovey married Miss Mary Ann Kingsley of Cambridge
Oct. 27, 1839. She was born in Boston Sept. —, 1816, and died
in Cambridge Dec. 26, 1891, at the age of seventy-five. Mr.
Hovey died at his home, 93 Otis street, East Cambridge, Jan. 18,
1899, at the age of ninety-three. On account of his venerable appearance and the esteem in which he was held he was known as
"Father." Many sought his confidence and advice, having trust
in his wisdom and sincerity. He was associated with the important charities of the city; and in his church always made it
his practice to welcome strangers and greet the brethren. He was
gentle and tender, and the children loved and trusted him. He
was absolutely independent in his thought and conviction; and
so religious, in both thought and deed, that to him God was the
great reality, and the future life as real and reasonable as the
present life. He was a member of the New England lodge,
I. O. O. F., and active in the affairs of the Trinity M. E. church
for fifty-two years.

Their children were born in Cambridge, as follows:—

1310—I. HORATIO NELSON[5],[*] born Aug. 21, 1840. *See family numbered
"1310."*

1311—II. ELIZABETH ALLISON[5], born Nov. 4, 1842; married Norman
Milleken Seelye of Winchester, Mass., Dec. 10, 1861. He was
born in St. George, N. B., April 28, 1834; and died in Millis,
Mass., Oct. 13, 1891, aged fifty-seven. He was a manufacturer of machinery. She survived him, and lives at 93
Main street, Winchester. Their children were born in Cambridge, as follows: 1. *Nelson Hovey[6]*, born Feb. 4, 1865;
is a manufacturer of machinery, and lives at 93 Main street,
Winchester. 2. *Norma Louise[6]*, born Dec. 9, 1869; stenographer; and lives, unmarried, at 93 Main street, in Winchester. 3. *Morton Chapin[6]*, born Nov. 16, 1876; manufacturer of machinery; and lives in Winchester.

1312—III. MARY KINSLEY[5], born Nov. 13, 1844; married George Washington Dearborn March 2, 1869, in Cambridge; lived at 93 Main
street, Winchester. Child: 1. *Edna May[6]*: married George
A. Tabor; and lives at 546 East 23d street, Brooklyn, N. Y.

1313—IV. MARIA LOUISA[5], born May 27, 1849; married Gardner Chapin
Nov. 24, 1870; he was born in Ogdensburg, N. Y., May 6,
1848. They live at 1 Mt. Vernon avenue, Melrose, Mass.
He is a merchant in Boston. Their children were born in
Cambridge, as follows: 1. *Gardner Hovey[6]*, born Feb. 3,
1873; died March 28, 1876. 2. *Myron Searles[6]*, born Dec. 4,
1874; died April 8, 1876. 3. *Myra Louise[6]*, born May 17,

* He was given the name of Nelson after the death of his brother
Nelson.

1878; and lives at her parents' home. 4. *Chester Laurence*[9], born Oct. 3, 1882; lives at his parents' home. 5. *Kenneth Seelye*[9], born April 19, 1884; died Aug. 9, 1884.

1314—V. NELSON[4], born Sept. 1, 1851; died March 17, 1853, aged one year.

801

JOSHUA HOVEY[7], born in Dracut, Mass., Jan. 8, 1808. He lived, first, in Dracut, and, when a young man, removed to Lowell, Mass., where he afterward lived, with the exception of a few years spent in Methuen. In 1835 he engaged in the shoe business, and in 1841 he became a grocer in the brick block on Bridge street, near Lakeview avenue. He conducted his grocery until 1857, when he again went into the shoe business, which he carried on until 1888. He was much respected, and a man of extremely temperate habits.

Mr. Hovey married, first, in 1836, Elizabeth Jane, daughter of Joshua L. and Jane Holt of Haverhill, Mass., where she was born in 1815. She died in Dracut July —, 1846. He married, second, his first wife's sister, Harriett Maria Holt of Haverhill Nov. —, 1850, in Nashua, N. H. She was born in Haverhill Nov. 11, 1821; and died in Lowell April 21, 1860, aged thirty-eight. He died in Lowell March 15, 1899, at the age of ninety-eight.

Mr. Hovey's children were born as follows:—

1315—I. SARAH ELIZABETH[8], born Aug. 14, 1843, in Dracut; lives, unmarried, at 4 Fifth street, Lowell.
1316—II. FREDERIC HOLT[8], born June 22, 1846; died, unmarried, in Lowell, July 3, 1871, aged twenty-five.
1317—III. MARIA LOUISE[8], born Nov. 6, 1851, in Lowell; died there Aug. 18, 1852(6?).
1318—IV. JAMES NELSON[8], born Nov. 8, 1853, at Lowell; died there Nov. 17, 1854.
1319—V. JAMES NELSON[8] (twin), born Oct. 19, 1856, in Lowell; is a wire worker; and lives, unmarried, at 4 Fifth street Lowell.
1320—VI. JOSHUA WARNER[8] (twin), born Oct. 19, 1856, in Lowell; clerk; lived in Lowell; and died there, unmarried, Nov. 5, 1908, at the age of fifty-two.

802

GEORGE HOVEY[7], born in Dracut, Mass., Nov. 26, 1810. He was a farmer, and lived in his native town, in the old tavern, at Hovey square. This house was bought when it was only a frame, with twenty-seven square rods of land, by his grandfather, Dea. Thomas Hovey (182), of Joseph Colburn of Dracut, husbandman, May 16, 1759.* Originally the house had a leanto the whole length of the back side, which was subsequently removed to make the gable even. Except for this change, the house still stands as it did when "we lived under the King." It has the same

* Middlesex Registry of Deeds, book 69, page 456.

great chimney, small windows with smaller panes of wavy, many
tinted glass. The room at the right of the front door as one entered the house was the bar and office of the tavern, and it was
said that Deacon Hovey could mix the best flip of anyone in all
the country round. Here was told the news of the Declaration of
Independence, and anxious men brought tidings of the conflicts
at Lexington and Concord. The first United States mail to the
town was delivered here. Three great buttonwood trees formerly
stood before the house.

George Hovey married Nancy Wood Dec. 30, 1841. She was
born in Vermont Feb. 9, 1820; and died in Dracut July 6, 1891.
at the age of seventy-one. Mr. Hovey died in Dracut June 27,
1905, at the age of ninety-four.

Their children were born in Dracut, as follows:—

1321—I.   JAMES SYLVESTER[8], born May 25, 1843. *See family numbered
            "1321."*

1322—II.   EDWIN[8], born Feb. 27, 1846; lives at the old homestead, 469
            Hildreth street, Dracut; is unmarried and a farmer.

1323—III.   GEORGE HOLBROOK[8], born Dec. 10, 1848; married Helen C. Var-
            num Sept. 6, 1876, in Dracut; lives in Chicago, Ill.; and is a
            clerk for Gage Bros. & Co., Michigan avenue, in Chicago.
            They have no children.

803

CYRUS HOVEY[7], born in Dracut, Mass., July 14, 1813. He
lived in Lowell, Mass., and was a silversmith. He married Dorcas
Maroe, daughter of Daniel and Dorcas Elliott in Lowell in 1852.
She was born in Rumney, N. H., May 31, 1832; and died there
in 1863. Mr. Hovey died in Lowell March 26, 1890, at the age
of seventy-six.

Their child was born in Lowell, as follows:—

1324—I.   MAROE ELIZA[8], born April 22, 1855; married Amasa, son of
            Capt. David and Caroline (Miller) Pratt Oct. 13, 1875, in
            Haverhill, N. H. He was born in Lowell July 28, 1842; and
            lives at 141 Mt. Vernon street, Lowell. Their children were
            born in Lowell as follows: 1. *Murray Hovey*[9], born April
            11, 1878; married Edith A. Nevers Jan. 30, 1899; and lives
            at 120 Mt. Vernon street, Lowell. 2. *Blanchard Earl*[9], born
            April 22, 1884; lives at home with his parents.

813

JOSEPH HOVEY[7], born in 18—; lived in Lowell, Mass.; and
died July —, 1902.

Child:—

1325—I.   ——————[8], died, without issue, before his father's death.

814

AUGUSTUS V. HOVEY[7], born in 18—. He lived in Dracut,
Mass.; and married Clarissa S. ——————. He died March 20.
1879. She survived him and lives in Lowell.

Children:—

1326—I. CLARA A.[8], born Sept. 26, 1840; married ———— Short; and
          lives at 583 Central street, Lowell.
1327—II. AUGUSTUS V.[8], born May 26, 1844; lives in Dracut, Mass.
1328—III. SARAH A.[8], born Oct. 21, 1850; married ———— Peabody; and
          lives at 23 Columbus avenue, Lowell, Mass.
1329—IV. HENRY E.[8], born April 23, 1853. *See family numbered "1329."*

816

DR. DANIEL HOVEY[7], born in Lyme, N. H., March 25, 1792.
He attended medical lectures at Dartmouth college, and studied
medicine with Doctor Hamilton. He established himself in practice in Guildhall, Vt., about 1814; and after about two years removed to Canaan, N. H., where he was one of the early settlers.
He remained there until his removal to Lyme, his native town, in
1826, and became the successor of Doctor Hamilton. He continued in practice in Lyme until the fall of 1842, when he removed
to Greenfield, Mass., where he afterward lived and practised his
profession extensively and with skill.

Doctor Hovey married Hannah Hough, daughter of Joshua
and Miriam (Johnson) Harris, of Canaan, N. H., Jan. 12, 1817;
and he died at Greenfield, Mass., May 6, 1874, at the age of
eighty-two. She was born in Canaan Feb. 13, 1793; and died in
Brooklyn, N. Y., at the residence of her daughter, Mrs. John K.
Hosmer, Aug. 15, 1877.

Their children were born as follows:—

1330—I. GEORGE HARRIS[8], born Sept. 24, 1817, in Canaan, N. H. He was
          a druggist, and lived in Greenfield, Mass. He married Nancy
          Maria, daughter of David and Sarah (Dickman) Willard
          Oct. 23, 1855, in Bernardston, Mass. She was born in
          Greenfield June 27, 1830. They had no children.
1331—II. EDWARD OLCOTT[8], born June 23, 1824, in Canaan; died July 6,
          1824.
1332—III. LUTHER SHELDON[8], born Aug. 14, 1825, in Canaan; died Dec. 14,
          1875, unmarried, at the age of fifty.
1333—IV. MARIA LUTHERA[8], born April 6, 1828, in Lyme, N. H.; married
          John Kingsbury, son of James D. and Dorothy (Leavens)
          Hosmer April 2, 1850, in Hartford, Conn. He was born in
          Willimantic, Conn., Nov. 30, 1825; and lived at 460 Vander-
          bilt avenue, Brooklyn, N. Y. They had no children.

824

REV. GEORGE LEWIS HOVEY[7], born Aug. 20, 1810, in Lyme,
N. H. When he became of age, in 1831, he joined the Congregational church in his native town. Having commenced studies at
Thetford Academy, in Vermont, and felt a strong desire to be a
clergyman, the claims of the West in 1832 being pressed upon the
Eastern churches, calling for their young people to go there as
teachers and preachers, Mr. Hovey was drawn toward the work.

and he went to Oberlin, O., to attend the new college there, in
the autumn of 1833. The colony then consisted of a half dozen
log houses and one frame building, all being located in a dense
forest, some six miles from any town. In 1837, while a member
of the theological class, he was licensed to preach, by the Loraine
County Association; and the next year was ordained as a missionary by the same body. In November, 1839, in company with
his wife and several friends, he went as a missionary to the eman-
cipated negroes on the island of Jamaica, in the West Indies.
They were not sent by any society, but depended for their support
upon the people to whom they ministered. His wife died Feb. 1,
following, and in July, 1842, he returned to the United States,
worn out by his labors in that climate, but hoping to return after
a season of rest. For the next four years, he was able to do but
little, except to present the case of his people to the churches and
individuals. In 1846, he received an appointment from the
American Missionary Association to raise six thousand dollars
for the Jamaica Mission; and in the fall of the next year he became an agent of the Foreign Evangelical society, in connection
with Doctors Baird, Kirk and others, having his office in Boston.
In May, 1850, the Foreign Evangelical Society united with the
American Protestant Society and the Christian Alliance, under
the name of the American and Foreign Christian Union; and he
remained from that time till the fall of 1871 with the society as
its agent or district secretary, for New England, though in 1851
he spent six months in Europe and twice made extensive tours
through the South in the interest of the society. In 1871, his
health having again broken down, he went to Bricksburg, N. J.,
and subsequently for a short time acted as agent for Lincoln
university. In 1878, he was financial agent of the American and
Foreign Christian Union, with special reference to raising money
for its evangelical work in France.

Mr. Hovey married, first, Sarah Gilbert, daughter of Asa
and Sarah (Gilbert) Nelson Dec. 25, 1836, in Lyme. She was
born in Lyme Sept. 12, 1812; and died at Kingston, Jamaica,
W. I., Feb. 22, 1840, at the age of twenty-seven. He married,
second, Anna Maria, daughter of Royal and Lucretia Cargill
(Carter) Sibley Feb. 6, 1849, in Providence, R. I. She was born
in Uxbridge, Mass., Nov. 3, 1822; and died in Deerfield, Mass.,
April 2, 1865, aged forty-two. He married, third, Olivia Capron,
daughter of Augustus and Sally Williams (Carter) Marcy Aug.
8, 1867, in Providence, R. I. She was born in Dudley, Mass.,
Oct. 18, 1839. They lived in Bricksburg, N. J., in 1878.

His only child was born as follows:—

1334—1. ————⁸ (daughter), born April 27, 1872; died April 27,
        1872.

827

SAMUEL HOVEY[7], born in Lyme, N. H., March 9, 1795. He married Lucy Walker, daughter of John and Sarah (Kimball) Bishop May 10, 1816, in Lyme, where she was born May 24. 1798, and died April 24, 1852. at the age of fifty-three. Mr. Hovey died in Waupaca, Wis., July 9, 1878, at the age of eighty-three.

Their children were born in Lyme, as follows:—

1335—I.   JOHN DUDLEY[8], born June 5, 1817; died June 10, 1817.
1336—II.   SAMUEL LEWIS[8], born Oct. 11, 1818; drowned July 3, 1831, aged twelve.
1337—III. JOHN BISHOP[8], born Aug. 20, 1820. See family numbered "1337."
1338—IV.   SYLVANUS SUMNER[8], born July 12, 1822. See family numbered "1338."
1339—V.   ABNER BINGHAM[8], born Nov. 12, 1825. See family numbered "1339."
1340—VI.   LUCY LOUISE[8], born May 9, 1828; died Jan. 6, 1847, aged eighteen.
1341—VII. ——[8] (son), born April 5, 1831; died April 26, 1831.
1342—VIII. ——[8] (son), born April 1, 1834; died April 1, 1834.
1343—IX.   SARAH LORINDA[8], born March 12, 1835; married Charles, son of James and Fanny (Blunt) Johnson May 10, 1853. in Elba, Wis. He was born in Bulwick, Northamptonshire, England, in 1802; and lived in Waupaca, Wis. Children: 1. Silas Samuel[9], born Oct. 18, 1854. 2. Lucy Ann[9], born April 10, 1856; married Taylor, son of Stephen and Margaret (House) Looker Aug. 6, 1876, in Waupaca. He was born near Utica, N. Y., Jan. 26, 1850. They had one child.
1344—X.   RHODA LUCINDA[8], born April 3, 1841: married John Frederic, son of John and Erimunda (Kuen) Wiedman, Jan. 26, 1862, in Elba, Wis. He was born in Posen (near Eain), Prussia, June 21, 1835. He was a farmer, and lived in Waupaca. Children: 1. Hattie Amelia[9], born March 21, 1863. 2. Frederic Albert[9], born Oct. 31, 1872. 3. Mary Alice[9], born Dec. 25, 1875.

828

DUDLEY HOVEY[7], born in Lyme, N. H., Jan. 31, 1797. He was a farmer, and lived in Lyme, N. H., Newbury and Bradford, Vt., and Haverhill, N. H. He married Rubie, daughter of Pelatiah and Letitia (Knapp) Allen April 17, 1820, in Lyme, where she was born Jan. 25, 1799. Mr. Hovey died in Haverhill Oct. 28, 1865, at the age of sixty-eight. She survived him, and died in Haverhill Dec. 15, 1869.

Their children were born as follows:—

1345—I.   SIMEON ALLEN[8], born Jan. 2, 1821, in Lyme. See family numbered "1345."
1346—II. EBER DAVIS[8], born Nov. 23, 1822, in Lyme. See family numbered "1346."

1347—III.   ALVAN SEABURY[8], born June 5, 1824, in Lyme. When he be-
             came of age, in 1845, he engaged in successful land spec-
             ulation in Maine. Having closed up his affairs there, he
             started for home, with a considerable aamount of money,
             drafts, etc., but was never heard from.

1348—IV.   JOSEPH MILTON[8], born July 3, 1826, in Lyme. *See family num-
             bered "1348."*

1349—V.   MARY LUCINDA[8], born May 29, 1828, in Lyme; married Hiram
             Frederic, son of Joseph and Susan (Mitchell) Herbert
             Sept. 9, 1857, in East Abington, Mass. He was born in
             Haverhill, N. H., Nov. 4, 1823; and died in Waco, Texas,
             June 25, 1869, aged forty-five. He was a daguerrean artist.
             She survived him, and lived in Haverhill, N. H., in 1877.
             They had no children.

1350—VI.   JOHN NELSON[8], born June 5, 1830, in Newbury, Vt. He was
             a farmer, residing in Otterville, Iowa, in 1878. He married
             Sophia Sarepta, daughter of John and Betsey (Erwin)
             Johnson Nov. 30, 1856, in Haverhill, N. H., where she was
             born Jan. 13, 1832. They had no children.

1351—VII.   SAMUEL LEWIS[8], born Sept. 21, 1831, in Newbury. *See family
             numbered "1351."*

1352—VIII.   GEORGE IDE[8], born Feb. 21, 1834, in Bradford, Vt.; died April
             19, 1834.

1353—IX.   ISABELLA BARRON[8], born Aug. 1, 1836, in Bradford; married
             Nathan Hammond, son of David and Sally T. (Willard)
             Batchelder Dec. 21, 1856, in Bradford. He was born in
             Bridgewater, N. H., April 20, 1823; was a carriage builder;
             and lived in Haverhill, N. H., in 1878. Children: 1. *Fred-
             eric Perkins[9]*, born Dec. 17, 1864. 2. *Mary Allen[9]*, born
             Sept. 13, 1869; died Oct. 26, 1869.

1354—X.   WILLIAM BARRON[8], born July 4, 1844, in Bradford. *See family
             numbered "1354."*

838

RUFUS BILLINGS HOVEY[7], born in Lyme, N. H., Nov. 17,
1794. He married Polly, daughter of Timothy and Eunice
(Houghton) Kendall Jan. 14, 1819, in Williamstown, Vt., where
she was born July 7, 1797. He died in Albany, Vt., Jan. 9, 1844,
at the age of forty-nine. She survived him, and died in Albany,
his widow, Sept. 20, 1885, at the age of eighty-eight. He was
widely known and eminently esteemed for his devotion to every
good work and conscientious performance of duty.

Their children were born as follows:—

1355—I.   GEORGE[8], born Nov. 6, 1819, in Brookfield, Vt. *See family
             numbered "1355."*

1356—II.   ———[8] (son), born Aug. 2, 1821; died Aug. 2, 1821.

1357—III.   ———[8] (daughter), born July 23, 1822; died July 23, 1822.

1358—IV.   ELIAS SEABURY[8], born Oct. 4, 1823, in Brookfield. *See family
             numbered "1358."*

1359—V.   JOHN BILLINGS[8], born Nov. 27, 1825, in Brookfield. *See family
             numbered "1359."*

1360—VI.   ALVIN[8], born Aug. 7, 1827, in Albany, Vt. *See family num-
             bered "1360."*

1361—VII.   ———[8] (son), born July 9, 1829; died July 9, 1829.

1362—VIII. LEWIS[8], born Jan. 3, 1831, in Albany. *See family numbered "1362."*

1363—IX. ELIJAH ADAMS[8], born Feb. 13, 1833, in Albany. *See family numbered "1363."*

1364—X. TIMOTHY KENDALL[8], born Oct. 20, 1835, in Albany. *See family numbered "1364."*

1365—XI. MARY ANN[8], born Aug. 30, 1837, in Albany; married Madison, son of Charles and Anna (Metcalf) Cowles Dec. 27, 1858, in Albany. He was born in Irasburgh, Vt., April 7, 1833; and was a farmer and carpenter, living in Albany, where he died Feb. 9, 1894, aged sixty. She survives him, and lives in Albany. Their children were born in Albany, as follows: 1. ————[9] (daughter), born Dec. 30, 1862; died Dec. 30, 1862. 2. *Almira Howard*[9], born March 21, 1864; married George Glines April 9, 1896; and lives in Portland, Ore. 3. ————[9] (son), born Dec. 2, 1865; died Dec. 2, 1865. 4. *Archie Billings*[9], born Jan. 5, 1870; died Sept. 11, 1870. 5. *Roscoe Madison*[9], born March 4, 1871; married Bertha Aiken June 5, 1895; merchant; lives in Albany. 6. *Clarence Porter*[9], born Aug. 30, 1875; married Laura Golden June 21, 1905; lawyer; and lives in Burlington, Vt. 7. *Herbert Hayes*[9], born Aug. 10, 1877; married Lillian Hill Feb. 26, 1901; merchant; lives in Mansfield, Mass.

1366—XII. EMILY DARLING[8], born July 4, 1839, in Albany; married Jesse Rogers, son of Nathan and Mary Jane (Rogers) Beede Jan. 10, 1871, in Independence, Iowa. He was born in Albany Aug. 28, 1837; served as a private in company F, First Vermont heavy artillery in the Civil war, 1862-1865; was a farmer, and lived in Vermillion, S. D. He died in Gayville, S. D., Dec. 29, 1889, aged fifty-two. She lives at Fort Totten, N. Y. Their child was born in Vermillion, as follows: 1. *Adelaide Electa*[9], born Sept. 1, 1875; married Capt. Elmer J. Wallace July 29, 1897. He is an instructor in coast defence gunnery in the United States navy. They live in Honolulu, Hawaii.

1367—XIII. SARAH LIVINGSTON[8], born Jan. 14, 1842, in Albany; married Jesse Rogers Beede, husband of her sister Emily, as his first wife, Aug. 10, 1862. She died in Vermillion Sept. 8, 1870, at the age of twenty-eight. Their child was born in Albany, as follows: 1. *William Hovey*[9], born July 30, 1867; lumber dealer; lives in Vermillion; married Rosa E. Hyde Oct. 28, 1890.

840

ORANGE HOVEY[7], born in Brookfield, Vt., Feb. 5, 1797. He was a farmer, and lived in Craftsbury, Vt. He married, first, Clarissa, daughter of Charles and Ann (Perry) Williams Feb. 5, 1818, in Chelsea, Vt., where she was born April 15, 1799. She died in Albany, Vt., June 4, 1855, at the age of fifty-six. He married, second, Mrs. Louisa Maria, widow of Oliver Hidden, and daughter of Dexter and Mary (Lines) Wood Dec. 12, 1855, in Craftsbury, where she was born Jan. 20, 1800, and where she dropped dead a few years after her marriage to Mr. Hovey. Mr. Hovey died at Craftsbury about 1880.

Mr. Hovey's children were born as follows:—

1368—I. ORANGE⁶, born Oct. 9, 1818, in Brookfield, Vt. *See family numbered "1368."*

1369—II. CLARISSA ANN⁶, born Sept. 8, 1820, in Brookfield; married Jonathan Hartwell, son of Jonathan and Polly (McClure) Wheeler Feb. 12, 1851, in Albany, Vt. He was born in Amherst, N. H., Nov. 5, 1821; was a sash and blind manufacturer; and lived in Oshkosh, Wis. Children: 1. *George Hartwell⁷*, born March 23, 1852, in Nashua, N. H.; was an accountant, residing in Milwaukee, Wis., unmarried, in 1878. 2. *Frank Hovey⁷*, born March 20, 1859, in Merrimac, N. H.; was an accountant, residing in Milwaukee, in 1878.

1370—III. ABIEL⁶, born Jan. 23, 1822, in Brookfield; died in Northfield, Vt., Sept. 8, 1826, aged four years.

1371—IV. OLIVER PERRY⁶, born July 22, 1825, in Northfield, Vt. *See family numbered "1371."*

1372—V. LUCINDA⁶, born Sept. 4, 1828, in Northfield; married Josiah D., son of Amos and Sally (Smith) Hood Aug. 30, 1846, in Albany, Vt. He was born in Chelsea, Vt., June 9, 1817; and died there Jan. 6, 1878, at the age of sixty. She survived him, and died in Vermont many years ago. Children: 1. *Oliver Perry⁷*, born March 11, 1849, in Albany; married Abbie Louisa Tucker Feb. 19, 1873, in Chelsea. 2. *Clara Amanda⁷*, born Jan. 3, 1851, in Albany; died in Chelsea June 4, 1863. 3. *Alice Mary⁷*, born June 11, 1858, in Chelsea; and died there May 29, 1863. 4. *Emma Minnie⁷*, born Oct. 8, 1867, in Washington, Vt.

1373—VI. WILLIAM PALMER⁶, born Oct. 8, 1831, in Northfield; lived in Downieville, Cal., in 1871; and died many years ago.

1374—VII. AMANDA MALVINA⁶, born Jan. 10, 1837, in Northfield; married George Stephen, son of Stephen and Dorothy (Smith) Fogg March 3, 1862, in Albany. He was born in Chelsea, Vt., June 30, 1838. She died in Albany Aug. 10, 1875, at the age of thirty-eight. He lived in North Tunbridge, Vt., in 1878. Child: 1. ————⁷ (daughter), born Aug. 31, 1872; died Aug. 31, 1872.

842

SILAS HOVEY⁵, born in Brookfield, Vt., March 5, 1801. He was a farmer, and lived in Albany, Vt. He married Polly, daughter of Solomon and Susan (Bosworth) Annis April —, 1823, in Chelsea, Vt., where she was born March 8, 1801. She died in Albany Aug. 21, 1859, at the age of fifty-eight; and he died there July 29, 1868, at the age of sixty-seven.

Their children were born as follows:—

1375—I. WILLIAM⁶, born May 23, 1824, in Brookfield, Vt. *See family numbered "1375."*

1376—II. MARY⁶, born July 26, 1826, in Albany; died March 9, 1832, aged five.

1377—III. ABIEL BURNHAM⁶, born Feb. 9, 1829, in Albany. *See family numbered "1377."*

1378—IV. LAURA⁶, born Feb. 21, 1831, in Albany; died April 14, 1831.

1379—V. SILAS⁶, born Feb. 2, 1833, in Albany; died Aug. 15, 1841, aged eight.

1380—VI.   MARY[8], born July 17, 1835, in Albany; died Aug. 16, 1841, aged six.

1381—VII.   ZIBA[8], born May 26, 1838, in Albany; died July 13, 1844, aged six.

1382—VIII. LAURETTA P.[8], born Nov. 14, 1840, in Albany; married Henry Lathrop, son of Austin and Maria (Harrington) Kendall Aug. 27, 1859, in Albany. He was born in Cavendish, Vt., Sept. 17, 1836; was a jeweller; and lived in Tiffin, O., in 1878. Children: 1. *Willie*[9], born Oct. 24, 1861, in Albany; died March 1, 1864. 2. *George Woodward*[9], born Dec. 21, 1865, in Albany; died March 29, 1866. 3. *Ella May*[9], born May 7, 1871, in Tiffin.

846

SIMEON SKINNER HOVEY[7], born in Brookfield, Vt., Nov. 13, 1809. He was a merchant, and lived in Albany, Vt. He was a member of the state legislature in 1841. He married, first, Emeline, daughter of Eli and Sally (Stanley) Chamberlain Nov. 26, 1833, in Albany, where she was born Nov. 10, 1812. She died there, without children, July 4, 1834, at the age of twenty-one. He married, second, Ann Bliss, daughter of Col. Gilbert and Esther Burgess (Hilliard) Gross Nov. 28, 1835, in Brownington, Vt., where she was born April 3, 1818. Mr. Hovey died in Albany Feb. 15, 1842, at the age of thirty-two. He was much esteemed for his amiability. His wife Ann survived him, and died in Newbury, Vt., March 17, 1865, at the age of forty-six.

Mr. Hovey's children were born as follows:—

1383—I.   HENRY LA FAYETTE[8], born Jan. 25, 1838; died Feb. 25, 1841, aged three years.

1384—II.   HELEN MAR[8], born Oct. 29, 1840; married William, son of Joseph D. and Charlotte (Mitchell) Jondro July 7, 1862, in Derby Line, Vt., where he was born July 18, 1837. They lived in Derby Line, without children, in 1878.

1385—III.   HARRIET ALMIRA[8], born May 17, 1842; married Joseph Addison, son of Horatio Nelson and Maria Salome (Brown) Carter May 12, 1864, in Chicopee, Mass. He was born in Plymouth, Vt., Sept. 12, 1835; and lived in Chicopee in 1878. She died there May 16, 1878, at the age of thirty-six. Their children were born in Chicopee, as follows: 1. *Mary Ella*[9], born March 10, 1866. 2. *Belle*[9], born Jan. 29, 1868. 3. *Addison Hovey*[9], born March 13, 1869; died Sept. 8, 1869. 4. *Edith Hovey*[9], born Aug. 13, 1870. 5. *Helen Gertrude*[9], born Feb. 25, 1872. 6. *Nelson Brown*[9], born June 1, 1876. 7. *George William*[9], born April 26, 1878.

849

REV. HORACE NELSON HOVEY[7], born in Brookfield, Vt., Jan. 28, 1815. He lived in Albany and Lowell, Vt., and was a Baptist clergyman of force and talent. He was a farmer in Albany until 1843, when he removed from his farm to the village of Albany, where he had begun to preach the preceding year, and fully en-

tered upon his ministerial work. He had the charge of the
church until the autumn of 1866. During that time he also had
the pastoral charge of the church in Newport for eight years, and
of the church in Irasburgh for three years, preaching at those
places one-half of the time and at Albany the other half. In July,
1876, he removed to Lowell, Vt., and had charge of the small
Baptist church there.

Mr. Hovey married, first, Fanny Caroline, daughter of John
and Deborah (Haines) Kellum May 26, 1836, in Irasburgh, Vt.,
where she was born Oct. 29, 1814. She died in Lowell Feb. 12,
1873, at the age of fifty-eight, and her remains lie in the cemetery at West Albany, Vt. He married, second, Myrtilla Eglan-
tine, daughter of Newton and Submit (Perkins) Hitchcock Dec.
23, 1873, in Bethel, Vt. She was born in Westfield, Vt., Sept. 29,
1837. Mr. Hovey died in Lowell May —, 1882, at the age of
sixty-seven.

Mr. Hovey's children were born in Albany, as follows :—

1386—I.   CHARLES KELLUM[6], born July 14, 1837. He was a farmer in
            Lowell, and unmarried, in 1879.
1387—II.   ARTHUR JUDSON[6], born April 3, 1842. *See family numbered*
            "1387."
1388—III.   LAURA ELIZABETH[6], born March 12, 1847; graduated at New-
            hampton Institute, Fairfax, Vt.; lives at 86 Centre street,
            Dorchester, Mass., unmarried, having been a teacher in the
            Dorchester high school since 1875.
1389—IV.   ANNIE CATHERINE (twin), born Aug. 6, 1852; lived at Lowell,
            Vt., in 1878, and now at 86 Centre street, Dorchester, Mass.
1390—V.   FANNIE CAROLINE[6] (twin), born Aug. 6, 1852; married Dr.
            Anson Joseph, son of Warden and Eliza Elizabeth (Moffet)
            Golden May 5, 1874, in Stoneham, Mass. He was born in
            Sutton, P. Q., May 15, 1848; is a physician and surgeon;
            and lived at Maiden Rock, Wis., in 1878, and now at 3019
            Lyndale avenue, Minneapolis, Minn. Their children were
            born as follows: 1. *Verna Jennie[6]*, born April 30, 1876, in
            River Falls, Wis. 2. *Laura Elizabeth[6]*, born Nov. 3, 1878,
            in Maiden Rock, Wis.
1391—VI.   ALBERT SILAS[6], born Sept. 28, 1856. *See family numbered*
            "1391."

852

SAMUEL WILLIS HOVEY[5], born in Brookfield, Vt., Sept. 25,
1801. He was a farmer, and lived in Merrimack, Wis. He mar-
ried Betsey, daughter of Timothy and Eunice (Houghton)
Kendall Dec. 5, 1822, in Williamstown, Vt. She was born in
Alstead, N. H., July 2, 1795; and died in Merrimack, Wis.,
April 24, 1865, at the age of sixty-nine. He died in Merrimack
March 17, 1866, at the age of sixty-four.

Their children were born as follows :—

1392—I.   SAMUEL KENDALL[6], born Nov. 30, 1823, in Brookfield, Vt. *See*
            family numbered "1392."

1393—II.   EUNICE PERMELIA[8], born April 20, 1832, in Albany, Vt.; married Isaac, son of Matthew and Sarah (Willis) Emerson Feb. 5, 1854, in Merrimack, Wis. He was born in Lincolnshire, England, Dec. 7, 1827; was a farmer; and lived in Merrimack, Wis., and Westside, Minn., where he was living in 1878. Their children were born in Merrimack, as follows: 1. *Matthew James[9]*, born May 25, 1854. 2. *Betsey Lovina[9]*, born Nov. 26, 1860; married Dr. Henry Paine, son of Dr. John Bunce April 5, 1877, in Westside, Minn. He was born in Janesville, Wis., May 22, 1847; and lived in Luverne, Minn., in 1878. 3. *Sarah Amelia[9]*, born Sept. 10, 1864.

854

ALVAN HOVEY[7], born in Brookfield, Vt., Dec. 4, 1804. He was a thrifty farmer, and lived in East Brookfield. He married Mary Dodge, daughter of Ebenezer and Abigail (Dodge) Trask in Hartland, Vt., Feb. 26, 1827. She was born in Beverly, Mass., June 10, 1805. Mr. Hovey was a sturdy Democrat.

Their children were born in Brookfield, as follows :—

1394—I.   ABIGAIL LIBBY[8], born May 18, 1828; died May 29, 1828.
1395—II.   MARY ANN NANCY[8], born June 15, 1829; married Urban Lathrop, son of Nathan and Lydia (Lathrop) Bixby April 22, 1849, in East Brookfield. He was born in Chelsea, Vt., Dec. 18, 1824; was a farmer, and lived in East Brookfield in 1878. Their children were born in East Brookfield, as follows: 1. *Ida Alelia[9]*, born June 23, 1851; married Everett Clifton, son of Joseph and Sarah Davison (Hibbard) Newell March 14, 1869, in Randolph, Vt. He was born in Oxford, Vt., May 13, 1847; was a farmer, and lived in Chelsea, Vt. They had several children. 2. *Mary Eva[9]*, born June 20, 1853. 3. *Alvan Hovey[9]*, born Jan. 28, 1859. 4. *Charles Hunter[9]*, born Aug. 4, 1862. 5. *Urban Willis[9]*, born Dec. 26, 1865.
1396—III. EBENEZER TRASK[8], born May 24, 1832; married Emily, daughter of Jesse W. and Julia (Libby) Downing Dec. 6, 1855, in Williamstown, Vt. She was born in Chelsea, Vt., Jan. 30, 1839. He died in East Brookfield, Vt., Sept. 23, 1862, at the age of thirty. They had no children.
1397—IV.   EMELINE[8], born Aug. 27, 1834; married Hiram Wells, son of Hiram and Asenath (Kendall) Chafey Jan. 1, 1855, in East Brookfield. He was born in Brookfield Oct. 22, 1830; and she died there Aug. 13, 1856, at the age of twenty-one. They had one child: 1. *Flora Emeline[9]*, born Dec. 5, 1855; died Aug. 20, 1896.

857

JAMES HARVEY HOVEY[7], born in Brookfield, Vt., July 28, 1811. He married Rachel, daughter of Rufus and Polly (Wills) Downing Dec. 5, 1832, in Brookfield. She was born in Chelsea, Vt., May 2, 1811. He died in Brookfield Jan. 3, 1857, at the age of forty-five. She survived him, and lived in Hartford, Vt., in 1878.

Their children were born as follows:—

1398—I.   LEWIS WILLIAM⁸, born June 6, 1835. *See family numbered* "*1398.*"

1399—II. CORDELIA⁸, born Oct. 10, 1840; died April 20, 1842, aged one year.

1400—III. CHARLES WILBER⁸, born May 7, 1843; died, while a soldier in the army, in the winter of 1863, unmarried.

858

RUFUS CLEVELAND HOVEY⁷, born in Brookfield, Vt., Oct. 15, 1816. He was a farmer, and lived in East Brookfield. He married Caroline Mary, daughter of Hyde and Caroline (Brooks) Clark March 6, 1844, in Hartford, Vt., where she was born May 24, 1810. He died in East Brookfield July 12, 1872, at the age of fifty-five. She survived him, and was living at East Brookfield in 1878.

Their children were born as follows:—

1401—I.   SARAH EMILY⁸, born Aug. 6, 1845, in Brookfield; died March 11, 1863, at the age of seventeen.

1402—II. CAROLINE ELLA⁸, born Sept. 7, 1849, in Chelsea, Vt.; died March 19, 1863, at the age of thirteen.

867

CHARLES HOVEY⁷, born in Middlebury, Vt., April 19, 1815. He married Lucinda, daughter of Christopher and Sarah (Dunn) Nesler Oct. 9, 1836, in Mount Vernon. Ind., where she was born July 25, 1822. He was killed by a cannon in Mount Vernon Jan. 9, 1862, in his forty-seventh year. She survived him, and was living in Mount Vernon in 1878.

Their children were born in Mount Vernon, as follows:—

1403—I.   ALVINA⁸, born Sept. 26, 1837; died April 5, 1838.

1404—II. LIZZIE⁸, born May 28, 1839; married Isaac, son of John and America (Montgomery) Baker in 1859, in Black, Ind. He was born in Mount Vernon Jan. 8, 1838. Their children were born as follows: 1. *Charles⁹*, born June 10, 1860; died July 5, 1860. 2. *Edward⁹*, born Dec. 21, 1861; died Oct. 9, 1862. 3. *Frank⁹*, born March 28, 1863. 4. *Nellie⁹*, born April 18, 1865. 5. *Jesse⁹*, born June 17, 1867. 6. *Isa⁹*, born Feb. 8, 1869; died Oct. 19, 1869.

1405—III. HENRY⁸, born April 20, 1841; died June 4, 1841.

1406—IV. JEROME⁸, born June 1, 1842; died June 19, 1858, at the age of sixteen.

1407—V.   FANNIE⁸, born Aug. 1, 1845; married Robert Fulton, son of James and Mary (Hintchell) Dunn March 27, 1865, in Mount Vernon, where she died July 9, 1872, at the age of twenty-six. He was a pilot. Children: 1. *Lulie⁹*, born Jan. 1, 1866; died Sept. 18, 1869. 2. *Mary⁹*, born Nov. 28, 1868. 3. *Robert⁹*, born April 4, 1869; died April 20, 1870, aged one year.

1408—VI. CHARLES⁸, born Dec. 29, 1847. *See family numbered "1408."*

1409—VII. HELEN⁶, born March 4, 1850; married Thomas Jefferson, son
           of Samuel and Lucilla (Herald) Gardom Oct. 29, 1868, in
           Mount Vernon. He was born in Illinois April 27, 1847; and
           is a blacksmith by occupation. She died at Mount Vernon
           July 12, 1873, at the age of twenty-three. Their children
           were born as follows: 1. *Samuel⁶*, born March 4, 1869;
           died Aug. 1, 1873. 2. *Eva⁶*, born April 7, 1871. 3. *Helen⁶*,
           born Dec. 21, 1872; died Jan. —, 1874, aged one year.
1410—VIII. ALVIN⁶, born Sept. 5, 1852; died July 11, 1873, at the age of
           twenty.
1411—IX.   GRACE⁶, born July 4, 1854; married William Craw Nov. 19,
           1870, at Mount Vernon. He died in Morley, Mo., March
           7, 1871; and she died in Mount Vernon July 22, 1873, at
           the age of nineteen.
1412—X.   EVA⁶, born June 15, 1856; died July 22, 1873, aged seventeen.
1413—XI.   MARY⁶, born March 26, 1858; died Jan. 5, 1866, at the age
           of seven.
1414—XII. JOSEPHINE⁶, born Aug. 26, 1859.
1415—XIII. LUCY⁶, born July 2, 1862; died Sept. 23, 1863, aged one
           year.

869

Gov. ALVIN PETERSON HOVEY⁵, born in Mount Vernon, Ind.,
Sept. 6, 1821. He always lived in his native town; and was
a distinguished citizen. He was a delegate to the convention
which framed the new constitution of the state of Indiana, in
1850; judge of the circuit court for the judicial circuit comprising
Posey and ten other counties in the southwestern part of the state,
from May, 1851, to May, 1854; and judge of the supreme court of
Indiana from May, 1854, to 1855. He next served as United
States district attorney for the district of Indiana, from 1856 to
1858, when President Buchanan removed him because he supported Stephen A. Douglas for president.

When the Civil war broke out, Mr. Hovey became colonel of
the Twenty-fourth Indiana regiment of volunteers; and was
promoted to brigadier-general of volunteers April 13, 1862, and
afterwards, July 9, 1864, to brevet major-general of United
States volunteers "for distinguished and meritorious service during the present war." He commanded at the celebrated battle
of Champion Hill, which was the key engagement of the Vicksburg campaign, opening the way to the capture of Vicksburg;
and General Grant gave him great credit for the conduct of the
battle. In May, 1864, he was brigadier-general in command of
the First Division Twenty-third Army Corps, in Tennessee, and
it was in that position that he won the promotion to brevet
major-general.

General Hovey was appointed Envoy Extraordinary and
Minister Plenipotentiary of the United States to the government
of Peru, South America, Aug. 12, 1865, and resigned in 1870.
Afterwards, he became a member of congress, which position he

resigned to become governor of Indiana, dying in the office of governor Nov. 23, 1891, at the age of seventy.

Governor Hovey married, first, Mary Ann, daughter of Hon. Enoch Randolph and Esther (Lowry) James Nov. 24, 1844, in Mount Vernon. She was born in Baton Rouge, La., Feb. 22, 1825; and died in Mount Vernon Nov. 16, 1863, at the age of thirty-eight. He married, second, Rosa Alice, widow of Maj. William F. Carey of Cleveland, O., and daughter of Hon. Caleb Blood Smith of Indiana, in Grace church, New York. She was a native of Indiana; and died in New York City soon after their marriage.

Governor Hovey's children were born at Mount Vernon, as follows:—

1416—I.   ESTHER[8], born Jan. 8, 1846; she finished her education at Madam Hoffman's school, in New York City; married Maj. Gustavus Varsa, son of Samuel Garber and Sally Ann (Winston) Menzies Nov. 11, 1869, in New York City. He was born in Boone county, Ky., Dec. 25, 1844, and at the time of his marriage was lieutenant-commander in the United States navy. In 1878, he was practising law with his father-in-law under the style of Hovey & Menzies. Their children were born as follows: 1. ————[9] (daughter), born Aug. 26, 1870; died Aug. 26, 1870. 2. *Mary*[9], born Oct. 5, 1872. 3. *Juliette*[9], born April 22, 1874. 4. *Winston*[9], born Nov. 22, 1875.

1417—II.   ENOCH JAMES[8], born Feb. 7, 1848; died Aug. 4, 1854, at the age of six years.

1418—III. CHARLES JAMES[8], born Jan. 8, 1850. *See family numbered "1418."*

1419—IV.   MARY[8], born Jan. 13, 1854; died March 30, 1855, aged one year.

1420—V.   MARY ANN[8], born April 1, 1857; died April 7, 1858.

880

SAMUEL BENJAMIN HOVEY[7], born in Milton, Vt., Sept. 21, 1818. He was a farmer, and lived in Fremont, Mich. He married Dorinda, daughter of Milton and Fanny (Evans) Pierce Oct. 28, 1843, in Eden, O. She was born in Sunbury, O., April 15, 1827.

Their children were born in Delaware county, O., as follows:—

1421—I.   VICTOR[8], born April 13, 1845; died Jan. 8, 1850, aged four years.

1422—II.   TILDEN[8], born Oct. 30, 1846; died Sept. 10, 1848, aged one year.

1423—III. FANNY ELIZABETH[8], born March 20, 1848; died Jan. 10, 1850.

1424—IV.   JONAS[8], born Jan. 18, 1850; died July 8, 1851, aged one year.

1425—V.   JUDSON WATERMAN[8], born Oct. 27, 1852. *See family numbered "1425."*

1426—VI.   ELLA[8], born April 13, 1855.

1427—VII. IDA[8], born May 20, 1858; married Ralph Immer, son of Rodney and Delilah (Reynolds) Smith Dec. 24, 1877, in Fremont, Mich. He was born in Berlin, O., Sept. 4, 1856; was a farmer; and lived in Alum Creek, Delaware county, O., in 1878.

881

JOHN KEAN HOVEY[7], born in Milton, Vt., March 3, 1821. He was a farmer, and lived in Townville, Pa., in 1878. He married Mary Elvira, daughter of William and Sarah (Hamilton) Bunce March 23, 1843, in Brighton, O. She was born in Hanover, N. Y., July 10, 1821.

Their children were born as follows:—

1428—I.   EDWIN HAMILTON[8], born June 26, 1844, in Brighton, O. *See family numbered "1428."*

1429—II.   LAURA JANE[8], born Oct. 2, 1846, in Freedonia, Wis.; died in Camden, O., Dec. 22, 1852, aged six years.

1430—III.   SARAH ELIZABETH[8], born Jan. 29, 1849, in Freedonia.

1431—IV.   ELLEN JANETTE[8], born July 4, 1851, in Freedonia; married Enos Ames, son of Daniel and Roby Ann (Ames) Scott Sept. 1, 1872, in Randolph, Pa. He was born in Rockdale, Pa., Feb. 11, 1849; and was a farmer. Children: 1. *Jennie May*[9], born July 4, 1873; died Nov. 15, 1878. 2. *Carrie Elizabeth*[9], born June 20, 1876.

1432—V.   HARRIET EMELIA[8], born May 22, 1853, in Richard, Pa.; died in Randolph, Pa., April 7, 1857, aged three years.

882

ALVAN SEABURY HOVEY[7], born in Milton, Vt., March 31, 1823. He was a farmer, and lived in Holland, O., in 1878. He married Sarah Ann, daughter of Newell and Esther L. (Shattuck) Cook Oct. 28, 1849, in Birmingham, O. She was born in Scriba, N. Y., Jan. 13, 1831.

Their children were born in Lorain county, O., as follows:—

1433—?.   LUELLA CLARETTE[8], born June 22, 1852; married William Washington, son of George Points and Mary Ann Thomas Nov. 15, 1876, in Holland, O. He was born in Centerville, N. Y., April 27, 1853; was a farmer; and lived in Farmersville, N. Y., in 1878. Child: 1. *Clarence Hovey*[9], born July 8, 1878.

1434—II.   GEORGE ELBERT[8], born Nov. 24, 1855. *See family numbered "1434."*

883

PHILEMON HENRY HOVEY[7], born in Milton, Vt., March 17, 1826. He was a farmer, and lived in Union City, Tenn., in 1878. He married Rachel Ruthea, daughter of Ezekiel and Martha (Beck) Indman Oct. 12, 1854, in Paris, Tenn. She was born in Pleasant Garden, Burke county, N. C., May 8, 1826.

Their children were born as follows:—

1435—I.   SARAH PAULINE[8], born Aug. 19, 1855, in Henry county, Tenn.

1436—II.   JOSEPH NEWTON[8], born Jan. 20, 1858, in Henry county, Tenn.

1437—III.   MARTHA ANN EUDORA[8], born Feb. 4, 1860, in Henry county, Tenn.

1438—IV.   HENRY HORACE[8], born Nov. 12, 1861, in Metropolis City, Ill.

1439—V.   JOHN WILLIAM[8], born Dec. 14, 1863, in Metropolis City.

1440—VI.   MARY ELIZABETH[8], born July 20, 1865, in Camden, O.

1441—VII.   JAMES ALVIN[8], born Aug. 6, 1871, in Metropolis City.

884

DANIEL HILL HOVEY[7], born in Milton Vt., March 23, 1828. He was a farmer, and lived in McPherson, Kas., in 1878. He married Jane, daughter of Cornelius and Eliza (Walker) Ellis Nov. 8, 1851, in Sandusky O. She was born in Florence, O., Sept. 11, 1830.

Their children were born as follows:—

1442—I.   EDGAR WILLIS[8], born March 8, 1853, in Eden, O.
1443—II.   MARY ELIZABETH[8], born Feb. 8, 1856, in Wakeman, O.; married Simon Peter, son of Isaac D. and Keturah (Rhoadermel) Fisher Feb. 20, 1875, in Harper, Kas. He was born in Northumberland county, Pa., Sept. 9, 1848; is a farmer; and lived in Lindsburg, Kas., in 1878. Their children were born as follows: 1. *Maud Alice*[9], born Sept. 7, 1876. 2. *Lottie*[9], born April 18, 1878.
1444—III.   JAMES ANDREW[8], born April 27, 1860, in Ottumwa, Kas.
1445—IV.   JOHN CORNELIUS[8], born April 1, 1862, in Ottumwa.
1446—V.   IDA MAY[8], born Jan. 25, 1866, in Ottumwa.
1447—VI.   EVA ELLEN[8], born Feb. 17, 1868, in Ottumwa.

886

JAMES MONROE PROUTY HOVEY[7], born in Milton, Vt., Oct. 29, 1833. He married Nancy Melissa, daughter of Newell and Esther Lucinda (Shattuck) Cook June 15, 1856, in Clarksfield, O. She was born in Scriba, N. Y., March 22, 1834. He died in Clarksfield June 14, 1877, at the age of forty-three; and she was living there in 1879.

Their children were born as follows:—

1448—I.   WILBERT NEWELL[8], born Jan. 30, 1860.
1449—II.   ESTHER ELIZABETH[8], born Dec. 19, 1870.

892

HARDEN HOVEY[7], born in Woodstock, O., Jan. 15, 1829. He married Eliza Jane Houch of Shepherdstown, Jefferson county, West Virginia, in Texas, Champaign county, O. They died in Atchison, Kansas.

Their children were born as follows:—

1450—I.   EDWIN MORTIMER[8], married Emma Ridge.
1451—II.   ZETTA[8], married Joseph McCord.
1452—III.   IDA MAY[8], died Feb. 4, 1863.
1453—IV.   CLARA[8], married ———— Crandell.

894

WILLIAM WIRT HOVEY[7], born Nov. 8, 1835, in Champaign county, O. He was employed by a railroad company. He married Isadella Gibens, in Urbana, June 26, 1860, and he died in Grand Rapids, Mich., Dec. 20, 1901, at the age of sixty-six.

Their children were born as follows:—

1454—I.   MARY ELIZABETH[8], born Dec. 13, 1862; married Edward Butler.
1455—II.   EDWARD HARNSON[8], born Sept. 15, 1864.

895

LEWIS COOK HOVEY[7], born in Urbana, Champaign county, O., Dec. 2, 1837. He was a contractor; and married, first, Sarah Ryan, a native of Ireland, who died in Urbana in 1871. He married, second, Louise Margaret Cox, who was a native of Champaign county.

His children were all by the first marriage, and were born as follows:—

1456—I.   ALBERTINE SARAH[8], born Aug. 14, 1864; married George Frederick Harpster.

1457—II.   MARGARET INAN[8], born Aug. 24, 1867; married John Harnson Olmes Dec. 22, 1886, in Pueblo, Col., where they live at 2028 Greenwood street. Their children were born in Pueblo, as follows: 1. *Albertine Meta*[9], born March 4, 1888. 2. *Ruth Verginia*[9], born Sept. 5. 1895.

1458—III.   JOHN EMERSON[8], born Oct. 14, 1870.

899

SOLON GILBERT HOVEY[7], born in Urbana, Champaign county, O., Feb. 16, 1851. He is a grocer; and married Alma Rachel Tracy.

Their children were born as follows:—

1459—I.   CLARENCE L.[8], born Aug. 24, 1877.

1460—II.   HARRIS ALTON[8], born July 20, 1887.

900

CHARLES HOVEY[7], born in Windham, Conn., Nov. 22, 1822. He removed from Scotland (a part of Windham), Conn., to New York City about 1840, worked diligently, and finally established a good and remunerative business as refolder and repacker of goods at 39 West Broadway. Owing to a combination of circumstances, he lost his business and his prosperity, and became very poor.

Mr. Hovey married Anna L. Kerr July 2, 1859, in New York City, where she was born May 4, 1834. He died there April 10, 1877, at the age of fifty-four; and she died there Dec. —, 1897, at the age of sixty-three.

Their children were born in New York City, as follows:—

1461—I.   MATILDA COULTER[8], born May 6, 1860; married, and lives in Elmsford, N. Y.

1462—II.   CHARLES BENJAMIN[8], born Jan. 12, 1862, at 9 a. m. He lives, unmarried, at 137 East 46th street, New York City, being a commission merchant. With adversity to commence with, he struggled, after his father's death, to support his mother and sisters and brother, and having a good nerve managed to pay some of his father's unsecured debts, and get his own footing in the business world.

1463—III.   FANNY BAKER[8], born Oct. 11, 1866; died in New York City.

1464—IV.   FRANK MACMULKIN[8], born Aug. 10, 1871; lives at Mamaroneck, N. Y.; married; and is receiving teller in a New York bank.

901

GEORGE HOVEY[7], born in Windham, Conn., July 10, 1824. He was a carpenter, and lived in Scotland (Norwich), Conn. He married Cornelia Bass May 20, 1848, in Scotland; and was a private in company G, Twenty-sixth regiment of Connecticut volunteers in the Civil war.

Their children were born in Windham, as follows:—

1465—I.   FRANK[8], born March 1, 1849.
1466—II.   MARTHA[8], born Oct. 6, 1850.
1467—III. FREDERICK[8], born Nov. 10, 1856.

903

LEWIS HOVEY[7], born in Windham, Conn., May 20, 1828. He was a sergeant in Company A, Eighteenth regiment of Connecticut volunteers in the Civil war, being severely wounded. He married Sarah Parker Jan. 16, 1857 (1866?); and is now retired from business, residing at 110 Prospect street, Norwich (Greenville?). Conn.

Their child was born as follows:—

1468—I.   LOUISE PARKER[8], born May 2, 1870.

906

HENRY HOVEY[7], born in Windham, Conn., Dec. 18, 1839. He was a merchant, and now has retired and lives at 6 Cliff street, Norwich, Conn. He was commissary and quartermaster-sergeant of the eighteenth regiment of Connecticut volunteers in the Rebellion, and also served three years in the War department in Washington, D. C. He married Emma Frances Joslin Sept. 26, 1872, in Webster, Mass.

Their children were born as follows:—

1469—I.   MABEL ESTELLE[8], born Jan. 18, 1874.
1470—II.   NATHAN JOSLIN[8], born May 24, 1877; died May 20, 1885, at age of eight years.
1471—III. GRACE ELEANOR[8], born June 9, 1884.
1472—IV.   ————[8] (son), born Nov. —, 1889; died Nov. —, 1889, one day old.

927

JOHN HOVEY[7], born in Ipswich, Mass., March 17, 1811. He married Mary Ann Carr of Newburyport Nov. 8, 1846. She was born there in 1828. He left Ipswich when young and went to California, and was never heard from.

Child:—

1473—I.   ————[8] (dau.), born April 14, 1848; and died in Ipswich, of canker, April 24, 1848.

933

NATHANIEL FULLER HOVEY[7], born in Ipswich, Mass., Jan. 27, 1824. He was a bricklayer and mason; and lived in his native town. He married Lydia Spiller, daughter of Thomas C. and Lydia C. (Spiller) Boardman Nov. 14, 1847. She was born Feb. 7, 1829. He died in Ipswich June 15, 1890, at the age of sixty-six; and she died April 19, 1892, in Ipswich, at the age of sixty-three. Their remains lie on Burying hill, in Ipswich.

Their children were born as follows:—

1474—I.	WILLIAM B.[8], born Oct. 18, 1848; died June 7, 1852.
1475—II.	ELIZABETH FULLER[8], married Edwin A. Howes; she died May —, 1886, in Ipswich. Child: 1. *Edwin Alliston*[9]; a lawyer in Boston.
1476—III.	WILLETTA BURNETT[8], born March 20, 1852, in Ipswich; married George Spencer Spiller July —, 1868; and lived in Ipswich. Their children were born in Ipswich, as follows: 1. *Annie Mabel*[9], born in 1869; died in 1869. 2. *George Albert*[9], born March 15, 1871; physician, formerly in Haverhill, Mass., but now in Sacramento, Cal.; married Elizabeth George Jan. 1, 1905. 3. *John Iliffe*[9], born April 17, 1873; died Feb. 7, 1880. in Ipswich, at the age of six.
1477—IV.	ABBIE SWEET[8], born May 29, 1856; married Harlan Ward, son of Allen and Juliena (Goodale) Gould; lived in Beverly, where she died April 15, 1906, aged forty-nine.
1478—V.	LUELLA[8], married ——— Roberts.
1479—VI.	LEWIS HOWARD[8], born March 30, 1864; died Dec. 29, 1887, at the age of twenty-three.
1480—VII.	ANNIE MABEL[8], born Sept. 30, 1866; died Aug. 17, 1867.
1481—VIII.	NATHANIEL[8], born Jan. 19, 1873; died Oct. 19, 1874, aged one year.

945

DAVID HOVEY[7], born in Peterborough, N. H., Feb. 28, 1785. He was a carpenter by trade, and succeeded his father on the farm in Peterborough. when the latter removed to Ackworth. He remained in Peterborough until 1832, when he bought a farm in Francestown, N. H., to which he removed. He settled in 1866 or 1867 in Greenfield, N. H., where he afterwards lived. He married Betsey Gregg of Jaffrey, N. H. She was born July 9, 1791. He died in North Lyndeboro, of ossification of the heart, May 5, 1868. at the age of eighty-three. She survived him, and died, his widow, June —, 1869, at the age of seventy-seven.

Their children were born in Peterborough, as follows:—

1482—I.	SARAH[8], born April 12, 1814; married Sylvester Proctor of North Lyndeboro. They had four children. She was living in 1865.
1483—II.	ELIZA A.[8], born Aug. 24, 1818; married Franklin Center of North Lyndeboro. They had one child. She was living in 1865.
1484—III.	PHEBE F.[8], born March 19, 1825; married Josiah Swinington; and lived in Lyndeboro. They had five children. She was living in 1865.

954

STEPHEN HOVEY[7], born in Peterborough, N. H., June 19. 1794. He was a yeoman, and lived in Francestown, N. H. He married Martha Ferson of Francestown Feb. 18, 1819; and died in Lancaster March 15, 1849, at the age of fifty-four.

Children:—

1485—I. ————[8].
1486—II. ————[8].
1487—III. ————[8].
1488—IV. ————[8].
1489—V. ————[8].
1490—VI. ————[8].
1491—VII. ————[8].

955

JOSEPH HOVEY[7], born in Peterborough, N. H., Oct. 19, 1800. He lived in Pepperell, Mass.; and married Dolly Shattuck in 1827. He was living in 1836.

Children:—

1492—I. ————[8].
1493—II. ————[8].
1494—III. ————[8].
1495—IV. ————[8].

957

ROBERTS HOVEY[7], born in Peterborough, N. H., May 17, 1807. He was a farmer, living in Swanzey, N. H., first on the C. Whitcomb farm, and afterward on the farm where he died. He married Elizabeth, daughter of Francis and Sally (Ames) Smiley of Peterborough Dec. 4, 1833. She was born in Peterborough May 22, 1813; and died in Swanzey, of meningitis. July 21, 1882, at the age of sixty-nine. He died in Swanzey, of paralysis, April 13, 1891, at the age of eighty-three.

Their children were born in Swanzey, as follows:—

1496—I. LUCINDA MELISSA[8], born Oct. 29. 1834; married David Allen, son of Charles and Betsey Pratt of Westmoreland, N. H., Oct. 26, 1854; he was born Jan. —, 1828; and died at Two Rivers, Wis., Aug. 17, 1858, at the age of twenty-three. They had no children.

1497—II. FRANCIS ALONZO[8], born Oct. 20, 1836. *See family numbered "1497."*

1498—III. SARAH ELIZABETH[8], born Aug. 11, 1838; and died, unmarried, in Swanzey Aug. 9, 1864, at the age of twenty-six.

1499—IV. ELLEN VICTORIA[8], born April 17, 1840; married Joseph E., son of Joseph and Gillias A. (Rice) Long of Swanzey, as his first wife, Dec. 31, 1861. He was born in Swanzey April 30, 1836. She died June 14, 1864, at the age of twenty-four. He married, second, Lois A. Taft Jan. 1, 1867, and by her had four children. The children of Joseph E. and Ellen V. (Hovey) Long were born in Swanzey, as follows: 1. *Nellie Melissa[9]*, born Aug. 2, 1862; married Ellery, son of

Aaron and Lura (Davis) Leborveau; and they live in Swanzey. 2. *George E.*, born June 12, 1864; married; and lives in Keene, N. H.

1500—v. THEODORE⁴, born Aug. 7, 1842. He was mustered into service in the Civil war Oct. 23, 1862, in the Sixteenth New Hampshire regiment of infantry, and was mustered out Aug. 20, 1863. He died June 16, 1864, at the age of twenty-one, in Swanzey, unmarried.

1501—vi. SYLVANDER⁴, born June 4, 1844; was a soldier in the Civil war, being mustered Oct. 23, 1862, in the Sixteenth New Hampshire regiment of infantry; mustered out Aug. 20, 1863; mustered into the Eighteenth New Hampshire regiment of infantry Sept. 13, 1864; promoted to corporal; discharged June 10, 1865; and died April 27, 1866, at the age of twenty-two.

1502—vii. FERNANDO SMILEY⁴, born Aug. 27, 1846. He was a soldier in the Civil war, being mustered into the United States service from Dublin, N. H., March 29, 1864, into the First regiment of the New Hampshire cavalry; and discharged for disability March 15, 1865. He died in Swanzey March 3, 1866, at nineteen years of age.

1503—viii. RUTH CLEMENTINE⁴, born Aug. 4, 1848; married Willard I. Thomas of Swanzey. He was born Sept. 3, 1844; and died May 13, 1873, at the age of twenty-eight. She is his widow, living in Swanzey. Child: 1. ———⁵, born in 18—; died ——— ———, being two days old.

1504—ix. HARRIET ASENATH⁴, born Dec. 22, 1850; died Sept. 1, 1866, at the age of fifteen.

1505—x. FLORA A.⁴, born Nov. 28, 1852; died Jan. 8, 1867, at the age of fourteen.

1506—xi. EMMA JENNETTE⁴, born Nov. 18, 1854; married George Henry Taylor of Richmond, N. H., Nov. 19, 1878; and both are now living. Their children were born as follows: 1. *Blanche E.*, born May 30, 1880. 2. ———⁵; living. 3. ———⁵; living.

1507—xii. IDA ISABELLE⁴, born Nov. 23, 1857; married Frank E., son of Josephus and Rowena A. (Woodward) Handy Oct. 9, 1875. He was born in Swanzey Feb. 19, 1855; and they live there. Their children were born as follows: 1. *Theodore F.*, born April 23, 1876; lives in Springfield, Mass.; married Jennie Clark of Springfield. 2. *Wayland L.*, born Oct. 5, 1881; married Alice Tarbox; and lives in Marlborough. 3. *Leland*; lives in Springfield, Mass., unmarried.

959

TIMOTHY L. HOVEY⁷, born in Peterborough, N. H., Aug. 9, 1813. He was a farmer, and lived on his father's homestead in Peterborough. He married, first, Ruth, daughter of Dea. Timothy and Lydia (Holt) Holt of Peterborough Nov. 17, 1836. She was born in Peterborough May 12, 1812; and died there July 29, 1874, at the age of sixty-two. He married, second, widow Myra Hutchinson, daughter of J. and A. Parker of Peterborough July 1, 1875. She was born in Dracut, Mass., about 1814. He married, third, Margaret, widow of ——— Vickery of Brookline, N. H., and daughter of J. and J. Ballantyne, about 1883.

She was born in Southbridge, Mass., about 1836. Mr. Hovey
died in Peterborough, of acute splenitis, March 31, 1887, at the
age of seventy-three. His wife Margaret survived him.

Mr. Hovey's children were born in Peterborough, as follows:—

1508—I.   LYDIA JANE[8], born June 2, 1838; died Sept. 18, 1854, aged
          sixteen.
1509—II. ASENATH B.[8], born Oct. 20, 1840; married George W. Marden
          Sept. 3, 1862. Children: 1. *Cora A.[9]*, born Aug. 9, 1863.
          2. *Jennie S.[9]*, born Sept. 21, 1865. 3. *Walter H.[9]*, born
          May 30, 1867.
1510—III. JOHN A.[8], born March 19, 1845. *See family numbered
          "1510."*
1511—IV. ALMON T.[8], born Sept. 17, 1846; married Mary A., daughter
          of Franklin and Pamelia Center of Lyndeboro June 5, 1870;
          and she died in Peterborough, of phthisis pulmonalis, Feb.
          18, 1882, aged thirty-five. He was living in 1889.
1512—V.   JOSEPHINE R.[8], born Sept. 22, 1849; married Albert O. Smith
          Nov. 1, 1871. He is a trader in Peterborough. She was
          living in 1889.

969

SAMUEL C. HOVEY[7], born July 16, 1805. He was a cordwainer and farmer, and lived in Boxford and Groveland. He
married Miriam F. Chace Oct. 5, 1826; and, as the result of
being hit by a freight train, died in Haverhill, at the home of his
son, Dec. 29, 1890, at the age of eighty-five. She died April 6,
1888, aged eighty-five years.

Their children were born as follows:—

1513—I.   SUSAN[8], born Nov. 11, 1827; married John W. Libby of
          Groveland; and died Sept. 5, 1880. He was a well-known
          "Forty-Niner," and for years engineer of the Hale mills
          in South Groveland and many years chief of the Groveland
          fire department. He married, secondly, Lizzie Banks;
          and died March 26, 1898. His second wife survived him.
          The children of John W. and Susan (Hovey) Libby were
          born as follows: 1. *William Parker[9]*, born July 20, 1848,
          in Groveland; shoemaker; lives in Groveland; married
          Asenath Parker July 20, 1869. They have one child. 2.
          Mary Ella[9], born Jan. 8, 1851; married Nathaniel Donnell
          July 15, 1871; he is a contractor; and she died March
          10, 1907; they had two children. 3. *Blanche[9]*, born March
          16, 1872; died Aug. 8, 1872.
1514—II. RUFUS A.[8], born Nov. 16, 1831; died March 10, 1837, aged five.
1515—III. HENRY L.[8], born Sept. 30, 1833. *See family numbered "1515."*
1516—IV. RUFUS A.[8], born June 22, 1837. *See family numbered "1516."*
1517—V.   LEONARD[8], born July 9, 1840; died March 25, 1842.
1518—VI. ELLEN S.[8], born Aug. 10, 1843; married Alonzo Quimby at
          Newton, N. H., Dec. 24, 1868; lived in Groveland. He
          died June 11, 1912. Their only child is: 1. *Alice[9]*, born
          Nov. 25, 1874; married John Esterly of Albany, N. Y., June
          20, 1910; lives at Albany.
1519—VII. BENJAMIN L.[8], born Jan. 16, 1851. *See family numbered
          "1519."*

971

CHARLES HOVEY[7], born Nov. 22, 1871. He was a cord-wainer; and lived in Groveland. He married, first, Mary Stevens Savary April 21, 1836; and she died April 21, 1864. He married, second, Julia P. Hopkinson June 27, 1867; and she died Feb. 9, 1883. He died in 1899.

Mr. Hovey's children were born as follows:—

1520—I. CHARLES F.[8], born April 15, 1837; died Feb. —, 1861.
1521—II. HENRY L.[8], born Nov. 22, 1840; died Aug. —, 1851.
1522.—III. EDWARD F.[8], born Feb. 15, 1845; lived and died in Groveland.
1523—IV. GEORGE S.[8], born Dec. 16, 1839; married Mary Morse; and they lived in Groveland in 1912.

973

WILLIAM C. HOVEY[7], born in Bradford, Mass., Dec. 19, 1820. He married Mary F. Simpson Sept. 5, 1846, in Lowell, Mass. She was born in Concord, Mass., May 6, 1822; and he died in Salem, Mass., Nov. 20, 1855. She died in Salem June 21, 1856. Their children were born as follows:—

1524—I. ROBERT LEONARD[8], born May 15, 1847, in Charlestown, Mass.; died Aug. 17, 1847.
1525—II. ABBY FRANCES[8], born Sept. 5, 1848, in Salem, Mass.; married Rev. James Vila Blake, minister of the First Unitarian parish in Haverhill, Mass., June 22, 1869. They lived in Chicago in 1909. Their children were born as follows: 1. *Clinton Frederick*[9], born May 4, 1871, at Forest Hills, in Boston, Mass.; married Vida Clement, in Chicago, Feb. 17, 1899. He is a mechanical engineer; and they have two children, both born in Michigan. 2. *Amos Carleton*[9], born April 29, 1873, in Englewood, N. J.; died in Englewood Oct. 12, 1874. 3. *Rachel Frazier*[9] (twin), born June 8, 1876, in Boston; married Jerome Mahoney in Chicago; and lived there in 1912. 4. *Ruth Deering*[9] (twin), born June 8, 1876; married Frederick A. Thompson, in Chicago, Feb. 28, 1901; and lived in New York in 1912. 5. *Alice*[9], born July 26, 1880, in Quincy, Ill.; died in Boston Sept. 19, 1882.
1526—III. MARY CARLETON[8], born Feb. 21, 1856, in Salem; married Charles F. Priest of Haverhill Jan. 24, 1876; and lived at 8 Lawrence street, Haverhill, in 1912. Their children were born as follows: 1. *E. Blanche*[9], born Aug. 1, 1876, in Haverhill; died Nov. 13, 1878. 2. *Ethel F.*[9] (twin), born Jan. 8, 1878; died July 24, 1878. 3. *Edith F.*[9] (twin), born Jan. 8, 1878; died July 31, 1878.

975

HENRY PORTER HOVEY[7], born in East Machias, Me., Sept. 4, 1810. In early manhood he went to Canada, then to Ohio, and in 1839 settled as a farmer, first at Freedom, and subsequently at Ottawa, Ill., which place then contained few settlers, and Chicago was a small village. He married Mary Ann Sinclair Jan. —, 1850, near Ottawa. She was born in Kentucky Sept. 16, 1826. He was a great reader, well informed, and a good citizen, as well as a Christian and a student of the Bible. He died at Freedom, Ill., July 2, 1885, at the age of seventy-four. She survived him, and died at Ottawa Feb. 2, 1893, at the age of sixty-six.

Their only child was born at Freedom, as follows:—

1527—1.   SUSAN ELIZABETH[8], born Jan. 3, 1851; lives at 919 Paul street, Ottawa, unmarried.

981

RUFUS PORTER HOVEY[7], born in 18—. He was a wheelwright, and lived in Bradford, Mass., in that part of the town which was incorporated as Groveland in 1850. He married Jane, daughter of Phineas and Betsey C. Ayer of Haverhill, Mass., before 1844. She was born in Methuen. He died in Groveland Dec. 27, 1850; and she survived him.

Children:—

1528—1.   ELIZABETH C.[8], born March 23, 1834, in Groveland; married Charles Byron Hopkinson of Groveland before 1850; and she died Sept. 23, 1853. Their children were born in Groveland, as follows: 1. *Mary Jane[9]*, born Dec. 24, 1850; died in Groveland April 27, 1851. 2. *Frank Byron[9]*, born March 11, 1852; paper hanger; lived in Amesbury, Mass.; married Bertha Edna Burrill July 29, 1869; and she died in Amesbury June 25, 1897, aged forty-six.
1529—11.   MIRANTHA ANN[8], died at the age of nine months.

986

JOSEPH HENRY HOVEY[7], born in Boxford, Mass., April 30, 1830. He was for many years a last manufacturer, but is retired (1913), living in Haverhill, Mass., at 38 Fountain street. He married, first, Hannah C. Weeks Oct. 31, 1858, in Lawrence. She was born in Oakland, Me., and died Aug. 27, 1870. Mr. Hovey married, second, Sarah Learnard Oct. 15, 1879.

The children of Mr. Hovey were:—

1530—1.   ALBERT P.[8], born Oct. 15, 1856; lived in Haverhill; last maker; married Christine Fisher April 11, 1892; and died in 1905. They had one son: 1. *Henry F.[9]*, born Feb. 2, 1893; living in Haverhill in 1913.
1531—11.   EDWARD L.[8], born Aug. 1, 1859, in Haverhill. *See family numbered "1531."*
1532—111. CLARENCE S.[8], born Feb. 8, 1869, in Haverhill; last maker; married Hattie Cammet April 6, 1896; and both were living in Haverhill in 1913.

987

EDWARD BEECHER HOVEY[7], born in Boxford, Mass., April 3, 1832. He was a shoemaker, and lived in Lynn. He married Emeline Eaton Holt of North Andover before 1857; and died in the insane hospital at Ipswich July 6, 1878, at the age of forty-six. She survived him, and died about 1900.

Their children were born as follows:—

1533—i. HELEN HASTINGS[8], born in 1857; dress-maker; unmarried; lives in Lynn.
1534—ii. LUCY E. PORTER[8], born in 1868; married Louis M. Winslow; and lives in Lynn.

988

CHARLES P. HOVEY[7], born in 18—. He married Mary E. ————. She lived at 171 Congdon street, Providence, R. I., in 1900.
Children:—

1535—i. ————[8].
1536—ii. ————[8].
1537—iii. WILLIAM[8]; lives at 2715 Sacramento street, San Francisco, Cal.
1538—iv. FREDERIC E.[8]. He bought the Hovey homestead at East Machias, Me., for a summer residence.
1539—v. EMILY R.[8]; married ———— Spaulding.
1540—vi. SOPHIA F.[8]; married ———— Sweat; and lives at 372 Broadway, Providence, R. I.

989

STEPHEN HOVEY[7], born in 18—. He died before 1900.
Children:—

1541—i. ————[8]; lives in Oregon.
1542—ii. ————[8]; lives in Oregon.

990

WARREN F. HOVEY[7], born in 18—. He lived in Machias, Me.; and married Angelica H. Hovey (1005) May 11, 1835. She died in Machias July 16, 1853.
Their children were born as follows:—

1543—i. URBAN HITCHCOCK[8]. See family numbered "1543."
1544—ii. ————[8]; died young.
1545—iii. ————[8]; died young.
1546—iv. ————[8]; died young.

1013

SOLOMON HOVEY[7], born in Charlestown, Mass., Nov. 6, 1806. He attended the Bunker Hill grammar school of Charlestown and the private school of Master Gates on Bow street, and spent the years 1822 and 1823 at Bradford Academy. He lived in Charlestown until 1857, when he removed to Boston, and from there to Roxbury in 1862. In 1869 he settled in Hyde Park.

He was collector of taxes for Charlestown from 1827 to 1836, a member of the city council in 1851, and of the school committee. For several years he was a member of the firm of Stover & Hovey, tanners. In 1837, he entered the insurance business, and served as secretary of the Mechanics Mutual Fire Insurance Company of Boston from that date until 1857, when he became president of the company. He continued its president until 1877, when the company was dissolved on account of the losses sustained in the great Boston fire. They paid in full all the claims, which amounted to nearly one and one-half millions of dollars. Mr. Hovey was also for many years president of the Massachusetts Charitable Fire Insurance Society.

He married Joanna Augusta, daughter of George Stillman and Joanna (Sylvester) Flint of Rutland, Mass., Sept. 10, 1833. She was born in Charlestown April 15, 1810; and died at Hyde Park Dec. 22, 1892, at the age of eighty-two. He died June 21, 1897, at the age of ninety.

Their children were born in Charlestown, as follows:—

1547—I. HELEN AUGUSTA[6], born Dec. 14, 1834; married Thomas, son of Gen. Thomas and Hannah (Blair) Chamberlain of Worcester, Mass., Aug. 31, 1858. He was born in Worcester June 4, 1835. They resided in Peoria, Ill., and Roxbury, Mass., until 1872, when they removed to their present residence in Hyde Park, Mass. Mr. Chamberlain has been connected with the State National Bank of Boston since April, 1861. Their children were born as follows: 1. *Harry Richardson*[7], born Aug. 25, 1859, at Peoria; lives in London, England; was editor of the *New York Press* from 1888 to 1891 and of the *Boston Journal* in 1891 and 1892, and since the latter date he has been the London correspondent of the *New York Sun*, with his office in London. He married Abigail Louise, daughter of Charles K. and Eliza A. Sawyer Sept. 10, 1883. 2. *Alfred Thomas*[7], born Dec. 22, 1862, at Roxbury; died in Roxbury Nov. 26, 1868. 3. *Helen Clare*[7], born May 7, 1866, in Roxbury; and lives at Hyde Park. 4. *Alice Louise*[7], born Jan. 29, 1872, in Roxbury; was a kindergarten teacher; and married Nestor Wilbur, son of Charles Franklin and Sarah Abigail (Drew) Davis of Somerville, Mass., Feb. 12, 1903. He was born at Newmarket Feb. 15, 1869. They live in Winchester, Mass.

1548—II. MARTHA SKILTON[6], born May 24, 1836; married Henry W. Adams of Charlestown Nov. 10, 1857. They lived in Peoria, Ill., from the time of their marriage, and subsequently removed to Brooklyn, N. Y., and then to Chicago, Ill., where she died May 25, 1863, at the age of twenty-seven. He married, secondly, Susan Steele of Chicago; and removed to St. Joseph, Mo. The child of Henry W. and Martha Skilton (Hovey) Adams was born in Peoria, as follows: 1. *Emma Hovey*[7], born Oct. 13, 1858; married George Buchanan Kerr of Hyde Park Sept. 12, 1877; and she died in Chicago Jan. 16, 1906, aged forty-seven. They had four children.

1549—III. SOLOMON[6], born July 22, 1837. He was a soldier in the Civil war, being commissioned first lieutenant of company E, Twenty-first regiment, Massachusetts volunteer infantry, Aug. 21, 1861. He was promoted to captain March 3, 1862, and made lieutenant-colonel of the regiment July 2, 1864.

At the expiration of his term, Aug. 23, 1864, he re-entered the service as captain in the Seventh regiment, United States Veteran volunteers, and remained with that organization until the end of the war. He participated in the battles of Roanoke Island, New Bern, Camden, Second Bull Run, Chantilly, South Mountain, Antietam, Fredericksburg, Vicksburg, Jackson, The Wilderness, Spottsylvania, North Anna, Cold Harbor and The Crater. For special acts of bravery he received the honors of membership in the Loyal Legion of the G. A. R. He was never married, and lived in Charlestown and Boston. He died at Hyde Park Oct. 21, 1884, at the age of forty-seven.

1550—IV.   BATHSHEBA THAXTER[6], born Nov. 10, 1842; married Lt. James McDaniel, son of Newman and Sally Bennett (Osborne) Durell of Newmarket, N. H., Feb. 10, 1864, in Boston. He was born in Newmarket June 2, 1832. He recruited the larger part of company E of the Thirteenth regiment, New Hampshire volunteer infantry, of which he was commissioned first lieutenant Sept. 27, 1862. He served throughout the war, and received wounds at Fredericksburg and Cold Harbor. July 19, 1864, he was promoted to captain of company C, Thirteenth regiment, New Hampshire volunteer infantry, and was detailed in September of that year as acting aide-de-camp on the staff of Gen. Charles K. Graham at Bermuda Hundreds. After the war, Captain Durell resided in Boston and Roxbury, Mass., until 1870, when he removed to his present residence in Hyde Park, Mass. Their children were born as follows: 1. *Edward Hovey[6]*, born Feb. 10, 1866, in Boston; graduated from the United States Naval Academy at Annapolis, Md., in 1887; and was commissioned ensign in 1889, junior-lieutenant in 1897, lieutenant in 1899, lieutenant-commander in 1905 and commander in 1909. He served on the warships Santee, Constellation, Dale, Pensacola, Kearsarge, Eagre, Spy, Bache, Monongahela, San Francisco, Bancroft, Oregon, Wheeling, Independence, Philadelphia, Zafiro, Solace, Newport, Dixie, Panther, Columbia, Boxer, New Jersey, West Virginia and Indiana. He was also instructor at the naval academy at Annapolis in the departments of discipline and of history and law, and head of the English department; and was also a member of the Academic Board. He married Annie Hartwell, daughter of Edward Alonzo and Matilda (Pooley) Kendall June 9, 1890. She was born in Chicopee, Mass., Nov. 20, 1863; and died at Annapolis March 11, 1910, aged forty-six. They had one child. 2. *Isabelle[6]*, born April 11, 1869, in Roxbury; married Sumner Leavis, son of Charles Henry and Sarah Emily (Holmes) Osborne of Hyde Park Oct. 29, 1894. He was born in Gorham, Me., June 20, 1867. They have had two children. 3. *Mildred[6]*, born Sept. 9, 1871, in Hyde Park; married Ferdinand Alexander of New York City Nov. 30, 1891. 4. *Louis Flint[6]*, born Nov. 21, 1877, in Hyde Park. 5. *Wallace Osborne*, born March 20, 1883, in Hyde Park.

1551—V.   FRANCES FLINT[6], born Dec. 10, 1844; and died March 10, 1846.

1552—VI.   FRANCES FLINT[6], born July 19, 1848; married Lawrence O'Brien in New York; and died there June 28, 1899, at the age of fifty.

1025

WILLIAM HOVEY[7], born in Cambridge, Mass., Dec. 3, 1812. He lived in Grand Rapids, Mich.; and married Sarah Stone. He died at Grand Rapids Nov. 21, 1881.

Their children were born as follows:—

1553—I.   HELEN M.[8], born July 17, 1835; married George W., son of Joel and Amanda (Sweet) Gay of Grand Rapids Sept. 3, 1861. He was born in Washington county, N. Y., March 17, 1837; and lived in Grand Rapids, where she died April —, 1898. He died there Sept. 13, 1899. Children, born in Grand Rapids: 1. *William H.[9]*, born May 30, 1863; lives in Grand Rapids; and is engaged in the manufacture of furniture, being at the head of the Birkey & Gay Furniture Company of that place. He married Netta Cole June 12, 1888. 2. *Gertrude A.[9]*, born Dec. 6, 1868; married Charles Whitney Carman June 27, 1899; and lives in Grand Rapids.

1554—II.   MELANIA P.[8], born Dec. 18, 1836, in Cambridge; died there March 6, 1838.

1555—III. HANNAH AMANDA[8], born Feb. 27, 1839, in Cambridgeport; married John Prescott, son of Capt. Thomas and Jane (Greenough) Rand Nov. 23, 1863, in Grand Rapids. He was born in Maine March 25, 1835. They lived in Grand Rapids, where she died April —, 1873. Their children were born in Grand Rapids, as follows: 1. *Bertha Sarah[9]*, born July 19, 1863; married Arthur Gifford Graham Oct. 18, 1887. He is a manufacturer of fireless cookers, and they live at Evanston, Ill. 2. *Jennie Greenough[9]*, born July 5, 1865; died at Grand Rapids May 20, 1884, at the age of eighteen. 3. *Hannah Aurelia[9]*, born March 31, 1873; died Aug. 21, 1873.

1556—IV.   SARAH M.[8], born Nov. 8, 1840, in Cambridge; died there Sept. 18, 1841.

1557—V.   WILLIAM STONE[8], born Oct. 1, 1842, in Cambridge. *See family numbered "1557."*

1027

CHARLES HOVEY[7], born in Acton, Mass., Nov. 17, 1817. When quite young he went to Cambridge, Mass., where he was educated in the public schools. He went to Lowell in 1832, at the age of fifteen, and entered the employ of George H. Carlton in the drug business. When he became of age he was invited to enter into partnership with Mr. Carlton, and the invitation was accepted. The name of the firm, Carlton & Hovey, was continued as long as Mr. Hovey lived, although Mr. Carlton died in 1857. Mr. Hovey then conducted the business alone until 1865, when J. G. Tweed became a partner.

Mr. Hovey had large interests outside of his drug business. He was a director of the Railroad National Bank from 1846; and in 1867 was treasurer of the Lowell Gas Light Company. From 1861 to 1879 he was a trustee of the Mechanics' Savings Bank; for many years treasurer of the Lowell Cemetery company; clerk of the Stony Brook Railroad company from 1851 to 1862; and a trustee and clerk of the board of St. Mark's school in Southboro from the time of its opening until the time of his death.

His busy life allowed no time for political aspiration, and he never sought nor held public office. For some years before his decease he was much interested in the Old Residents' Historical Association, of which he was a valued member. He contributed much of the valuable information which is possessed in its archives and probably no citizen of Lowell was better informed relative to the prominent events or the actors in the history of the city during his lifetime.

Mr. Hovey became identified with St. Anne's church, and was clerk of the parish from 1839 to 1843, and treasurer from 1844 until his death. At the time the chime of bells was placed in the tower of the church edifice he contributed a bell to the collection dedicated to the memory of his deceased partner.

Mr. Hovey married Catherine, daughter of Col. Joseph Smith of Dover, N. H., Nov. 7, 1843. She was born in Dover Sept. 15, 18—. Mr. Hovey died, suddenly, in Lowell, May 4, 1886, at the age of sixty-eight. His wife survived him, and died in Lowell Aug. 6, 1907.

Their children were born in Lowell, as follows:—

1558—I.   HENRY EMERSON[6], born Nov. 23, 1844. *See family numbered* "1558."

1559—II. ALICE[6], born Oct. 22, 1847; died in Lowell March 14, 1850.

1560—III. KATE SMITH[6], born Jan. 21, 1849; was educated at Miss Dana's private school in Lowell; married Laurin, son of Leonard and Priscilla (Abbott) Martin of Dixville, Province of Quebec, Canada, Nov. 17, 1870, in Lowell. He was born at Coaticook, Province of Quebec, Aug. 27, 1843; and was educated at Hatfield academy, in Canada, and at Eastman college at Poughkeepsie, N. Y. He served in the Civil war in 1864. He was cashier in a bank in Lowell, where they lived, and he died April 25, 1878. She survives him and lives at 14 Park street, in Lowell. Their children were born in Lowell, as follows: 1. *Charles Abbott[6]*, born Aug. 24, 1873; was educated at Phillips academy in Andover, and at Harvard college; and lives, unmarried, at Berlin, N. H., where he is a sulphite pulp manufacturer. 2. *Laurin Hovey[6]*, born May 30, 1875; was educated in the Lowell public schools, Cowles Art school of Boston and the Birmingham School of Art, in England. He won a medal at the National exhibition held at South Kensington, England, in 1899, for excellence of design and workmanship. He lives in Lowell, engaged in arts and crafts; and teaches at the Massachusetts Normal Art school at Boston and at the Rogers Hall school in Lowell. He married Harriet Nesmith Greenhalge Sept. 19, 1904. 3. *Louise Hovey[6]*, born April 17, 1878; was educated at private schools, Rogers Hall school in Lowell and Miss Low's school at Stamford, Conn. She married, first, Waldo Kennard of Colorado Springs March 3, 1898. They separated, and she married, second, I. Hasbrook Chahoon of Au Sable Forks, N. Y., Sept. 22, 1902. He is a paper manufacturer. They lived at Au

Sable Forks, where she died May 31, 1908, at thirty years of age.

1561—IV.   CHARLES WILLIAM⁸, born Aug. 9, 1853; died in Lowell Oct. 9, 1855, aged two.
1562—V.   WILLIAM CHARLES⁸, born Jan. 31, 1861; died Feb. 23, 1861.

1028

DEA. ALBERT HENRY HOVEY⁷ born in Acton, Mass., Oct. 5, 1820. He removed from Boston to Grand Rapids, Mich., in 1856, before any railroad communication had been established nearer than Kalamazoo. He plotted and laid out a large portion of the west side of Grand Rapids; and in 1860 he removed to Chicago, Ill. There he conducted a successful business until the great fire of 1871, which crippled it so much that he never recovered the position he had had in his line. He was always very active in church and Sunday-school work, holding the office of deacon in the First Baptist church of Chicago for many years, and also in Los Angeles, Cal., where he latterly lived.

Deacon Hovey married Rebecca, daughter of John P. and Betsey (Griffin) Valentine Jan. 1, 1845. She was born in Hopkinton, Mass., Aug. 21, 1822. He died in Los Angeles June 9, 1890; and she died in New York City Aug. 21, 1898, on her seventy-sixth birthday.

Their children were born as follows:—

1563—I.   JAMES ALBERT⁸, born May 13, 1847, in Boston, Mass. See family numbered "1563."
1564—II. ELIZABETH DANA⁸, born Jan. 23, 1851, in Brookline, Mass.; married William A., son of Harwood and ——— (Adams) Morgan June 24, 1873. He was born in England Oct. 3, 1849; and lived in Chicago, Ill. She died in Los Angeles, Cal., Dec. 10, 1884, at the age of thirty-three. He died there June —, 1902. Their children were born in Chicago, as follows: 1. Grace Valentine⁹, born March 16, 1874; died Aug. 10, 1874, in Chicago. 2. Mabel Adams⁹, born April 26, 1876; married Haswell J. Ramsey; and lives in Seattle, Wash. 3. Robert Henry⁹, born July 10, 1878; married Edna Hanscom in 1903; and lives in Tacoma, Wash. 4. Minnie Florence⁹, born Feb. 12, 1882; lives in Boston.

1038

JOSIAH CLARK HOVEY⁷, born in Plymouth, Mass., June 25, 1806. He married Judith, daughter of Charles and Anne (Weston) Witherell Dec. 2, 1830, in Plymouth. She was born in Duxbury, Mass., May 20, 1803. They both died at Plymouth, he in 1870; and she in 1884.

Their children were born at Manomet, in Plymouth, as follows:—

1565—I.   DOMINICUS⁸, born Nov. 13, 1831. See family numbered "1565."
1566—II. FRANCES ELIZABETH⁸, born Sept. 9, 1833; lives in Plymouth, where she taught school forty years, having never married.

1567—III.   ADELAIDE ANN⁴, born Jan. 7, 1836; married Austin, son of Ichabod and Betsey (Holbrook) Morton; and lived in Plymouth, where they both died. They had two children.

1568—IV.   JOSIAH CLARK⁴, born March 13, 1842; was a master-mariner, went on whaling cruises, and subsequently voyages to China. He lived in Plymouth; and died, unmarried, about 1870, at the age of twenty-eight.

1569—V.   FREELOVE SCOTT BARDEN⁴, born Feb. 29, 1844; married Ezra, son of Trueman and Laurette* (Blackmer) Holmes Sept. 28, 1870. He was formerly on apothecary, but for the last twenty-five years has been turnkey in the house of correction at New Bedford, Mass., where they live. Their children were born in New Bedford, as follows: 1. *Margaret Hovey*, born Sept. 3, 1871; married Arthur Stanley, son of Benjamin Spooner and Sarah Elizabeth (Cobb) Briggs of New Bedford, a bookkeeper. 2. *Elizabeth Clarke*, born Jan. 22, 1874; married Henry Dean, son of Charles D. and Demaris Waldron of Fairhaven, a reporter. 3. *Joseph Buckminster*, born July 22, 1876; baker; lives in New Bedford. 4. *Philip Curtis*, lives in New Bedford; and is a textile manufacturer. 5. *Edward Winslow*, born Dec. 20, 1880; is a lawyer, and lives in New Bedford.

1039

EDMUND HOVEY⁷, born in Mirimachi, N. B.; and married Dolly Price.

Child:—

1570—1.   WILLIAM⁸, born in Mirimachi. *See family numbered "1570."*

1041

DANIEL HOVEY⁷, born May 26, 1793. He was a scythe maker, and lived in Oxford, Mass., until about 1823, when he removed to Bristol, Ill. He married Reliance Smith; and died in Bristol.

Children:—

1571—I.   GEORGE DANIEL⁸; died in 1850.
1572—II.   MARY CRANE⁸; lived in Bristol.

1042

PEREZ G. HOVEY⁷, born Sept. 25, 1795. He was a scythe maker, and lived in Oxford on the homestead, and removed to Charlton about 1827. He subsequently returned to Oxford, and removed to Troy, Ill., about 1840. He married Hannah J., daughter of Mayo Packard Dec. 4, 1821. She was born Dec. 2, 1803. He died at Bunker Hill, Ill., July 26, 1851, at the age of fifty-five.

Their children were born as follows:—

1573—1.   CALPURNIA⁸, born June 17, 1822, at Oxford; died at Charlton, in 1831.

* Granddaughter of Sarah Hovey (536).

1574—II.   MILO⁴, born Oct. 6, 1824, in Oxford. *See family numbered*
           "1574."
1575—III. LUCIUS⁴, born in 1826, in Oxford; died in 1826.
1576—IV.   MARCIA ANN⁴, born Dec. 24, 1826, in Oxford; died at Bunker
           Hill, Ill., July —, 1848, at the age of twenty-one.
1577—V.   CALISTA⁴, born March 12, 1827, at Charlton; married David
           Cavender of Bunker Hill; and she died in 1846, childless.
1578—VI.   LURA⁴, born April 4, 1828; died at Bunker Hill July 23, 1851,
           at the age of twenty-three.
1579—VII. DANIEL W.⁴, born Oct. —, 1829. *See family numbered "1579."*
1580—VIII. GIDEON⁴. *See family numbered "1580."*
1581—IX.   MARY G.⁴, born Sept. 28, 1834; married William Lancaster;
           and had seven children.
1582—X.   CLARISSA H.⁴; married George E. Barnes; and had five chil-
           dren.
1583—XI.   JAMES H.⁴, born July 23, 1837; married Mary A. Griffin of
           Salem, Ill.; and had no children.
1584—XII. ELIZA J.⁴, born June 8, 1839, at Oxford; married John M.
           Ness; and had six children.
1585—XIII. OLIVE J.⁴, born March 15, 1841, at Troy, Ill.; married James
           M. Wilson of Bethalto, Ill.; and he died Dec. 8, 1872. They
           had no children.
1586—XIV. SARAH H.⁴, born Jan. 28, 1844, at Bunker Hill; married John
           L. Manley; and had three children.

1049

FREDERICK HOVEY³, born in Hanover, N. H., Aug. 6, 1796.
He married Harriet Ellis Jan. 12, 1825; and lived at Thetford,
Vt. She died Feb. 28, 1770; and he died at Berlin, Vt., March
1, 1876, at the age of seventy-nine.

Their children were born as follows:—

1587—I.   FREDERICK FREEMAN⁴, born Jan. 16, 1826, in Thetford. *See*
           family numbered "1587."
1588—II.   HARRIET MARIA⁴, born Nov. 9, 1828, in Thetford; died May
           25, 1880.
1589—III. OTIS ELLIS⁴, born July 13, 1831; was graduated from Wabash
           college in 1856; was an attorney-at-law; died at Crawfords-
           ville, Ind., June 14, 1857, at the age of twenty-five.
1590—IV.   JABEZ WADSWORTH⁴, born May 3, 1833, in Thetford. *See*
           family numbered "1590."
1591—V.   EDWARD PAYSON⁴, born June 1, 1835. *See family numbered*
           "1591."
1592—VI.   MARY EDNA⁴, born Dec. 29, 1837.

1051

REV. EDMUND OTIS HOVEY, D. D.³, son of Roger Hovey
(573) and Martha Freeman, was born July 15, 1801, at Hanover,
N. H., the ninth in a family of ten, five of them dying in childhood, and the other five living to be more than 70 years of age.
All of them were baptized by Dr. Eden Burroughs, pastor of the
Presbyterian church in Hanover. The family removed to Thetford, Vt., in 1814, but Edmund remained a while longer at

Hanover as the pupil of his uncle Jonathan Freeman. When he rejoined the family he found plenty to do on his father's farm of 160 acres; but time enough was taken for family worship, and after six days of farm-work and shop-work always came a quiet unbroken Sabbath. Much reading was done in the long winter evenings by the firelight or the dim illumination of dip candles. Standard works of history, travel and science were preferred to lighter literature. The American Journal of Science and Art found here a group of eager readers and gave to Edmund his first impulse toward a scientific career. For a while he went to a school taught by a Mr. Hubbard; but later to the Thetford Academy, of which Rev. John Fitch was the principal.

In 1821 Edmund joined the Congregational church of which Dr. Asa Burton was the pastor, who relied on him to help bring forward the hundred or more converts of the great revival marking that year. His mind being turned toward the ministry the church adopted him as its beneficiary, "boarding him around," buying his text-books, etc., and the "Ladies' Cent Society" undertook to clothe him. His father did not really approve of all this; but finally "gave him his freedom" and ten dollars; while his uncle Otis gave him a calf that was sold and the money applied to his tuition. So zealously did the young man apply himself to study that his health gave way and his physician advised him to take a long journey on horseback. Accordingly he went first to Saratoga, and thence to Sandwich, on Cape Cod, where he was for six months the guest and patient of his uncle, Dr. Nathaniel Freeman, who had been a member of Congress and a general in the Revolutionary army, and was the father of twenty children, yet generously made room for his invalid nephew.

Having regained his health Mr. Hovey entered Dartmouth College in the spring of 1825, and was graduated in 1828, being aided financially by Judge Joseph Reed and others. He was made a member of the Phi Beta Kappa Society by reason of his degree of scholarship. In his junior year his devotion to a classmate, Horace Ezra Carter, who died of typhoid fever, led to an acquaintance with Mr. Carter's sister Mary which later ripened into a marriage engagement. With another classmate, Caleb Mills, a friendship was formed that lasted through life. Other classmates were strong men who made their mark on the age; and more than half of them entered the ministry. Mr. Hovey worked his way through Andover Seminary by his skill as a box-maker and by vacation mission-work in Vermont and Canada. His license is dated Nov. 27. 1830; and he was duly ordained Sept. 26, 1831, by the old Presbytery of Newburyport, at East Bradford (now Groveland), the parts being taken by Rev. Messrs. Perry, Hunt, Dana, Storrs and Phelps. The record is that on that day seven young men were ordained "to go into the Western country"; namely, Messrs. Hovey, Larabee, Blood, Chapin, Tenney, Bowtell and Folsom.*

On Oct. 5, 1831, Mr. Hovey married Miss Mary Carter, daughter of Ezra Carter, Esq., principal of the Peacham Academy, an alumnus of Dartmouth, and a relative and friend of Daniel Webster. Her grandfather, Ephraim Carter, was an ensign in the Revolutionary army and "Constable of Canterbury." Her great-grandfather, Ezra Carter, was both a physician and a magistrate; hence the inscription on his tomb, "Dr. Ezra Carter, Esquire." He married Ruth Eastman, daughter of Capt. Ebenezer Eastman, who commanded a company at the taking of Louisburg, June 16, 1746.† The immigrant ancestor of the name was Thomas Carter, one of the early settlers of Ipswich, then of Newbury, and in 1640 of Salisbury, Mass.‡ On the maternal side Miss Carter came from the families of Ellsworth, Edwards and Stoddard, names illustrious in colonial annals.

As soon as the marriage ceremony had been performed by Dr. Leonard Worcester, the wedded pair started for the West, with "a roving commission," like Abraham, "not knowing whither they were going." Crossing Lake Champlain by boat, they went by canal to Troy and Buffalo, spent a day at Niagara, and took the steamboat "Henry Clay" for Detroit, then a village of 3,500 inhabitants. According to their diary "railroads were, as yet, a subject of contemplation." Mr. Hovey started the first temperance society in Michigan, enlisting for its support Hon. Lewis Cass, then governor of the territory, but made that year Secretary of War under Jackson, and by his order "grog" was banished from the U. S. army. After a short stay at a village of Pottawattomy Indians, they went by ox-cart to the Maumee rapids, and thence by pirogue to Fort Wayne, where they met Judge Hanna, who advised them to go to a small town just started at the foot of Lake Michigan, a "right smart place of 300 inhabitants and no minister; they call it 'Chicago.'" But by this time their hearts were set on doing mission work in Indiana. Floating down the Wabash in a canoe they were stranded on shoals one night. Curling for sleep on the boxes aboard, they sang, "Thus far the Lord hath led us on," and waited till with daylight help came to set them afloat again. At Logansport they met friends with whom Mrs. Hovey remained while her husband, with the Rev. James Carnahan, "rode and tied" to Lafayette, where the latter had a parish.

* See records of Presbytery; records of Groveland Church; diary of Mr. Nathaniel Ladd; and the Home Missionary Magazine, Vol. iv, No. 7.
† See Bouton's History of Concord, pages 531-555.
‡ See Hoyt's "Old Families of Salisbury and Amesbury," Part Two, pages 87 and 88.

Fountain county attracted Mr. Hovey, where there were 10,000 people and no minister, no meeting-house, no school-house or newspaper. Returning for his wife, they began to keep house in a log-cabin near Rob Roy, with a log floor, a stick chimney, and near by a log stable that sheltered "Barney" a reformed race-horse that carried his missionary-master 2,000 miles the next two years, never letting him miss a single appointment. Mr. Hovey started four churches, several Sunday schools, day schools and temperance societies, and promoted the first newspaper in the county. He helped form the Wabash Presbytery, covering six-teen counties, whose four ministers and eight elders once met in the Hovey cabin and at night lodged on the straw-strewn pun-cheon floor of its single room.

A new chapter was opened on Nov. 21, 1832, when five min-isters and four elders met at Crawfordsville, in Montgomery county, in the only brick house within fifty miles, and voted to found a college. The ministers present were Rev. John M. Ellis, who presided; Mr. Hovey, who was secretary, James and John Thomson, and James A. Carnahan. Hon. Williamson Dunn gave them a forest lot of fifteen acres, where they drove the corner stake for Forest Hall, and kneeling in the newly fallen snow they solemnly dedicated the institution to God, and then voted to secure Caleb Mills as its first principal. The charter name was "Wabash Manual Labor College and Teachers' Institute" afterwards abridged to simply "Wabash College." With it Mr. Hovey be-came identified for life.

First, he took an appointment as its financial agent. Em-barking at Covington he descended the Wabash to its mouth, then went up the Ohio to Louisville, Cincinnati and Pittsburg. Few encouraged him. Dr. Lyman Beecher "frowned on the in-fant weakling of a college." Appeals were in vain at Philadel-phia, New York, Boston, Hartford and New Haven. At the latter city he reported himself as "with an empty purse, no hope and every door closed." He wrote resigning all connection with the college, and signed his letter, "Yours at the point of despera-tion." Had that letter been sent the college would have perished; but it was not sent and the college lived and finally became one of the strongest of the interior colleges. The faculty of Yale College spoke words of encouragement to the agent and ad-vised an appeal to the smaller towns in New England. The first effort in this direction was at Amesbury, where $50 were given. A visit to Newburyport was rewarded by gifts of money and supplies amounting to $425. The crisis was past. Several thou-sand dollars were obtained. Then, one day, Mr. Hovey intro-duced himself to the most successful minister in New York City, saying, "Dr. Baldwin, you are asked to be the first president of Wabash College." The map of Indiana was spread out and the claims of the new state, "as large as all New England, aside from Maine," were urged, till consent was gained, and the Hoosier agent returned home with $40,000 and the promise of a president. After the death of Dr. Baldwin, in 1840, Mr. Hovey secured Dr. White as his successor; and again, after White's death, he obtained Dr. Tuttle to follow him. Other officers of the college were secured by Mr. Hovey. His services as treasurer enabled him to turn over to his successor in that office the sum of $100,000. He personally superintended the erection of Forest Hall, South Hall and Centre Hall. He bought of Major Whitlock the grounds for a new campus, selling at auction what was not needed for a college reserve. The Major was a hard-money man and refused payment unless in coin. Mr. Hovey went to Cincinnati and brought home, by "mud-wagon," the sum of $6,000, in six boxes, each box containing $1,000 in silver. A tenant of the college named Tom Kelly took the precious boxes by wheelbarrow through the public streets to the Major, who counted the contents, dollar by dollar and then gave his receipt for the sum. The new campus was densely covered by a virgin forest. Allowing the best trees to stand, the less desirable were felled and the underbrush cleared away, mainly by the professors and students, and in the clearing a building was erected that was burned before it was finished; but the recitations were hindered for only one day, and the rebuilding was begun at once.

At the outset Mr. Hovey was offered the chair of the Natural Sciences, which, after some deliberation he accepted and retained till his death. From first to last he was a trustee; for several years he was the librarian. He is said to have had at various times classes in everything taught in the college curriculum. His professorship was amply endowed by the late Chauncey Rose, of Terre Haute, who also entrusted large sums to him to be spent in acts of benevolence.

On a lot of the college reserve the Hovey house was built in 1837, which remained in the family till it was recently sold as a site for a fine presidential mansion; the old dwelling being removed and used for occupancy by the curator of the campus. Within its hospitable walls were welcomed scores of youth who were treated like sons and who carried forth with them impressions felt for life.

Amid such diversity of duty Mr. Hovey found scant time for special studies or for authorship. He amassed a cabinet of 25,000 specimens, 10,000 of which were numbered and catalogued. He made a few contributions to scientific periodicals, published a few sermons, and wrote a history of Wabash College in 1857. Frequently he occupied the pulpits in the vicinity, and always won fixed attention, though his appeals were intellectual instead of emotional. At its centennial celebration Dartmouth College gave him the degree of Doctor of Divinity. Public-spirited, patriotic, upright and conscientious in all things, he wrought out faithfully the problems that fell to his lot. The end came suddenly, March 10, 1877, and after commending his spirit to his Maker, his expiring words were "God bless Wabash College." Over the main window in Centre church, which he helped to found, a memorial window has been placed in his honor, and a monument of Quincy granite marks his final resting-place in the Oakhill cemetery at Crawfordsville, with the simple yet sufficient legend, "Faithful in the Lord." Mrs. Hovey survived him, ending her useful and beautiful life July 12, 1886, at the age of seventy-seven.*

The children of Dr. and Mrs. Hovey were as follows:—

1593—i. HORACE CARTER⁷, born near Rob Roy, Indiana, Jan. 28, 1833.
See family numbered "1593."

1594—ii. MARY FREEMAN⁷, born at Crawfordsville, Indiana, Sept. 28, 1838, and died there, June 4, 1897, of heart-failure. Her girlhood education was by private tutors, followed by a course at the Ohio Female College, near Cincinnati. Soon after the founding of the Agricultural College at Manhattan, Kansas, the chair of English Language and Literature was offered to Miss Hovey, who is said to have been the first lady in America to hold a college professorship. After occupying this place for several years she resigned in order to care for her venerable parents; and accordingly opened a school for young ladies at Crawfordsville, where, first and last, she instructed more than 250 young women. After her father's death, in 1877, she taught in the public schools of New Haven, where her brother then resided, and with whom she and her widowed mother made their home till in 1880, when they returned to Crawfordsville, where her school for young ladies was resumed, in which she continued with occasional interruptions till the work was relinquished on account of impaired health. Miss Hovey joined the Centre Presbyterian church at an early age and remained in its fellowship through her life. She was a tireless religious worker and was for many years president of the Ladies' Missionary Society. She also belonged to the Athenian Literary Society, to which she made frequent literary contributions. She most tenderly cared for her parents in their declining years, and aided her father in cataloguing the college cabinet, and in compiling a voluminous scrap-book of college history. She was never married. Her remains rest beside those of her parents at Crawfordsville. By will she left $500 to the Presbyterian Board of Home Missions, and the remainder of her estate to her brother and his family.*

1052

HORACE HOVEY⁷, born in Hanover, N. H., Aug. 1, 1805. He was a farmer, and lived in Thetford, Vt., and, after his marriage, in Worcester, Vt. He married Alpa, daughter of Dr. Elijah and

* Rev. Horace C. Hovey, D. D.

Lydia (Hutchinson) Hammond of Thetford Jan. 5, 1836;
and died in Worcester Jan. 25, 1883, at the age of seventy-
seven.

Their children were born in Worcester, as follows:—

1595—I.   MARTHA FREEMAN[8], born Dec. 2, 1836; married (as his second
           wife) Socrates Udall Jan. 10, 1866. He was born April 20,
           1827; and was a farmer in Craftsbury, Vt. He died Oct. 5,
           1899; and she died Dec. 17, 1905. Their children were born
           in Craftsbury, as follows: 1. *Bertren Rufus*[9], born July
           30, 1868; was a farmer; married Elsbeth Marguerite Peter-
           son of Craftsbury Aug. 4, 1904; and had a daughter. 2.
           Denny Hammond[9], born Feb. 9, 1874; graduated at Uni-
           versity of Vermont, 1898, and at Veterinary University of
           Cornell; and he is assistant professor of veterinary surgery
           and clinics, University of Ohio, Columbus, O. He married
           Mary E. Taylor of Craftsbury Sept. 10, 1903; and they
           have one child.

1596—II.   ROGER[8], born Sept. 7, 1839. *See family numbered "1596."*
1597—III. HORACE WILSON[8], born Sept. 26, 1841. *See family numbered
           "1597."*

1598—IV.   JULIA MARIA[8], born Sept. 2, 1843; married Lyman L. Udall of
           Buchanan county, Iowa, Jan. —, 1867; and they live at
           Strafford, Vt. Their children were born as follows: 1.
           William Selden[9], born Oct. 19, 1869, in Buchanan county; he
           is a salesman, and lives in Haverhill, N. H. He married,
           first, Belle Grose of Strafford, Vt., in 1890; she died in
           Washington, D. C., Sept. 2, 1891; and he married, second,
           Madeline E. Child of Malden, Mass., May 12, 1897. 2.
           Rufus Jesse[9], born Nov. 24, 1869; died Aug. 26, 1872. 3.
           Horace Hovey[9], born July 12, 1872, in Wolcott, Vt.; is a
           merchant, and lives in Strafford. He married Avis Julia
           Simmons of Woodstock, Vt., Sept. 3, 1901; and they had
           one child. 4. *Mary Abbie*[9], born March 17, 1874, in Wol-
           cott; married Fred W. Preston Sept. 1, 1894. He is a
           farmer, and they live in Strafford. 5. *John Lucknow*[9],
           born Feb. 8, 1876, in Wolcott; is a salesman, and lives in
           Haverhill, N. H. He married Bertha M. Wardner of Ran-
           dolph, Vt., Sept. 6, 1899; and they have two children.

1599—V.   MARY ABBIE[8], born Oct. 15, 1846; married Dudley B. Jones of
           Middlesex, Vt., March 17, 1880. He was born in 1829; was
           a farmer; and died Dec. 21, 1898, at the age of sixty-
           nine.

1057

EDMUND CLARK HOVEY[7], born in Norwich, Vt., Oct. 16,
1791. He was a merchant, and lived in his native town. He
married Lavinia, daughter of Rev. Timothy and Phalle (Richardson) Grow Dec. 31, 1819. She was born in Hartland, Vt.,
July 17, 1799. He died at Hardwick, Vt., Nov. 28, 1846, at the
age of fifty-five; and she died at New Rochelle, N. Y., Oct. 5,
1854, aged fifty-five.

Their children were born in Norwich, as follows:—

1600—I.   JANE AMANDA[8], born Nov. 8, 1820; died June 6, 1823, at two
           years of age.

1601—II. EUNICE SOPHRONIA[4], born Oct. 1, 1822; married Rev. Franklin A., son of Adonijah and Rebecca (Mansfield) Slater Dec. 5, 1850, in Coventry, Vt. He was a Baptist clergyman; and lived at Matawan, N. J. She died at Greenport, L. I., April 11, 1863; and he died at Matawan Aug. 3, 1900. Their children were born as follows: *1. Ida E.[5]*, born Nov. 24, 1852, in Mystic, Conn.; lives at Matawan, unmarried. *2. Frank Hovey[5]*, born May 15, 1855, in Rome, N. Y.; druggist; lives in Matawan, unmarried. *3. Myron E.[5]*, born Dec. 8, 1857, in Keyport, N. J.; he is a salesman; and lives at Red Bank, N. J. He married, first, Ella V. Cadmus Dec. 3, 1884; second, Laura, daughter of James and Elsie M. (Wolford) Van Wickle Jan. 6, 1897; she died Jan. 20, 1904, in Matawan; and he married, third, Mrs. Charlotte Hickok Williams May 22, 1906. He has one child. *4. Henry G.[5]*, born Aug. 26, 1861, in Keyport; died Dec. 29, 1863, in Greenport, L. I.

1602—III. MARVIN GROW[4], born March 27, 1824; died April 12, 1842.
1603—IV. BETSEY JANE[4], born Feb. 25, 1826; died Nov. 2, 1828.
1604—V. EDMUND OTIS[4], born May 24, 1829. *See family numbered "1604."*

1605—VI. LUMAN BRUNSON[4], born Nov. 15, 1830; died April 19, 1843.
1606—VII. GEORGE BORDMAN[4], born Sept. 9, 1834; died April 29, 1842.
1607—VIII. PERSIS ALMINA[4], born July 12, 1837; died Jan. 31, 1840.
1608—IX. ARABELLA IOLA[4], born Sept. 9, 1845; married Dr. Rush Wilmot, son of Baxter P. and Mary Tetherly (Stone) Kimball April 15, 1891. He was born July 26, 1862, and they live in Norwich, Conn.

1061

OLIVER KNOWLTON HOVEY[5], born in Norwich, Vt., Aug. 25, 1799. He married Fannie Martin.

Children:—

1609—I. BETSEY[4], born in 1828; married Samuel Merrill; and lived in Windsor, Vt. He died March 4, 1894, in Claremont, N. H., where she died May 19, 1900.
1610—II. CHARLES L.[4], born in 18—; lived in Windsor, Vt., being a farmer, married ———— ————; and died in Windsor. His widow lived there.
1611—III. ROSALINE LUCY[4], born April 30, 1832, in Perkinsville, Vt.; married James Franklin, son of James and Diantha (Chapin) Weston Sept. 14, 1856, at Weathersfield; he was born in Hooksett, N. H., Aug. 16, 1832. They lived in Lawrence and Lowell, Mass. He was a belt maker; and died in Lowell, Mass., June 23, 1892, at the age of fifty-nine. She survived him, and died there Oct. 31, 1896, at the age of sixty-four. Their children were born in Lawrence, as follows: *1. Jennie Colvin[5]*, born Dec. 25, 1857; married Jesse F., son of John C. and Hannah (Allen) Knowlton Oct. 27, 1881, in Lowell. He was born in Gloucester, Mass., Sept. 3, 1856. He is engaged in the leather business; and lives in Chelsea, Mass. They have three children. *2. Lillian Marie[5]*, born March 30, 1860; clerk; lives in Lowell, unmarried. *3. Charles Franklin[5]*, born Feb. 14, 1862; married Alice Perham Oct. 10, 1888, in Lowell. He is a belt maker, and lives in Lowell. They have no children.

1063

ANDREW L. HOVEY[7], born in Norwich, Vt., July 11, 1805.
He married ——— ———; and lived in Craftsbury, Vt.
    Child :—

1612—I.   DWIGHT[8]; lived in Craftsbury.

1068

CAPT. HENRY RUSSELL HOVEY[7], son of Rev. Aaron and
Huldah (Ely) Hovey, was "a collateral descendant" of Rev. John
Russell of Hadley, Mass., who secreted the regicides, Goffe and
Whalley.* He was born in Saybrook (now Centerbrook), Conn.,
Jan. 27, 1816. His brother-in-law was Capt. Henry L. Champlin
of Essex, Conn., at that time in command of one of the clipper
ships of the "Black X" line, sailing between New York and
London, to whom he was much attached, with the result that, at
the age of eighteen, he made a passage with Capt. Champlin as
cabin boy. At twenty-one he had become first mate; but, feeling
that his education was not complete, he left the service and for
two years attended the Colchester, Conn., seminary, making a
special study of navigation. At twenty-three he followed the sea
again, and at twenty-four was in command of the ship "President"; and he successively commanded the "Philadelphia," the
"Westminster," the "Devonshire" and the "Amazon," all of the
"Black X" or, as it was then known, the Morgan Line.

The "Amazon" was burned in the English Channel in 1863.
Some "infernal machine" was probably shipped in her cargo. In
this year the privateers "Alabama" and "Tallahassee" were fitted
out in Europe for the purpose of destroying United States ship-
ping. Captain Hovey's estate, some years later, proved their
claim and participated in the "Alabama Award."

On returning to America, Captain Hovey became part owner
and commander of the steamer "Lodona" of the Mallory line,
sailing between New York and New Orleans, which was lost on
the Florida coast August 16, 1871. Captain Hovey was among
those who perished.

Several rescues at sea were made by him; notably of the
passengers and crew of the steamer "Helena Sloman," bound
from Hamburg for New York, which had lost her rudder and
was leaking badly, having been in that condition for eight days.
Captain Hovey, of the ship "Devonshire," answered her signals of
distress, and transferred to his ship fifty-four cabin and eighty-
six steerage passengers and the crew of forty men, the sinking
vessel being left to her fate.† Fir this timely rescue, Captain

* See History of Hadley, Mass.
† See New York Herald, Dec. 6, 1850.

Hovey had the thanks of two continents, and many testimonials of esteem.

The mayor and common council of the City of New York sent him, in token of their high appreciation, the following finely engrossed resolution :—

By the Corporation of the City of New York—
Resolved, That the thanks of the Common Council be, and the same are hereby tendered to Captain Henry R. Hovey, of the ship Devonshire, of New York, for his humane and daring efforts in rescuing from imminent peril, and safely conveying to this port the crew and passengers, numbering 175 persons of the steamer Helena Sloman, Captain P. U. Paulsen, of Hamburg, fallen in with at sea on the 28th of November, 1850, in a sinking condition; also that a grateful recognition is due to the heroic services of his gallant officers and crew, of whom his third mate, John G. Johnson, of this city, and three seamen, nobly perished in their endeavors to save others from the fate which they themselves so suddenly experienced. Also, that as a further mark of appreciation of the City of New York of the noble conduct of Capt. Hovey, a Gold Box, suitably inscribed, be presented him.

This testimonial is now in the family collection of Henry Russell Hovey of Hartford, Conn.

The box is of fine gold, about four inches long by two and one-half wide and about an inch thick, and bears on the outside of the cover the inscription, "HOVEY," and inside the following :—

"Presented by the Corporation of the City of New York to Capt. Henry R. Hovey, of the ship Devonshire, of the same place, as a testimonial of their appreciation of his heroic conduct on the occasion of his rescuing the crew and passengers of the steamer Helena Sloman, at sea, on the 28th Nov., 1850."

This relic is now owned by Mrs. W. S. Lines, a daughter of Captain Hovey, of Hartford, Conn.

A gold medal was also presented to Captain Hovey by the senate of Hamburg. On one side is a view of the harbor of Hamburg, on the reverse, the Exchange, the Bank, the Berlin railway station, the Opera house, the building of the Patriotic Society, Music hall and Theatre. The medal was in a box, superbly ornamented with silver mountings. On the lid is the following inscription :—

THE SENATE OF HAMBURG
To Capt. HENRY R. HOVEY, for
the gallant rescue of the
passengers of the
Hamburg Ship
Helena Sloman,
Nov. 29,
1850.

This medal is now in the possession of Roger Huntley
Hovey, of Hartford, Conn., a grandson of Capt. Henry Russell
Hovey.

The following correspondence passed between the consul of
Hamburg and Captain Hovey:—

CONSULATE OF HAMBURG, 4 William-st., April 16, 1845.

DEAR SIR—It affords me great satisfaction to renew my correspondence with you, and in referring to my note of 7th December last, to have it
in my power to say, that the government of Hamburg has not only approved of my having expressed to you officially *my* thanks for the assistance rendered to the passengers and crew of the Hamburg steamship
"Helena Sloman," but has also directed me to express to you the high
appreciation with which has been viewed by the Senate of the free and
Hanseatic city of Hamburg, your humanity and gallantry, and the courage and devotion displayed by the officers and crew of the noble ship,
Devonshire, under you on that lamentable occasion, lamentable on account
of the loss of life sustained in the act of transferring passengers to your
rescue ship.

I am instructed to present to you and to Mr. Moore, your efficient
first officer, a memorial of the acknowledgments of the city of Hamburg,
consisting of a gold medal in an ornamented case, and to pay the sum of
one hundred dollars to the families (if in needy circumstances) of the
late third mate, Mr. John G. Johnson, and the three seamen of the ship
Devonshire; also, to distribute the some of other hundred dollars among
the other part of the crew at that time under your command; and in the
hope that you will lend me your assistance in the carrying out of these
instructions as far as practicable, I request you to grant me an interview
on board of your vessel tomorrow (Thursday) afternoon, and to induce
Mr. Moore to be present at that time, also, in order to meet me.

With assurance of my high regard,

I remain sir,

Your obd't serv't.

(Signed)   FERDINAND KARCK, CONSUL.

HENRY R. HOVEY, Esq., Commander of ship Devonshire.

——————

NEW YORK, April 21 1851.

FERDINAND KARCK, Esq., Consul for the City of Hamburg.

DEAR SIR: I have this day had the honor of receiving through you
a gold medal, also a beautifully engrossed document expressing the pleasure you feel in being made the medium through which the Senate of Hamburg has seen fit to present me with the above memorial.

In return, allow me to tender, through you, to the honorable Senate,
my most sincere and heartfelt thanks for the notice is has been pleased to
take of a transaction upon which I shall ever look back with gratitude.

This testimonal will recall to me and mine an occasion in which
Providence enabled me to aid my suffering fellow-creatures and will
remind us of the generous appreciation of my conduct at that time, in
such a manner as to incite to new efforts for others.

I did no more than my duty, and trust that the notice which has
been taken of the rescue of the passengers of the "Helena Sloman," may
stimulate others of my profession to still greater exertions for those who
are in danger.

Allow me, also, to express my thanks to you personally, for the cordial and flattering interest you have manifested in this matter. The gift has been made more valuable by all the accompanying circumstances of its presentation.

Mr. Moore, first officer of the "Devonshire," has also received a medal, and unites with me in thanks to the honorable Senate.

With the highest respect I remain, yours truly,

(Signed)   HENRY R. HOVEY,

Captain of the American Packet-Ship Devonshire.

A superb silver speaking trumpet was given to Captain Hovey by cabin passengers on the rescued vessel. It weighed forty-two ounces and was inlaid with gold, having on it an embossed representation of the act of rescue and the loss of the mate, three seamen and five passengers by the upsetting of the boat which they were in. The trumpet bears the following inscription:—

Presented to Captain Henry R. Hovey of the ship Devonshire, by some of the cabin passengers of the steamer Helena Sloman and others, as a token of esteem for saving the passengers and crew of said steamer while in a sinking condition on the twenty-eighth November, 1850.

This relic is owned by Henry Russell Hovey of Hartford, Conn.

As an indication of the esteem in which Captain Hovey was held by the passengers of the ship "Devonshire," very interesting letters are on file with the family, testifying to the constant courtesy and elegant hospitality of the commander, as well as the superior order kept on board his vessel. His reply to these words of thanks and appreciation is also on file.

Captain Hovey was a devout christian. Even as a boy his mind was trained to religious thought; but it was not until he had seen something of the world and become convinced that, while "in the world" he was "not of it" that he confessed Christ and joined the church of which his father (Rev. Aaron Hovey) was pastor. When ashore he always attended church meetings and the writer of this sketch (Henry Russell Hovey, jr.) has been present at many prayer meetings in which he took part,— always in prayer and always (as was customary then) kneeling during its offering. His death, at the age of fifty-five years (August 16, 1871), was an event that called for elaborate notices from pulpit and press of two continents, as may be found from a perusal of New York and London papers of that date. It was truly said of him: "Here was a man, a nobleman."

Captain Hovey married Mary Emma Kutz, daughter of Erasmus A. Kutz, for forty years (1810-1850) a manufacturer of nautical instruments on Water street, in New York. She was born in Brooklyn, N. Y., November 24, 1818, and died in Hartford, Conn., August 10, 1906. They were united in marriage

May 4, 1841, in Broolyn, N. Y., by Rev. Melancthon Jacobus, father of Rev. Melancthon W. Jacobus, the present dean of Hartford Theological Seminary. It is worthy of note to quote the lines written by Doctor Jacobus and given "His beloved Miss Mary," at the time he married them :—*

> Bonds, sweet and lasting may these be,
> In unalloyed felicity;
> And in this hallowed blest estate,
> Long live the CAPTAIN and his MATE;
> Aiding each other o'er life's sea,
> To reach a safe eternity.*

Their children were born as follows :—

1613—I. AMELIA LOUISA⁴, born April 28, 1843, in Brooklyn, N. Y.; married Roger Williams Love Dec. 21, 1865. He was born in Corfu, Greece, Feb. 14, 1842; and died in Saratoga, N. Y., July 30, 1878. She lives in Washington, D. C. Their children were born as follows: 1. Henry Hovey⁵, born Sept. 8, 1866, in Bristol, Conn.; lives in Boston, Mass.; married Virginia C. Aldridge in Rochester, N. Y. 2. Robert Harlow⁵, born July 30, 1868, in Windsor, Vt.; lives in Washington, D. C.; married, first, Katherine V. Bishop Jan. 16, 1890; she died Sept. —, 1894; married, second, Bertha M. Compet Sept. 6, 1898; and she died Oct. —, 1899. 3. Winifred⁵, born Aug. 26, 1870, in Claremont, N. H.; died Dec. 6, 1881. 4. Roger⁵, born Sept. 12, 1872, in Claremont; died in 1873. 5. Mabel⁵, born Aug. 22, 1874, in Claremont; died Dec. 25, 1881. 6. Maude Marion⁵, born March 12, 1876, in Claremont; married Harry B. Moore in Washington, D. C.

1614—II. MARY EMMA⁴, born April 26, 1845, in Newark, N. J.; married, first, James T. Curtin Dec. 25, 1863, in Essex, Conn. He was born in Richmond, England, in 1836; and died in Newark, N. J., April 2, 1865. She married, second, Andrew D. Ross May 4, 1871, in Essex, Conn. He was born in Brooklyn, N. Y., Dec. 24, 1844; and died in Aiken, S. C., Feb. 29, 1884. She died in Chicago July 17, 1907. Children of James T. and Mary E. (Hovey) Curtin: 1. James Hovey⁵, born Feb. 15, 1865, in Newark; lives in New Orleans, La.; married Georgie May Dixon April 3, 1890, in Chicago, Ill. She was born in New Orleans, La., Oct. 25, 1871. They had three children. Children of Andrew D. and Mary E. (Hovey) Ross: 1. Henry Russell⁵, born Aug. 9, 1872, in Brooklyn, N. Y.; lives in Chicago.

1615—III. CAROLINE SUSAN⁴, born Sept. 18, 1848, in Newark; married, first, Edward Anthon Smith of Essex, Conn., Aug. 31, 1867; he died in 1881; she married, second, William Samuel Lines of New York Nov. 18, 1886, in Hartford; he was born Feb. 16, 1837; and died Dec. 24, 1912. She lives in Hartford, Conn. Child of Edward A. and Caroline S. (Hovey) Smith: 1. Maude M.⁵, born May 20, 1869; died Oct. 2, 1870. Child of William S. and Caroline S. (Hovey) Lines: 1. William Samuel⁵, born Aug. 9, 1889, in Hartford,

---

* Henry Russell Hovey, jr.

Conn.; married Dorothy Kenyon of Hartford. She was born Nov. 10, 1889. They have two children: 1. Carolyn, born Sept. 22, 1911. 2. William Samuel, born Sept. 6, 1912. They reside in West Hartford, Conn.

1616—iv.   ADA LOUISE[6], born June 9, 1850, in New York, N. Y. Living in Broad Brook, Conn. She married, first, George Cone Richmond April 12, 1870. He was born in Moodus, Conn., Nov. 16, 1845; and died in Philadelphia, Pa., in 1889. She married, second, William B. Tifft Jan. 15, 1891, in Hartford, Conn., where he was born. Child of George C. and Ada L. (Hovey) Richmond: 1. *Mary Katherine*[7], born May 11, 1871, in Plainville, Conn.; married Frederick John, son of Rev. T. T. Lightbourne of Attleboro, Mass. He was born at St. George's, Bermuda. Child of William B. and Ada L. (Hovey) Tifft: 1. *Emerson Buckingham*[7], born March 12, 1892, in Hartford.

1617—v.   HENRY RUSSELL[6], born June 9, 1852, in Centerbrook, Conn. *See family numbered "1617."*

1618—vi.   CHAMPLIN ERASMUS[6], born May 5, 1854, in Centerbrook; died May 24, 1858, in Essex, Conn. The following lines upon his death were written by Amelia P. Champlin, wife of Capt. H. L. Champlin and half-sister of Captain Hovey:—

THE WITHERED FLOWER

Arrayed for the grave, lo! a fair child lies sleeping,
   From his cheeks, late so blooming, the roses have fled;
Beside him a mother in anguish is weeping—
   The pride of her garden lies withered and dead.

Far away on the ocean the father is tossing,
   Whose presence could lighten this burden of woe;
He knows not that Death hath his threshold been crossing.
   He hears not the wail o'er this loved one laid low.

How cold is this brow, by the silken locks shaded,
   And pale are those lips that once rival'd the rose;
The light of those eyes into darkness is faded,
   The lids are sealed up in eternal repose.

Thou fell spoiler Death; here thy triumph has ended.
   Though thy touch hath demolished this prison of clay,
The spirit released to its God hath ascended
   And angels have borne it rejoicing away.

What though, weeping mother, the grave must receive him,
   This thought should console thee, his sufferings are o'er;
Believing in Jesus, again thou shalt meet him,
   In yonder bright world, to be parted no more.

Then yield this loved form, let it rest on earth's bosom;
   Nor grieve that thus early he sank to his rest,—
Escaped from the storms of this life's troubled ocean,
   How sweetly he slumbers the sleep of the blest.
      ESSEX, CONN., May 31, 1858.

1619—vii.   FREDERICK EUGENE[6] (twin), born Sept. 26, 1856, in Centerbrook; lives in Hartford; married Bertha May Caswell Oct. 28, 1885, in Hartford. She was born in Bloomfield, Conn., Aug. 3, 1865; died in Philadelphia, Pa., Dec. 24, 1904.

1620—VIII. FLORENCE EUGENIA[8] (twin), born Sept. 26, 1856, in Center-
brook; married Everett L. Morse May 14, 1878, in Essex,
Conn. He was born in Chepacket, R. I., June 10, 1852.
They lived in Hartford, where he died April 25, 1898. Their
child was born in East Hartford, as follows: 1. *Everett
Hovey[9]*, born March 8, 1879.

1071

AARON HOVEY[7], born in Mansfield, Conn., March 31, 1812.
He was a farmer, and lived in Rockford, Ill. He married Fidelia
E., daughter of Gehial and Elizabeth (Westboth) Harmon of
Suffield, Conn., Nov. —, 1836. She was born in Suffield Nov. 21,
1807; and died at Rockford Nov. 6, 1886, at the age of seventy-
eight. He died at Rockford Feb. 3, 1894, at the age of eighty-one.
Their children were born as follows:—

1621—I.   MARY ELIZABETH[8], born Jan. 10, 1838, in Suffield; married
Dr. Harrison H. Guthrie of St. Charles, Minn., April 16,
1863, at Rockford, Ill.; she died at St. Charles in 1866; and
he died at San Bernardino, Cal., Nov. —, 1909. Their only
child was born at St. Charles, as follows: 1. *Florence[9]*,
born Jan. 5, 1865; married James Hutchings Aug. 7, 1895;
and resides at San Bernardino, Cal. They have two children.
1622—II.   JULIETTE BULKLEY[8], born March 16, 1840, in Rockford; married Stephen Hicks Sept. 2, 1868, at Rockford. He was a
farmer, and they live at Rockford. Their only child was
born in Rockford, as follows: 1. *Herbert[9]*, born April 12,
1872; a lawyer; lives in Rockford; married Florence Gautz
March 10, 1904; and has a daughter.
1623—III. EDMUND T.[8], born Dec. 1, 1842, in Rockford; a farmer; and
lives in his native town.
1624—IV.   ELLEN CLARISSA[8], born in 1845, in Rockford; married George
S. Martin Nov. 22, 1880, at Dixon, Cal. They live in
Pasadena, Cal. Their only child was born in Dixon, as
follows: 1. *Aaron Hovey[9]*, born Feb. 3, 1883; died March
29, 1883.
1625—V.   HUBERT HENRY[8], born Dec. 10, 1847, in Rockford. *See family
numbered "1625."*
1626—VI.   MELISSA E.[8], born Jan. 9, 1850, in Rockford; married Albert S.
Kidd Aug. 24, 1881; and lives in Pasadena, Cal. Their
children were born as follows: 1. *Oliv[9]*, born Aug. 24,
1882, at Rockford, Ill.; died Dec. 29, 1882. 2. *Emery
Hovey[9]*, born Jan. 3, 1885; lives at San Bernardino, Cal.;
married Rose Ann Graves June 6, 1907; and has one child.
3. *Irving Albert[9]*, born Aug. 3, 1887; lives in Pasadena.
4. *Ellen Fidelia[9]*, born Feb. 17, 1889; lives in Pasadena.
5. *Hubert Elmer[9]*, born Sept. 2, 1890; lives in Pasadena.

1072

EDMUND BULKLEY HOVEY, ESQ.[7], born in Mansfield, Conn.,
Aug. 3, 1814. He was a lawyer, and lived in Quincy, Ill. He
married, first, Abby Prior in 1839; and, second, Adelia Harrington Nov. —, 1846. He died at Quincy Jan. 14, 1890, at the age
of seventy-five.

Mr. Hovey's children were born in Quincy, as follows:—

1627—I.   FRANK[8], born Sept. 2, 1857; lives in Quincy.
1628—II.   DELLA[8], born March 14, 1866; married Elijah D. Young; and lives in Quincy.

1060

AMOS WHITE HOVEY[7], born in Greene, N. Y., July 5, 1818. He lived in Bristol Springs, N. Y., in 1893. He married, first, Josephine Mary, daughter of James Schofield June —, 1847, in Brandon, Vt. She was an intelligent and excellent woman, a consistent Christian, ready for every good work. She died in Wisconsin Oct. —, 1866. He married, second, Henrietta Brown Trembly Jan. 13, 1870, in Darlington, Wis. She was born in South Bristol, N. Y., April 11, 1841.

The children of Mr. Hovey were by his first wife, and born as follows:—

1629—I.   JAMES ALFRED[8], born March 28, 1848, in White Oak Springs, Ill.; married Laura S. DeForrest April 18, 1887, in New York City; and died in Oracle, Ariz., Aug. 2, 1891, at the age of forty-three.
1630—II.   EDGAR WALLACE[8], born March 30, 1859, in Darlington, Wis.; and died at Sacramento, Cal., Oct. 3, 1891, aged thirty-two.

1061

REV. ALVAH HOVEY, D. D., LL. D., S. T. D.[7], born in Greene, N. Y., March 5, 1820. His early years were passed on a farm in Thetford, Vt. He fitted for college at Brandon, Vt., and entered Dartmouth at the age of nineteen, leaving at the beginning of his junior year to become principal of Derby academy. After two years he returned to college, entered the senior class and was graduated in 1844. He then taught a private academy in New London, N. H., one year and three months; and entered Newton Theological Institution, at Newton Centre, Mass., in 1845, for the study of theology. At this Baptist institution, his teachers were Doctors Sears and Hackett. He graduated in 1848, and preached for a year (June, 1848, to June, 1849) in New Gloucester, Me., was ordained Jan. 13, 1850, and then returned to the Newton Theological Institution, where he was tutor in Hebrew for five years, librarian for three years, professor of Church History two years, and professor of Christian Theology forty-six years.

Doctor Hovey visited Europe in 1861-2, and Egypt and Palestine in 1897. He was elected president of the Newton Theological Institution in 1868, and remained its head until June 1, 1900, when he resigned, on account of ill-health. He had been professor of General Introduction and Apologetics since the pre-

vious year, and continued to occupy that chair until the year of
his death.

He was a trustee of Worcester academy and the New England Conservatory of Music; vice president and trustee of Wellesley college; fellow and trustee of Brown university; a corpo-
rate member of the General Theological Library of Boston; member of the board of managers of the American Tract Society,
Victoria Institute of London, the Theological Club "C. C." the
Harvard Biblical Club, the Theological Circle and of the Neighbors of Newton Centre, and an honorary member of the Boston
Social Union. Besides being its president, he was a trustee of the
Newton Theological Institution; and a member of the executive
committee of The American Baptist Missionary Union for fifteen
years, eight of which he was the chairman. He duly received the
degrees of S. T. D., D. D., and LL. D., from Brown University,
Richmond College and Denison University.

Dr. Hovey published "The Life and Times of Isaac Backus,
A. M.;" "The State of the Impenitent Dead;" "Miracles of
Christ;" "Biblical Eschatology;" "God with Us;" "Religion and
the State;" "Commentaries on the Gospel of John" and "The
Epistle to the Galations" in the "American Commentaries," of
which he was the general editor; "Manual of Christian Theology;" "Studies in Ethics and Theology;" and several other
volumes, beside numerous articles in various periodicals.

Doctor Hovey married Miss Augusta Maria Rice of Newton
Centre Sept. 24, 1852. She was born there Feb. 19, 1831. They
celebrated their golden wedding anniversary Sept. 24, 1902. The
next summer, he received a paralytic shock, and, failing in
health rapidly, died at his home, 91 Summer street, in Newton
Centre, Sept. 6, 1903, at the age of eighty-three. His funeral
was held at the First Baptist church on the following Wednes-
day, and was largely attended. His estate was valued at sixteen
thousand, three hundred and twenty dollars. Mrs. Hovey survives him, and lives in Newton Centre.

Their children were born in Newton Centre, as follows:—

1631—I. GEORGE RICE[2], born Jan. 17, 1860. *See family numbered
          "1631."*

1632—II. AGNES CURTIS[2], born Aug. 23, 1861; died Aug. 23, 1861.

1633—III. HELEN AUGUSTA[2], born May 13, 1863; married Rev. Wilbur
          Brown Parshley May 21, 1890; and lives in Yokohama,
          Japan.

1634—IV. HATTIE LEE[2], born March 22, 1865; married Rev. John Rus-
          sell Gow Sept. 10, 1884. He was born in Waterville, Me.,
          Oct. 20, 1855. In 1893, they lived at 275 Fifty-second street,
          Hyde Park, Chicago, Ill.; 1886-1889, in Bridgeport, Conn.,
          and 1900-1903 at 42 Franklin street, Somerville, Mass.
          Their children were born as follows: 1. *Lucy Augusta[3]*,
          born Sept. 1, 1885, in Fair Haven, Vt. 2. *Alvah Hovey[3]*,
          born April 25, 1887, in Bridgeport; died there July

12, 1887. 3. *Arthur Coleman*[8], born April 12, 1888, in Bridgeport. 4. *Dorothy*[9], born June 6, 1900, in Somerville. 5. *John Russell*[9], born March 1, 1903, in Somerville.

1635—V.   FREDERICK HOWARD[8], born Oct. 7, 1868. *See family numbered* "*1635.*"

1082

WILLIAM ASHLEY HOVEY[7], born in Thetford, Vt., Sept. 30, 1821. He is a wheelwright and undertaker, and lives in Yreka, Cal. He married Mary Caroline, daughter of William and Sarah (Conway) Wallace April 25, 1850, in Kendall, Wis. She was born in Trimble county, Ky., Aug. 28, 1825; and died in Yreka July 12, 1905, at the age of seventy-nine.

Their children were born as follows:—

1636—I.   EUGENE[8], born Jan. 30, 1852, in Centre, Wis.; killed by Modoc Indians near the Lava-beds, some eighty miles from Yreka, Cal., April 17, 1873, at the age of twenty-one. He was engaged in hauling supplies to the front in the war. He was unmarried.

1637—II.   ELLA MARSELLA[8], born March 30, 1855, in Yreka, Cal.; married George Herbert Peck Jan. 28, 1874, in Yreka. He was born in Oswego, N. Y., Sept. 28, 1846; and they lived in Sisson, Cal., in 1893, and now in Yreka. Their children were born as follows: 1. *Clara Hattie*[9], born April 29, 1879, in Yreka. 2. *George Byron*[9], born Sept. 14, 1881, in Yreka. 3. *Roy Morris*[9], born Dec. 21, 1883, in Yreka. 4. *Ramona Marguerite*[9], born Oct. 5, 1891, in Sisson.

1638—III.   MELVIN[8], born Feb. 8, 1858, in Yreka; was a printer and farmer in Yreka and San Francisco; and died, unmarried, in Yreka April 3, 1911, at the age of fifty-three.

1639—IV.   CLARA MILLY[8], born Sept. 2, 1860, in Yreka; she taught school; and married James Buchanan, son of James Howard and Ann Hazeltine (Hill) Russell June 2, 1885, in Yreka. He was born in Jackson county, Ore., Sept. 7, 1856. They live in Yreka, where he is a dealer in iron fencing, cement and stone, doing his own quarrying. Their children were born in Yreka, as follows: 1. *Lawrence Eugene*[9], born Jan. 3, 1886; married ———— ————; and died Feb. 25, 1893. 2. *Lelia Marguerite*[9], born Dec. 9, 1889; milliner; married Harry William Doggett of Sisson Aug. 3, 1908; they live in Yreka, where he is engaged in cement work and carpentry. They have two children. 3. *Mary Hazeltine*[9], born Sept. 15, 1892; married Elmer Ernest King July 1, 1911. He was born in Minneapolis, Minn., Jan. 1, 1887; and is cashier in the office of Wells, Fargo & Co.'s express at Salem, Ore., where they live. 4. *Howard Ashley*[9], born March 12, 1895. 5. *Mildred Dorothy*[9], born March 21, 1899. 6. *Claud Hovey*[9], born April 19, 1904.

1640—V.   FRANK[8], born May 14, 1863, in Yreka. *See family numbered* "*1640.*"

1641—VI.   WILLIAM GEORGE[8], born Dec. 22, 1866, in Yreka; is a teamster on railroad work, has lived in Yreka and Oakland, Cal.; and is unmarried.

1642—VII.   JENNIE IRENE[8], born Sept. 20, 1869; lives at home, unmarried.

1083

LELAND AARON HOVEY[7], born in Thetford, Vt., Sept. 21, 1823. He lived at first in Darlington, Wis., and then Bloomington, Ill., in 1893. He married, first, Joanna Miriam Allen in 184-, in Lyme, N. H., where she was born April 12, 1824. She died in Bloomington, Ill., March —, 1878(?) He married, second, Emma Mills Johnston in 1880, in Bloomington. She was born in Muskingum, O., June 15, 1840.

The children of Mr. Hovey were born in Darlington, as follows:—

1643—I.   ABBY MIRIAM[8], born Feb. 15, 1848; married William Russell Bascom in 187-, in Normal, Ill.; and he was born in West Halifax, Vt., Sept. 8, 1848. She died in Dubuque, Iowa, Oct. 1, 1891, at the age of forty-three; and he lived in Dubuque in 1893. Their children were born as follows: 1. *Russell*[9], born May 29, 1873, in Normal. 2. *Lelia*[9], born March 31, 1875, in Bloomington. 3. *Fred Thearle*[9], born July 29, 1877, in Bloomington. 4. *Harry Hovey*[9], born April 15, 1879, in Bloomington. 5. *George Rockwell*[9], born June 21, 1882, in Bloomington. 6. *Burton William*[9], born March 3, 1887, in Bloomington. 7. *Ellen Abby*[9], born Sept. 21, 1891, in Dubuque, Iowa.

1644—II.   CHARLES LELAND[8], born Nov. 15, 1851. *See family numbered "1644."*

1645—III. LELIA LEANTHA[8], born March 27, 1856; married Howard Wright Shriner in 18—, at Bloomington, Ill. He was born in Indianapolis, Ind., Dec. 10, 1857. They lived in Hutchinson, Kansas, in 1893. Their children were born as follows: 1. *Nellie May*[9], born Sept. 14, 1883, in Decatur, Ill. 2. *Charles Howard*[9], born Aug. 5, 1885, in Decatur. 3. *William Lelia*[9], born Jan. 23, 1888, in Wichita, Kansas. 4. *Lee Allen*[9], born Nov. 22, 1890, in Hutchinson, Kansas.

1646—IV.   EMMA JOANNA[8], born Aug. 5, 1859; married Henry Oliver Roberts in 188-. He was born in Wintersville, O., Dec. 31, 1855; and they live in Minneapolis, Minn. Their children were born in Minneapolis as follows: 1. *Earl Hovey*[9], born May 6, 1889. 2. *Jessie*[9], born March 14, 1891.

1084

ORAMEL FLETCHER HOVEY[7], born in Thetford, Vt., July 11, 1825. He married Sarah Jane Halstead April 12, 1850, in Darlington, Wis. She was born in Eagleville, Ohio, Sept. 24, 1833. They lived in Sheffield, Pleasant Valley, Iowa, in 1893.

Their children were born as follows:—

1647—I.   ALVAH FLETCHER[8], born Nov. 25, 1851, in Darlington, Wis. *See family numbered "1647."*

1648—II.   ALFRED EGBERT[8], born Oct. 17, 1853, in Darlington.

1649—III. EUGENIE JOSEPHINE[8], born July 19, 1857, in Darlington; married Lorenzo Waldo Fansler March 13, 1879, in Rockwell, Iowa. He was born in Conant, O., Oct. 9, 1855. They lived in Sheffield, Iowa, in 1893. Their children were born as follows: 1. *Milly May*[9], born Dec. 23, 1879, in Geneseo,

Iowa. 2. *Lou Leafy*[8], born Sept. 28, 1881, in Geneseo. 3. *Oramel William*[8], born Feb. 9, 1889, in Long Island, Kansas.

1650—IV. MILLY CLARA[8], born March 17, 1861, in Darlington; married Ansel Alonzo Perrin Jan. 25, 1888, in Pleasant Valley, Iowa. He was born in Pultneyville, N. Y., May —, 1854. They lived in Sheffield, Iowa, in 1893. Their children were born in Geneseo, Iowa, as follows: 1. *Mira Eugenie*[8], born Oct. 28, 1888. 2. *Alfred Ansel*[8], born Dec. 18, 1890.

1651—V. FRANCIS CHARLES[8], born March 21, 1866, in Yreka, Cal.

1652—V. JOHN HALSTEAD[8], born Feb. 10, 1874, in Darlington.

1085

GEN. CHARLES EDWARD HOVEY[7], born in Thetford, Vt., April 26, 1827. He was graduated at Dartmouth College, in 1852. He first studied law but became an educator. He was principal of the high school at South Framingham, Mass., 1852-1854, and of the high school at Peoria, Ill., 1854-1856; superintendent of the public schools of Peoria, 1856 and 1857; president of the State Teachers' Association, 1856; and organizer and first president of the Illinois State Normal University, at Normal, Ill., 1857-1861 When the Civil war came, he rallied a regiment of teachers, the Thirty-third regiment of Illinois, and by unanimous vote was its colonel, 1861 and 1862. He was promoted to be brigadier general in 1862. He resigned in 1863 on account of ill-health, but, in 1865, he was breveted major general of volunteers, "for gallantry and meritorious conduct in battle, particularly at Arkansas Post."

General Hovey married Harriet Farnham, daughter of Farnham and Lydia (Cogswell) Spofford of North Andover, Mass., Oct. 9, 1854. She was born on the island of Nantucket, Mass., July 5, 1834. They lived in Washington, D. C., for a number of years, and there he was admitted to the bar and practised law (1869-1897), while Mrs. Hovey also held an important place in the Department of Education. He died in Washington, D. C., Nov. 17, 1897, and his remains lie buried in the National cemetery at Arlington.

Their children were born as follows:—

1653—I. EDWARD[8], born April 9, 1857, in Peoria, Ill.; died in Bloomington. Ill., Nov. 9, 1859, aged two years.

1654—II. ALFRED[8], born June 16, 1859, in Bloomington. *See family numbered "1654."*

1655—III. RICHARD[8], born May 4, 1864, in Normal, Ill. *See family numbered "1655."*

1086

ELEAZER HOVEY[7], born in Thetford, Vt., June 8, 1829. He lived in Darlington, Wis., in 1893. He married Clara Augusta Scofield Aug. 3, 1855, in Darlington. She was born in Brandon, Vt., May 23, 1833.

Their child was born in Darlington, as follows:—

1656—1.   HARRY SCOFIELD⁸, born June 27, 1862. *See family numbered "1656."*

1088

PROF. SYLVESTER HOVEY⁷, born in Mansfield, Conn., June 17, 1797. He graduated at Yale college in 1819; and was tutor and professor of mathematics at Williams and Amherst colleges. He was skilled in several sciences, and devotedly religious. He published Letters from the West Indies. Mrs. Sigourney eulogized him as

> Sublime in science, yet with meekness clad,
> Clear-minded and eloquent in thought and speech,
> And full of love for truth.

He married Mary Jane Chester. She was born Nov. 10, 1804; and died Jan. 11, 1840. He died in Hartford, Conn., May 6, 1840, at the age of fifty-two.

Their child was:—

1657—1.   ——⁸.

1090

—— HOVEY⁷.

Child:—

1658—1.   GEORGE I.⁸, lives in Deansboro, Oneida county, N. Y.

1109

ENOCH HOVEY⁷, born in Mansfield, Conn., Jan. 18, 1800. He married Abigail Freeman May 29, 1821; and was a manufacturer of sewing silk. He died in Philadelphia, Pa.

Their children were born in Lisle, N. Y., as follows:—

1659—1.   FRANKLIN STORRS⁸, born Sept. 22, 1822. *See family numbered "1659."*

1660—11.   EMELINE MOORE⁸, born Oct. 2, 1832; married Rev. N. A. Prentiss Aug. 26, 1856, at South Coventry, Conn. They live in Chicago, Ill.

1661—111.   JOHN ADDISON⁸, born July 17, 1834. *See family numbered "1661."*

1110

JULIUS HOVEY⁷, born in Mansfield, Conn., May 29, 1805. He lived in Gurleyville, in his native town, and was a manufacturer of sewing silk. He married Mary, daughter of Seth and Martha (Wing) Conant of Mansfield Nov. 6, 1825. She was born in 1806. He died in Mansfield May 30, 1852, at the age of forty-seven; and she died July 23, 1868.

Their children were born in Mansfield, as follows :—

1662—I. MARY WING[6], born June 28, 1827; married John Clark Aug. 29, 1854, in Mansfield; and died in Windsor, Conn., Jan. 26, 1898, at the age of seventy.

1663—II. MARTHA ELIZABETH[6], born Oct. 26, 1830; married Rev. Dwight, son of Nicholas and Sally (Slate) Spencer, D. D., of Fairhaven, Vt., Nov. 26, 1850, in Mansfield. She died at Cheshire, Mass., Sept. 26, 1908, at the age of seventy-seven. Their children were born in Brooklyn, as follows: 1. *Julius Dwight*[6], born Sept. 18, 1852; insurance broker; lives in Brooklyn; married Nellie M. Shearman July 2, 1878. 2. *James Howcy*[6], born Feb. 17, 1860; Baptist clergyman; settled at North Adams, Mass.; married Cora S. Wishore March 26, 1894. 3. *Mary E.*[6], born Oct. 9, 1861; married John Metcalf Jan. 13, 1886; and lives in Fairhaven, Vt. 4. *Grace May*[6], born May 15, 1870; married T. L. Bingham; and lives at Richmond, Va.

1664—III. MARCIA DELIA[6], born Nov. 20, 1833; married T. W. Douglass April 20, 1870, in Brooklyn, N. Y.; and lives in West Thompson, Conn.

1112

HENRY HOVEY[7], born in Warsaw, N. Y., Sept. 1, 1804, being the first white male child born in that town. He married Lydia H. Maher Oct. 17, 1838; and they celebrated their golden wedding in 1888. He died in 1892.

Their children were born as follows :—

1665—I. HARRY L.[8]; living at Ashland, Neb.
1666—II. FRANCIS[8]; died at the age of twenty-two.
1667—III. EUGENE[8].
1668—IV. LAURA BELL[8]; married ———— Napes, a jeweler. They had one child: 1. *Harry Lea*[9]; lived, first at Knoxville, Tenn., and now at Warsaw, N. Y.
1669—V. WILBER H.[8]; lives in Warsaw.

1120

ENOCH WHITE HOVEY[7], born in Warsaw, N. Y., in 1819. He married Amelia A. Merrill. They removed to Janesville, Wis., and he was living in Texas in 1901, at the age of eighty-two. Children :—

1670—I. FREDERICK[8].
1671—II. CHARLES M.[8], born April 22, 1852, in Warsaw, N. Y. *See family numbered "1671."*
1672—III. LAURA[8].
1673—IV. LEROY[8].
1674—V. EDWARD[8].

1129

ALFRED HOVEY[7]. He married Polly Cleveland.
Children (five sons and two daughters) :—

1675—I. ————[8].
1676—II. ————[8].

1677—III.   ————[?].
1678—IV.   ————[?].
1679—V.   ————[?].
1680—VI.   ————[?].
1681—VII.   ————[?].

1134

JUSTUS HOVEY[7], born in 18—. He married Sarah Smith in Canada. He died in California, and she died at the West.
Child:—

1682—I.   MARIAN[8] (daughter).

1148

JOHN SUMNER HOVEY[7]. He lived in Rome, N. Y., in 1900.
Child:—

1683—I.   EDWARD P.[8]; lived in Brooklyn, N. Y., in 1900.

1183

MARLOW HOVEY[7], born in Lima, N. Y., Dec. 5, 1801. He was a farmer, and lived in LeRoy, O. He married, first, Belinda Bates Nov. 16, 1826, in LeRoy. She was born in Chesterfield, Mass., Sept. 9, 1804; and died in LeRoy Sept. 24, 1860, at the age of fifty-six. He married, second, Mrs. Lydia Goes Nov. 4, 1861, in Trumble, O. He died in LeRoy Aug. 23, 1882, at the age of eighty.

Mr. Hovey's children were born in LeRoy, as follows:—

1684—I.   MARIETTE[8], born Nov. 1, 1829, Sunday, at 4.30 o'clock; and died in LeRoy, unmarried, Nov. 22, 1865, at the age of thirty-six.

1685—II.   EMELINE[8], born Jan. 7, 1834, Tuesday; married William Tilley June 25, 1854. He was born Nov. 15, 1829; and died March 4, 1900, at the age of seventy. She survived him, and died Jan. 19, 1906, at the age of seventy-two. Their children were born as follows: 1. *Ina Alice*[9], born April 19, 1858; married Charles S. Adams Jan. 29, 1879. He was born Dec. 20, 1853. They have two children. 2. *Dell Belinda*[9], born May 1, 1860; died Oct. 2, 1887, aged twenty-seven. 3. *Winnie M.*[9], born Jan. 17, 1866; died Feb. 1, 1866. 4. *Wirt Addison*[9], born Jan. 26, 1868; married Birdie Emeline Fassett July 12, 1894. She was born Nov. 10, 1872. He is a merchant at Ashtabula, O. They have one child.

1686—III.   ADDISON LEVI[8], born Jan. 19, 1836, at one o'clock, Tuesday; died, unmarried, at LeRoy April 3, 1864, at the age of twenty-eight.

1185

PHILETUS HOVEY[7], born in Lima, N. Y., May 12, 1808. He was a farmer, and lived in LeRoy, O. He married Aurelia House Jan. 20, 1831. She was born Aug. 2, 1808. He died at Cleveland, O., Jan. 12, 1881, at the age of seventy-two. She died Feb. 19, 1890, at the age of eighty-one.

Their children were born as follows:—

1687—i. ELIZA JANE[8], born Jan. 4, 1832, in LeRoy, O.; married Pardon Brownell Smith Aug. 10, 1854. He was born Aug. 15, 1833. Their children were born as follows: 1. *Anna Ida[9]*, born July 11, 1855; married Elbert Hall Baker June 1, 1876. He was born July 25, 1854; and is business manager of the Plain Dealer, Cleveland, O. They have five children. 2. *Frank More[9]*, born Dec. 24, 1857; married, first, Susie Dickerson Nov. 12, 1884. She died April 14, 1886. He married, second, Helen Effie Ruple Oct. 2, 1889. She was born April 14, 1863. He had one child, by the second wife. 3. *Alton Hovey[9]*, born Aug. 24, 1860; married Nellie Northrop Aug. 29, 1883. She was born Nov. 20, 1863. They had two children. 4. *Harry Hawkins[9]*, born June 17, 1863; married Bessie Comstock Aug. 22, 1885. She was born April 2, 1867. They had one child. 5. *Pardon Hudson[9]*, born Oct. 25, 1867; married Jeannette L. Odell June 1, 1889. She was born March 28, 1873. 6. *Mary Helen[9]*, born Oct. 5, 1870. 7. *Harley Gibbs[9]*, born Dec. 10, 1874; married Charlotte Edith Ladd Sept. 5, 1900. She was born Nov. 25, 1877. They have two children.

1688—ii. ELLEN MARIA[8], born May 10, 1834, in LeRoy; married Harvey Daniel Greeley Dec. 25, 1861, at Cleveland, O. He was born in New York state Feb. 7, 1830; and died at Cleveland Aug. 13, 1900. Their children were born in Cleveland, as follows: 1. *Manie Eliza[9]*, born Nov. 13, 1862. 2. *Horace Ephraim[9]*, born Dec. 16, 1865. 3. *Alton Hovey[9]*, born Dec. 1, 1871; married, first, Julia Carnell July 7, 1892, at Cleveland; and, second, Mary Elizabeth Lowrey Oct. 24, 1894, at Cleveland. They were divorced in 1904; and he married, third, Ida A. Cox Aug. 23, 1906. She was born at Cleveland March 17, 1879. He lives in Cleveland, having one child.

1689—iii. MARY CHARLOTTE[8], born March 30, 1836; married Horace Ford Feb. —, 1883; lived at 2216 Euclid avenue, Cleveland, O.; and she died there Dec. 9, 1883, at the age of forty-seven. She was active in Sunday-school and missionary work.

1690—iv. ALTON PHILETUS[8], born April 22, 1838; died March 17, 1859, aged twenty.

1691—v. JOANNA WARNER[8], born Sept. 27, 1840; died Dec. 6, 1840.

1186

SYLVANUS HOVEY[7], born in Lima, N. Y., June 6, 1810. He was a farmer, and lived in LeRoy, O. He married Caroline House Oct. 10, 1833. She was born Feb. 5, 1819; and died Jan. 8, 1867, at the age of forty-seven. He died Jan. 17, 1881, in Hampden, O., at the age of seventy.

Their children were born in LeRoy, as follows:—

1692—i. FRANKLIN OSCAR[8], born July 29, 1836. *See family numbered "1692."*

1693—ii. CORNELIA BELINDA[8], born Aug. 7, 1838; married James R. Drake Oct. 10, 1858. She died June 24, 1875, at the age of thirty-six; and he died in 1902. Their children were as follows: 1. *Wilton Ernest[9]*; married. 2. *Walter Henry[9]*; married. 3. *Edmond[9]*; married. 4. *Alice Lucelia[9]*; died,

unmarried. 5. *Myrtle*[9]; unmarried. 6. *Carrie*[9]; died in
18—. 7. *Kittie*[9]; died in 18—.

1694—III. ADALINE FUDELIA[8], born April 4, 1841; married John H. Valentine Aug. 27, 1862. Their children were born as follows:
1. *Luna*[9], born July 21, 1865. 2. *Eugene Wakefield*[9], born
June 20, 1868. 3. *Ethlyn May*[9], born Dec. 29, 1869; married
Charles D. Stafford Aug. 24, 1891; and she died Nov. 5,
1902. They had one child. 4. *Josie Estella*[9], born Sept.
17, 1872; died May 4, 1893, aged twenty. 5. *Harry Clifton*[9],
born Sept. 5, 1876.

1695—IV. AMELIA CAROLINE[8], born Dec. 19, 1847; married Delos Rogers
Sept. 19, 1872. Their children were born as follows: 1.
Nellie Maud[9], born Dec. 23, 1874. 2. *Floyd Elwin*[9], born
April 18, 1879; married Flora Jane Hill Dec. 12, 1900.
They have children.

1696—V. HELEN ANNETTE[8], born Dec. 11, 1849; married Chalmers
Lamar Quine Sept. 26, 1872. Children: 1. *Dwight*[9], born
June 30, 1873; died June 22, 1874. 2. *Lynn*[9], born April
30, 1876; married Mabel McNutt March 20, 1901. She was
born July 17, 1878. 3. *Bernice*[9], born Jan. 21, 1887.

1697—VI. BYRON SYLVANUS[8], born June 18, 1853. *See family numbered
"1697."*

1188

REV. SIMEON HOVEY[7], born in Lima, N. Y., Aug. 12, 1814.
He went to Ohio in 1822, at the age of eight; and was ordained
a clergyman of the Universalist denomination Jan. 11, 1844,
preaching in Ohio and Michigan. He married Mary, daughter
of Jonathan and Betsey Corbin (Huntoon) Whipple April 16,
1840, in LeRoy, where she was born July 10, 1819. He died in
Collinwood, O., Jan. 17, 1895, at the age of eighty; and she died
at St. Clair, Mich., Feb. 17, 1895, at the age of seventy-five.
Their children were born as follows:—

1698—I. JAMES BYRON[8], born Dec. 22, 1840, at 6 o'clock a. m., in LeRoy,
O.; and died there Sept. 15, 1847, aged six years.

1699—II. ANN ELIZA[8], born April 5, 1842, at 3 p. m., in LeRoy; mar-
ried Henry Harrison Clark May 1, 1866, at China, Mich.
He was born July 19, 1836; and died April 20, 1888, at
Peru, O. She lives at Chautauqua, N. Y. (p. o. box 187).
Their children were born at Peru, as follows: 1. *Agnes
May*[9], born May 22, 1867; married Dudley Irving Badger
July 15, 1896. He was born May 17, 1851; and died at
Pasadena, Cal., June 10, 1903, at the age of fifty-two. They
had one child. 2. *Mabel Maggie*[9], born Sept. 6, 1868; died
at Akron, O., Feb. 28, 1899, at the age of thirty.

1700—III. PERMELIA JANE[8], born Feb. 6, 1845, at 11.30 a. m., in LeRoy;
married Oscar Hart May 1, 1866, at China, Mich. He was
born July 7, 1835. He is a farmer; and lives in St. Clair,
Mich. Child: 1. *Mae*[9], born Nov. 11, 1881, at St. Clair.

1701—IV. ALBERT SIMEON[8], born Sept. 8, 1850, at 10.30 a. m., in Perry, O.
He is a civil and mining engineer, and lives in Helena,
Mont. (p. o. box 777). He married Martha, daughter of
Birchard and Martha (Esbick) Tregonning April 2, 1895,
at Butte, Mont. She was born at Bristol, Eng., Dec. 17,
1872.

1189

Augustine Washington Hovey[7], born in Lima, N. Y., June 19, 1817. When his father went to New Orleans, he was taken by his maternal grandparents, to Grand Blanc, Mich. He learned to set type at the age of twelve, and worked on the *Detroit Free Press* as compositor. He also worked in the office of the *Livingston Journal*, at Genesee, N. Y., and of the *Niagara Courier*, at Lockport, N. Y.

He settled in Pontiac, Mich., being a pioneer, in the spring of 1836, and was first employed in the printing office of Samuel N. Gautt, editor of the *Pontiac Herald*. When he arrived at the age of twenty-one, in 1838, he became managing editor of that paper. He then formed a partnership with S. S. Denton, and published the *Pontiac Jacksonian*, which they continued to issue until the spring of 1844, when the firm of Denton & Hovey sold the paper and office.

Mr. Hovey then abandoned the newspaper business, and engaged in the drug trade, which he carried on for forty years, in Pontiac. For many years he was associated with a Mr. Dean, under the firm name of Dean & Hovey. Mr. Dean died some years later, but Mr. Hovey continued the business under the old firm name as long as he remained in the trade. He sold out, in 1883, to his clerk, Peter Schmitz.

Mr. Hovey was an ardent Democrat, and cast his first vote for Martin Van Buren, but his last for William McKinley, uniting his influence with the sound money Democrats in crushing out free silver.

Through his mother, he had some French characteristics, and possessed many sterling traits. He was thoroughly honest and of unquestioned integrity. A man of few words, he was seldom deceived in his estimate of a person, and with wonderful directness could detect sham, however genteelly it was concealed, and noble qualities of manhood, though clothed in tattered garments.

He held many positions of honor and trust. He was clerk of the house of representatives of Michigan in 1844, 1846, 1847, 1848 and 1849, and for three years was a member of the Pontiac school board. In 1852, he was made superintendent of the poor, and held the position more than thirty years. He was also the county purchasing agent.

For many years, Mr. Hovey's rotund figure made him a conspicuous person. He reduced his weight of three hundred pounds or more to less than two hundred by force of his will controlling his appetite, and this contributed to his health and comfort in his latter years.

Mr. Hovey married, first, Jeanette, daughter of Abner and Sally (Horton) Wilcox May 14, 1840. She was born in Livonia,

N. Y., May 18, 1822; and died at Pontiac Oct. 6, 1842, at the age of twenty. He married, second, Laura Merrill of Springfield, Mich., April —, 1847. He died at Detroit, Mich., at the house of his daughter, Nov. 29, 1897, at the age of eighty. His burial took place in the family lot in the attractive Oak Hill cemetery at Pontiac.

Mr. Hovey's children were born in Pontiac, as follows:—

1702—I.   GERTRUDE LAURA[8], born May 6, 1841, at midnight; married Stephen, son of Thomas and Hannah (Pickering) Baldwin of Pontiac Oct. 28, 1868. He was born in London, England, July 31, 1834; and came to America with his parents in babyhood, growing to manhood on a farm in Pontiac. He taught school in Oakland county, and in the fall of 1861 engaged in the produce and commission business in Pontiac. He removed to Detroit in 1870. He also became interested in lumber and paper interests; and as a member of the firm of Baldwin & Nelson he handled large tracts of pine forest in Michigan and Canada. He had large interests in real estate in and around Detroit, owning, at one time, the Whitney opera house, where he had his office. His farms at Dearborn, Royal Oak and Woodward avenue were his special pride. He was president of the Detroit Creamery company. He was wealthy, rugged and aggressive, of sterling integrity, and for forty years one of Detroit's foremost citizens. He resided at 3 Madison avenue, where he died April 7, 1909, at the age of seventy-four. They had no children. She survives him, and lives at the same number and street.

1703—II.   ————[8]; died in 18—.

1190

CHARLES HOVEY[7], born in Lima, N. Y., Aug. 2, 1821. He was a carpenter and builder, and lived at Port Huron, Mich. He married Maria, daughter of John and Ann (May) Prout Aug. 2, 1852, at Port Huron. She was born at Triligga, England Feb. 21, 1830. He died at Holly, Mich., May 23, 1903, at the age of eighty-one. She is still living.

Their children were born at Port Huron, as follows:—

1704—I.   GRACE[8], born Dec. 3, 1854; died March 8, 1857, at Port Hudson.

1705—II.   CLARA[8], born Jan. 2, 1860; married Fred, son of Carl and Louise (Ruhl) Hartwig Sept. 25, 1888. He was born in Battensthal, Germany, May 12, 1852. He is a farmer, and they live at Holly, Mich. Their children were born at Holly, as follows: 1. *Charles H.*[9], born Aug. 2, 1889; lives in Holly, being a farmer. 2. *Grace L.*[9], born Nov. 2, 1890; lives in Holly. 3. *William F.*[9], born Dec. 22, 1891; lives in Holly. 4. *Roy L.*[9] (twin), born April 13, 1894; lives in Holly. 5. *Richard P.*[9] (twin), born April 13, 1894; died Sept. 7, 1894. 6. *Clara H.*[9], born April 21, 1896. 7. *Clyde*[9], born Oct. 20, 1897. 8. *Ivory H.*[9], born Jan. 23, 1901. 9. *Jane E. H.*[9], born Dec. 7, 1902. 10. *Maria H.*[9], born May 31, 1904.

1195

THOMAS HOVEY[7], born June 7 (20?), 1796. He was a trader, and lived in Woburn. He married, first, Miss Clark ; and, second, Susan Townsend Hovey. He died Aug. 20, 1848, at the age of fifty-two ; and his wife Susan survived him.

Mr. Hovey's children were born in Cambridge, as follows :—

1706—I.   ISABELLA ELIZABETH[8], born July 4, 1824 ; died in Cambridge April 7, 1838, aged thirteen.
1707—II.   MARIA LOUISE[8], born June 26, 1826 ; married Daniel H. Horn.
1708—III.   FREDERICK AUGUSTA[8], born May 15, 1828 ; living in 1848.
1709—IV.   AGNES MCINTYRE[8], born April 9, 1830 ; living in 1848 ; and died in 18—.
1710—V.   GEORGE HENRY[8], born April 29, 1832 ; married Naomi Davis.
1711—VI.   SUSAN TOWNSEND[8], born about 1840 ; married Jeremiah Mower.
1712—VII.   MASON MOSS[8], born about 1842. When the Civil war opened he belonged to the National Guard, and went into the service of the Union. He was in the battle of Bull Run, and was first lieutenant at Fort Leavenworth, Kansas, before going to Denver, Col., where he subsequently lived. He went west about 1870. He married Miss Emma R. Auld. He died in 1—— ; and she survived him.
1713—VIII.   JAMES OSBORN[8], born in 18— ; living in 1848.
1714—IX.   ABEL W.[8], born in 18— ; living in 1848.

1198

SAMUEL SPARHAWK HOVEY[7], born in Newton, Mass., March 16, 1802. He was a merchant, and lived in Boston and Cambridge until 1839, when he removed to Chicago, Ill. He married Adelaide Low, daughter of Josiah and Hannah (Grant) Sept. 8, 1830, at Portsmouth ; and died in Chicago March 2, 1872, at the age of sixty-nine. She was born in Portsmouth Aug. 20, 1811 ; and died in Oakland, Cal., Nov. 15, 1878, aged sixty-seven.

Their children were born as follows :—

1715—I.   WILLIAM[8], born in 1830 ; died in 1830.
1716—II.   GEORGIANNA S.[8], born May 6, 1834, in Boston ; married George Waite, son of Nathaniel F. and Nancy (Waite) Deering of Portland, Me., July 5, 1853. They lived in Chicago until about 1870, and afterwards at Portland. He was an accountant ; and died at Berlin Falls, N. H., May 4, 1891. Their children were as follows : 1. *Dora Adelaide*[9], born April 6, 1854, in Chicago ; married W. Henry Moulton of the Cumberland National Bank ; lived at 93 High street, Portland ; and died there, of typhoid fever, June 21, 1904. 2. *Georgie Fullerton*[9], born April 25, 1857, in Chicago ; and died in Portland March 5, 1867. 3. *Josephine*[9], born Sept. 28, 1861, in Chicago ; married Amos W. S. Anderson Oct. 14, 1897 ; he is an accountant, and they live at 248 Goffe street, Quincy, Mass. 4. *Edward Preble*[9], born April 16, 1863, in Chicago ; accountant ; lives in Portland ; married Eugenie Wells Dec. 7, 1888. 5. *Eleonora Wildrege*[9], born July 15, 1873, in Portland ; married Harry A. Rounds Nov. 24, 1896 ; he is a banker ; and they live in Portland.

1717—III. FRANKLIN[8], born April 16, 1836, in Boston; and died in Cambridge June 8, 1837.

1718—IV. HELEN ADELAIDE[8], born Feb. 21, 1838, in Cambridge; married Edward Fitch of Chicago Aug. 8, 1853; and lived at 925 Chestnut street, San Francisco, Cal., until their removal to North Bridgton, Me. Their child was born in Chicago, as follows: 1. *Luther Edward[9]*, born March 3, 1856; married Ella Pierce; lives in San Francisco, where he is engaged in the newspaper business.

1719—V. ELIZABETH FRANKLYN[8], born Jan. 17, 1840, in Chicago; married James Milton, son of Herman and Cecilia (Abrahams) Spofford Nov. 15, 1862, in Chicago. He was born on Prince Edwards Island, Dominion of Canada; and was a merchant in San Francisco, where they lived. Mrs. Spofford is a Daughter of the American Revolution, and a member of the Society of Colonial Dames, being registrar of the California chapter. Mr. Spofford died July —, 1911, at the age of seventy-one. She resides at 322 Maple street, San Francisco. Their children were born as follows: 1. *Adelaide Spofford[9]*, born Nov. 15, 1862, in Chicago; married Gen. Victor Hugo Woods in 1898; and lives in San Francisco. They have three daughters. 2. *James Hovey[9]*, born Aug. 20, 1864, in Chicago; is unmarried. 3. *Helen E.[9]*, born April 16, 1866, in Chicago; is unmarried. 4. *George Deering[9]*, born March 14, 1868, in Chicago; is unmarried. 5. *Frances Hovey[9]*, born Nov. 14, 1875, in Oakland, Cal.; is unmarried. 6. *Dora D.[9]*, born April 29, 1878, in Oakland; is unmarried.

1720—VI. JOSEPHINE[8], born Jan. 1, 1842, in Chicago; and died there Jan. 21, 1860, at the age of eighteen.

1721—VII. FRANCES V.[8], born Dec. 22, 1846, in Chicago; married Malcom Waite Sept. 10, 1866; and lives in Chicago.

1204

DEA. WILLIAM BOWLES HOVEY[7], born in Newton, Mass., Sept. 3, 1795. He enlisted in the Mexican war at its beginning in 1816. He was later schoolmaster, and clerk in Deacon Brown's grocery at Harvard square, in Cambridge. He subsequently engaged in the grocery business for himself at Cambridge with Thomas Hovey, the firm-name being Thomas & William B. Hovey. Later he secured stall No. 32 in Faneuil Hall market, Boston, when it was opened, Aug. 26, 1826, and founded the business which is still conducted by his son William A. Hovey.

He lived in Cambridgeport and Brighton. He was a director of the Cambridge Bank, a deacon of the First Baptist church at Central square, in Cambridge, from 1849 to 1871, and was known as "Honest Hovey."

Deacon Hovey married, first, Susan, daughter of Daniel Lerned, esq., of Wayland Sept. 22, 1819. She was born in the old Lerned house on Main avenue June 10, 1796; and died May 1, 1849, at the age of fifty-two. He married, second, Mrs. Mary A. Davis, a widow, Dec. 5, 1857. He died in Cambridge July 4,

1871, at the age of seventy-nine. His estate was valued at $30,976.50. In his will, he remembered the Baptist church in Cambridge and the various societies. His wife Mary survived him some twenty years.

Children :—

1722—I.   HORATIO ATWELL⁸, born Sept. 1, 1820, in Cambridge. *See family numbered "1722."*

1723—II. ANNE ELIZABETH⁸, born Dec. 10, 1821, in Cambridge; attended Mary Livermore Rice's seminary, in Charlestown; married Jerediah, son of Capt. Aaron Ricker May 7, 1843, in Cambridgeport. He was born in Lebanon, Me., May 9, 1812; was a housebuilder; and lived in Cambridgeport. He died in Cambridgeport Sept. 11, 1888, at the age of seventy-six; and she died there June 17, 1890, at the age of sixty-eight. Their children were born in Cambridgeport, as follows: 1. *Emma Frances⁹*, born March 7, 1844; married, first, Manley S. Gay Nov. 30, 1867; and had a son. He died July 31, 1872. She married, second, John I. Carroll Feb. 20, 1876; and had four children. She died in Cambridgeport July 27, 1885, at the age of forty. 2. *Susan Hovey⁹*, born Sept. 20, 1847; married George Whitfield Canterbury July 3, 1876. He was born in 1852. No children. They live at 14 Lake street, in Cambridgeport. 3. *William Hovey⁹*, born Feb. 22, 1855; married Maud L. Fuller Sept. 19, 1883, in Cambridge. She was matron of the Cambridge hospital. He is an inventor and owner of several modern apartment houses in Cambridge. They live at The Dana, 991 Massachusetts avenue, Cambridge; and have no children.

1724—III. WILLIAM HENRY⁸, born Sept. 22, 1824, in Cambridge. *See family numbered "1724."*

1725—IV. WALTER⁸, born May 1, 1828, in Cambridge. *See family numbered "1725."*

1726—V.   FRANCIS WAYLAND⁸, born Sept. 13, 1835, in Cambridge. *See family numbered "1726."*

1727—VI. MARSHALL⁸, born Dec. 11, 1837, in Brighton; died Dec. 17, 1837.

1209

JAMES GARDNER HOVEY⁷, born in Brighton, Mass., April 14, 1813. He lived in Cambridge, on the corner of Main and Bay streets. He was a merchant, and for many years carried one an extensive business at one hundred and forty-nine Washington street, opposite the old South church, in Boston. He sold small and fancy goods, fire works, etc.; and manufactured fire works at a plant in Cambridgeport. He became noted for the magnificent displays he furnished the city of Boston each Fourth of July, on the Common, as well as many other cities. He was cashier for Bigelow & Kennard, and then, under Kennard, for many years, assistant sub-treasurer for the port of Boston.

Mr. Hovey was a member of the Boston Fusileers, a crack militia company, and, also, one time foreman of a fire-engine company. In 1851, while living in Boston, he served in the common council of that city. The next year he removed to

Cambridge, where he was a member of the city council in 1856 and until his death, in 1857.

He married Harriet, daughter of Noah and Sally (Howe) Lincoln of Boston May 14, 1840. She was born in Boston July 1, 1814; and died in Cambridge Feb. 18, 1856, at the age of forty-one. He died in Cambridge April 27, 1857, aged forty-one.

Their children were born as follows:—

1728—I. JAMES LEWIS⁸, born Feb. 27, 1841, in Boston. He enlisted Aug. —, 1862, in the Forty-fourth regiment of Massachusetts volunteers, which was known as the "seed cake" regiment, the average age of the members being only twenty-two years. The regiment became a part of the Eighteenth army corps in North Carolina, with headquarters at Newberne, and Maj.-gen. John G. Foster in command. It took part in a number of engagements, and withstood a three-weeks' siege in the town of Little Washington, N. C. On its return, in 1863, the regiment received a magnificent oration and feast on Boston Common.

In 1881, he was appointed to the position of money clerk in the United States sub-treasury, in Boston, and still retains it.

He became a member of Revere lodge of Freemasons in 1864, the Grand Army of the Republic and the Royal Arcanum at its institution, in 1877, having served as secretary of Council No. 4 since 1886.

Mr. Hovey married Susan Collins Lowden of Pawtucket, R. I., June 10, 1874, but have had no children. They reside at 22 Gaylord street, in Dorchester.

1729—II. HARRIET ANNA⁸, born Aug. 18, 1842, in Boston; died Aug. 19, 1843.

1730—III. EMMA FRANCES⁸, born Jan. 10, 1847, in Boston; married Thomas Wentworth, son of Samuel C. and Amy A. (Wentworth) Shapleigh of Boston March 3, 1869. He was born in Portland, Me., Feb. 28, 1841. They live at Newton Highlands, Mass., and is a clerk. He was interested, with his brother, in the coffee business; and then went into the business alone. Their children were born in Cambridge, as follows: 1. Bertram Lincoln⁹, born Jan. 15, 1871; composer of music; lives in Longfield, Kentshire, England; married Mabel Vilas Carpenter Feb. 25, 1898. 2. Emma Eda⁹, born Jan. 15, 1877; married George Wallace Barker April 14, 1909; and lives at 31 Dunckler street, Newton Highlands.

1731—IV. FRANKLIN CUSHMAN⁸, born Nov. 19, 1850, in Boston; died June 16, 1851.

1732—V. CHARLES LINCOLN⁸, born Jan. 2, 1853, in Cambridge. See family numbered "1732."

1210

EBENEZER HOVEY⁷, born in Cambridge, Mass., March 24, 1801. He was a victualer and bacon curer, and lived in his native town. He married Harriet Scott of Needham, Mass., Sept. 3, 1823. She was born in Bethel, Me. He died in Cambridge March 25, 1866, at the age of sixty-five. He possessed an estate valued at twenty thousand dollars. She survived him, and died in Chicago, Ill., in 1886.

Their children were born in Cambridge, as follows:—

1733—I.   CHARLES AUGUSTUS⁸, born June 12, 1824; died Aug. 23, 1825, aged one year.
1734—II.   CHARLES EBENEZER⁸, born Feb. 19, 1826; died in Needham Oct. 28, 1844, aged eighteen.
1735—III. HARRIET ELIZABETH⁸, born Oct. 2, 1827; died in Cambridge May 15, 1844, at the age of sixteen.
1736—IV.   AUGUSTUS HENRY⁸, born Jan. 27, 1830. *See family numbered "1736."*
1737—V.   EDWIN JUDSON⁸, born July 11, 1832; died in Needham Oct. 25, 1844, aged twelve.
1738—VI.   ELBRIDGE SCOTT⁸, born Jan. 9, 1837. *See family numbered "1738."*
1739—VII. JOSEPH WHITING PARKER⁸, born April 17, 1839. *See family numbered "1739."*
1740—VIII. SAMUEL DANA⁸, born Jan. 9, 1841. *See family numbered "1740."*

1216

FREEMAN HOVEY⁷, born in Cambridge, Mass., March 1, 1811. He was a housewright, and lived in Cambridge. He married, first, Harriet Stone Dec. —, 1831; and, second, Sophronia Walker in 1838. He died Jan. 28, 1843, at the age of thirty-two. His wife Sophronia survived him.

Children:—

1741—I.   ————⁸.
1742—II.   ————⁸.
1743—III. ————⁸.
1744—IV.   ————⁸.
1745—V.   ————⁸.

1218

GEORGE HOVEY⁷, born in Cambridge, Mass., Aug. 5. 1814. He married ———— Martin; and died Jan. (July?) 6, 1863, at the age of forty-eight.

Children:—

1746—I.   ————⁸.
1747—II.   ————⁸.
1748—III. ————⁸.
1749—IV.   ————⁸.

1219

THOMAS GREEN HOVEY⁷, born in Cambridge, Mass., Jan. 23, 1816. He lived in Cambridge until 1849, when he removed to Lexington. He married Ann Maria Hoping Nov. 3, 1841. She was born in Cambridge Nov. 13, 1822. He died March 20, 1880, at the age of sixty-four.

Their children were born as follows:—

1750—I.   EMMA MARIA⁶, born Dec. 26, 1842, in Cambridge.
1751—II. ELLEN AMANDA⁶, born Jan. 1, 1844, in Cambridge.
1752—III. THOMAS EBENEZER⁶, born June 26, 1845, in Cambridge.   *See family numbered "1752."*
1753—IV. WALTER SEWALL⁶, born May 7, 1847, in Cambridge.   *See family numbered "1753."*
1754—V.   GEORGIANNA⁶, born Feb. 7, 1849, in Cambridge.
1755—VI. STILMAN SOUTHWICK⁶, born April 15, 1850, in Lexington. He lives at 398 Main street, Woburn, Mass.
1756—VII. FRANK PIERCE⁶, born Dec. 3, 1852, in Lexington.
1757—VIII. ————⁶.

1237

ALONZO HOVEY⁷, born in Hatley, Province of Quebec, Canada, June 11, 1818. He was a farmer, and lived in North Hatley. He married Lydia Amanda, daughter of Philip and Lydia (Hall) Flanders, at Stanstead, Province of Quebec. She was born in Hatley Sept. 18, 1823. He died in Hatley Jan. 2, 1896, aged seventy-seven years; and she died in Springfield, Mass., Dec. 31, 1906, aged eighty-three.

Their children were born in Hatley, as follows:—

1758—I.   CHESTER LEROY⁸, born April 25, 1850.   *See family numbered "1758."*
1759—II. HENRY ALBERT⁸, born Feb. 15, 1852. Resides in Pittsfield, Mass., and is a provision dealer.
1760—III. WILLIAM (twin)⁸, born March 7, 1855; is a collector; lives in Seattle, Wash.; married Harriet Ackley June 2, 1885.
1761—IV. MARY (twin)⁸, born March 7, 1855; married Charles F. Margeson Dec. 27, 1881. He is in the express business, and they live in Springfield, Mass.
1762—V.   PHILIP ALLISON⁸, born April 30, 1857; is a manufacturer; lives at Sherbrooke, Province of Quebec; married Jennie F. Clapp Dec. 24, 1880.
1763—VI. FREDERICK⁸, born May 27, 1860; is a manufacturer; lives in Sherbrooke; married Etta Le Baron Dec. 27, 1881.
1764—VII. IDA HELEN⁸, born March 1, 1863; lives in Springfield, Mass., unmarried.

1239

WRIGHT HOVEY⁷, born in Hatley, Province of Quebec, Canada, July 23, 1833. He was a farmer, and lived in his native town. He married Lois Mehitable, daughter of Edward and Mehitable (Kezar) Hitchcock in Lenoxville, Province of Quebec, Oct. 24, 1860. He died in Hatley Oct. 22, 1884, at the age of fifty-one; and she lives, his widow, in Massawippi, Province of Quebec.

Their children were born in Hatley, as follows:—

1765—I.   EDWARD H.⁸, born Aug. 29, 1861; died in Hatley July 8, 1863.
1766—II. ALICE G.⁸, born Feb. 13, 1864; married Stephen Samuel, son of Pierre Poulin and Genevieve Colt May 10, 1887. He was born in Sherbrooke, Province of Quebec, May 24, 1858; and

lives in Hatley, where he is a farmer. Their children were born in Massawippi, as follows: 1. *Lois Gladys*[8], born Nov. 24, 1889. 2. *Alice Marion*[8], born Aug. 8, 1896. 3. *Genevieve*[8], born March 9, 1903; died May 1, 1903.

1767—III.   EDWARD WRIGHT[4], born July 21, 1867. *See family numbered "1767."*

1768—IV.   BERTHA[4], born Dec. 2, 1870; died April 26, 1871.
1769—V.   LESLIE ROY[4], born March 18, 1878. *See family numbered "1769."*

1241

HORACE MELVIN HOVEY, ESQ.[7], born in Hatley, Province of Quebec, Canada, Dec. 15, 1838. He is a lawyer, and lives at Rock Island, a small village, bounding on the Vermont line, in the Province of Quebec. He married Ruth Whitcomb, daughter of David and Thankful (Whitcomb) Chamberlin of Seabrooke, Province of Quebec, July 21, 1874, at Magog, Province of Quebec. She was born at Magog Aug. 25, 1846.

Their children were born as follows:—

1770—I.   HORACE WRIGHT[8], born April 19, 1875, in Derby Line, Vt. *See family numbered "1770."*
1771—II.   CLARA[8], born May —, 1876, in Derby Line; died Aug. —, 1876.
1772—III. CHARLES WALTER[8], born Oct. 28, 1878, at Rock Island; died there July 19, 1884.

1242

LESLIE PIERPONT HOVEY[7], born in Hatley, Canada, Oct. 29, 1842. He lives in Canaan, Vt.; and is engaged in the lumber business and the settlement of estates. He married Emeline Victoria, daughter of Mark and Praxana (Gordon) Beane, at Stanstead, Province of Quebec, Dec. 24, 1868. She was born in Hatley May 29, 1846.

Their children were born as follows:—

1773—I.   MILLIE ELLEN[8], born Dec. 11, 1869, in Yarmouth, N. S.; married, first, Enos James, son of Silas H. and Harriet F. (Le Barron) Hill June 7, 1892, at Hatley. He was born in Barnston, Province of Quebec, June 5, 1869; was a bookbinder; and lived in Holyoke, Mass. He died in Boston, Mass., Sept. 15, 1900, at the age of thirty-one. She married, second, Ira Allan, son of Ira Allen and Louise (Merrill) Ramsay, in Colebrook, N. H., Oct. 16, 1909. He was born in Colebrook March 18, 1862; and resides there, being postmaster. The children of Mr. and Mrs. Hill were born at Holyoke, as follows: 1. *Winthrop Ward*[9], born Aug. 11, 1893. 2. *Donald Hovey*[9], born May 13, 1895.

1774—II.   HORACE KIMBALL[8], born Jan. 31, 1872, in Yarmouth. He is a machinist, and lives in Southbridge, Mass. He married Charlotte Hoffman in 1905.

1775—III. MAUDE ELSIE[8], born Jan. 26, 1874, in Hatley; married Louis Ramsay in 1897; and lives in Colebrook, N. H.

1776—IV.   ALICE JANE[8], born Oct. 20, 1876, in Hatley; married Bryan McDonald in 1900; and lives at Beecher Falls, Vt.

1777—v.   RUTH VICTORIA[8], born Sept. 18, 1880, in Hatley; she is a
           teacher; and lives in Canaan, Vt.
1778—vi.   JOSEPHINE EDNA[8], born March 7, 1885, in Hatley; she is super-
           visor of music in the public schools; and lives in Canaan.
1779—vii. EDWIN DANIEL[8], born Aug. 10, 1887, in Hatley; lives in
           Canaan, having received a collegiate education.

1243

JACOB G. HOVEY[7], born in Waterford, Vt., June 24, 1834.
He was a farmer, and lived in St. Johnsbury, Vt. He married,
first, Elizabeth Chamberlain in Waterford. He married, second,
Sarah J. Graves of Lyndon. She was born in Lyndon April 26,
1837. He died in St. Johnsbury Aug. 5, 1897, at the age of
sixty-three.

Mr. Hovey's children were born as follows:—

1780—i.   WILLIAM C.[8], born in Waterford; merchant; and lives in
           Burton Harbor, Mich.
1781—ii.   ERASTUS G.[8], born in St. Johnsbury; lives at Denver, Col.,
           an invalid.
1782—iii. MARCUS J.[8], born in St. Johnsbury; ice dealer; and lives at
           St. Johnsbury.

1246

WILLIAM OREN HOVEY[7], born in Monson, Mass., Dec. 16,
1834. He lived in Palmer, Mass., and later returned to his native
place, where he was living in 1865. He married Lucy Ferry.

Their children were born in Monson, as follows:—

1783—i.   FRED W.[8], born Dec. 11, 1867; physician; lived in Spring-
           field, Mass.
1784—ii.   ALBERT E.[8], born Nov. 14, 1870; died Dec. 8, 1872.
1785—iii. ROBERT FERRY[8], born Feb. 19, 1875. Resides in Springfield,
           Mass.

1249

ALBERT HENRY HOVEY[7], born in Monson, Mass., March 22,
1840. He married Miss Sarah E. Heywood Jan. 28, 1885. She
was born in Springfield, Mass. They lived at Monson in 1862,
at Prince Edwards Island in 1865, in Willoughby, O., in 1870,
again in Monson in 1872 and 1905, and now in Springfield.

Their children were born as follows:—

1786—i.   ALBERT HEYWOOD[8], born June 16, 1892.
1787—ii.   WALTER READ[8], born July 21, 1895.

1250

CHARLES LOUIE HOVEY[7], born in Monson, Mass., Nov. 29,
1842. He married Louise, daughter of Edward W. and Sylvie
(Eager) Morey Nov. 28, 1866, in Chester, O., and lived there.
She was born Feb. 15, 1846, in Canton, N. Y., and now lives with
her daughter in Springfield, Mass.

Their children were born in Chester, as follows:—

1788—I. CARL HENRY², born Dec. 14, 1867. *See family numbered "1788."*

1789—II. BELLE LOUISE², born June 14, 1872; married Charles, son of Almon and Louise White July 3. 1895. They live at 52 Larone avenue, West Springfield, Mass. Children, born in West Springfield: 1. *Almon³*, born Aug. 16, 1898. 2. *Kenneth³*, born Dec. 30, 1905.

1790—III. GEORGE FOREST², born Feb. 24, 1876; lives in Chester, unmarried.

1791—IV. ADA MARIE², born March 28, 1879; married Charles, son of Theodore and Jennie Beardsley Aug. 4, 1897. He was born in Springfield, Mass., July 27, 1867. They live at 39 Bancroft street, in Springfield. Children: 1. *Sylvie Louise³*, born June 16, 1899, in Springfield. 2. *Jennie Hazel³*, born Dec. 5, 1902, in West Springfield.

1792—V. ARTHUR LEIGHTON², born Sept. 14, 1886; lives in Cleveland, unmarried.

1259

ELISHA FLINT HOVEY¹, born in Munson, O., Dece. 6, 1832. He married Hannah Philbrick of Chester, O., July 1, 1855. She was born in Chester Nov. 30, 1835. He died at Munson Sept. 17, 1905, at the age of seventy-two. She survived him, and lives at Munson.

Children:—

1793—I. FRED², born Nov. 24, 1856; married Myra Herrick Oct. 28, 1896; and lives at Chester.

1794—II. HORACE², born June 21, 1858; lives at Munson; married Della Maud Hinton July 22, 1908. They have no children.

1795—III. JENNIE MARIA², born June 20, 1860; married Eugene Dudley Aug. 21, 1884; and lives at Chardon, O. Their children were born as follows: 1. *Hugh³*, born Dec. 15, 1886. 2. *Anna Mary³*, born Nov. 1, 1891. 3. *Luke Philbrick³*, born June 18, 1894.

1796—IV. KATE², born Aug. 22, 1863; married William G. King, esq., June 18, 1891. He is a lawyer, and lives in Chardon. Their children were born as follows: 1. *Merrell³*, born June 10, 1892. 2. *Kenneth William³*, born Dec. 10, 1904.

1797—V. ROBERT ELIOT², born Feb. 2, 1867. *See family numbered "1797."*

1798—VI. CLARK SAMUEL², born March 2. 1873. *See family numbered "1798."*

1260

HIRAM ALMON HOVEY¹, born in Munson, O., Nov. 18, 1835. He lives at 2195 W. 29th street, Cleveland, O., having retired from business. He married, first, Mary Ann Cutting Sept. 12, 1864, at Munson, O., where she was born Oct. 26, 1838. She died July 8, 1889, at the age of fifty. He married, second, Celucia Dunning Oct. —, 1892, at Cleveland, O. By his second marriage he had no children.

Mr. Hovey's children, by his first wife, were born in Munson, as follows:—

1799—I.   SUSIE⁵, born June 2, 1865; married Edward Vanvalkenburg;
          and died June 25, 1898, at Russell, O., at the age of thirty-
          three. Children: 1. *Zetta⁶*, born in 1894. 2. *Ethel⁶*, born
          in 1896.
1800—II. MAMIE⁵, born July 2, 1874; married Melvin Robinson; and
          lives in Cleveland, O. Children: 1. *Loyd⁶*, born in 1893.
          2. *Marie⁶*, born in 1895.
1801—III. GLADYS⁵, born March 10, 1879; married Clayton A. Gibson;
          and lives in Denver, Col. They have no children.

1262

ORRIN UTLEY HOVEY⁴, born in Munson, O., Oct. 2, 1841.
He married Sarah Metcalf May —, 1883, at Chardon, O. She
was born Aug. —, 1850. They live at Hampden, O., he having
retired from business.

Children :—

1802—I.   PAULINE⁵, born Oct. 20, 1883, at Munson, O.; married ————
          Reed; and lives at Alaska.
1803—II. SIBYL⁵, born Aug. 31, 1885, at San Bernadino, Cal.
1804—III. NINETY⁵, born Sept. 20, 1887, at Troy, O.; died in ————.

1263

ALBERT D. HOVEY⁴, born in Munson, O., Nov. 7, 1845. He
is a druggist at 10 Main street, Chardon, O., where he lives. He
married Mary Foote of Chardon May 20, 1880. She was born
there May 14, 1850.

Their children were born in Chardon, as follows :—

1805—I.   CHARLES ALBERT⁵, born Sept. 7, 1884; married Laura Thacher
          Sept. 7, 1909; and lives in Cleveland, O.
1806—II. RALPH FOOTE⁵, born May 24, 1891; and lives at home in
          Chardon.

1267

WILLIAM ALFRED HOVEY⁴, born in Boston, Mass., Dec. 21,
1841. He was educated in the public schools of Boston,—the
Phillips grammar school and the English high school. Upon his
graduation from the high school, in 1860, he went to Europe,
and spent nearly two years in Italy, Germany and France, im-
proving his time in the study of languages and general culture.
In this experience was the foundation of his delightful and in-
structive conversational ability. Upon his return to this country
he became associated with the Sanitary Commission, through a
visit to the Army of the Potomac, and filled many positions of
responsibility in the field and in various offices in Washington,
rising to the position of assistant secretary. The excellence of
his work and the value of his reports and general services were
often commented on by his superiors in the Commission, and by
the many army officers with whom his duties brought him into
official relations.

At the end of the war, Mr. Hovey drifted to Pennsylvania, where, for several years, he was connected with coal mines in the capacity of engineer and also of superintendent. There, he became interested in journalism and wrote articles for several newspapers in that state on political and general economic subjects. He returned to Massachusetts, and established, in Chelsea, a weekly paper which proved to be a financial failure. In 1872 he became managing editor of the *Boston Commercial Bulletin,* and remained in that position until 1875, when, on the death of Daniel N. Haskell, he succeeded to the editorship of the *Boston Evening Transcript.* He continued his connection with this paper for six years, and his position brought him into contact with a large circle of men and women who recognized his integrity of thought, his fearlessness of opinion, and that general intelligent point of view of all large and important questions which stamped him a remarkable man among men.

In the *Transcript,* Mr. Hovey established a column entitled "Causerie," in which he was "delightfully dogmatic, brilliantly epigrammatic, extravagantly emphatic, and on all questions of ethics, politics and society gloriously democratic. . . A gentleman in the full old-world sense, no man's heart ever beat truer for equal rights or warmed with wrath quicker at sight of any social oppression. Naturally, along with this sort of feeling went an intense detestation for the petty frauds of custom, religious shams, the pretentions and affectations of society."*

He was a prince of good fellows, with great sense of humor and a fund of stories accumulated in smoking rooms with congenial spirits on land and sea. He was a founder of both the Papyrus and St. Botolph clubs, and became influential and widely esteemed within the membership of each.

He was twice invited to deliver a course of lectures on scientific subjects before the Lowell Institute.

The last twenty years of his life were passed in serving the American Bell Telephone Company with his wide acquaintance, his encyclopedic information and his general abilities.

He received the honorary degree of M. A. from Williams college in 1880.

Mr. Hovey married Frances Goodridge, daughter of Lowell Goodridge and Caroline Knox Morgan, Dec. 16, 1868, in Pennsylvania. She died in 1896. He died at Chestnut Hill, in Boston, Feb. 18, 1906, aged sixty-four.

Their children were born as follows:—

1807—i.   JANE DE PEYSTER²; married Edwin S. Webster of Boston.
1808—ii. MABEL²; married Henry W. Harris of New York.
1809—iii. CHANDLER²; married Dorothy Allen of Boston.

* "Listener" in *Boston Evening Transcript.*

1268

EDWARD CLARENCE HOVEY[7], born in Paris, France, April 13, 1854. He lives in Brookline, Mass.: and married Lucy Almira Cobb of Brookline. She was born there Feb. 26, 1856.

Their children were born as follows:—

1810—I.   MARY COBB[8], born Dec. 21, 1877, in Chicago, Ill.
1811—II. ALICE GARDINER[8], born Oct. 22, 1879, in Brookline, Mass.
1812—III. EDWARD CLARENCE[8], born March 29, 1883.

1276

DOUGLASS HOVEY[7], born in Hampton, Conn., Feb. 22, 1828. He was a manufacturer. In his early manhood, he was a photographic artist in New York City, and the inventor of an albumen paper. He married, first, Clara L. Kelsey Nov. 6, 1856, at Homer, N. Y. She was born April 7, 1833; and died April 2, 1858, at Rochester, N. Y., aged twenty-four years. He married, second, Frances Marion Pixley April 12, 1860, at Rochester. She was born in Springwater, N. Y., April 20, 1838. He died in Rochester Feb. 8, 1886, at the age of fifty-seven. He was a man of character. His wife Frances survived him, and lives in Rochester.

The children of Mr. Hovey were born in Rochester, as follows:—

1813—I.   CHARLES FREDERICK[8], born Nov. 8, 1857. *See family numbered "1813."*
1814—II. GEORGE CARLTON[8], born Aug. 15, 1866; died Oct. 14, 1866.
1815—III. JOHN FITCH[8], born June 5, 1868; married Jessie Z. Holley April 12, 1892, in Milwaukee, Wis., where she was born March 19, 1870. He died in Rochester, N. Y., Aug. 4, 1894, at the age of twenty-six. She survived him, and lives in Milwaukee, his widow.

1277

JOHN DUSTIN HOVEY, ESQ.[8], born in Londonderry, N. H., June 19, 1821. He was a teacher and lawyer. He married Susan Cotton, daughter of Norman and Lydia Payne in Marietta, O., April 27, 1845. She was born in Marietta Oct. 10, 1825; and died at Milford, O., Jan. 14, 1888, aged sixty-two. He died in Milford Dec. 19, 1898, at the age of seventy-seven.

Their children were born as follows:—

1816—I.   LAURA DUSTIN[9], born March 20, 1846, near Cincinnati, O.: married John Yakey at Goshen, O.; died Feb. 5, 1902, and was buried at Milford, O.
1817—II. JOHN PAYNE[9], born Aug. 31, 1847, near Milford, a suburb of Cincinnati. *See family numbered "1817."*
1818—III. MARIA RHODA[9], born Feb. 12, 1850, near Cincinnati; married Isaac Jefferson Grimes at Belton, Mo.; and died at Waverly, Kan., Nov. 21, 1899, aged forty-nine.

1819—IV.   ANNIE CUSHING[9], born Sept. 17, 1852, at New Albany, O.; married Isaac Newton Anderson at Goshen, O.; and died at Madisonville, O., Sept. 27, 1897, aged forty-five.

1820—V.   FRANKLIN STARK[9], born Aug. 21, 1855, at New Albany; married Sadie Baldwin at Belton, Mo.; and lives at Alexandria, Minn.

1821—VI.   NANNIE[9], born Nov. 20, 1857, at New Albany; married Anson Henry Baldwin at Ottawa, Kan.; and lives at Long Beach, Cal.

1822—VII.   CHARLES[9], born April 23, 1860, at Batavia, O.; died Aug. 12, 1860.

1823—VIII.   GEORGE MILTON[9], born Aug. 10, 1861, at Batavia; died at Perins Mills Sept. 23, 1865, and buried at Zion Church, Clermont county, O.

1824—IX.   VIRGINIA E.[9], born April 3, 1864, at Zion Church; and died there April 3, 1865.

1825—X.   FLORENCE A.[9], born Feb. 2, 1866, at New Boston, O.; married William J. Alford at Ottawa, Kan.; and lives at Winfield, Kan.

1293

FRANK ADELBERT HOVEY[8], born in Oxford, N. Y., Feb. 28, 1859. He is a coal dealer, and lived in Bainbridge, Afton and Union and now at Endicott, N. Y. He married Flora Elgin, daughter of Peter Francis and Eliza Empy Feb. 12, 1879, in Deposit, N. Y. She was born in Churchville, N. Y., Sept. 1, 1860.

Their children were born as follows:—

1826—I.   CHARLES FRANCIS[9], born Sept. 25, 1882, at Cannonsville, N. Y.; was reared on a farm and attended the district school at Bennettsville, N. Y., and the high school at Afton, whither his parents had removed in 1896; graduated from the high school in 1900; took a two-years' post-graduate course; and graduated at Harvard College in 1906, with the degree of Bachelor of Arts and distinction in political science, having specialized in economics and other commercial subjects in preparation for a business career. He went to New York City immediately after leaving college, and engaged in the piano and player piano manufacturing industry. In 1910, he became vice-president of the Milton Piano Company, and has been interested in the manufacture of fountain pens and other business enterprises. April 16, 1912, he patented a sockless self-filling fountain pen (U. S. patent No. 1,023,447). He is a close student of modern business methods and the application of the principles of efficiency to manufacturing and industrial pursuits. He is a member of the Efficiency Society and Harvard Club of New York City; and resides at 27 West 44th street, New York City. He is connected in business with the Mason Fountain Pen Company, makers of fountain, stylo and gold pens, their place of business being located at 1777 Broadway, New York City.

1827—II.   JESSIE MAY[9], born Aug. 1, 1885, in Bainbridge; she is a stenographer, and lives at home in Endicott.

1828—III.   HATTIE AMANDA[9], born May 28, 1889, in Bainbridge; and died there Oct. 7, 1897, at the age of eight.

1294

HENRY MORRIS HOVEY[8], born in Oxford, N. Y., Aug. 2, 1860. He is a salesman, and lives at 4 Judson street, in Binghampton, N. Y. He married Helen Eunice, daughter of Benjamin B. and Emily (Shepherd) Bennett Feb. 2, 1887, at Guilford, N. Y. She was born at Masonville, N. Y., Sept. 14, 1866.

Their child was born in Binghampton, as follows:—

1820—1.   LENA MAE[9], born April 3, 1898.

1299

COL. CHARLES HENRY HOVEY[8], born in Boston, Mass., March 28, 1830. He attended the Brimmer school in Boston, and received a Franklin medal. He was employed as a boy in Jos. T. Brown's drug store, at the corner of Washington and Bedford streets, and learned the business. He then had a store of his own in Lowell, but subsequently returned to Brown's, where he was at the beginning of the Civil war. He enlisted into the service, being mustered in as first lieutenant in company D, Thirteenth regiment of Massachusetts volunteers, July 16, 1861; promoted to captain of company K (a Westboro company) Nov. 6, 1861; and to lieutenant-colonel of the regiment April 16, 1864. He was wounded in the face at the battle of Antietam, while in command of company K, Sept. 17, 1862, and in the thigh at Gettysburg July 1, 1863. He was captured while acting as division inspector on General Robinson's staff, and recaptured July 4, 1863. He was detailed from the regiment as brigade inspector on General Taylor's staff, Third brigade, Second division, First corps, Jan. 15, 1863; and promoted May 7, 1863, on the retreat from Chancellorsville, to division inspector on the staff of General Robinson. He served until he was wounded at Gettysburg as above stated; and was mustered out of service Aug. 1, 1864.

Shortly after the war he opened a drug store at the corner of Walnut avenue and Warren street, in Roxbury, and during the years he conducted it, the store was the rendezvous of the solid and influential men of the city. He was elected to the state legislature during this period, serving for many years; and subsequently was an inspector in the custom house at Boston.

He was a member of the old Boston light infantry, the Thirteenth Regiment association, the Ancient and Honorable Artillery Company, member and past commander of Stevenson Post 26 G. A. R., and of John A. Andrew Post 15, G. A. R., member of Abadour lodge A. F. & A. Masons and of the Loyal Legion.

Colonel Hovey married Louise Caroline, daughter of Emery and Arabella (Wheeler) Perry July 25, 1861, in Boston. She was born in Worcester, Mass., May 30, 1839. He died at Boston

May 11, 1900, at the age of seventy. She survives him and lives at "The Warren," in Roxbury.

He was an ideal soldier, beloved by all who knew him, and gladly welcomed on all occasions. He was tall, remarkably erect in form, handsome and dignified, with marked ease and polish of manner, a keen eye and sense of humor, deliberate but clear and decided in speech, simple tastes, and domestic. A bronze tablet was placed to his memory by the Loyal Legion in the public library at Westboro.

Their children were born in Roxbury district, Boston, as follows:—

1830—I.   FREDERICK SAMPSON[8], born March 22, 1866; was a Franklin medal scholar, and, immediately after graduation from the English high school, was drowned at Wells Beach, Me., while camping out there, in an endeavor to save a boy from drowning, July 25, 1884, at the age of eighteen.

1831—II. EDITH[7], born Nov. 20, 1868; married Guy Harold, son of William and Margaret Ann (Maguire) Holliday of Boston June 12, 1895. He was born in Roxbury Aug. 17, 1866; attended the Roxbury Latin school; graduated at Harvard college, with the degree of Bachelor of Arts, in 1869, and at the Harvard Law school, with the degree of Bachelor of Laws, in 1892; admitted to the bar of the United States Circuit court in 1899, practised law in Boston from 1892 to 1901; and has been since the latter date assistant clerk of the superior court, for Suffolk county, for civil business. He is a member of the Harvard club of Boston, Boston City club, Joseph Webb Lodge and St. Paul's Chapter A. F. & A. M., of Boston. They live at 26 Fountain street, Roxbury district, Boston; and their children were born as follows: 1. Harold[10], born June 15, 1898, in Boston. 2. Beatrice[10], born Feb. 1, 1901, in Sharon, Mass. 3. Rebecca Frances[10], born Dec. 13, 1902, in Boston.

1832—III. REBECCA FRANCES[8], born July 2, 1870; married George Fernald Reed Sept. —, 1891; he died ————; and she lives at 27 Livermore Road, Wellesley Hills, Mass. Children: 1. Paul S.[10], born in 1892. 2. Helen S.[10], born in 1894.

1833—IV. CARL[8], born Oct. 2, 1875. See family numbered "1833."

1309

LEROY FARLEY HOVEY[8], born in Waldoboro, Me., Nov. 19, 1847. He is a merchant; and lived formerly at East Orange, N. J., and now at 249 W 104th street, New York City. He married Sarah Frances, daughter of James Winthrop and Lydia Maria Tewksbury of Lynn, Mass., April 25, 1877. She was born in Lynn Oct. 14, 1850.

Their children were born in East Orange, as follows:—

1834—I.   JAMES[8], born July 2, 1880; died in New York City June 26, 1905, aged twenty-four.

1835—II. LEROY FARLEY[9], born March 21, 1882; salesman; lives in New York City.

1836—III.   WINTHROP TEWKSBURY[9], born Sept. 14, 1885; employed in
            banking; and lives in San Francisco, Cal.
1837—IV.   MARGARET[9], born Jan. 25, 1887; lives in New York City.
1838—V.   MYRON[9], born Jan. 7, 1890; clerk with the New York Tele-
            graph Company; and lives in New York City.

1310

HORATIO NELSON HOVEY[8], born in Cambridge, Mass., Aug.
21, 1840. He lives at 8 Mystic avenue, Winchester, Mass. He
married Mehitabel Ann Eaton April 7, 1864, in Cambridge. She
was born in Alfred, Me., April 6, 1841; and died in Cambridge
Jan. 13, 1873, at the age of thirty-one.

Their children were born in Cambridge, as follows:—

1839—I.   FREELAND EATON[9], born Feb. 22, 1866. *See family numbered
            "1839."*
1840—II.   ETHEL[9], born Aug. 1, 1871; married Austin Bradstreet Fletcher
            of Cambridge March 1, 1894; and lives at West Medford,
            Mass.

1321

JAMES SYLVESTER HOVEY[8], born in Dracut, Mass., May 25,
1843. He was a bank cashier, and lived in Lowell, Mass., at 481
Beacon street. He married Annie Elizabeth, daughter of Artemas and Mary J. (Durgin) Dillingham of Lowell Nov. 29,
1865. She was born in Lowell July 19, 1842. He died there Oct.
22, 1885, at the age of forty-two; and she survives him.

Their children were born in Lowell, as follows:—

1841—I.   PHILIP ROGERS[9], born July 28, 1871; lives, unmarried, at 481
            Beacon street, Lowell.
1842—II.   ELIZABETH DILLINGHAM[9], born Jan. 23, 1877; married Rev.
            Charles Thomas, son of Thomas and Louisa (Dudley)
            Baylis May 24, 1899, at Lowell. He was born in Liverpool,
            England, April 17, 1869. They live at 85 Homer street,
            Newton Center, Mass. Their children were born as fol-
            lows: 1. *Marjorie Elizabeth[10]*, born May 22, 1900, in
            Brecksville, O. 2. *Gertrude Louise[10]*, born May 27, 1901,
            in New York City. 3. *Esther Victoria[10]*, born June 19,
            1906. 4. *Miriam Joy[10]*, born Jan. 23, 1908.
1843—III.   MARION[9], born Feb. 13, 1882; lives, unmarried, at 481 Beacon
            street, Lowell.

1329

HENRY E. HOVEY[8], born in Dracut, Mass., April 23, 1853.
He lived in Lowell, and married Mary E., daughter of William
and Mary Locke of Lowell Jan. 17, 1877. He died in Lowell
March 4, 1903, at the age of forty-nine. She survived him; and
lives at 99 Concord street, Lowell, Mass.

Child, born in Lowell:—

1844—I.   CLARA V.[9], born Jan. 26, 1877; is unmarried; and lives at 99
            Concord street, Lowell.

1337

JOHN BISHOP HOVEY[8], born in Lyme, N. H., Aug. 20, 1820. He lived in Stoneham, Mass.; and married Melissa Mack, daughter of John and Polly (Moses) Hall Nov. 24, 1842, in Newbury, Vt., where she was born April 10, 1823. He died in 1——; and she survived him. Her home is at 6 Pearl street, in Stoneham.

Their children were born as follows:—

1845—I.   MELISSA ANN[9], born Nov. 28, 1843, in Lyme, N. H.; married Philip Leon, son of Leander and Emily (Story) King March 15, 1872, in Stoneham, Mass. He was born in Philadelphia, Pa., July 16, 1837. Their children were born in Stoneham, as follows: 1. *Hubert Leon*[10], born Jan. 16, 1873. 2. *Frank Warren*[10], born Sept. 4, 1874.

1846—II. JOHN LEWIS[9], born March 31, 1847, in Springfield, N. H.; died in Stoneham, Mass., June 11, 1865, aged eighteen.

1847—III. IDA JOSEPHINE[9], born Sept. 22, 1855, in Stoneham; married Warren Nathan, son of Abiel and Sarah Anna (Smith) James June 24, 1875, in Stoneham. He was born in Eastport, Me., Sept. 14, 1849; and lived in Stoneham, Mass. Children: 1. *Charles Warren*[10], born Jan. 12, 1876; died Feb. 21, 1876. 2. *Josephine Hovey*[10], born Sept. 10, 1877, in Stoneham; married Benjamin R. Davis July 21, 1900; he is a civil engineer. They have four children; and live in Somerville. 3. *Alice Mabel* (twin)[10], born April 14, 1879, in Brooklyn; married Harvey D. Symonds March 15, 1902; he is a civil engineer. They have two children; and live in Chicago. 4. *Annie Maud* (twin)[10], born April 14, 1879, in Brooklyn; married John Roscoe Bokaker Jan. 30, 1907; he is a secretary; they live in Swampscott, Mass. 5. *Lewis Warren*[10], born June 14, 1883, in Stoneham; lives in Stoneham.

1338

SYLVANUS SUMNER HOVEY[8], born in Lyme, N. H., July 12, 1822. He married, first, Lydia, daughter of Kimball and Charlotte (Noyes) Tyler March 31, 1853, in Medford, Mass. She was born in North Haverhill, N. H., July 18, 1838; and died in Lynn, Mass., Feb. 15, 1866, at the age of twenty-seven. He married, second, Mary Jane Tyler, sister to his first wife, Oct. 22, 1868, in Lynn. She was born in Warren, N. H., June 25, 1835; and died in Lynn March 27, 1874, at the age of thirty-eight. Mr. Hovey died in Lynn April 28, 1877, at the age of fifty-four.

His children were born as follows:—

1848—I.   ALBINI SUMNER[9], born Jan. 12, 1854, in Stoneham, Mass. *See family numbered "1848."*

1849—II. EFFIE BLANCHE[9], born March 12, 1858, in North Haverhill, N. H.; married George William, son of William Harrison and Annette (Stickney) Ingalls Nov. 8, 1876, in Lynn. He was born in Medford, Mass., Nov. 3, 1856; and lived in Lynn, where he was an express agent in 1878.

1339

ABNER BINGHAM HOVEY[8], born in Lyme, N. H., Nov. 12, 1825. He lived in Stoneham, Mass.; and married Malvina Lydia, daughter of Ebenezer and Sophia (Bryant) Bryant March 4, 1849, in Stoneham. She was born in South Reading (now Wakefield), Mass., Aug. 11, 1832.

Their children were born in Stoneham, as follows:—

1850—I.   LOUISA SOPHIA[9], born Sept. 20, 1851; married Gustavus, son of James and Rebecca (Stubbs) Bryant Jan. 4, 1873, in Stoneham. He was born in Portland, Me., March 28, 1848; and lived in Stoneham in 1878. Children: 1. *Malvina Lydia[10]*, born Nov. 9, 1873. 2. *Frank[10]*, born Dec. 21, 1876.

1851—II.   FRANK ABNER[9], born Dec. 31, 1857.

1852—III. CHARLES SUMNER ALPHONSO[9], born Sept. 29, 1865.

1345

REV. SIMEON ALLEN HOVEY[8], born in Lyme, N. H., Jan. 2, 1821. He became a Disciple preacher, and was a chaplain in the Confederate army in the Civil war. In January, 1870, he was in Memphis, Tenn., on business, and nothing has been learned of him since. It is supposed that he was killed shortly afterward at Johnsonville, Tenn. He was a man of fine appearance and of ability.

Mr. Hovey married Melissa, daughter of Robert and Sarah (Wright) Scanlon Dec. 15, 1842, in Jackson county, Tenn., where she was born Nov. 19, 1827. She was living at Nashville, Tenn., in 1877.

Their children were born as follows:—

1853—I.   SARAH LOUANN[9], born Aug. 8, 1844, in Franklin county, Ill.; married Granville Bowman, son of David and Elizabeth (Cruise) Turner Dec. 22, 1857, in Linden, Tenn. He was born in Monroe county, Ky., Jan. 14, 1841; and was a farmer in Gamaliel, Ky., in 1878. Children: 1. *Simeon Allen[10]*, born Feb. 16, 1866. 2. *Virginia[10]*, born Jan. 15, 1869. 3. *Bettie Scanlon[10]*, born Sept. 10, 1871. 4. *Mary Isabella[10]*, born Dec. 21, 1874. 5. *Ruth Ellen[10]*, born July 1, 1876.

1854—II.   ISABELLA[9], born Sept. 3, 1847, in Franklin county; married, first, Benjamin Franklin, son of Green H. and Susan (Allen) Dillehay, Dec. 25, 1869, in Linden. He was born in Murray county, Tenn., Nov. 28, 1848; and died from a railway accident near Nashville, Tenn., Nov. 10, 1873, at the age of twenty-four. She married, second, John Calvin, son of Levi and Susan Caroline (Holden) West July 10, 1876, in Nashville. He was born in Lauderdale county, Ala., Nov. 27, 1853.

Her children by her first husband, Benjamin F. Dillehay, were born as follows: 1. *Edward Franklin[10]*, born Aug. 8, 1869. 2. *Allen[10]*, born Aug. 15, 1872; died Oct. 30, 1874.

Her child by her second husband, John C. West, was born as follows: 1. *Herbert[10]*, born April 25, 1877.

1855—III. MARY LOUISE[8], born Feb. 13, 1849, in Clinton county, Tenn.;
married George Washington, son of William H. and Mary
L. (Mayfield) Boyce March 5, 1867, in Perry county, Tenn.
He was born in Palestine, Tenn., March 27, 1846. He was
a farmer, and lived in Farmer's Valley, Tenn., in 1878.
Children: 1. ———[10] (son), born in 1868; died in 1868.
2. *William Henry*[10], born Nov. 7, 1871. 3. *John Granville*[10], born May 10, 1874.

1856—IV. ELLEN RUBIE[8], born Jan. 20, 1851, in Gainesborough, Tenn.;
married Marshall Andrew, son of Marshall and Emily
(Brown) Dodson Sept. 29, 1867, in Linden. He was born
in Williamson county, Tenn., Jan. 8, 1849. She died in
Linden Feb. 13, 1868, at the age of seventeen, and a bride
of four months. They had no children.

1857—V. MELISSA ALLEN[8], born Oct. 8, 1864, in Gainesborough; died
there March 20, 1865.

1346

CAPT. EBER DAVIS HOVEY[8], born in Lyme, N. H., Nov. 23,
1822. He was a sea captain; and married Amanda B., daughter
of Washington and Abigail (Lane) Preston Oct. 16, 1848, in
Bradford, Vt. She was born in Concord, N. H., July 24, 1824.
Captain Hovey sailed, in 1852, as mate of the steamship "Independence," which was wrecked off Montigordia Bay. While
heroically endeavoring to save a lady passenger who had been
washed overboard, he was drowned, March 26, 1852, at the age
of twenty-nine. His wife survived him, and was living in
Charlestown, Mass., his widow, in 1877.

They had one child:—

1858—I. ———[9] (son), born March —, 1851; died April —, 1851.

1348

JOSEPH MILTON HOVEY[8], born in Lyme, N. H., July 3, 1826.
He lived in Bristol, N. H.; and married Alma Elizabeth, daughter
of Alpheus and Sarah (Hovey) (819) Hibbard Jan. 20, 1850, in
Brookfield, Vt., where she was born Oct. 20, 1832.

They had one child:—

1859—I. CARROLL MILTON[9], born June 11, 1870, in Jesup, Iowa.

1351

SAMUEL LEWIS HOVEY[8], born in Newbury, Vt., Sept. 21,
1831. He was a farmer, and lived in Jesup, Iowa. He married
Julia Frances, daughter of Amos S. and Lucy (Piper) Hatch
May 3, 1853, in Chelsea, Vt., where she was born May 20, 1834.

Their children were born as follows:—

1860—I. CHARLES EBER[9], born Aug. 27, 1855; died May 17, 1875, at the
age of nineteen.
1861—II. MARY BELLE[9], born March 16, 1862.
1862—III. NELLIE MARCIA[9], born Feb. 11, 1864.
1863—IV. LUCY RUBIE[9], born April 4, 1869.

1354

WILLIAM BARRON HOVEY⁸, born in Bradford, Vt., July 4. 1844. He was a florist, and lived in Norwich, Conn. He married Luella Ann, daughter of James and Elmira (Greenleaf) Page July 31, 1867, in Haverhill, N. H., where she was born Dec. 20, 1844.

Their child was born as follows:—

1864—I.   HELEN ALLEN⁹, born Nov. 11, 1869.

1355

GEORGE HOVEY⁸, born in Brookfield, Vt., Nov. 6, 1819. He was a farmer, and lived in Independence, Iowa. He married Maryetta, daughter of Barzillai H. and Betsey (Sweetland) Reed March 24, 1842, in Albany, Vt. She was born in Vernon, Vt., Oct. 30, 1819.

Their children were born as follows:—

1865—I.   NELSON KING⁹, born Dec. 19, 1842. *See family numbered "1865."*

1866—II.   BETSEY MARIA⁹, born Oct. 2, 1844; married William S., son of Ichabod and Almira (Gifford) Richmond March 7, 1863. He was born in ————, C. W., in 1841; is a farmer, and lived in Jesup, Iowa, in 1878. Their children were born as follows: 1. *Alice Almira¹⁰*, born June 12, 1864. 2. *Adelaide¹⁰*, born May 10, 1866. 3. *Albert¹⁰*, born Aug. —. 1868.

1867—III. GEORGE BILLINGS⁹, born Dec. 6, 1846. *See family numbered "1867."*

1868—IV.   DANA WELLINGTON⁹, born Nov. 20, 1849; merchant; and lived in Winthrop, Iowa, in 1878.

1869—V.   BARZILLAI REED⁹, born Sept. 12, 1851. *See family numbered "1869."*

1870—VI.   FRANK WASHINGTON⁹, born May 24, 1854. *See family numbered "1870."*

1356

ELIAS SEABURY HOVEY⁸, born in Brookfield, Vt., Oct. 4, 1823. He was a farmer, and lived in Swanton, Iowa, in 1878. He married Martha Maria, daughter of Artemas and Catherine (Colt) Fish Jan. 26, 1847, in Brookfield, Vt., where she was born Dec. 30, 1827.

Their children were born as follows:—

1871—I.   ALMIRA MARTHA⁹, born Dec. 11, 1849, in Albany, Vt.; married Charles Henry, son of Moses and Sarah (Cook) Little in 1869, in Independence, Iowa. Children: 1. *Sarah Climena⁹*, born Aug. 17, 1870. 2. *Charles Herbert¹⁰*, born Dec. 9, 1873. 3. *Martha Alice¹⁰*, born Jan. 20, 1879.

1872—II.   RUFUS BILLINGS⁹, born Feb. 13, 1852; died Sept. —, 1855. aged three years.

1873—III. CATHERINE⁹, born Nov. 21, 1858; died Feb. 17, 1859.

1874—IV.   HORACE NELSON⁹, born Feb. 1, 1860.

1875—V.   CAROLINE ALLEN⁹, born Sept. 18, 1862.

1359

JOHN BILLINGS HOVEY[8], born in Brookfield, Vt., Nov. 27, 1825. He was a farmer, and lived in Albany, Vt., in 1878. He married Ellen, daughter of Eli and Achsah (Delano) Chamberlin May 26, 1853, in Albany, where she was born Nov. 4, 1824.

Their children were born in Albany, as follows:—

1876—I.   WALLACE HENRY[9], born Oct. 13, 1854.
1877—II.   LILLIE ELLEN[9], born Aug. 17, 1858; died Aug. 25, 1869, aged eleven.
1878—III. SELMA VIOLET[9], born Feb. 1, 1861.

1360

ALVIN HOVEY[8], born in Albany, Vt., Aug. 7, 1827. He was a photographer, and lived at Burr Oak, Kansas. He married, first, Lydia Abby, daughter of Silas and Lucy (White) Smith Jan. 18, 1853, in Albany. She was born in Vershire, Vt., Feb. 4, 1827; and died in Albany April 20, 1870, at the age of forty-three. He married, second, Susan Eliza, daughter of Wesley and Lucretia (Smith) Clemons March 14, 1871, in Coral, Ill. She was born in Wells, Vt., Feb. 23, 1836. He died in Burr Oak Nov. 1, 1903, aged seventy-five. She lives at Kansas City, Mo.

His children were born as follows:—

1879—I.   ————[9] (son), died in infancy.
1880—II.   ————[9] (son), died in infancy.
1881—III. ————[9] (daughter), died in infancy.
1882—IV.   ————[9] (daughter), died in infancy.
1883—V.   ————[9] (daughter), born Oct. 8, 1872, in Coral; died Oct. 8, 1872.
1884—VI.   WILLIAM ALVIN[9], born Feb. 8, 1874, in Evanston, Ill. *See family numbered "1884."*

1362

LEWIS HOVEY[8], born in Albany, Vt., Jan. 3, 1831. He was a farmer, and lived in Swanton, Iowa. He married Marcia A., daughter of Thomas J. and Sophia H. (Culter) Ufford June 15, 1855, in Linn county, Iowa. She was born in Glover, Vt., June 28, 1832. He died in Swanton April 5, 1877, at the age of forty-six. She survived him, and died, his widow, at Heron Lake, Minn., Nov. 18, 1900, at the age of sixty-nine.

Their children were born as follows:—

1885—I.   CLARA SOPHIA[9], born July 5, 1862, near Littleton, Iowa; died March 15, 1867, at Swanton, at the age of four.
1886—II.   JULIA IDELLA[9], born Oct. 3, 1864, in Swanton; married S. S. Striker June 26, 1844; they live in Lesneur, Minn.; and he is engaged in banking. Children: 1. *Maud*[10], born Oct. 2, 1887, at Meriden, Iowa; lives at home. 2. *Wayne*[10], born Nov. —, 1904, at Des Moines.
1887—III. HATTIE ELLSWORTH[9], born Oct. 19, 1866, in Swanton; died Sept. 9, 1870, in Swanton, at the age of three.

1888—IV. EMMA POLLY[6], born Oct. 17, 1868, in Swanton; married Benona P. St. John Oct. 1, 1890; they live at Heron Lake; and he is engaged in the grain business. Their children were born as follows: 1. *Kathleen*[2], born Aug. 7, 1891, at Claghorn, Iowa. 2. *Clair Hovey*[4], born Feb. 2, 1898, at Heron Lake. 3. *Idelia*[10], born Sept. 23, 1900, at Heron Lake. 4. *Matthew*[12], born Jan. 11, 1907, at Heron Lake; died Oct. 25, 1908, at the age of one year.

1363

DEA. ELIJAH ADAMS HOVEY[6], born in Albany, Vt., Feb. 13, 1833. His father died when Elijah was eleven years old and he lived with his brother Elias on the old homestead near Albany until he was about nineteen, when, being in poor health and believing that salt water and fresh air would be beneficial to him, he went to Boston and for two years served in fishing boats plying the coast from Maine to Virginia. He then spent about two years in Boston, being employed as collector in a rental agency, janitor of the old Park Street church and as overseer of forestry and keeping the lawns on the Common. On leaving Boston, he returned to his home in Albany.

In 1855, for his brother Elias, he drove a four-horse team, heavily loaded with goods, from Albany to Littleton, Iowa, driving to Ogdensburg, N. Y., then coming by boat to Milwaukee, Wis., and overland to Littleton. This was before the railroad was built west of Dubuque. He took up a quarter section of land, now within the city limits of Jesup. He made some improvements on the claim, and then returned to Vermont. From 1857 to 1867 he spent in mercantile business in Albany.

He went west again in the latter year, and at Independence, Iowa, engaged, with his brother Elias, in driving wells, under the firm-name of Hovey Bros. Eight years later, after the people in their neighborhood had been well supplied with wells, they removed to Tampico, Ill. This was in the fall of 1874. They followed the same kind of business in this new section until the summer of 1877. At that time, Elijah dislocated his right shoulder, and subsequently broke his collar-bone and fractured his left arm near the shoulder. He retired from all business, and in the spring of 1882 removed to Independence, where he afterward lived.

Mr. Hovey was a deacon of the First Baptist church in Independence. While living at Tampico he organized the First Baptist church in that place. Wherever he lived or was, he did what he could to uplift men, doing at one time considerable evangelistic work.

He married Rhoda Savage, daughter of Timothy and Maria E. (Hazen) Lyman of Glover, Vt., July 4, 1857, in Albany. She was born in Glover March 6, 1834. He died in Independence

April 11, 1908, aged seventy-five; and she died there, his widow, Jan. 19, 1910, at the age of seventy-five.

Their children were born in Albany, as follows: —

1888—I.   ADELE², born June 12, 1858; died Dec. 24, 1869.
1889—II.   SILAS BILLINGS², born March 29, 1861. *See family numbered "1889."*
1890—III. MAURICE WALLBRIDGE², born Jan. 8, 1866. *See family numbered "1890."*

1364

TIMOTHY KENDALL HOVEY², born in Albany, Vt., Oct. 20. 1835. He was a farmer and miller, and lived in Littleton and Swanton, Iowa, then in Vermillion, S. D., and subsequently in Oelwein, Iowa. He married, first, Electa Bartlett, daughter of Moses and Sarah (Cook) Little Dec. 15, 1860, in Littleton. She was born in Lowell, Ill., Jan. 20, 1844. He married, second, Belle M. Balluff Sept. 6, 1904; and died in Oelwein July 15, 1906, at the age of seventy.

His children were born as follows: —

1891—I.   SARAH ALICE², born April 18, 1862, in Swanton; died Sept. 6, 1863 (1873?).
1892—II.   NELLIE M.², born Feb. 9, 1864, in Swanton; married George H. Washburn Dec. 23, 1887; and died Oct. 13, 1888.
1893—III. SUSIE², born March 14, 1871, in Vermillion, S. D.; married A. S. Hoffman May 1, 1890; music teacher; they live in Hankinson, N. D.
1894—IV.   EDMUND S.², born July 30, 1873, in Vermillion; mechanic; lives in Oelwein; married Mertie H. Stevenson May 24, 1899; and she died Sept. 15, 1900, at the age of twenty-seven.

1368

ORANGE HOVEY², born in Brookfield, Vt., Oct. 9, 1818. He was a scythe polisher by occupation; and lived in West Waterville, Me., in 1878. He married Matilda Abbie, daughter of George Hamilton and Jane (Bickford) Penney March 2, 1845, in Belgrade, Me., where she was born Dec. 4, 1825. He died in Oakland, Me., July 2, 1882, aged sixty-three; and she died in North Anson, Me., Jan. 26, 1904, aged seventy-eight.

Their children were born as follows: —

1895—I.   ———² (son), born Sept. 22, 1846; died Sept. 22, 1846.
1896—II.   ———² (son), born Oct. 31, 1849; died Oct. 31, 1849.
1897—III. GEORGE LORIN², born Nov. 7, 1855, in North Wayne, Me. *See family numbered "1897."*

1371

OLIVER PERRY HOVEY², born in Northfield, Vt., July 22, 1825. He learned the printer's trade in Lowell, Mass., and worked at it. He married a Mexican lady in Santa Fe, N. M., where he lived. He served in the Mexican war; and was with the troops when they confiscated a printing establishment in Santa Fe, and he published a war paper with it. After the war was over he owned and continued the office, editing and publishing The Santa Fe Republican as long as he lived. He was a representative of New Mexico, when it was a territory, to the national government; and died in Santa Fe Aug. 9, 1862, at the age of thirty-seven, having accumulated a considerable estate.

Their children were born as follows:—

1898—I.   JAMES⁹, born in 1863; was employed by the government as teacher to the Indians in Albuqurque, N. M.; and died a few years ago.

1899—II.   O. P.⁹, was a postmaster in Cuba; lived in Algodones, N. M.

1900—III. ————⁹ (daughter), died in ————.

1901—IV.   ————⁹ (daughter), died in ————.

1375

WILLIAM HOVEY⁸, born in Brookfield, Vt., May 23, 1824. He was a merchant, and lived in Oberlin, O. He married Philena, daughter of Wells and Martha (Paine) Allen Aug. 30, 1847, in Albany, Vt., where she was born March 5, 1826. He died in Oberlin July 25, 1868, at the age of forty-four. She survived him, and was living at Oberlin in 1878.

Their children were born as follows:—

1902—I.   FRANK⁹, born April 28, 1853. *See family numbered "1902."*

1903—II.   WILLIE⁹, born Dec. 3, 1863.

1377

DR. ARIEL BURNHAM HOVEY⁸, born in Albany, Vt., Feb. 9, 1829. He was a surgeon and physician, and resided in Tiffin, O. He married Susan, daughter of William and Anna (Johnson) Boyce June 20, 1849, in Sandusky, O. She was born in Danville, Canada West, April 11, 1827.

Their children were born as follows:—

1904—I.   ZENOBIA IRENE⁹, born May 16, 1851, in Oberlin, O.; died in Tiffin Nov. 17, 1854.

1905—II.   LOLA IRENE⁹, born Sept. 17, 1854, in Tiffin; married Charles Van Tyne of Sandusky, O., Sept. 17, 1873, in Tiffin. Children: 1. *Orvilla*¹⁰, born in 1875. 2. *Charles Hovey*¹⁰, born in 1877.

1906—III. ORVILLA ARIEL⁹ (twin), born March 11, 1860, in Tiffin; died Aug. 1, 1860.

1907—IV.   ORVILLA SUSAN⁹ (twin), born March 11, 1860, in Tiffin; died Aug. 2, 1860.

1908—V.   EARL BURNHAM⁹, born Dec. 22, 1861, in Tiffin; died Oct. 16, 1875, at the age of thirteen.

1387

REV. ARTHUR JUDSON HOVEY⁸, born in Albany, Vt., April 3, 1842. He was educated at Brown University; was pastor of the Baptist church in Stoneham, Mass., in 1878; and now resides at

Caloosa, Fla. He married, first, Ella Experience, daughter of Nathan and Emeline (Armington) Mason June 27, 1872, in Providence, R. I., where she was born Jan. 4, 1840. He married, second, ———— ———— in 1886, at Providence.

Mr. Hovey's children were born as follows:—

1909—I. ————[9] (daughter), born April 15, 1873; died June 19, 1873.
1910—II. HORACE MASON[9], born April 6, 1877.

1391

ALBERT SILAS HOVEY[8], born in Albany, Vt., Sept. 28, 1856. He has resided in Stoneham, Mass., since he became of age, and been engaged in the grocery and provision business. His present address is 63 Franklin street, Stoneham. Mr. Hovey married Ella Adella Harris July 9, 1879, in Stoneham. She was born in Charlemont, Mass., March 23, 1856.

Their children were born in Stoneham, as follows:—

1911—I. ARTHUR ERNEST[9], born Dec. 16, 1880; clerk; lives in Stoneham.
1912—II. MAUD ELLA[9], born Oct. 23, 1885.
1913—III. ROY ALBERT[9], born Feb. 23, 1888.
1914—IV. HARLOW HARRIS[9], born May 20, 1893.

1392

SAMUEL KENDALL HOVEY[8], born in Brookfield, Vt., Nov. 30, 1823. He was a farmer, and lived in Westside, Minn. He married, first, Melvina, daughter of David and Maria (Hunt) Sutton Jan. 28, 1851, in Merrimack, Wis. She was born in Sparta, N. Y., Aug. 1, 1831; and died in Merrimack March 31, 1855, at the age of twenty-two. He married, second, Rebecca Ann, daughter of Charles and Mary (Delargee) Bostwick Nov. 25, 1855, in Merrimack. She was born in Norfolk, N. Y., May 11, 1834.

Mr. Hovey's children were born as follows: —

1915—I. DAVID WILLIS[9], born Jan. 21, 1852.
1916—II. MELVAINE[9], born March 3, 1855; married Emma Ralph April 11, 1877, in Austin, Minn.
1917—III. MARY MELVINA[9], born July 24, 1859.
1918—IV. AMY JANE[9], born Sept. 30, 1861.
1919—V. CAROLINE ELLA[9], born April 26, 1865.
1920—VI. BETSEY ANN[9], born April 2, 1868.

1398

LEWIS WILLIAM HOVEY[8], born June 6, 1835. He resided in Boston, Mass., in 1878. He married Matilda Frances, daughter of Albert and Rachel (Goodrich) Hixon Feb. 2, 1864, in Williamstown, Vt. She was born in Brookfield, Vt., June 30, 1844.

Their child was born as follows:—

1921—I. ALBERT HARVEY[9], born May 15, 1867.

1408

CHARLES HOVEY⁸, born in Mount Vernon, Ind., Dec. 29. 1847. He was a blacksmith; and married Louisa, daughter of Wyndar and Amanda (McKenzie) Bailey Sept. 5, 1870, in New Haven, Ill. She was born in Shawneetown, Ill., March 11, 1850.
Child:—

1922—I.   LILLIE⁹, born Oct. 7, 1872.

1418

CHARLES JAMES HOVEY⁸, born in Mount Vernon, Ind., Jan. 8, 1850. He has been a shoe merchant, banker, farmer, justice of the peace and twice postmaster of his native town, where he lives. He married Lillie, daughter of Jonathan and Parna (Whittlesey) Jaquess March 16, 1871, in Evansville, Ind. She was born in Poseyville, Ind., May 6, 1850.
Their children were born in Mount Vernon, as follows:—

1923—I.   ALVIN JAQUESS⁸, born Dec. 27, 1871. *See family numbered "1923."*

1924—II. MABEL⁹, born Sept. 1, 1873; died at Lakeside Farms, Ind., Aug. 26, 1876, aged two years.

1925—III. MARY⁹, born Aug. 17, 1875; married Otis Theo Brinkman Oct. 18, 1898. He was born in Mount Vernon Oct. 23, 1871; and lives at Mount Vernon, being a hardware dealer. Their children were born in Mount Vernon, as follows: 1. *Charlotte H.*¹⁰, born Aug. 24, 1899. 2. *Lillie J.*¹⁰, born Nov. 8, 1903. 3. *Margaret Bernice*¹⁰, born March 29, 1908.

1926—IV. RANDOLPH JAQUESS⁸, born March 23, 1879. *See family numbered "1926."*

1927—V.   NINA⁹, born June 23, 1881; married Edward M. Daniel March 30, 1898. He was born in Mount Vernon Dec. 26, 1875; and lives there, being a printer. Their child was born in Mount Vernon, as follows: 1. *Helen H.*¹⁰, born Jan. 7, 1899.

1425

JUDSON WATERMAN HOVEY⁸, born in Delaware county, O., Oct. 27, 1852. He was a farmer, and liver at May, Mich., in 1878. He married Lucy Brewster, daughter of Elijah and Emeline (Potter) Shade Oct. 8, 1872. She was born in Logan county, O., Sept. 25, 1852.
Their children were born as follows:—

1928—I.   HILLIARD DE WAYNE⁸, born May 3, 1875.

1929—II. BERTHA EMELINE⁸, born April 11, 1877.

1428

REV. EDWIN HAMILTON HOVEY⁸, born in Brighton, O., June 26, 1844. He was a Baptist clergyman; and lived, in 1878, in Stoneboro, Pa. He married, first, Diantha, daughter of Horace and Eliza (Hatch) Hunt Sept. 24, 1865, in Randolph, Pa., where she was born June 22, 1845, and where she died Dec. 4, 1867, at the age of twenty-two. He married, second, Mary Jane, daughter of Franklin Rice May 3, 1871, near Lancaster, Wis. She was born in Vermont Sept. 16, 1841.

The children of Mr. Hovey were born as follows:—

1930—I.   MARY ELIZA⁹, born Dec. 3, 1867; died Dec. 3, 1867.
1931—II.   MARY ADDIE⁹, born March —, 1872; died March —, 1872.
1932—III. IONA ESTELLE⁹, born Aug. 8, 1874; died July —, 1875.
1933—IV.   JOHN FRANKLIN⁹, born June 22, 1876.

1434

GEORGE ELBERT HOVEY⁸, born in Lorain county, O., Nov. 24, 1855. He married Adelaide Louise, daughter of John and Rosette (Ackland) Barnsey Jan. 1, 1878. She was born in Richfield, O.

Their child was born as follows:—

1934—I.   MABEL ELLEN⁹, born Oct. 9, 1878.

1497

FRANCIS ALONZO HOVEY⁸, born in Swanzey, N. H., Oct. 20, 1836. He was a farmer, and lived in Swanzey. He married, first, Helen Belinda, daughter of Jonathan W. Whitcom and Belinda Capron of Keene Nov. 26, 1857. She was born in Swanzey Aug. 25, 1839; and died Jan. 6, 1863, at the age of twenty-three. He married, second, Lucina Holbrook, daughter of John H. and Lemira (Crossett) Matthews March 3, 1864. She was born in Swanzey Nov. 6, 1843. He died in Swanzey, of consumption, Feb. 9, 1868, at the age of thirty-one; and she survives him, living at 85 Wilson street, in Keene.

The children of Mr. Hovey were born in Swanzey, as follows:—

1935—I.   FRANK EDRICK⁹, born July 21, 1860; and died Oct. 10, 1866,
           at the age of six years.
1936—II.   HERBERT CAPRON⁹, born Dec. 22, 1862; married Alice M.
           Blodgett of Swanzey, where she now lives, his widow. She
           was born in Leominster. He died, of consumption, Aug 4,
           1887, at the age of twenty-four.
1937—III. JOHN MATTHEWS⁹, born July 29, 1865. *See family numbered
           "1937."*
1938—IV.   ELIZABETH JANE⁹, born March 4, 1867; lives at home, 85
           Wilson street, Keene, N. H., unmarried. She is book-
           keeper for the Cheshire Beef and Produce Company in
           Keene.

1510

JOHN A. HOVEY⁸, born in Peterborough, N. H., March 19, 1845. He lived on his father's farm in Peterborough, being a farmer. He married Julia E. Center of Lyndeboro Oct. 24,

1869; and he died in Peterborough, of heart disease, Oct. 6, 1881, at the age of thirty-six.

Children:—

1939—I. GEORGE W.[9]: living in 1882, and was probably dead in 1887.
1940—II. GRACE M.[9], born in or before 1877, and was living in 1899.

1515

HENRY L. HOVEY[8], born Sept. 30, 1833. He lived in Groveland; and married Mary Henry. He died March 3, 1883; and his widow married, secondly, Charles N. Hardy, a carpenter and contractor.

The children of Henry L. and Mary (Henry) Hovey were born as follows:—

1941—I. LEE A.[9], born Sept. 23, 1857. He is a shoe cutter and lives in Groveland. He married Carrie M., daughter of Joseph R. and Ellen M. Brown of Haverhill Sept. 29, 1886.
1942—II. FRED C.[9] *See family numbered "1942."*
1943—III. WILLIAM[9].

1516

RUFUS A. HOVEY[8], born June 22, 1837. He lived in Groveland and Lynn, Mass.; and married Mary E. Renton Oct. 7, 1859. He died April 13, 1872; and she was living in Lynn, his widow, in 1909.

Their children were born as follows:—

1944—I. EDWARD L.[9], born April 14, 1861, in Lynn. *See family numbered "1944."*
1945—II. ANNIE M.[9], born in 1863, at Lynn; died in 1864.
1946—III. ELLA R.[9], born June 10, 1865, in Lynn; bookkeeper; living, unmarried, with her mother, at High Rock avenue, in Lynn, in 1909.
1947—IV. RALPH CREIGHTON[9], born Nov. 20, 1867, in Groveland; pharmacist; manufacturer of Hovey's dental polish; lives with his mother in Lynn, unmarried.
1948—V. GUY CARLETON[9], born May 5, 1869, in Groveland; photographer; lived in Lynn until 18—, when he removed to San Diego, Cal., because of ill health; and now lives at Palm Beach, Cal. He married Clara W. Page Oct. 6, 1898, in San Diego. He is one of the most noted photographers on the Pacific coast.

1519

BENJAMIN L. HOVEY[8], born Jan. 16, 1851. He is a shoe cutter, and lives in Haverhill. He married Mae Sophia, daughter of Richard and Susan (Davis) Peaslee of Haverhill July 31, 1873. She died at 47 Baltimore street, in Haverhill, after many years of patient suffering, a noble and devoted mother and wife.

Their child was born in Haverhill, as follows:—

1949—I. LEWIS RICHARD[9], born May 17, 1874. *See family numbered "1949."*

1531

EDWARD L. HOVEY[8], born in Haverhill, Mass., Aug. 1, 1859. He lives in Haverhill, and is manager of his father's last manufacturing business. He married Abbie Emerson Oct. 9, 1893; and she died Nov. 2, 1910, at the age of forty-one.

Their child was born as follows :—

1950—I.   LUCY LEARNARD[9], born March 2, 1894; and is now (1913) a student at Bradford Academy.

1543

URBAN HITCHCOCK HOVEY[8]. His parents died when he was fourteen, and he went to Warren, Me., and lived with his mother's father. He died before 1890.

Children :—

1951—I.   FANNY M.[9], born July 19, 1861; unmarried; lives in Newburyport.
1952—II.   JOSEPHINE BUXTON[9], born Aug. 19, 1873; married ———— Brooks; and lived in Warren until 1900, when they removed to Newburyport, Mass., where they live, at 291 High street.

1557

WILLIAM STONE HOVEY[8], born in Cambridge, Mass., Oct. 1, 1842. He lives at Grand Rapids, Mich.; and married, first, Aurelia H., daughter of Charles Hatch and Abigail Morgan (Safford) Taylor Oct. 16, 1866. She was born in Grand Rapids July 15, 1844; and died there Feb. 28, 1887. He married, second, Gertrude (Fitch) Storrs, daughter of James O. and Minerva (Gager) Fitch Dec. 5, 1888. She was born in Rockville, Conn., June 2, 1845.

Mr. Hovey's children were born at Grand Rapids, as follows :—

1953—I.   JULIA ABBY[9], born Dec. 5, 1867; married Edgar Miller Metheany Dec. 5, 1887; and lives in Grand Rapids.
1954—II.   CHARLES TAYLOR[9], born Jan. 25, 1869. *See family numbered "1954."*

1558

REV. HENRY EMERSON HOVEY[8], born in Lowell, Mass., Nov. 23, 1844. He prepared for college in the public schools of Lowell, and graduated at Trinity college, in Hartford, Conn., in 1866, at the head of his class, and from the General Theological seminary, at New York City, in 1869. He was ordained a deacon the same year, and shortly after went abroad, passing much of his time at Oxford, England. During the period of his deaconate he was rector of St. John's church, Fort Hamilton, New York harbor. He was ordained a priest of the Episcopal church in

1870; and was rector of the Church of the Ascension, at Fall River, Mass., the next two years. He was then rector of the new parish of St. Barnabas, Brooklyn, N. Y., from 1873 to 1883, leaving the parish firmly established and a centre of power and influence in that ward.

In 1880, he spent a vacation on the continent of Europe, and, in 1882, received calls simultaneously to the rectorship of the American Episcopal church in Geneva, Switzerland, and to St. John's and Christ churches in Portsmouth, N. H. He chose the latter churches, and entered upon his duties in February, 1883. During his rectorship at Portsmouth, St. John's church was largely restored and beautified and the Portsmouth hospital founded.

In 1884, Mr. Hovey delivered the address of welcome in behalf of the citizens of Portsmouth to the Greeley survivors on their return from the Arctic region; and in 1885 he gave the civic oration at the local commemoration of the death of General Grant.

In 1885, he was elected a trustee of the Home for Aged Women in Portsmouth, and was its president from 1886. He was a trustee of St. Mary's Diocesan school of Concord from 1886, and from 1887 of the Portsmouth Board of Instruction. He held many other local positions of trust and responsibility.

He was president of the New Hampshire Society of the Sons of the Revolution, and much interested in its work and progress.

Mr. Hovey was a man of wide reading, of strong convictions and generous sympathies, an accurate scholar, admirable organizer, staunch churchman and an affectionate rector. As a preacher, he was unusually simple, direct and logical. His sermons were graphic, tender and earnest.

He married Sarah Louise, daughter of Charles James and Sarah Carmen (Downing) Folsom of New York City April 19, 1871, in St. George's church. She was born in New York City Aug. 23, 1844.

He was of strong, vigorous constitution, but in the year 1908 valvular disease of the heart developed, and on August 6, 1909, Feast of the Transfiguration, he passed away while seated in his chair at the rectory. An elegant memorial window has been placed in St. John's church, and dedicated an Sunday, Sept. 17, 1911. It represents Christ and his beloved disciple, and bears the following inscription:—

This window is in loving memory of the Reverend Henry Emerson Hovey, 1844-1909, for twenty-six years rector of this parish, 1883-1909. Presented by his parishioners and friends.

Their children were born as follows:—

1955—I. SARAH WHITTIER[6], born March 2, 1872, at Fall River. She resides, unmarried, with her mother in Portsmouth.

1956—II. KATHARINE EMERSON[6], born July 28, 1876, in Brooklyn, N. Y.; married William Marston, son of Rev. Dr. William Jones and Alice (Beare) Seabury Nov. 10, 1900. Mr. Seabury is a lawyer and for twelve years practised law in New York City, when ill health forced him to leave New York and go to Arizona. He recovered his health at once, and now practises law in both California and Arizona. He resides at Phoenix, Arizona. Their children are: 1. *Katharine Lispenard*[10], born April 1, 1902. 2. *Etheldreda Winthrop*[10], born March 5, 1904. 3. *Muriel Gurdon*[10], born May 3, 1910.

1957—III. LOUISE FOLSOM[6], born April 19, 1879, at Brooklyn; married Lieutenant-Commander Austin, son of Gen. August V. and Frances (Markbreit) Kautz, of the United States navy, June 6, 1903; and lives at Portsmouth. Their child was born in Portsmouth, as follows: 1. *Leopold Markbreit*[10], born May 22, 1905.

1958—IV. ETHELDREDA DOWNING[6], born Oct. 18, 1880, in Brooklyn; married Lieutenant Scudder, son of James Romulus and Cora Virginia (Binford) Klyce, of the United States navy, Nov. 21, 1908. He was born in Friendship, Tenn., Nov. 7, 1879; and lives in Portsmouth. Their child was born at Portsmouth, as follows: 1. *Scudder*[10], born Dec. 12, 1909.

1959—V. CHARLES EMERSON[6], born Jan. 10, 1885, at Portsmouth. He graduated from the Portsmouth high school, and entered the Massachusetts Institute of Technology, in Boston, in 1902, where he was admitted to the fraternity of Delta Psi. He was appointed to the Naval Academy in 1903 and graduated "with credit" in 1907. He was on the U. S. S. Ohio on the battleship cruise around the world in 1908-09. In 1910, then ensign, he was ordered to the Asiatic station. He was second in command on the gunboat Pampauga when the governor of the islands requested him to co-operate with the scouts in subduing outlaw Moros. In conflict with them he was killed in action Sept. 24, 1911, aged twenty-six. He was buried in Portsmouth, with military honors, Nov. 25, 1911. In the last year of his life he compiled a "Watch Officers' Manual," which supplied a long-felt need for a test and reference book for naval officers, and it has been very successful. A drinking fountain of bronze and Carara marble has been ordered by the family to be set up near the postoffice in his memory.

1563

JAMES ALBERT HOVEY[8], born in Boston, Mass., May 13, 1847. He is a florist, in Cambridge, and resides in Newton Centre, Mass., at 41 Chase street. He married Amelia A., daughter of Edward and Hannah (Worthington) Howe Oct. 18, 1876, in Chicago. She was born in Key West, Florida, Nov. 21, 1856.

Their children were born in Chicago, as follows:—

1960—I. FRANK AUGUSTINE[9], born April 28, 1878; married Nellie Saunders Johnson Dec. 8, 1908; and lives in Boston.

1961—II. DAISY[9], born Sept. 4, 1880; died Sept. 4, 1880.

1565

DOMINICUS HOVEY[5], born in Plymouth, Mass., Nov. 13, 1831.
He formerly lived at Nokomis, Ill., but now in Cromwell, Iowa,
being a retired railroad man. He married Orissa A. Barrows
Dec. 25, 1860, in Buder, Ill. She was from Maine. She died in
———, and he survives her, unmarried.

Their children were as follows:—

1962—I.   WALTER C.[6], died young.
1963—II.   ANNIE B.[6], born June 10, 1862, in Rockland, Me.; lives at
            home, unmarried.
1964—III.   MINNIE F.[6], born March 12, 1864, in Rockland; married M.
            E. Tuohey, in Nokomis; and lives in Cromwell. Child:
            1. *Margery*[7]; married William A. Stevens Feb. 19, 1908;
            he was born in Nokomis Oct. 17, 1887; and died Jan. —,
            1909.
1965—IV.   WALTER CLARK[6], born March 15, 1873, in Chicago, Ill. *See
            family numbered "1965."*

1570

WILLIAM HOVEY[5], born in Mirimachi, N. B. He is a farmer,
and has lived in Houlton, Me., since about 1870. He married
Elizabeth Brown in 1861. She was born on Bare Island, and died
Oct. 1, 1896.

Their children were born as follows:—

1966—I.   IVORY[6]; died in infancy.
1967—II.   FRANK W.[6], born March 9, 1863, on Bare Island(?). *See
            family numbered "1967."*
1968—III.   EMMA J.[6], born April 9, 1864, on Bare Island (?); married
            ———— Hill in 1884; and lives in Houlton, Me.
1969—IV.   JAMES F.[6], born Oct. 22, 1865, on Bare Island (?); grocery
            clerk; married ———— ———— in 1890; and lives in West
            Somerville, Mass.
1970—V.   ANNIE[6], born Sept. —, 1867, on Bare Island (?); married
            ———— Hagerman in 1892; and lives in Houlton.
1971—VI.   ELDORA[6], born in 1869; married ———— Burbank in 1886;
            saleswoman; lives in Augusta, Me.
1972—VII.   FRANCES E.[6], born in 1871, in Houlton; married ————
            Hagerman in 1892; and lives in Keswick, N. B.
1973—VIII. GRACE E.[6], born in 1873, in Houlton; teacher; lives in Houlton.
1974—IX.   GERTRUDE[6], born in 1878, in Houlton; teacher; lives in Houlton.
1975—X.   MABEL[6], born in 1880; lives in Houlton.

1574

MILO HOVEY[5], born in Oxford, Mass., Oct. 6, 1824. He
married Sarah Goodwin of Bunker Hill, Ill.; and died July 27,
1881, at the age of fifty-six.

Children:—

1976—I.   ————[6].
1977—II.   ————[6].
1978—III.   ————[6].
1979—IV.   ————[6].

1980—V.   ———[2].
1981—VI.   ———[2].

1579

DANIEL W. HOVEY[8], born Oct. —, 1829. He lived at Forest City, Ill.; and married Rebecca A. Barnes.

    Children:—

1982—I.   ———[2].
1983—II.   ———[2].
1984—III.   ———[2].

1580

GIDEON HOVEY[8]. He married Kate Herder of Bunker Hill, Ill.

    Children:—

1985—I.   ———[2].
1986—II.   ———[2].
1987—III.   ———[2].

1587

DR. FREDERICK FREEMAN HOVEY[8], born in Thetford, Vt., Jan. 16, 1826. He married Harriet G. Field March 14, 1854; and died March 7, 1872, at the age of forty-six. She died Dec. 9, 1900.

    Their children were born as follows:—

1988—I.   HARRIET R.[9], born June 12, 1858; married Charles F. Higgins. He died Dec. —, 1900. She lived at 67 Church street, Springfield, Mass., in the summer of 1901 and taught the Plummer Farm School, Salem, Mass. Their only child: 1. *Frederic Marshall*[10]; died Dec. —, 1900.

1989—II.   GERTRUDE FREEMAN[9], born Aug. 17, 1862; married Eugene B. Jardine March 31, 1886. Their children were born as follows: 1. *Hovey Jardine*[10], born Feb. 26, 1891. 2. *Constance Ruth*[10], born Sept. 8, 1895.

1590

JABEZ WADSWORTH HOVEY[8], born in Thetford, Vt., May 3, 1833. He married Hannah Catherine Montgomery May 14, 1862, at East Hardwick, Vt.; and lives at East Harwick. He was a farmer and had what was regraded as the model farm in Vermont. He was also a magistrate, and in all respects held in high esteem.

    Their children were born as follows:—

1990—I.   OTIS ELLIS[9], born April 9, 1864, in East Hardwick. *See family numbered "1990."*

1991—II.   FREDERICK M.[9], born Aug. 13, 1865; was a quiet and unassuming man, of sterling character. He was greatly esteemed, and a member of the Congregational church at East Hardwick. He was a sufferer from consumption a long time; and died at the home of his parents, in East Hardwick, May 23, 1901, at the age of thirty-five.

1992—III.   ELWYN G.⁴, born July 23, 1867. *See family numbered "1992."*
1993—IV.   MARY EDNA⁴, born Dec. 3, 1872.
1994—V.   ABBA MARIAH⁴, born May 4, 1879.

1591

EDWARD PAYSON HOVEY⁸, born June 1, 1835. He married
Libbie Jackson Oct. 25, 1876. He has been a hardware merchant
in Cincinnati, Wichita and elsewhere.
  Child:—

1995—I.   EDWARD JACKSON⁴, born July 3, 1881.

1593

REV. HORACE CARTER HOVEY, D. D.⁸, born in a log cabin near
Rob Roy, in Fountain county, Indiana, Jan. 28, 1833, was the
son of Edmund Otis Hovey and Mary (Carter) Hovey. His
father was for 47 years identified with Wabash College as
founder, trustee and professor. (See No. 1051.) Mr. Hovey
was graduated from Wabash College in 1853, and was subsequently honored by election to the Phi Beta Kappa society. He
joined the Centre Presbyterian church of Crawfordsville, Ind.,
when twelve years of age, and was a teacher in its Sunday school,
and for several years a member and then a director of its large
chorus choir. For two years he was a tutor in college. He
served one summer as Sunday school missionary in Fountain
county, where he organized twenty schools and devised a method
of Sunday school map-making that has since been generally
adopted throughout the country. While fitting for the ministry
at Lane Theological Seminary, from which he was graduated in
1857, he taught music in the public schools of Cincinnati, and
directed a chorus choir in what is now known as the Third Presbyterian church of that city. He was ordained by the Presbytery
of Madison, April 16, 1858, within whose bounds he labored
for three years as a home missionary, followed by a year as field
secretary of the American and Foreign Christian Union in Indiana, Michigan and Wisconsin. Declining a call to the pastorate
of a church at Coldwater, Michigan, and also an offer to serve
as chaplain in the U. S. Army, Mr. Hovey accepted as his first
settled pastorate the care of the Florence Church of Christ, in
Northampton, Mass., where he remained from 1863 to 1866.
While there he served for two terms of two months each, as a
delegate of the U. S. Christian Commission. The first term he
did what was styled "battlefield duty" amid the perils of the
Wilderness, North Anna and Cold Harbor. The second term
was more quietly spent amid the hospitals at Washington, and
after the fall of Richmond in aiding its starving citizens.
  Dr. Hovey held several other pastorates as follows: Second
Presbyterian Church, New Albany, Ind., (1866-69); Fulton

Street Presbyterian Church, Peoria, Ill., (1869-73) ; First Presbyterian Church, Kansas City, Mo., (1873-75) ; Pilgrim Congregational Church, New Haven, Conn., (1876-83) ; Park Avenue Congregational Church, Minneapolis, Minn., (1883-87) ; Park Street Congregational Church, Bridgeport, Conn., (1887-91) ; South Church, Middletown, Conn., as supply, (1892) ; First Presbyterian Church (Old South) Newburyport, Mass., (1893-1909). On resigning the latter charge, at the age of seventy-five years, and after more than fifty years of active service, he retired from public life in order to devote himself to special literary, scientific and theological pursuits, though frequently answering invitations to occupy the pulpit or the platform.

Dr. Hovey received in course the degree of Master of Arts from Wabash College in 1856; and the honorary degree of Doctor of Divinity, first from Gale University, Wis., in 1883, and again from Wabash College in 1907. He is a fellow of the A. A. A. S., a member of the Geological Society of America, and of the International Geological Congress, of the National Geographic Society, of La Societe de Speleologie (France), a charter member of the Conn. S. A. R., has been for fifteen years president of the Merrimac Bible Society, is an honorary member of the local G. A. R., and was one of the founders of the Daniel Hovey Association, of which he has been the president since its inception in 1900. He has also held numerous offices in the ecclesiastical bodies with which he has been connected. In 1897, with his son, Dr. Edmund Otis Hovey, he attended a meeting of the International Geological Congress at St. Petersburg; previous to which, with a select party, they made explorations in European Russia and across the Ural mountains into Asia, and later made an excursion into Finland. Subsequently Dr. Hovey returned to Paris and accompanied members of the Societe de Speleologie on an exploring tour through the caverns and canyons of the region of the Causses and gorges of the Tarn, Jonte and Durbais, with remarkable results.

Although not claiming to be a professional geologist, Dr. Hovey has been interested in geological research from boyhood. When but nine years old he found the first of all the myriads of Crawfordsville crinoids that have since been sent by Corey, Bassett, Springer, and others beside himself, to the leading museums of America and Europe; and the original crinoid-bank known as Corey's Bluff is still owned in the family. In the summer of 1854 he made an independent reconnaissance of the geological features of southern Indiana, and was among the first to call attention to the marble quarries and coal fields of that state. During that year he explored a number of Indiana caverns, including the famous Wyandotte Cave, which he mapped, and of which he

published an account at the time in the *New York Tribune* and
the *Indianapolis Journal*. He has since explored many other
caves and grottoes, and is a recognized authority on the subject.
He has lectured in the principal cities of the United States and
Canada on his travels and on popular science. He has been a
frequent contributor to the leading magazines, and more than a
hundred articles from his pen have appeared in the *Scientific
American*. Articles by him have been published in the Ninth,
Tenth and Eleventh editions of the Encyclopaedia Britannica.
He is the author of "Celebrated American Caverns" (1882);
"Guide-Book to Mammoth Cave" (fifteen editions); "Mammoth
Cave Illustrated," jointly with Dr. R. E. Call (1897), and a new
edition of the same greatly enlarged by him (1912); "On the
Banks of the Quinnipiac," an historical poem, (1889); "The
Origin and Annals of the First Presbyterian Church of New-
buryport" (1897); and a new "Hand-book of the Mammoth
Cave," with new maps, (1909); and more than thirty of his
sermons and addresses have been published in pamphlet form.
A complete Bibliography of works about Mammoth Cave has
been prepared by him and will shortly be published in *Spelunca,*
a scientific magazine issued in Paris, France.

Dr. Hovey married, Nov. 18, 1857, Helen Lavinia Blatchley,
of New Haven, Conn., a daughter of Samuel Loper Blatchley,
descendant of William Blatchley, an early merchant in Boston
and Hartford; and on her maternal side she came from Ebenezer
and James Robinson, both Revolutionary soldiers, and through
them from the Spelman family, famous in early English annals.
(See Spelman Genealogy, published by Frank Allaben, 1910.)
She was born at North Madison, Conn., and was a teacher at
New Haven, and in both the Cincinnati High schools until the
time of her marriage. Dr. and Mrs. Hovey celebrated their
golden wedding, Nov. 18, 1907, and a large delegation from the
Daniel Hovey Association were among the many guests. Testimonials were presented by the Essex North Ministerial Association, and by the Presbytery of Boston. The latter is as follows:—

"To the Rev. Horace Carter Hovey, D. D. The Presbytery of
Boston takes pleasure in presenting to you this testimonial, containing a
brief expression of their esteem for you on having completed the Jubilee
of ministry for Christ and His Church. In doing so we wish to acknowl-
edge the unfailing goodness of Almighty God, our Heavenly Father, whose
hand has sustained your beloved wife and yourself in all your varied
life and work. We also recognize with profound gratitude His signal
honor conferred on you by His grace, in permitting you to serve as an
ambassador of Christ for the exceptional period of fifty years. We
realize that, for the ripe scholarship which has adorned your preaching,
the pastoral care which has nourished it, the irenic spirit which has
sweetened it, the consistent godly life which has enforced it, and the
large measure of success which has attended it, the whole Church of God.

and the land you love are your debtors. Your work as a Presbyter has been characterized by loyalty to Presbyterian principles; your zeal for and unremitting toil in their advancement have been tempered with sweet reasonableness and charity to Christians in other flocks. Your knowledge of church law has made you a safe counsellor and leader in her courts; for all of which we tender you our most hearty thanks and this small tribute to your worth. We congratulate you and Mrs. Hovey upon this exceptional consummation together of fifty years' service in the vineyard of our Lord. It is the earnest prayer of our Presbytery that you and your life-partner may be long spared to enjoy in health and peace the evening of life among your family and many friends; and when the dawn of the Endless Day shall break and the shadows of this life shall flee away, that you may have abundant entrance into the inheritance of the saints in light, and receive life's crowning benediction from Him whose name is Love, in His own immortal words, 'Well done thou good and faithful servant, enter thou into the joy of thy Lord.' "

Dr. and Mrs. Hovey reside at 71 Lime street, Newburyport, in which city they have had their home for the last twenty years. Their children were born as follows:—

1996—I. HELEN CARTER*, born Jan. 4, 1859, in Madison, Ind.; educated at Mount Holyoke College and Claverack College and approved by the New York State Regents; studied vocal music with Dr. Barnett of New Haven and Hugh Clarke of New York; married Rev. Henry Feld Ellinwood April 6, 1891, at Anniston, Alabama. He is the son of Henry P. and Helen Ellinwood of East Pembroke, N. Y.; was graduated from Williams College; after teaching a short time he studied theology for two years at Andover and one year at Auburn Seminary whence he was graduated, and was ordained as a Presbyterian minister. His pastorates have been at Victor, N. Y. (six years); Medina, N. Y. (ten years; and at Hamlet, N. C., where they now reside. During an interval caused by his impaired health they spent a season amid the Bahamas. In all these varied localities Mrs. Ellinwood has shared faithfully in pastoral work as opportunity offered, especially in connection with social and musical service.

1997—II. EDMUND OTIS*, born Sept. 15, 1862, at New Haven, Conn. *See family numbered "1997."*

1998—III. SAMUEL BLATCHLEY*, born Aug. 29, 1864, in Florence, Mass.; died, after a short illness, at Peoria, Ill., Aug. 8, 1869, in the fifth year of his age; a singularly spiritual child.

1999—IV. CLARA LOUISE*, born Nov. 27, 1872, in Peoria; graduated at the Bridgeport (Conn.) high school in June, 1891; was a student at Wellesley College, 1891 to 1893; studied piano with Junius W. Hill of Boston and with Madame Minna Sites Severn of New York City; married Rev. Royal Wilkins, son of Franklin M. and Elizabeth (Wilkins) Raymond of Westport, Conn., Sept. 15, 1896, at Newburyport, Mass. He was a clergyman of the Methodist Episcopal church, and is now in business in Portland, Oregon. Since 1909 Mrs. Raymond's residence has been in Newburyport, where she is organist, choir-director and teacher of the piano. Their child was born in Newburyport, as follows: 1. *Horace Hovey*[18], born June 29, 1897; resides with his mother in Newburyport.

1596

ROGER HOVEY[6], born in Worcester. Vt., Sept. 7, 1839. He was a farmer; and lives in Worcester, Vt. He was a soldier in company A, Eighth regiment of Vermont volunteers, in the war of the Rebellion, 1861-1865, serving in Louisiana and Virginia.

He married, first, Caroline C. Hatch Jan. 1, 1866. She was born in 1839; and died Oct. 20, 1882. He married, second, Mary Ann Pope of Lower Province of Quebec Jan. 1, 1884; and died Dec. 1, 1907. at the age of sixty-eight.

The children of Mr. Hovey were born as follows:—

2000—I.   MARY EDNA[9], born Feb. 26, 1867; died Oct. 4, 1892, at the age of twenty-five.
2001—II.   FREDERICK WILSON[6], born Nov. 17, 1868, in Worcester. *See family numbered "2001."*
2002—III. HELEN MARION[9], born Oct. 9, 1870.
2003—IV.   ABBIE CAISIA[6], born Feb. 28, 1873, in Worcester; married Chester J. Wood of Mansfield, Vt., Sept. 24, 1895. He is a manufacturer; and moved to Swift River, N. H., in 1904. Their children were born as follows: 1. *Beatrice Mildred*[10], born Oct. 15, 1897. 2. *Carl Chester*[10], born July 5, 1900. 3. *Ruby May*[10], born Feb. 15, 1906.

1597

HORACE WATERS HOVEY[6], born in Worcester, Vt., Sept. 26, 1841. He lived on his father's farm, in his native town, until his twenty-fifth year, and then spent seven years in Wabash College, at Crawfordsville, Ind. In 1868, he settled in business as a druggist in Independence, Iowa, and is still there and engaged in the same business. He married Harriet Marial Barnhart of Independence June 20, 1872. She was born in Mayville, N. Y., Oct. 16, 1832.

Their children were born as follows:—

2004—I.   ROYAL BARNHART[6], born March 20, 1874. *See family numbered "2004."*

1604

PROF. EDMUND OTIS HOVEY[6], born in Norwich, Vt., May 24, 1829. He was educated at Madison university, and received the degrees of A. B., A. M. and Ph. D. from his alma mater, the last in 1884. He was professor of Latin, Greek and Hebrew. After his graduation, he began teaching in small schools in Vermont and later held several positions in Central New York. He left the Ontario Female Seminary in Canandaigua, N. Y., to enter upon the principalship of the high school at Newark, N. J., where he remained for twenty-nine years. He brought the Newark high school from a very small school to a large size and of the highest standing. He also had charge of the normal and training school at Newark. Upon the twenty-fifth anniversary of his position at Newark many of the leading men of the state gathered at a banquet, at which a solid silver tea service was presented to him.

Doctor Hovey was a member of the New Jersey State Teachers' Association, the Teachers' Provident Association of the United States, the High School Teachers' Association, the New York Alumni Association of Madison University and a number of other similar organizations, in all of which he held office at various times. He also belonged to the Bureau of Associated Charities, the Essex Art Association, of which he was a director, and the Harmonic Singing Society.

He was a member of St. John's lodge of freemasons, and deeply interested in the Masonic secret ritual. He often took part in conferring degrees and frequently made addresses at Masonic gatherings.

Doctor Hovey joined the Baptist church in New York in 1843, being baptized in mid-winter in the Black river, near Albany, when the weather was so cold that a hole had to be cut through the ice for the immersion. In Newark, he was admitted to the First Baptist church, and was deacon of it for four years. In 1897 he was admitted to the South Baptist church of Newark, and was deacon of that church at the time of his death. He was a man of optimistic temperament, literary in his tastes, nearly six feet in height, courtly in manner, with blue eyes and dark hair.

He married Julia Bennett, daughter of James Calkins and Laura (Wood) Huntley Dec. 29, 1858, in West Winfield, N. Y. She was born in Plainfield, N. J., Feb. 18, 1835. He died in Newark Feb. 23, 1902, at the age of seventy-two; and she died there Oct. 4, 1906, aged seventy-one.

Their children were born as follows:—

2005—I.   LEON L.[9], born Feb. 21, 1861, in West Winfield; died Feb. 27, 1861.

2006—II.   CLARA MILABELL[9], born May 23, 1863, in West Winfield; married Charles Jones, son of Michael Miller and Elizabeth G. (Caldwell) Riter Dec. 6, 1888, in Newark. He was born in Philadelphia, Pa., Dec. 29, 1859. He is a merchant, and they live at 4819 Trinity Place, West Philadelphia. Their child was born in Philadelphia, as follows: 1. *Michael Miller*[10], born Oct. 13, 1889.

2007—III. LAURA FINNETT[9], born April 7, 1866, in Rome, N. Y.; married Wilbur Todd Sayre of Newark June 6, 1888. He was born in Brooklyn, N. Y., May 27, 1860. He is a druggist, and lives in Newark. Their child was born in Newark, as follows: 1. *Maugerite*[10], born Oct. 11, 1889.

1617

HENRY RUSSELL HOVEY[9], born in Centerbrook, Conn., June 9, 1852, at the Hovey homestead. In 1860, the family removed to Essex, Conn., and his father built the house known as the "Yellow mansion," being a large house, with cupola, set on the

highest point of land about Essex and painted a bright yellow.
From the Cupola is a view of Long Island Sound, and the arrival
of Captain Hovey from London was always announced by flying
the American and English flags.

Henry attended the public schools and Essex high school,
and in 1868 went to the Highland Military Academy at Worcester, Mass., from which he graduated in 1870. He began
business with his brother-in-law, Roger Williams Love, at Claremont, N. H., but in a few years went to Boston, remaining there
two years with the publishing house of James R. Osgood & Co.
He then removed to Hartford, Conn., where he has since lived,
with the exception of eight years (1903-1911) when he was in
New York City. He is connected with the Aetna Life Insurance
Company.

Mr. Hovey married Alice Eliza, daughter of Elisha A. and
Ruth (Gee) Huntley of Alstead, N. H., March 18, 1880. She is
a lineal desendant of Gen. Nathan Huntley of Revolutionary
fame, and was born in Charlestown, Mass., Jan. 27, 1856.

Their children were born as follows :—

2008—I.   MARY EMILIE³, born Dec. 25, 1880, in Alstead, N. H.; grad-
            uated at the Hartford high school, Madam Lefebure's
            school for girls (Edgeworth school) of Baltimore, Md.,
            and Simmons College, Boston, Mass.; and she is now in
            charge of the Domestic Science Department of Salisbury
            School at Salisbury, Conn.

2009—II.   ROGER HUNTLEY³, born June 8, 1886, in Hartford, Conn.;
            graduated from Hartford high school; and from his grad-
            uation until 1905, was engaged in the safe deposit depart-
            ment of the Hartford Trust Co. At the latter date, he was
            offered the position of assistant manager for Connecticut
            by the American Surety Company of New York City and
            in 1912 was sent to Providence, as manager for Rhode
            Island, where he now resides.

2010—III.   RUTH³, born March 12, 1890, in Hartford; graduated from
            the Hartford high school, Madam Lefebure's School, Bal-
            timore (Edgeworth school), and is now taking a course as
            a trained nurse in the Presbyterian Hospital, in New York
            City.

1625

HUBERT HENRY HOVEY³, born in Rockford, Ill., Dec. 10,
1847. He is a farmer, and lives in Cambridge, Kansas. He
married Martha Ella Brooks Feb. 19, 1878, in Joplin, Mo. She
was born in Iowa March 30, 1863.

Their children were born as follows :—

2011—I.   FLORENCE MELISSA⁴, born March 6, 1880, in Winfield, Kansas;
            lives in Cambridge, Kansas.

2012—II.   MARY FIDELIA⁴, born Oct. 13, 1885, in Cambridge; lives in
            Cambridge.

2013—III.   JULIA B.⁴, born Jan. 20, 1888, in Cambridge; lives in Cam-
            bridge.

2014—IV.   CORA[8], born May 30, 1890, in Cambridge; lives in Cambridge.
2015—V.   EDMUND H.[8], born Aug. 7, 1893, in Cambridge; lives in
           Cambridge.
2016—VL.   GRACE ELLA[8], born June 26, 1896, in Cambridge; lives in
           Cambridge.
2017—VII. HUBERT BROOKS[8], born Aug. 19, 1898, in Cambridge; lives in
           Cambridge.
2018—VIII. RALPH AARON[8], born Sept. 1, 1903, in Cambridge; lives in
           Cambridge.

1631

PROF. GEORGE RICE HOVEY[8], born in Newton Centre, Mass., Jan. 17, 1860. He is professor in Virginia Union University, Richmond, Va. He married Clara Kelsey Brewer Sept. 15, 1890.
Child:—

2019—L.   ALVAH BREWER[9], born March 3, 1897, in Newton Centre, Mass.

1635

FREDERICK HOWARD HOVEY[8], born in Newton Centre, Mass., Oct. 7, 1868. He resides at 16 Chestnut Terrace, Newton Centre; and was at one time the champion tennis player. He married Sara Hayes Sanborn April 29, 1896, in Newton Centre.
Child:—

2020—I.   FREDERICK HOWARD[9], born May 26, 1900, at Newton Centre.

1640

FRANK HOVEY[8], born in Yreka, Cal., May 14, 1863. He lives in his native town, and is a farmer and proprietor of a livery stable. He married Laura, daughter of James R. and Sarah E. (McCrary) Courts Aug. 24, 1898, at Fort Jones. She was born at Scott's Bar Sept. 10, 1866.
Their children were born at Fort Jones, as follows:—

2021—I.   MYRTLE ELIZABETH[9], born Aug. 24, 1902.
2022—II.   CARL FRANK[9], born Jan. 5, 1906.

1644

CHARLES LELAND HOVEY[8], born in Darlington, Wis., Nov. 15, 1851. He lived in Decatur, Ill., in 1893. He married Anna Lowe Wilmarth in Bloomington, Ill. She was born Dec. 5, 1862.
Their children were born as follows:—

2023—I.   AMY KELLOGG[9], born June 11, 1882.
2024—II.   CHARLES LELAND[9], born Dec. 5, 1885.

1647

ALVAH FLETCHER HOVEY[8], born in Darlington, Wis., Nov. 25, 1851. He married Mary Susan Lillie Dec. 25, 1877, in Darlington. She was born in Careyville, N. Y., April 25, 1857.

Their children were born as follows:—

2025—I.   ORAMEL TRACY[9], born July 24, 1879, in Pleasant Valley,
             Iowa.
2026—II.   SHIRLEY SEYMOUR[9], born April 3, 1882, in Grimes, Iowa.

1654

ALFRED HOVEY[8], born in Bloomington, Ill., June 16, 1859.
He resided at Kooskia, Idaho, in 1913. He married Ada Brown
Oct. 7, 1885, in Mt. Idaho, where she was born Dec. 10, 1866.
       Their children were born in Mt. Idaho, as follows:—

2027—I.   RENA[9], born Sept. 2, 1886.
2028—II.   HELEN[9], born April 12, 1889.
2029—III.   ADA[9].
2030—IV.   CHARLES R[9].

1655

RICHARD HOVEY[8], born in Normal, Ill., May 4, 1864. His
childhood was passed chiefly in Washington, D. C., the summers
being spent at the old Spofford place, in North Andover, Mass.,
then owned by his grandfather, Farnham Spofford. His constitution was so delicate that he was not sent to school, but prepared
for college privately. He was graduated at Dartmouth college in
1885; and was one of the speakers at the commencement and
class poet. He took honors in English literature; and secured
prizes for dramatic speaking in 1884 and 1885. He was a Phi
Beta Kappa man, and a member of the Psi Upsilon fraternity,
being its delegate to the convention at Hartford in 1885. He
was editor of *The Dartmouth* in his freshman, sophomore and
junior years, and managing editor of the 1885 *Aegis*. He, also,
wrote the sophomore history of his class, under the title, "Hanover by Gaslight; or, Ways that are Dark."

He spent the years 1885 and 1886 in Washington, studying
drawing and painting in the Art Students' League of that city.
In 1886, he studied Hebrew at Professor Harper's summer school
of Hebrew at Newton Centre. Mass.

In 1886 and spring of 1887 he was a junior at the General
Theological Seminary of the Episcopal church at Chelsea Square,
N. Y., being at the same time an assistant of Father Brown at
the Church of St. Mary the Virgin; but at the end of the school
year he left the seminary, by the advice of the bishop, to pursue
his studies under the bishop's direction. Mr. Hovey said that
"practical necessity" compelled his attention in other directions,
and he gradually drifted away from the career of a clergyman.

In the summer of 1887 he was again at Newton Centre; and
then met Tom Breford Meteyard, the painter, and Bliss Carman,
the poet, who became his dearest friends, and were associated
with him in the "Songs from Vagabondia." That fall he lived in

Boston and did some newspaper work. He also then and there made his first appearance on the stage as a "super" in the production of "Julius Cæsar," by Booth and Barrett.

He returned to Washington that winter, and the next spring, as he was coming away from a lecture on "Sappho" at the Columbian University, he heard some one shouting behind him, "Hi! Halloa, there!" Turning around, he saw Hon. Horatio King (postmaster-general under President Buchanan) running after him and gesticulating incomprehensibly. Mr. Hovey was not acquainted with Mr. King, but stopped until he came up, when the latter said that Mr. Hovey looked like Giotto's portrait of Dante, and that he wanted to meet him. Mr. Hovey returned with Mr. King, met Mr. Davidson, and was engaged that day to lecture for him the next June at his summer school of philosophy at Farmington, Conn. The lecture was on Mephistopheles of Goethe and Marlowe. At Farmington, he met the widow of Sidney Lanier, who presented to him a wreath of laurel which she had just received from the south. This was the occasion of his writing "The Laurel." In the summer of 1889, he lectured again at the same school, on the "Relations between Ethics and Aesthetics."

In the spring of 1890, he went on the stage, primarily to complete his education as a playwright. His first part was with Mary Shaw in "A Drop of Poison," as "Counsellor Fabricus," a diplomatist at the court of Berlin.

In 1891, he went to Europe and spent a year in England and France, the greater part of his time being spent among the impressionistes and symbolistes painters in France, etc.

Mr. Hovey began to write poetry when a mere child, and at the age of eleven he printed and bound some of his verse. The first recognition of merit in his writings was received from Prof. C. F. Richardson, on the occasion of printing in The Dartmouth some of his sonnets to Swinburne. He was the author of a famous song,—the strongest belonging to any American college, entitled

THE MEN OF DARTMOUTH.

Men of Dartmouth, give a rouse
For the college on the hill!
For the Lone Pine above her
And the loyal men who love her,—
Give a rouse, give a rouse, with a will!
  For the sons of old Dartmouth,
  The sturdy sons of Dartmouth—
Though round the girdled earth they roam,
  Her spell on them remains;
They have the still North in their hearts,
  The hill-winds in their veins,
And the granite of New Hampshire
  In their muscles and their brains.

They were mighty men of old
That she nurtured at her side,
Till like Vikings they went forth
From the lone and silent North,—
And they strove, and they wrought, and they died.
But—the sons of old Dartmouth,
The laurelled sons of Dartmouth—
The mother keeps them in her heart
And guards their altar-flame;
The still North remembers them,
The hill-winds know their name,
And the granite of New Hampshire
Keeps the record of their fame.

Men of Dartmouth, set a watch
Lest the old traditions fail!
Stand as brother stands by brother!
Dare a deed for the old Mother!
Greet the world, from the hills, with a hail!
For the sons of old Dartmouth,
The loyal sons of Dartmouth—
Around the world they keep for her
Their old chivalric faith;
They have the still North in their souls,
The hill-winds in their breath;
And the granite of New Hampshire
Is made part of them till death.

Mr. Hovey's Stein Song, the most popular college song in existence, has a lilt and a swing to it that satisfies the college youth as few songs do. The music was written by Frederic Field Bullard. The words are as follows:—

A STEIN SONG.

Give a rouse, then, in the Maytime
For a life that knows no fear!
Turn night-time into day-time
With the sunlight of good cheer!
For it's always fair weather
When good fellows get together
With a stein on the table and a good song ringing clear.

When the wind comes up from Cuba
And the birds are on the wing,
And our hearts are patting juba
To the banjo of the spring,
Then there's no wonder whether
The boys will get together,
With a stein on the table and a cheer for everything.

For we're all frank-and-twenty
When the spring is in the air,
And we've faith and hope a-plenty,
And we've life and love to spare;
And it's birds of a feather
When we all get together,
With a stein on the table and a heart without a care.

For we know the world is glorious
 And the goal a golden thing,
And that God is not censorious
 When his children have their fling;
 And life slips its tether
 When the boys get together,
With a stein on the table in the fellowship of spring.

Mr. Hovey was intensely human. He worshipped comrade-ship, loyalty, brotherhood, with a profound faith that is an in-spiration. Sham and hypocrisy irked him beyond endurance. To his alma mater he gave his frankest loyalty and love. The following lines are characteristic of his jubilant spirit, which knew no bounds :—

HANOVER WINTER-SONG.

Ho, a song by the fire!
(Pass the pipes, fill the bowl!)
Ho, a song by the fire!
—With a Skoal! . . .
For the wolf wind is whining in the doorways,
And the snow drifts deep along the road,
And the ice-gnomes are marching from their Norways,
And the great white cold walks abroad.
(Boo-oo-o! pass the bowl!)
 For here by the fire
 We defy frost and storm.
 Ha, ha! we are warm
 And we have our heart's desire;
 For here's four good fellows
 And the beechwood and the bellows,
 And the cup is at the lip
 In the pledge of fellowship.
  Skoal!

In the spring of 1893, he read a poem at the Psi Upsilon Fraternity reunion in Hanover, which is instinct with his own love of the college. These opening lines quicken one with their exultation :—

Again among the hills!
The shaggy hills!
The clear arousing air comes like a call
Of bugle notes across the pines, and thrills
My heart as if a hero had just spoken.
Again among the hills!
The jubilant unbroken
Long dreaming of the hills!
Far off, Ascutney smiles as one at peace;
And over all
The golden sunlight pours and fills
The hollow of the earth, like a God's joy.
Again among the hills!
The tranquil hills
That took me as a boy
And filled my spirit with the silences!

The poem reaches its climax in the parting lyric :—

> Comrades, pour the wine to-night,
>   For the parting is with dawn.
> Oh, the clink of cups together,
>   With the daylight coming on!
>   Greet the morn
>   With a double horn,
> When strong men drink together!
>
> Comrades, gird your swords to-night,
>   For the battle is with dawn.
> Oh, the clash of shields together,
>   With the triumph coming on!
>   Greet the foe
>   And lay him low,
> When strong men fight together.
>
> Comrades, watch the tides to-night,
>   For the sailing is with dawn.
> Oh, to face the spray together,
>   With the tempest coming on!
>   Greet the sea
>   With a shout of glee,
> When strong men roam together.
>
> Comrades, give a cheer to-night,
>   For the dying is with dawn.
> Oh, to meet the stars together,
>   With the silence coming on!
>   Greet the end
>   As a friend a friend,
> When strong men die together.

Richard Hovey's "Seaward" was an elegy on his friend, Thomas William Parsons, an American poet, "The hermit thrush of singers," who gave thirty years to the study and interpretation of Dante. *The Independent* said it excelled any elegiac verse since John Milton. A few selected stanzas as specimens of the forty-five that make up this marvelous monody follow :—

> The tide is in the marshes. Far away
>   In Nova Scotia's woods they follow me,
> Marshes of distant Massachusetts Bay,
>   Dear marshes, where the dead once loved to be.
> I see them lying yellow in the sun,
>   And hear the mighty tremor of the sea
> Beyond the dunes where blue cloud-shadows run.
>
> The fanfare of the trumpets of the sea
>   Assaults the air with jubilant foray;
> The intolerable exigence of glee,
>   Shouts to the sun and leaps in radiant spray;
> The laughter of the breakers on the shore
>   Shakes like the mirth of Titans heard at play,
> With thunders of tumultuous uproar.

Playmate of terrors! Intimate of Doom!
   Fellow of Fate and Death! Exultant Sea!
Thou strong companion of the Sun, make room!
   Let me make one with you, rough comrade, Sea!
Sea of the boisterous sport of wind and spray!
   Sea of the lion mirth! Sonorous Sea!
I hear thy shout, I know what thou wouldst say.

Poet thou hast adventured in the roar
   Of mighty seas with one that never failed
To make the havens of the further shore.
   Beyond that vaster Ocean thou hast sailed
What old immortal world of beauty lies!
   What land where light for matter has prevailed!
What strange Atlantic dreams of Paradise!

Then the author of the elegy fancies Parsons as being greeted
by numerous other poets in order to lead the new arrival "To the
eternal company of song." Mightiest among them emerges
Dante from the shades to greet his best and latest interpreter:—

His feet are in thy courts, O Lord; his ways
   Are in the City of the Living God.
Beside the eternal sources of the days
   He dwells, his thought with timeless lightnings shod;
His hours are exaltations and desires,
   The soul itself its only period,
And life unmeasured save as it aspires.

About his paths the tall swift angels are,
   Whose motion is like music but more sweet;
The centuries for him their gates unbar;
   He hears the stars their *Glorias* repeat;
And in high moments when the fervid soul
   Burns white with love, lo! on his gaze replete
The vision of the Godhead shall unroll.

A biographical sketch of Richard Hovey was prepared in
1912 by Herbert D. Foster, secretary of the class of 1885; to
which was appended a bibliography by Harold Goddard Rugg.
Nineteen separate volumes by Mr. Hovey are catalogued, including four that were published after his death. The first in the
list was a book of poems for which Richard, in his boyhood, set
the type, did the printing and binding, and had it copyrighted
before even his parents knew about it.

Among his published works may be especially mentioned,
"The Laurel," in 1889; "Launcelot and Guenevere," in 1891;
"Seaward, an Elegy," in 1895; "Songs from Vagabondia," with
Bliss Carman, in 1894; "Maeterlink's Plays" (translated) in
1894; "The Marriage of Guenevere," in 1895; "More Songs from
Vagabondia," in 1896; "The Birth of Galahad," in 1898; "Along
the Trail," in 1898; "The Quest of Merlin," in 1900; "Taliesin,
a Masque," in 1896, and again in Poet Lore in 1900.

Mr. Rugg gives the titles of ninety of Mr. Hovey's poems and sketches that appeared in various literary magazines and a list of his songs that had been set to music. He also lists the more prominent book reviews of his works; and gives a list of the portraits of the poet, from which Mrs. Hovey has selected the one found in this volume as the best.

Mr. Hovey married Mrs. Henrietta Russell Jan. 17, 1893, in Boston. From the time of their marriage until 1896 they were in Europe, living most of the time in London. After their return to America, they lived in New York and Washington, where he was engaged in literary work. He was subsequently lecturer on literature in Columbia college and professor of English literature in Barnard college, New York City. About Feb. 10, 1900, Mr. Hovey entered the Post Graduate hospital, at Barnard college, to prepare for a serious operation which was performed successfully a few days later. A week after the operation he was up and walking about the building, and was suddenly stricken with appoplexy, while walking in one of the wards, Feb. 24, 1900, dying almost immediately. His age was thirty-five. Mrs. Hovey lived in New York City until 1909, when she removed to Los Angeles, Cal., where she now resides. She was the leading representative of the philosophy and art teaching of Francois Delsarte; having sutdied with the younger Delsarte in Paris, where she was his assistant.

Child :—

2031—I.   JULIAN RICHARD HOVEY[9], born in 1893, in France; graduated from the Central high school, Washington, D. C., in 1912, and now resides at Pasadena, Cal.

1656

HARRY SCHOFIELD HOVEY[8], born in Darlington, Wis., June 27, 1862. He married Lydia Blackburn Dec. 10, 1887, in Darlington. She was born in Toronto, Canada, Feb. 7, 1866. They lived in Darlington in 1893.

Their child was born in Darlington, as follows :—

2032—I.   HELEN[9], born Oct. 17, 1890.

1659

FRANKLIN STORRS HOVEY[8], born in Lisle, N. Y., Sept. 22, 1822. He was a silk merchant in Philadelphia, Pa. He married Jane Palmer Barrows of Mansfield, Conn., Nov. 1, 1848. She died in Beverly, N. J., May 5, 1890; and he died in Pennsylvania July 21, 1896, at the age of seventy-three.

Their children were born as follows :—

2033—I.   JANE ELIZABETH[9], born Sept. 12, 1849, in Cambridge, Mass.; married ————— Allen Sept. 1, 1874, in Beverly, N. J., where they reside.

2034—II.   FRANKLIN HENRY[9], born Nov. 27, 1851, in Mansfield, Conn.; married ———— Nov. 19, 1884, in Philadelphia. He lives in Beverly, N. J., and is interested in the American Thread Company.

2035—III.   EDWIN DWIGHT[9], born Oct. 8, 1854, in Philadelphia; lives in Trenton, N. J.

2036—IV.   CLARA BINGHAM[9], born Sept. 5, 1856, in Mansfield, Conn.; married ———— Chipman Nov. 21, 1878, in Beverly, N. J.; and died at Mt. Washington, Ind., April 25, 1891.

2037—V.   ABBIE MANSFIELD[9], born Jan. 24, 1859, in Philadelphia; married ———— Kile April 24, 1884, in Beverly, N. J., where they live.

2038—VI.   MARY FREEMAN[9], born Sept. 7, 1862, in Beverly, N. J.; married ———— Hall Nov. 11, 1886, in Beverly, where they live.

2039—VII.   FREDERIC SHERMAN[9], born Dec. 21, 1865, in Beverly; married ———— Sept. 6, 1900, in Hagerstown, Md. He is a banker, and lives in Philadelphia.

2040—VIII.   JOHN JULIUS[9], born Nov. 17, 1867, in Beverly; married ———— March 27, 1894, in Philadelphia, where they live. He is a wholesale dealer in jewelry.

1661

JOHN ADDISON HOVEY[8], born in Lisle, N. Y., July 17, 1834. He married Annie E. Cade of Philadelphia, Pa., Feb. 19, 186–; and died March 21, 1871, at the age of thirty-six. She lives in Edgewater Park, N. J.

Their children were born as follows:—

2041—I.   HARRIET LOUISE[9], born in Moorestown, N. J.; married ———— June 20, 1899; and lives in Glen Ridge, N. J.

2042—II.   JOHN ADDISON[9], born July 28, 1869, in Philadelphia; unmarried; lives in Edgewater Park, N. J.; address, 23 South Front street, Philadelphia, Pa. He is a soap manufacturer.

1671

CHARLES M. HOVEY[8], born in Warsaw, N. Y., April 22, 1852. He married Clara Adella Burling of Muskegon, Mich., Nov. 19, 1880. They live at 283 Oakley boulevard.

Their children were born as follows:—

2043—I.   FRED B.[9], born July 29, 1882.

2044—II.   CHARLES M.[9], born June —, 1885.

2045—III.   RALPH J.[9], born July 13, 1888.

1692

FRANKLIN OSCAR HOVEY[8], born in LeRoy, O., July 29, 1836. He married Lucy Knapp Feb. —, 1873; and lives in Midland City, Mich.

Children:—

2046—I.   ————[9].

2047—II.   ————[9].

1697

BYRON SYLVANUS HOVEY[8], born in LeRoy, O., June 18, 1853. He married Emma Jane Rogers.

Child:—

2048—I.   ALTON[9]. *See family numbered "2048."*

1722

HORATIO ATWELL HOVEY[8], born in Cambridge, Mass., Sept. 1, 1820. He lived in Brighton, Brookline and Boston and returned to his native town, living at the corner of Chester and Massachusetts avenues. He worked for several years in the butter trade in his father's stall in the Faneuil Hall market in Boston, and at twenty-one became a partner with his father. He continued the business under the old firm-name of H. A. Hovey & Co. in the same stall for more than sixty years, supplying some of the largest hotels and prominent Back Bay families of Boston with butter and eggs. He was highly respected, and was one of the best known butter dealers in the United States. He was a trustee of the lay college at Revere beach, and a member of the Chamber of Commerce.

Mr. Hovey married, first, Mary Elizabeth, daughter of Emery Rice of Brighton Nov. 25, 1841. She was born in Brighton; and died in Boston Feb. 10, 1868, at the age of forty-eight. He married, second, Laura, daughter of Charles and Sarah (Cook) Janes of Charlestown Sept. 1, 1872. She was born in Charlestown.

He died March 31, 1906, aged eighty-five. She survives him. The children of Mr. Hovey were born as follows:—

2049—I.   SUSAN ANNA[9], born Nov. 17, 1842, in Cambridge; died Aug.
             31, 1847, aged four years.
2050—II.   BESSIE ROSE[9], born July 7, 1875, in Charlestown. This was an
             adopted daughter.

1724

WILLIAM HENRY HOVEY[8], born in Cambridge, Mass., Sept. 22, 1824. When a boy he ran away to New Bedford to go to sea, but the vessel sailed before his arrival. His father permitted him afterward to go several voyages, to England and the Indian Ocean, about five years in all. He subsequently took up lands in Lawrence, Kansas, where he lived about twelve years. He then sold out and removed to Clinton, Mass., and before 1871, returned to his native town, where he spent the remainder of his life, except for a short time when he lived in Brighton. In the latter part of his life, he was at 32 Faneuil Hall market, in Boston. He engaged in many valueless speculations.

Mr. Hovey married his cousin Susan Augusta Gerry June 18, 1846, in Sterling, Mass., where she was born Aug. 8, 1825.

She died July 11, 1885 (9?); and he died Feb. 6, 1899, at the age of seventy-four. He was highly respected.

Their children were born as follows:—

2051—I.   SUSAN HENRIETTA[9], born Sept. 2, 1847, in Cambridgeport; died in Cambridge Aug. 21, 1848.

2052—II.   CHARLES SUMNER[9], born May 20, 1856, in Lawrence, Kan.; died June 25, 1856.

2053—III.   WILLIAM[9], born April 28, 1857, in Lawrence; died July 15, 1857.

2054—IV.   CLARA[9], born Oct. 10, 1858, in Lawrence; died April 4, 1859.

2055—V.   RUTH[9], born Jan. 9, 1863, in Lawrence; died Dec. 19, 1864, in Lawrence, one year old.

2056—VI.   MARY[9], born April 29, 1866, in Clinton, Mass.,; died in Clinton Jan. 19, 1867.

2057—VII.   ANNA[9], born Nov. 11, 1868, in Cambridge, Mass.; died Aug. 10, 1869.

2058—VIII.   SUSAN AUGUSTA[9], born April 3, 1861, in Sterling, Mass. This was an adopted child, daughter of Thomas L. and Sarah E. Gerry of Sterling, being Mrs. Hovey's niece. She resides at 67 Pleasant street, Cambridgeport, Mass., unmarried.

1725

WALTER HOVEY[8], born in Cambridge, Mass., May 1, 1828. He was, at one time, at the silk department in Warren's, Washington street, Boston. He went to Europe on business for that firm; and afterwards was general superintendent at Jordan & Marsh's, and remained in that position about thirty years. He was dignified and conservative and highly respected.

Mr. Hovey married Mary Ann Elizabeth Bruce Feb. 16, 1851, in the First Baptist church in Cambridge. She was born Aug. 14, 1829. He died in Cambridge Jan. 21, 1888, at the age of fifty-nine. She survived him, and lives at 29 Lancaster street, North Cambridge.

Their children were born as follows:—

2059—I.   CHARLES WALTER[9], born May 27, 1852, in Cambridge; died Jan. 7, 1853, in Hingham.

2060—II.   WILLIAM BOWLES[9], born Nov. 10, 1854, in Head Place, Boston. *See family numbered "2058."*

2061—III.   ALICE WHITNEY[9], born Dec. 11, 1856, in Cambridge; lives at 29 Lancaster street, North Cambridge, unmarried.

2062—IV.   MARY ELIZABETH[9], born Oct. 13, 1862, in Cambridge; died in Cambridge Oct. 17, 1878, aged fifteen.

2063—V.   RICHARD WALTER[9], born Dec. 18, 1871, in Cambridge. He is in the wool business, having charge of a Boston office; lives at 991 Massachusetts avenue, Cambridge, unmarried.

1726

FRANCIS WAYLAND HOVEY[8], born in Cambridge, Mass., Sept. 13, 1835. When a boy, living with his parents in Cambridge, he borrowed a gun, and, while firing at a buoy or log in Charles river, fatally shot a young man up the river. He did not know it until his arrival home; but trouble about it ensued.

He removed from Cambridge to Brighton when quite young, then, his father having married a second wife, he went west and lived in Lawrence, Kansas, seven years. He returned to Massachusetts about 1868, and his since lived at 76 Merrick street in Worcester.

He married Delia A. Coolidge in 1868, in Worcester. She was born in 1848.

Their children were born in Worcester, as follows:—

2064—I.   NELLIE F.[9], born in 1869; died in Worcester in 1874.
2065—II.   FRANCIS IRVING[9], born in 1870; died in Worcester in 1870.
2066—III. LILLIAN[9], born May 28, 1875.
2067—IV. FRANCIS W.[9], born Sept. 2, 1877; lives in Worcester; salesman in wholesale crockery and furniture store.

1732

CHARLES LINCOLN HOVEY[8], born in Cambridge, Mass., Jan. 2, 1853. He is ingaged in fine tailoring, on Avon street, in Boston, and lives at Waban, Newton, Mass. He was twice married.

Children:—

2068—I.   ———[9] (son).
2069—II. ———[9] (son).
2070—III. ———[9] (son).

1736

AUGUSTUS HENRY HOVEY[8], born in Cambridge, Mass., Jan. 27, 1830. He lived in Cambridge until 1856, in Malden until 1858, in Cambridge until 1862, in Waltham until 1867, in Evanston, Ill., until 1871, in Glencoe, Ill., until after 1875, and lived in Morgan Park, Ill., in 1901. He now lives in Hollywood, Los Angeles, Cal., having retired from business.

Mr. Hovey married Alice Maria Kennison May 20, 1852, in Leominster, Mass.; and she died at Morgan Park, July 30, 1905.

Their children were born as follows:—

2071—I.   HARRIET MARIA[9], born July 2, 1853, in Cambridge; married William Oliver, son of Andrew B. and Mary (Bassett) Jackson Feb. 6, 1879. He is a capitalist, and lives at 902 E. Hollywood boulevard, Los Angeles. Their children were born as follows: 1. *Augustus William*[10], born Sept. 6, 1880, in Glencoe, Ill.; graduated at Armour Institute of Technology, in Chicago; electrical engineer and manager of the Ornamental Iron Works, in Los Angeles. 2. *Irving Foster*[10], born April 9, 1883, at Glencoe; graduated at Armour Institute of Technology, in Chicago; mechanical engineer; lives in Los Angeles; married Ruth E. Swan Sept. 2, 1909. 3. *Wayne Bassett*[10], born July 8, 1886, in Evanston, Ill.; lives in Hollywood, Cal. 4. *Herbert Ladd*[10], born Aug. 2, 1889, in Merrill, Wis.; lives in Hollywood.

2072—II. ABBY ANNETTE[9], born Aug. 22, 1855, in Cambridge; died Nov. 6, 1856, aged one year.

2073—III. ALICE BICKFORD[9], born March 4, 1857, in Malden, Mass.; died April 12, 1857.

2074—IV. WALTER AUGUSTUS[9], born March 22, 1858, in Malden. *See family numbered "2074."*

2075—V. SARAH JOSEPHINE[9], born Aug. 21, 1859, in Cambridge; married Robert H. Nutt Aug. 18, 1881. He lives at Cliffside, N. J.; and is superintendent of the Wilcox L. R. They have eight children.

2076—VI. MARY AMELIA[9], born Oct. 3, 1861, in Cambridge; died March 4, 1885, at the age of twenty-three.

2077—VII. ADELAIDE LOUISE[9], born Aug. 28, 1865, in Waltham, Mass.; married Frederick Arthur, son of Frederick W. and Eliza (Mist) Brookes July —, 1899 (?). He was born in Chicago, Ill., June 7, 1866; served in Cuba in the Spanish war; and lives at Delcino, Cal., being a rancher. Their child was born in Chicago as follows: 1. *Kenneson Hovey[10]*, born Dec. 8, 1901.

2078—VIII. FRANK EBENEZER[9], born March 1, 1868, in Evanston, Ill.; lives at Hollywood.

2079—IX. ALFRED KENNESON[9], born Dec. 18, 1869, at Evanston. *See family numbered "2079."*

2080—X. ALICE AUGUSTA[9], born April 14, 1873, at Glencoe, Ill.; and lives at Hollywood.

2081—XI. HERBERT DANA[9], born Jan. 21, 1875, at Glencoe; clerk; lives at Hollywood.

1738

ELBRIDGE SCOTT HOVEY[8], born in Cambridge. Mass., Jan. 9, 1837. He was a merchant and manufacturer, and lived in his native town until about 1876, when he went to Chicago, Ill., and subsequently to Alameda, Cal., where he now lives at 2037 San Jose avenue. He married Mary Elizabeth, daughter of Timothy and Mary (Winn) Newell Oct. 21, 1858, in Cambridge, Mass., where she was born Sept. 9, 1838.

Their children were born in Cambridge, as follows: —

2082—I. CHARLES ELBRIDGE[9], born Nov. 20, 1859. *See family numbered "2082."*

2083—II. HENRY NEWELL[9], born Oct. 13, 1862; and died in Chicago Sept. 1, 1882, at the age of nineteen.

2084—III. MARY LOUISE[9], born Jan. 11, 1868; married Gilmore M. Agnew Jan. 28, 1895; and lives in Alameda. Their children were born in Alameda as follows: 1. *Florence Hovey[10]*, born Oct. —, 1895; lives at home. 2. *Ruth Hovey[10]*, born Sept. —, 1896; lives at home.

2085—IV. HATTIE WINN[9], born July 21, 1872; and died in Cambridge July 10, 1873.

2086—V. FRED WINN[9], born Dec. 12, 1875; died in Chicago July 22, 1877, aged one year.

1739

JOSEPH WHITING PARKER HOVEY[8], born in Cambridge. Mass., April 17, 1839. He lived at Evanston, Ill., in 1862; and

married Pamelia Snow Sept. 13, 1861. He died at Evanston
March 10, 1876, at the age of thirty-six.

Children :—

2087—I.   ————[5].
2088—II.   ————[5].
2089—III.   ————[5].
2090—IV.   ————[5].
2091—V.   ————[5].

1740

MAJ. SAMUEL DANA HOVEY[6], born in Cambridge, Mass.,
Jan. 9, 1841. He was in the service in the Civil war as lieutenant in the Nineteenth regiment of Massachusetts infantry;
was at New Orleans as captain under General Butler; and at
siege of Port Hudson under General Banks, who breveted him
major of storming party.

Mr. Hovey married Louise Cogswell April 22, 1865. He
lived in New York City in 1866; and now resides at Los Angeles,
Cal.

Children :—

2092—I.   ————[5]; died.
2093—II.   ————[5]; died.
2094—III.   ————[5]; died.

1752

THOMAS EBENEZER HOVEY[6], born in Cambridge, Mass., June
26, 1845. He married Matilda Elizabeth, daughter of Charles
Garrard and Elizabeth (Kent) English; and she lives at 64
Chestnut avenue, Jamaica Plain, Mass.

Children :—

2095—I.   ARTHUR THOMAS[7]. He lives at home.
2096—II.   HERBERT LEROY[7]. He lives at home.

1753

WALTER SEWALL HOVEY[6], born in Cambridge, Mass., May
7, 1847. He lived in Somerville, Mass.; and married Martha J.
————. She died in 1905.

Children :—

2097—I.   CORA B.[7]; married ———— Evans.
2098—II.   DAISY M.[7]; married ———— Butterfield.
2099—III.   HERBERT L.[7]
2100—IV.   WALTER S.[7]
2101—V.   OSCAR C.[7]

1758

CHESTER LEROY HOVEY[6], born in Hatley, Province of Quebec, Canada, April 25, 1850. He is a capitalist, and engaged in
the real estate business in San Francisco, Cal., where he lives.
He married Annie Elsie, daughter of Jacob and Rachel (Coombs)

Hoffman Aug. 21, 1872, in Portsmouth, N. H. She was born in Boston, Mass., Sept. 22, 1850.

Their children were born as follows:—

2102—I. FREDERICK[2], born June 16, 1873, in Boston, Mass.; died Aug. 23, 1873, in Boston.

2103—II. RICHARD HOFFMAN[2], born May 6, 1878, in San Francisco, Cal.; lives in San Francisco; is in the lumber business; and married Grace Garoutte Nov. 24, 1903.

2104—III. RACHEL AMANDA[2], born July 19, 1881, in San Francisco; married Stewart Fairweather; lives in San Francisco. He is an architect.

1767

EDWARD WRIGHT HOVEY[8], born in Hatley, Province of Quebec, Canada, July 21, 1867. He lives at Rock Island, Province of Quebec, where he is an insurance agent and town secretary and treasurer. He married Susanna Mary, daughter of William V. and Mary A. C. (West) Carter June 21, 1893, in East Hatley. She was born in Waterloo, Province of Quebec, Oct. 30, 1869.

Their children were born at Rock Island, as follows:—

2105—I. LOIS MARY[9], born April 20, 1894.
2106—II. DORIS CHARLOTTE[9], born Sept. 7, 1896.
2107—III. ALAN CARTER[9], born Dec. 31, 1897.

1769

LESLIE ROY HOVEY[8], born in Hatley, Province of Quebec, Canada, March 18, 1878. He lived in Massachusetts, first in Lynn and now in Dorchester, and is a department manager of the business of Swift & Co., produce dealers, in Boston. He married Phœbe Elizabeth, daughter of W. H. and Jane Davidson June 28, 1905, in Province of Quebec. She was born there June 17, 1877.

Their child was born in Dorchester, as follows:—

2108—I. JANIE RUTH[9], born July 24, 1906.

1770

HORACE WRIGHT HOVEY[8], born in Derby Line, Vt., April 19, 1875. He is a manufacturer, and lives at Rock Island, Province of Quebec. He married Mary W., daughter of David and Maria (Clark) Mansur of Stanstead Plain, Province of Quebec, Sept. 25, 1901. She was born at Stanstead Plain July 4, 1870.

Their children were born at Rock Island, as follows:—

2109—I. LINDSAY MANSUR[9], born July 8, 1902.
2110—II. FRANCIS WRIGHT[9], born May 29, 1905.
2111—III. HORACE MANSUR[9], born March 21, 1907.

1788

CARL HENRY HOVEY[8], born in Chester, O., Dec. 14, 1867. He lives in Chardon, O.; and married Elizabeth, daughter of William Whiston. She was born in Chardon April 13, 1871.

Their children were born in Chardon, as follows:—

2112—I.   DOROTHY BELLE[9], born Jan. 5, 1899.
2113—II.   FOREST WHISTON[9], born Nov. 13, 1901.
2114—III. NELSON[9], born Aug. 15, 1905.

1797

ROBERT ELIOT HOVEY[8], born Feb. 2, 1867. He married Nora Herrington June 4, 1889; and lived in Munson, O.

Their children were born as follows:—

2115—I.   ROBERT HILTON[9], born Nov. 19, 1891.
2116—II.   WALTER STEWART[9], born Dec. 28, 1894.

1798

CLARK SAMUEL HOVEY, ESQ.[8], born at Fowler's Mill, O., March 2, 1873. He attended the district school at Fowler's Mill till twelve years of age, and subsequently graded schools at Chardon, O., where he was graduated in 1890. He then spent a year at home with his parents on the farm. At the end of that period he entered the freshman class at Buchtel College, at Akron, O., from which he graduated with the degree of Bachelor of Arts in 1895. He was awarded the Senior Ashton first prize of forty dollar for dramatic reading in competition with other members of his class, and also the first prize of forty dollars, for a law essay, competing with his class in the senior year. He entered the law office of Sadler, Atterholt and Marvin, of Akron, in 1895, as a student and maintained himself by work at collections and as proprietor of a small book and stationery store. In September, 1897, he entered the senior law class at the law college of Ohio State University, at Columbus, O., and graduated with the class the next year, with the degree of Bachelor of Laws. He was admitted to the bar in March, 1898, in examination with one hundred and thirty-six other law students by the State board of examiners, being third highest. He removed to Minneapolis, Minn., in June, 1898, and opened an office for the practice of law, spending his spare time in preparing a thesis in competition with other members of the law class of the Ohio State University, on the subject of "Proximate Cause." In this contest he was awarded the first Edward Thompson law prize of the second edition of American and English Encyclopedia of Law, consisting of thirty-two volumes. In January, 1899, he was admitted to the bar of Minnesota by examination; and practised law at Minneapolis until February, 1901, when he removed to Donnybrook, N. Dak. At Donnybrook he practised law and edited *The Donnybrook Mirror*, a newspaper, till 1904, when he disposed of the paper to give his time wholly to his practice. He formed a law partnership with Floyd White. This contract continued only one year, and he continued to practice at Donnybrook till March,

1906, when he located at Minot, N. Dak., where he is now practising his profession.

In November, 1908, he was elected to the office of public administrator for the county of Ward, N. Dak., on the Republican ticket. He now holds the office.

Mr. Hovey married Alice Maude, daughter of David R. and Susanna (Maris) Hoopes June 17, 1903, at Friends Meeting, in Minneapolis, the wedding ceremony being in accord with the custom of the Quaker church. She was born in Oskaloosa, Ia., Feb. 21, 1875. He is a member of the Knights of Pythias, and Past Chancellor of his (Minot) lodge and also of I. O. O. F. lodge and encampment.

Their children were born as follows:—

2117—I.   DAVID FLINT⁹, born Sept. 3, 1905, at Donnybrook.
2118—II. ELWYN PAUL⁹, born Feb. 24, 1908, at Minot.

1813

CHARLES FREDERICK HOVEY⁸, born in Rochester, N. Y., Nov. 8, 1857. He is a correspondent; and lives in his native city. He married Millicent A. Atherton Nov. 22, 1887, in Rochester. She was born in Henrietta, N. Y., March 19, 1861.

Their children were born in Rochester, as follows:—

2119—I.   CARLTON FITCH⁹, born March 6, 1889.
2120—II. JOHN ATHERTON⁹, born Dec. 6, 1893.

1817

JOHN PAYNE HOVEY⁹, born near Milford, Ohio, Aug. 31, 1847. His early education was obtained at Batavia, O., and in the high school at Russellville, O. At the age of sixteen, he went to Nashville, Tenn., and was appointed messenger in the department of quartermaster of the Union army, under Gen. George H. Thomas. He continued in the service until the close of the war, when he returned to Russellville, and finished his education. He then went to Frankfort, Ky., where he taught school for about two years. Returning again to Ohio, he accepted a position in the store of W. F. Curtis & Company at Marietta, and two years later went back to Russellville. There he formed a partnership with John D. Seip, in the general mercantile business. In 1871, he removed from there to Lafayette, Ind., and engaged in the dry-goods business until 1877, when he went to Kansas. He located in Wichita and engaged in the loan business, being appointed agent for the Kansas Loan & Trust Company of Boston, and was later connected with the mercantile establishment of George Y. Smith & Company. In the spring of 1881, he removed to Tacoma, Wash., traveling by steamer from San Francisco, and has lived there ever since. At Tacoma he was employed by the Tacoma Mill Company as manager of its store,

which was operated as an adjunct to its extensive lumber mills.
Mr. Hovey built up the business to large proportions, not only
locally, among the retail trade, but also an extensive jobbing
business throughout the Puget Sound country. In 1887, he
withdrew from mercantile business, and engaged in the real
estate and loan business, which he still carries on. For some
time he was in a partnership in this line with Thomas L. Nixon
and A. C. Brokaw. Buying Mr. Nixon's interest in the business,
Hovey & Brokaw conducted a successful business until 1898,
and since that date Mr. Hovey has carried on the business alone.
Having made large purchases of city property, farms and timber
lands throughout the state, his operations of late years have
been mostly in his own property. He was one of the organizers
of the National Bank of Commerce of Tacoma, and has at various times held the office of director.

Mr. Hovey married Rebecca Meharry, daughter of John A.
and Margaret (Bower) Miller at Russellville March 12, 1871.
She was born in Russellville Aug. 9, 1850. They worship at
the First Presbyterian church of Tacoma.

Their children were born as follows:—

2121—I.   ARTHUR MILLER[16], born Jan. 10, 1873, at Russellville. *See
            family numbered "2121."*
2122—II.   IVY SUSAN[16], born March 27, 1879, at Wichita; graduated
            from the University School of Music, Ann Arbor, Mich.,
            in 1902; married James Grimes, son of Capt. Asa Betts and
            Amelia (Grimes) Fitch of Los Angeles, Cal., Oct. 31, 1906,
            at Tacoma. He was a student of the University of Michi-
            gan. Child: 1. *Robert Hovey[17]*, born July 12, 1907, at
            El Paso, Texas.
2123—III. JOHN MILES[16], born July 19, 1887, at Tacoma.

1833

CARL HOVEY[9], born in Roxbury district, Boston, Mass., Oct.
2, 1875. He attended the Boston Latin school, and graduated at
Harvard college, A. B., in 1897. He contributed articles to the
"Readers department" of *The Youth's Companion*, and was reporter for *The Commercial Advertiser*, New York City, and of
The Independent, and has published numerous magazine articles. He lives on Far View avenue, New Brighton, Staten
Island, New York City; and married Jean Egerton June —,
1898, at Charleston, S. C., where she was born.

Their children were born in New York City, as follows:—

2124—I.   COPELAND[10], born April —, 1899.
2125—II.   BETTINA[10], born Sept. —, 1900.

1839

FREELAND EATON HOVEY[9], born in Cambridge, Mass., Feb.
22, 1866. He lives in Winchester, Mass., and is a manufacturer

of fancy goods. He married Emma Marie Jacobson June 7, 1893, in Cambridge.

Their children were born as follows:—

2126—I.   MADGE[19], born March 1, 1894.
2127—II. ALAN[19], born April 3, 1896.

1848

ALBINI SUMNER HOVEY[9], born in Stoneham, Mass., Jan. 12, 1854. He married Henrietta Janette, daughter of Enoch Russell and Mary Jane (Bubier) Quimby Dec. 23, 1874, in Lynn, Mass. She was born in Freeport, Iowa, Oct. 31, 1856.

Child:—

2128—I.   ARTHUR SUMNER[10], born May 13, 1877.

1865

NELSON KING HOVEY[9], born Dec. 19, 1842. He was a farmer, and lived in Jesup, Iowa, and Vermillion, S. Dak. He married Nancy, daughter of Charles and Hester (Price) Melrose Nov. 17, 1870. She was born in Perry, Iowa, March 29, 1850.

Their children were born in Jesup, Iowa, as follows:—

2129—I.   WILLIE RICHMOND[10], born Sept. 18, 1871.
2130—II. FANNIE MAY[10], born Sept. 6, 1873.
2131—III. EFFIE[10], born Feb. 20, 1875.
2132—IV. JENNIE[10], born May 12, 1877.

1867

GEORGE BILLINGS HOVEY[9], born Dec. 6, 1846. He married Emily Jane, daughter of William Samuel and Harriet Adelia Ross July 3, 1872, in Coral, Ill. She was born in Sherman, N. Y., June 24, 1851.

Their children were born as follows:—

2133—I.   EDMUND LEE[10], born June 7, 1873.
2134—II. MARY ADELIA[10], born Aug. 10, 1875.

1869

BARZILLAI REED HOVEY[9], born Sept. 12, 1851. He married Susan Strickland, daughter of Charles Cotesworth Pinkney and Sarah Ann (Woodward) Baldwin Feb. 4, 1874, in Buchanan county, Iowa. She was born in Bradford, Vt., April 21, 1852.

Their child was born in Jesup, Iowa, as follows:—

2135—I.   JAY BALDWIN[10], born Oct. 15, 1876.

1870

FRANK WASHINGTON HOVEY[9], born May 24, 1854. He lives in Council Bluffs, Iowa; and married Helen Maria, daughter of John Henry and Hannah Maria (Ross) Freeman Dec. 5, 1877, in Coral, Ill. She was born in Waterloo, Iowa, Sept. 24, 1857.

Their children were born as follows:—

2136—I. GEORGE F.[10], born Sept. 7, 1881, in Union, Ill.; married Myrtle M. Shadduck June 22, 1902; and lives in Council Bluffs.
2137—II. CLARENCE F.[10], born April 15, 1887, in Independence, Iowa; died in Perry, Iowa, Jan. 10, 1908, at the age of twenty.
2138—III. FRANK W.[10], born Feb. 7, 1897, in Independence; lives in Council Bluffs.

1884

WILLIAM ALVIN HOVEY[9], born in Evanston, Ill., Feb. 8, 1874. He is a railway postal clerk, Kansas City and Colorado Springs; and lives in Kansas City. He married Jessie M. Bragg May 5, 1898.

Their child was born in Kan., as follows:—

2139—I. JESSIE LUCILE[10], born May 5, 1899; lives at home.

1889

SILAS BILLINGS HOVEY[9], born in Albany, Vt., March 29, 1861. He lives at Independence, Iowa, being secretary and one of the Jones & Hovey Company, builders and operators of five large electric and gas plants in Iowa and Missouri. He married Mary, daughter of John W. and Olive (Johnston) Glassburn Sept. 19, 1883, at Tampico, Ill.

Their children were born in Independence, as follows:—

2140—I. GLENN GLASSBURN[10], born March 20, 1892; lives at home.
2141—II. SHERMAN PLAYFUL[10], born Jan. 19, 1897; lives at home.
2142—III. FERN[10], born Nov. 7, 1899.

1890

MAURICE WALLBRIDGE HOVEY[9], born in Albany, Vt., Jan. 8, 1866. He is superintendent of the Marshalltown Light, Power & Railway Company at Marshalltown, Iowa, where he resides. He married Ida Leonora, daughter of G. A. and Cynthia (Andrews) Coulter Nov. 26, 1891, in Macon, Mo.

Their children were born in Marshalltown, as follows:—

2143—I. MAURICE GERTRUDE[10], born Jan. 18, 1894; lives at home.
2144—II. MARGARET LOUISE[10], born April 24, 1900.
2145—III. MARIAN ELIZABETH[10], born May 23, 1902.

1897

GEORGE LORIN HOVEY[9], born in North Wayne, Me., Nov. 7, 1855. He was an express messenger on the Somerset Railroad, living at West Waterville, Me., in 1878; and now lives in North Anson. Me., where he is the postmaster.

Mr. Hovey married Annie, daughter of Asa and Catherine (Thompson) Parlin Oct. 5, 1881. She was born in North Anson Jan. 22, 1858.

Their children were born as follows:—

2146—I.   MARION FRANCES[10], born July 13, 1882, in Oakland, Me.; married Ernest Parker Barnaby of North Anson Sept. 25, 1905. They have one son: 1. *George Hovey*[11], born July 11, 1906, at North Anson.

2147—II.   EDNA ANNIE[10], born May 22, 1888, in North Anson, where she lives.

1902

FRANK HOVEY[9], born April 28, 1853. He lived in Oberlin, O., in 1878. He married Mary Etta, daughter of Amos Warner and Catherine (Beeman) Harnet Sept. 25, 1874, in Oberlin. She was born in LaGrange, O., May 25, 1856.

Child:—

2148—I.   LENA CARLOTTA[10], born Oct. 24, 1875.

1923

ALVIN JAQUESS HOVEY[9], born in Mount Vernon, Ind., Dec. 27, 1871. He was clerk to his grandfather Hovey, while the latter was governor of Indiana. He is now a dentist, and resides in Mount Vernon. He married Anna Louise Williams Jan. 11, 1904, at Mount Vernon. She was born Jan. 23, 1877.

Their children were born in Mount Vernon, as follows:—

2149—I.   HELEN LOUISE[10], born Oct. 24, 1904.
2150—II.   FLORENCE[10], born March 1, 1906.
2151—III.   ESTHER[10], born March 1, 1908.

1926

RANDOLPH JAQUESS HOVEY[9], born in Mount Vernon, Ind., March 23, 1879. He is employed by the Electric Railroad company, and lives in Evansville, Ind. He was a sergeant in a company of the one hundred and sixty-first regiment of Indiana volunteers in the Spanish-American war, and served in Cuba. He married Ruth Nepper May 12, 1901, at Mount Vernon. She was born Feb. —, 1877.

Their children were born in Mount Vernon, as follows:—

2152—I.   ISABELLA[10], born June 16, 1902.
2153—II.   RANDOLPH NEPPER[10], born Dec. 24, 1903.
2154—III.   CHARLES NEPPER[10], born Dec. 7, 1905.
2155—IV.   ROSEMOND[10], born Nov. 1, 1907.

1937

JOHN MATTHEWS HOVEY[9], born in Swanzey, N. H., July 29, 1865. He was a druggists' clerk in Keene, N. H., from sixteen to twenty-five years of age; for the next two years hotel clerk for his uncle at Milford, Mass.; and then, for a year, he ran an express with William C. Coughlin of Holliston, under the name of Hovey & Co.'s express. He then began his meat and produce business in Keene, it being now the Cheshire Beef and Produce

Co. He has now been engaged in this business about twenty years.

Mr. Hovey married Alice Mary, daughter of Albert and Mary Belinda (Davis) Hutchinson of Keene Jan. 8, 1889. She was born in Harrisville, N. H., Nov. 24, 1866. They have a delightful home at 222 Main street, in Keene.

Their children were born in Keene, as follows:—

2156—I.   DOROTHY AGNES[8], born March 4, 1890; graduated at Mount Holyoke College in 1912.
2157—II. ———[18], born March 10, 1894.

1942

FRED C. HOVEY[9], born in Groveland, Mass., ——— ———. He was a talented musician, playing the cornet, and a member of several famous orchestras. He married Carrie M., daughter of Charles and Jennie (Bachelor) Clark of Hampstead, N. H., Feb. 3, 1889, at Groveland, Mass. He died at Haverhill, Mass., Jan. 5, 1891; and she died in 1909.

Their only child was born in Haverhill, as follows:—

2158—I.   EVERETT COLLINS[10], born Oct. 7, 1889. He is an electrician, and lives at 8 Lawrence street, in Haverhill. He married Bertha Josephine O'Neil Jan. 4, 1908, at Haverhill.

1944

EDWARD L. HOVEY[9], born in Lynn, Mass., April 14, 1861. He married Elizabeth K. Messervy in Lynn in 1884; and lived in Lynn until about 1900, when he removed to South Peabody, where he now lives at 44 Bartholomew street. She died in Peabody March 4, 1912. Mr. Hovey is a stockfitter.

Their children were born in Lynn, as follows: —

2159—I.   LEROY T.[10], born April —, 1885; and died Sept. —, 1885.
2160—II.   MILA D.[10], born June —, 1887; is a stenographer; and lives at home.
2161—III. CLARA L.[10], born Oct. —, 1890; and died June —, 1902.
2162—IV.   HAROLD[10], born Feb. —, 1893; is a driver; and lives at home.
2163—V.   MARION[10] (daughter), born Feb. —, 1896; living in 1912.

1949

LEWIS RICHARD HOVEY[9], born in Haverhill, Mass., May 17, 1874. He lived in Haverhill and Groveland in childhood, being educated in the public schools of Haverhill, except for two years in the Groveland high school. He was president of his class (1893) in the Haverhill high school.

Mr. Hovey married Helen Cleveland, daughter of Dr. Laurance Sumner and Abbie A. (Eldridge) Smith of Haverhill April 19, 1899. He spent the summer of 1893 at the World's Columbian exposition in Chicago in charge of the shoe and leather exhibits.

He entered the employ of *Haverhill Daily Bulletin* as reporter in September, 1893; and was city editor in 1894 and 1895. He was editor of *The Shoe and Leather Journal* of Lynn and Boston in 1895 and 1896. He bought the *Ipswich Independent* and its newspaper and job printing office, at Ipswich, Mass., May 1, 1896, and lived there until May 1, 1900, when he removed the plant to Haverhill. He added to it, and, with his father-in-law, Dr. L. S. Smith, established the *Saturday Evening Criterion* at 4 Main street. For four months, in 1902, he published a daily paper called the *Haverhill Daily Press*. With Dennis A. Long of Lowell, in September of that year, he started the *Haverhill Sunday Record,* and later secured the controlling interest in it. This business grew rapidly, and larger quarters were secured at the rear of 108 Merrimack street in 1904, and at 15 West street in 1909. The office now has a modern equipment, consisting of a double Hoe perfecting press, linotype machines, etc.

Mr. Hovey lives at 217 Main street, in Bradford district, Haverhill; and he is a member of Merrimack lodge of Free and Accepted Masons, Haverhill lodge No. 165, B. P. O. E., Massachusetts Press Association, Boston Press Club, Merrimack council, Junior Order United American Mechanics, Haverhill Board of Trade, etc.

In 1912 he was appointed by Governor Foss a member of the Merrimack Valley Waterway Board and helped to develop a plan for a deep-water channel in the Merrimack river.

He has been secretary of the Daniel Hovey Association from its founding and had direct charge of printing this book.

Their children were born in Haverhill, as follows:—

2164—I.   MARTIN RICHARD[10], born Aug. 3, 1901.
2165—II.   MIRIAM BRADFORD[10], born July 5, 1903.
2166—III. LAURANCE SMITH[10], born Jan. 30, 1905.
2167—IV.   CHARLES LEWIS[10], born March 12, 1909; died Aug. 13, 1909,
           of infantile paralysis.
2168—V.   CARLETON BEECHER[10], born Aug. 25, 1912.

1954

CHARLES TAYLOR HOVEY[9], born in Grand Rapids, Mich., Jan. 25, 1869. He lives in his native city; and married Stella Rebecca Davis June 5, 1894.

Their children were born as follows:—

2169—I.   GERTRUDE HELEN[10], born March 14, 1895.
2170—II.   ADELAIDE DAVIS[10], born March 6, 1897.

1965

DR. WALTER CLARK HOVEY[9], born in Chicago, Ill., March 15, 1873. He graduated at St. Louis Medical College in 1897; is a physician; and lives in Nokomis, Ill. He married Miss Effie Leuce April 26, 1899, in Jonesboro, Ill.

Their children were born in Nokomis, as follows:—

2171—I.   ALFRED DOMINICUS[10], born July 11, 1900.
2172—II.   GERALDINE ELIZABETH[10], born Aug. 30, 1907.

1967

HON. FRANK W. HOVEY[8], born on Bare Island (?) March 9, 1863. He is a lawyer, and resided in Biddeford, Me., until recently and is now living in Los Angeles, Cal. In Biddeford, he had a good practice, trying more cases than any other attorney in York county. He graduated from the Boston University Law School in 1887; was district attorney for Somerset county, Me., from 1890 to 1894; member of the Maine legislature, representative in 1889, and senator in 1895; was city solicitor of Biddeford, and chairman of the Republican City committee, having always been an active Republican. He has also taken a prominent part in Odd-Fellowship, in both the subordinate and encampment branches.

Mr. Hovey married Gertrude ———————— June 3, 1887.
Child:—

2173—I.   BYRON PRICE[10].

1990

OTIS ELLIS HOVEY[9], born in East Hardwick, Vt., April 9, 1864. He received the degree of Bachelor of Science from Dartmouth College in 1885, and Civil Engineer from the Thayer School of Civil Engineering of the same college in 1889. He was the engineer of the Hoosac Tunnel and Wilmington Railroad in 1885 and 1886; draughtsman for the Edge Moor Iron Co., Wilmington, Del., in 1887; assistant engineer for D. H. & A. B. Tower, Holyoke, Mass., in charge of the dam at Chicopee, Mass., and various improvements in paper mills in 1888; instructor in civil engineering in Washington University, St. Louis, Mo., in 1889 and 1890; assistant engineer with George S. Morrison, engaged in bridge designs in the Mississippi valley and other engineering work from 1890 to 1896; engineer of Union Bridge Company, New York and Athens, Pa., from 1896 to 1900; in engineering department since 1900, and since June, 1907, assistant-chief-engineer in the American Bridge Co., New York. He is a member of the American Society of Civil Engineers; and on the board of overseers of the Thayer School of Civil Engineering of Dartmouth College. He belonged to the Beta Theta Pi Society; is a Republican in politics; and a Presbyterian in religion.

Mr. Hovey married Miss Martha Wilson Owen of La Fayette, Mich., Sept. 15, 1891. He lives in Plainfield, N. J., and has his office at 30 Church street, New York City. He belongs to the Park Club in Plainfield and to the Dartmouth in New York City.

Their children were born as follows :—

2174—I.   OTIS WADSWORTH[18], born May 25, 1893, at Chicago, Ill.; stu-
            dent at Dartmouth College.
2175—II.   ELLEN CATHERINE[19], born April 11, 1896.

1992

ELWYN G. HOVEY[9], born July 23, 1867.. He married Bessie
A. Shepard June 12, 1895.

Their children were born as follows :—

2176—I.   FREDERICK F.[18], born June 22, 1897.
2177—II.   HERBERT S.[18], born Sept. 20, 1899.
2178—III.   ALLAN M.[18], born Oct. 19, 1901.

1997

EDMUND OTIS HOVEY, PH. D.[9], born in New Haven, Conn.,
Sept. 15, 1862. He was educated in the public schools of Peoria,
Ill., Kansas City, Mo., and New Haven. He prepared for college at Hillhouse high school in New Haven, from which he was
graduated in 1880; and graduated with honor at Yale in 1884.
He taught in the evening schools of New Haven from 1882 to
1884; was principal of the high school and superintendent of
schools at Janesville, Minn., in 1884-5, and at Elk River, Minn.,
in 1885-6. He returned to Yale in the fall of 1886 to take up
graduate work, majoring in geology, with chemistry and min-
eralogy as minor subjects. He was assistant in the mineralogical
laboratory, Sheffield Scientific school, at New Haven, 1886,1887,
assistant-principal of the high school in Waterbury, Conn., 1888-
1889, and its principal in 1891-1892. He received his degree of
Doctor of Philosophy in June, 1889, his thesis being "Observations on the Trap Rock Ridges of the East Haven-Branford
(Connecticut) Region."

In the summer of 1890, Dr. Hovey was one of Professor
W. M. Davis' assistants in the United States geological survey
work in the New Haven region; and that fall he went to Heidel-
berg (Germany) University where he studied two semesters
under Professor H. Rosenbusch, the leading petrographer of the
world. The vacation seasons were spent in geological and other
excursions in central Europe. Returning to this country in the
fall of 1891, Dr. Hovey was elected principal of the Waterbury
high school, a position which he resigned at the end of June, 1892,
to become assistant on the State geological survey of Missouri in
charge of the assembling and installation of the state mineral ex-
hibit at the Chicago Columbia exposition. Finishing this work in
July, 1893, he returned to New Haven. Jan. 1, 1894, he entered
the service of the American Museum of Natural History as assistant curator of the Department of Geology and Invertebrate Pa-
leontology, under the curatorship of the noted paleontologist Rob-

ert P. Whitfield. Jan. 1, 1901, Dr. Hovey was advanced to the grade of associate curator, and Jan. 1, 1910, was made curator of the department, Mr. Whitfield having been retired on account of old age. He was an assistant on the United States geological survey in 1890, 1892 and 1902-1906 (mineral resources).

Dr. Hovey's principal publications have been on the geology of the New Haven region, on the type specimens of fossils in his department at the museum (in collaboration with R. P. Whitfield), on the geology and petrography of the western Sierra Madre of Chihuahua, Mexico, on meteorites and particularly on the 1902-1903 eruptions of Mt. Pele, Martinique, and the Soufriere, St. Vincent. He was editor of the *American Museum Journal*, 1902-1910, contributing many pages of its text. He has been editor of the New York Academy of Sciences since Jan. 1, 1908. He is a fellow of the Geological Society of America (secretary since 1907) and of the New York Academy of Sciences (vice-president, 1905-1906, recording secretary, 1907-19—, editor, 1908-19—), and a member of the American Institute of Mining Engineers, the Association of American Geographers, the American and National Geographical societies, the International Geological congresses of 1897, 1900, 1903, 1906, 1910 and 1913; the Century Association and the Explorers' club. He is a corresponding member of the Sociedad Cientifica "Antonio Alzate" of Mexico.

He married Esther Amanda, daughter of Henry Samuel and Cornelia Harriet (Tuttle) Lancraft of New Haven Sept. 13, 1888. She was born in New Haven Aug. 21, 1863; is a graduate of Hillhouse high school, in New Haven, in 1882, and of Mount Holyoke College in 1886. Mrs. Hovey has been prominent in the affairs of her college, having served its national alumnæ association in several offices from 1901 to 1909 and the New York Mt. Holyoke Alumnæ Association as president for three terms, 1909-1912. She is now an alumna trustee of the college. They reside at 115 West 84th street, New York City.

Their children were born as follows:—

2179—I.   HENRY LANCRAFT[30], born July 7, 1893, in New Haven; died
                July 7, 1893.
2180—II.   OTIS LANCRAFT[30], born Oct. 17, 1894, in New Haven; died in
                New York City Sept. 17, 1896.
2181—III. CORNELIA HELEN[30], born Oct. 25, 1896, in New York City; died
                there Oct. 25, 1896.

2001

FREDERICK WILSON HOVEY[9], born in Worcester, Vt., Nov. 17, 1868. He was a farmer; and lived in Worcester. He married Matilda King of Worcester Dec. —, 1889.

Their children were born as follows:—

2182—I.   HARRY[16], born Sept. —, 1890.
2183—II.   ANNIE CAISIA[16], born Nov. 23, 1892.
2184—III.   ROGER[16], born July 13, 1894.
2185—IV.   ALPA MAY[16], born July 23, 1896.
2186—V.   JOHN[16], born April 27, 1898.
2187—VI.   HORACE[16], born Aug. 17, 1900.
2188—VII.   CORA ELLEN[16], born April 8, 1902; died June —, 1904.
2189—VIII.   WILLIAM[16], born July 6, 1903.
2190—IX.   GEORGE[16], born Sept. —, 1906.

2004

ROYAL BARNHART HOVEY[9], born March 20, 1874. He graduated, with the degree of B. S. in the chemistry course, at the University of Michigan in 1899. He has lived in Independence, Iowa, and Chicago, Ill., and now resides at Winnetka, Ill., where he is now a member of the firm of Barnhart Bros. & Spindler, 185 Monroe street, typefounders. He married Nellie E. Willey of Independence Oct. 31, 1905.

Their children were born at Winnetka, as follows:—

2191—I.   RUTH MARIAL[10], born Jan. 20, 1907.
2192—II.   SARAH ELIZABETH[10], born June 23, 1908.
2193—III.   EUGENIA[10], born Aug. 23, 1912.

2048

ALTON HOVEY[9]. He married ——— ————.
Child:—

2194—I.   ———[10] (son).

2060

WILLIAM BOWLES HOVEY[9], born in Boston, Mass., Nov. 10, 1854. He lives at 29 Lancaster street, Cambridge, Mass., and is superintendent of J. S. Paine's furniture store, in Boston. He married Marion, daughter of William Frothingham and Margaret (Jones) Bradbury Dec. 1, 1891, in Cambridge.

Their children were born in Cambridge, as follows:—

2195—I.   LEON BRADBURY[10], born Aug. 31, 1892.
2196—II.   GRACE[10], born Nov. 12, 1893.
2197—III.   EDITH[10], born July 2, 1901.

2074

WALTER AUGUSTUS HOVEY[9], born in Malden, Mass., March 22, 1858. He is a broker, and lives in Chicago, Ill. He married Carrie E., daughter of Alpheus and Sarah Elizabeth (Willard) Dean May —, 1883.

Their children were born in Glencoe, Ill., as follows:—

2198—I.   HELEN DEAN[10], born March 2, 1884; died Nov. 6, 1884.
2199—II.   MARGARET ALICE[10], born March 17, 1886; lives at 811 N. Pine avenue, Austin, Chicago.
2200—III.   MARY[10], born July 27, 1887; lives at 811 N. Pine avenue, Austin, Chicago.

2201—IV.   DONALD DEAN[19], born June 5, 1889; is an undertaker; and
             lives at Great Falls, Mont.
2202—V.   CARRIE NEWHALL[19], born June 20, 1890; died at Glencoe Aug.
             2, 1891.

2079

ALFRED KENNESON HOVEY[9], born in Evanston, Ill.,, Dec. 18,
1869. He is a broker, and lives at Morgan Park, Chicago. He
married Lulu, daughter of Porter J. and Mattie A. (Gilligan)
Walker April 19, 1894. She was born in Peru, Vt., Oct. 3, 1872.
Their children were born in Morgan Park, as follows:—

2203—I.   JEANNETTE ADELAIDE[10], born Jan. 19, 1900.
2204—II.   VIRGINIA E.[10], born Jan. 10, 1909.

2082

CHARLES ELBRIDGE HOVEY[9], born in Cambridge, Mass., Nov.
20, 1859. He is a dealer in bonds, and lives at 1831 San Jose
avenue, Alameda, Cal. He married Marion Elizabeth, daughter
of Walter R. and Marion Man (Loraine) Blake of Chicago, Ill.,
Jan. 8, 1885.
Their children were born in Chicago, as follows:—

2205—I.   WALTER HENRY[10], born March 12, 1887; traveling salesman;
             lives at home; unmarried.
2206—II.   MARION NEWELL[10], born Jan. 6, 1890; engaged in music; lives
             at home; unmarried.

2121

ARTHUR MILLER HOVEY[10], born in Russellville, Ohio, Jan.
10, 1873. He graduated from the University of Michigan in
1898; and married Louetta, daughter of Arthur Brewer and Rebecca Artemiss (Hamrick) Brobst Jan. 1, 1903, at Knoxville,
Iowa, where they now live.
Their children were born in Knoxville, as follows:—

2207—I.   DONALD BROBST[11], born Nov. 7, 1903.
2208—II.   VICTOR MILLER[11], born March 21, 1908.

2209

SAMUEL HOVEY was an Antipedobaptist preacher at Newton,
N. H., who visited Weare, N. H., in 1766, and was so well
pleased that he began his settlement, on Barnard hill, and came
to reside there April 19, 1768. He, together with Elder Smith
and Elder Greenleaf and others, organized the Second Baptist
church in the state (the first Baptist church was formed at New-

ton in 1755).* Rev. Samuel Hovey had some difficulty with some of the brethren and led a second party to form a new covenant. He often preached sermons two hours long. People carried their dinners and had their noonings, after which they held meetings for conference and prayers. August 1, 1773, Elder Hovey preached a sermon which came upon the people "like a thunderbolt from a clear sky." The result was a church meeting on August 6, followed by another, Sept. 12, when the church voted not to allow "Hovey's followers to commune or act with it as members in good standing, because they held that it (the church) has got the Devil's counterfeit gospel." The church met again October 31, and ex-communicated all of "Hovey's followers." The schism which broke the church in pieces was as to whether "sinners should be exhorted to repent and believe whether they did or not." Elder Hovey taught that "the true Gospel proclaims justice fully satisfied, and God fit to be trusted." He held that it was "safe to exhort all mankind to act toward God, to trust in Him and be ready for every good work." The historian remarks: "Thus we see that Elder Hovey was a remarkably bright man and had a large share of common sense."

Those who are descended from this extremely interesting and picturesque personage, have always regarded him as a descendant of Daniel Hovey of Ipswich and there seems to be no sufficient reason for calling in question this family tradition.

2210

LEVI HOVEY, lived in Weare, N. H., and was the son of Rev. Samuel Hovey.† He married Miriam, daughter of Timothy and Hannah (Hoyt) George, of Weare, July 2, 1777.

Their children were as follows:—

2211—I.   TIMOTHY, born Dec. 27, 1781, in Weare. *See family num-bered "2211."*

2212—II.   HANNAH, born in 1789; married Clarke, son of Samuel and Hannah (Clarke) Bailey of Weare; farmer; he died sud-denly March 18, 1830. Children: 1. *Benjamin Franklin,* born in 1817; married Catharine Ann Block of New Phila-delphia, O.; removed to Millers Ford, O. 2. *James Monroe,* born in 1819; died in 1843. 3. *Levi Hovey,* born

* See History of Weare, N. H., by William Little, chapter 13. This Samuel Hovey has been regarded as identical with Rev. Samuel Hovey (No. 189), who "was living in Weare, N. H., Jan. 31, 1777, but later settled in Lyme, N. H., on Grant's Island." But the latter was a resident of Canterbury, Conn., from 1765 to 1773, where several of his children were born. He was a Presbyterian elder until after his settlement in East Brookfield, Vt., in 1794, when he became a Baptist minister, and re-mained such until his death May 12, 1833, at the age of 90 years.—*H. C. Hovey.*

† See William Little's "History of Weare," page 905.

in 1821. 4. *Samuel Clarke*, born in 1823; died in 1840.
5. *George Evans*, born in 1824. 6. *Sarah Buzzell*, born in
1826; married Stephen Kimball.

2211

TIMOTHY HOVEY, born in Weare, N. H., Dec. 27, 1781. He
was a carpenter, and lived at East Weare, N. H. He married
Sarah, daughter of Daniel Gould of Weare Aug. 26, 1802. She
was born in Newton Sept. 17, 1782. He died March 30, 1844;
and she died March 8, 1869.

Children:—

2214—I.　JOHN, born Oct. 20, 1802, in Weare. *See family numbered*
　　　　"2214."
2215—II.　DIANTHA, born Oct. 28, 1804; married John Edmunds.
2216—III.　LAVINIA, born in 1807; married John Cross.
B217—IV.　LEVI ARTHUR, born Dec. 22, 1809. *See family numbered*
　　　　"2217."
2218—V.　HANNAH B., born in 1813; married Charles H. Chase.
2219—VI.　NATHAN, born in 1815; died, unmarried.
2220—VII.　LUCIAN B., born in 1817; died Sept. 2, 1831.
2221—VIII.　DAVID D., died young.
2222—IX.　STANFORD, born Feb. 24, 1823, in Weare.
2223—X.　MARY ANN, born Oct. 29, 1825; married Moses F., son of
　　　　Thomas and Eunice (Fox) Currier; he was born Aug. 2,
　　　　1821; was a machinist, and made a specialty of manufac-
　　　　turing the peculiar tools used by wheelwrights. Child: 1.
　　　　Herbert Hovey.

2214

JOHN HOVEY, born in Weare, N. H., Oct. 20, 1802. He was
a carpenter, and lived in his native town. He married Alice
Jones Oct. 21, 1875; and died Jan —, 1869. She was born in
Chelsea, Mass.

Child, born in Weare:—

2224—I.　J. CARROLL; wheelwright; lived in Weare and Boston; mar-
　　　　ried Mary Jeannette, daughter of William and Mary E.
　　　　Worthley. She was born in Weare.

2217

LEVI ARTHUR HOVEY, born Dec. 22, 1809. He was a cabinet-
maker by trade, and lived at East Weare until his marriage, when
he settled in Lowell, Mass. He married Huldah Dow, daughter
of Thomas and Eunice (Fox) Currier of Weare Nov. 11, 1835.
She was born Dec. 11, 1818. He died in Lowell Jan. 18, 1839.
She married, secondly, Albert Haven Emerson; and died July
16, 1894.

Child, born in Lowell:—

2225—I.　HAMBLIN LEVI, born June 17, 1838. *See family numbered*
　　　　"2225."

2225

HAMBLIN LEVI HOVEY, born June 17, 1838. When six months old, his father died, and with his mother he went to East Weare to live with her parents. He lived there with them until he was ten years old, when his mother married Mr. Emerson, and with her he removed to Gilmanton, N. H., where he lived until he was fifteen. He then went to live with his uncle Daniel Gove Currier in Waltham, Mass., where he attended the high school. He became a clerk in his uncle's retail clothing store and subsequently with Bean & Clayton and later with J. W. Smith, Dock square, in Boston. He was a quiet boy with studious tastes and early became a member of the Everett Literary Society, which was composed of some of the best young men in the town, with whom he formed some close friendships which continued through life.

In 1861 he enlisted in Company M., of the First regiment of Massachusetts cavalry, and went with the regiment to Hilton Head, S. C.; was made corporal; and was discharged on account of ill-health in 1863. In the autumn of that year he went to Springfield, Ill., where he engaged in the commission business until the "Fall of Richmond," Va, in 1865, when he went thither. After a few months in the office of the Special Treasury agent of the United States he became one of the founders of the Powhatan Granite Company in Richmond, Va. He remained there until October, 1867, when he returned to Waltham, and entered the office of J. W. Parmenter, coal, wood and brick dealer.

He married Harriet Adelaide, daughter of his employer Jonas Willis and Harriet (Kingsbury) Parmenter June 3, 1868, in Waltham. He succeeded Mr. Parmenter in the business upon the latter's retirement in 1870 Although not a communicant he was a constant attendant of Christ Church in Waltham, and served it for many years as a vestryman. He was a life member of the Monitor Lodge of Free Masons, a member of the F. P. H. Rogers, Post 29, G. A. R., of the Pencil and Brush Art Club and of several social clubs in Waltham and of the Middlesex and Home Market Clubs of Boston. He was a staunch Republican in politics, but never desired office. He was a chairman of the board of water commissioners for a number of years, and an original member of the sewer commission. He was a trustee and chairman of the investment committee of the Waltham Savings Bank for many years, and a director of the Newton and Watertown Gas and Electric Light Company for twenty-five years and its president for twelve years, until its consolidation, when he declined to hold the office longer. He was a director of the Waltham National Bank for twenty-five years, and its president the last ten years of his life. He served as treasurer of the

Leland Home for Aged Women for many years, and as its president the last six years of his life. He was president of the Waltham Crayon Company for several years, and vice president of the Waltham Hospital. Mr. Hovey had a pure, cheerful, helpful nature, his presence spreading sunshine wherever he went; and he was always interested in and freely supported every thing that was for the social, religious and public welfare of the community. Mr. Hovey died suddenly, May 12, 1904.

His wife survives him and resides at 542 Main street in Waltham, Mass. Both Mr. and Mrs. Hovey were among the earliest members and most generous supporters of the Daniel Hovey Association; and they contributed largely to the success of this volume.

2226

Mrs. EMILY STEELMAN FISHER, of Reedville, Virginia, furnishes the following data, too late to be inserted in the proper place. Her ancestor, John Hovey, (see family numbered 149, page 142), married Rachel Kidder. (See Kidder Genealogy for particulars). Their daughter, Rachel Hovey, married Andrew McIntire, by Rev. Samuel Stillman, D. D., and their children were given under number 149. Nancy Hovey McIntire, their sixth child, married Amos Lewis, and they had the following named children:—

1. ANNA MARIA, born in Boston, Oct. 22, 1825, died Jan. 8, 1907; unmarried.
2. ADELAIDE, born May 27, 1827; married John Ingersoll Steelman Jan. 27, 1849, and is still living at the age of 86 years. He was born July 17, 1822; died March 24, 1899.
3. THOMAS K., born July 20, 1829; married Mary A. Lake June 29, 1856; died Dec. 25, 1896.
4. AMOS, born Dec. 11, 1831; married Annie Smallwood; had four children; died Sept., 1908.
5. CAROLINE W., born March 25, 1834; died June 16, 1912, unmarried.
6. MARY W., born July 17, 1836; married, first, Matthew Fife; and, second, Abram Jaque; died Dec., 1908.

The children of Adelaide Lewis and John Ingersoll Steelman, were:

1. EMILY STEELMAN (compiler of this data), born Oct. 2, 1850; married James Clark Fisher Nov. 21, 1871. Children: A son, born and died July 21, 1873.
2. ANNA HOVEY, born March 19, 1853; married Albert Morris Nov. 23, 1873; died, without issue, Oct. 12, 1908.
3. ADELAIDE, born June 2, 1855; died Oct. 4, 1873.
4. LEWIS S., born March 30, 1859; married Eva Blackman July 4, 1885. Children: 1. *Adelaide*, born Aug. 29, 1886. 2. *Vera*, born Sept. 9, 1888. 3. *Stanley*, born March 3, 1893.
5. JOHN C., born Dec. 9, 1862; married Lillie D. Hickman Dec. 24, 1888. Children: 1. *Marion*, born Sept. 8, 1896; died Dec. 17, 1896. 2. *Freda E.*, born May 21, 1905.

APPENDIX.

In this Appendix are included a few family records which, for want of evidence, have not been connected with the family of Daniel Hovey as given in the preceding pages. It is hoped that the place they should have taken in the genealogy of the family will soon be ascertained so that, in any future edition of this work, they may be properly inserted. Of course, it is not known that any of the families mentioned in this Appendix are descendants of Daniel Hovey; but it is probable that they are all of one kindred.

I

SILAS HOVEY[1], born in Connecticut in 1781; was engaged in the potash business in Lockport, N. Y., where he resided. He married widow Anna Marie (Crysler) Schiemerhorn* of Lockport.

Children:—

2—I.   CHARLOTTE[2], born about 1812, in Connecticut; married ———— Crotzer.

3—II.   ABIGAIL[2], born about 1814, in Connecticut; married ———— Still; children: 1. *George*[3], served in the Federal army during the Rebellion, and was killed at Charleston. 2. *James*[3], lived at St. Thomas, Ontario, Canada; and died about 1902. 3. *Charles*[3], lives in Michigan. 4. *John*[3], lives in Michigan. 5. *Alice*[3], married Joseph W. Eldon; and lives in Chicago, Ill.

4—III.   MATHIAS CRYSLER[2], born in the autumn of 1816, in Schoharie county, N. Y. *See family numbered "4."*

5—IV.   JOHN[2], born April 11, 1819, in Schoharie county. *See family numbered "5."*

6—V.   JACOB PHILANDER[2], born Sept. —, 1821, in Schoharie county. *See family numbered "6."*

7—VI.   MATHILDA[2], born about 1823, in Schoharie county; married, first, ———— Reynolds; and, second, John Hawk; and died in 1894.

4

MATHIAS CRYSLER HOVEY[2], born in the county of Schoharie, N. Y., in the autumn of 1816. He removed to Canada about 1849, and lived at St. Thomas, Province of Ontario. He married Phebe Hill in 1836, at Lockport, N. Y. She was born Jan. 24, 1820; and died Jan. 18, 1892. He died Aug. 19, 1903.

* By her first husband, Mrs. Schiemerhorn had two children: Anna Marie Schiemerhorn, who married Mathus Barnes, and Sophia Schiemerhorn, who married Ira Pratt.

Children:—

8—I. ASENATH[3], born June 29, 1837, at Lockport; married ———— Polluck; and lives, a widow, on Lafayette avenue, Detroit, Mich.

9—II. CHARLES EDWARD[3], born Oct. 9, 1840, at Lockport. *See family numbered "9."*

10—III. MARY EMILY[3], born March 27, 1844, at Lockport; married Allen Macdonald, a lawyer, who died about 1906, in St. Thomas. She lives in Winnipeg, Manitoba.

11—IV. JAMES TABER[3], born Feb. 4, 1847, at Lockport; died Feb. 23, 1869, at the age of twenty-two.

12—V. JOANNA[3], born March 1, 1855, in Fingal, Province of Ontario; married Edwin Orchard (Birchard?) Aug. 22, 1877; he was born Oct. 12, 1848; and he died May 1, 1880. She lives born Oct. 12, 1848; and died May 1, 1880; she lives at St. Thomas; children: 1. *Wilfred*[4], born Aug. 3, 1878. 2. *Edwin*[4], born June 20, 1880.

5

JOHN HOVEY[2], born in Schoharie county, N. Y., April 11, 1819. He lived in Cleveland, O.; and married, first, Maria Hamm in 1841. She was born in Rome, N. Y., in 1814; and died in 1847. He married, second, Caroline Ford in 1849, in Rochester, N. Y. She was born in Rome in 1814; and died at Cleveland May 20, 1873. Mr. Hovey died in Cleveland April 1, 1893.

Children:—

13—I. FRANK EUGENE[3], born Sept. 25, 1852, at Port Buswell, Province of Ontario. *See family numbered "13."*

14—II. LOUISE[3], born Nov. 26, 1855; died May 16, 1858.

15—III. JOHN[3], born April 21, 1857, at Cleveland. *See family numbered "15."*

6

JACOB PHILANDER HOVEY[2], born in Schoharie county, N. Y., Sept. —, 1821. He married, first, Jane Ham; second, Nancy Birch; and, third, Caroline Birch. He died in Wichita, Kas., Dec. 16, 1906. His third wife is still living.

Children:—

16—I. ETHYL[3]; married ———— Richards; and lives at 2406 Troost avenue, Kansas City, Mo.

17—II. MARGARET[3]; married Edward Dickenson; and lives at 1116 Pasco street, Kansas City.

18—III. ELLA[3].

9

CHARLES EDWARD HOVEY[2], born in Lockport, N. Y., Oct. 9, 1840. He married Mary E. Weldon, who was born in Fingal, Province of Ontario, in 1844. She died in 1902; and he lives at Clinton, Province of Ontario.

Their children were born at Clinton, as follows:—

19—I. JAMES ERNEST[4], born in 1872; druggist.

20—II. HERBERT ALLAN[4], born in 1877; druggist.

21—III. FRANK WELDON[4], born in 1880. *See family numbered "21."*

13

FRANK EUGENE HOVEY[3], born at Port Buswell, Province of Ontario, Canada, Sept. 25, 1852. He married Mattie J. Camp June 15, 1876, at Cleveland, O . She was born at Ashtabula, O., Nov. 23, 1854; and died June 20, 1902, at the age of forty-seven. He lives in Madison, O.

Their children were born in Cleveland, as follows:—

22—I.   CARRIE MAUDE[4], born Oct. 5, 1877.
23—II.   JENNIE[4], born Feb. 2, 1879; died July 5, 1879.
24—III.   MATTIE MAY[4], born Feb. 27, 1880; married Lawrence Rood June 6, 1900, at Warren, O.; he was born July 25, 1850, at Warren; they live at Madison; children: 1. *Lawrence Elmer[5]*, born Aug. 14, 1902. 2. *Ellen Beatrice[5]*, born March 23, 1905.
25—IV.   BESSIE EMELINE[4], born June 12, 1882; married George Bank Feb. 14, 1904, at Cleveland; he was born Nov. —, 1879; children: 1. *Lillian Catherine[5]*, born July 5, 1905. 2. *Mattie Emeline[5]*, born Aug. 19, 1906.
26—V.   EDWARD EUGENE[4], born Jan. 30, 1885.
27—VI.   JOHN CAMP[4], born May 17, 1887; died July 4, 1888.
28—VII.   JAMES CAMP[4], born July 4, 1892.
29—VIII.   CLARENCE WILLIAM[4], born July 6, 1896.

15

JOHN HOVEY[3], born in Cleveland, O., April 21, 1857. He married Anna Jacobs, who was born May 8, 1860, at Mt. Vernon, O. They live at 63 Nevada street, in Cleveland.

Their children were born in Cleveland, as follows:—

30—I.   WINFIELD EUGENE[4], born Nov. 22, 1881; married Katherine Thacher Oct. 10, 1906. She was born Sept. —, 1881.
31—II.   EDYTHE LOUISE[4], born Aug. 4, 1883.
32—III.   GEORGE LARKIN[4], born July 6, 1886; lives in Cleveland; and is of the Cleveland Window Glass Company.
33—IV.   IDA MAY[4], born May 3, 1890.

21

REV. FRANK WELDON HOVEY, M. A.[4], born in Clinton, Province of Ontario, Canada, in 1880. He is a rector of St. Luke's parish, Burlington, Province of Ontario; and married Rena Billings.

Child:—

34—I.   CHARLES[5], born in 1905.

II

JOHN HOVEY[1], died March 17, 1852, at the home of his son Isaac Hovey, in Francestown, N. H., where he had spent the last years of his life.

Children:—

2—I.   JOSEPH[2].
3—II.   ISAAC[2], born March 1, 1808, in Boxford, Mass. He is said to have been a relative of David Hovey. *See family numbered "3."*

3

ISAAC HOVEY[2], born in Boxford, Mass., March 1, 1808. He settled in Francestown, N. H., in 1834, on the Cressey place, Driscoll hill. He removed to Dunbarton, N. H., where he remained a few years, and returned to Francestown. He subsequently went to California, and during his absence his house was destroyed by fire. He finally established himself in Ayer, Mass.

Mr. Hovey married, first, Margaret Perkins of Dunbarton, who died in Ayer Feb. 8, 1865. She was buried in Dunbarton. He married, second, Susan S. (Lakin) Freeman, a widow, Jan. 1, 1866. She was born in Durham, N. H., Aug. 31, 1821. Mr. Hovey died Jan. 10, 1888, and was buried in Dunbarton. His wife Susan survived him, and died in West Acton, Mass., July 10, 1907.

Children:—

4—I.   PERKINS D.[3], born Jan. 6, 1835; died ———— ————.
5—II.   ISAAC JAMESON[3], born March 4, 1837; resides in California.
6—III. HORACE CLOUSTON[3], born Nov 16, 1843, in Dunbarton. *See family numbered "6."*
7—IV.   WILLIAM J. C.[3], born Sept. —, 1844; died Feb. 24, 1845.

6

HORACE CLOUSTON HOVEY[3], born in Dunbarton, N. H., Nov. 16, 1843. He was a civil engineer and an inventor. He married, first, Flora Clapp; and, second, Ella F. Freeman Sept. 11, 1872. He died in Ayer, Mass., Oct. 28, 1904, and was buried in Newburyport.

Child:—

8—I.   SUSIE F.[4], born June 25, 1874, in Ayer; married Stafford N. MacWilliams Sept. 4, 1897; and lives in Newburyport; children: 1. *Margaret Jean*[5], born April 4, 1898; died in Newburyport Nov. 14, 1902. 2. *Ruth Hovey*[5], born Feb. 10, 1900. 3. *Harold Freeman*[5], born June 9, 1901. 4. *.Dorothy*[5], born July 17, 1902; died Aug. 15, 1902. 5. *Stafford*[5], born April 28, 1904; died April 28, 1904. 6. ————[5], died at birth. 7. ————[5], died at birth. 8. *Dorothy Jean*[5], born Aug. 8, 1909. 9. *Marjorie*[5], born Sept. 19, 1911. 10. *Elizabeth Tigh*[5], born Aug. 11, 1913.

III

EBENEZER HOVEY[1], born Nov. 24, 1786, probably in Grafton county, N. H. He had a brother Jacob, who had a son Jacob. Ebenezer Hovey married Mary Smith at Niagara Falls Oct. 2, 1808. She was born in Braintree, Mass., March 10, 1792. He was a furniture manufacturer and held the office of assessor and supervisor at Niagara Falls, and in the War of 1812 removed to Canandaigua, N. Y. He became a farmer and about a score of years later removed to Townsend Settlement, N. Y., where he died Sept. 23, 1852. His wife died there Feb. 20, 1862.

Their children were born as follows:—

2—I. ALBERT JAMES², born Aug. 23, 1809, at Niagara Falls; engaged in insurance and real estate business; and died at Chicago in 1880.

3—II. BETSEY SCRIBNER², born April 29, 1812, at Niagara; died at Townsend Settlement (?).

4—III. HARRIET², born Sept. 25, 1813, at Niagara Falls; died at Townsend Settlement Sept. 7.1870.

5—IV. EDMUND S.², born Sept. 25, 1815, at Canandaigua. *See family numbered "5."*

6—V. WALTER SEYMOUR², born April 15, 1819, at Canandaigua; died at Rochester, N. Y., Mar. 23, 1821.

7—VI. HIRAM², born March 13, 1822, at Canandaigua; owned a fur store; and died at Lyone Jan. 2, 1880.

8—VII. EBENEZER BURTON², born Oct. 24, 1826, at Canandaigua.

5

EDMUND S. HOVEY², born in Canandaigua, N. Y., Sept. 25, 1815. He lived at Rockford, N. Y., where he was a contractor. He married Harriet M. Dikeman April 21, 1850. She was born Nov. 22, 1830. He and his wife separated, and he died at Elkhart, Ind., Jan. 10, 1885.

Their children were born as follows:—

9—I. HATTIE ABIGAIL³, born Feb. 20, 1851, at Niles, Mich.; married George A. Mix; lived at Oregon, Ill.; and in 1901 at Roswell, N. M.

10—II. HELEN MARY³, born July 8, 1852, at Cleveland, O.; married David Griffin Janes Dec. 26, 1877; he was born in Racine, Wis., April 2, 1852; and always lived there, being mayor of the city; children: 1. *David Griffin*⁴, born Oct. 3, 1878; died Aug. 3, 1879. 2. *Henry Lorenzo*⁴, born Dec. 24, 1879, at Racine; graduated at Madison University; and subsequently studied at Berlin and Paris. 3. *Helen Estelle*⁴, born May 23, 1881; graduated at Rockford College. 4. *Leila Abigail*⁴, born July 7, 1883; studied at Rockford College, and graduated at Mt. Holyoke College in 1909. 5. *Arthur R.*⁴, born March 2, 1885; graduated at Wisconsin University; then at the close of another year's study there took degree of Master of Arts; then studied on a scholarship at Columbia University for a year; went to Europe, studied a year at Berlin and Sorbonne, Paris; then served as second secretary of the Legation, Havana, one year; then went to Santiago, Chili, as first secretary in the spring of 1908; and while on a vacation took the degree of Doctor of Philosophy, his thesis being published in the *American Historical Review* for January, 1909. 6. *George Alfred*⁴, born Oct. 20, 1886; died at Racine Dec. 6, 1892. 7. *Elvenah Juanita*⁴, born Jan. 29, 1893.

IV

THOMAS HOVEY¹, lived in Nottingham and Stapleford, Notts, England. He had a brother George who left England for America about 1850. Miss Mary Hovey of Liverpool (see below No. 8) has a miniature painted on ivory of their father, who resided in Nottingham, and the style of his dress indicates its date as early as 1800. She believes that he was a descendant of a brother of Daniel Hovey who remained in England. Mr.

Hovey married Anna ――――. She was born Jan. 16, 1825. He died Dec. 29, 1849; and she died Aug. 12, 1854.

Children:—

2—I. JOHN THOMAS², born July 19, 1826, in Nottingham; eldest son. *See family numbered "2."*
3—II. ――――― (daughter)²; is deceased.
D—III. GEORGE HENRY², born June 3, 1830, in Nottingham. *See family numbered "4."*
5—IV. ――――― (daughter)²; is deceased.

2

JOHN THOMAS HOVEY², born in Nottingham, England, July 19, 1826. He was a lace manufacturer. He married Fanny Samuels in St. Mary's church, in Nottingham, Feb. 8, 1848. She was born in Nottingham Jan. 6, 1824. He died there Sept. 17, 1898; and she died there Nov. 19, 1900.

Their children were born in Nottingham, as follows:—

2—I. ANNE MARY², born Dec. 11, 1849; is a professor of music; and resides at 2 St. Maur Place, Livingston avenue, Sefton Park, Liverpool.
3—II. FANNY KATE², born May 19, 1851; died June 7, 1851.
4—III. AGNES², born Dec. 25, 1853; died April 30, 1859, in Nottingham.
5—IV. ROSE², born Aug. 29, 1855; lives, unmarried, at 14 Hope Drive, The Park, Nottingham.
6—V. EDITH³, born Aug. 7, 1857; married Francis William Stanley Aug 17, 1882, in High Pavement Chapel, in Nottingham; Mr. Stanley died, of diphtheria, April 15, 1907; and she lives at 14 Montrell Road, Sheatham Hill, London, S. W.; children: 1. *Edith Winifred⁴*, born Sept. 13, 1883. 2. *Muriel Hovey⁴*, born Dec. 21, 1884. 3. *Evelyn Hilda⁴*, born Sept. 14, 1887.
7—VI. JOHN THOMAS³, born Aug. 3, 1859. He is a lace manufacturer's manager, having been connected with the lace trade all his life. He first served an apprenticeship to lace machine building, and then traveled in the wholesale lace trade in the United Kingdom. He lives at 14 Hope Drive, Nottingham.
8—VI. MARY³, born Aug. 13, 1862; she received a musical education, at first in Nottingham, and subsequently at the National Training in Music, London, where she held the scholarship founded by Nottingham citizens, in memory of Samuel Morley, Esq., their late member of parliament; at the expiration of this scholarship she completed her training under Herr Ludwig Straus; and since that time has held an appointment in the Liverpool schools, and professor of music of the Girls' Public Day Schools Company Limited, London. She resides at 2 St. Maur Place, Livingston avenue, Sefton Park, Liverpool.

4

REV. GEORGE HENRY HOVEY², born in Nottingham, England, June 3, 1830.* He was a Wesleyan Methodist local preacher for fifty years, and in business as a draper and general house furnisher. He married Frances ――――; and died in Sheffield June 1, 1897. His widow survived him; and lived in Sheffield.

---

* Mr. Hovey's great-grandmother was a Clement.

Their children were born as follows:—

9—I.   GEORGE HENRY[2]; was partner with his father.
10—II.   ERNEST BALDWIN[2]; lost his life by the blow of a crickett ball, at the age of thirty-two, leaving a widow and two boys.
11—III.   ANNIE FRANCES[2], born in 1854; married ———— Styring, a lawyer.
12—VI.   KATE[2], born in 1856; lives at home, unmarried.
13—V.   FLORENCE[2]; married Abel C. Sykes.
14—VI.   LILLIAN[2]; is a singer and recitationist.
15—VII.   ROSA[2]; is a lady principal of Penrhos College, Colwyn Bay, North Wales.
16—VIII.   ETHEL MAY[2]; is lady matron of Peurhos College.
17—IX.   BEATRICE[2]; married Raymond E. Crawshaw.
18—X.   ARTHUR CLEMENT[2]; is a gas engineer.
19—XI.   CHARLES HOWELL[2], born in 1874; is an accountant.

V

AZEL HOVEY[1], born in New Lebanon, N. Y., Nov. 5, 1764.* He was a soldier of the Revolution. He married Lucy Rockwell March 4, 1795. She was born in Stockbridge, Mass., May 8, 1778. They settled in Tioga county, N. Y., and removed from there to Maine, N. Y., in 1809, and in 1825 to Newark, Tioga county, where he died Sept. 14, 1838. She survived him, and removed to Belvidere, Ill., where she died Feb. 29, 1860.

Their children were born as follows:—

2—I.   JULIA M.[2], born Feb. 7, 1796; married Harlow King Jan. 18, 1826; and died Dec. 1, 1865.
3—II.   ELIZA C.[2], born April 11, 1798; married David Councilman Oct. 27, 1819; and died Feb. 9, 1885, at the age of eighty-six.
4—III.   GEORGE[2], born June 24, 1899; married Rhoda Bacon June 2, 1824; his wife died Jan. 16, 1870; and he died Jan. 8, 1879.
5—IV.   AZEL[2], born Oct. 24, 1800; died July 12, 1826.
6—V.   HANNAH[2], born Aug. 8, 1802; married Allan Watkins Feb. 2, 1832.
7—VI.   CLARINDA[2], born Nov. 8, 1804; married Newell Watkins Oct. 9, 1828; and died Sept. 4, 1850.
8—VII.   JEDEDIAH[2], born Sept. 30, 1906; died Oct. 3, 1808.
9—VIII.   CALVIN[2], born April 20, 1809, in Maine, N. Y. *See family numbered "9."*
10—IX.   LUCY ANN[2], born Dec. 24, 1811; married Leander King Dec. 3, 1829; she died Feb. 21, 1884; and he died Dec. 11, 1891.
11—X.   SABRINA[2], born June 24, 1814; married Edward Brown Dec. 25, 1855.
12—XI.   FRANCIS H.[2], born Sept. 22, 1816; married Sarah Swain July 4, 1855.
13—XII.   AMANDA M.[2], born Nov. 12, 1819; married Franklin Payne July 4, 1855; she died Nov. 10, 1879; and he died Oct 4, 1892.
14—XIII.   WILLIAM F.[2], born March 14, 1822; married Belinda B. Foster May 7, 1850; and died Nov. 22, 1900.

9

CALVIN HOVEY[2], born in Maine, N. Y., April 20, 1809. In

* This is probably No. 628, page 194, of the genealogy.

1825, he removed with his parents to Newark, N. Y., where he spent his boyhood and young manhood. About 1850, he returned to his native town, and in 1866 removed to Belvidere, Ill. He married Mary Smith Wheeler May 7, 1844. She was born July 18, 1824; and died Dec. 4, 1902. He died, twenty-five days later, Dec. 29, 1902.

Their children were born as follows:—

15—I. FREDERICK W.[3], born Sept. 3, 1845. *See family numbered "15."*
16—II. SMITH B.[3], born Feb. 13, 1848. *See family numbered "16."*
17—III. WILLIS W.[3], born March 5, 1851. *See family numbered "17."*
18—IV. STELLA[3], born Jan. 30, 1862; died Sept. 3, 1867.

15

FREDERICK W. HOVEY[3], born Sept. 3, 1845. He married Josephine C. Bell Sept. 29, 1869.

Their children were born as follows:—

19—I. ALBERT F.[4], born June 19, 1872.
20—II. THEODORE C.[4], born Sept. 12, 1876.
21—III. ETHEL B.[4], born April 19, 1882; lives in Troy, Pa.

16

SMITH B. HOVEY[3], born Feb. 13, 1848. He married Libbie J Onderdonk March 23, 1869.

Their children were born as follows:—

22—I. BERNICE JUANITA[4], born March 28, 1870; married Dr. William A. Duringer April 14, 1897; children: 1. *Elizabeth Hovey*[5], born Feb. 16, 1898. 2. *Havey William*[5], born Sept. 29, 1902.

17

WILLIS W. HOVEY[3], born March 5, 1851. He married Georgina M. Bainard March 6, 1878.

Their children were born as follows:—

23—I. VERNA MAY[4], born March 15, 1881; married Donald A. Cowan Nov. 2, 1904; children: 1. *Georgina Elizabeth*[5], born Sept. 30, 1905. 2. *Juanita Irvine*[5], born March 8, 1907. 3. *Dorothy May*[5], born June 19, 1909. 4. *Ruth Winogene*[5], born Oct. 27, 1910. 5. *Vernabel*[5], born Aug. 21, 1912.
24—II. STELLA WINOGENE[4], born Dec. 8, 1888.

VI

JOHN HOVEY[1], born in Cambridge. He was a bricklayer. He married Mary Ann Gould; and died in Griggsville, Ill.

Children:—

2—I. JOHN[2], born March 20, 1806; died in Griggsville.
3—II. JAMES GOULD[2], born March 30, 1807.
4—III. WILLIAM[2], born March 25, 1810; died young.
5—IV. MARY ANN[2], born March 4, 1813.
6—V. HENRY[2], born July 13, 1815, in Charlestown, Mass. *See family numbered "6."*
7—VI. WILLIAM[2], born Feb. 16, 1824.

6

HENRY HOVEY[2], born in Charlestown, Mass., July 13, 1815. He was a carpenter. He married Eliza Swett Allds Oct. 26, 1837. She was born in Hollis, Me., Sept. 4, 1821. He died Aug. 15, 1852; and she died Nov. 25, 1877.

Their children were born as follows:—

8—I.   HENRY ALONZO[3], born Dec. 11, 183-; died Sept 22, 1850.

9—II.   MARY GOULD[3], born April 19, 1840; married Alonzo H. Foss Oct. 1, 1862; died July 28, 1896; children, born in Charlestown: 1. *George Albert*, born Dec. 7, 1863; died Jan. —, 1875. 2. *Viola Caldwell*, born Sept. 6, 1865; married Alonzo G. Long Oct. —, 1897.

10—III.   JAMES FRANCIS[3], born Jan. 27, 1843, in Hollis, Me. *See family numbered "10."*

11—IV.   SARAH ALLD[3], born June 21, 1846; died July 14, 1896.

10

JAMES FRANCIS HOVEY[3], born in Hollis, Me., Jan. 27, 1843. He married Amanda Wilson Jewett Nov. 1, 1876. She was born at Alton Bay April 29, 1841. They live at 28 Cortes street, Boston, Mass.

Their child was born in Boston, as follows:—

12—I.   EDNA JEWETT[4], born Dec. 16, 1877.

VII

SIMEON HOVEY[1], a surgeon in the Revolution.

Child:—

2—I.   SIMEON[2]. *See family numbered "2."*

2

SIMEON HOVEY[2], who was a soldier in the War of 1812. He married Mary Judd, widow of William Barrett.

Children:—

3—I.   WILLIAM B.[3], born Feb. 8, 1809 (1812?), in Ashford, Conn. *See family numbered "3."*

4—II.   SIMEON[3].

5—III.   MARY[3]; married Joel B. Green of Hartford, Conn.; he was a superintendent of roads; children: 1. *Mary*[4]; married —— Pollard of Brooklyn, N. Y. 2. *Charles*[4]; probably died in a Southern prison.

6—IV.   LUCIUS[3]; trunk maker; lived in Saginaw, Mich.; married Lucy ——. They had at least seven sons, two of whom were circus performers.

7—V.   ROSWELL[3]. *See family numbered "7."*

3

WILLIAM B. HOVEY[3], born in Ashford, Conn., Feb. 8, 1809 (1812?). He removed with his family to North Haven, Conn., in 1853, and was a mechanic and inventor. He served in company C, Tenth Connecticut regiment from Aug. 11, 1862, to Feb. 22, 1863, being discharged for disability.

He married Charlotte E. Sillaman, daughter of Elisha and ———— (Tuttle) Turner of North Haven Dec. 29, 1833. She was born in New Haven, Conn., July 15, 1815. He died at the Soldiers' Home hospital, Noroton, Feb. —, 1894.

Their children were born as follows:—

8—I.   WILLIAM I.[1], born March 7, 1835; died July 2, 1837.

9—II.   MARY M.[1], born Nov. 10, 1836; died July 22, 1838.

10—III.   WALTER P.[1], born Nov. 9, 1838; enlisted in company C, Tenth Connecticut regiment Oct. 22, 1861; re-enlisted as a veteran Jan. 1, 1864, being acting adjutant of regiment in 1865, and in command of company K, at return of regiment. He was present at all of the engagements of the regiment,—Roanoke Island, Newberne, Cove Creek, Trenton, Rauls Mills, West Creek, Kingston, Whitehall, Goldsboro, Seabrook Island, Siege of Charleston, James Island, Ford Wagner, Fort Sumpter, Walthall Junction, Wathall and Chester Stations, Salem Church, Proctor's Creek, Drury's Bluff, Bermuda Hundred, Srtawberry Plains, R. & P. Railroad, Wirebottom Church, Deep Run (twice), Deep Bottom, Laurel Hill, Petersburg and the assault on Fort Gregg April 2, 1865. At that time he was hit by a minnie ball and left on the field for dead, but reached his regiment again and continued in service att Newmarket Heights, Newmarket crossroads, Darley Town, Charles City Road, Hatchers Run, Fort Gregg and Appomattox until the end of the war. After the war he married Mrs. Mary Terry, a widow with two children. The last twenty years of his life he served in the fire department of New Haven, and while in that service he was injured by one of the horses. He was then transferred to night duty on the telephone, and held that office for two years. He was found dead at the post of duty July 12, 1899.

11—IV.   MARY L.[1], born Dec. 6, 1840; married Charles Bishop; lived in New York and North Haven; he was with Perry when the latter made the treaty with Japan, and served with General Faragut in the War of the Rebellion. He died in Norfolk, Va.; and she is also deceased.

12—V.   ARMETHA M.[1], born April 6, 1843; married Ebenezer R. Davis, a sailor, of New Haven; and both are dead.

13—VI.   SARAH JANE[1], born Oct. 8, 1845; married Capt. William R. Marihugh, a sailor, Jan. 20, 1864; lived in North Haven; and she died June —, 1887.

14—VII.   EMILY W.[1], born Sept. 3, 1849; married Rufus E. Hine, a sailor; lived in New Haven; and she died in May, 1907.

15—VIII. CATHERINE A.[1], born Aug. 2, 1853, in North Haven; married Franklin, son of George Lewis and Martha (Smith) Thorpe of North Haven, a farmer, Jan. 24, 1874. He was born in North Haven Feb. 26, 1844; children, born in North Haven: 1. *Harriette Louise*[8], born Jan. 24, 1875; married Herbert Lyon Nov. 18, 1903; stenographer; lives in New York City (Bronx). 2. *Lillian Armetha*[8], born March 30, 1877; died Jan. 22, 1878. 3. *Walter Franklin*[8], born Nov. 25, 1878; teacher in Commercial school; lives in Auburn, N. Y.; married Margaret Young. 4. *Ruby Vernelia*[8], born May 17, 1882; married Dea. Meres Stoddard Aug. 26, 1907; lived in Bridgeport, Conn. 5. *Gertrude Leila*[6], born March 21, 1884; married Rev. William Finney Tyler June 26, 1907; Congregational clergyman at East Northfield, Mass. 6. *William Lewis*, born March 17, 1886; lives in North Haven; married Emma Valentine June 28, 1911.

16—IX. WILLIAM FREDERIC[4], born July 27, 1858, in North Haven; died June —, 1860.

17—X. ESTHER IRENE[4], born March 4, 1861, in North Haven; died March 26, 1864.

7

ROSWELL HOVEY[3]. He lived in New York or Brooklyn; and married Mary ————.

Child:—

18—I. MARY[4].

VIII

IRA C. HOVEY[1], born in Salem, N. H., Nov. 1, 1815. He was a shoemaker. He married Mary A. ———— July 22, 1839, in Albany, N. Y. She was born in Troy, N. Y., Dec. 8, 1820; and died in Philadelphia, Pa., June 19, 1895. He died in Philadelphia March 25, 1900, having been a sufferer from Bright's disease for many years.

Their children were born as follows:—

2—I. ELIZA B.[2], born June 11, 1840, in Troy, N. Y.; died June 23, 1841, in Albany, N. Y.

3—II. IRA M.[2], born Nov. 3, 1841, in Albany; machinist; died Oct. 23, 1867, in Philadelphia.

4—III. LYDIA A.[2], born June 20, 1843, in Albany; married ———— Young Sept. 16, 1873, in Philadelphia; and lives at 704 Belgrade street, Philadelphia.

5—IV. JOHN W.[2], born May 23, 1845, in Albany. *See family numbered "5."*

6—V. MARY W.[2], born June 17, 1848, in Philadelphia; lives, unmarried, at 704 Belgrade street, Philadelphia.

7—VI. MARIA B.[2], born Oct. 7, 1850, in Philadelphia; married ———— Husted Oct. 19, 1868; and lives at 622 Belgrade street, Philadelphia.

8—VII. RUTH[2], born Feb. 26, 1852, in Philadelphia; died Aug. 25, 1852, in Utica, N. Y.

5

JOHN W. HOVEY[2], born May 28, 1845, in Albany, N. Y. He is a carpenter, and lives at Philadelphia. He married Lucy A. ———— Oct. 11, 1868, in Philadelphia, where she was born.

Their children were born as follows:—

9—V. IRA M.[3], born July 25, 1870, in Philadelphia; lives at 7 C street, Echota, Niagara Falls, N. Y.; machinist; married ———— ———— Nov. 22, 1898, in Buffalo, N. Y.

10—II. LYDIA A.[3], born Feb. 3, 1873, in Philadelphia; died there June 15, 1877.

11—III. LUCY A.[3], born Sept. 6, 1875, in Philadelphia; died there May 23, 1877.

12—IV.   JOHN W.[3], born April 9, 1878, in Philadelphia; bookkeeper; lives
          on Sergeant street, Philadelphia.
13—V.   GEORGE W.[3], born Dec. 4, 1880, in Philadelphia; died Jan. 4.
          1884, in Camden, N. J.
14—VI.   CLARA A.[3], born July 13, 1883, in Camden, N. J.; lives on Ser-
          geant street, Philadelphia.

IX

————— HOVEY[1].

Children:—

2—I.   MARY[2], born April 16, 1782, in Brimfield, Mass.; married Shubal
          Conant Hovey (No. 649) Nov. 16, 1800 in Lima, N. Y.; and
          died April 9, 1866, in LeRoy, O.
3—II.   EBENEZER[2].   *See family numbered "3."*
4—III.   BENJAMIN[2].   *See family numbered "4."*
5—IV.   JAMES[2].
6—V.   SOLOMON[2].

3

EBENEZER HOVEY[2].

Children:—

7—I.   ARNOLD[3].
8—II.   SPARFORD[3].
9—III.   LOVICY[3].
10—IV.   MINDWILL[3].
11—V.   DIANTHA[3].
12—VI.   POLACE[3].
13—VII.   ELVIRA[3].

4

BENJAMIN HOVEY[2].

Children:—

14—I.   LYMAN[3].
15—II.   SOLOMON[3].
16—III.   CALVIN[3].
17—IV.   GURNSEY[3].
18—V.   MARION[3].
19—VI.   ELIJAH[3].
20—VII.   LUCY[3].
21—VIII. BETSEY[3].

X

ABEL HOVEY[1], lived in Maine, and married Lydia Libbey.
Children:—

2—I.   JOSEPH[2], born about 1828. *See family numbered "2."*
3—II.   JOHN C.[2]; lives in Millbridge.

2

JOSEPH HOVEY[2], born about 1828. He married Hepsy
Stevens in Gouldsboro, Me. She died in 1889; and he died in
1892, at the age of sixty-four.
     Children:—

4—I.   WILLIAM G.³, born in 1861, at Gouldsboro. *See family numbered "4."*

5—II.   HENRY J.³; lived in Evanston, Ill.

4

WILLIAM G. HOVEY³, born in Gouldsboro, Me., in 1861. He is superintendent of the Taylor Signal Company, having its general office and works at Buffalo, N. Y. Mr. Hovey is to be found at the Chicago office, 1223 Monadnock Block. He married, first. Edith Handy in Maine; and, second, Lizzie Mullen in Chicago.

Children:—

6—I.   MARY⁴, born in 1880.
7—II.   HELEN⁴, born in 1882.

XI

WILLIAM HOVEY¹, lived in Worcester, and married Prudence ————.

Child:—

2—I.   FRANCIS², born in 1819, in Massachusetts. *See family numbered "2."*

2

FRANCIS HOVEY², born in Massachusetts in 1819. He was a machinist, and lived in Worcester. He married Ellen ————, who was born in New York in 1830, and lived in Worcester at the time of her marriage. Mr. Hovey died in New York Jan. 23, 1885; and she died in Worcester April 8, 1900.

Children:—

3—I.   FRANK A.³, born in 1850, in Worcester; clerk; lives at 152 E. 20th St., New York City, unmarried.
4—II.   GEORGE A.³, born in 1852, in Worcester.
5—III. CHARLES W.³, born in 1854, in Worcester; died in New York April 3, 1887.
6—IV.   HENRY R.³, born in 1858, in New York; clerk; and lives at 145 E 15th Street, New York City.
7—V.   E. J.³, born in 1861, in New York; clerk; and lives at 152 E 20th street, New York City.

XII

ICHABOD HOVEY, born in Troy, Vt., June 24, 1781. He died in Ulysses, Pa., in 1847. He married Helen Smith Torrance June 6, 1808. She was born in Scotland April 26, 1790; and died Oct 10, 1827.

Their children were born as follows:—

I.   SARAH JENETTE, born Feb. 10, 1810; died, unmarried, in Chicago, July 31, 1890.
II.   SAMUEL TORRANCE, born July 1, 1812; married in Tioga county, N. Y.; and died at Quasqueton, Iowa, Feb. 1, 1871.
III.   WILLIAM PROCTOR, born May 13, 1814; married in Freeport, Ill.; and died there Sept. 20, 1849.

IV.   JAMES GROSS, born Nov. 18, 1818; died at Waverly, Iowa, May 18,
        1865.
V.   JACOB TURNER, born March 10, 1822; married in Tioga county, N.
        Y.; and died at Ulysses, Pa., in 1899.
VI.   EDWARD DODGE, born in Tioga county, N. Y., May 22, 1825; married
        in Independence, Iowa, Jan. 15, 1857; and lives at Quasqueton,
        Iowa.

INDEX.

Elwyn Paul, 389.
Emeline, 252, 283, 285, 328.
Emeline Eaton, 298.
Emeline Moore, 326.
Emeline Victoria, 339.
Emily, 256, 268, 285.
Emily Ann, 230.
Emily Darling, 281.
Emily Jane, 391.
Emily R., 299.
Emily W., 414.
Emma, 290, 357.
Emma Frances, 292, 336.
Emma J., 364.
Emma Jane, 382.
Emma Jennette, 295.
Emma Joanna, 324.
Emma Maria, 338.
Emma Marie, 391.
Emma Mills, 324.
Emma Polly, 354.
Emma R., 333.
Enoch, 135, 194, 196, 252, 253, 326.
Enoch James, 288.
Enoch White, 253, 327.
Erastus Franklin, 213.
Erastus G., 340.
Ernest Baldwin, 411.
Esther, 16-18, 33, 35, 36, 78, 88,
  101-103, 105, 132, 133, 140, 222,
  253, 288, 393.
Esther Amanda, 398.
Esther Elizabeth, 290.
Esther Irene, 415.
Ethel, 348.
Ethel B., 411.
Ethel May, 411.
Etheldreda Downing, 363.
Ethyl, 406.
Etta, 338.
Eugene, 323, 327.
Eugenia, 399.
Eugenie Josephine, 324.
Eunice, 134, 140, 147, 163, 164, 185,
  192-194, 212, 252, 253, 262.
Eunice Permilia, 285.
Eunice Sophronia, 313.
Eunice Woodward, 209.
Eva, 287.
Eva Ellen, 290.
Everett Collins, 394.
Experience, 141, 142, 192, 203.
Ezra, 180, 194.
Fannie, 286.
Fannie May, 391.
Fanny, 162, 181, 232, 246, 313, 410.
Fanny Baker, 291.
Fanny Caroline, 284.
Fanny Elizabeth, 288.

Fanny Kate, 410.
Fanny M., 361.
Fanny Pope, 267.
Farnham, 235.
Fern, 392.
Fernando Smiley, 295.
Fidelia, 213.
Fidelia E., 320.
Fina, 195.
Flora, 408.
Flora A., 295.
Flora Elgin, 345.
Florence, 393, 411.
Florence A., 345.
Florence Eugenia, 320.
Florence Melissa, 372.
Florilla, 196.
Forest Whiston, 388.
Frances, 181, 209, 227, 410.
Frances E., 364.
Frances Elizabeth, 304.
Frances Flint, 301.
Frances Goodridge, 343.
Frances Marion, 344.
Frances Mary Ann, 251.
Frances V., 344.
Francis, 4, 5, 43, 100, 164, 165, 203,
  233, 241, 327, 417.
Francis Alonzo, 294, 359.
Francis Charles, 325.
Francis H., 411.
Francis Irving, 384.
Francis Wayland, 335, 383, 384.
Francis Wright, 387.
Frank, 292, 321, 323, 336, 373, 393.
Frank A., 417.
Frank Abner, 350.
Frank Adelbert, 270, 345.
Frank Augustus, 363.
Frank Ebenezer, 385.
Frank Edrick, 359.
Frank Eugene, 272, 406, 407.
Frank MacMulkin, 291.
Frank Pierce, 338.
Frank W., 364, 392, 396.
Frank Washington, 352, 391.
Frank Weldon, 406, 407.
Franklin, 334.
Franklin C., 256.
Franklin Cushman, 336.
Franklin Henry, 381.
Franklin Oscar, 329, 381.
Franklin Stark, 269, 345.
Franklin Storrs, 326, 380.
Fred, 341.
Fred B., 381.
Fred C., 360, 394.
Fred W., 340.
Fred Winn, 385.